ORSON WELLES

Simon Callow is an actor, director and writer. He has appeared on the stage and in many films, including the hugely popular *Four Weddings and a Funeral*. Callow's books include *Being an Actor*, *Shooting the Actor*, a highly acclaimed biography of Charles Laughton, and *Love is Where it Falls*, an account of his friendship with Peggy Ramsay.

ALSO BY SIMON CALLOW

Being an Actor
Shooting the Actor
Charles Laughton: A Difficult Actor
Orson Welles: The Road to Xanadu
Love is Where it Falls

'Callow's finely-balanced judgement, enhanced by his own observations as an actor, ensures that this not only ranks as one of the best Welles biographies, but of film biographies full-stop'

Empire

'This is an attractive and persuasive view of an ocean-sized talent for which there is still no finished map. One can only hope that Callow continues the voyage'

Times Literary Supplement

'The facts of this remarkable period [in Welles' career] are well established, but *Hello Americans* offers a novel lens through which to view them afresh'

Sight and Sound

'Almost every page throws up nuggets of interest . . . This is a rich, meaty and ultimately rewarding banquet'

Scotsman

'Admirably level-headed'

New Statesman

'A universal story of hubris, wasted talent, and celebrity achieved at much too young an age'

Spectator

SIMON CALLOW

Orson Welles

Hello Americans

VINTAGE BOOKS
London

Published by Vintage 2007

2 4 6 8 10 9 7 5 3

First published in Great Britain in 2006 by Jonathan Cape

Vintage
Random House, 20 Vauxhall Bridge Road,
London SW1V 2SA

www.vintage-books.co.uk

Addresses for companies within The Random House Group
Limited can be found at: www.randomhouse.co.uk/offices.htm

The Random House Group Limited Reg. No. 954009

A CIP catalogue record for this book
is available from the British Library

ISBN 9780099462613

The Random House Group Limited supports The Forest Stewardship
Council® (FSC®), the leading international forest-certification organisation.
Our books carrying the FSC label are printed on FSC®-certified paper.
FSC is the only forest-certification scheme supported by the leading
environmental organisations, including Greenpeace. Our
paper procurement policy can be found at
www.randomhouse.co.uk/environment

Typeset in Bembo by Palimpsest Book Production Limited,
Grangemouth, Stirlingshire

Printed and bound in the UK by
Clays Ltd, St Ives plc

To Paula Laurence (1916–2005)

Helen of Troy to Welles's Faustus, and
this book's guardian angel.

Contents

PART THREE

WELLESCHMERZ

Illustrations

Picture credits

Preface

FROM THE mid-nineteen-fifties Orson Welles was working on a version of Cervantes's great novel *Don Quixote*, snatching days where he could, borrowing equipment, staging sequences, slowly assembling his footage. Young actors grew old, old actors died. And still he shot, quietly pursuing his private passion, never with a thought to completion, or, God forbid, to showing it to anyone. And over the years, whenever they came across him, people would ask Welles the question, 'When are you going to finish *Don Quixote*?' Finally, out of amused exasperation, he changed the title of his film to *When are you going to finish Don Quixote?* Sometimes, in the over ten years since the publication of *The Road to Xanadu*, it has occurred to me to call its successor *When are you going to deliver Volume Two?*

I hasten to disclaim any larger similarities between myself and Welles, but it has seemed to take an awfully long time to determine what would be the most useful way to continue the investigation into one of the most extraordinary figures of twentieth-century art begun in the earlier book. The problem is a simple one: *The Road to Xanadu* took 600 pages to cover Welles's first twenty-five years, culminating in the release of *Citizen Kane*. He was professionally active for only seven of those twenty-five years, and I devoted most of my pages to a close scrutiny of the legendary work that he did in the theatre and the radio of the nineteen-thirties – Unit 691, the Mercury Theatre, the Mercury Theatre on the Air: *Dr Faustus*, *Julius Caesar*, *The War of the Worlds* – ending with an account of the depressing period in limbo in Hollywood before the making of *Kane* and its subsequent delayed release. It was, I believe, the unusually detailed examination of the work and the circumstances that gave rise to it, as well as the attendant myths that surrounded everything to do with Welles, that gave the book its value. The patina of legend – placed there partly by Welles, partly by various interested parties who sought to prove their own points of view, and mostly by journalists happy to be handed colourful copy on a plate – had often obscured what was really remarkable about the man and his achievements, at the same time presenting a false image of his work in the various media in which he was engaged – theatre, radio, cinema. Only the closest scrutiny, it seemed to me, could restore the living reality, both of Welles and his world. The context was almost as important as the event. And that meant time and space; it meant length. My publisher was kind enough to see the point of this, as he showed by commissioning a two-volume biography.

In approaching the rest of Welles's life, I had no intention of reverting to the synoptic method inevitably adopted by the writers of most one-volume biographies (many of which, I hasten to say, are nonetheless full of exceptional interest and insight). But to write in the same sort of detail about the remaining forty-five years of Welles's life – during which time, as I said in *The Road to Xanadu*, he had become a one-man diaspora, hurling himself across the globe, exploring virtually every performance art known to man (he even staged a ballet, *The Lady in the Ice*), was a logistical impossibility. I spent some of the years between the publication of the first book and the one you have in your hands trying to devise cunning postmodern structures that would enable me, as I kept telling interested parties, to adopt a cinematic – perhaps even, I modestly suggested, a Wellesian – approach, offering first a panoramic wide-shot, giving an overview of a whole decade, say, and then suddenly swooping in for a close-up examination of a particular event or period. It all sounded very brilliant, but in the end I couldn't come up with a structure that actually made sense. Nor, in truth, did I want to. It seemed to me that the only way I could even attempt to do justice to the wonderful singularity of my subject was to focus ever more closely on the individual strands in the increasingly complex fabric of his life.

In particular, I was fascinated by the years between *Citizen Kane* and *Macbeth*, a period in which, even by his standards, Welles extended himself in a remarkable number of new directions with an intensity and almost a desperation that reveal him in an entirely unfamiliar light. Here the biographical enterprise was not to dispel myths, but to reconstruct a part of his life that has very nearly disappeared without trace, warranting references of only a few paragraphs here or there in most accounts. I was concerned to try to do justice to the political pursuits that so engaged him during the nineteen-forties, and to trace in some detail his evolving relations with Hollywood, including the nightmarish catastrophe of his

Brazilian film, *It's All True*. The difficulty remained, however, how to write at such exhaustive length and still encompass the rest of his life in a second and final volume. It seemed clear that what was needed was a separate volume which focused on these few but astonishingly abundant years. A very close examination indeed was possible: his life during this period is prodigiously well documented, to the degree that it can be determined with some precision exactly what he was doing every day of his life for nearly five years. As I studied the material, it became increasingly clear that it could go a long way to answering the most persistent question asked about Orson Welles: what went wrong after *Citizen Kane*?

I began to see that Welles's departure from his own country in 1947, for what was in effect an occasionally interrupted exile of a little over twenty years, was a critical break in his career, releasing him to develop into the sort of artist he essentially was. It also signalled the end of a period of intense engagement with the culture from which he had sprung. During the period from the premiere of *Citizen Kane* to the beginning of his extended European sojourn, he had continued to try to grapple unequally with Hollywood, but he also – passionately, persistently and with huge expenditure of time and money – came back to the question of what it was to be an American, assessing the results of what he called 'our American experiment'. He was not, of course, the only person doing this at the time. America's involvement in the war brought into sudden focus the matter of how it would deal with the rest of the world after victory; it also transformed the situation of the black population, who for the first time found that they had some bargaining power, which in turn compelled the white population to reconsider its own position. They were, to put it mildly, stirring times. But Welles, more than most of his contemporaries, seemed driven to find a satisfactory answer to the issue of how Americans were to live.

He did this directly in his speeches, in his radio commentaries and in his political and popular journalism. He did it, more subtly, in his films of the period, *The Magnificent Ambersons*, *Journey into Fear*, *The Stranger* and *The Lady from Shanghai*, each of which presents a problem in American life, and he did it in the unfinished *It's All True*, which seeks to redefine the parameters of being American. (As it happens, one of the original titles of *Citizen Kane* was *American*.) Finally, he did it in his wholehearted embrace of American popular culture, in the vaudevillian extravaganzas *The Mercury Wonder Show* and *Around the World*, and in his really very serious attempt to become a radio comedian in the mould of Jack Benny. In giving my study of these years the name of one of his radio programmes of the period, I am suggesting that his work of the time was an extended attempt to address his audience as fellow-citizens. Eventually, he gave up what seemed to him a doomed struggle to get America to listen to him. In a sense, the book might have been called *Goodbye, Americans*, which is certainly what he was saying in 1947; significantly, the film he left behind him was *Macbeth*, his first film not to have a single American character in it, or any American resonance.

The catalogue of work contained in the preceding paragraph is enough to give a glimpse of the almost bewildering diversity of Welles's output; many of these activities were pursued simultaneously. Virtually everything Welles ever did was done in the fullest glare of publicity, and he was ceaselessly and increasingly mercilessly judged by a relentless press, which from early on had his scent in its nostrils. Even during the eighteen months of this period in which he did not act or direct, he was rarely out of the newspapers. I have tried to show what was actually going on behind the image of Welles that the press was busy manufacturing, generally abetted by Welles himself. It is a period of his life strikingly characterised by bad luck, just as the period documented in *The Road to Xanadu* represented a phase of extraordinary and continuing good fortune. Of the earlier period, it may be said that Welles's temperament capitalised wonderfully on the good fortune he experienced; of the later, that the bad luck exposed his weaknesses. It is without apology that I write of Welles's weaknesses. There is a faction among the supporters of Welles – the Wellesolators – who will hear no criticism of their hero. They seem to identify with him, to project themselves onto him. The Welles they have created is a fearless independent, punished by the world for being too talented, too original, too visionary. He is cinema's sacrificial victim, too good to be allowed to flourish. If only Welles's sublime plans had not been viciously frustrated by the studio pygmies, they imply, the world would have been the better off by dozens of flawless masterpieces. They refuse to countenance any complicity on his part in what went wrong, and they are unable to see him for what he was – an individual of immense gifts, filled with contradictory and often self-defeating impulses, a man who failed to find a way to put his gifts to their best use, one who had very little talent for having the enormous talent he possessed.

Some of Welles's most fervent supporters are those who came

to know him in later life; the directors Peter Bogdanovich and Henry Jaglom and the cinematographer Gary Graver are among the most notable of these. To them, Welles was mellow, wry and wise, viewing the events of his life and career from a lofty position of irony, amused at the follies of the world. It is entirely understandable that, having fallen under the irresistible spell of this Orson Welles, they should wish to fight his corner, propagating his interpretation of what happened to him. But neither they nor he had troubled to look at the actual record, which is freely available to scrutiny in the Lilly Library of the University of Indiana in Bloomington and in a number of individual archives spread across the libraries of America. Perhaps the most revealing source of all is the RKO archive, wherein are to be found not only Welles's letters, telegrams and memoranda, but those of everyone else, both from the studio and from the Mercury offices, who was involved in the breakdown of Welles's Unit within RKO: executives, press representatives, production managers, writers, cameramen, secretaries, friends, enemies and those who crossed from one camp to the other. Particularly in the case of Welles's great lost film, *It's All True*, the record amounts to an account of almost Proustian detail, offering a picture of Welles at work and at play, inspired and indulgent, deeply sensitive and grossly indifferent, mature and infantile, admired and despised, which provokes both admiration and compassion for a man in the grip of a temperament that was often fundamentally at war with his gifts.

It is, above all, a very human record. In this, it will not please the other faction of Orsonolators, the army of theoretical academics who have moved in on him like locusts, seeing rich pickings in that very substantial body. For them he is a cornucopia, a gift from heaven; nothing that he did is less than profound from a phenomenological perspective. Whole conferences discuss his every filmed frame: their debates are polysemous, polyvalent, polymorphous, above all polysyllabic, although 'debate' is hardly the word for such one-sided activity. Fastidiously, they refuse to attribute value, to assess worth; or rather, they see equal value and equal worth everywhere, converting everything into their hermetic formulas. Welles would have found their activities incomprehensible and intolerable; he told Peter Bogdanovich that 'everyone under thirty-five has gone to film school and they've learned this terrible lingo. They don't think, just repeat these terrible little slogans.' That was in the early nineteen-sixties. He was lucky enough not to live to witness the crimes against intelligibility committed in his name. 'By enlarging the field of causal explanation beyond the studio career of Orson Welles (a sort of "zoom-out" and "rack focus" of historical procedure),' writes one prominent Welles scholar:

> I have tried to show how the impossibility of a single filmic representation can serve as a refractory surface against which a series of analogies, paradigmatic shifts, and disarticulations located within distinct yet convergent planes of historical actualisation come into view. It is in turn, across the strata of this unstable causal field (the discontinuities of which have been reconciled or reduced within the binary logic of the dominant supratext) that the reconstitution of the various ontogenetic stages of *It's All True* (planning, production, dispersion) can be sketched.

The author of this remarkable passage, which, as far as I am aware, has not yet been translated into English, is a serious researcher who no doubt has much to tell us about Orson Welles, but we will never know what it is. The same author, Catherine Benamou – who, it must be stressed, has read wider and deeper than anyone alive into the *It's All True* material – justifies Welles's fanciful claim to have appeared as an extra in Robert Flaherty's film *Man of Aran* during his Irish sojourn in 1931 with the remarkable phrase: 'what matters is the homage Welles rendered to Flaherty in this claim, not its "truth".' In the Lewis Carroll world of the structuralists, of course, there is no such thing as truth: there is merely 'truth'.

My view is different. It seems to me that there is a plain, if many-layered, truth to be told. Orson Welles was a real man, if an exceptional one, confronting real and recognisable problems, making real and very human mistakes with real consequences. He sought to make his way in a world that often failed to accommodate his temperament; for the most part he refused to accommodate the world. He therefore needed to make a world of his own, a context in which he could flourish. His personality, like that of most human beings, was complex and often contradictory, but, unlike most human beings, he pushed these contradictions to such extremes that it sometimes seems that he had no centre at all. It sometimes seemed that way to him, and he sought many antidotes to eliminate the sense of a vacuum at the core; the most frequently deployed of these antidotes was the most effective of all, more reliable than alcohol, food, sex or love: work. He never ceased to want to tell stories in ever newer ways. There is a widely held view that Welles was self-destructive. A recent writer has suggested that what he said about John Barrymore was in fact autobiographical: after the supreme performance Barrymore gave at the dress rehearsal of his first *Hamlet*, 'the rest of his life,' says Welles, 'was anti-climax':

> There wasn't anything left to do except go on imitating, as accurately as possible, that one great evening . . . the truth is that after that dress rehearsal, Jack began to fear that he couldn't do anything else as good again. I think he was afraid to find out for certain, so he set about destroying himself, as publicly and as entertainingly as possible . . . he used to tell me that he hated theatre. But he couldn't kid either one of us. We spent hundreds of hours together, planning the production of a dozen plays. And I began to guess that what he hated was the responsibility of his own genius. Jack wanted to keep it a secret from both of us.

To apply this to Welles is sheer romanticism. *Citizen Kane* is not perfect; Welles did not feel daunted by it. Unlike Barrymore, he was driven by a desire to transform the medium in which he worked, both in terms of its form and its content. His 'incomparable bravura personality', as Kenneth Tynan described it, was often a burden to him; it is no accident that amnesia features so strongly in his output. But at core he was an artist; the problem was to find the way in which he could be true to his own art. That search was to occupy him for the rest of his life, a never-ending quest to tell the stories he wanted to tell in the way he wanted to tell them. In doing so, he left an astonishing corpus of work, some of it successful, some not, but all of it vital. If you attempt a different genre with each venture, you will not always master it. *Citizen Kane* was *sui generis*, a form of which Welles was of course the undisputed and never successfully imitated master. In seeking new forms he was not avoiding responsibility to his own genius: he was trying to find out what precisely it was, and to fulfil it as best he could. This is, it seems to me, a tale of heroism, not of self-destruction, and it will occupy the third and final volume of this Life.

In this volume, as in the previous one, I have focused on why and how Welles made his films, and why they turned out the way they did. I have not attempted frame-by-frame analyses of the work, an enterprise which has been superbly undertaken elsewhere.

It remains for me to thank those whose unstinting generosity and input have so richly fed the present volume: Charles Higham, Richard France, James Naremore, Robert Fischer-Ettel, Kent Hägglund, René Hagenhauer, Alcides da Costa. I am deeply indebted, too, to the work of the Wellesian scholars: the endlessly perceptive Jonathan Rosenbaum, and the quite phenomenally industrious Bret Wood; a fuller list of individual acknowledgements will be found at the end of the book. During the fifteen years since I started work on Welles, so many of those who not merely helped but also befriended me have disappeared from our lives; I think especially of George Fanto, Welles's cameraman on *It's All True* (and *Othello*), and Dick Wilson, who was pretty well the first witness I cross-examined and whose generosity not only to me, but also to Welles's posterity in preserving the Mercury archive, is memorialised elsewhere in this volume. Beyond his great gifts as a film-maker, Welles was a phenomenon, a remarkable member of the human race, and I have been especially grateful for the testimony of those who made him more vivid as a man. I hope I have been able to do justice to what I have been told.

Simon Callow
London, 2005

For the paperback edition, I have incorporated a number of factual corrections furnished me by my friends and colleagues Kent Hägglund, Charles Higham, Miles Kreuger, Sam Leiter and François Thomas. My deep gratitude to each of these gentlemen for sharing the fruits of their long years of immersion in Welles's life and work; the precision and generosity of their contributions means that the present edition owes even more to their work than the first one did. One or two reviewers of the book also made useful suggestions which I have gratefully incorporated, though I was amused to note that many of them thought that the punning chapter titles were my own invention: it may be worth noting that they all derive from contemporary articles on Welles, who seemed to inspire journalists to uncommon heights of playfulness.

Simon Callow
London, 2007

Part One

TARZAN TRIUMPHS

CHAPTER ONE

Orson Ascendant

THE LOS Angeles premiere of *Citizen Kane* on 2 May 1941 was one of the greatest and most brilliant occasions Hollywood had ever mounted: a celebration of cinematic audacity, a slap in the face for William Randolph Hearst and his cohorts in the press and within the industry who had sought to suppress the film, and a very public vindication of RKO's controversial championship of Orson Welles. The film's not quite twenty-six-year-old director-writer-producer-star had, it seemed, confounded his critics and laid down a marker for what would surely be a spectacular career in motion pictures.

As it happens, Welles would never again know anything remotely like the premiere of *Citizen Kane*, nor ever again direct a film like it. Indeed, no film of his ever again had a premiere, even on the most modest scale. *Kane* proved to be the end of a chapter, not the beginning of one, though Welles would have been forgiven for not knowing so at the time. Just before the film's release there had been a black few months when it seemed that it might never be seen – might indeed be physically destroyed – a prospect that drove him back, filled with rage against Hollywood, to the theatre, where he staged the most radical play he ever directed, *Native Son*; and to radio, where he wrote, directed and performed the most politically provocative programme he ever produced, *His Honor the Mayor*. But in May 1941, he appeared poised to resume his self-appointed task of transforming the movie industry. The reviews for *Citizen Kane* had almost unanimously acclaimed him as the most original, the most intelligent, the most important film-maker of the day – perhaps of all time. Such big talk is always dangerous to the recipient, particularly when (as all too soon proved the case) the acclaim is not matched by box-office performance. But for the time being, as far as Welles knew, his situation could scarcely have been better; he and his Mercury unit within RKO were raring to go, smiled on by company president George J. Schaefer, who had, at a shaky moment in the company's fortunes, risked everything in backing

Kane against powerful and ruthless forces, and who now felt triumphantly vindicated.

The film's critical success was a much-needed boost for Schaefer, who was determined, against the advice of the hard-headed businessmen who had hired him in 1938, to make RKO Hollywood's artistic leader. With some imagination, he had contracted, albeit with notably less generous deals than Welles's, outstanding talents like Pare Lorentz, the sturdily original director of the documentary *The Plow that Broke the Plains*, and Jed Harris, Broadway's most admired (and most feared) director. From the start, Schaefer's artistically ambitious policy had surprised and alarmed his board, but he had convinced them of the efficacy of his business plan, founded on the establishment of independent units within the RKO fold. Schaefer's background was in sales, and sales is what RKO expected. At Paramount, he had driven his team, as Betty Lasky put it, 'like a Prussian riding master'; at United Artists, where he had been before his RKO appointment, he was known as 'The Tiger'.

In his dealings with distributors and the press over *Citizen Kane*, Schaefer had certainly justified that sobriquet, displaying the fierce tenacity of an animal protecting its young. In his personal dealings with Orson Welles, however, it was the reverse: he had become, to the astonishment of his colleagues, a doting parent. The tiger turned pussycat. His sponsorship of the twenty-six-year-old still known, more or less ironically, as the Boy Wonder had been a personal gamble, incurring many enmities and not a little ridicule. Welles as head of Mercury Productions dealt directly with Schaefer and was answerable only to him. From Welles's point of view, this relationship with an older man, like so many in Welles's early life, was of a curious intensity, emotional and tender: boyishly trusting, vulnerable, sometimes hot-headed on his part; protective, solicitous, occasionally strict on Schaefer's. This 'big, robust bulldog' of a man (Lasky's phrase; obviously he made a powerful, if zoologically complex, impact on his beholders) vied with Welles's former headmaster 'Skipper' Hill and his official guardian Dr Maurice Bernstein in absolute and very public devotion to him and his talent. 'Thank you Orson Welles!' read Schaefer's unprecedented personal message in the colour supplement of the *Hollywood Reporter* at the time of *Kane*'s release. 'Your triumph is one of the greatest accomplishments in motion picture history, and proof that America is still the land of opportunity, where there will always be room for those with dreams and the courage to bring them to reality.'

In the light of such unqualified and highly visible support, why would Welles, as he contemplated his next moves, not have expected absolute support from Schaefer in whatever he chose to do? And he was not wrong. What he misjudged was the strength of the older man's position.

Despite the noisy acclaim for *Citizen Kane*, Schaefer, in May 1941, was particularly vulnerable. Those he had personally appointed to crucial positions – the heads of programming and of studio – had failed to deliver the results he needed: their activities in 1939–40 left the company $1.25m in the red. In February of 1941, Schaefer had personally taken charge of the whole studio, a decision that led to widespread firings and walk-outs. 'I just had a hot tip,' quipped Garson Kanin, directing the current Ginger Rogers vehicle for the studio, 'that R is pulling out, leaving the company only the KO.' There were vigorously denied rumours that Joseph Kennedy, recently relieved of his controversial position as ambassador to Britain, might be called in to mount an investigation of the company's corporate structure, possibly even to take it over; maybe, it was suggested, he had an option to acquire a major slice of the company's stock. The independent production units – 'top-bracket specialists' – of which Welles's Mercury unit was one (and a very expensive one at that) were failing; while even critical successes like William Dieterle's *All That Money Can Buy* had done poor business. In April of 1941, while *Kane* was still in limbo, Schaefer had signed a deal with the most dynamic of the independent producers, Sam Goldwyn; the deal brought prestige, but was scarcely going to produce any financial windfalls. In renegotiating Welles's contract, Schaefer had offered him the same generous financial terms as before, but with one highly significant omission: Welles no longer had absolute approval of the final cut. He was also informally given to understand that budgets were to be very tight.

Later that summer, against this financial background, and shortly after *Kane*'s rip-roaring premiere, Schaefer unveiled a new team. It was a surprising one. As head of production, he appointed Joseph Breen, the fiercely Roman Catholic former director of the industry's morality watchdog, the so-called Hays Code Administration Office; while head of 'A' pictures was Sol Lesser, who will inevitably go down in history as producer of the *Tarzan* series rather than as the organiser of several valiant, if controversial, attempts at salvaging Sergei Mikhailovich Eisenstein's abandoned American masterpiece, *Que Viva Mexico!* In July, Breen gave his first press conference to announce the new programme. He made a point both of confirming Welles's importance to the company – 'the Wizard of RKO', Breen called him – and at the same time suggesting a new direction for his work: his new three-picture deal would include 'a Mexican picture' and another, unnamed, 'which will not follow the pattern of shocking Hollywood'. Finally, said Breen, there was the possibility of a film of Eric Ambler's highly successful bestseller *Journey into Fear*. Despite the ringing endorsement, it was a slightly foggy announcement, which failed to offer a satisfactory answer to the pressing question: whither Welles?

Welles and Schaefer both knew that the success of *Citizen Kane* had been a close-run thing. The quest to determine what to follow it with would be every bit as urgent and as full of anxiety as it had been in the desperate two years after Welles's arrival in Hollywood and his discovery in Herman Mankiewicz of an ideal collaborator. Both Welles and Schaefer were sharply aware that they needed to succeed *Kane* with something different: they were not going to follow 'the pattern of shocking Hollywood'. Both of them had been taken aback by the virulence of Hearst's response to the film that he insisted was his portrait. Not only had the studio bosses been threatened with exposure by Hearst's hit-woman, Louella Parsons, but so (far more dangerously from Schaefer's point of view) had majority shareholders of RKO. Parsons had threatened Nelson Rockefeller, art-loving head of Standard Oil, and an early and enthusiastic supporter of Schaefer's recruitment of Welles, with exposing supposed dirt on his father, John D. Rockefeller, Junior; David Sarnoff, head of RCA, a co-founder of RKO, had been similarly menaced. It had been an ugly and frightening experience, one that Welles was intent on not repeating. For all his radicalism, and his pleasure in cocking a snook at vested interests, Welles had no desire to destroy his future. Nor did he wish to be typecast as a controversialist. He was determined not to be confined to one persona, one genre, or one career. With the harrowing and health-wrecking period in limbo before the release of *Citizen Kane* behind him, his sense of illimitability had returned in full force. He was ready to reinvent himself.

The search for new subjects was in play, on all fronts. The next period of Welles's working life, from May 1941 to July 1942, and the termination of his contract with RKO, resembles one of his own films in the multiplicity of its narratives. There was never a moment during this time when he was not engaged, full-time, on at least three absolutely separate projects, to say nothing of innumerable extra-curricular activities. On a purely quantitative level, his productivity is almost impossible to grasp. Finding himself in command of substantial (if finite) resources, and driven by the need to compete with himself, the word 'genius' still echoing unendingly and tauntingly in his ears, Welles's personal dynamo, fuelled by a characteristic mixture of idealism and sheer raging appetite – greed, to put it less politely – generated waves of simultaneous activity whose breadth of address is surely without parallel in the annals of Hollywood. That the breadth should sometimes be at the expense of depth is scarcely surprising. Under his inspiration, and with the swaggering sense of having just pulled off the most audacious coup imaginable by the skin of their teeth, the high-spirited young men of the office of Mercury Productions started generating ideas for films with unstoppable energy: they were registering so many titles that by the end of the year Breen had delicately to enquire whether they really wanted them all, since RKO was only allowed to register a hundred a year.

Welles was an early sufferer from the condition that the Yugoslavian film-maker Dusan Makavejev has described as *projectitis*. His fertility in engendering ideas was astonishing. He was able to conceive an entire film within minutes; in the incubator of his mind, the germ of the idea rapidly grew to full-fledged maturity, demanding to be announced immediately. Once exposed to the light of common day, the project would, generally speaking, and in the nature of things, almost immediately expire. In 1940, Welles told the press that he was going to film the *Life of Christ*, though he modestly demurred from saying who would be playing the title role; in 1942, he proclaimed that he would be filming *Mein Kampf*. This time no inhibition prevented his claiming the part of Hitler. Of neither project, divine or diabolic, was another word ever heard. Some forty or so other properties were considered, encompassing the peaks of world literature, from Balzac to Mark Twain, and all, for one reason or another, discarded.

In May of 1941, he entertained an idea of some promise. Mercury registered a brace of titles, *The Life of Desiré Landru* and *Bluebeard*, which related to the same idea. Dick Wilson, Mercury's manager, had read some articles about the notorious serial wife-killer, and enthused Welles with the subject; Welles conceived the remarkable notion that Charlie Chaplin would be ideally suited for the part of the murderer (a bold and, as it turned out, very shrewd idea). Meeting Chaplin by chance at supper in Hollywood, Welles had proposed that he should write and direct a film in which the great comedian would play the part of Landru. He had a brilliant title: *The Lady Killer*. Chaplin was interested, but on reflection decided that he preferred to direct and write the film himself, as was his wont; he had, after all, more or less invented the category of actor-writer-director-producer of which Welles was the newest example. He proceeded with due propriety, being very careful about matters of copyright, having recently had his fingers burnt in an ugly dispute. A document was accordingly drawn up in July in which Welles stated: 'I hereby sell, assign and transfer to you my original story of Henri Desiré Landru, conceived by me originally for you, and also my original title for the subject . . . for the sum of $5,000 which you agree to pay me concurrently with the signing of this agreement. You shall have full and complete rights in and to the idea and may use the same without limitation or restriction.' The agreement also sought to involve Welles artistically in the film:

> I agree that at such reasonable times as you may request, I will read and criticise such scripts as may be prepared by you or for you based upon said idea or referring thereto; provided I am able to do so without serious interference with my own work, and I will offer suggestions to you with reference to such scripts, which said suggestions and all ideas that may be embodied therein shall, of course, be included in the grant hereinabove provided for, without additional compensation. You agree that in any photoplay made by you based on said idea, I shall be given screen credit.

The agreed formula for this was typed out: the phrase 'Suggested by Orson Welles' was deleted and replaced with (handwritten) 'Based on an idea by Orson Welles'. (When Chaplin finally made the film, some six years later, this agreement would come back to haunt him: perhaps thinking that the $5,000 had been quite enough reward for a suggestion over supper, he omitted Welles's credit. Interestingly, Welles, veteran of so many authorship disputes, instructed his lawyers to sue unless the matter was rectified. It was.) But in May 1941, it was simply one of many ideas Welles threw out like so much spume as he sailed forth on the high seas of his imagination.

A further clutch of titles from that year were to have more concrete results: notably a project initially dubbed *Pan-America*, which rapidly metamorphosed into *It's All True*, a compendium movie in four sections whose titles were *Jam Session*, *Love Story*,

Bonito the Bull – also known as *My Friend Bonito* – and *The Captain's Chair*. The project was typical of Welles's desire to break away from the established format of movie-going. It also exemplifies his conviction that certain very interesting ideas, though lacking the potential for full-length features, are nevertheless well worth realising. Above all, though still very loose in conception, it expressed a central part of Welles's personal political philosophy: his insistence that there was more to American life than the narrow norms and gauzy escapism of white Anglo-Saxon existence as promoted by Hollywood. American life in its totality was what he wanted to address. His own inclination to the heterogeneous, his appetite for the unofficial, his desire to escape the bourgeois confines of his own class, all informed his desire to dramatise unseen America, North and South. Two of the original stories (*Bonito* and *The Captain's Chair*) were written by Robert Flaherty, the director-poet of *Nanook of the North* and *Man of Aran*, in which latter film Welles imaginatively claimed to have done some extra work as a fifteen-year-old during his boyhood sojourn in Ireland; the director was something of an idol of his. Flaherty's two stories are radically different. *Bonito* concerns bull-fighting, an abiding fascination of Welles's since his boyhood stay in Seville, and is set in Mexico; *The Captain's Chair*, which in Flaherty's story takes place in the Arctic, was to be relocated to Hudson Bay, so the two films would encompass the alpha and omega of America's experience of itself. *Love Story* by John Fante (author of a recently acclaimed novel, *Ask the Dust*) told of the courtship of his immigrant parents, a tale of love triumphant, in which the traditions of the lovers' country of origin – Italy – are awkwardly transposed into their new American life. (An important part of the premise for *It's All True* was embodied in its title. 'All the stories we do for Welles are supposed to be *true* stories,' wrote Fante. *Love Story*, as it happens, was not, but he persuaded his mother to sign a document for RKO saying that it was.) The final sequence, *Jam Session*, which before long became *The Story of Jazz*, was to follow jazz from its African roots to its central place in modern American music, asserting its origins in the real lives of the people who created it.

The project as a whole was, in fact, a perfect manifestation of the artistic ideals of the Popular Front, a loose grouping of radical but non-doctrinaire writers, actors, singers and directors, of which Welles was a prominent and growingly articulate (if non-aligned) supporter; he enthusiastically endorsed its radical social-democratic policies, 'forged around anti-fascism,' as its historian Michael

Denning says, 'anti-lynching, and the industrial unionism of the CIO [Congress of Industrial Organisations]'. Denning cites *Ballad for Americans* as sung by Paul Robeson as the anthem of the movement, its lyrics defining the nation as 'everybody who's nobody . . . Irish, Negro, Jewish, Italian, French and English, Spanish, Russian, Chinese, Polish, Scotch, Hungarian, Litvak, Swedish, Finnish, Canadian, Greek and Turk, and Czech and double Czech American'. Robeson's words celebrate the multifariousness of America; they include rather than narrow down. This ideology was precisely what Welles wanted to embody in *It's All True*.

It was instinctive for him to align himself with the underdog. Inspired by the example of his socially conscious mother, Beatrice – head of the Kenosha School Board and energetic cultural missionary – he had from childhood been imbued with the tenets of radical social action; while from his stage-door-Johnny father, Dick, who revelled in the louche company of variety artists, jazzmen, conjurors and chorus girls, he had acquired a taste for diversity in his human contacts. His political education proper had started in the mid-thirties with the left-wing playwright and poet Archibald MacLeish, when the very young Welles appeared in MacLeish's anti-capitalist play *Panic*; it continued with his passionate friendship with the Marxist composer Marc Blitzstein, whose frankly syndicalist musical *The Cradle Will Rock* Welles, then working with the Federal Theatre Project, had staged in defiance of a government prohibition, in the process losing his job. Although he was never tempted to join Earl Browder's Communist Party of America, he made common cause with it, introducing a New Masses concert, participating in the Workers' Bookshop Symposium and backing the American Student Union's Peace Ball; along with the radical academic F. O. Mathiessen and the innovative music producer John Hammond, he was on the high-profile Citizens' Committee against the deportation of the Australian longshoreman union activist, Harry Bridges. The dramatist Clare Luce Booth (author of *The Women* and wife of Henry Luce, proprietor of *Time* magazine) had brusquely dismissed Welles as 'part of the whole Broadway–Browder axis'. Her husband's support of *Citizen Kane* – in some ways a quintessential Popular Front movie – had more to do with his desire to lock horns with a rival press baron than to endorse either the film or Welles's political position. As Welles became increasingly outspoken, he would have occasion to attack Luce's own political platform with some vigour, but that time was not yet.

Nor was it time for *It's All True* in the form in which it was first conceived. Like every other Mercury project of the period, it was in constant evolution, changing in response to the needs of the studio and to the degree of Welles's personal involvement in it, jostling for attention with all the other projects. Mercury was less a unit within RKO than a laboratory in a state of ceaseless experimentation, a heuristic enterprise in quest of what might prove ultimately to be interesting, rather than an organisation narrowly dedicated to the achievement of a particular result. Writers were attached, researchers commissioned, composers hired. Welles had the autodidact's passion for accumulating information, and the prodigy's sense of unlimited possibilities. He saw himself as engaged on a mission. Radio and film, he said, were 'a modern form of education . . . to dramatise the art of imparting knowledge, so that people will listen to what I have to say politically'. He believed messianically in the importance of what he was doing, and had to an exceptional degree the ability to convince his collaborators of its importance, too. Mercury Productions was, they all felt, the workshop of the coming dispensation. He strode around his little empire, like a Pharaoh or a Caesar, a Rameses or a Napoleon, building a new world of the imagination, supervising, inspiring, cajoling, charming, berating. His brain was working at full stretch during every waking moment, and the hours of sleep were few, for him or for his collaborators.

In the summer of 1941, while *It's All True* was in the forefront of Welles's mind, Duke Ellington, involved in the triumphant run of *Jump for Joy* in Los Angeles, suddenly found himself swept up in the Orsonic tornado. A message came to him backstage: he was to meet Welles at RKO the following morning at nine. Ellington was on time ('I've never been anywhere else on time in my life'); Welles was an hour late. When he finally arrived, not allowing the by now thoroughly grumpy musician to draw breath, he plunged straight into an account of his impressions of Ellington's show 'from the first curtain to the last curtain, blow by blow, every number, every sketch, all of it coming out of his mind without notes – and he saw it once! It was both a review and a mass of suggestions. It was the most impressive display of mental power I've ever experienced – just pure genius.' There and then, Welles asked him to do *The Story of Jazz*. 'I want it to be written by Duke Ellington and Orson Welles,' he said, 'directed by Duke Ellington and Orson Welles, music written by Duke Ellington.' Ellington's reminiscence ends with a detail that gives an idea of the lordly munificence that would contribute to Welles's undoing. 'You're on salary at a thousand dollars a week,' he told Ellington, 'and if you don't take it, you're a sucker!' 'I accept,' Ellington replied. 'In the end,' he confesses in his autobiography, 'I took $12,500, for which I wrote a total of 28 bars.'

Clearly *It's All True*, still in the impulsive stage, was unlikely to be the next Mercury production, not in its entirety, at any rate. One section of the compendium, however, stood on its own: Flaherty's story of a boy who raises a bull for fighting, a simple tale that Welles in his narration was to place in an epic context: 'This is the story of a little boy who loved a great fighting bull,' the screenplay reads. 'The boy's name was Chico and the bull's name was Bonito. As you probably know, a bullfight is not a contest between men and beast: it is a predestined tragedy. All bulls die, as all men die. Some men meet death ignominiously, while others die gloriously in battle. Like all brave bulls, Bonito was destined to fight and die in the *Corrida de Toros*.' The final words of the script (by John Fante and Norman Foster) are very much in the spirit of the ebullient Mercury team: 'The authors hope that somewhere in Mexico there can be found a bull so intelligent, so literate, and so movie-struck that he will perform the miracles that are required of Bonito in this script.' It was intended that the film should be shot with Flaherty-like simplicity of means; Gregg Toland, Welles's closest mentor and inspired collaborator on *Citizen Kane*, was to be cinematographer. But then Toland enlisted in the Navy's photography unit, and Welles impulsively decided to shoot two other films, the already tentatively announced *Journey into Fear* and – something new – a remake of Booth Tarkington's *The Magnificent Ambersons*, first filmed in 1924 under the suggestive title of *Pampered Youth*.

Bonito was not shelved, however. Somewhat surprisingly, in view of the importance to him of his actor-writer-director-producer credit on *Kane*, Welles informally assigned the direction of *Bonito the Bull* (under his supervision) to the co-author of the screenplay, Norman Foster. He and Fante had both signed up earlier that year (for $300 a week) as part of the writing team for *It's All True*. Foster had written for Welles before, contributing to the Mercury Theatre on the Air. He was a well-established journeyman film director, notably on the *Charlie Chan* and *Mr Moto* series, of which he had directed six each; some of his work rose above routine: *Thank You, Mr Moto* of 1938, as James Naremore points out, has considerable visual distinction of an unmistakably *noir* character. When he joined the Mercury group at RKO, he had just branched out, ethnically speaking, with *Viva Cisco Kid* and *Ride, Kelly, Ride*; in addition, he had the considerable advantage of speaking fluent Spanish. It wasn't Foster's track record, however, that got him the job; Welles simply took to him, which was the essential condition for being part of the team, more important even than having talent. Welles's relationship with his collaborators was not unlike that of Bertolt Brecht with his. Like Brecht, he had no difficulty in sharing the artistic – and indeed the practical – work of creating a film (or mounting a radio show or putting on a play in the theatre). Also like Brecht, he was less enthusiastic about sharing the credit, but both men had the attitude of Renaissance painters; they maintained studios, in the painterly sense, where everyone was expected to pitch in, though there was no question of whose studio it was. In Welles's case, he was also perfectly happy to help out with other people's jobs, even with menial tasks – painting a wall or making a prop. And he was ready to thrash out a problem on the floor. He had no preciousness or anxiety as an artist, possessing immense innate authority – as he had from childhood, when he ruthlessly disciplined his troupe of fourteen-year-old thespians at the Todd School in Woodstock, Illinois. He was wholly secure in his own work.

There would certainly have to be some considerable division of labour of the workload he was lining up. RKO had now bought the rights in *Journey into Fear* for Welles from the writer Ben Hecht, who owned them. Hecht had already done a screenplay from the book; there had been fierce competition for the rights, with both Gary Cooper and Charles Boyer eager to play the central character. The plan now was for Welles to act in the film, opposite Michele Morgan, with the Englishman Robert Stevenson, fresh from *Tom Brown's Schooldays*, as director. This project was quite separate from the Mercury unit: David Hempstead was originally slated as producer. An internal studio deal was struck between Mercury and RKO that linked *Journey into Fear* with *The Magnificent Ambersons*: Welles would receive $20,000 (payable at $2,000 per week, a very substantial sum in 1941) to direct the latter, while his acting performance in the former would be given gratis. But by July, Welles had clearly become personally enamoured of the project. He no longer wanted to work on Hecht's version, he informed Joe Breen, and was working with the writers on the new version they had made for Hempstead, since 'my own conception of the picture is so thoroughly developed'. It thus became a Mercury project.

It is scarcely surprising that Welles should have been so engaged by Eric Ambler's dark, laconic thriller. The genre was among his favourites – his more or less undiscriminating consumption of thrillers was remarked on by everyone who knew him – and would continue to fascinate him to the very end. Quite apart from his pleasure in forceful narrative, he was strongly drawn to the characteristic Ambler hero: the sophisticated innocent, a type to which Welles could warmly relate. In the case of *Journey into Fear* the hero was engineer Winston Graham, trying to ply his trade during the period of the phoney war, finding himself caught up in a disturbing web of largely incomprehensible intrigue. A sense of bewilderment, of the uselessness of intelligence and talent in a ruthlessly brutal universe, is common to many of Welles's heroes; even Charles Foster Kane can scarcely comprehend how his life became what it did. The parallels with Welles's own life hardly need to be underlined.

His fascination with the genre led him to attempt to turn two other such novels into films during his time at RKO: before *Kane*, Nicholas Blake's *The Smiler with a Knife* and, immediately after it, *The Way to Santiago*, by Arthur Calder-Marshall. This latter project, sometimes known as *Mexican Melodrama*, is one of the most remarkable and experimental of Welles's unfilmed projects; the screenplay (radically transformed from the novel that is its source) expresses with startling vividness the sense of the central character's Pirandellian dislocation. In the script he is simply identified as ME, explicitly underlining the overlap with Welles himself. 'MY FACE FILLS THE FRAME,' the script opens. And then ME says: 'I don't know who I am.' Soon enough this central character is given – wrongly, of course – another identity, that of Lindsey Keller, a British pro-fascist broadcaster known as 'Mr England'. The script continues: 'the camera pulls back to reveal ME seated in the middle of a big bare white-washed room, dressed only in a sheet. I am surrounded by a lot of men, representatives of nearly every race. With a sudden rush of sound, they begin firing questions at me. "Where did you come from? When did you arrive? Who attacked you? How did you get into the country?"' A reporter – in some versions of the screenplay a Mexican, Gonzales; in others an American, Johnson – takes the amnesiac ME/Keller/Mr England to a party given by the President. The President is killed, and ME is swept up in a sequence of events in which he discovers that he is not Mr England, after all, though he has just made an anti-fascist broadcast as Mr England in an attempt to expiate his past errors. Finally, at the climax of a dense farrago of events, he is reunited with his girl Elena, after this suggestive exchange:

ME:
Hello, Elena! – Hello! I'm not Mr England!
ELENA:
What? . . .
ME:
I'm somebody else!
ELENA:
I don't understand!
ME:
I don't either, but I'm somebody else! I'm somebody else!

As soon as ME reaches her arms, 'I am motionless. Elena turns to Roberto. A beautiful little smile on her face. "ROBERTO: What's wrong with him? ELENA: He's asleep." CLOSE SHOT: Elena's tender expression as she puts her face next to mine. FADE OUT.' The problem of identity is resolved by sleep.

Bret Wood has acutely observed that the question of identity is Welles's great theme. Ambler's *Journey into Fear* contains no such explicit ontological explorations, but its hero is certainly baffled, from first almost to last. The world in which he finds himself is exotically menacing, the political atmosphere poisoned by covert (and sometimes overt) fascism. Though the work of an Englishman, the novel falls precisely into the category of Popular Front art, as Michael Denning points out, quoting Ambler's own words: 'I took the right-wing and often downright fascist thriller and turned it upside down' – turning the heroes into left-wing and often Popular Front figures. In the novel, the excitable socialist, Mathis, expresses himself unequivocally: obsessed with an incident in the First World War, in which an iron foundry was seized by the Germans but never bombed by the French because the owner would not allow it, he cries, 'We were fighting for our lives, but our lives were less important than the property of Monsieur de Wendel . . . it is not for us to ask questions. And why? Because the only people who can give us the answers are the bankers and the politicians at the top, the boys with the shares in the big factories who make the war materials. They will not give us answers. Why? Because they know that if the soldiers of France and England knew those answers, they would not fight.' Later he tells his wife: 'Monsieur [Graham] and I have made a plot to blow up the Bank of France, seize the chamber of deputies, shoot the two hundred families and set up a communist government.' 'You should not say such things,' she protests, 'even for a joke.' 'A joke!' He scowls malevolently. 'You will see if it is a joke or not when we drag these capitalist reptiles from their great houses and cut them to pieces with machine guns.' Even more tellingly, Josette, the dancer with whom Graham almost has an affair, defends the Turks: 'Most armies commit what are called atrocities at some time or another. They usually call them reprisals.' 'Including the British army, perhaps?' enquires Graham, stiffly. 'You would have to ask an Indian or an Afrikaner about that. But every country has its madmen.'

Deeper and darker than these explicitly made political points, Ambler conveys an undercurrent of romantic pessimism about society. Josette quotes the philosophy of her brooding husband, José: 'José would say that you are as much a murderer as Landru or Weidmann and that it is just that fortune has not made it necessary for you to murder anyone. Someone once told him that there was a German proverb that says that man is just an ape in velvet. He likes to repeat that.' At a later juncture, Graham is studying the lifeboat instructions in his cabin. They start: *In case of danger*. 'In case!' he thinks:

> But you couldn't get away from danger! It was all about you, all the time. You could live in ignorance of it for years. You might go to the end of your days believing that it couldn't happen to *you*, that death could only come to you with the sweet reason of disease or 'an act of God', but it was there just the same, waiting to make nonsense of all your comfortable ideas about your relations with time and chance – ready to remind you – in case you had forgotten – that civilisation was a word and that you still lived in the jungle.

From *Bright Lucifer*, written when he was seventeen, through the sensational Harlem *Macbeth* to the even more provocative *War of the Worlds*, Welles had sought to express the fragility of civilisation and the darkness within us all; he was no stranger to the universe of *Journey into Fear*. Welles had a taste for pulp fiction, but he was not indulging it in choosing to film this particular book: his aim was to combine the stylishness of the genre with his own anti-fascist agenda, creating a vehicle at once for actors and for ideas, for which Ambler's novel was ideal.

So it was very much a Mercury project, although at the beginning David Hempstead was still slated as producer and Michele Morgan was still wanted for the leading female role. The director was to be the distinguished former playwright and character actor,

Thomas Mitchell (shortly to become immortal as Uncle Billy in Capra's *It's a Wonderful Life*). This erratic notion – Mitchell had never directed a film – came and went very quickly; Welles would, of course, direct. The great Karl Struss, fresh from shooting *The Great Dictator* for Chaplin, and laden with honour from his years with Griffith and DeMille, was appointed cinematographer. For the rest, it was to be the old team reunited, certainly as far as the acting company was concerned: veterans of Welles's stage, screen and radio companies. Joseph Cotten was to play Graham, Ruth Warrick his wife, Welles himself would be the charming and sinister Colonel Haki. Everett Sloane, Eustace Wyatt, Edgar Barrier and other stalwarts were to take various more or less sinister parts, while the crucial role of the killer, Petre Banat, was to be played by the new business manager of Mercury Productions, Jack Moss. Moss was a sometime conjuror whose appointment as manager had been characteristically quixotic – Welles had once appeared on the same variety bill as Moss and had been impressed, not only by his act, but also by his personal suavity and elegance. Who better than a magician, he must have thought, to deal with the tiresome and mundane facts of money and management? And who better to relieve Welles himself of the tedium of dealing with the studio apparatchiks? Welles would be able to perform his favourite trick – vanishing – under a smokescreen provided by his fellow-thaumaturge.

As well as Moss, in casting the film, the Mercury office was plundered for the press officer Herb Drake (former drama critic of the *New York Herald Tribune*), who appears as a steward, as does Robert Meltzer, writer and researcher. This habit of casting anybody who happened to be around was typical of Welles, and became more and more common in his movies. It indicates an interestingly cavalier attitude to acting on film. If the face fitted and the quality was right, then he saw no objection. This is wholly consonant with his fascination with texture; a particular face or voice or silhouette is simply another strand in that texture. It does not conduce to depth of expression or complex interchanges, but it can lead to strikingly vivid and effective results. As if to contribute to the gleeful sense of free-for-all, Jo Cotten, with no experience whatever of writing, except for a few youthful drama reviews (good training, no doubt, for playing Jedediah Leland in *Citizen Kane*), was now appointed screenwriter, the attached writers having walked out because 'an unnamed picture has taken precedence'.

CHAPTER TWO

Pampered Youth

THE UNNAMED picture for which *Journey into Fear* was put on hold was *The Magnificent Ambersons*, a project that had suddenly materialised out of thin air – almost literally: Welles's 1939 radio version of Booth Tarkington's novel (transmitted when he was already under contract to RKO) had been one of the most striking of his Campbell Playhouse productions, and it was a recording of that performance that he played to George Schaefer, who duly gave him the go-ahead for the project. It may perhaps have been *The Magnificent Ambersons* to which Breen was making veiled reference in his press conference, when he spoke of a film that would not follow the pattern of shocking Hollywood – and indeed, there was nothing remotely contentious in Tarkington's epic of the decline of a Mid-Western family, unless its elegy for a vanished world and its criticism of the values promulgated by the rise of the auto-mobile could be taken for anti-capitalist subversion. (The RKO lawyers did shudder at the possibility that the car-manufacturing Morgans might be taken as a version of the Fords or the Chryslers, but they were overruled.) What is more surprising is, firstly, that the adrenalin-crazed young Welles should have wanted to engage with so sober and sombre a subject, and secondly, that he and Schaefer – or anyone else at RKO – should have thought it a suit-able film to make at a time when half the world was at war, with America poised between ardent isolationism and fervent anti-fascism. It did, however, perfectly fit into Welles's over-arching fascination with what it is to be an American, a question given some urgency by the war. America's values would have to be defended, either by isolation or by taking up arms.

The novel, written in 1918, had been an immediate bestseller on publication, confirming the Indiana-born Tarkington (already famous for *Monsieur Beaucaire* and *Seventeen*) as the Hoosier laureate, a serious analyst of American mores. It forms part of *Growth*, a non-continuous trilogy of chronicles of Midland family life. The book, a sort of Mid-Western *Forsyte Saga*, is a pessimistic elegy, depicting the destruction by industrialisation of the intricate fabric of the life of the upper middle classes, tracing through the decline of one family, the eponymous Ambersons, the growth of the unnamed Midland town in which the action takes place as it 'spreads and darkens into a city'. Like Lampedusa's *The Leopard*, it is a record of a doomed class, but in this case it is a class that has scarcely flourished at all. The novel has a curiously short sense of history, a deep nostalgia for a very recent past, and the saga of the Ambersons is largely passive. Major Amberson makes his fortune after the Civil War – we never learn how – but none of his offspring knows what to do with it; he himself makes a series of disastrous investments. His daughter Isabel quite casually, it seems, decides against marrying the spirited Eugene Morgan because he has drunkenly fallen into his bass viol while serenading her, and instead pledges herself to the unremarkable Wilbur Minafer: this is the mainspring of the plot. Having no passion for her husband, she idolises her son George; their only child, he is monstrously indulged and grows up loathed by the entire terrorised community, which ardently desires his comeuppance. He is given no boundaries to his behaviour, but equally has no sense of identity outside the rigid notions of the class that his family has so recently joined.

When, some years after his rejection by Isabel, the widowed Eugene turns up again, filled with plans for the development of his new automobile, George is dimly aware of the fact that he represents an entrepreneurial spirit that is inherently inimical to the caste interests of the Ambersons, but also that there is some unfinished emotional business with his mother. Meanwhile George himself has fallen blindly, hopelessly in love with Eugene's daughter, Lucy, who – though she never reveals it – has fallen equally deeply in love with him. Lucy knows at a profound level that George would not make a good husband for her, unequipped as he is to survive in the modern world; she constantly puts off his offer of marriage. When Wilbur, the father George has scarcely been aware of, dies, Eugene – now a highly successful industrialist – declares his love for Isabel and asks for her hand, which reduces George to incoherent rage; he forces her to refuse, taking her away from her only hope of happiness (to say nothing of his own, in the shape of Lucy), and embarking with her on unending pointless travels rather than submit to his rival. In effect George kills his mother by refusing to acknowledge that she is ill; ever after, he is racked by guilt. All this is paralleled by the desperate passion of Wilbur's sister Fanny for Eugene, which, denied expression, turns to mischief.

After Isabel's death, the flimsy financial foundations of the Ambersons give way completely and George is finally forced to become a realist; he and Fanny take rooms in a boarding house while he works as an explosives supervisor. The town, meanwhile, has changed beyond recognition:

> the town was growing and changing as it had never grown and changed before. It was heaving up in the middle incredibly; it was spreading incredibly; and as it heaved and spread, it befouled itself and darkened its sky. Its boundary was mere shapelessness on the run . . . a new Midlander – in fact a new American – was dimly beginning to emerge . . . they were optimists – optimists to the point of belligerence – their motto being 'Boost! Don't knock.' And they were hustlers, believing in hustling and in honesty because both paid. They loved their city and they worked for it with a plutonic energy which was always ardently vocal . . .

The book takes off into overt symbolism when George is knocked down in the street by the very thing that has blighted his life: an automobile hits him, running over him as he stands idly dreaming of Lucy in a carriage. In his hospital bed, he is obliged by circumstances to think for the first time about life; he finally understands that his determination to preserve the rigid patterns of his class is pointless, coming to the conclusion – 'somehow . . . vaguely but truly' – that 'nothing stays or holds where there is growth'. His generosity and sense of responsibility towards his aunt, which have never faltered, only become stronger. The book's final resolution is effected by a somewhat unsatisfactory contrivance, a gauche mystical intervention, *deus ex machina*, wherein Eugene, who has sworn never to speak to George again, visits a clairvoyant, whose spirit guide, Lopa, tells him that Isabel wants him to visit the boy; he does, and finds Lucy at the bedside. Reconciliation all round.

This was the wide-ranging novel that Welles had squeezed into sixty minutes of radio in 1939, and it was a recording of this that he played to George Schaefer in the spring of 1941, when they were urgently looking for Welles Project Two. Welles later claimed that Schaefer fell asleep while listening to the discs of the radio transmission and, hearing the show today, his slumber is pardonable. Not that the show, and particularly Welles's performance as George, is anything less than deeply felt; on the contrary, it is the barely contained emotionalism that becomes monotonous, especially in the context of the dying fall of the Ambersons' inexorably dwindling fortunes.

In his introduction to the programme, Welles calls the novel 'the truest, cruellest picture of the growth of the Middle West and the liveliest portrait of the people who made it grow', but the cruelty and the liveliness are both subdued in this radio version, with distinctly stagy and rather stiff performances. An elderly, quavery Walter Huston plays Eugene; his wife Nan Sunderland plays Isabel on a single note of gracious pathos. For Welles's own performance as George he uses his uncomfortable upper register, and seems constantly on the brink of hysteria. It is not good acting, but it seems to be strongly felt; the scene with his mother is distinctly overwrought, unlike anything Welles ever did, on film or on radio – almost out of control. The result is alienating rather than affecting. It is as if the actor's identification with the brattish, arrogant boy whose comeuppance forms the narrative spine of the novel is too strong; he is unable to present the character. Welles's great skills as an actor lay in the realm of the rhetorical, in which the actor is absolutely in command of himself and his material; when he touches the personal, which he does rarely, he seems to lose his judgement, and so it is here. His narration, except for the opening, is uncharacteristically leaden, too, intending to be elegiac, but instead becoming simply morbid; the adaptation omits the character of Aunt Fanny, which might have varied the emotional palette a little. The great success of the production is, as so often with Welles, in the texture, the virtuoso use of evocative sounds, the integration with the music, in which Bernard Herrmann uses some of Welles's favourite waltzes by Waldteufel with impeccable timing and ingenuity. The sudden bustle of group scenes is exhilarating; the opening narrated sequence (using almost exactly the same text as subsequently appears in the film) is immensely engaging and elegant. But, in the end, even these elements are overcome by the sickly, turgid tone, as of a grief imperfectly discharged.

It is clear from the radio production that the subject was perilously close to Welles's own heart and experience. The death scenes, in particular, are dwelt on with positively Victorian emotionalism; mortality was an uneffaceable component of Welles's mental landscape, the deaths of both his parents – and especially, perhaps, that of his mother, when he was nine – branded on his consciousness. The sense of guilt and shame that so informed his early manhood no doubt contributed to his obvious identification with the character of the intolerably arrogant and selfish (if bewildered) George Amberson Minafer. There were other points of contact, too. In his imagination, the Welleses of Kenosha had been a family like the

Ambersons; and indeed, the Gottfredsons, his paternal grandparents, had known a certain magnificence in their big, ugly mansion in Kenosha, though their wealth was scarcely on the scale of Tarkington's heroes. Welles always claimed that his father had been Tarkington's best friend, and that the character of Eugene Morgan ('a mechanical genius', according to the novel) was based on the happy-go-lucky, modestly inventive secretary of Badger Brass, but no evidence for this claim exists. Nor does it matter, one way or the other; what is significant is that Welles believed it to be true, and wanted it to be true, and his conception of Gene Morgan is certainly an idealised version of his father. The general tone of lament for a vanished Golden Age – for what he calls 'the Merrie Englands' – was from an early age central to Welles's inner life; this feeling too was associated in his imagination with his father and with what Welles fondly recollected as a semi-feudal existence in the tiny Illinois retreat of Grand Detour, where Richard Welles for a while ran a hotel. The pull of the past was a mighty one for Welles, which partly accounts for the immense force of his thrust towards the future.

Robert L. Carringer, in a celebrated, if somewhat tortuous, essay 'Oedipus in Indianapolis', makes an explicit autobiographical connection between Welles himself and George Amberson Minafer. There are certain trivial similarities that are quite striking – George, like Welles himself as a boy, is known as Georgie; at school, as with Welles at Todd, 'they did not like him – he was too arrogant for that – but he kept them in such a state of emotion that they thought more about him than they did about all of the other [ten] pupils'. George has an overwhelmingly intense relationship with his mother, as did Welles, and endures a heart-rending death-bed scene, as did Welles. But all resemblances stop there. Beatrice was tough and demanding, refusing to indulge her son, to the point of watching with equanimity as he climbed out onto the ledge of a fifth-floor window to throw himself off rather than take his piano lessons. All Welles's memories of her indicate a severity in her demeanour and an expectation, indeed an insistence, on her part that Welles would distinguish himself in her eyes. This is the precise opposite of the infinitely idolising indulgence, at whatever cost to herself, her health or her happiness, that the novel's Isabel Minafer so doggedly displays towards her only son. No doubt there may have been some element of Oedipal outrage for the young Orson when Beatrice Welles began her affair with Maurice Bernstein, just as George Minafer reacts so traumatically when Eugene Morgan begins to court Isabel; but in Welles's case it soon modified into something considerably more complex, as Dick Welles slipped away into alcoholic absence and Bernstein became the boy's de facto parent.

Carringer insists that Welles's affectionate accounts of his father – 'Dickensian caricatures' – mask violent hostility towards him, and that what drove Welles was 'a furious need to prove himself in the eyes of a man who was no longer there'. This is a surprising analysis. In an important sense Dick Welles, like Wilbur Minafer, was no longer there long before his actual death; as with Wilbur, it was his death that gave him real significance. Welles was certainly deeply guilty about Dick Welles's subsequent lonely, booze-sodden death after he had abandoned him at the behest of Skipper Hill and Dr Bernstein, but he hadn't disappointed his father: his father had disappointed him, and Welles had rejected him in favour of Hill. In the short autobiographical sketch entitled 'My Father Wore Spats' published in *Vogue* towards the end of his life, Welles memorably states without further elaboration that he killed his father. Carringer dismisses this statement as melodramatic. Obviously it is not literally true, but it seems a clear indication that guilt (not revenge) was the fuel of Welles's psyche, although it is certainly possible that the guilt bred a degree of resentment. The stories that he told about his father, and his conception of Eugene Morgan, amount to an idealised reinvention of a man who, good-humoured to a fault, had frittered away on booze and girls the large sum of money that had come to him by a combination of solid clerkship and good luck. (Interestingly enough, Dick Welles's modest contribution to the progress of engineering science had been the development of a headlight, and in Tarkington's novel, it is as a result of being unwisely invested in a company manufacturing headlights that the last dribble of the Ambersons' fortune dries up.)

Carringer also makes great play of the parallels to *Hamlet* in the central relationship of the novel, and marvels at the fact that Welles never took the central role in that play (though he had played both the Ghost and Claudius when he was, respectively, sixteen and seventeen, to Micheál macLiammóir's Prince). Although Welles certainly airily mentioned that he should have left Hollywood after *Citizen Kane* and played Hamlet on Broadway, this can be nothing but shorthand for saying that he should have pursued a serious career as a classical stage actor. Of all great Shakespearean roles, Hamlet is the least suited to his particular gifts, physical and temperamental. The character's mercurial thought processes, his indecisiveness and vulnerability, his neurotic sensibility, and above all his restless self-questioning, would have been very elusive for Welles, a natural

King actor, as he said of himself, not a Prince actor at all. It is true that Tarkington draws attention to an aspect of Hamlet in the character of George Amberson Minafer; he has him, indeed, consciously – self-consciously – quoting the play. But his point is not that George identifies with Hamlet (as well he might), but that there is an element in his behaviour that is play-acted. After his first confrontation with his mother, he puts on his long black dressing-gown. He glimpses himself in the mirror. 'Happening to catch sight in his pier glass of the picturesque and medieval figure thus presented, he paused to regard it; and something profoundly theatrical in his nature came to the surface. His lips moved; he whispered, half-aloud, some famous fragments: "'Tis not alone my inky cloak, good mother,/Nor customary suits of solemn black" . . . no less like Hamlet did he feel and look as he sat gauntly at the dinner table with Fanny to partake of a meal throughout which neither spoke.' The 'something profoundly theatrical in his nature' is a crucial insight into George's behaviour: he is enacting a role – the role of a gentleman, as he understands it – as a purely cerebral imperative, in defence of a code that only he seems to recognise. Earlier, he has spoken of the importance of 'being' over 'doing'; he sees himself as a kind of totem of his tribe, the living embodiment of its values. In so doing he cuts himself off from everything that sustains human life: love, work, the future. This, more than any centrally unresolved Sophoclean or Shakespearean conflict, is at the heart of George's profoundly negative journey through life, until comeuppance teaches him sanity.

It is worth dwelling on these matters, because *The Magnificent Ambersons* is a book that mattered greatly to Welles at many levels. The film that he made from it is a problem film, perhaps for that very reason, and Carringer is absolutely right to say that this is by no means only as a result of what the studio did to it before it was released. It is a measure of Welles's complexity both as man and artist that he should decide not only to take on such charged and difficult material at such a critical moment in his own career, but simultaneously to work full out on two other films as different from it as can reasonably be imagined: a witty and radical political thriller and a wildly ambitious pan-American compendium film. Perhaps to focus on *The Magnificent Ambersons* to the exclusion of anything else would have been simply too disturbing, too painful. All of which may well explain why he chose not to appear in the film, although he liked to say that it was simply because he was too fat. Of equal significance, he knew that he would be speaking the narration, which would form such an important part of the film's effect;

and George Minafer could scarcely be the narrator. In fact, for George he cast an actor as different from himself as could be imagined, Tim Holt, noted for his appearances in cowboy films. Welles was certainly familiar with the actor's work in at least one film, John Ford's *Stagecoach*, which had been his celluloid bible in learning the rudiments of his craft as a film-maker; he claimed to have watched it more than a hundred times. He may also have seen him playing a spoiled rich boy in Gregory La Cava's *Fifth Avenue Girl* of the same year. There is no question that Holt is the actor Welles wanted for the part: he was booked as soon as the project was given a start date; none of the Mercury regulars was even considered. Welles told Peter Bogdanovich that Holt was 'extraordinary . . . one of the most interesting actors that's ever been in American movies, and he *decided* to be just a cowboy actor', which is a most generous view of the talents of a serviceable actor, the apogee of whose career was his appearance as Humphrey Bogart's dogged, conscientious sidekick partner in John Huston's *The Treasure of the Sierra Madre* in 1948. Disappointed by his experience of acting (perhaps understandably: his last film was *The Monster that Changed the World*), Holt retired from the profession at the age of forty until making an ill-judged comeback in *This Stuff'll Killya*. But Welles clearly felt that he was the embodiment of his conception of George Minafer.

It is doubtful whether Tarkington would have recognised him as such. At all times – even after his fall – George is described in terms of his exceptional elegance and nobility of bearing. 'George's imperious good looks were altogether manly, yet approached actual beauty as closely as a boy's good looks should dare.' He is 'the magnificent youth', his manners *de haut en bas*. When he comes home from university, 'it was as if M. le Duc had returned from the gay life of the capital to show himself for a week among the loyal peasants belonging to the old château, and their quaint habits and costumes afforded him mild amusement'. At the celebrated ball in the Ambersons' mansion, 'it is to be doubted if anybody felt more illustrious or more negligently grand than George Amberson Minafer felt at this party'.

There is nothing negligent, grand or magnificent about Tim Holt's George: he is stocky, plebeian in manner, sulky and impetuous. In the Arthur William Brown illustrations to the original edition (which, as it happens, the artist sent to Welles during the preparations for the film), George appears almost as a young Basil Rathbone, soigné, unsmiling, impeccably elegant. This is not a quibble: in the novel, his appearance expresses everything that he stands for, his features frozen in the attitudes of his class. Even in the boarding house, when he and Fanny have to scrabble for their very subsistence, he insists on dressing for dinner. Tim Holt could never play this character, even if he were more versatile – and he was not versatile. He was essentially a one-performance actor, a performance with which Welles was very familiar. This must have been the way he wanted George portrayed. Perhaps he thought that a more patrician performance would have alienated the audience; or perhaps he thought that expressing the baffled, emotionally strangled soul of George Amberson Minafer was more important than realising his external characteristics. Either way, the whole sense of the story is changed by this decision: this is the point at which casting becomes narrative. At the centre of Welles's *The Magnificent Ambersons* is a pettish lout; at the centre of Tarkington's is a gilded youth who seeks to arrest history.

To cast the roles of George's mother and his grandfather, Welles also stepped out of the fold of the Mercurians. In the pivotal role of Isabel Amberson, he cast Dolores Costello. Here sentimental factors governed his choice: she had been a great star of the silent movies, and she had once been married to Welles's hero (and, latterly, friend) the once-great, now ruined, John Barrymore. Again, she was not quite Tarkington's Isabel, and again, that is neither here nor there, except in so far as it affects the balance of the story. Isabel, the universally adored, is characterised throughout the novel for her uncanny youthfulness: as often as not, says Tarkington, she seems to be fourteen years old, vivacious and girlish. (Again, Brown's illustrations are an interesting pointer: his Isabel looks more like George's sister than his mother.) Costello, though only thirty-seven at the time, seems matronly and elegiac from the start, anticipating Isabel's physical decline and making her relationship with both George and Eugene less vivid, less dangerous. The morbid tone starts early in the film; in the book, it only makes its appearance with Isabel's illness and death.

For the casting of Major Amberson, Welles again turned to the silent movies: Richard Bennett had been a considerable film star from the time of *Damaged Goods* (1914), though it was on the Chicago stage that Welles had first encountered him: 'I'd been such a breathless fan of his in the theatre,' he told Peter Bogdanovich. 'He had the greatest lyric power of any actor I ever saw on the English speaking stage. There's no way of describing the beauty of that man in the theatre.' Welles might certainly have seen Bennett in *Winterset* in New York (his last stage performance); it is conceivable that he saw him in his greatest role, the title character in Andreyev's expressionist fantasy *He Who Gets Slapped*, in which his performance was thought to be the culmination of romantic acting. Despite being the father of a famous trio of actresses (Joan, Constance and Barbara Bennett), his circumstances had declined to the point at which Welles had discovered him – he said – living alone in a Catalina boarding house. This, of course, was the stuff of theatre romance for Welles: his genuine and practical love of elderly performers was a constant in his life, and entirely reciprocal; they knew he was one of them. Bennett later wrote to him with affectionate *esprit de corps* in the parlance of his generation of theatre folk: 'You have made me – happy – with sweet potentialities – I hope my meagre epistles have not bored you – they are only to remind you that you are still making people happy this side of the equator – Bless you, boy – R.B.' In this piece of casting, Tarkington's conception of the character and Welles's are identical; Tarkington (no mean playwright himself) may well have seen Bennett's work in the Chicago theatre; Bennett, like the author, was of good Hoosier stock.

For Lucy, the object of George's unwavering but perennially unrequited passion, Welles cast the eighteen-year-old Anne Baxter, who was perfectly able to realise the charm, intelligence and independence of the character. She may sometimes fail to go much beyond the limits of a conventionally high-spirited young woman of the period – Tarkington suggests something a little deeper – and is hard-pressed to convey the strength of her feelings for George, but one never questions her ability to provoke the love he feels for her, which is perhaps the more crucial matter. She very credibly creates the relationship with her father, who is played by that key figure in Welles's life and that of the Mercury, Joseph Cotten, who was thirty-six, exactly ten years older than Welles, and probably ten years younger than Eugene Morgan. Casting Cotten in the role ensured that it would be sympathetically played; his easy Virginian charm and soft handsomeness, allied to his perfect deportment, ideally convey the elegance and restraint of Gene Morgan and the chivalrous romanticism of his *tendresse* for Isabel Minafer. His attempt to play a part ten years older than he was – always a very difficult transformation, much harder than playing extreme old age – would inevitably tend to create a slightly muted impression, and here he and Welles would start to part company with Tarkington, whose Eugene is a more forceful and more reckless character than Cotten would be able to suggest. Morgan has suffered two financial collapses already by the time he returns to his home town, ready to invest everything in a newfangled and widely suspected invention, the automobile. 'There was something of the sixteenth-century buccaneer,' Tarkington observes, 'about Eugene Morgan', but that was not in Joseph Cotten's repertory. George Minafer accuses him of being a businessman and Lucy ripostes that he is a genius. He must of course be both, an inspired entrepreneur who ends up as one of the wealthiest men of his era. He has not achieved this by charm alone: Cotten's casting would make it seem as if he had, which somewhat diminishes the force of George's intuitive reaction against him. Gene stands for everything that George rejects: doing is his natural mode; being is neither here nor there. The balance between Tim Holt and Joseph Cotten as actors is almost the reverse of Tarkington's. Holt's turbulent, slightly brutish energy makes his claims to epitomise the ideals of American aristocracy unconvincing, while Cotten's natural relaxed amiability and languidness scarcely suggest the restless spirit of capitalist enterprise. Whether from filial piety or from a more general desire to create a sepia-tinted vision of the recent American past, Welles's casting here again conspires to rob the narrative of some of its meaning and a great deal of its energy.

Where the book and the casting are again triumphantly at one is in the role of Fanny Minafer, Isabel's deeply disappointed sister-in-law. The character is Tarkington's most compelling creation, self-defeating and desperate, at war with George, pathetic and sometimes malign in her attempts to deal with her hopeless passion for Eugene. Agnes Moorehead was perhaps the most remarkable of all the actors in the Mercury stable. Like many of the others, she had first worked with Welles on radio; as early as 1937 she had been in *The Shadow*, playing the long-suffering secretary Margot to his Lamont Cranston. She joined the Mercury Theatre on the Air the following year, appeared in the very first programme, *Dracula*, in the notorious *War of the Worlds* and, to startling effect, in *Rebecca*. In addition to the high spirits and technical skill of the other actors, she brought an extraordinary emotional depth and a transforming imagination to her work, which made each of her roles uniquely expressive; like the very greatest actors, she forged a mask that both liberated her and imprinted itself indelibly on the spectator's mind. Welles took her to Hollywood with him, and in *Citizen Kane* cast her in the small role of the mother of the young Charles Foster Kane. Noting the terrifyingly intense determination she brought to the part, allied to and expressed by the American Primitive gauntness of her appearance – hair tautly swept back, cheeks lined, waist tightly nipped – he and Toland shot her in such a way as to give her work maximum impact: these brief scenes become the fulcrum of the film. Now, in *The Magnificent Ambersons*, he cast Moorehead in the part that would be the high point of her early career. There was in the actress a latent (and sometimes naked) neediness, a disappointment in herself and, especially, her physical appearance, that can often be the source of exceptional power. Her greatest admirers as directors – and the directors whom she most admired – were Orson Welles and Charles Laughton, and both of them had a particular protective affection for her beyond their respect for her work. On any consideration – in terms of age (thirty-six at the time of filming), physically, vocally, emotionally – Moorehead was perfectly placed to play Fanny Minafer.

The rest of the roles were cast very much from Mercury ranks, the most prominent of them being that radio stalwart, Ray Collins, the powerful Boss Jim Gettys in *Citizen Kane*, here set down to play George's Uncle Jack (renamed, presumably to avoid confusion, from the Uncle George of the novel). Once again, the casting is slightly off. The novel's Uncle George is a failed congressman, a failed businessman, a failed lover – useless, in fact, for anything at all except the distant colonial embassy to which he is despatched at the end of the book. He is a Turgenevian superfluous man, unfitted for the modern world. Welles's Uncle Jack is inevitably a sturdier type, because Collins was. There is nothing of the exquisite or the aristocratic about him, nor could there be.

Having cast the film, Welles went away, in July of 1941, with Amalia Kent, his trusty amanuensis and erstwhile tutor in screenwriting, and wrote the screenplay on King Vidor's yacht; perhaps some of the vision of the great experimentalist of the silent cinema rubbed off on him. Working from the novel, two earlier screenplays and the script of his own radio broadcast, he selected with immense flair from the vast array of incident and character, adding little of his own, but emphasising the epic backdrop to the characters' lives. His fidelity to the book is extraordinary. He changes Uncle George into Uncle Jack, as we have seen; he gives George's line after he's been run over ('Riff-raff') to the policeman, which is a little odd since it is George's catchphrase. But in almost every other way his approach has been to realise the book as faithfully and literally as possible – instead of asking, as with the other projects on which he was working at the time, how can this material be used for cinematic purposes? He places the film at the disposal of the novel, rather than vice versa; in the narrations – a direct transposition of his familiar radio techniques – Welles allows the author's characteristic cadences to be heard, unmediated. Tarkington is nobly served. Only in the last reel, no doubt embarrassed by the spiritualist contrivances of the book – Eugene's highly uncharacteristic visit to a clairvoyant – does Welles offer a radical rewrite; but even then, in translating the final scene in the hospital into a reported one, in which Eugene visits Fanny in the boarding house, Welles tells precisely the same story, omitting only the mediumistic element. He also gives a proper (if perhaps slightly unTarkingtonian) end to Fanny's story. The original screenplay, with its collage of distant comedy records, squeaking rocking chair, heavy shadows passing across faces and extreme close-ups, gives a striking sense of unease, of things unresolved, of deepening bitterness and perhaps incipient insanity, where the novel speaks only of healing. This is clearly a vast improvement over Tarkington.

Fine and intelligent though it is, the screenplay suggests a less radical form of film-making than *Citizen Kane* – or indeed than *Journey into Fear*, to say nothing of the planned *Way to Santiago/Mexican Melodrama*, which is a complete reinvention of the book for cinematic purposes. It is, however, a profound, very grown-up, and somewhat sombre subject for a mainstream Hollywood film to address head-on, and in the screenplay, for all the charm and affection of Welles's version, he does not for a moment shy away from his theme. No faithful treatment of *The Magnificent Ambersons* could be anything other than a sobering experience; it describes the *dégringolade* of a class, and the growth of what Michael Denning in *The Cultural Front* calls 'Fordism': the triumph of the automobile, with all that that implies. Welles the missionary for the reform of Hollywood insisted that 'audiences are more intelligent than the people who create their entertainment'. While he was shooting *The Magnificent Ambersons*, he told students at the University of California Los Angeles: 'I can think of nothing that an audience won't understand. The only problem is to interest them; once they are interested they understand anything in the world. That must be the feeling of the movie maker.' In his preparations for the film, he was governed by his conviction that 'the movies are the nearest thing to reality . . . if the production is intelligent you could find out more about life from a movie screen than you can from theatre or radio'.

In his quest for reality, he became obsessed by historical accuracy to a degree scarcely rivalled until Michael Cimino's 1980 Western, *Heaven's Gate*. He demanded 125 turn-of-the-century vehicles to be commandeered and put into working order, and was overjoyed to find a 1905 model exactly as shown in the Sears catalogue of that year. Like David Selznick before him in *Since You Went Away*, he built an entire house in the studio. He also set aside a period for systematic rehearsals, not to stage the film, but to work intensively on character, background and relationships. This is fairly uncommon now, and was almost unheard of in 1941, to the extent that Welles's colleague Richard Wilson, running the office, received a letter from Robert Gessner of New York University congratulating Welles on the plan: 'It can be chalked up as another innovation that Mr Welles has brought to the screen in an attempt to raise its quality.' Welles had done a little of this sort of work on *Citizen Kane*, but clearly thought that *The Magnificent Ambersons*, as an essentially realistic piece, required detailed psychological consideration. In this sense, despite a pattern of discernibly Wellesian themes in his work over the years, and an immediately recognisable manner or style, he responded individually to the material in hand, just as he had done in the theatre: *The Shoemaker's Holiday*, after all, was not staged like *Julius Caesar*. And the material of *The Magnificent Ambersons* dictated its form.

During this period of rehearsal, he recorded the actors' performances. His plan was to play the recordings on the set, while they mimed to them; he favoured this technique, he told Barbara Leaming, 'so the actors would listen to the way they played it in rehearsal. Because the tendency of all actors in front of the camera is to slow up. I wanted them to hear how quickly and brilliantly they played it in rehearsal.' This explanation is bewildering. Almost all American actors of the period speak at lightning speed – Cary Grant, Edward G. Robinson, James Cagney; American actors, indeed, were known and admired in England above all for the rapidity of their delivery. Speed and brilliance could hardly have been the issue. No doubt Welles believed that the recordings would speed up the process of filming: he wouldn't have to worry about sound. Needless to say, the effect was the opposite; the procedure proved absolutely unworkable, a nightmare for the actors, robbing them of the freedom to respond naturally in the situation or to vary their rhythms by as much as a millimetre. The simplest explanation is that it gave him greater control over the performances, not necessarily in a tyrannical sense, but simply in assembling the elements he required.

*

Shooting of *Ambersons* began in October of 1941, somewhat later than planned; juggling the three films – *Journey into Fear* as well as *It's All True* – had demanded adjustments to the schedule. Before the rehearsal period for *Ambersons*, Welles had gone with Norman Foster and the cameraman Al Gilks to Mexico for a few days to set up the production of *Bonito the Bull*, which he then intended to supervise at long distance; his girlfriend, Dolores del Rio, had travelled with him. They had both been involved in the edition of *The Lady Esther Show* transmitted only the day before their flight (Jiminy Cricket was a fellow-guest); Welles had to be back in time for the next episode a week later. It is an entirely typical week from this period of Welles's life. *Lady Esther*, for CBS, of which he had produced weekly broadcasts since September, was no great strain on him. It consisted of a pot-pourri of literary adaptations, musical interludes, poetry readings and vaudevillian turns, presided over by a high-spirited Welles, who did a little of everything, appearing now boyish, now suddenly serious; he never entirely abandons his self-imposed mission to inform and affirm the values in which he believes, but cheerfulness keeps breaking in. Sometimes the effort shows in a false note of gaiety; his vaudevillian skills are limited, and his serious tone inclines to piety. The attempt to be all things to all men is inevitably doomed. But part of his nature demanded this sort of exposure, and would continue to demand it almost to the day he died. In his sixties, he gave an interview to Kathleen Tynan in which he confided that the desire to please was paramount in him; in *The Lady Esther Show*, and in later radio programmes of a similar kind, this need to be popular is rather touching. He makes a bit of a fool of himself, and his vulnerability is like that of a teenager trying hard to impress and amuse. He continued to present the programme every Monday night throughout the filming of *The Magnificent Ambersons* and *Journey into Fear;* he only gave it up when he went to Brazil. Of course he had a team of writers and technicians, but he had nonetheless to take decisions unceasingly, and it was his responsibility on the night to pull everything together. This is how he liked it: no time for reflection. He had secretaries, assistants, managers, associates. Every idea, every inspiration would be written down and acted upon. In George Amberson Minafer's terms, he was doing, doing, doing; being would have to look after itself.

Bonito the Bull meanwhile was approaching the commencement of principal photography. The cast was in place – Jesús Solorzáno as the bull-fighter and Jesús Vasquez (dubbed Hamlet by Welles) as Chico, Bonito's young friend; so were the locations. Foster wrote regularly to Welles from Mexico describing the problems and sending screen tests. The two men had formed the sort of relationship that Welles was always able to inspire in his fellow-workers – one of extraordinary familiarity and affection, playful, rather saucy, but with an unmistakable undertow of real emotion. Foster was fully fifteen years older than Welles – he had been acting since the early twenties and had more experience than Welles in every department of film-making

– but he instantly accepted the younger man's leadership. In response to Foster's anxious first telegram, Welles wired back simply: I LOVE YOU. But the crisis was real – difficulties with the weather, the bulls, the locals, the actors, the cameras. 'Personally,' Foster writes back, 'I shall never feel sorry for a bull in the *corrida de toros*. I hate the bastards now – we love you so much that it's killing us that we aren't having better luck. But we're doing everything we can and by God and by Jesus we'll get it yet.' Welles replies by telegram: WE ALL MISS YOU TERRIBLY, and adds: BELIEVE ME OUR TROUBLES HERE ARE AS NUMEROUS AND AS BITTER AS YOURS WITHOUT THE DIALECT. Money seems to be the main problem. MOSS PROMISES TO SEND MONEY STOP HE IS PRINTING IT THIS AFTERNOON STOP LOVED LAST BATCH OF FILM . . . MUCH LOVE ORSON. Even in a telegram one catches his electrical effect – the sense of fun and urgency and everything being possible that he generates; as soon as things cease to be possible, it is, naturally, a different story.

The situation at RKO was increasingly tense. Richard Wilson, as head of the Mercury office, had received an anxious phone call from Reg Armour, who was in charge of overseas sales and a nervously cautious man: he reported that the board was worried about Welles going to Mexico on account of 'the tremendous investment the company had in Orson and his present projects' and was deeply disturbed that the cost of *The Magnificent Ambersons* had risen so sharply – now $853,000, much higher than the agreed ceiling of $600,000, though less than the $1m originally projected. The start date, moreover, had been deferred. Armour reluctantly approved a requisition for Welles to leave the country for another short visit to Mexico. His anxiety, and that of his colleagues, is forgivable: their investment in Welles was indeed enormous; as the overall financial position worsened, he seemed only to expand, functioning like a one-man studio, setting more and more plates spinning like one of his admired vaudevillians, always adding yet one more when it seemed that the whole thing was about to collapse. It was dazzling; and deeply unnerving.

Meanwhile, the situation of *Bonito*, starved of funds, was equally troubled: in desperation José Noriega, the executive producer, wired Jack Moss for more money. In addition, the cameraman, Al Gilks, was summoned to Washington to work for the Federal government, and Floyd Crosby took over. This at least was positive: Crosby had been Robert Flaherty's cameraman, receiving an Academy Award for *Tabu*, the curious drama documentary that Flaherty and F. W. Murnau had co-directed; he was a free spirit, not associated with any major studio, and had worked extensively with the outstanding documentary film-makers of the day, Pare Lorentz and Joris Ivens. Welles briefly visited the set in mid-October, again with del Rio; he brought back footage with him, and when he showed it to the RKO executives, they were thrilled. YOU ASKED ME TO BE BRUTALLY FRANK, Welles telegrammed Foster. OKAY STOP THE FILM IS ABSOLUTELY WONDERFUL STOP I WILL REPEAT THAT THE FILM IS COMPLETELY MARVELLOUS, VERY VERY EXCITING AND AS BEAU-TIFUL AS ANYTHING YOU EVER SAW IN YOUR LIFE STOP FROM NOW ON YOU ARE OFFICIAL CREDITED CO-DIRECTOR OF BONITO & GOD BLESS YOU ORSON. Foster wired back, clearly touched: YOU ARE REALLY A SWEET GUY THANKS FROM ALL OF US. Excitement over rushes is common; but for someone as demanding as Welles – and as concerned about his image as an *auteur* – to have awarded a co-directing credit to a colleague could scarcely be a greater affirmation of the quality of what Foster was shooting.

*

By late October, *The Magnificent Ambersons* was finally under way. Welles had assembled his production staff – Robert Wise and Mark Robson, the *Citizen Kane* team, as editors; James Stewart as sound editor; Mark-Lee Kirk as production designer; Bernard Herrmann to write the score. These had all been obvious choices. The decision about who should be the director of photography had been delayed almost until the last moment. Clearly, Toland's defection to the Naval Photographic Unit was a blow to Welles: Toland had been his closest collaborator on *Kane*, teacher, friend and co-conspirator. He had given Welles courage, while Welles gave Toland permission. Together they had gone further than anyone in Hollywood in pushing the boundaries of what could be done with film. What could they not do together? Without Toland, Welles was stranded. Charles Higham reports that he had wanted to shoot *The Magnificent Ambersons* without a director of photography, as such: he would use Toland's team and together they would evolve the cinematography. But even Welles, self-confident and quick to learn as he was, must have realised that he was not yet quite the absolute master of the myriad technical demands of film and light; more importantly, had he followed (or been allowed to follow) such a disastrous policy, he would have been depriving himself of the creative and imaginative input of a fellow-artist, someone who could not merely realise his visions but exceed them, contradict them, be stimulated by them to completely unexpected – but richer – alternatives. He would, in short, have lost a partner who could surprise him.

The appointment of the director of photography was made suddenly, and at the very last moment, but destiny provided Welles with the ideal cinematographer for his project. Stanley Cortez was a man as unlike the swift, no-nonsense Toland as could be imagined, as *The Magnificent Ambersons* was unlike *Citizen Kane*, in fact. Seven years older than Welles, Cortez (whose real name was Kranz) had started his career as assistant to the great portrait photographer Edward Steichen, and had a lifelong preoccupation with formal experiment. Known as 'the Baron', he cut an elegant, dandyish figure, seeing himself, unashamedly, as an artist; he enjoyed holding forth about what he was doing, often with reference to the Great Masters of painting and to classical music, of which he was a passionate devotee. As the very young head of photography at Universal Studios, he had carried out his experiments with a remarkable lack of interference; he later worked for various studios in a fairly low-profile way. One day, when he happened to be doing some work at RKO, he sneaked onto Stage Three to watch Welles rehearsing on the massive set he had had built for *The Magnificent Ambersons*. 'He had eight sets upstairs and downstairs, and Orson was rehearsing on all these actual sets. And I said to myself: "I feel sorry for the guy who has to photograph the damn thing."' That Sunday he was in New York and had a call from Jack Moss; Welles had seen some of his work – *Danger on the Air* and *Black Cat* – and wanted him to shoot the movie for him. David Selznick, to whom Cortez was currently under contract, had to be tracked down to be asked to release him, which he did, at a price. Cortez arrived in Los Angeles at noon on Monday, met Welles that night 'for the first time in my life', and started shooting the film the following morning. He had no chance to make a test of anybody.

This is an extraordinary sequence of events. Preliminary discussions between the director and the cinematographer are indispensable: the whole approach to the shooting of the scenes has to be mutually evolved and agreed. By deciding on a particular shooting style, a cinematographer can, purposely or otherwise, completely undermine the director's work (or greatly improve it, of course); in appointing Cortez at such short notice, Welles was taking an enormous gamble. (The front office bitterly resented the salary Welles had agreed to pay him: $450 per week, plus compensation to Selznick for taking him off the other project; on his previous film Cortez had been working for basic studio rate. 'This is the second case of the Welles company giving a cameraman a big leap in salary,' scolded a front-office memo.) As Cortez describes it, the first day of shooting – the dinner-table scene at which George Minafer denounces Eugene – was something of an audition for him. It was also a first trial for the playback dialogue system, one which ended in conspicuous disaster, with the speakers blaring raucously across the studio as the actors attempted to maintain some degree of truth and spontaneity, desperately trying to synchronise their lips with the recording. The playback was abandoned; but the cinematography was a success. After seeing the rushes, Welles embraced Cortez: 'You're in,' he said. 'Immediately,' said Cortez, 'there was a *rapport*. From then on, to work with Orson was a fantastic experience.' Welles gave him complete freedom, he said, 'but every one of his suggestions was of enormous significance'. Cortez was keenly sympathetic to Welles's desire to re-create the look and feel of the late-Victorian and Edwardian Mid-West; he it was who proposed the Currier and Ives look for the snow scene. But it would take time: his approach to his work was meditative and reflective; the detail was everything. 'People said I was much too arty,' he observed, happily. In later life, he would fondly recollect his earlier career, describing with admiration how he and Busby Berkeley would sit around playing cards for two or three days at a time until the master became inspired. This was not the Welles method. Welles liked to attack a problem with blazing energy and high adrenalin, in Oliver Cromwell's phrase not simply striking while the iron was hot, but making the iron hot by striking it. Gregg Toland was of the same persuasion, and Welles began to miss his presence, becoming ever less tolerant of what he took to be Cortez's self-indulgence.

The persistent comparison with Toland was inevitable, not least in terms of experience. Cortez had never shot an A-feature before, while Toland was veteran of a dozen superb mainstream films made by masters – Hawks, Wyler and above all Ford; Cortez's last three films had been *Moonlight in Hawaii*, *Bombay Clipper* and *Eagle Squadron*, not films that will be found in the Hollywood Hall of Fame. What is remarkable about Cortez is that neither his confidence nor his artistry had been affected by the dull screenplays he had been called on to shoot. He continued to develop, quietly, almost unnoticed. Welles also took no account of the fact that shooting *Citizen Kane* was in a sense a less demanding job than shooting *The Magnificent Ambersons*. *Kane* is to a large extent about myth and a man's relationship with his own image. The screenplay and the subject called for stylised imagery and conscious visual metaphor; the bolder the solution, the better. Bold solutions, once conceived, are always easier to implement. *The Magnificent Ambersons* is about the disintegration of a class; it had to be detailed and textured and real, which is a different and in some ways more difficult challenge, both for Welles and for Cortez (and, indeed, for the actors). Creating the illusion of reality is inevitably much more laborious and more expensive; the cost of the sets had been staggering. The sort of *trompe l'oeil* approach in which Welles and Toland had so revelled in shooting *Kane* had no place here; Toland's adrenalised camera alone would have had been entirely inappropriate. In much the same way, the cunning use of existing sets in *Citizen Kane*, the brilliant optical sequences, were irrelevant to *The Magnificent Ambersons* and Welles's approach to it. But Welles seemed unwilling to accept the price of the approach that he himself had adopted. He wanted Cortez's results by Toland's methods.

Part of Welles's frustration was due to the fact that he was not acting in the movie. His staggering energies were not fully used. To demonstrate his frustration with the slowness of Cortez's modus operandi, he used the gaps between takes to have Jack Moss ostentatiously teach him new conjuring tricks; his general demeanour became more and more explosive, though he managed, as usual, to maintain good relations with his cast. Dolores Costello as Isabel Minafer (his second choice after Mary Pickford) proved a little disappointing because, Welles told Bogdanovich, 'she was quite unfocused – nothing naughty; just not wanting to be an actress'. He had supposed that she might have been interested in the process of filming; not a bit of it. For his Major Amberson, Richard Bennett, his affection was limitless, though the old chap was unable to remember a single line of his part (this had been a problem for him on stage: as early as 1935 he had been replaced on Broadway for not knowing his text). On the set of *Ambersons*, Welles was very happy personally to feed him each of his lines off-camera, one by one; his tenderness for old troupers – especially old men – must surely be associated with those childhood years during which he had looked after his drunken father. Welles's feelings for Anne Baxter were tender in a different way: their working relationship somehow survived an incident in a car when, seriously the worse for wear, he had made a determined lunge for the nineteen-year-old actress: he, and Baxter's brassiere, ended up in the gutter. His physical appetites remained enormous: though he no longer needed to appear slim as he had for *Kane*, he continued to take amphetamines, as well as ingesting his habitually vast quantities of alcohol and food.

With the dinner-table scene in the can, the snow scene was the next great sequence that he and Cortez attempted. For absolute verisimilitude, Welles had hired the same ice-plant in downtown Los Angeles at 6th and Pedro Streets that Frank Capra had used for *Lost Horizon*; there would be nothing artificial in the film, not even the actors' breath standing on the air. Welles insisted on real snow, too, so the art department supplied a panorama of the snow-covered Indiana countryside by feeding 5,000-pound cakes of ice into a cruncher. Cortez used massive arc lights of 500 and then 1,000 watts to create the glare of the winter sun; in the cold of the ice-house the bulbs kept shattering. Welles strode around this icy universe that he had summoned up in a leather suit and a hat with a pompom, swigging brandy – when he was there, that is. His other projects, including the weekly *Lady Esther Show*, meant that he was a frequent absentee; on such occasions he would record his instructions to the actors and crew on disc. Campbell Dixon, visiting Hollywood for the London *Daily Telegraph*, had hoped to interview him. 'There I was to meet him and watch the young maestro at work. And but for players catching cold, and the frozen oil stopping the camera, and Mr Welles being absent for reasons unknown, I would have.' Instead, Dixon had to resign himself to being photographed with 'the furred survivors' as consolation. The furred survivors themselves – the actors – were close to mutiny: the cold, the smell of dead fish, and finally the infernal playback, which was again attempted and again disastrous, and again abandoned (at least on this film; it was an *idée fixe* of Welles's and lived on to torment actors on more than one of his other films). In the event, all the sound on the film had to be post-synched. When Welles heard the dialogue for the sleigh-ride scene, which had been recorded in a sound studio, he told Stewart, 'Jim, it's too static.' Stewart dubbed it all again. Again Welles found it too static. Finally Stewart re-recorded it once more, with the actors standing on a shaking platform, and this at last found favour with Welles. Meanwhile, Ray Collins succumbed to pneumonia.

*

Through all this, Welles continued to co-direct *Bonito the Bull* at long distance and with high exuberance. CROSBY IS INDULGING IN TOO MUCH REFLECTOR, he wired José Noriega. KISS NORMAN ON ALL FOUR CHEEKS. LOVE ORSON; he joshingly complained that Norman Foster's new wife Sally was coming between them. High-spirited though his missives were, they contain precise and detailed instructions: RETAKE HEAD-ON CLOSE SHOT OF LITTLE BOY SITTING ON GATE AND GETTING OFF STOP THE BACKGROUND IS TOO FUZZY STOP CROSBY'S TEXTURE IS BEAUTIFUL BUT HE TENDS IN THIS

DIRECTION AND MUST BE WATCHED. Sharp definition was the core of the celluloid aesthetic that Welles and Toland had evolved. ALSO LET US HAVE SOME CLOSE-UPS OF HAMLET REACTING TO BRANDING OF BULL WITH SMOKE FROM BRANDING CROSSING FILM STOP ALSO A COUPLE OF SIMILAR SHOTS OF OTHER CHARACTERS INVOLVED IN BRANDING STOP EXTREME CLOSE-UPS I REPEAT EXTREME EXTREME CLOSE-UPS OF SWEATING FACES, SMOKE OF BURNING FLESH YUM YUM STOP I CAN'T STAND IT STOP WHY DON'T I HEAR FROM YOU STOP I CAN'T STAND IT STOP SALLY HAS COME BETWEEN US STOP ORSON. Foster replied in similarly exuberant vein: SENOR ORSON WELLES DEAR PATRON WILL MAKE BRANDING SHOTS WITH SIZZLE DESPITE TREMENDOUS ODDS . . . SALLY HAS NOT COME BETWEEN US BONITO & HAMLET HAVE LOVE – NORMAN.

Despite the characteristic hilarity and excitement that Welles generated among his collaborators, filming was very tough. The bull-fighter, Solorzáno, was temperamental, as were the rancheros and indeed the bull itself. The shoot was physically dangerous on several levels. One of the fighters got badly gored; then his brother was held up by gangsters, stripped and had his face slashed with a machete. 'Several times we've been afraid we were going to be held up,' wrote Foster. Noriega wrote to Welles proposing to shut the film down over the winter, to resume in February or March, at which point Welles would take the helm to shoot the bull-fight sequence and the scene in which Bonito gets away and rampages through the village. Welles wrote back to reassure them of 'how really and truly beautiful and important is the picture you're making. I hope you believe me.'

He had reason to be exhilarated by the progress on *The Magnificent Ambersons*, too. They had filmed the ball sequence in the Ambersons' mansion, which, as planned and shot, he described to Barbara Leaming as 'the greatest tour-de-force of my career'. In this pivotal section of the film, the camera – as if it were itself a guest – glided from room to room of the great house, apparently without cutting, eavesdropping on conversations, plunging into the middle of a dance, stopping for a moment on the stairs to take in the whole scene in all its splendour, luxuriantly surveying the Ambersons at their most magnificent. It is the crucial (and more or less the only) demonstration of their sumptuous wealth in the film, the glory from which everything else is a decline. Welles intended it to be much more than simply a piece of virtuoso shooting: the point of it was to express the seamlessness of the life that George Minafer believed would endure for ever, but which would so shortly be unravelled.

That long, long tracking shot was to be the cinematic metaphor for the smoothly sustained elegance of upper-middle-class life at the turn of the nineteenth century. It is a brilliantly conceived idea, but whose was it? Cortez, not an unduly boastful man, claimed it was his. He told at least two different versions of the story, however: in the first, he claims to have suggested it to Robert Wise before he was part of the project, when he was simply watching Welles rehearse on the set. 'Orson must have overheard.' In the second, he claims to have suggested it in the course of planning how to shoot the party scene: he thought of it, he said, as 'a symphony of movement, noise withstanding'. This is almost exactly the phrase that Welles himself used: he wanted, he said, 'a symphonic effect'. As so often in the practical and pragmatic arts of theatre and film, it scarcely matters who had the idea: making it work was the point, and here Cortez and Welles collaborated to brilliant effect, Welles superbly choreographing the actors, Cortez solving the technical logistics. In his stockinged feet – Cortez had him remove his shoes – the operator of the hand-held camera (a Mitchell equipped with periscopic finder and a thirty-one-inch lens) padded upstairs, through doors and across rooms with the heavy camera. Walls flew in and out as the camera and the actors wove their way through. Some rooms had mirrors, which had to be turned around on cue and turned back on a second cue, according to Cortez. Unsurprisingly, the sequence took nine ten-hour days to shoot; the crew consisted of nearly a hundred men, a huge number for the period. It took epic forces to shoot Tarkington's understated literary saga.

After this triumph of cinematic audacity, Welles shot the scene in the kitchen between Fanny and George. Agnes Moorehead gave an account of working with him that illuminates the way he collaborated with actors. She felt that the scene, as written and played, needed something more. Welles accordingly encouraged her to improvise, he would then shape the results, and then they would improvise more, and Welles would make further suggestions 'while poor Tim Holt,' remembered Moorehead, 'eats more and more cake and turns green'. This was how Welles had always liked to work in the theatre. 'From a little over a minute, we had ad libbed until the scene was almost four minutes in length. And the effect was like peering through or listening at a keyhole because Fanny was suddenly stripped of her pretensions and her sad truth revealed. And that was what it was like to work for Orson.' The scene is devastating, for exactly the reason she gives: the ugly nakedness of the character's need is simply shocking. It is, in fact, considerably more powerful than the equivalent scene in the novel; it may indeed be that her great performance is in danger of over-balancing the film (as the character very nearly over-balances the book). Fanny's neurotic and irrational journey through the novel offers a jagged and tragic counterpoint to the stiff upper lips more generally on display. Her terror of being abandoned and her desperate attempts to claw back some sort of support haunt and disturb almost disproportionately: in a sense, the film becomes about her; she is seen to be the family's sacrificial offering. It is a supreme example of an actor's creativity, as much Agnes Moorehead as Fanny Minafer, and greater than either.

George Schaefer, who with certain selected executives had been shown about an hour's worth of the footage, immediately saw the power of her work: AGNES MOOREHEAD DOES ONE OF THE FINEST PIECES OF WORK I HAVE EVER SEEN ON THE SCREEN, he wired Welles. EVEN THOUGH I HAVE SEEN ONLY A PART OF IT, continued a clearly relieved Schaefer, THERE IS EVERY INDICATION THAT IT IS CHUCK FULL OF HEART-THROBS, HEARTACHES AND HUMAN INTEREST. ('Unlike *Citizen Kane*' is perhaps the grateful subtext.) Schaefer was struck by the 'startling' technique of the film and insisted: I AM VERY HAPPY AND PROUD OF OUR ASSOCIATION. Joe Breen, head of production, 'hastened to thank you, to congratulate you, and to tell you that I have not been so impressed for years . . . though you know me to be a chronic kicker, in this instance I have nought but praise – from my heart. – God love you' (the final phrase, from the devoutly Roman Catholic Breen, was considerably more than a form of words). And one of the younger vice-presidents, Phil Reismann, a drinking pal of Welles's, said exactly what Welles wanted and needed to hear. 'This film will be one of the outstanding pictures of the year . . . produced with an intelligence that only a few people in show business are gifted with. I am certain that it will be a commercial success.'

From within Mercury came a shrewd and striking assessment of Welles's work in progress: Herb Drake, the witty and worldly-wise publicist who had so cleverly handled the press over the campaign to get *Citizen Kane* released, wrote to Welles's lawyer, Arnold Weissberger: 'It is extraordinarily dramatic and beautiful to look at,' adding that it was 'full of Orson's personal violence. As usual with Welles, the cast is perfectly co-ordinated, after all, we can always count on Orson being the puppet master.' 'Personal violence' is a very acute description of the explosive energy of both the man and his work. If Welles was a puppet master, it was only with those who needed to be manipulated; as we have seen, with a powerful creative personality like Agnes Moorehead, he was as much midwife as martinet. 'Orson is full of beans personally,' Drake continues, 'and seems happy with the picture.'

At this point, on the morning of 7 December 1941, Admiral Chuichi Nagumo's taskforce launched a first wave of 184 aeroplanes and then a second of 169 on Pearl Harbor in Hawaii, killing 2,000, wounding 1,700 and sinking eight battleships. The United States government immediately declared war on Japan; Germany declared war on the US on 11 December, and the Second World War commenced.

CHAPTER THREE

The Best Man in Hollywood

O N THE afternoon of 7 December, Welles was writing a letter to Norman Foster on the set of *The Magnificent Ambersons*. 'First, thanks for your wonderful long letter, and if this reply doesn't make much sense remember that I'm writing it on the set between takes . . . forgive me.' He says that he knows and admires the bullfighter Perez, that they should keep hold of him in case Chucho (Solorzáno) stumbles again. There is a break, and then the letter continues: 'My god three days have gone by since I started writing this letter. What did I want to tell you? I can't really think. War has broken out and I have broken down. I think I'll phone you. I send this on, as testimony, however feeble, of my good intentions as a correspondent. Also may I remind you that your heart is god's little garden. Ever lovingly.'

The pause in the letter signifies a turning point in Welles's life. He was undoubtedly deeply shaken by the declaration of war. His social–democratic Popular Front allegiances were profoundly antifascist. In common with his fellow-liberals, though he held the warmest regard for Britain and its people in their current plight two years into their war with Germany, he had little sympathy with the British Empire and its perceived objectives; indeed, as reported by the FBI (which from now on took a lively interest in his activities), he had signed, as late as June of 1941, the call of the Fourth International Congress of the League of American Writers to keep out of the European War, 'an imperialistic war for world markets and not a war to serve democracy'. But he had been convinced for some years, especially after the Spanish Civil War, of the urgent threat to democracy posed by Hitler, and was now increasingly inclined to the belief that the only way to stop him was by means of war. Like all radicals, Welles had been momentarily poleaxed by the Nazi–Soviet Non-Aggression Pact of 1939; like most liberals, he supported Roosevelt – in theory. As an employee of the Federal

Theatre Project in the late thirties, he had, of course, been a direct beneficiary of New Deal policies, and he instinctively approved of Roosevelt's determination to commit America to the war against fascism in the face of powerful resistance from the American Right, a resistance noisily promulgated by, among others, Senator Joseph Kennedy and his friends, who were prepared to spend large sums of money to leave Germany alone. Welles's support for Roosevelt was by no means unconditional, however. In accord with the rest of liberal opinion, he was somewhat suspicious of the President, distrusting his political subtlety and seeming indecisiveness; nonetheless, he endorsed Roosevelt's support for Britain, his extension of Lend-Lease to Russia, his signing of the Atlantic Charter with Churchill, and the more or less clandestine preparations he had instigated for joining the fight against Hitler.

Welles was by no means passive politically: he had become increasingly fascinated by politics – engaged by its ideas, convinced of the possibility of effecting fundamental change, excited by the notion of appealing directly to large numbers of his fellow-citizens. If there was a national politician he really admired, it was Roosevelt's Vice-President, the visionary agricultural reformer, Henry Wallace, by whose uncompromised radicalism and blazing oratory Welles had been deeply stirred. In Wallace's utterances he glimpsed the vision for the future of mankind that seemed to him lacking in Roosevelt. He took his responsibilities as a prominent citizen very seriously: even in the midst of filming *Ambersons*, doing *The Lady Esther Show* and co-directing *Bonito*, he had participated in a combined benefit for refugees, the Exiled Writers' Committee and Spanish Aid; on the very morning of the attack on Pearl Harbor, he had sent telegrams to the President and Secretary of State Cordell Hull in support of three Soviet citizens arrested in Vichy France, urging action to prevent their being handed over to the Italian or German governments.

The suddenness of the Japanese attack electrified him as it did everyone on the Left. The long-awaited moment demanded commitment of some sort from each individual: in Welles's case – at twenty-six, apparently an eminently able-bodied male – this would normally have meant the draft. His eligibility for call-up was the subject of constant press interest: in May 1941, the *Los Angeles Herald Examiner* reported on his draft status – somewhat humiliatingly, his fallen arches and spinal irregularities were noted, without comment. It was not Welles's destiny to be a foot soldier. Instead he received a telegram – on 10 December, the same day as his interrupted letter to Norman Foster was finally completed – from John Hay Whitney, head of the Motion Picture Division of the Office of Inter-American Affairs, asking him, as a matter of some urgency, if he would go as soon as possible to Brazil to make a film to promote pan-American unity; the subject would be Rio de Janeiro's famous Carnival.

One of the first objectives of a shocked America as it swung into action after Pearl Harbor was to secure its relations with South America; several Latin American leaders were energetically pro-fascist, posing a considerable threat to the United States at its own back door. The co-ordinator and prime mover of the Office of Inter-American Affairs (I-AA) was the energetic Nelson Rockefeller, 'the eager beaver to end all eager beavers', in Vice-President Wallace's phrase, who had convinced the administration to transform the Office's budget of $3.5m per annum to $140m, a mark not only of his persuasiveness, but of the importance of what came to be known as hemispheric unity. It is more than likely that the suggestion that Welles should direct the proposed film came from him. As a major shareholder in RKO and an early and vigorous supporter of Welles's original contract with the company, Rockefeller had reason to know his work, and would certainly have known of the slated projects, *Bonito the Bull*, set in Mexico, and the other South American parts of *It's All True*, whose outline was still quite vague. Rockefeller may also, as Frank Brady suggests, have been helping RKO out at a difficult moment.

It took Welles twenty-four hours to make up his mind about 'Jock' Whitney's offer. His decision was a popular one. On 11 December, Phil Reismann was writing to Joseph Breen:

> They [the Brazilians] feel that the sending of Orson Welles by RKO to cover the Carnival which is so close to them and so near to their hearts, was a most magnificent gesture and it is highly appreciated by the Brazilian people and the Brazilian government . . . Orson Welles is looked upon by the Brazilian people as one of the great theatre and picture personalities in the United States, and he has in his make-up exactly what these people like . . . the compliment that we are paying them by sending the best man in Hollywood to cover this, is greatly appreciated.

It seemed that the Brazilians did indeed know all about Welles, though his amatory arrangements were of at least equal interest to his cinematic achievements. 'Here is sensational news which we divulge as a scoop,' proclaimed the Rio evening paper *A Noite*. 'Orson Welles, the revolutionary of the movies, the extraordinary actor and creator of *Citizen Kane*, the most complex and fascinating figure of the American artistic world today, has his trunks packed to come to the city, in company with Dolores del Rio, with whom he will be married within a few weeks.' The prospect of his presence in Rio was seen as a huge endorsement and a hope for the future; the native film industry perceived it as a step towards its emergence from obscurity. It is worth recalling that these statements made in Brazilian newspapers appeared a bare six months after the release of *Kane*; it is doubtful whether there has ever been any figure in the history of cinema who has created such an instant and overwhelming impact with a single film.

It's All True, having been part of RKO's programme, now became an official part of the war effort. The world of Mercury Productions was transformed overnight by Welles's commitment to the new project. Swift decisions were made. *Journey into Fear* – RKO's best hope for a commercial success – was given a start date (6 January 1942) and Norman Foster was nominated as its director, transferred from *Bonito*, which was now summarily closed down. *Bonito*'s twelve-year-old star Jesús Vasquez – 'Hamlet' – was to come to America with the crew for an indefinite period, during which the company would assume responsibility for his safe-keeping and his education; his mother would come too. GIVE ASSURANCES TO ALL CONCERNED, wrote Norman Foster to José Noriega, THAT WHEN WE RETURN TO COMPLETE PRODUCTION WE WILL MAKE EVERY EFFORT TO RETAIN SAME CREW AND PERSONNEL. A VERY MERRY CHRISTMAS TO ALL. By this time 80 per cent of the movie had been filmed, and, as indicated in Noriega's letter above, the production team had in any case been keen on a temporary lay-off during the winter months. There was certainly no doubt in anyone's mind that the film would be completed; the footage had been universally admired.

The pressure to complete *The Magnificent Ambersons*, meanwhile, inevitably increased, creating renewed tension between Welles and Cortez, whose leisurely approach now seemed not merely irritating, but actually unpatriotic; Welles would later accuse him of being 'criminally slow' and took no trouble to conceal his impatience, which sometimes became ugly as the pace of his life rapidly accelerated. At the same time as he was shooting the last couple of weeks on *The Magnificent Ambersons*, and preparing *Journey into Fear* (which would soon be shooting alongside it), the radio shows for CBS continued, though the *Lady Esther* format had given way to a more straightforward mixture of dramatisations and readings. The vaudevillian element, no doubt to Welles's intense disappointment, quietly evaporated. One week it was *The Hitch-Hiker* by Bernard Herrmann's wife, Louise Fletcher, a huge popular hit; the next *A Farewell to Arms*. He was also involved in one of the first major wartime broadcasts, Norman Corwin's *The President's Bill of Rights (We Hold These Truths)*, with, among others, Edward G. Robinson, Walter Huston, James Stewart and Roosevelt himself; programmes of this nature would henceforward be a significant part of his life, identifying and celebrating the virtues of American democracy, while convincing a nation that had by no means been unanimously eager to go to war of its necessity.

Welles also continued to pursue his educational ideals. His old mentor Roger Hill, who was never absent from his life for long, ever urging him on in his social mission, had come forward with the notion of Todd Scholarships. Dick Wilson wrote to Hill that Welles was not keen on that particular notion: *Orson Welles* scholarships, on the other hand, he said, were very possible. 'That is good publicity for the school, for us, for everybody.' He then went on to suggest subsidising a chair, a department, a project. Hill was thrilled with the response: PLEASE SHUT UP FOR A FEW DAYS, he wired, UNTIL I CAN GET THE MISTINESS OUT OF MY EYES AND WRITE COHERENTLY ABOUT THE GENUINE EDUCATIONAL SIGNIFICANCE AND NATIONAL IMPORTANCE OF WHAT YOU WILL DO. Just as Dadda Bernstein, another surrogate parental voice that was rarely still, had murmured the word 'Genius' in Welles's ear from birth, so Roger Hill, encountering the boy in his adolescence, had from the start urged on him the notion of Greatness, by which he meant greatness as a leader, as a prophet, as a teacher. There was huge, almost overwhelming personal emotion involved: praising Welles's initiative, he says: 'Everybody talks about it but no one does anything about it. Except you, my love. And except Todd. And we're going to do something about it so significant that it will be recognised in every history of education in the next five hundred years as the Turning Point . . . yours, this side – but not far – idolatry, R.' The key word in Hill's letter was 'significant': he wanted Welles to use his influence for the good of mankind, and he thought that he was uniquely placed to do so. Nor was he alone in encouraging this. In December of 1941, Welles had received a letter typical of many others from a teacher at Long Island University: 'It is probably difficult for you to realise,' she said, 'what weight your word carries with the youth of Brooklyn. They have not heard of Jeremiah, Deuteronomy, nor Cardinal Newman, but they become alive with the mention of Orson Welles.' Not many twenty-six-year-old film-makers were spoken of, or to, in such a fashion. Despite the frustrations of working with Cortez, Welles ended the year in a state of some exhilaration: on the last day of December, *Citizen Kane* won the New York Critics' Best Picture Award for 1941; the same day he received a telegram from H. G. Wells, whom he had met the year before when they shared a good chortle over *The War of the Worlds* broadcast, reporting on the film's British premiere: CITIZEN KANE MAGNIFICENT. PRESS HERE EMBARRASSED. RELUCTANT TO RECOGNISE OUR PRESS BARONS. SALUTATIONS. The footage from both *Bonito* and *The Magnificent Ambersons* had been greeted with delight by the studio. The radio show continued successfully in its new Reader's Digest format, with readings from the Gospel of St Luke, and Wilde's *The Happy Prince* and Walt Whitman; while the *It's All True* project was being hailed on all sides. George Schaefer had sent Welles a carefully worded letter, which was released to the press: '. . . this goes to you as an expression of our government's deep appreciation of your patriotic service to the cause of hemisphere solidarity. Your service in this work is fully as important to the national cause as would your service in any other phase of national endeavour'– no doubt pointedly phrased to deflect any criticism of his failure to enlist. And finally, as a harbinger of delights to come, on the last *Lady Esther Show* of the year (*There Are Frenchmen and There Are Frenchmen*) he had met the woman who, on the strength of having seen her photograph on the cover of a famous edition of *Life* magazine five months earlier, he had vowed he would marry: Rita Hayworth. Between Miss Hayworth (née Margaret Cansino) and Miss Del Rio, he was doing his bit for hemispheric solidarity in more arenas than one.

As well as Hayworth, the broadcast starred Joseph Cotten, who had also adapted the original story. It was Cotten's adaptation of *Journey into Fear* – presumably with fraternal input from Welles – that was now about to start shooting alongside *The Magnificent Ambersons*. The declaration of war had added new levels of interference from the front office. In addition to the usual prissinesses from the Hays Office ('there should be nothing sex-suggestive in the line: "Maybe he thought the sea air would do him good"'), the production team was inundated with memoranda from various RKO functionaries, offering strictures and advice. 'For your information and guidance, the war department is now exceedingly critical of any mention of itself,' wrote one, William Gordon, always happy to share the fruits of his polymathy with them. 'It is suggested that Josette refer to Rio rather than to Buenos Aires . . . I will be glad to give a dozen reasons why, if you want them.' Another memorandum urged them: 'Please please have Gogo speak French or even possibly in the Basque dialect which no one on this earth can understand except another Basque. (This is one language which even the Russians cannot learn, unless raised in the Basque district.)' Another from a different source suggests the diplomatic challenges of wartime filming: 'if Haki is overplayed as a ladies' man . . . he will be most offensive to the sensibilities of the Turkish people . . . The Turkish Secret Police is considered one of the best in the world . . . Mme Matthis' reference to the Reds and their having violated nuns and murdered priests is particularly unfortunate . . . not only to Spaniards – and some might not think it a better world if the Reds *had* won – but also the Russians whom we certainly don't wish to offend today.' As a parting shot, Gordon picks holes in the archaeologist's speech, citing Leonard Woolley's *Ur of the Chaldees* as his authority. Between wartime censorship, industry censorship, expert pomposities and studio panic, the film was severely challenged to maintain any sort of identity, but that it does manage to achieve, albeit of a somewhat quirky kind.

The authorship – in the wider sense of the word – of *Journey into Fear* is something of a mystery. 'There was a Mercury style of acting,' Welles told Peter Bogdanovich, 'and both Jo Cotten and I worked together perfectly in establishing that look and feel.' The film evolved in an improvisatory manner out of the relationship between Welles and Cotten, Norman Foster and Karl Struss, the art directors Mark-Lee Kirk and Albert D'Agostino. A large number of the cast were also appearing in *The Magnificent Ambersons* and, like Welles, shuttled between the two sets. Both films were shot almost in repertory: in addition to Cotten and Welles, Agnes Moorehead and Richard Bennett (as a drunken sea captain) appear, as well as the non-actors Moss, Meltzer and Drake from the Mercury office, and Welles's long-suffering secretary, Shifra Haran. The Mercury stalwarts – Ruth Warrick, Eustace Wyatt and Everett Sloane – are joined by other chums of Welles's, like Hans Conried (later to become something of a cult star as Dr Seuss's Dr Terwilliker) and Frank Readick (Welles's predecessor as the Shadow); Dolores del Rio plays the role originally intended for Michele Morgan. All in all, it has the feeling of a party about it, a high-spirited jape, in which the cast must have been on the point of breaking up at pretty well any time.

Cotten, in fact, is very well cast, much in the mould of Ambler's Winston Graham: 'He was a quiet, likeable sort of chap, and generous with his whisky. You couldn't, of course, imagine yourself getting to know him very well . . . he was always friendly. Nothing effusive, just friendly, a bit like an expensive dentist trying to take your mind off things.' Cotten is perhaps a little more glamorous than Ambler's character, whom 'it is difficult to imagine a woman like Stephanie marrying . . . for anything except his salary', but his even temper is well suited to the baffled, somewhat passive central character. Naturally, Graham has become American in the film, and his first name is no longer Winston – which would have seemed, in 1941, the quintessential English name – but Howard. Dolores del Rio, too, is admirably suited to the part of Josette, the Serbian femme fatale, a dancer locked in a joyless marriage with her surly dancing partner, José. 'She was a slim woman with beautiful arms and shoulders and a mass of gleaming fair hair,' says Ambler. 'Her heavily lidded eyes, almost closed as she danced, fixed in a theatrical half-smile, contradicted in a curious way the swift neatness of her performance.' (By odd chance, the character's background is oddly similar to that of Rita Hayworth: she has been dancing since childhood, dominated by a bullying father who is also a dancer.) At a certain moment in the book, Josette's expression is described as changing very quickly: 'She became an international beauty humouring with a tolerant smile the extravagances of a love-sick boy.' Del Rio perfectly finds the equivalent moment in the film; she had some practice at it.

As for Welles in the role of Colonel Haki (a character who had already made an appearance in Ambler's earlier *The Mask of Dimitrios*), it was just the sort of part that Welles was drawn to and which he should have resisted at all costs. Given the opportunity to play the charming but wicked *raisonneur*, he was irresistibly impelled to go for a theatrical stereotype, the exact opposite of what Ambler created. 'He was a tall man with lean, muscular cheeks, a small mouth and grey hair cropped Prussian fashion,' according to the author. 'A narrow frontal bone, a long beak of a nose, and a slight stoop gave him a somewhat vultural air . . . his eyes were grey and very wide awake.' Ambler's 'somewhat vultural' figure becomes, in Welles's hands, and with all the lavish resources of his make-up box, a mountain eagle crossed with Count Dracula. One is reminded how inexperienced a film actor he was: this was only his second excursion into the medium, and he is cruelly exposed in a way that he was not, paradoxically, in the much larger role of

Kane. That role consisted of shards of character, pieces in a mosaic; for the younger Kane, moreover, he was able to draw extensively on himself. Here, he has only the stock types of the stage to turn to; one is very aware of a young man's assumption of middle age. In the novel there is a droll moment in one of his exchanges with Graham. 'A little melodramatic, aren't you?' asks Graham. 'We have no proof that what you say is true. After all, this is real life, not . . .' Graham hesitates. 'Not what, Mr Graham?' demands Haki. 'The cinema, I was going to say, only it sounded a little impolite.' It is not the cinema to which Welles's Haki belongs, but the theatre – specifically the theatre of Victorian melodrama to which Welles, in his atavistic heart, belonged. The characterisation might well have caused raised eyebrows at the Gate Theatre in Dublin in 1930, but would have made his career at Henry Irving's Lyceum fifty years earlier. Seeing the film by chance on television thirty years later, Welles was not proud of the performance. 'I'm pretty awful in it,' he told Bogdanovich. 'The character was supposed to be a cynical sort, and that's the way I played it – but I think I missed.'

The final, crucial character in the story is Petre Banat, the killer; even here, in his description of him, Ambler the radical is unable to resist a dig at capitalism: 'His approach to the business of killing would be that of the lavatory attendant to the business of attending to his lavatories or of the stockbroker to taking his commission – purely practical.' The physical description fits Moss admirably: 'short, broad-shouldered and unkempt, with a heavy jowl and a fringe of scurfy grey hair round a bald pate'. Welles identified a certain sinister quality in his manager, which he was to exploit brilliantly. ('He had a smile,' continues Ambler, in a characteristic aside, 'fixed like that of a ventriloquist's doll: a standing apology for the iniquity of his existence.') Moss had agreed to play the role on the condition that he would say nothing, a limitation that only increased his disturbing presence. In his hat, staring huge-eyed through his pebble spectacles, he is both disturbing and utterly commonplace. He almost steals the film. For the rest, there is a certain almost Expressionist character to Richard Bennett's bunk-bound soused and roaring captain; Ruth Warrick's glamorous Stephanie Graham is pleasingly scatty; Hans Conried brings real vaudevillian flair to the part of the conjuror; and Welles's chum Bob Meltzer is drily witty as the steward. As a group, they cohere into the sort of exotic ensemble that Warner Brothers so effortlessly fielded, and perhaps had the slight advantage that they were for the most part unknown, and thus apparently not acting, simply being.

Filming was more than usually chaotic, a striking contrast to the stately pace imposed by Stanley Cortez on *The Magnificent Ambersons*. The atmosphere was Welles's favourite: one for all and all for one. When Bogdanovich asked Welles who was responsible for the penultimate scene in the film – Banat and Graham crawling round the highest ledge of a tall building in driving rain – he answered: 'Whoever was nearest the camera.' Everyone involved, he remembered, had been up for twenty-four hours and was light-headed with exhaustion – 'rocked', he says. Welles's own deadline to start work on *It's All True* created huge pressure to finish the sequences in which he was involved – he had to be in Rio in advance of the start of Carnival, on 9 February. 'It was very dangerous but we were feeling no pain, and we were all helping . . . it was a collaborative effort.' Everyone involved in the creative team had strong opinions and they freely pooled their ideas; a film duly evolved that is full of flair and talent, but narratively uncertain and stylistically unfulfilled. (It was, however, certainly Welles's idea to open the film with a long pre-credit sequence that features Banat, silent apart from the scratchy old gramophone churning out the tune that becomes the hired killer's leitmotiv. Welles thought, he charmingly confessed, that he was making film history in so doing, until he found out, long afterwards, that Lewis Milestone had got there before him, in *Of Mice and Men*'s opening sequence two years earlier.) On the whole, though, apart from its set-pieces, the film lacks visual ambition. Politically neutered by wartime restrictions, manically pressured because of Welles's need to get to South America, its narrative all but incomprehensible, *Journey into Fear* turned into a quickie done with intermittent flair, a mere shaving off the Wellesian woodblock.

Principal photography on *The Magnificent Ambersons* ended on 20 January 1942; Cortez had been released from the film a day before. Neither he nor Welles ever commented on this petty slight. Indeed, Cortez only ever spoke well of his time working with Welles, whom he pronounced (along with Charles Laughton) the only director he had worked with who understood light. The whole visual gesture of the film is Cortez's; the few additional shots scarcely amount to a major contribution to the cinematographic achievement. But Cortez had certainly riled Welles; the moment he could be dumped, he was. Robert Wise told Carringer that by the end of the shoot Cortez had been demoted to the second unit. There is some evidence that later sequences, including the death of Isobel, were at least in part shot by Harry J Wild, a staff cameraman, and some by Russell Metty; Wise's memory of events, if not strictly accurate, is an indication of Cortez's low standing within the team. Certainly when in the months ahead scenes were reshot, there was never any attempt to use him to execute them. After the completion of principal photography, there were pick-up shots over the remaining ten days; the cameraman for these was the solid RKO staffer, Harry Wild. The last shots of *The Magnificent Ambersons* that Welles himself directed were taken on 31 January, just two days before his departure for Brazil.

Earlier in the month, he had had his first production meeting for *It's All True*, and it was a stormy affair; one catches a glimpse of quite how combative Welles could be in establishing his authority. It was a formidable group. Those present included representatives of the United States government (Harry Hopkins, Roosevelt's right-hand man no less, creator of the Works Progress Administration and hence the Federal Theatre Project, there in his capacity as Special Advisor on Foreign Affairs), of RKO and of Technicolor. Welles immediately establishes that the film is to be an RKO production, facilitated by the government, and not the other way round. His prime anxiety is about the use of Technicolor. Hopkins insists that it is very important to the government that the carnival section should be in colour; clearly their expectation of the movie – which had so far only one idea, simply to catch the Carnival on film – is that it will celebrate, in the most vivid and attractive way possible, the famously flamboyant climax of a neighbour's year. The purpose is to flatter. Welles reluctantly submits to their insistence on the use of colour in this sequence, but refuses to commit himself as to how much of the rest will be; he was to remain sceptical about colour until the mid-sixties, and even then only used it for a television film. The question of 'the Color Technician' is raised. 'Who's he?' asks Welles. The Technicolor representative explains that he is 'trained and knows interpretation', but Welles will have none of it: he hates the idea of this man. 'If you know anything about colour –' he erupts. 'I used to be a painter. I can crib now and then . . . I think we can do without this fellow.' The last thing he wants is an expert telling him what he can and can't do. In fact, Technicolor had just taken a leap forward with their new monopack system, using only one negative instead of three, which resulted in much lighter equipment altogether, but it was a new system and one that they were understandably keen to monitor. None of this impressed Welles in the least.

The committee next considers the technical complications of an almost unprecedented operation, far from home – 'It's easier,' says

Welles, 'to get to the Far East or London' – and the problem of
the amount of stock needed; film in South America is not up to
Hollywood standards, so they have to bring it with them. Welles
returns to the question of personnel: he will not, he insists, put
up with organisation men. The one thing not discussed, inevitably,
is the film itself. The meeting is adjourned with several major questions unanswered: the matter of the Technicolor technicians, the
amount of stock needed, and finally, crucially, the nature of the
film they are about to make. Harry Hopkins suggests that they
should make an interesting, instructive, visually exciting travelogue,
called *Orson Welles Sees South America*. No comment is recorded.
Hopkins obviously hadn't got the measure of Welles at all. That
the Office of Inter-American Affairs, if not the government, wanted
something more than a travelogue is indicated in a memo written
to Jock Whitney by the Brazilian division a mere day after Welles
had agreed to direct the film. Reporting the great excitement in
Brazil at the idea of Welles coming to Rio, the writer suggests as
a possible subject the heroic journey recently made by some fishermen (*jangadeiros*) from Fortaleza, in the far north of the country.
They had travelled an astonishing 3,000 miles of rough coastal seas
on a raft to deliver a petition to the President, Getúlio Vargas, in
Rio de Janeiro, demanding the right to form unions and receive
pensions. 'These *jangadeiros* are almost legendary figures in Brazil
. . . and a well-executed short subject of the type suggested should
have an enthusiastic following both in Brazil and in the United
States.' How this could fit into the Carnival sequence was unclear,
but the idea no doubt sowed a seed in Welles's mind.

In the weeks before his departure, Welles continued to shoot
pick-ups on *The Magnificent Ambersons* and to act in and advise on
Journey into Fear, while still producing and fronting *The Lady Esther
Show*. One of these broadcasts featured an adaptation of a Carl
Ewald story, *My Little Boy*, which had been one of the Mercury
Theatre on the Air's greatest triumphs. By some curious
synchronicity, two days later Welles was reported in the *Los Angeles
Times* as having adopted a seven-year-old Czech boy, Peter
Neuschul. His paintings had been shown in Prague and London;
both his parents were painters. Of this child, little more is ever
heard; perhaps the adoption was a mere formality, involving a
payment for subsistence (though Welles was notoriously dilatory in
paying the legally binding sums prescribed by the divorce courts
for the maintenance of his own daughter Christopher). Young
Neuschul wrote to him on a regular basis for a year or so, then

there was silence. Welles was an intermittent correspondent at best, but loving messages flooded in to him during this time in an unbroken stream – from Thornton Wilder, Alexander Woollcott, the Mexican composer Carlos Chavez. To reverse Oscar Wilde's comment on Shaw, Orson Welles had many enemies, but his friends most certainly loved him.

Before flying to Brazil via Washington, he arranged to meet Robert Wise in Miami with the footage of *The Magnificent Ambersons*. He stayed up all night to record the narration for the film and to shoot the penultimate scene of *Journey into Fear*, and on the following evening, 1 February, he introduced the final *Lady Esther Show* of the season, *Between Americans*. It ended with a rather solemn farewell speech: 'Tomorrow night the Mercury Theatre starts for South America.' He reports that he's been asked to do a motion picture 'especially for Americans in all the Americas, a movie which in its particular way might strengthen the good relations now binding the continents of the Western Hemisphere'. Increasingly preoccupied with the question of what it was to be an American, he was moving towards a more inclusive notion, which would dominate much of his thinking over the next few years. The people of these 'United Nations of America', he says in this farewell broadcast, now stand together. 'We're going to have to know each other better than we do. My job – the Mercury's – job is to help with the introductions . . . and now it's time for goodbyes. As always, we remain *obediently* yours.' The plan was to release *The Magnificent Ambersons* in time for Easter, which in 1942 was at the beginning of April, in eight weeks' time; there was no possibility of the filming on *It's All True* taking less than that, and thus no possibility of Welles being involved in detailed post-production.

In effect, Welles was handing the film over to his associates at the most delicate stage in its life. A rough-cut is like a suit at a final fitting: the raw materials are in place, the shape is essentially there, but all kinds of vital alterations can still be made, while perhaps the most striking aspect of the garment – its finish – is, as the word implies, the very last stage of the process. Nearly 30 per cent of *Citizen Kane* was made after the end of principal photography; many of the most famous sequences in that film were achieved by the use of special effects, all contrived in post-production. During that period of the process, Welles had made radical use in particular of sound (including music); his minutely detailed work with Bernard Herrmann was one of the most striking elements in the film, but much of this work – and the work with special effects – had been done, slowly and painstakingly, after the end of shooting.

In leaving the country (no matter how complex and specific the instructions he left behind), Welles was forgoing these possibilities. Only by watching the film take shape at the Movieola could Welles discover what he needed, and make arrangements for its urgent implementation. Vern Walker, who had created so many of the effects in *Citizen Kane*, prepared a final list of outstanding trick and matte shots for *The Magnificent Ambersons* on 4 February – two days after Welles had left Hollywood for Brazil. Most unusually, the bulk of Herrmann's musical score had been recorded by the end of principal photography, but Welles now had no opportunity to work on the critical process of mixing the music and sound. Herrmann had written an immensely sophisticated score, mirroring and counterpointing the grand themes of the film, the courtly elegance of the world of the Ambersons versus the growing power of the machine, the whole made organic by its use throughout (as in the radio broadcast) of a motif from the Waldteufel waltz *Toujours ou jamais* – initially gracious, later boisterous, until it finally disintegrates altogether. As he had shown both in his radio work and in *Citizen Kane*, Herrmann conceived of music not as a duplication or an underlining of the mood of the images and the text, but as an additional element, making its own comment, creating space by its absence as much as by its presence. Every bar, every orchestral colour, every rhythmic transformation was closely linked to the frame for which it was composed. This being the case, the closest collaboration between director and composer was indispensable. But Welles would be thousands of miles away, with all the complications of wartime communication. So what? He had already directed *Bonito* at long distance; why not post-produce *The Magnificent Ambersons* by telegram and telephone? The answer to that question would soon be given, and in no uncertain terms.

CHAPTER FOUR

Carnival

*I*T'S ALL *True*, Welles's great new venture, was informed by a characteristic mixture of political idealism, artistic excitement and calculating self-promotion. Alongside his loftier ambitions, Welles never lost sight of his public profile. Shortly after his departure, Herb Drake wrote to his associate Tom Pettey, who was already in Brazil as part of the advance guard, to tell him that Welles had called him from Pittsburgh en route to Washington. 'He has left the country furious with yours truly because he has exaggerated expectation of newspaper response.' The Brazil story had made little impact on columnists and trade papers; Welles had been over-sold. 'Newspapers are a little tired of Welles activity, we need a lull.' Another problem was that Drake knew next to nothing about the venture. 'He left me with only limited notion of what he is doing. Please get from him as much theory as possible. He tells me he wants to plug the expedition rather than the picture.' Drake was a particularly shrewd observer of his volatile boss, and in their exchanges over the Brazilian episode he and Pettey offer sharp, sometimes acid analyses of his behaviour. 'OW has certain unpleasant habits such as reading your mail so be circumspect,' advises Drake. 'Don't mind him any if he is rude, he regards this as a time-saving expedient. You will find it difficult getting a logical answer from him about what he is going to do. He trusts always his genius or his charm to get him out of any situation. Sometimes irresistible force meets the immovable object. At such times, go into bomb shelter.' How to handle Orson is their daily study. Clearly the whole organisation is similarly preoccupied: Drake recommends that Pettey should show Dick Wilson 'this letter and all others I send you'.

The advance guard of which Pettey was part had left for Brazil in high spirits, ten days before Welles. In his first letter back to Drake, Pettey describes the perils of travelling during war without papers and with the bare minimum of comforts: in the plane, on the way to Puerto Rico, it is, he says, 'colder than a producer's heart'. Their arrival in Rio was timed to enable Under-Secretary of State Sumner Welles, who had been negotiating with the Brazilian government, to return to Washington on one of their two planes, a Clipper, which had carried the crew and the bulk of the equipment – eighty-six cases and 4,500 pounds of Technicolor equipment, including two cameras and 50,000 feet of film. Later equipment went by army bomber, with the passengers sitting on the floor and hanging on through the curves. The rest went by freighter: a boom, a dolly, black-and-white cameras, two portable generators mounted on truck-trailers and arc lamps. They were in effect moving a small studio to Brazil.

But if travelling was strange, arriving was even stranger. Nothing in the past experience of any of the team prepared them for the startling novelty of life in Rio de Janeiro. 'The first thing on arrival everyone went out and bought white linen suits and we all look like a bunch of broken-down Ambassadors,' wrote Lynn Shores, the hard-bitten RKO production manager, who filed regular reports to his bosses at the studio. 'It is practically impossible to get tight here as it comes out under your arms as fast as you pour it in,' adding a comment that set the tone for his subsequent dealings with the local population: 'We can expect nothing from down here as the countries are virtually as far apart in relations as can be.' The team had nearly two weeks to fill before Welles's arrival. During that time they had a sort of crash course in Brazilian life, under the guidance of Raymundo Magalhaes, a local newspaper magnate: they were shown motion pictures of the previous year's Carnival, of life in the interior, and of the customs and lives of the *jangadeiros*. The government, Pettey's first press release concluded, 'would like for Orson Welles to film some of the daring exploits of these hardy fisherfolks'. *It's All True* was already beginning to look rather more complex than anything Harry Hopkins or RKO had in mind.

Meanwhile the various departments of this somewhat uneasily mixed group – the Mercurians, the Technicolor cameramen, the regular camera crew and sound people, and the RKO production functionaries – staked out their own territories as they waited for Welles to arrive. No one had any experience of making documentaries, which is a vastly different undertaking from making a film in a studio, with its controlled environment, its pre-existent screenplay and its trained actors; no one knew much about Brazil, or even Rio; few of them really understood why they were there; and there was no clear chain of command. 'We already have 22 generals here now,' wrote Lynn Shores to William Daniels of the

RKO front office. Shores was a cynical old pro with no illusions about art, endowed with the full complement of prejudices – racial, sexual and political – of his breed. He just wanted to be able to get on with the job and get the hell out of there, and was already restless, as was Ned Scott, the stills photographer. 'I'll go nuts with another inactive week ahead of me,' he wrote. But the temporary lull was congenial enough to some members of the crew, who were charmed by the country and its people and delighted to be away from the conventions of North American life. Some of the crew started shooting at random: 'We were on our own,' recalled the second cameraman, Joe Biroc. 'We photographed what we wanted, where we wanted. Worked 24 hours for 4 days – then took a week off. One crew member shacked up with a red-headed girl. At the end of the shoot he went back to his wife, but he couldn't stay away. He left the wife, and came back to Brazil.'

Welles, meanwhile, had first flown to Washington to be briefed by the State Department, then to Miami where he was met, as agreed, by Robert Wise with the footage of *The Magnificent Ambersons*. Working round the clock for three days and nights at the Fleischer Cartoon Studio, he and Wise put together a rough-cut of the film; then he dictated a telegram to Jack Moss: BECAUSE OF THE ENORMOUS AMOUNT OF WORK BOB WISE HAS TO DO ON *AMBERSONS*, BECAUSE OF THE NECESSITY OF SPEED AND OF SOME CENTRAL AUTHORITY, I WOULD LIKE YOU TO MAKE CLEAR TO ALL DEPARTMENT HEADS THAT HIS IS THE FINAL WORD. HE IS TO HAVE A FREE HAND . . . I WANT TO KNOW THAT HE WON'T BE SLOWED DOWN AT ANY POINT BECAUSE HIS AUTHORITY IS QUESTIONED. I DICTATE THIS AT THE AIRPORT JUST BEFORE DEPARTING. Meanwhile Wise, in the hope that he might come to Rio at some later point, sped back to Hollywood with the rough-cut while Welles headed off for Brazil, on, of all aptly named vehicles, a Mars Flying Boat.

Tom Pettey had prepared thoroughly for Welles's arrival, ensuring that it had maximum coverage and impact: among other things, he made certain there was a large crowd waiting for him at the airport. Welles was duly fêted; and he readily submitted to the adulation that greeted him. It made a pleasant change, no doubt, from the sniping and pettiness of Hollywood, as did the opportunity – always eagerly seized by Welles – of immersing himself in another culture, another life. He had been thoroughly prepared by his office, with digests of books on Brazilian history, geography, culture and politics; he had begun to learn Portuguese, by no means the easiest of languages. His capacity to absorb essential information rapidly had never been more effectively deployed than it was here, and he immediately seduced his hosts with his well-informed curiosity and his boyish delight in what he discovered. RECEPTION OF ORSON WELLES RIO NOT ONLY EQUAL TO BUT SURPASSED DISNEY'S SUCCESS HERE STOP ORSON CAN QUALIFY FOR MY MONEY AS A GREAT AMBASSADOR, wired Phil Reismann, who had travelled with Welles, to George Schaefer within a few days of their arrival. KNOW THAT IT IS NO SURPRISE TO YOU THAT HIS OUTLOOK AND UNDERSTANDING ARE INTELLIGENT AND COMPREHENSIVE AND THAT HE HAS A COMPLETE GRASP OF THE IMPORTANCE OF THIS JOB. Reismann was convinced, he said, that despite the handicap of a lack of equipment, they were going to get 'a great and unusual picture'. THE ONLY THING THAT KEEPS US FROM BEING EXTREMELY HAPPY, he added, in the same flirtatious tone that Welles employed when communicating with Schaefer, IS THE FACT THAT YOU ARE NOT HERE.

Welles had arrived five days before Carnival, in the midst of a pre-Lenten debauch, which was if anything more feverish than the event itself. His hedonistic impulses needed little encouragement; he plunged right in. The day after he arrived, *A Noite* published a photograph of him partying at a rehearsal of one of the numbers. He was immediately adopted as an honorary citizen of Rio, his appetite and his sense of fun warmly approved of: CARIOCA CITIZEN KANE, said the headline: 'this enormously sympathetic big boy who's being seen around the streets of our metropolis is without doubt an authentic first-rate Carioca', making him an honorary citizen of Rio. Apart from the sheer indulgent joy of it, this immersion in the life of the streets was essential to discovering the spirit of Carnival, where to be merely a spectator is to miss the point; it is, indeed, scarcely an option. The samba rhythm – insistent, hypnotic – that overtakes the city cannot be resisted.

The daunting task of capturing the true Carnival, as it wended its way across the whole city like a frisky, many-headed dragon, called for a novel strategy. 'The moment the Producer-Director-Writer arrived,' reported Herb Drake a little breathlessly, 'Technicolor cameras began to turn out test shots among some of the most beautiful scenery in the world.' Recounting 'what might be called a day with Orson Welles in Rio', Drake describes a cycle of filming, eating, drinking, meeting the press, more eating, drinking, clubbing, and out-of-hours location scouting: '3 a.m. found Welles inspecting the photographic possibilities of the Municipal Theatre where one of the biggest balls of the carnival will be held. You can bet there will be some changes made. Doors will come down, walls will be opened and there will be entrances where no entrances existed before.' There is more clubbing: Welles crowns a beauty queen – 'and that is a story in itself'. He was in bed by dawn – with or without the beauty queen, Drake fails to record. In a private memo to his boss, Tom Pettey reported that 'Welles and Phil Reismann have been playing all the time and I've had a hell of a job protecting them.' All his young life (he was now twenty-six) Orson Welles had been instinctively drawn to the underbelly – Harlem, the dives of Chicago – and here it came straight for him. Then as now, Brazil had a singularly uncomplicated attitude to sex; it had been the country's good fortune to have been colonised by the lax (not to say lethargic) Portuguese, whose administrators had utterly failed to instil the slightest sense of Catholic guilt in the native population. Welles ate, he drank, he smoked, he blithely shovelled amphetamines down his throat in the belief that they were helping him to lose weight, and he reached out for all the flesh he could get his hands on, which was a great deal.

For all the frolicking, the immediate pressure on the RKO team was immense: in so far as they knew what they had come to Brazil to do, it was, at the very minimum, to capture the Carnival on film. Carnival lasts exactly four days, during which short period the bulk of the material had to be shot. Despite Welles's thorough briefing on the background, neither he nor anyone else on his team was familiar with the city of Rio de Janeiro, or had any experience of a comparable phenomenon – let alone of filming it. Moreover, they were severely limited technically, both in terms of the equipment they had brought with them and the available local back-up. 'It must be remembered,' Welles wrote in a memorandum to RKO a couple of weeks after Carnival, 'that our group was practically pioneering in the motion picture business in Brazil', which is not strictly true, although it must certainly have felt as if it was. They had the cooperation and the commitment of officials (Dr Assis Figuereido, head of the State Propaganda Department – the DIP – was particularly keen to help), but there was nothing even they could do in the face of national temperament. At least ten days before Carnival, the production had informed the DIP that they wanted to get shots of Rio at Carnival time and were assured that it could be arranged without much difficulty. When it came to the day actually scheduled for the aerial shots, William 'Duke' Greene, the chief Technicolor cameraman, went to the airport to inspect the plane, and was informed they were not allowed to make use of it. 'We were told that perhaps later we would be able to get a plane.'

Everything that makes the Brazilian Carnival extraordinary was inimical to the process of film-making. Welles and his team soon became acquainted with the two quintessential Carioca types: *moleque*, the street urchin, witty and fleet of foot, and *malandro*, the fixer, avoiding work at all costs, opinionated, pugnacious, lascivious, bibulous, boastful. Welles wrote in his memorandum:

> The human element in particular, the people untrained in the industry and ignorant of its problems, were many times quite impossible to control. Other headaches included the general Brazilian tempo of business activity, such simple hazards as key people lacking telephone service, two-hour lunch periods for business establishments, gasoline shortage . . . things a Hollywood studio through its equipment and organisation could achieve in a matter of hours required as many weeks. None of the organisations on which we could rely was accustomed to actual production problems, the North American tempo of work, or especially professional motion picture discipline.

Here was the paradox: their purpose was to catch the exuberance, the anarchy, the formlessness and the sheer foreignness of Carnival, but to do so they needed to be brilliantly organised. The team's attitude towards the event and the people they were filming – Welles's, in particular – was by definition affirmative, but from a practical angle it was hard not to see both event and people as simply a problem. Up to a point, every film shot on location assumes the character of a war fought against the indigenous people; this one was no exception, even though the commander-in-chief was temperamentally inclined to go native. Inevitably they would not be able to capture everything they needed during the Carnival itself; unquestionably there would have to be subsequent reconstructions of sequences or parts of sequences. 'Even had our information been the most accurate, and our equipment the most effective,' Welles wrote, 'we should have been unable to get a thorough coverage of carnival during the actual days that it lasted. To do this,' he added, 'would have required us to be everywhere at once, at all hours of every day and night.' The scale of the thing was vast: there were something like two million participants involved. Clearly, though, however fraught with difficulties it might be, it was essential to film as much of the live event as was humanly possible.

They duly threw themselves at it. Three years later, on one of his *Orson Welles Almanac* radio programmes, Welles delivered an account of Carnival that vividly expresses his view of what he was about to film:

Carnival isn't a religious observance, but it is fundamentally the celebration of a religious people. Wherever the money changers have taken over, carnival is no more. Wherever work is so hard that a holiday means a rest instead of a good time, carnival is only a word for a tent show. You have to save up for carnival. You have to save something yourself out of the business year. You have to play hard at carnival – not in contest with anybody, not for points in a score – carnival calls for the aimless exuberance of childhood. And if you never felt like dancing around and making a fool of yourself in a funny hat, you won't know what I'm talking about and you won't care. There are some who disapprove of carnival because they think it's only an excuse for getting drunk. I'm glad to say that I was in Rio three years ago for the last great carnival in that greatest of carnival cities and I saw with these two eyes a couple of million people dancing and singing in the streets (most of them don't even go to bed for three days) and nobody anywhere in that enormous jamboree stopped celebrating long enough to take a drink . . . it's brighter than a circus, bigger than the world series, and louder than the Fourth of July. It is all of those times rolled into one. It's New Year's Eve, Halloween night and Christmas morning. It's wild and gay and it's absolutely sober because in carnival you don't need liquor to help you forget you're growing old. You're too busy remembering what it was like when you were young.

In truth, the booze never stops flowing and the dope never stops being puffed and the coupling is pretty much non-stop, but though Welles somewhat sanitises it, his point about the youthfulness of the experience is particularly pertinent here. The whole city becomes a child again – a sexy, exuberant child. And so did Welles.

Tom Pettey of the press office was reporting everything to Herb Drake while it was happening; his description of what he saw is a record not only of the young Orson Welles in action – half teenage delinquent, half inspired artist – but of a Rio Carnival that no longer exists, one that spread everywhere, possessing the city, not confined, as now, to the Sambodromo, the official stadium. Pettey's report also shows not only the degree to which the Carnival affected Welles, but the degree to which he affected it; the filmed event becomes something else, lit, staged, observed. On the Saturday they kicked off by shooting, under lowering skies, the formal opening of the proceedings, the triumphant entrance of King Momo, the Carnival's Lord of Misrule. After this, Welles and the crew immediately dashed in their cars to the elegant suburb of Petropolis on the hillside, for the official opening party, colourful but restrained. The following day, they were out shooting whatever moved. The mood of the 1942 Carnival was particularly explosive: the war hovered over everything. The Rio press insisted: 'for 1942 the order is FORGET THE WAR! We may have the noisiest carnival of all time,' though one of the most popular sambas was the defiant *We Know How to Fight*: 'We will fight in the blue skies that cover South America'; the underlying text was: 'Eat, drink, and be merry, for tomorrow we die.'

The RKO convoy, cheered on by the revellers, itself became part of the revelry. For Technicolor night-shooting there were six army searchlights, manned by eighty Brazilian officers and soldiers, and supervised by the RKO technicians. Simply trying to get through the thousands of people 'who behave abnormally all during carnival', as Pettey said, with all that equipment was a major problem for the crew; the soldiers had no experience and little knowledge of what was demanded of them, piling mayhem on chaos. Five huge lights were set up near the Palace Hotel on Avenida Rio Branco. 'It was difficult to shoot anything except upturned faces and waving arms, as the crowd was so dense there was hardly an inch between the persons.' None of the crew had the slightest idea whether what they were shooting was good or bad. For hours the four great Carnival clubs filed past the Technicolor cameras and moved on down the Avenida amidst the applause of the throng. Welles set up cameras to photograph the floats as they turned across the plaza; one float that they focused on closely depicted Pan-American Unity. Somewhere in the midst of all this Welles had spotted the great black singer-dancer known as Grande Otelo and they followed him whenever they could on his riotous, eccentric path through the throng.

On Monday night, the crew took over the Municipal Theatre where the Grand Ball was to take place, installing lights, strategically placing them all over the theatre to make it possible to obtain shots from every conceivable angle of the dance floor and interior; the chief colour cameraman, Duke Greene, had worked for two weeks in advance to ensure the proper colour combinations. Welles, Pettey notes, had a particular flair for doing three or four things at once. That night he was 'a director of the movie production, a judge of costumes, a good-will envoy, and last but not least, a participant in virtually every one of the dances'. The air-conditioning was primitive: a dance floor packed with a hundred tons of ice. They might just as well have been on the set of *The Magnificent Ambersons*.

It carried on like this for two more days. On the fourth and last day, the crew moved to the Republic Theatre, again struggling to convey tons of equipment across the heaving city, the downtown streets jammed with decorated cars, 'many of them convertibles of ancient vintage . . . filled with ten to twelve costumed boys and girls, and how they held together is a mystery . . . Welles's boys have their cameras pointed at the children whenever it was possible.' Everywhere people were wearing papier mâché masks, no mere item of fancy dress but serious disguise, liberating the wearer into behaviour that would be inconceivable at any other time of the year: to lift a mask or false face from the person wearing it was, Pettey reports, a statutory crime. At midnight, the cameras moved to Avenue Republic where they found the wildest of all the Carnival dancers. 'Here the fun was unrestrained, the only regulation being that women seated at boxes must remove their hats. No one seemed to care whether they removed anything else or not.' Bonhomie was all-pervading. 'Every single one of the million or more revellers tried to be as helpful as possible, even,' he drily notes, 'when their help served only to make things more difficult.'

On this final night, Welles 'suddenly became enthusiastic, grabbed a 16mm camera and moved onto the dance floor at the Republic Theatre. Surrounded by the dancers who were at the height of their revelry, Orson joined in photographing close-ups of the milling mob. When he returned to the camera platform, he was as wet as if he had just emerged from the sea.' To say that Welles was entering into the spirit of things is to understate. 'Perfume battles, exhausting innumerable atomisers, have been daily occurrences around the Copacabana Hotel between Orson Welles and Phil Reismann. They have chased one another around the swimming pool, into the lobby, behind posts, and through the salon. At the present time it is a draw, but Welles expects to win eventually as he apparently has the largest supply of atomisers.' He and his aides made their way across Rio in an old seven-passenger convertible with two motorcycle escorts, their sirens screaming.

'Whenever the sound of a siren is heard they scream "Orson is coming! Orson is coming!"' Finally, the crew shot King Momo's retirement ceremony, the official end of Carnival, and then – and only then – the rain, which had threatened when Momo entered the Carnival four days earlier, fell, as if to wash clean the licentiousness excess in preparation for Ash Wednesday. Pettey was not the only journalist covering the shoot: *Life* magazine had chosen it as the subject of its regular '*Life* Goes to a Party' feature. The photo–essay – like Welles's film, in both colour and black and white – gives a vivid impression of the different strands of the Carnival, focusing on the samba schools, bluntly delineating the upper class, the low class and the poor white and black sections, noting the themes (Swiss mountaineering, Egyptian, Hawaiian), not batting an eyelid at the transvestism and the near-nakedness. Here are the giant backdrop at the Praça Paris – 'a combination of crinolines and samba under a big guitar' – and the jam-packed crowds at the ball at the Teatro Municipal. And here is Welles, 'calling everything *empolgante* (terrific), *assombrosa* (stunning) or *encantadora* (adorable)'. He is photographed 'sweating like all Cariocas', pointing his 16mm camera at the revellers, roaring with laughter, 'feeling good' in the midst of 'one of the low-class "people's dances"', trying to organise poor whites and blacks who are 'too dazed to respond to Welles's direction'.

Life catches him in the act of squirting ethyl chloride over another guest with Phil Reismann at the Copacabana Hotel. The accompanying photographs reveal a striking aspect of the phenomenon of Orson Welles, his extraordinary mutability. In one picture, he is a handsome, dashing, raffish young man; in another, he looks like a fat, mischievous, rather ugly youth; in yet another, the concentrated artist, willing his listeners to do his bidding. Perhaps it was his desire to control his image that led to the falling out with *Life*'s representatives, which Tom Pettey relayed to Herb Drake. Pettey was desperately trying to get the local press not to focus entirely on shots of Welles in nightclubs. There was a near-miss when he had arranged a press conference at which Welles had failed to make an appearance; eventually, though, he arrived and 'came through nobly'.

Yet another, particularly beady, pair of eyes was trained on Welles as he improvised his way through the Carnival shoot: those of Lynn Shores, the RKO production manager. He offers a view untouched by the euphoria of the journalists. 'I am enclosing a sort of day-to-day report on this junket to date,' he writes to his masters. 'We have been shooting a certain amount of film during carnival, but I am afraid the results on the screen are not going to be terribly impressive from what I have seen so far.' Here is one man, at any rate, who is in no danger of going native. 'What with the heat, the strange food, our inability to get anything moving in the speedy American way, and' – the nub – 'the fast shuffles that Welles cooks up, everyone is pretty much at each other's throats in our organi-sation down here. However, he can't complain as we have given him everything we have.' The problem, and it was an all-pervading one, was that in the aftermath of Carnival no one knew exactly what they were shooting. 'As to the plans of this set-up, I am entirely in the dark. Harry Wild is also trying to get something out of Mr Welles. Each time Orson just shows him the cuff of his shirt.' Clearly the team was not a team at all. A division was already evident. Dick Wilson, Shores complains, 'sticks so close to Welles over at the beach that we are entirely without any information here at any time'. Welles's natural resistance to any form of corporate control was only enhanced by his physical distance from the studio, and he now began an elaborate game of cat and mouse, which would last for the length of the shoot. 'I get along swell with Orson and Reismann,' Shores reports, 'and in their saner moments we sometimes have a business-like conversation lasting at least a minute or so.' Signing off, he drily notes, in a sardonic reference to the pious Catholic Joe Breen, RKO's head of productions, that 'conduct throughout has been up to the high standard Mr Breen hoped for'.

Welles was now able to stand back a little after the whirlwind of Carnival and take stock of the film he was making or, more precisely, the film that was being made. 'The problem of shooting carnival may be compared to the problem of shooting a storm,' he wrote in his memorandum to RKO. 'We shot without a script. We were forced to. A script was impossible. Even in those sequences in which it was possible to exercise directorial control, *I as a director was always the one to be informed rather than the people working under me.* In other words, I couldn't tell them what to do. They had to tell me.' This was an alarming experience for a man accustomed to being obeyed. He had as little idea as anyone else of the value or quality of what he had just shot, working as they all were 'without the critical advantage of nightly sessions in projection and cutting rooms'. He defends the large quantity of footage shot. 'Put it this way: we've had to take out all the paying dirt and ship it halfway round the world from the place where it was mined. We won't get the gold till we go back to where operations are possible.' This was his brief, he says (his italics): '*It was understood by all concerned before I left that carnival would be shot on the cuff*,' but 'none of us knew anything about it before we came here, nor were there any sources of information available'. Because, he says, the film he had been despatched to Brazil to make was to be 'unrelieved by story (or what is generally considered story)', their treatment of the Carnival subject of Brazilian music had to be 'definitive, and beyond reproach. Above all, it had to be entertainment.' Accordingly, in the midst of filming the pick-up shots from Carnival – and still with little more than a vague intuition about a unifying narrative – he set about investigating an entire culture. Thinking big was the only kind of thinking Welles knew. Largely at his own expense, under the direction of his friend the radical writer Robert Meltzer (a member of the Communist Party, and formerly Chaplin's assistant on *The Great Dictator*), with input from his other Mercury colleagues, he assembled a remarkable team, including two of Brazil's best newspapermen, Rio's leading historian, and one of Brazil's leading playwrights. Their task was to provide both an overview of Brazilian culture and a detailed analysis of its individual manifestations, especially in so far as they related to Carnival.

Welles wrote Meltzer a memorandum that suggests the scope of his intellectual curiosity, but also the charismatic authority that he exercised over his colleagues, many of whom were older and rather better educated than he was. The memo is a rare example of Welles's approach to film-making in action. He manifests a surprisingly detailed and almost academic interest in the origins of the different forms of samba – *bateria, cuica, ganza, surdu, tamborim, pandeiro* – issuing bossy demands for more and more information about origin, meaning and the future of Carnival:

What made carnival what it was? Is it what it was? Make a full report of the element of competition in carnival . . . Brazil is a country of clubs. Samba is a manifestation of this national tendency. What are the social, economic and moral motives behind all this organisation? Does the old potency of Masonry relate to this? . . . all this requires absolute reams of written material to be composed by yourself *now*. Generalise, please, as little as you can. Particularise and specify as much as may be in this land of *mas* or *menos*. Above all, I beg of you don't try to write well. Just notes.

Welles's instinctive prelapsarianism rightly suggests to him that 'carnival began raucous . . . now it's going commercial . . . if they don't stop they're going to turn it into Mardi Gras and the floats are going to end up as commercials'. Perhaps, he muses, the dilution of Carnival commenced with the emergence in Rio of a middle class, the *granfinos*. 'Carnival,' he says, 'is a creation by somebodies and less than nobodies.' His instincts as story-teller overcoming his socio-economic analyses lead him to urge Meltzer to make 'Mr and Mrs Granfino and Mr and Mrs Malandro' real as characters: 'Surround them with their worlds – their entire worlds complete with props – sights and smells and sounds, and even a couple of ideas. Do this thoroughly as though you were writing a good novel, and carnival will be better defined than it has been.' Unrelentingly, he demands engravings, lithographs, photographs and designs, which, like Napoleon returning from Egypt, he plans to take back to Hollywood with him. Once past the immediate intoxication of shooting the Carnival itself, he is beginning to edge towards a new sort of film: an anthropological, cultural, historical, musical, comical survey of a whole country. 'The picture progresses,' he ends. 'Everything is just as it ought to be and our subject is more perfect than I hoped. You are all I need – you and a woman – I need you both.'

Who would not follow such a man to the ends of the earth? This letter reveals the full force of Welles's exploding mind and the overpowering immediacy of his personal engagement with individuals. As Geraldine Fitzgerald said of him, 'he was like a lighthouse. When you were caught in the beam it was utterly dazzling. When the beam moved on, you were plunged into darkness.' Driven on by the need to articulate the substance of the film they wanted to make, Meltzer's little unit produced a plethora of learned, colourful and often witty papers on, among many themes, Brazilian legends and folklore, 'how different races and peoples contributed to carnival' and 'the whys of Rio's carnival'. It is worth quoting some of the contributions, offering as they do a strong indication of what Welles's film might have dealt with. 'The humiliated, the timid, the unsatisfied constitute the majority of this crowd of badly-mixed races that dances, sings, yells and drinks and shows costumes of violent colours, in a mad search for dizziness and vertigo,' writes Rui Costa in his exuberant essay about Carnival. 'It's the Negro that can't be a white man, the woman still waiting for her great love affair, the poor that can't be a maharajah – and he brings on his head a cheap imitation of a turban.'

Professor Ghiaroni, in a paper entitled 'Carnival and Respectable Gentlemen', describes the *Gafieira* ('the cheap public ballroom where people with little means and great desire for fun find all the consolation they need for their hard work'), underlining its socially levelling aspect: 'In Rio the customers are a mixed-up throng of white, blacks and half-breeds. But there is always a predominance of the latter, so that white men, even those on the same economic and social level, are looked upon with little sympathy. At the carnival, all these psychological boundaries fall and everybody puts hands on the shoulders of everybody else, thanks to carnival's roaring enlargement of the freedom idea, rather unsure during the rest of the year.' Someone else anatomises the *chôro*, the classic Brazilian instrumental form; others, in great detail, analyse the samba. Meltzer himself writes a piece for this running symposium that he drolly calls 'The Genealogy of Samba and Other Aspects of an Unquiet Life'; it is entirely characteristic of the Mercurians' jokey manner with each other: 'Since it's very probably true that nothing comes from nothing, you can say right to begin with that Samba must have had specific origins in time and space . . . it has a pedigree, ancestry, roots. The problem is to find out what the hell they are, exactly. Unfortunately there doesn't seem to be any single authority competent to give this information in one-two-three form.' His method, for all its playfulness, is essentially dialectical; he was, after all, a well-trained Marxist:

Whether or not an article or a book on Samba would be necessarily true in all its details, it would at least make enough of a stir to serve as a focal point for a real clash between the various claims and theories. In the absence of such a focal point, it's necessary to create one if you want to find out anything. One way to do this is the way you outlined: see as many people as will respond, ask as many questions as possible, and stir up a maximum of contradiction. Since no two people agree entirely, this is comparatively easy. After a while . . . you find yourself with a residue which might be called The Truth about Samba.

An anonymous piece on the samba schools, the *escolas*, suggests a more passionate view: 'The rivalry of different schools has its roots in old Portuguese dances, in which Moors and Christians sparred . . . to obtain . . . victory, the poor washerwoman or cook gets herself into debt for the whole year . . . the samba school is a world for psychologists: the father, who drivels with joy at seeing his daughter half-dressed in front of the floats; the jealous sweetheart who takes shots at anyone who makes a remark to the leader of the *cordão*; the mother who works day and night on her daughter's fancy dress so that she can shine in the ballrooms of the "United Heart".'

The idea of the samba begins to pervade all the discussions. Phil Reismann, in a letter to Jock Whitney immediately after the shooting of Carnival had ended, takes credit for pushing it to the fore. '[Welles] will carry a story through the carnival film and an idea which I gave him showing the birth of the Samba in the hills of Rio and carrying it right down through the carnival using this as a thread to tie up all of his action.' On the face of it, this idea was perfectly within the terms of Welles's brief. The specific remit of the I-AA's Motion Picture Division was 'to remove sources of irritation and misunderstanding in the US as when our motion pictures burlesque Central and South American characters'; *Girl of the Rio* and *Cuban Love Song* were particularly glaring examples of this. The Brazilian division had already made documentaries such as *Americans All* and *Good Neighbor Family*, but no Latin Americans had been involved in their production. The I-AA wanted a film that avoided the crude ethnic stereotypes, but nonetheless promoted a positive, 'colourful' image; if it helped to promote tourism, so much the better (the year before, 700 Americans had come to Rio for the Carnival, in 'a swirling four day and four night bender of lights, noise, tinsel and music, that makes New Orleans Mardi Gras look like a meeting of the Modern Language Association'). The trade cut both ways: Latin America was an important market, now that a large part of the European one had for all practical purposes disappeared. The origins of the I-AA give a clue to its policy. Roosevelt had created its immediate predecessor, the revealingly named Office of Commercial and Cultural Relations with the Americas, after reading a paper on 'Hemispheric Economic Policy' from Nelson Rockefeller's informal think-tank on Latin America, the so-called *junta*, created in the wake of the left-wing Mexican government's expropriation of all foreign oil holdings in 1938. Rockefeller had become convinced during his travels on behalf of Standard Oil in Latin America (where he was dubbed 'El Principe de Gasolina') that instability in the region was a threat to his family's oil holdings and that economic prosperity was the only effective means of protecting foreign investment. This form of 'missionary capitalism', in Darlene Rivas's suggestive phrase, informed all the activities of what soon became known as the

Office of Inter-American Affairs, whose declared aim was not to build up a large government organisation, but to handle as many activities as possible through private organisations – hence the initial approach to RKO to make the propaganda film they wanted. It was a delicate mission, which Welles, now that he was fully intellectually and artistically engaged, was about to sabotage.

Phil Reismann's letter to Whitney reported that 'the important and welcome surprise to me is Welles's frame of mind, his willingness to forget that he is a motion picture producer alone, and that he has an important mission to perform'. Welles unquestionably believed that, but Reismann's suggestion of the history of the samba itself as a possible spine for the Carnival section of the movie (if it was his suggestion) opened up innumerable avenues of interest to Welles, who sensed an opportunity to do something revolutionary, striking a blow for popular culture at the same time as creating a new kind of film, far beyond the scope of the ramshackle compendium he had originally talked about in Hollywood, and way beyond the travelogue envisioned by Harry Hopkins. To focus on the samba's origins in Rio's *favelas*, the shanty towns with their largely black population huddled together on the hillside in apparent squalor just beyond the smart centre of President Getúlio Vargas's capital city with its aspirations to Parisian elegance, would inevitably involve an exploration not only of the city's underbelly, but also of its African element. Neither the Office of Inter-American Affairs nor the Brazilian government was in the least interested in any such exploration. But Welles was compulsively drawn to this other Rio, where he was more and more often to be found, visiting the *escolas de Samba*, dabbling with the musical instruments, hanging out with the players, far from the posh salons of the cultural attachés; he gave in to the Cheapside part of his nature, his somewhat romanticised sense of a life without constraints or obligations, which seemed to him more real than the bourgeois world from which he came. As always, popular music enchanted and transported him. He was understandably greeted with open arms by the *favelistas*, ignored and despised as they were by the middle classes, who were somewhat embarrassed by their existence. 'To give you some idea of Welles's popularity,' wrote Reismann, 'he seems to be especially great with the masses; he has mingled with them and danced with them, and wherever we go in the car, the children yell out his name and applaud.' In making the film, it was to these people that he felt his principal loyalty – to them and to those popular heroes, the boatmen, who had travelled on their *jangadas* from their home in the far north of Brazil's vast domain to deliver to the President himself their petition, and whose story the government was so keen to have told. Increasingly, that modern Homeric epic began to assume equal narrative importance in Welles's mind to the Carnival and the history of the samba.

The government of Getúlio Vargas was a highly significant factor in the situation with which Welles was dealing. On the face of it, this remarkable and somewhat paradoxical figure would scarcely seem likely to feature on a list of Welles's political heroes: President since 1930, when he had been imposed by the army, he governed by decree, until four years later the Constituent Assembly, under the army's influence, officially increased his formal powers. In 1937 Vargas had used the excuse of an imaginary communist uprising to declare a state of siege, imposing a new constitution, declaring in Brazil what he called *Estado nôvo* – the new state – which was essentially a totalitarian corporate state, heavily centralised, rigidly policed, highly undemocratic. Nonetheless, he was the most popular leader the country had known since the reign of Pedro II in the previous century. Champion of the urban middle and lower classes, he stood against the hitherto all-powerful coffee barons and their rural, semi-feudal empires. Before the creation of the *Estado nôvo*, he had endeared himself to his countrymen and women by instituting the secret ballot, vastly expanding the electorate (giving women the vote for the first time), enacting substantial social-security legislation, establishing a minimum wage and initiating a vigorous programme of industrialisation; he remained on good terms with the labour movement even after 1937, though political unrest was widespread.

Vargas continued to press forward with his modernising programmes during the internationally tense period of the European war. Skilfully, he avoided committing himself to either Axis powers or Allies: his essential sympathies might have been assumed to lie with the fascists (the population of Brazil, moreover, has always had a very strong German component), but he was mindful of his relationship with his Latin American neighbours, as well as with the United States. He had personally expressed his support for *It's All True* when it was first mooted, and had caused the full (if sometimes ineffective) weight of the government Motion Picture Division under Assis Figueiredo to be thrown behind it; a couple of weeks after Welles's arrival, Vargas had personally hosted a reception for him in Petropolis, at which he expressed his delight that the *jangadeiros*'s story would be told. He had his own purpose in encouraging the film: he saw it as an advertisement for his modern Brazil, where even illiterate fishermen in the far north could be unionised and receive benefits. And he could show off his capital, Rio, in a permanent state of reconstruction, the rival of any European city with its fine hotels, its parks and its massive boulevards. The geographical heart of the Carnival, the old Praça Onze, had indeed recently been swept away and replaced, somehow inevitably, by Avenidad Getúlio Vargas. Grande Otelo's samba in the 1942 Carnival, which became the *enredo*, the featured song of the year, lamented this:

> They're closing down
> There will be no more samba school
> The shanty towns cry
> Favela, Salguiero
> Marquera, Estaçao Primera
> Put away your instruments
> The samba schools won't be parading today.

The song perfectly embodies one of Welles's central themes, the disappearance of paradise – in this case not the gracious life of *The Magnificent Ambersons*, but the people's pleasures. This theme would feature strongly in the film that was forming in his mind.

This was not, of course, a theme that Vargas or his government wanted aired. As time went on, it became apparent that what Welles intended to film was very different from what any of his three masters – the I-AA, RKO and the Brazilian government – expected from him. For the moment, Welles was smiled on, and by way of return was happy to write to Getúlio Vargas to inform him that he would be doing a series of broadcasts from Brazil in which he intended to tell the story of *The March on the West*, 'a true civic epic of your great political movement', an extraordinary piece of ideological flexibility on his part, but one that was certainly in accord with US government policy – that is, to encourage Brazil by all means to declare war on Germany. The tension was at its height during the spring and summer of 1942: Catherine Benamou reports that during the period of the shooting of *It's All True*, more than fifteen Brazilian vessels were torpedoed by Axis forces.

Meanwhile Welles and the crew, having captured the actual Carnival from every possible angle, now set about the task of reconstructing large portions of it, in the hope of creating a coherent narrative. The central sequence of the Carnival section was to be the famous entertainment at the Urca Casino, which required restaging, relighting and strenuous organisation both of the performers and the audience. In effect, they found that they were now filming a musical, another form of which none of them had the slightest experience. Moreover the weather had turned. Distracted by social and formal engagements and absorbed in plans for the larger movie he was evolving, Welles himself seemed to be only partly focused on the work in hand. 'On location 8 p.m., waited for Mr Welles until 9.30 p.m.' is a fairly typical entry in the daily log of activities. Surprisingly, Lynn Shores, the production manager, was entrusted with responsibility for taking a large number of shots, mostly process and montage, but sometimes more than that. Unsurprisingly, he was not best pleased. On one occasion, having been told that Welles wanted to take certain shots, Shores secured, with some difficulty, the army searchlights they had just returned; Welles never showed up. Shores shot anyway ('neither Harry Greene nor myself had the vaguest idea of exactly what he was after'); the following day Welles phoned to tell him to carry on for the next two days, which he did. At no point, Shores said, did he or anyone else know what they were shooting or why:

> I will not go into detail of my various attempts at trying to pin
> Welles down as to future plans. In a vague way he has given me
> to understand that we are to travel over most of South America
> with the Mercury Players, various units of Technicolor and black
> and white, radio set-ups, goodwill speeches, and general messing
> around for the next two or three months . . . it has become a
> horrible nightmare to me personally. I am carrying not only the
> working but the personal problems of practically twenty-seven
> individuals, each one with an axe to grind and a grievance of
> some sort at every hour of the day.

He works, he says, twenty-hour days. Welles, it appears, wants him to carry on shooting, and will continue to want him to carry on shooting because of the radio shows he is planning. If so, Shores fulminates, he wants a new deal.

While Shores and the crew were baffled and resentful (Duke Greene, the Technicolor cameraman, was drinking heavily and 'certainly does not make for N American goodwill in Rio', according to a memorandum), Welles himself was investigating the Brazilian cinema; he saw some shorts that contained, according to Tom Pettey, 'ideas he might wish to look into'. At the same time, the Brazilian cinema was investigating Welles; and it liked what it found. *Kane* was given a special showing in Rio; Welles got awards for best actor, best director, best picture. At supper with some journalists afterwards he was told that it was he who had really been King of the Carnival in Rio, and that 'no other personality from the United States, especially from Hollywood, had won so many friends in Rio'. A group of artists and intellectuals gave a dinner in his honour, a *Homenagem a Orson Welles*: he was, they declared, 'the outstanding figure in the motion picture world' (he had at this point completed exactly one film). He gave every appearance of exhilaration in his reports back to George Schaefer.

> We're working too hard down here for good letter writing, or even one good long letter. Since you are my most understanding friend, I won't even attempt to explain my silence or alibi the brevity of this. I have great hopes for the film itself. Quite apart from its importance as a documentary, its entertainment value promises to be great. The carnival sequence alone . . . is going to mark a totally new departure in musicals. Indeed every aspect of this picture is as fresh as even you could ask for. – This is a big job and a tough one, and I am truly and deeply grateful for the opportunity. I do think our rewards will be great. This is real pioneering and – after all – [he added in the special tone he reserved for Schaefer] pioneering is what we like best. Fondest regards.

In stark contrast to the evidence of the production reports or the admittedly biased letters of Lynn Shores, Welles wrote to Jock Whitney that they were definitely on schedule and – if anything – doing a little better than might have been expected. A certain amount of string-pulling had been deployed. 'You may have heard that the city of Rio – and, for all I know, the United States of Brazil – was without anti-aircraft searchlights for more than a week. How we got them is a matter between Dr Assis Figuerido and his God. How they were transformed into plausible Technicolor units is a wonder of absolutely Old Testament proportions.' He praises the ingenuity and resourcefulness of the team – 'reflectors gleam and everywhere things buzz and hum and click' – but they are still in desperate need of the promised supplies: 'that boat's got to come or we'll all run screaming into the jungle'. Phil Reismann wrote to Whitney that Welles's good humour was 'positively Brazilian; his enthusiasm always informed; his tact is limitless. Besides which,' he added, 'he's rare good company', something no one had ever disputed about Orson Welles.

George Schaefer, meanwhile, quietly reminded Welles on 27 February that *The Magnificent Ambersons* – from which this Brazilian venture was, in RKO's eyes, a mere (if worthy) diversion – was due for an Easter release. Easter Sunday that year fell on 3 April: a print would be with him for his approval by 15 March and must be immediately returned. PLEASE ORSON, Schaefer begged Welles, in the slightly pleading tone he so often adopted in their exchanges, DO EVERYTHING MAKE THIS POSSIBLE; and he added: HAVE HEARD OF EXCELLENT PROGRESS VERY HAPPY EVERYTHING WORKING OUT SO WELL. KIND PERSONAL REGARDS. Schaefer, with exceptional restraint, made no attempt to convey the precariousness of his situation. The studio was haemorrhaging money, by no means exclusively on the independent units such as the Mercury. Its star-packed *Sing Your Worries Away* lost $225,000; *Valley of the Sun*, a Western, lost $185,000. The board had been reluctant to renew George Schaefer's contract: a new board was about to take over, and the old board was eager not to tie its hands. Schaefer had been allowed to continue as head of studio on an informal basis, but there had been ominous visits from New York, culminating in the sacking of two of Schaefer's lieutenants, McDonough and Lesser. Joe Breen was on vacation, and Charles Koerner, also from head office, a famously tough cookie, stepped in for him; he never stepped out. The tumbrils were rolling; the days of Schaefer's *ancien régime* were numbered.

Far removed from all this, at the beginning of March, Orson Welles wrote, in his unmistakably open hand, a curious kind of a haiku, half reminder, half reassurance, placed firmly in the centre of a blank foolscap sheet of paper: somewhere, deeply buried beneath all that talent, arrogance and charisma, there was in Welles an unexpected vein of deep humility.

> Nothing has ever been too good for the public.
> Nothing has ever been good enough for the public.

CHAPTER FIVE

Only Orson and God

WELLES'S RESPONSE to Schaefer's telegram of 27 February was to put everyone working on *The Magnificent Ambersons* at RKO on triple shifts. He had wired Robert Wise to make as many alternate cuts of dissolves, sound and music as possible, and now asked Jack Moss, in charge of the Mercury office in Hollywood, to start running the film nightly, and to take active command of the production. GET IN NORMAN JO DOLORES FOR JURY AS MANY TIMES AS POSSIBLE EVERY OPINION MUST BE COVERED BY AN ALTERNATE, he told Moss. This was, in the most literal sense, editing by committee, Moss being the chairman. YOU HAVE BEEN AWAY FROM AMBERSONS LONG ENOUGH TO BE FRESH AND YOU KNOW I TRUST YOU COMPLETELY – an extraordinary act of faith in a man who, until two years before, had been an obscure vaudevillian, one who, moreover, had never written, directed or produced a film in his life, and whose only appearance in one had been mute. The note of panic in Welles's communication and in the many that followed is unmistakable. He telegrammed Schaefer to reassure him that he was in almost daily contact with the office, and that the studio was working on the film 'at breakneck speed'. He had, he said, conceived an idea that the world premiere should be in Buenos Aires, the day before the Hollywood premiere; he wanted to do the narration himself in Spanish and Portuguese. RESULTANT INTERNATIONAL PUBLICITY WILL BE ENORMOUS SHOWMANSHIP TERRIFIC, he insisted, continuing with a touch of deluded grandeur, MAGNIFICENT PAN–AMERICAN GESTURE BESIDES KEEPING ARGENTINE FROM FEELING LEFT OUT OF OUR S AMERICAN PICTURE.

Schaefer replied with understandable exasperation that he had no objection to a Rio world premiere of *The Magnificent Ambersons* (he wired Phil Reismann to the effect that a Buenos Aires opening was out of the question), but he was absolutely desperate to get on with the American one since the picture had already cost more than $1m – $150,000 more than the strict limit he and Welles had agreed. His own position at RKO was now vulnerable in the extreme. The ruthless Charles Koerner was daily strengthening his position there, laying plans for the studio's return to financial health. His first target was the Mercury. 'With respect to Orson Welles or Mercury Productions in which we are interested,' he stated in a crisp memorandum, 'please make sure that no commitments of any nature whatsoever are entered into without first checking with the writer.' In so far as the erratic communications system, now rendered even more unreliable by wartime restrictions, would allow, Welles was in constant contact with the Mercury office, not only about *The Magnificent Ambersons*, but also about *Journey into Fear*. In the light of the current international situation, he now felt that the latter film required some reshooting; to this end he proposed to shoot cutaways of himself in Rio, for which he would need the full Colonel Haki wardrobe and, most importantly, his false nose. In the meantime, he hastened to assure Schaefer: EVERYTHING HERE PROCEEDING BEAUTIFULLY IN SPITE OF NON ARRIVAL OF BOAT STOP CANNOT OVERSTATE OUR ENTHUSIASM CONFIDENCE EFFECTIVENESS BEAUTY SOLID ENTERTAINMENT VALUE SHOWMANSHIP THIS PICTURE.

He was the only person who thought so. In the absence of the boat bearing the additional equipment required, the team's activities were at best desultory, at worst non-existent. The weather, which had broken at the end of Carnival, had never recovered and continued to be appalling, bitterly cold with rain and thunderstorms. They shot the samba clubs in Technicolor in the afternoons and at night; Welles was not present for this work, which would have been second-unit material, if they had had a second unit, and was generally supervised by the grossly disaffected Lynn Shores. Despite the fact that Welles had arranged a rise in salary for him – AS FAVOR TO ME, he had wired the front office – Shores's festering resentment continued to inform his reports back to RKO's Walter Daniels. 'I have a lot of things in my mind which may explode before you receive this letter,' he wrote to his master. 'We have not made a shot worth while this week, and if we had been shooting continually all week, the shot would still not have been worth while. I do not like to be pessimistic on this trip but the longer we are here the more involved we get and seem to be working toward no end . . . Welles is definitely throwing the shooting of this picture onto my lap. Confidentially I believe there is nothing promising here. The shooting of the carnival was a big disappointment to all of us, and I know to him personally.' The crew was unhappy. 'I am working under continuous pressure from both ends. Welles wants me all night for meaningless conferences, and the boys want me all day for shooting and general lending ear to their beefs. Whatever they feel about Welles they are taking out on me.' He hoped that on arrival at the studio 'the lights and equipment will keep the boys occupied to the extent of keeping them out of too much unoccupied mischief . . . I am doing everything humanly possible to preserve law, order, morale and progress.' Almost any human group has its Lynn Shores, grimly rejoicing in the prospect of disaster; here he had material in abundance to feed his *schaden-freude.* 'I hate to continually bombard you with pessimistic letters,' he avers. 'Someone has got to be a little truthful about this jaunt . . . the details of the daily manoeuvre down here would fill a book and be most amusing. Someday I may write that book.' Tom Pettey was writing to Herb Drake to much the same effect. The crew was deeply unhappy, not only about the work or lack of it in Rio, but about the low profile of the venture: 'everyone in Hollywood will forget about us and we will become forgotten men'.

Partly to counteract this, early in March, Pettey concocted one of his striking press releases, which does not entirely dispel the impression that no one really knows what he's doing, least of all Welles: 'The glimpse into the future that follows may go through as outlined, may be changed, may be done altogether or in part. No one can tell as no one knows what difficulties may be encountered in a war-ridden world. Anyhow, here's the story as it stands today. A big smiling man in a plum-coloured suit – easily the most stared-at man in the salon of the Copacabana Hotel in Rio de Janeiro – leaned across the coffee table and began talking with a couple of newsmen . . .' The picture, the much-stared-at Welles tells them, will be a long one. 'We don't know how much it will cost because we don't know what difficulties we may have to face in the way of delays and transportation.' Then he outlines a general plan: 'Devices – pictorial, musical and by sound – will be utilised at the opening to establish a mood, bring all sections of South and Latin America to the screen.' Over it all, apparently, will be 'the Welles voice'. *Bonito* will follow, and lead into the *jangadeiros's* story. There will be sequences shot in countries other than Brazil, including, for example, a short account of the conquest of Peru, to be shot around Lima. More than half the picture will be shot in Brazil. 'I'm not trying to make a documentary film,' Welles concluded, 'nor am I interested in making a travelogue. I want to tell some of the stories of South America in an interesting manner and bring certain phases of Latin entertainment to the movie-going world. The picture will have music, colour, romance, and will be of the land, the sea and the cities.' Pettey reports that Welles is fully aware that he is facing tremendous difficulties. 'It's a safe bet that out of Welles's South American trek will come a new and novel production. It will be a great production if he gets an even break with fate,' says Pettey, gamely. 'In a few weeks Rio will have a first class movie studio. It may result in fine pictures being made right here in Brazil . . . the Welles crew and the man will be remembered in Brazil for years to come. They brought something to the country and are taking nothing away except pictures . . .'

The horror with which George Schaefer and the heads of production at RKO must have read this press release may well be imagined, the prospect of restaging the conquest of Peru perhaps bringing a touch of the surreal to the situation. In fact, Welles's extrapolation of the possible contents of the film hark back to his radio past, where the conquest of Peru could be easily and effectively knocked off in fifteen minutes of air time, and everything could be changed on the floor (indeed, only a few months hence he was to produce just such a sequence for his programme *Hello Americans*). But if Welles was still unclear about the film he wanted to make, he was by no means unengaged by its possibilities. Tom Pettey described seeing him one evening, apparently set up for 'a night of relaxation'. But no: as he passed Welles's hotel room much later, 'the lights were burning at 3 a.m. and the typewriters going'. Welles's thoughts were turning increasingly to the story of the *jangadeiros* and their charismatic leader, Mandel Olimpio Meira, known as Jacaré. He was planning a reconnaissance trip to the far north, to Fortaleza, to the town from which the rafters' odyssey had set out. Lynn Shores was darkly suspicious: 'I believe Welles's intentions are to leave me at Fortaleza to finish the *jangada* picture and bring one complete unit back to Rio where he will start filming dips and dabs of the carnival cut-in. The trip is assuming all the proportions of a typical Orson Welles production in that we are attempting to start three or four different things at once instead of sticking on one till it is accomplished. Welles has not seen a camera since the finish of carnival two weeks ago.'

In fact, the Carnival, even the account of the origins of the samba, was beginning to seem very small beer next to the heroic story of the *jangadeiros*, which had a particular advantage over the Carnival material: it was a reconstruction of an event that had already happened, and was therefore available to interpretation, reinvention and control. Documentary was a medium of which Welles had still not quite got the hang; this was drama. Even with the *jangadeiros* material, he was uncertain as to what he wanted to do with it until he had gone north, though he now had a title for it, which gave an immediate sense of the epically simple manner he proposed for the sequence: *Four Men on a Raft*. He was sure of one thing: the film must be shot in Technicolor. An increasingly frantic George Schaefer was equally sure that it must not: the expense would be prohibitive, to say nothing of the logistical problems of transporting a Technicolor crew to the north. He cabled Phil Reismann to that effect: MOST IMPORTANT THIS BE THOROUGHLY UNDERSTOOD BY WELLES AND YOURSELF. YOU CAN SHOW THIS CABLE TO WELLES. PLEASE EXPLAIN TO HIM THAT BECAUSE OF CERTAIN BOARD AND GOVERNMENT RESTRICTIONS I HAVE NO ALTERNATIVE. Reismann replied with an emollient and cleverly calculated letter, assuring Schaefer that the cost of shooting the rest of the Carnival picture would not go much beyond the salaries of crew and the very nominal studio rental; even Shores admitted that filming had been cheap: 'money really does go a long way down here'. The whole movie to date, claimed Reismann, had cost a mere $19,000. Welles insisted, Reismann added, that the *jangadeiros* story was always part of the theme (which was true enough) and that Hollywood always knew it was going to be in Technicolor (which was not); without the *jangadeiros*, the Carnival story would not be much more than newspaper coverage.

What was undeniable was that the unit was sinking into despair. Welles was planning broadcasts, waiting for a sponsor to materialise. He spoke constantly about a tour of South America, and personal appearances with *The Magnificent Ambersons* in (among other places) Peru, which no doubt he saw himself conquering effortlessly. 'It is all very grand and exciting,' grumbled Shores, 'but everyone is feeling pretty low thinking of the monotony of the months that are to follow here with little accomplishment in the way of direct picture progress.' Tom Pettey was no more cheerful. 'The weather remains quite cloudy, the boat remains unreported, the studio we are to rent remains unoccupied, most of the time the cameras are idle,' he told Herb Drake. 'Actually we've done remarkably little toward making a picture since the close of carnival . . . as for the picture we are trying to make, only Orson and God knows anything about it and neither are in town at this writing. So many difficulties to overcome. Most of all we lack aggressive leadership.'

The leader himself and his inner circle had flown to Fortaleza, capital of the state of Ceará, the wind-swept home of the *jangadeiros*, with its limitless succession of beaches and its quiet colonial elegance, now quite disappeared, but which, in 1942, made the town a particularly charming contrast to Rio's metropolitan swagger. Despite the restaurants, the ballroom and the Tiffany-decorated interiors and grand façade of the Teatro José de Alencar, the heart of the city remained its fishing trade, symbolised by the great pillar surmounted by a monumental statue of Christ blessing the fishermen, erected in 1922 in the city centre. The *jangada* – a primitive raft as old as the Phoenician barques it so strongly resembles, invented by the Indians, whose blood flows in the veins of so many of the inhabitants of the north-east – was at the core of the subsistence economy that sustained 80 per cent of the population. In the five days of their voyage, Welles and his team travelled 4,000 miles across Brazil, visiting Natal, San Luise, Bahia and other cities once thought to be, according to Tom Pettey's excited report, LOST JUNGLES. In Fortaleza (where he was accompanied by Bob Meltzer and Augusta Weissberger, who kept a diary), Welles took part in a *jangada* race during which a fisherman was seriously injured, giving him a keen sense of the dangers the *jangadeiros* had courted in their heroic journey to Rio. He found, here in the north-east, a life and a people very different from the heterodox, multiracial, cynical, occasionally sleazy Cariocas; Fortaleza was tougher and simpler, an outdoor world; and it powerfully appealed to that aspect of Welles – every bit as powerful in him as the *goût de la boue*, which had been so generously indulged in Rio – that relished and honoured the life of working communities in direct contact with nature, governed by strictly regulated codes of behaviour. He had been moved in the same way by the fishing communities he had seen in the west of Ireland as a schoolboy traveller, and only a little later by the Berbers in the Atlas Mountains and the bull-fighters of Andalusia. They were, *mutatis mutandis*, yet other versions of the Merrie England that so haunted him: the Edenic paradises where, in Welles's dream, decency, dignity and a franker, truer understanding of human nature prevailed.

Contact with the fishermen had a revivifying effect on him. Tom Pettey reported Welles's enthusiasm, wiring Herb Drake that the *jangadeiros* were the MOST COLORFUL ADVENTUROUS TRULY BRAZILIAN PEOPLE HE'S SEEN. With some flourish, Welles brought back Jacaré and the other three *jangadeiros* with him to Rio, installing them in the Copacabana, the most famous and expensive hotel in the whole of South America, to thrash out the script of *Four Men on a Raft*. Welles and the fishermen bonded fiercely, their admiration for his capacity for Scotch whisky knowing no bounds. Welles himself, according to Pettey, looked BETTER THINNER HEALTHIER ANYTIME SINCE WE LEFT HOME. The day after their arrival, he sketched out his first ideas for the sequence. It starts with Welles talking direct to camera: 'Beautiful shots Rio, and I start kind of travelogue, looks like going to be boring and I say a few words, lush expensive music, Copacabana crowds of bathing girls and suddenly close shot of couple girls under umbrella looking out at water . . .' He describes the triumphant arrival of the *jangadeiros*, their reception by President Vargas and their immersion in the Carnival. The camera follows the fishermen: 'one of them turns to camera – OW picks up story – fade to village. Tell about Dragon of the Sea and whole life – return to Rio – petition – they excuse themselves – want to go to carnival – last shots of morning after.' The sense of actuality, of reportage – all to be reconstructed, of course – plus the direct address to camera, represent a glimpse of the sort of photo-essay Welles was to develop in later years. This off-the-cuff preliminary sketch, dictated at high speed, was clearly intended as the roughest of outlines for his restive crew; on it Lynn Shores has laconically written: 'this is the original script for me to plan the picture *Four in a Boat*'.

Welles remained convinced that the sequence needed to be shot in Technicolor, and larkily wired Phil Reismann, who was en route for Hollywood to persuade Schaefer of its importance; the tone is of one smart schoolboy to another. THAT THERE IS NOTHING IN THE WORLD I WON'T DO FOR GEORGE IS A SECRET IT IS SOMETIMES TEMPORARILY ADVISABLE TO WITHHOLD FROM HIM STOP THE TRULY HISTORICAL IMPORTANCE OF WHAT WE TOGETHER PROJECT FOR THE SOUTH AMERICAN CONTINENT IS A VISTA I LEAVE TO YOUR OWN GOOD SELF TO OPEN TO HIM STOP NEED I SAY THAT HIS OWN COURAGE AND FORESIGHT IN THIS MATTER ARE WORTH MENTIONING TO HIM AT THIS POINT STOP DON'T WORRY I AM PAYING FOR THIS TELEGRAM MYSELF. But Welles's chum Reismann was already on his way back to Hollywood in more senses than one. Even before leaving, he had wired Schaefer that *The Magnificent Ambersons* could not be premiered in Buenos Aires because it would need Spanish subtitles, for which they would need the negative; they only had an answer print. That, he tells Schaefer, might give Welles the idea of going to the Argentine and shooting a picture there. This must have been part of the subject of their private conversations. Reismann urges Schaefer to wire Welles direct: THAT HE IS NOT TO MAKE ANY PICTURE IN ANY S AMERICAN COUNTRIES ON THIS STOP.

Oblivious, Welles was still planning to record the *Ambersons* narration in Portuguese and Spanish: 'Line up translators of real merit and see that we get a script for them,' he wrote to Dick Wilson in a memo. 'Later, speech experts, that they may devil me into understandability.' Welles's lack of urgency is remarkable, as if he felt that everything – both in Hollywood and in Brazil – was essentially on course, and that things would sort themselves out in their own good time. He wants to finish a Walt Whitman recording started in Los Angeles; he writes thank-you letters; makes observations about the history of the samba and Bob Meltzer's latest draft; is happy to 'lecture anywhere and everywhere anyone says'. The critical situation in Rio is dealt with whimsically: 'It is my intention,' he writes to Wilson, 'to report to you my own daily activities. Of yesterday it can truly be said that I dreamed largely and accomplished little . . . by way of criticism, I would like to suggest that it would have been strategic for you or Meltzer or both to have turned up, as Pettey did, at the airport this morning. I was there and spent the dog watches proceeding [*sic*: Welles's charmingly wayward spelling] that solemn event filling Phil's brain with those large dreams to which I have already made reference.' Those large dreams (which Reismann was busily conveying to Schaefer) were now in the forefront of his mind, with the real world – the world of war, the world of movie politics – a vague backdrop. 'Let nothing slip through our fingers. Fill every golden hour with something done. Do it now. Keep smiling. Obrigado. – Remember all our watchwords. Abide by them. And it must follow, as the night the day, that I will sleep till after lunch.'

Schaefer, desperate to try to control his favourite son of art, and to restore some sense of his own authority, wired Welles to ask him whether he could release Bob Meltzer from his duties: SURE YOU REALISE IMPORTANCE OF CURTAILING EXPENSES REGARDS. Welles replied with the usual soft soap: HASTEN ASSURE YOU MY ONLY POSSIBLE DESIRE HERE IS TO MAKE THIS BEST POSSIBLE PICTURE AT LOWEST POSSIBLE COST STOP HOPE YOU BELIEVE I WISH NOTHING MORE THAN TO BE FULLY CO-OPERATIVE IN EVERY RESPECT TO MAKE YOU PROUD OF ME MUCH LOVE. A couple of days later, on 18 March, Welles defended Meltzer again, indicating that overheads would be radically reduced once the Carnival reshoots were finished, and adding nonchalantly, almost as an afterthought: EAGER HEAR REACTIONS AMBERSONS PREVIEW LOVE ORSON WELLES. He would not be nonchalant again for some while – if ever.

CHAPTER SIX

Pomona

IN THE career of Orson Welles, the name of Pomona, one of the smaller cities of Los Angeles County, rings horribly down the decades. It was here that RKO (breaking with their strategy for *Citizen Kane*, which had been widely but privately exposed to informed and influential individuals) decided to test *The Magnificent Ambersons* on an unsuspecting public. A less happy choice of venue could scarcely have been made, even from a symbolic point of view. Named after the Roman goddess of fruit, the city had rapidly outgrown its agricultural roots to become a major industrial conurbation – the very form of social existence that the novel (and the film) so eloquently deplores. In 1942, the city was a bustling and impatient place, vigorously expanding, home of a principal branch of the California State Polytechnic University, with a large young population, both indigenous and student; and it was from these that the film's first audience was drawn. They had no idea what to expect: it was a sneak preview. They were delighted by the first half of the double bill on offer that night: *The Fleet's In*, a musical from Paramount starring Eddie Bracken and Betty Hutton. 'Gobs of glee!' the posters would later proclaim, 'A boatload of beauties! A shipload of songs!' Among that shipload of songs were 'Arthur Murray taught me dancing in a hurry', 'Conga from Honga' and, topically, 'Tomorrow you belong to Uncle Sam'. The gung-ho young audience had a further delight in store: James Cagney was to make a personal appearance at the end of the evening. In between was the small matter of *The Magnificent Ambersons*.

Welles had had exactly a day's notice of the preview. Robert Wise wired on 16 March to inform him that George Schaefer had unexpectedly requested running *Ambersons* for himself and Charles Koerner and four other men unknown to him: PROBABLY EASTERN EXECUTIVES. Following the showing, Schaefer asked about the possibilities of reducing the length of the film. 'He ordered me to prepare picture for sneak preview Tuesday nite with following cuts: both porch scenes and factory.' Wise did not say it, but there was no question about it: they had taken Welles's film away from him. The long-drawn-out surgery that followed over the subsequent five months was simply a matter of degree. The principle was established: 'they' would do what 'they' thought was necessary; just for starters, three crucial scenes had been arbitrarily removed from the film without Welles's consultation. Simply reading Wise's wire makes one's stomach tighten: it is every film-maker's worst nightmare, one that in Welles's case was to prove recurrent; indeed, he never really woke from it. The active hand of Charles W. Koerner is evident in this manoeuvre; George Schaefer was losing the power struggle. Apart from Koerner's natural animus against Welles, the Mercury and everything they stood for, he had a mission: he believed that the double bill was the commercial answer to an executive's prayer. It was no more than simple logic, therefore, that *The Magnificent Ambersons* must be reduced to an appropriate length, something just on either side of ninety minutes. The print that Wise showed to Koerner, Schaefer and the executives lasted 125 minutes; the one seen at Pomona was 110 minutes. The process of attrition had just begun.

Predictably, the boisterous preview audience, high on the Conga from Honga and its own hormones, viewed Welles's film with bewilderment and boredom. It is impossible to believe that RKO's motives in showing the film in this context were anything other than Machiavellian. Certainly the report cards perfectly duplicated Koerner's general view of Welles's work: the violence of the reaction is still somewhat shocking to read. 'It should be shelved as it is a crime to take people's well-earned money for such *artistic* trash as Mr Welles would have us think. There just isn't room here to tell how disgusted everyone was. Mr Welles had better go back to radio I hope.' 'It stinks – too dark – too slow, and too mixed up.' 'Who cares about that junk.' 'It was putrid.' 'It was slow, morbid, and not exactly good entertainment for people in a world in the condition ours is in.' 'We do not need trouble pictures, especially now. Make pictures to make us forget, not remember.' The lighting was greatly animadverted on: 'Please have pity on our poor strained eyes.' A number of the comments were addressed to 'you producers', perceived as a tyrannous clique forcing their highbrow tastes on the public, which is nicely ironic. 'I don't see why, in times of trouble, bloodshed and hate, movie producers have to add to it by making dreary pictures. I wish you producers could see how much more the audience enjoyed *The Fleet's In* than *The Magnificent Ambersons*.' As far as the acting performances were concerned, there was general admiration for Dolores Costello, Anne Baxter and Tim Holt, with little mention of Joseph Cotten or Agnes Moorhead. One report would have given particular satisfaction to the Koernerites: 'It's as bad if not worse than *Citizen Kane*.' The few favourable responses also predicted commercial disaster for the film, which played into Koerner's hands too: 'This picture is magnificent. The direction, acting, photography, and special effects are the best the cinema has yet offered. It is unfortunate that the American public, as represented at this theatre, are unable to appreciate fine art. It might be, perhaps, criticised for being a little too long.'

Two days later, at the second preview in Pasadena, the film was 1,500 feet shorter. The reaction of the infinitely more sophisticated audience in that city of playhouses and museums was commensurately warmer: 'Much better than *Citizen Kane*. Orson Welles is a genius.' 'This preview cannot be praised too highly. Depressing but better than any propaganda picture.' 'Definitely 10 times better than *Citizen Kane*.' 'Orson Welles is the most tremendous director of the day. This is by far one of the finest pictures I have ever seen.' Generally the reaction in Pasadena focused on Welles, for or against. It is notable how much personal feeling he provoked: 'I do not like Orson Welles "running his shows". He should "keep quiet".' 'The G—d— thing stunk/only Orson Welles could think up a thing like that.' There are more lighting comments, including, quite wittily: 'The blackout doesn't have to be observed on the screen. Turn on the lights!' And then there are the sort of reports that would have pleased Welles: 'The setting accurately portrayed the scenes of my own childhood and I saw some of my unlovely relatives.' The Mercurians were all delighted, feeling vindicated; but Pomona could not be undone.

Two days after Pasadena, Schaefer wrote to Welles:

I did not want to cable you with respect to *The Magnificent Ambersons* as indicated in your cable of the 18th only because I wanted to write to you under confidential cover. Of course, when you ask me for my reaction, I know you want it straight, and though it is difficult to write to you this way, you should hear from me. Never in all my experience in the industry have I taken so much punishment or suffered as I did at the Pomona preview . . . they laughed at the wrong places, talked at the picture, kidded it, and did everything that you can possibly imagine. I don't have to tell you how I suffered, especially in the realisation that we have over $1m tied up. It was just like getting

one sock in the jaw after another for over two hours. The
picture was too slow, heavy, and topped off with sombre music,
never did register. It started off well, but it just went to pieces . . .
I queried many of those present and they all seemed to feel that
the party who made the picture was trying to be 'arty', was out
for camera angles, lights and shadows, and as a matter of fact,
one remarked that 'the man who made that picture was camera
crazy'.

Pasadena did not change Schaefer's opinion. It was 'better; but
not enough. The Pomona audience was young – it is the younger
element who contribute the biggest part of the revenue. If you
cannot satisfy that group, you just cannot bail yourself out with a
$1m investment.' Their initial discussions, he reminds Welles, were
all about making low-cost movies – and here they are with two
pictures having cost $2m. They won't make a dollar on *Citizen
Kane* and will probably not break even. 'All of which reminds me
of only one thing – that we must have a "heart to heart" talk.
Orson Welles has got to do something commercial. We have got
to get away from "arty" pictures and get back to earth. Educating
the people is expensive, and your next picture must be made for
the box-office.' At least he was talking about a next picture. 'God
knows, you have all the talent and the ability for writing, producing,
directing – everything in *Citizen Kane* and *Ambersons* confirms that.
We should apply all that talent and effort in the right direction and
make a picture on which "we can get well". – That's the story,
Orson, and I feel very miserable to have to write you this. My
very best as always. Sincerely yours.'
    This is a noble letter, written entirely in sorrow, not in the least
in anger. But it is the letter of a beaten man, and a confused one.
Schaefer, like Welles, believed that The People would lap up quality;
now, the moment he meets rejection, his only concern is for the
box office, for which the adolescents of Pomona are to be the
arbiters. He approvingly quotes the amateur critic who accuses
Welles of being 'arty' and 'camera crazy'. He was, of course, running
scared: the corporate dogs were yapping at his heels. Jack Moss had
wired Welles after what he called the UNSATISFACTORY REACTION in
Pomona; he attributed it to the audience's youthfulness and impatience with the film's length, but nonetheless, he insists, THEY
WERE OVER AND OVER HELD BY THE DRAMA. Welles's other colleagues
were less inclined to spare him. Bob Wise wrote to him somewhat
wearily, 'You asked for a more detailed report of preview audience

reactions and I have never tackled a more difficult chore. What I mean is it's so damn hard to put on paper in cold type the many times you die through the showing – the too few moments you are repaid for all the blood and suffering that goes into a show. With God's help and a sigh, here's a rough breakdown of the previews.' The audience, he says, were restless during the first three or four reels; there were few laughs until the second half of the snow scene: 'The really important thing is the length of the film and the definite audience disinterest and inattention during all this.' There was, too, growing resentment at 'the hysterical sort of boy that George seems to be in these scenes'. In the scene of George reading Eugene's letter to his mother, there was 'not a laugh but a reaction that said: "Oh God here he is again."' On Welles's final line, 'That's the end of the story,' Wise reports that there was a round of applause 'and what seemed to be a sigh of relief'. At both previews, many people walked out throughout the showing. 'The picture,' he says, in a striking phrase, 'does seem to bear down on people.' Nonetheless, he adds, 'we are all certain that the basic quality of the show was appreciated and it is merely a matter of gentle, tireless and careful study and work to resolve *The Magnificent Ambersons* into a real proud Mercury production.' The very things, in other words, that Welles wasn't able or willing to give it; the very things he lavished on *Citizen Kane* in such profusion.

Worse was to come. Welles had a professional respect for Wise, but Joseph Cotten was perhaps his closest friend, a core Mercurian, his second self. Cotten's report suggested a general unease with the whole enterprise. Welles had written, he said, 'doubtless the most faithful adaptation any book has ever had', and when he finished reading it he had had the same reaction as when he read the book. 'The picture on the screen seems to mean something else. It is filled with some deep though vague psychological significance that I think you never meant it to have. Dramatically, it is like a play full of wonderful strong second acts all coming down on the same curtain line, all proving the same tragic point. Then suddenly someone appears on the apron and says the play is over without there having been enacted a concluding third act.' He reiterates Wise's prescription: 'It's all there in my opinion, with some trans-positions, revisions and some points made clearer.' He thinks that Welles doesn't realise that he's made 'a dark sort of movie. It's more Chekhov than Tarkington.' The situation was clearly absolute hell for everyone involved. All who had seen the film knew that something was wrong, and were unable in conscience to say, hand on chest, 'It's a masterpiece, leave it alone'; nor were they able to say exactly what was wrong, though they all made suggestions as to what to cut, what to shift. Conscious that Welles was feeling usurped, Cotten sought to reassure him: 'Jack [Moss], I know, is doing all he can . . . his opinions about the cuts, right or wrong, I know are the results of sincere, thoughtful, harassed days and nights, Sundays, holidays. *Nobody in the Mercury* is trying in any way to take advantage of your absence. *Nobody anywhere* thinks you haven't made a wonderful, beautiful inspiring picture. Everybody in the Mercury is on your side always . . . we all love you . . . and until then remain forever as all of us do. Obediently yours.'

Welles was not so certain. SURE I MUST BE AT LEAST PARTLY WRONG, he wired Jack Moss, BUT CANNOT SEE REMOTEST SENSE IN ANY SINGLE SUGGESTED CUT OF YOURS, BOB'S, JOE'S. He was convinced that the crucial new scene he had suggested, in which George discusses Eugene, cannot have been well enough shot by Wise, and he 'absolutely insisted' that Norman Foster reshoot it. He proposed new music for it; and a redub of Fanny's line 'George, George', which had earned such a big laugh at Pomona. SURE THIS WILL KILL LAUGH OR I'M CRAZY STOP I GUESS I AM ANYWAY MUCH LOVE ORSON. Nothing could better demonstrate the impossibility of Welles's situation. Any or all of what he had suggested might have been perfectly sensible or effective, but to do it by remote control, as he had done with *Bonito*, was doomed. He was working from the answer print, but had no means other than guesswork of judging the effect of his proposed changes. Nonetheless (or perhaps because of this), he kept up a steady bombardment of suggestions, some of which were effected. According to the assistant editor Mark Robson, he and Wise would work '100 – 110 – 120 hours a week . . . we were so overwhelmed by the amount of work that we both moved away from our houses and our homes and into a motel in Culver City. There were endless hours and I don't think we were paid any more for the 100th hour than for the first.' Among their many re-edits was the destruction of the lovingly planned and superbly executed seamless tracking shot at the Ambersons' ball, which now, with cutaways, became a conventional sequence – still beautiful and absorbing, but no longer a metaphor for a way of life; no longer a unique artistic gesture.

Meanwhile, in Brazil, the work seemed to have ground almost to a standstill. 'Events change from day to day and nothing – not even life and death – means very much here,' wrote Tom Pettey. 'It is a lazy land and I'm afraid the germ has got into the company.'

Curiously, his faith in the venture had grown, certain that they were going to get 'a real pix', and he added: 'I will stake my money on Welles coming out of this with added fame.' Welles had told him that he would take thirty days to complete the Carnival reshoots and the Urca sequence; then he was off to the north, to Fortaleza, while – dreams of Peruvian conquest still in the air – another crew went to Lima. Such desultory shooting as there was, was done by Lynn Shores; when he was absent, Dick Wilson or Bob Meltzer took over. Shores struggled with the fact that what they were trying to shoot no longer existed. Rio was a different city from the thronged, colourful, sexy metropolis of February. 'Once a year in December there is a packed house at the Jockey Club, otherwise it looks like Pomona fairgrounds on a blue Monday' – an unfor-·tunate reference whose significance he could not have known.

The entire front entrance of the Copacabana was being rebuilt and was thus a mass of scaffolding and unfinished masonry. 'The beaches are full of little black children except on Sundays when sometimes there is a turnout for about an hour. This turnout we are trying to get for ourselves.' The weather was atrocious, and the natives uncooperative. Sailors enlisted as extras simply didn't turn up. 'I can only do what one individual in a foreign land can try to do under conditions where getting a cup of coffee is almost a Federal deal.' There were problems with fuel for the generators: they needed 20,000 gallons of the stuff. 'At present there is not this much gas in all Brazil.' No one was any closer to knowing what the film was supposed to be. Welles changed his mind all the time: 'That is all we seem to be doing – getting ready to shoot something but we never shoot it . . . we would all like to work if somebody would please tell us what to do.' Shores himself had been writing scenes, then shooting them, 'and it still isn't any good'. Tom Pettey bemoaned that 'We still haven't done any of the script stuff. The studio has been ready and waiting for 10 days or so. Urca nightclub could have been done weeks ago. We made a couple of abortive stabs at the Rio *Jangadeiro* shots, but they will have to be done over as Orson didn't like the set-ups and walked out.'

Where was Welles? What was he doing? Partly, he was simply having a very good time. Cy Enfield recollects Jack Moss showing him some of the Brazilian footage at around this time. It showed chorus girls in a line. Welles had told Moss, 'I fucked her, and her, and her.' He was also planning his radio broadcasts. He was giving lectures. He was dreaming his *jangadeiros* sequence. Above all, he was trying to influence the reworking of *The Magnificent Ambersons*.

During this period, he was running up telephone and cable bills of $1,000 a week, a phenomenal figure for 1942.

Back in Hollywood, Lynn Shores's reports had spread panic. Walter Daniels, Shores's spymaster, noted in a memo to Reg Armour that there was 'no assurance that our trek is paying off as we had hoped'. The Carnival footage, he says, is no good; 'The picture will be salvaged at the studio here – as all location pictures are – by shooting additional scenes in colour to bridge and point up action.' He tells Armour 'to *instruct* Mr Welles' to give Shores an outline of *Four Men on a Raft* and let him film such long shots and location shots as may be necessary, while returning himself to finish the film in the studio. 'I feel that Shores is capable of doing a good job on his own with less cost in time than can be accomplished by the present set-up.' This astounding suggestion was not followed through, though Welles did indeed give Shores a further outline of *Four Men on a Raft*. Reg Armour nonetheless forwarded the memo to his superior, Charles Koerner, with Shores's latest letter. The noose was tightening around Welles's neck. It seems that he had no inkling of the gravity of his situation. The 'large dreams' of which he had spoken to Phil Reismann were becoming more real to him than Hollywood's reality; and Rio was providing him with a very satisfactory lifestyle. Shores reported that he had taken a year's lease on an apartment. 'Just why I cannot seem to find out.' Shores had taken a small apartment, too, 'in self-defense'. Tom Pettey reported the same thing to Herb Drake: 'it looks like Orson is going to make Rio his home and I'll be damned if I am . . . I'll continue to give you all the news that's safe to print. There really are some swell stories here, but not the sort a press agent does. I've killed more stories than Sgt York killed Germans since I've been here and some of them died hard.'

Phil Reismann, back at his desk in Hollywood, tried to give Welles a broad hint of the way things were developing for Schaefer at RKO. BE SURE AND LEAVE HIM A REASONABLE OUT, wired Reismann, AS CONFIDENTIALLY HE HAS HAD TERRIFIC PROBLEMS WITH BOARD AND I MEAN TERRIFIC. There was a new pressure, Reismann told him: Columbia was shooting a film called *Carnival in Rio* in the first or second week in April. Apart from Schaefer, Reismann was the only real friend Welles had at RKO; Koerner was now moving in on the Mercury's financial affairs. In a memo to Jack Moss he berates him in schoolmasterly terms for over-spending by $3,500 on Haki's new last line and other retakes for *Journey into Fear*. As far as that film was concerned, Welles was still convinced that he needed a better last appearance and telegrammed Norman Foster to that effect, urging him to come to Rio to shoot it. Astonishingly he adds: TELL JACK ITS MORE IMPORTANT FOR YOU TO COME TO RIO THAN BOB WISE, suggesting that Welles still failed to grasp the importance of his personal involvement in the reworking of *The Magnificent Ambersons*. Brazil seems to have changed his perspectives. ALL EXPECTATIONS SURPASSED AND EVERY DAY BRINGS A NEW EXPECTATION, he wired exuberantly to Phil Reismann.

George Schaefer's anxieties spill over in yet another minatory cable, this time more personal: I WANT YOU TO BELIEVE THAT I AM PERSONALLY ON THE HOOK FOR THE WHOLE SOUTH AMERICAN VENTURE . . . CLEARLY OUTLINED TO MY BOARD THAT CERTAIN EXTENT (OF GOVT FUNDING) DID NOT PERMIT US TO ALLOT FOUR MEN TECHNICOLOR. He no longer attempts to conceal from Welles the growing amount of animosity he inspires: IT WOULD CAUSE YOUR MAN FRIDAY TREMENDOUS AMOUNT OF PERSONAL EMBAR-RASSMENT AND EVERYONE IN PARTICULAR TAKING KEEN DELIGHT THAT YOU HAD NOT LIVED UP TO WHAT I HAD EXPECTED AND WHAT I HAD STATED WOULD BE DONE. The attempts at humour, and the fatherly concern for Welles's professional standing, continue to modify Schaefer's rising panic. By contrast, other executives of RKO were taking action without troubling to consult Welles, or indeed Schaefer. From the beginning of April, by decree of Reg Armour, all funds were to be administered from Hollywood on a weekly basis. Cash flow immediately became difficult; Shores started cancelling shooting days because of lack of money, telling Dick Wilson that 'he neither wished to go to jail or to go through another day like yesterday'. Welles furiously cabled Schaefer: THESE COMMITMENTS VALID AND AS PRODUCER I SHOULD BE CONSULTED BEFORE THEIR VALIDITY IS QUESTIONED. He insisted that if he did not hear from Schaefer personally in these matters, he must hear FROM WHOMEVER IS ISSUING THE ORDERS.

It is clear that he had no grasp of the real position. His daily battles with Lynn Shores were more real to him. They continued unabated, to the extent that Dick Wilson wrote a frank memo-randum for RKO's head office entitled 'On the Lynn Shores matter', little knowing that head office was 100 per cent united behind Shores and must have laughed hollowly on receipt of Wilson's complaints. The memorandum discloses the childishness of behaviour on both sides. From the start, Wilson says, Shores has over-stated the poor morale on the film. Resentful of the work he has had to do, he has voluntarily taken on more of it, for which he demanded and got more money. He is temperamental: once, after being kept waiting for half a hour, he walked off the set; Welles phoned him again and again till 3 a.m., but he 'absolutely and profanely' refused to come back. Shores has freely expressed his dislike of Bob Meltzer, and has openly stated that Welles doesn't know what he is doing. He constantly states, says Wilson, that the film is 'nothing but a Goddam nigger picture' and that they ought to drop the whole thing; he is particularly opposed to the *jangadeiros* sequence, asserting that 'nobody wants to look at a bunch of niggers'. Just to be helpful, the cameraman Harry Wild told Shores that Welles considered him a spy and a double-crosser (which of course is precisely what he was). When confronted with this, Welles told Wilson that he had a 'sincere and basic dislike' for Shores and 'that type of man' and that, if and when he had a dinner for the group, he was going to invite everybody but him. They could think what they wanted; Shores was to be the fall guy for everything he could pin on him. Wilson disagreed (silently), feeling that Shores could do them a great deal of harm; but nothing would have discouraged Welles. If he disliked someone upon whom he depended, he was constitutionally incapable of dealing cleverly with them.

Shores's behaviour was in fact far worse than Wilson knew. On his own initiative, Shores had directly contacted Dr Alberto Pessao of the Press and Propaganda Department of the Brazilian government, to warn him that Welles was continuing to concentrate on 'the negro and low class element' in and around Rio, adding that the scenes filmed in the Teatro Republica were all 'in very bad taste. This letter,' he concludes, 'is personal and I feel that I am expressing the feelings of the majority of our working crew here in Rio.' He is anxious, he unctuously claims, about the effect the footage will have on 'the good relations existing between our country and yours . . . I am holding the negative of this film and not shipping it through for development until I can perhaps have a talk with you on this subject to be sure that I am not unduly alarmed over its possible consequences.' The immediate outcome of this breathtaking act of disloyalty was a visit to Wilson from Dr Pessao, who courteously regretted the shooting in the *favelas*: 'Mr Welles knows what to do with his own picture, but here it is not like in the U.S., where you can show everything including ugly things.' He quoted the Prefetura of Rio, who had said, 'We are trying so hard to change the condition of the *favelas*, it isn't characteristic of Brazil.' Wilson replied, somewhat disingenuously, that 'Very possibly that was exactly what Mr Welles wanted to show – how beautiful and modern Brazil is.' The Rio newspapers were full of it, too: 'CARIOCA CARNIVAL IS GOING TO BE VERY DARK ON THE SCREEN' complained *A Noite*. RKO was even more perturbed, on purely commercial grounds. Reg Armour of the finance department reported to Phil Reismann that the production department had informed him that out of 67,000 feet of 35mm film, plus fifty-nine rolls of 16mm, only two reels could be used 'for entertainment purposes in this country'. Technicolor, he said, had heightened the effect of dark-skinned Brazilians. 'There is much footage showing people of the negroid type either dancing with or in close proximity to people with lighter skins, and this in our opinion will seriously militate against the showing of this film in certain sections of this country, particularly the South.'

Armour was equally implacable on the matter of the budget: unless Welles could shoot the Urca Casino sequence for nothing, he said in an internal memorandum, it would be better to shoot it in Hollywood – for technical reasons, apart from anything else. So far the Rio sequence had cost $241,000; he calculated that a further $288,000 was needed to complete it, adding up to $529,000, even without the Mexican sequence; with that and post-production (which might involve reshoots) the total cost of the film would be $1.3m – as much as *Citizen Kane*. Both *The Magnificent Ambersons* and *Journey into Fear*, he claimed, 'are destined to end up in the red'; *Citizen Kane* itself would at very best only break even. 'If Welles keeps on the way he is going, he can very easily wreck this company and it would be my recommendation that his operations as far as RKO is concerned be brought to a termination immediately.' Armour was a quintessential corporation man: sound money was his only criterion, and he was still quaking with rage and disapproval fifty years later when he was interviewed for a BBC documentary on RKO. 'I cannot understand his wanton waste of money,' his 1942 memorandum continued. 'Welles for all his failings is a very capable producer-director and his record to date in Rio, in our opinion, shows that he has not made an effort to lick the story problem or place his activities on a basis where the corporation has a chance of breaking even.'

Armour and many of his colleagues at RKO felt that Welles was deliberately and consciously dragging the company to ruin – and their living with it. One of Schaefer's increasingly desperate telegrams said that he was rapidly coming to the conclusion that

Welles had: NO REALISATION OF MONEY YOU SPEND AND HOW DIFFICULT IT IS TO RECOUP COST. It is hard not to agree that Welles had come to believe that *It's All True* was a project whose importance was beyond financial computation; from an artistic and cultural point of view, this may or may not have been the case, but it reveals a deep ignorance of, and indifference to, the realities of the company's parlous position. WHEN I FINISH THIS PICTURE YOU WILL SEE WHAT I MEAN, Welles cabled. UNLESS I CAN FINISH FILM AS IT MUST BE FINISHED FOR ENTERTAINMENT VALUE THE ENTIRE EXPENDITURE OF TIME AND EFFORT WILL BE TOTAL LOSS. Schaefer slammed back: THIS IS OUT OF ALL PROPORTION TO WHAT WE EVER ESTIMATED AND WE CANNOT GO ALONG ON THAT BASIS EVEN IF WE HAVE TO CLOSE DOWN SHOW AND ASK YOU TO RETURN . . . THERE ARE SOME DEVELOPMENTS THAT LOOK VERY UNPLEASANT IN ALL DIRECTIONS.

But Welles was now fully adrenalised and nothing was going to stop him. 'The seasons change but Orson goes on forever,' wrote Tom Pettey. 'You think you know Orson. Well wait until you see him directing a color scene in a low key. Man, that's something. This is the first week he has done any directing at all and he's busy making up for lost time. He has a caned-bottom rocking chair which is liable to turn over at any moment, loose bowels and the disposition of a teething baby – and that's in the mornings . . . members of the crew have been known to dash out of the place and race down six flights of stairs to the bar to calm their shattered nerves,' continued Pettey. 'I think you had better order a couple of beds for the fellows in a first-class madhouse if they ever return. Shores and Wilson,' he added, 'have so many worries and troubles that they practice voodism and chatter in gibberish.'

Welles was anxious that the outside world should give due weight to what he was doing. Incensed by a slighting reference to the film – 'our work and mission here', as he put it – in a recent edition of *Time* magazine, he angrily cabled Herb Drake to get Jock Whitney or Nelson Rockefeller to write a letter in his support. Meanwhile Dick Wilson had asked Berent Friele of the I-AA office similarly to endorse the importance of what he was doing in Brazil, which Friele duly did, in the most fulsome terms (despite an earlier anxious private conversation with Wilson). Friele details Welles's ambassadorial contribution, citing interviews, receptions, galas, awards, speeches and high-level meetings with politicians, artists and scientists. 'The fact that Welles is enough of an authority on so many subjects has been of much fundamental value to the work done here aside from the picture.' The range of extra-curricular activities that Friele describes (quite apart from the film) is almost bewildering: in March alone, Welles gives a lecture on 'The Brazilian Subject in Motion Pictures'; a month later he gives the first of four lectures (Literature, Painting, Graphic Arts, Music) on 'The Development of Art and Literature in America'. Brazilians, says Friele, were impressed by his trip up north (a journey rarely made by visitors to the country), and by the friendships Welles had struck up there; the visit to Buenos Aires, where he received an award for *Citizen Kane*, had been a huge success from the point of view of international relations. He had made two highly successful broadcasts from Rio, *Pan-American Day* and a curious programme celebrating Getúlio Vargas's birthday, both forerunners of the *Hello Americans* series he would later develop.

The Vargas broadcast is Welles's love-letter to Brazil. It comes from the Urca Casino, where he has been filming – 'one of last truly gay places in the world'. He introduces the bands, translates the samba *Todo es Brazil* ('Everything is Brazil'), his voice throbbing, and finally delivers a paean to the achievements of modern Brazil – all thanks, he says, to Vargas. 'There has been no American visitor,' says Friele, 'who has understood the country, its people and its problems so quickly and so well as Welles.' 'What energy, what vitality, what ubiquity is in this great Brazilian!' wrote the poet and cinéaste, Vinicius De Moraes (later inspiration of *Orfeu Negro*). 'Brazilian, yes; Orson Welles is beginning to know Brazil, or at least an important side of the soul of Brazil, better than many sociologists, novelists, critics and poets. His vision is at times raw, but he never sins through injustice. Knowing better than anyone how to understand our character, our foibles, our easygoing ways, our so-to-speak "negative" qualities . . . Welles has felt Brazil and the Brazilian people in a deeper, richer way than the vast majority of foreigners who have lived among us.' He is still the darling of the intellectuals. This urban, canapé-nibbling, cocktail-sipping Welles is a very different Welles from the one his film crew knew. There is no contradiction here. There are at least as many Welleses as there are Charles Foster Kanes; the problem was to find time for them all. It was congenial to Welles during a great deal of his time in Brazil to fulfil what he thought of as his mission as a roving polymath, interpreting North America to the South, and vice versa. What, in time of war, could be more important than hemispheric solidarity? Was it not government policy, specifically endorsed by Roosevelt and even more explicitly by his Vice-President, Henry Wallace, to whom Welles was if anything even closer, politically? And no doubt the work he was doing *was* valuable, in its way. But it was not the primary purpose for which he was there, as he suddenly seemed to realise after his return from Buenos Aires, when *It's All True* seemed at last to come into focus for him; thereafter, he devoted himself exclusively to filming it.

What he was now filming was highly contentious, however. His run-in with Shores and Dr Pessao had done nothing to modify his approach. 'I have had to lie and lie for the last two or three weeks to keep the local reporters away from the studio,' wrote Tom Pettey. 'If they ever got in and saw some of the shanty life we are doing they would write Orson out of town.' Welles was shooting sequences – 'dynamite in Rio' – involving *macumba*, the Brazilian version of voodoo. 'We have a closed set full of jigiboos and a little set depicting a hut in the hills,' added Pettey. 'Relations between Welles and the crew are still bad. There are days when it looks like everything is going to be happy and then he will pull some sudden stunt such as picking up a gal and vanishing in his car for a couple of hours or getting in a row with the person nearest to him and everything is bad for the rest of the day.' Welles had fired the first assistant director, Leo Reislor, for causing trouble with the Brazilians with 'dictatorial tactics'. Shores retaliated by keeping Reislor on the payroll for office work, a carefully calculated piece of provocation. The atmosphere was heavy with suspicion and counter-suspicion. 'Somebody has been turning in a detailed report on Welles in Rio and it has not been flattering, I am told,' continued Pettey. 'Everyone is a suspect . . . and I am of the opinion that I'm on the list.' His job, he tells Drake, is becoming almost impossible. Welles has had so much publicity 'that he feels he can push any of the newspapermen – Brazilian and American – around and that he is above criticism. He'll find out.' Now even Pettey wants to go home. 'Apparently he wants to handle his own public relations with the aid of Dick and Meltzer. I never did get into the family. My knees creak too loudly when I bend them.'

The atmosphere had become poisonous, on the brink of physical violence. Lynn Shores had told Meltzer, 'if he didn't stop doing things he wasn't supposed to do that he was going to "punch him in the nose"'. Then he told Dick Wilson that 'this whole thing has gone far enough', adding, for good measure, that Welles was trying to prolong his stay in Brazil just to avoid the draft. Welles,

Shores continued – the gloves now off for good and all – was 'just a vagabond who could live out of a trunk, but the rest of the men in the group had responsibilities and homes and people they cared about and no one gave a damn about Welles'. He'd seen fifteen directors like Welles, he said; he'd seen them come and go. He was feeding half of them right now in Hollywood.

The them-and-us division was now complete. The Mercurians – 'the family' – were indeed drawing ever closer together, newly invigorated by Welles's sudden clarity about the project, evolving the film day by day during gaps in shooting and without reference to any of the crew. Shifra Haran kept the minutes of a series of their brainstorming sessions (those 'meaningless conferences' so despised by Lynn Shores), which give a vivid account of how Welles worked with his team. The atmosphere was entirely democratic, with Welles functioning as a sort of chairman. The occasion for this particular set of meetings was to discuss the use of *chôros* in the film. Are they to be heard during Carnival time? Welles argues that 'since all of our sex appeal so far is presented in violent and vigorous form, one interlude is required presenting element of straight *romance*. If this can be included legitimately in a carnival sequence, it should be.' Meltzer is assigned the task of collecting all available *chôro* recordings and, where possible, sheet music. Since Welles's point in wanting *chôros* will be visual, his job is to figure out the location for this sequence. The group then breaks up to continue filming; the discussion resumes the following night. Meltzer spends two hours giving examples of suitable *chôros* with records and at the piano. The evening after, Welles outlines his idea for the proposed sequence, feeling strongly that romance is an absolutely necessary element. He wants an opportunity to show 'spooners in the moonlight, young people holding hands, equivalent to couples drifting away from country club dance back in the States'. Later that evening, Welles and Meltzer continue the discussion. Welles has had further ideas about the sequence: 'orchestra playing at Clube Baile during carnival breaks for a smoke; part of band moves into garden, starts idly playing. Work into Carinhoso.' Welles has found a girl in Minaes, he says, who has just arrived in Rio at her own expense. He suggests that she should sing the vocal: 'not actually singing it, lipping it'. She starts to sing with the combo. Elsewhere in the garden a good-looking boy hears her voice, deserts his girl to look for the girl singer, singing himself as he goes. The boy and the girl join up and complete the first chorus; the girl singer deserts her boyfriend to sing with the boy singer. The jilted boy and girl then join up for a fast *chôro* dance. The orchestra – now complete – changes tempo.

The scene they are evolving is a very conventional Hollywood one; it could be from almost any Fred and Ginger movie. The only significant difference – and it is an all-important one – is authenticity. Welles and his team are trying to make an old form new, but also to honour the culture they are depicting. The use of non-professional local talent (even if, as here, there might seem to be some ulterior motive) suggests a very different kind of film from the studio-made RKO musical romances, with their stock casts and conventional sets. The search for suitable locations was a crucial part of the discussion, too: apart from anything else, they could not afford to build sets. Welles was deputed to check in the files which clubs had extended invitations to them during Carnival – or perhaps, Welles suggests, they can use the Cinedia studio buildings and gardens, choosing camera angles carefully and putting up a sign saying 'Petropolis Tennis Clube'; all that's needed is to decorate the gardens with bunting and string up brightly coloured lights. Welles will spend a couple of hours late the following night, after shooting, working out the angles. There is nothing earth-shaking about these discussions, nothing startlingly visionary: it is a highly recognisable process of group work, collaboration at its most useful and democratic. No doubt Welles made the final decisions and strongly articulated the overall gesture of the film, but he had to do his share of leg-work, checking the list of clubs that had extended invitations to them for example; as the visual aspect is what concerns him most, he must, likewise, sort out locations. In the discussions, he's trying to save money and improvise cleverly, something with which during the rest of his career he would become very familiar. Everyone in the group has his say; there is no sign of Lynn Shores, of course, or even Harry Wild. This is the kitchen cabinet, the cabal, the inner sanctum. Welles is scarcely slacking, either: the meetings take place all day; then he shoots; then he works out angles. Improvisation was second nature to Welles; the adrenalin engendered was intoxicating to him, and it was an elusive commodity in a studio.

At about this point, at the beginning of May 1942, two months after Welles's arrival in Brazil, the group put down in writing for the first time what kind of film they thought *It's All True* might turn out to be. Herb Drake had already had a few stabs at it: this was the official version that they passed on to the front office. The film, the blurb said, would mix comedy and drama. 'Fact and fiction are served forth in unusual combination in Orson Welles's *It's All True*. This screen anthology of varied themes and stories marks a new departure. For the first time a full evening's entertainment, arranged with the diverse themes and subjects of a popular magazine's make-up, is combined in one picture . . .' In their recapitulation of the story of *Bonito*, the blurb stresses again the original notion of veracity contained in the film's title:

'It's a true story, this story of Bonito and the little boy who loves him. And the story of the *jangadeiros* who sailed a raft from the Equator to the Tropic of Capricorn is also true – a matter of recent history . . . burned black from the sun, worn thin as skeletons by hardship and privation, the four fishermen of Fortaleza find themselves heroes. They obtain instant audience with President Vargas, and through his intervention, they win full union rights and pensions. The Carnival becomes a fête in their honour. Then their mission accomplished, the four *jangadeiros* return to their little fishing village by train, their fares paid by the republic of Brazil. *My Friend Bonito* and *Jangadeiros of Fortaleza* are stories of people. *Carnaval* is music and colour, song and gaiety; a cross section of what goes on in the very hottest latitude of human hilarity.

The blurb is at great pains to emphasise the film's accessibility. 'It is cinema in the grand manner, combining the entertainment features of real life in Brazil with musical comedy, human interest values and constant action . . . the music of carnival is samba – it's the soul of the city in hot licks.' In the film, Welles will follow the course of the samba:

He takes us to the hills from where the samba comes, the hills above Rio where the poor people of the city have their homes . . . then comes the opening day of carnival and this samba and other sambas, take possession of the city . . . the city rocks to their dancing and roars with the reverberations of the drums and the sound of singing. It's carnival. It is the Samba . . . in the street outside is Otelo, the gamin leader of a samba band, who has for these four days of merriment dedicated every fibre of his being to singing and to partisanship.

The cameras follow a little boy around the carnival. As darkness comes over the city, the samba music subsides. The crowds trickle away and, in the deserted square of Praça Onze, Otelo and the little boy are left alone. They are sleeping. The little boy's cheeks are wet with tears and Otelo, exhausted, lies beside a broken drum. It is the end of Carnival. 'Next year it will have its rebirth, with new sambas and new crowds and new frenzy to make wild the streets of Rio.' All in all, it is a plain, coherent account of an entertaining but scarcely radical film. The core of the film – its claim to importance – would have to be the epic of the *jangadeiros*, and that was all to come, still being dreamed of.

Meanwhile, a thousand miles away, *The Magnificent Ambersons* and *Journey into Fear*, which Armour had so confidently written off from a financial viewpoint even before they were released, were being respectively mutilated and abandoned by RKO.

CHAPTER SEVEN

Turning a Bad Koerner

WELLES CONTINUED to regard *Journey into Fear* as a rather stylish *jeu d'esprit*. Herb Drake had reported to him enthusiastically that the film was 'a 100% natural and Dolores is marvellous, which I may as well confess is a surprise to me . . . I think you will be proud of Norman's work. Altogether, everything looks successful, elegant and happy.' But Welles knew that everything wasn't quite working as it should have been, and felt that the ending still needed something – that elusive 'tag', which would have to be shot in Rio. He communicated his suggestions directly to Norman Foster, praising him extravagantly – THERE ISN'T A BETTER DIRECTOR ON EARTH THAN YOU ARE AND I LOVE YOU – and ending by asking Foster with unexpected plaintiveness to record a track where they all say hello to him when they do the reshoot. I'M LONELY. Foster replied compliantly – COMPLETELY AGREE WITH CABLED INSTRUCTIONS FORTUNATELY HAVE ALTERNATE SHOTS COVERING EVERYTHING – and playfully, as was their wont: I KNOW A BETTER DIRECTOR AND HOW CAN YOU BE LONELY WITH SO MANY REFLECTORS. To Jo Cotten, Welles wrote: 'Everything I have seen of *Journey into Fear* surpasses anything we had any right to expect for it. You are even better than you were supposed to be . . . I miss you disastrously.' By the same post he wrote to Norman Foster with his proposed rewrite: 'The dialogue, you will immediately note, is as flawless and sparkling as a rich diamond. There is really nothing to be said of this by way of criticism except, perhaps, that it stinks. In case you think so, wire what you think and see what that gets you.' His spirits are obviously high. 'Why don't you ever write me long persuasive and informative letters like this one? I miss you seriously and I love you more than I let on.'

The new end he suggested has an interesting, classically Wellesian flourish: after some outrageous new plot twists, Haki is found in a lobby with Josette ('This is just a corner of the lobby such as comes within the capacities of Brazilian set-builders,' states the stage direction.) A journalist 'who resembles nobody so much as Richard

Wilson' asks Haki who she is. 'A young lady who's been sporting enough at the last minute to consent to join me for dinner,' he replies. ('Need I promise that all this will flow along at a pleasant clip?' Welles interjects.) 'Is that the story?' asks the journalist. 'No,' Haki says, 'that's not the story' – at which he steps into an elevator, turns to the camera and continues, 'but I sincerely hope it's a good enough end for the story'. Looks at the audience for a minute, then smiles: 'Good night, everyone!' This cheeky little sequence, whose success would entirely depend on Welles's own outrageous charm, was never shot.

What is striking about the letter is its merriness, at a point when *The Magnificent Ambersons* was beginning to slip completely out of his control and the Brazilian shoot was in the grip of all-pervading tension and panic. Meanwhile the preview of *Journey into Fear* in Pasadena, as part of a Koernerian double bill with the whimsical Charles Laughton comedy *The Tuttles of Tahiti*, produced an excellent response. Jack Moss wired Welles that he had overheard very favourable comments. THEY LOVED EVERYBODY, he said, EVEN BANAT (the part he played himself); one card-filler cited 'fat man with glasses' as his favourite character. 'We should have more pictures like these,' another had said; 'it is a relief to see something besides army and navy pictures.' Foster, in a measured letter after the preview, suggested that some cuts might be in order: the audience seemed to want 'Jo to turn into Dick Tracey and outwit the Gestapo single-handed'. He was also unenthusiastic about Welles's proposed ending, which he found simply too long. En passant he remarks, quite casually, that he liked *Ambersons* very much at a preview, and is sure that it will be a fine picture – a worryingly cool response from such a warm and expressive collaborator. 'We all really miss you every minute,' Foster continues, lightly slipping in the information that he has been off salary since 26 March. 'Not that I care as long as I'm a Mercury jerkery. Will you please make a tag of Col Haki, nose and all . . . but keep it brief unlike this letter.' Welles replied, 'I can't be very intelligent about *Journey* because I haven't seen it . . . also it does seem to me as though I can't agree with anybody about anything any more. The rest of the world must be going crazy. I think the tag I sent you was a perfect catharsis, but then as I say I haven't seen the film put together . . . I love you with all my heart.'

The freely expressed love with which Welles showered his collaborators was as fulsomely returned. The degree of it is striking, uncommon even today, in our much more touchy-feely world, even in show business; in 1942 it is almost shocking, and rather touching, especially since they are all men. It has nothing to do with sex, but it is remarkably intimate. 'I love you, more than I even realised. And I miss you like the devil,' Norman Foster wrote to him in one of their exchanges. 'Jesus, what a letter. All I really wanted to say was that I miss you very much, and love you very much, and that I have been happier since I've been with you than ever before, and that if you're going to stay down there long, I'm going to bum my way down too.' Welles's reply to this exuberant letter of Foster's shows him unexpectedly subdued, private and vulnerable: 'At dinner tonight I complained to Bob and Dick that nobody I loved had written me since I left. This observation was followed by a lengthy and morose silence. We finally paid the check and came home where I found your letter.'

John Berry, later a film director in his own right, but then touring *Native Son* around America, wrote to Welles at about the same time: 'I think constantly of being with you and there is nothing I would rather do than work with you. This is a thing that becomes more obvious every time I see the work of the so-called "artistic theatre" directors' (he names Elia Kazan and Robert Lewis). 'Not only is the theatre dead this season, it is spinning in its grave. So if I may say it, how wonderful it would be if you came back and did a show. *Five Kings* is always in my mind – sometimes I even dream of it – I loved it more than anything you ever did.' And a couple of days before, the hard-bitten Phil Reismann had wired Welles: NEVER REALISED I WOULD MISS ANY MALE COMPANION AS MUCH AS I HAVE MISSED YOU SINCE I LEFT RIO STOP YOU SORT OF GROW ON ME LIKE A WART. With his male collaborators – especially those ten or more years older than him – Welles was at the same time one of the boys, an inspiring leader and a vulnerable youngster. He was able to be simultaneously father, brother and son to them. He looked after them; he relied on them; he looked up to them. He made his working partners feel they were all in it together and that heaven and earth were there for the winning. Everything, in fact, that Foster meant by being a Mercury jerkery.

On 6 May 1942, his twenty-seventh birthday, Welles was inundated with affectionate telegrams, from Dadda Bernstein, Jo Cotten (BIRTHDAY GREETINGS TO AN OLD FRIEND FROM AN OLD MAN), Herb Drake (SO ITS YOUR BIRTHDAY WHAT WILL YOU THINK OF NEXT), various telegrams from actors and twenty-seven kisses from Dick Wilson's wife, Catherine. There was a telegram from George Schaefer, too, with a not entirely light-hearted message: DEAR

ORSON MANY HAPPY RETURNS OF THE DAY I KNOW YOU HAVE MANY PROBLEMS BUT BE YOUR AGE. The real world was not half so nice. Just three days after Foster's loving letter to Welles, Reg Armour sent a memo to Jack Moss refusing to authorise retakes for *Journey into Fear*. 'We have now finally decided to complete the picture with the film we have on hand without incurring any further expenses of any nature whatever.' A few days later, Charles Koerner, furious that Everett Sloane and Eustace Wyatt had been brought in from New York for reshoots, decreed that every penny by which *Journey into Fear* exceeded its budget was to be deducted from Welles's salary cheques. At this point, that amounted to some $150,000. But Welles, oblivious, continued to offer new solutions to the problem of the ending: HAVE VERY SWELL NEW FAST CHEAP JOURNEY FINISH, he wired Jack Moss exuberantly a month after Armour's official termination of reshooting.

All this while *The Magnificent Ambersons* was being hacked up by a bunch of amateurs and studio journeymen. Welles had never ceased to engender new proposals to overcome what everyone told him were the film's shortcomings. Robert Carringer, who has closely analysed Welles's proposals, rightly observes that some of his suggested cuts seem more brutal than any of the studio's, and his belief that the answer to the film's problems was a cheery end-credit sequence is bewilderingly irrelevant, the merest rearrangement of deckchairs on the *Titanic*. In any case, it appears from a shocking but unverifiable anecdote of Cy Enfield's that even the Mercury office was unable to deal with his flood of suggestions. Enfield was employed as a dogsbody by Jack Moss because he knew magic, and Moss wanted him to teach him a few tricks to impress Welles on his return:

A telephone with a private line had been installed in Moss's office in the Mercury bungalow that had a number known only to Orson in Brazil. For the first few days he had discussions with Orson and tried to placate him: then they had started arguing because there were more changes than Orson was prepared to acknowledge. After a few days of this, the phone was just allowed to ring and ring. I conducted many magic lessons with Moss when the phone was ringing uninterruptedly for hours at a time. I saw Jack enter carrying 35 and 45 page cables that had arrived from Brazil; he'd riffle through the cables, say, 'This is what Orson wants us to do today,' and then, without bothering to read them, toss them into the wastebasket.

Whatever the truth of this dark little story (and since a number of thirty- and forty-five-page cables survive, along with the replies to them, there seems to be a grain of truth in it), Moss – along with Robert Wise, Joseph Cotten and Freddie Fleck, the assistant director – was certainly a central figure in the reshaping of *The Magnificent Ambersons*. As we have seen, Welles reposed an astonishing amount of artistic authority in the hands of this failed conjuror-turned-business-manager. The little Mercury team he led was under immense pressure from Schaefer and, increasingly, Koerner, first of all to lighten the tone and secondly to shorten the film. Each of the team, in his own way, was trying to preserve the essence of Welles's work, but they started from the premise that serious surgery was required. Jo Cotten had expressed his dismay when he saw the film at the first preview (which, with two cuts, was essentially the film that Welles and Wise had put together) and sought to mitigate what he regarded as its gratuitous sombreness. The focus of their anxieties was on the bitter, ironic end of the film, and especially on the element that so strongly reinforced this bleakness, the brilliantly crafted score provided by Bernard Herrmann.

Herrmann was not the man for artistic compromise; not the man, indeed, for compromise of any sort. He was scarcely capable of calm conversation under the most easy-going circumstances: his biographer Steven Smith quotes an interview that Herrmann gave to a journalist called Zador, who transcribed it meticulously; it gives a fine flavour of his temperament:

ZADOR:
Did you find [Welles] easy to get along with?
HERRMANN:
I always find difficult people easy to get along with. I only find glad-Harrys difficult and vacuous. Nice guys are difficult. It's because they're a bunch of empty-heads, that's why they're nice guys! They pretend to be nice guys, but it's a disguise. They're not nice. They're vicious, vindictive people who try to make sure that anything good HASN'T GOT A CHANCE!
ZADOR:
Then Orson Welles, who's a difficult person, gave you a chance . . .
HERRMANN:
HE DIDN'T GIVE ME ANY CHANCE! I gave HIM a chance! I had a job and he was just an actor who we used . . . what the hell . . . he didn't give me any JOB.

ZADOR:

Well, for *Citizen Kane* and *Magnificent Ambersons* . . .

HERRMANN:

He didn't give me a job. It was his advantage to have me do the music for him! He didn't give me a job or a break or anything . . . for chrissakes, what's working in there, an accounting department?

ZADOR:

Did you select the various passages to be scored?

HERRMANN:

Yes, I do that. It's my profession and not theirs.

ZADOR:

Well, you're sure good at it.

HERRMANN:

WELL THAT'S MY TALENT. WHADDYA THINK I NEED SOME HALF-WIT TO TELL ME WHAT HE THINKS . . . I like music that is proud of itself. I don't like a guy who says, 'It's a good idea, but it's too good for those creeps who come in and look at a movie, so I'll debase it.'

ZADOR:

Well, that's not always done by choice.

HERRMANN:

NO! It IS done by choice. You don't *have*-ta do it! You say, I'm not your man, get somebody else. Don't tell ME that he has to make a buck — look what Schubert put up with.

The head of RKO's music department, the lustrously named Constantin Bakaleinikoff, had already had an incendiary encounter with this uniquely rebarbative individual at the beginning of work on *The Magnificent Ambersons*, trying to push him away from quoting the music of Waldteufel, which was still in copyright, towards that of Johann Strauss, which was not. Herrmann immediately referred the matter to Welles, who just as swiftly issued a curt memo: 'Use *Toujours ou jamais* as directed by Herrmann.' At Welles's behest, he was given unique freedom within the music department; he was in fact almost entirely independent from it. Amongst other things, he had the right (shared by Korngold, for example, but by very few others) to orchestrate his own music, which he did to revolutionary effect, scarcely endearing himself to the studio orchestrators in the process. The score he wrote for *The Magnificent Ambersons* was even more striking than that for *Citizen Kane* in its interaction with the dramatic life of the film. Since the film itself was destroyed, we can never know exactly how the score might have worked, but fortunately the music was not destroyed, and the highly sophisticated compositional procedures that Herrmann employed can be heard.

The Waldteufel waltz, or part of it, is used as a paradigm of the Ambersons themselves. It is first heard gently and delicately on muted solo violin joined by harps; then, in richly enhanced form, even plusher than in the original orchestration, it reaches its apotheosis in the chain of period dances that accompany the ball. From then on its increasingly rare appearances are fragmentary and often dissonant as the Ambersons' world breaks up. The future, so inimical to the Ambersons, is evoked in music (as Kathryn Kalinak notes in her elegant analysis of the score) made of short, non-melodic phrases, often highly chromatic and devoid of harmonic support; the instrumentation is increasingly percussive. The score contained an entirely characteristic instruction from Herrmann to his brass players for the scene in which George Minafer meets his comeuppance: 'cup mute more nasal; mechanical; reed-like; music should sound like [the] character', which is as good an example as may be found of Herrmann's absolute engagement with the specific work in hand. The gleeful music of the sleigh ride in the snow scene wholly eschews the generic, presenting an a-thematic impression of perpetual motion: 'absence of melody, gravitation towards atonality, repetition of key motifs, and unusual instrumental colour', as Miss Kalinak says. It was not this sequence, of course, with which the revisionists took issue: it was the grim, spare music of the final reels of the film, music of alienation, of despair, of failure – a long, bleak organ solo under the garden scene, a murky elegy in the old people's home, with harsh brass and edgy strings, and finally a sombre, Mahlerian threnody for the end titles, reprising the earlier love music in anguished form, topped off with a bitter, ironic allusion on vibraphone to Waldteufel's genial little waltz tune: *Toujours ou jamais*, indeed.

This is music of quite uncommon imagination, but it is undeniably sombre, as both Herrmann and Welles intended it to be. This is the element that had to be extirpated, and, after Pomona – the watershed of catastrophe for *Ambersons* – extirpated it was. More than half of all the music Herrmann had written was replaced by anodyne schlock, all golden harmonies and surging emotions, imbecilically replicating the feelings of the characters on the screen. It was written by RKO's resident composer, Roy Webb, the sort of stuff he ran up by the yard. It is a musically incontinent ramble, garrulous where Herrmann was terse (and, as often, daringly silent), designed to put a smile on the audience's face where none belonged. Herrmann was neither consulted about this nor informed of it; the moment he did find out, he demanded that his name be removed from the credits. At first RKO resisted, but studio executive Gordon Youngman was clearly shocked by his forthrightness – as who would not be. 'Am convinced,' he wrote in a memo, 'in view of man's temperament he will bring injunction proceeding and cause all other trouble he can. His theory is that statement is made score is by BH while it is not entirely so and that this is deception to public and injurious his reputation.' Herrmann passionately urged the studio to reconsider the desirability of making cuts in the film. He won the battle for his own integrity, though the battle for that of the film was lost. If he felt betrayed by Welles, whose job it was to shield him from this sort of thing as he had so often done in the past, he never said so; but this is what happens when the director is absent. Had some of Welles's other collaborators been equally obdurate, *The Magnificent Ambersons* might exist in something like its original form, though it is equally true that RKO, and especially Charles W. Koerner, had long ago made up their minds to cut it down to size, in every sense.

Previews continued, with rather more encouraging responses, at Inglewood, then, after substantial recutting and some reshooting, at Long Beach. But for every comment saying, 'new style of direction is very fascinating', there were three saying, 'it would take an IQ of 120 or more to really enjoy it', '75 minutes of gloom and camera acrobatics' or, rather more bluntly 'much too boresome'. The feeling was not entirely negative, but neither was it positive. Mark Robson commented that 'it reached a point where we had to pick up the film at the booth, people were waiting for us as if they were going to beat us up. They were so angered and annoyed.' All the brutal surgery had scarcely altered the general reaction. The same phrases recur, as if they were part of a popular critical vocabulary. The overall gist is highly consistent – the film is: a) out of tune with the country's mood; b) too arty; c) too dark. The actors most often praised are now Costello, Cotten, Holt and the artist endearingly referred to in one questionnaire as 'Fanny Moorehead'. Clearly something even more radical was called for. In the absence of Welles's personal presence, Moss and his team sought some kind of lodestone, some point of reference for what they were trying to do, and they came back, perhaps inevitably, to the novel, and above all its end, that curious modulation into mysticism that seems so out of line with the realism of the rest of the book, with the characters as we have come to know them and with Tarkington's solid prose style; he seems to abandon the grand themes he has so powerfully pursued in favour of unearned extra-terrestrial uplift. Welles's final scene, his single most creative contribution to the screenplay, is equally out of line with the rest of the book, but it progresses the characters much more satisfyingly, providing a vivid final illustration of the Ambersons' terminal decline; and it is cinema, not literature. This was the scene that particularly stuck in the audience's craw, and so Jack Moss – book-keeper, office manager, sometime conjuror – took pen and paper and adapted the scene with which Tarkington had ended the book and then directed Anne Baxter, Jo Cotten and Agnes Moorehead in it, finally ensuring the obliteration of Welles's vision.

That was on 19 May. The same day, a thousand miles away, in Rio de Janeiro, while filming a reconstruction for Orson Welles's film *It's All True*, showing the triumphant arrival of himself and his fellow *jangadeiros* in the capital to deliver their famous petition to President Getúlio Vargas, Mandel Olimpio Meira, the great popular hero known as Jacaré, drowned.

CHAPTER EIGHT

Four Men on a Raft

WITH BITTER timing, the day before Jacaré drowned, the *Life* magazine photo-spread shot during the Carnival, at the very beginning of the Brazilian escapade, three long months earlier, finally appeared under the jaunty banner '*Life* Goes to a Party in Rio'. For the group of film-makers still slogging it out in Rio, the party had long been over. The bonhomie and cross-cultural excitement of Carnival had been replaced by exhaustion, frustration and resentment; relations between the film and the community had cooled. The official attitude to the film that Welles was making, despite various broadcasts in which members of the Brazilian government (including Vargas himself) had participated, had abruptly changed in the face of his determination to show the reality of Brazilian life, giving due prominence to the 70 per cent of the population who were working-class and black. The popular press had become equally disenchanted with the image of their city that Welles was filming. He was showing things that they preferred not to be reminded of, things they lived with, but which were not for general consumption. 'Each time the robust and handsome fiancé of Del Rio points his camera at the so-called "picturesque" spots of the city we feel a slight sense of uneasiness,' observed *Rio Cine-Radio Jornal*. Instead of filming 'the lovely edge of the lake, where there is so much beauty and so many marvellous angles for filming', Welles was promoting the shabby image of the *malandro*, 'a good-for-nothing in a striped shirt, dirty straw hat over his eye, who comes in dancing an out-of-joint samba'. He seemed intent on shooting 'scenes of the hills, of no good half-breeds . . . and the filthy huts of the *favelas* . . . dances of Negroes covered with *aracatu* feathers, reminiscent of the temples of the African wilds, as though our not always edifying street carnival were not already sufficient'.

But if bourgeois opinion was turning against Welles, the film's day-to-day relations with the black working-class population whose lives he sought to celebrate were not of the best, either. The extras

were largely drawn from their ranks and proved to be only inter-
mittently interested in the process of filming. Day after day was
written off because they failed to show up, or drifted off in the
course of filming. The *Diary of Welles Group Activities* to 27 April
is a dismaying record of days lost due to weather, religious festivals,
Welles's illness, Welles's absence and above all, at the beginning,
lack of equipment, which had taken two whole weeks to clear
customs; but highest on the list of causes of days lost was 'no-
shows of extras', disastrous for continuity. Welles was particularly
piqued by this behaviour, and would often walk off the set when
it occurred. Even on his birthday, 6 May, when there was to have
been a party after shooting, the report tersely recorded: 'rehearsal,
shooting Urca; wrap 1 a.m. Loss of time because of non-attendance
and lateness of extras and singers'; the following day: 'more problems
with extras etc. Welles stays up finishing designs for decoration that
night and morning because of limited budget and project's inability
to contract'. In some cases there was open hostility: 'our period of
wholehearted co-operation was over,' wrote Dick Wilson. 'We were
being greeted in the streets with jeers, and – in the case of our
shooting of the coloured people – with beer bottles.'

Work had been proceeding erratically for all the reasons detailed
above, but now, in mid-May, after another long period of drift,
Welles was enthusiastically at work on the *jangadeiros* sequence. His
personal relationship with the fishermen was warm, the story was
heroic and clearly defined, with none of the attendant complications
of personnel and staging involved in the nightclub sequences or
the reconstruction of the Carnival, though even here there were
logistical difficulties. The first Sunday they had attempted to shoot
the arrival of *jangadeiros* in Rio, the crew on half the boats grew
impatient and sailed away in the middle of the most difficult portion
of the work. 'No threats, bribes, or payments could hold them. A
whole shooting day was lost and a long period of preparatory work
went for nothing. This has occurred many many times with varying
degrees of disaster in the course of production,' ended the
exasperated report. Welles's own crew were scarcely happier. When
the schedule was given to Harry Wild, 'he blew up completely',
refusing to shoot on a Sunday, Dick Wilson reported to the Office
of Inter-American Affairs. 'He didn't feel well from the previous
night's shooting, saying that it was very dangerous, everyone had
got sick, the men had openly rebelled against him about picking
up the cables covered with garbage and slop. People had gathered
around him and threatened him etc.' His general complaint was

that they had no one in authority with them. 'The men are talking night and day,' Wild said, 'about how slow we were working and that they would never get home.' Even the casting department, Wilson noted, was deeply unhappy, due to 'a conflict of personalities'. A disaffected film crew is like its naval equivalent; mutiny is never far away.

Welles was under pressure from every angle, personal and professional. Phil Reismann had been despatched to Rio by George Schaefer to bring things to a swift conclusion; he brought with him a letter from Schaefer so severe that he felt the need to forewarn Welles: I HAVE NEVER READ ANYTHING AS STRONG IN MY LIFE AND MY REASON FOR SENDING THIS CABLE IN ADVANCE IS TO PLEAD WITH YOU TO FINISH UP AS QUICKLY AS POSSIBLE TO AVOID CLOSING OUT THE PRODUCTION COMPLETELY BEFORE IT IS FINISHED. Reismann at least remained loyal to Welles; or so it seemed. The minutes of a conversation about Welles between Reismann and Reg Armour from that same week suggest the levels of duplicity that were at work in the Borgia Palace that RKO had become:

PR:
[Welles] is a tough baby – he has done a magnificent job of selling himself to Nelson Rockefeller.
RA:
George [Schaefer] will lose his job out of this . . . I think Orson wants to stay out of the country . . . he wants to duck military service.
PR:
I think I could get the authorities to take him off our hands.

The Mercury office itself was not free from infection.

PR:
Have you talked to Moss at all?
RA:
They're beginning to rat on Welles . . . they say 'we told Welles so and so – and now we're being disloyal to him – but we'll do it'.

Reismann had not misled Welles about the severity of Schaefer's letter, the culmination of a series of missed phone calls and enraged telegrams. But the letter Reismann finally delivered to Welles ten days after it had been written was different in tone and intent from the calls and the wires. It was a soberly comprehensive indictment from the quarter from which he least expected it.

'Here I am in New York,' Schaefer wrote, 'endeavouring against all odds to maintain the same confidence in you as I have had in the past. Facts and developments come so fast and are so overwhelming that it is no longer possible for me to maintain that frame of mind.' He writes of 'the crisis which has arisen in my relationship with my company and my relationship with you . . . you were chosen,' he says, 'as the man in whom we could place our confidence'. But that confidence, he continues, detailing the delays, the mendacities and the rising costs, 'has been betrayed. The thing that disturbs me more than anything else is that people in your unit don't know from one day to another what they are supposed to do, and that, to me, seems to be the crux of the situation.' The Brazil sequence is, he says, only one section of *It's All True*; the rest of it is equally unfinished. He's looked at the *Bonito the Bull* material: they only have 40 per cent of what's needed, though the accumulated expenses are $400,000 – 'we are just pouring money down the drainpipe'. Welles has his own writers (several of them) on the payroll, Schaefer says, but there has never been a script. 'I was astonished to the point of thinking that even you would have the audacity to turn over such a disgraceful synopsis to Lynn Shores . . . how in the world with such an outline you expect Shores or even your own men to carry on and give any loyalty to this company and yourself is beyond me to comprehend.' The whole thing, he says, is a catastrophe, quite apart from the financial aspect: Schaefer placed his confidence in Welles because of his 'fervid desire' to do something for his country. It could also have paved the way for future production by the industry in South American countries. 'They will come to the conclusion that you, the one person in whom they have had confidence, have spoiled all their future possibilities of motion picture production.' Everyone, he says, admires Welles's work as ambassador. 'But, quite evidently, you have come to the conclusion that you are down there representing the Coordinator's office and not RKO.'

The technicians all want to come home:

> The way I feel right now, I am wondering if the boys will be
> out of the trenches by Christmas. If there are any personal
> reasons why you want to stay down till August, or longer, at least
> get through with the picture, send the men back and stay as long

as you wish. That is your personal affair . . . I am now again put in the painful position where I have to write you a letter which I never, in God's world, thought I would have to write wherein I am begging you to fulfil in an honourable way your obligations and not put such a terrific load on my shoulders. In respect to the latter, I think I have carried that load a long time.

He writes of *Citizen Kane*:

What it cost this organisation, and me, personally, never can be measured in dollars . . . the abuse that was heaped on myself and the company will never be forgotten. I was about as punch-drunk as a man ever was. I made my decision to stand by you and I saw it through. I have never asked anything in return, but in common decency I should expect that I would at least have your loyalty and gratitude. To the extent that I have received it with respect to the Brazilian enterprise up to the present time, I would say it has merely been lip service.

He reviews Welles's four films, all of them over budget. 'It was one problem on *Citizen Kane*; sickness on *Ambersons*; $150,000 over on *Journey into Fear*; now what is the answer in Brazil? Here was a real opportunity to show the industry that without adequate equipment and with a most difficult problem, you were able to come through.' He is sending Phil Reismann to Rio: 'I have instructed him that he must forget his friendship for you . . . he has the authority to stop production immediately and call the whole production off and instruct everyone to return. That of course I would dislike to see – particularly because you left in a blaze of glory and made such a fine showing on your arrival. It would be painful to share with you the closing of the show and your instructions to return. Sincerely.'

This guilt-inducing battering was neatly backed up at almost exactly the same moment by a letter from Welles's ex-guardian, Dr Maurice Bernstein ('Dadda'), his mother's lover and the principal promoter of the infant Welles's status as a prodigy. His relationship to Welles – now, after all, a world-famous twenty-seven-year-old millionaire, the white hope of the movie industry – remained what it had always been: nagging, loving, censuring, demanding, intensely emotional and comprehensively invasive, resembling the music-hall idea of a Jewish mother, with a touch of nastiness all his own. 'Did you get my birthday cable? It was all we could send – just love. So far I have not received your promised compliance with my request' – for $1,000 – 'and I am hanging on to the last link now, so don't wait too long it may break and I'll sink!' he writes, adding a hand-written account of how his car needs new valves, $75 worth. 'Not a good way to start the week and I will walk as long as my arches hold out. PS Did you notice how much it costs me to write to you? I have to go without my meager lunch to mail this.' When not bombarding Welles with requests for money (he ran a very successful medical practice in Beverly Hills), he was blubbering over his former ward's – very rare – letters, passing on salacious gossip about Welles's ex-wife, Virginia, or admonishing him for the flaws in his character.

The letter Welles received early in May 1942, while he was in the midst of crisis in Rio, is quintessential Dadda. Welles had called him on his birthday: 'You have made me happy beyond words. I felt like embracing the janitor, the garage man, the garbage collector, the whole world, except the Japs and Hitler! Today, Monday, still back at the office and still happy. Let the old flat smelly feet come in for treatment, what do I care about their feet – I got your call today and their feet will not smell so badly.' He asks coyly about Welles's love life: 'so you hear no more from "a certain party"?' (a reference, presumably, to Dolores del Rio, from whom Welles had drifted apart during his long absence) and proffers homely advice: 'please don't stir up the embers. When the fire dies out, it shows there was little fuel.' He relays the RKO gossip – all of which is startlingly precise and accurate – and even goes to the heart of the studio's chief anxiety about the material Welles was shooting: 'your mixing of the black and the whites cannot be accepted by Iowa, Missouri, not to mention all the people the other side of the Mason Dixon line'. Everyone is convinced, he informs Welles, that Koerner will not renew his contract, then he helpfully recounts a meeting he has just had with Charlie Chaplin, who also, it appears, has strong views on Welles. 'He like everyone else thinks you have no appreciation of the value of money! Ever hear that before? He thinks you are a great artist, though still young in your conception of human emotion. He had much to say about *Kane* which he was crazy about, with only the above reservation, of emotional value. He believes in you 100%. I do wish that you could form some sort of alliance with him. You would complement each other.' Presumably he was fully aware of the *Landru* debacle. Dr Bernstein presses his advantage, probing Welles's weaknesses with surgical skill: 'You need mature minds in your associations, not mere "bulk".

The trouble with your associates has been that you have no respect for them. Most of them have need of you either financially or to help them climb. They therefore all flatter you, try to read your mind, and agree with you without giving you an honest opinion.' Then he goes for the jugular: 'I except Jack Houseman. He is the one person I am sorry you broke with.'

Of all names to taunt Welles with, Bernstein unerringly selects the one that is calculated to drive him into paroxysms of rage – Houseman, who had given him all his early opportunities, but whose attempts to rein him in had provoked Welles's undying hostility. 'I know that you do not like to face reality when it comes to business, and so your affairs are generally in a muddle,' Dr Bernstein continues unrelentingly. 'I wish too that you would have a little confidence in me. I guided *you* in a way which I have never regretted. And you STILL need a guardian! The proof of this is that you have little to show after all your tremendous success. You are now a man, and I am talking to you man to man. I am alarmed when I think of the mercenary people who surround you – Moss – his lawyer, and others who have sucked you dry.' It requires an effort of imagination to envisage anybody talking to Welles in these terms and getting away with it, but his two surrogate fathers, Skipper and Dadda, hold a critical key to Welles's psychology. A considerable part of him remained emotionally immature, even dependent: he was writing to and communicating with both these men until the day they died, accepting without complaint their steady stream of alternating cajolement and exaltation. To these semi-familial figures may be added that of Arnold Weissberger, the canny lawyer who was the engineer of the superb contract that brought Welles to RKO in the first place, and who had saved his bacon more than once. Welles's personal finances were looking shaky: Weissberger was having difficulty in raising royalties on *Native Son*; the Internal Revenue Service was about to move on the Mercury Theatre's outstanding Social Security contributions, as well as Welles's back taxes. 'A three-fold attack by the State, the Federal government against you personally and the Federal government against the Mercury, would not be a very good idea at this time.' The spread in *Life* magazine had been valuable, Weissberger says, but urges him to get Herb Drake to engender some publicity 'to counteract the flood of rumours about your relations with RKO'. Apart from an equivocal Phil Reismann and a deeply embattled George Schaefer (who had relented to the extent of authorising a final final allocation of $30,000 to complete shooting on *It's All True*), Welles was without support in Hollywood. Koerner's RKO was close to washing its hands of him, and his operation in Rio was grinding to a halt. A crowing Lynn Shores laconically wired Walter Daniels of the front office: OUT OF FILM AND OUT OF MONEY.

It was at exactly that point that Jacaré drowned. There have been innumerable conflicting versions of the events of 19 May; what follows is drawn directly from the daily report, under the usual heading, WELLES ACTIVITIES. Its veracity can scarcely be doubted, and nothing so well conveys the immediacy and horror of what happened. At 7.30 a.m. on the Tuesday morning, the report states, the unit went to the location at Barra Da Tijuca: there was a heavy mist, so the *jangada* was tied to the launch with two ropes. All four *jangadeiros* rode on the raft as it was towed into Guanabara Bay and past the spot chosen for the day's shooting. For some reason, Jacaré ordered the launch to go still further; despite the mist, people on shore could see what was happening and tried to attract the *jangadeiros'* attention, to get them to stop. Welles ordered two of the drivers to go ahead and signal to them, which they did by taking their shirts off and waving them; seeing this, Jacaré ordered the captain of the launch to approach the coast. At exactly that moment, a tremendous breaker caught the launch and the tow lines broke, freeing the *jangada*, which rolled over. Two of the *jangadeiros*, Jeronimo and Jacaré, started to swim to the shore. The other two, Tátá and Manuel Preto, stayed close to the raft, and managed to turn it upright. Jeronimo caught hold of the *jangada*'s rudder and, since he was nearest, the other two pulled him aboard. They heard Jacaré's calls for help, but by the time they went to look for him, he was gone. A second breaker righted the launch and the captain took it out of danger, whereupon the drivers took off their shoes and dived in; the *jangada* turned over again, and once more the *jangadeiros* were thrown into the water. The chauffeurs pulled the three surviving *jangadeiros* out of the water by rope; they were taken to Joá, and the drivers returned to tell Welles and the company what had happened. Lynn Shores and Dick Wilson were also informed, and they called the harbour police. Welles returned with the three *jangadeiros* to the Filumense *clube* and then to the Palace Hotel, and spent the rest of the day with various newspapermen in conferences with Assis Figuereido, Phil Reismann, Lynn Shores, Dick Wilson, Bob Meltzer and Fernando Pinto, president of the *jangada clube* in Fortaleza. The mood was sombre: death had come to the party.

The shock was immense, and not only in Brazil. The story of the *jangadeiros* created a considerable sensation. The incident made the front page of the *New York Times*: LEADING BRAZIL RAFTMAN DIES STARRING FOR MOVIE – an interesting turn of phrase: not *in* but *for* the movie. It also reported an incident that was to become part of folklore, though the evidence for it is slender: Jacaré, the *Times* said, was 'tipped from his raft today during the filming of a battle between a shark and an octopus. The fisherman swam away from the fighting monsters into a whirlpool, where he was drowned.' The Brazilian press was considerably less inclined to mythologize, sharply aware as they were of the bitter ironies of the situation: 'They got drunk with the fame,' proclaimed a leader in *Aino Da Noite*:

> Confused with rich presents, going back to Ceara, they could find
> no fun in their obscure work. Never again did they go back to
> their *jangada*, to earn their daily bread with their simple boat. The
> big city, the news in the press and the chance to be movie actors,
> gaining abundant and easy luxuries, killed the simple impulse of
> their triumphal trip. This is the way the *jangadeiros* ended. Jacaré
> died at the edge of the beach, in an adventure without grandeur
> . . . they should have stayed on their own sand dunes, in their
> small houses made of Carnauba straw, without ever glimpsing the
> seductions of Babylon, without ever meeting the American movie
> men. They should have stayed there far away, as *jangadeiros*, in the
> land of Itacema, without ever meeting Orson Welles.

A somewhat disingenuous piece – if the *jangadeiros* had never left the land of Itacema, they would never have made their heroic journey, they would never presented their petition to President Vargas, and they would never have been the subject of a film; Welles had little to do with it. He was, of course, racked with guilt. Prominent Brazilians hastened to comfort him in his distress: Antonio Ferreira assured him that he still had Brazil's support.

RKO was immediately alerted to what had happened by a blunt telegram from Lynn Shores: WHAT AMOUNT WE COVERED IN STATES SETTLEMENT ANSWER IMMEDIATELY. It transpired that the studio had cancelled the policy that would have covered Jacaré; RKO was obliged to pay his family something between $2,000 and $3,000, as opposed to the $10,000 that the policy would have given him. But there could be no question of cancelling the filming of *Four Men on a Raft* in Fortaleza; said Reismann. Welles was 'working like a dog'. They now had a rigid deadline to finish the Rio sequence. 'I have come to the conclusion that this is the only way to handle Orson, otherwise he has a very bad habit of putting off his daily work as long as possible.' As the activities reports reveal, whenever he wasn't shooting the remains of the Urca Casino material, he was working on the script for the Fortaleza sequence. Reismann reports that Dick Wilson had estimated a further expenditure of $32,500, but he, Reismann, reckons another five or six thousand. He immediately placed $10,000 in Dick Wilson's personal account, which would provide one Mitchell camera, 40,000 feet of film and a local cameraman: the utter minimum.

Lynn Shores put this into effect. His reports continued to bridle at Welles's capriciousness, noting that although Reismann was doing a good job keeping Welles under control, 'he still stays awake nights trying to think up fast ones . . . he has the boys up at 4 o'clock every morning shooting sunrise for no reason except he himself stays up all night and seems to want company around 4 o'clock in the morning'. There may be a certain element of truth in this; more importantly, Welles was becoming ever more exploratory in cinematic terms, still assembling material for some as-yet-unarticulated response to the extraordinary culture and country in which he found himself, now personified in his mind by the drowned *jangadeiro*. Reismann reported that Welles had many problems in Rio, 'but it all gets back to the main difficulty' – the core friction between the RKO and Mercury factions within the unit. To the crew, filming seemed interminable, but Welles – despite the letter from Schaefer – appeared to feel no real pressure to leave. Reismann believed that Welles planned to stay in Brazil until 1 August, 'the reasons for which I will tell you when I see you'. (Shores, the eternal grouse, ends a letter dated mid-June, 'Best wishes for a merry Xmas and a Happy New Year.')

Despite the catastrophe of Jacaré's death, life had gone on: even Welles was starting to think of life beyond *It's All True*. The day after the accident, he received another award for *Citizen Kane* at the Museum Nacional de Belas Artas, and wrote to Katharine Cornell in reply to a telegram from her that yes, of course he'd love to play Vershinin to her Masha, but when? Herb Drake, back in Hollywood, was actively planning for Welles's return: 'You have got to come home the right way, hugely, not sneak in on a plane. You must return with trumpets and banners because the campaign needs a good hot fillip of the old Welles personality (with quotes).' There have been two other Welles pictures to keep alive 'and the

RKO anti-Welles battle to fight. (It has never been so virulent.)'
He is nonetheless confident that 'a real bang-up arrival' can focus
the limelight on Welles. He outlines a four-point plan, including
stops in Miami, Washington, New York, Chicago. Then he should
arrive in Los Angeles 'on a tidal wave of wire stories and throw a
party before the studio issues its own story. There is a widespread,
nurtured campaign to prove you have been spending too much
time and money in Brazil, that *Ambersons* is no good and *Fear* ditto.'
Koerner has made a personal visit to William Wilkerson of the
Hollywood Reporter. 'The heat is definitely on. The RKO executives have been as busy as Goebbels putting the pan on your pictures
and on you.' There is, Drake tells him, a problem in stressing the
pan-American cooperation angle: 'Disney took the cream off the
idea. However, if someone in Washington will come out with a
thank you statement to you, you will return a conquering hero.'

This now became a major preoccupation: Berent Friele was
wheeled out yet again to affirm the importance of Welles's contribution. He telegraphed Phil Reismann: FACT IS THAT ORSON IS
DOING AN OUTSTANDING JOB IN BRAZIL WHICH DESERVES
GREATER RECOGNITION IN UNITED STATES. The Brazilian division
duly reported that Welles's knowledge of Brazil and its customs would
be invaluable even after his return, adding, somewhat mysteriously,
'as can be seen, it is already possible to measure the success of his
being here in many obvious ways, and to look forward to the important reinterpretation of it for other purposes and compound interests
at a later time'. In the absence of a completed film or a clear sense
of what any such film might be like, the nature of his contribution
was indeed somewhat in the realm of the mystic. Meanwhile the
apparently interminable casino sequence had been completed (at a
total cost of $17,000, by no means a large sum for a comparable
sequence shot in Hollywood) and the crew finally planned their
return, while preparations were made for the departure north of the
tiny core team that would shoot the Fortaleza footage.

In Hollywood, all those many hundreds of miles away, the
Mercury office was fighting a rearguard action to protect what was
left of *Journey into Fear* and *The Magnificent Ambersons.* Herb Drake,
with his usual sharp grasp of the situation, had written to Schaefer
urging him to mount a vigorous press campaign on behalf of
Ambersons. 'About a year ago you came to the rescue of *Citizen
Kane* with an exciting advertising insert in the trade papers.' The
same situation now exists, he says, with *The Magnificent Ambersons.*
'Not enough press people have seen the film yet to counteract the

irresponsible chatter of the anti-Ambersons element.' He knows what they're up against: envy and resentment. 'There is always a ready audience for anti-Welles talk. The current belief is that Welles has muffed his opportunity and that he is a flash in the pan and does not justify RKO's faith in his talents . . . only a statement on the picture's great worth from the very top can untie our hands and allow us to get the picture the attention it deserves. A powerful trade ad from you will set us right with the rest of the press.' Welles found himself again in the extraordinary position of begging the studio to back its own movie; this time, it didn't happen. Jack Moss was fighting a different battle, desperate to end the constant process of trimming, nipping, tucking, adding and subtracting, which had now been going on for nearly three months. The latest preview at Long Beach (which included his own new rewritten ending) had been, he told George Schaefer, 'amazing and gratifying'; at private screenings critics from *Life*, *Time* and *United Press* had 'unanimously rave[d]', vindicating, he said, Schaefer's judgement and faith. 'I cannot stress too urgently, George, the deep belief that the picture should be left as it is since we have had such phenomenal luck with last previews and critical showings. We have expended so much work and time and care and together have fought this problem through. I ask you to review this message and make your final consideration an all-round agreement not just with me but with unanimous opinion. May I hear from you?'

Small hope. That same day, Charles Koerner had written to Schaefer detailing further proposed changes to *The Magnificent Ambersons*, stating bluntly, 'we will eliminate the so-called kitchen scene', the astonishing scene between Fanny and George Minafer on which Welles and Moorehead had lavished so much attention and Tim Holt had turned green from eating too many cakes. As it happens, the scene was not removed, but others were, despite protests from the Mercury office. Ross Hastings checked with Reg Armour whether RKO was required to give notice before completing the final cutting of *The Magnificent Ambersons* and shipping the picture 'in a form not approved by Mr Jack Moss'. With evident satisfaction, Armour replied: 'No notice is necessary . . . after the first rough-cut and the first sneak preview, RKO has the right to have Mr Welles cut the picture as RKO directs. Because of the fact that Mr Welles is not present to cut the picture as directed, I think RKO is justified in having the picture cut as it desires.' The front-office men who had loathed Welles from the very beginning now had their revenge, and it was sweet. Jack Moss

TARZAN
TRIUMPHS

George Schaeffer, Dolores del Rio and Orson Welles when the going was good. At the Los Angeles premiere of *Citizen Kane*, May 1941.

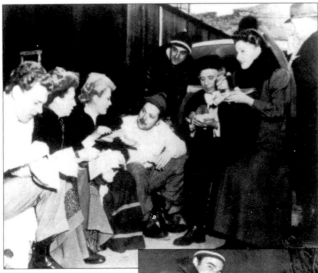

Left: Lunch in the ice factory: a brief break in filming *The Magnificent Ambersons*.

Right: The 'criminally slow cameraman', Stanley Cortez, with the actors Ann Baxter, Agnes Moorehead and Ray Collins, shooting in the downtown Los Angeles ice plant.

Left: Welles in conference with his manager, Jack Moss, sometime conjuror and, for one appearance only, actor.

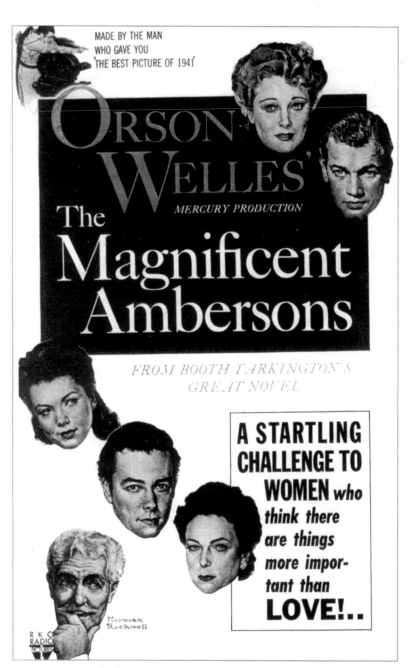

The poster for *The Magnificent Ambersons*, drawn, under Welles's direction, by the great Norman Rockwell.

THE MASTER DRAMATIST TURNS HIS HAND TO MYSTERY..

ORSON WELLES'
MERCURY PRODUCTION

JOURNEY INTO FEAR

STARRING

JOSEPH COTTEN · DOLORES DEL RIO
RUTH WARRICK
AND
ORSON WELLES

RKO RADIO PICTURES

Above: Welles goes to a party: Rio Carnival, February 1942.

Left: Welles being inter-preted. *It's All True.*

Above: Welles on the beach in Fortaleza.

Right: Welles framing a shot in Fortaleza for *Four Men on a Raft*, the key sequence of *It's All True*.

Above: Jangadeiros,
photographed by
Chico Albuquerque.

Left: Welles in Fortaleza
lining up a shot for
Four Men on a Raft
with George Fanto,
the cameraman.

was forced into whimpering, abjectly begging Schaefer to leave well alone: I AM ENTITLED TO BETTER CONSIDERATION AND CERTAINLY A REPLY. I'LL PUT IT THIS WAY: I BEG YOU TO CONSIDER MY COMMENTS REGARDING THE CHANGES IN AMBERSONS. When Schaefer, instinctively the most courteous of men, did reply, he apologised, offering his illness as an excuse, and politely passed Moss on to Koerner. Gordon E. Youngman, hearing of this exchange, wired his colleague Ned Depinet to get hold of Moss's original telegram: PLEASE TRY TO FIND IT IN SCHAEFER'S FILES AND BE SURE PRESERVE AS PROBABLY STRONG EVIDENCE IN CASE IF WE EVER HAVE WELLES LAWSUIT. Koerner himself had already written that same day to Schaefer discussing various further changes he planned to make to the movie. In a chilling note, he informed the man he was about to replace: 'Wise tells me this in no way will hurt the picture and will fit in that spot to really clean up the scene.' The studio's chief executive, the company president and the film's editor were blithely determining the film's final form without reference to its director at all. This of course was the common experience of many (perhaps of most) Hollywood directors, but it was the mould Welles was supposed to have broken. For Schaefer, at least, things had come to a sad pass. He wrote a troubled, uncomfortable letter to Reg Armour – the person on whose ears his request was least likely to fall favourably. 'I think it important, in the scheme of things, that you save the extra negative and positive cuts that we made on *The Magnificent Ambersons*. Some day someone may want to know what was done with the original picture Welles shot.' Still saddened by the waywardness of his protégé, and hopeful that he might one day be taught the error of his ways, he adds, 'it might be a good idea to put all cuts together and show him all the useless material he shot and the improvement that was made by the elimination'. There is no suspicion whatsoever in his mind that the film as directed by Welles, even though less commercial, might actually have been better than the one he and his partners in crime had cobbled together.

Journey into Fear was equally embattled, although, as George Schaefer might say, 'in the scheme of things' it is hard to feel so deeply about its fate. Koerner had confiscated the film from the Mercury office for re-editing. Moss appealed directly to him for its return: 'The natural conclusion can only be: Mercury can go – fishing . . . I'll not introduce any argument of rights, moral or legal. Courtesy alone should be enough to cause Mercury to be included in any function concerning *Journey into Fear*.' Koerner replied with aristocratic disdain, brooking no further discussion: 'Dear Jack, Believe me I realise your situation very definitely and clearly. Nevertheless, never for a moment can I imagine that RKO has at any time failed to extend every possible courtesy to Mercury Productions. In fact, the extent of RKO's help to Orson Welles and Mercury Productions would in many circumstances be considered somewhat fantastic. In regard to *Journey into Fear*, I simply followed definite and clear-cut instructions. There was no other alternative, and as far as I am concerned the matter is permanently closed. Sincerely CWK.' Jo Cotten, with slightly more clout than Moss (apart from anything else, he was the screenwriter), now weighed in, vigorously defending ending the picture with the scene in the rain, sharply and accurately delineating the arbitrariness of the studio's judgements: 'The editing and the cutting of the picture up to now has always been guided by audience reactions at the previews, and certainly we all know that the ending in the rain was more favourably received than any other ending ever screened. Since we started out accepting the opinion of the public to guide us in our own opinions, let us stick to this policy and not at this late date make the mistake of deciding that after all the audience is wrong.' All such civilised interventions were pointless. For Mercury at RKO, the game was up; they could go, as Moss so pointedly put it, '– fishing'.

On 26 June, hopelessly outflanked, George Schaefer resigned from the presidency of RKO. His departure was a formality; he had been among the living dead for some weeks. No mourners appeared. There is no record anywhere, in any document, letter, statement, interview, of one word of regret or condolence from anyone – let alone anyone at Mercury, least of all from Welles – at the forced departure of the man who had staked his career and his reputation on the great adventure that Welles's three-year sojourn at RKO represented. But for him, *Citizen Kane* might have been destroyed; but for him, indeed, it would never have been made. It is shocking that he received so little acknowledgement at the time, and continues to do so. Schaefer's unstinting support of Welles gives the lie to the suggestion, widely promoted by certain of Welles's apologists, that he was the victim of a cynical and ruthless studio system, which wanted to destroy him because of his independence and originality. This was precisely so in the case of Charles W. Koerner, who was quite explicit to that effect, but the case of George J. Schaefer shows the other side of the coin. Having assiduously courted Welles, he instantly fell under the young wizard's spell, immediately putting fabulous resources at his disposal with an absolute minimum of restraint. Schaefer believed in Welles unconditionally and sought to incorporate him into the system, hoping with his aid to transform Hollywood (or his patch of it) from a mere money-making enterprise into a place that was both artistically enlightened and commercially viable. Together they would do it. He wanted, in a nutshell, an equal partnership with Welles, an astonishing initiative on his part, considering that he had all the power in his hands. All he required from Welles – in addition to what he had to offer artistically – was a degree of responsibility for the consequences of his choices, and an acknowledgement that Schaefer was the head of a company that needed to make profits in order to survive.

Welles, young and flushed with the sense of his own talents, paid lip service to these small qualifications, seeing RKO as an inexhaustible milch cow. He rejoiced in Schaefer's enthusiasm for him, and thought that by a combination of charm, bluster and a sly implication of complicity he could get exactly what he wanted, often saying one thing and doing the opposite, in the belief that he would always come up with the goods and that they would always be worth whatever they cost. But he was at the mercy of the nature of his own talent, depending on adrenalin and inspiration to bring off his effects. He had enormous difficulty in engendering material: his real gift was for editing, interpreting, transforming. A screenplay only existed, for him, as a suggestion of a starting point, which would then acquire its character, its tone, its form and to a large extent its meaning from what he did with it in the act of creation. He could never supply anything to order. But Schaefer, as a businessman – an investor, so to speak, in Welles – had to believe that he could. The aggrieved letter that Schaefer sent him in Rio was an acknowledgement that the two men were not, in fact, partners at all. The terrible phrase 'lip service' sums up the older man's sense of betrayal and disappointment. Had Welles been straight with Schaefer, had he listened to him, had he understood what a peerless and indomitable ally he had in him, had he grasped that there were limits to any enterprise funded by Hollywood, his history and that of Hollywood – to say nothing of that of George Schaefer – might have been very different. Instead of being remembered merely as *Citizen Kane*'s midwife (who then heroically saved it from an untimely death), Schaefer might have been remembered – as he had dreamed of being – as usher-in of an altogether extraordinary period in the history of cinema.

His departure was without the slightest vestige of the glory he had dreamed of. Louella Parsons, William Randolph Hearst's avenging angel, gloated that despite Schaefer's having violently denied – when questioned by representatives of Hearst Newspapers in the east – that he had any intention of leaving his post, 'the moment Schaefer's resignation was received it was accepted', adding coyly, 'far be it from me to hazard what changed his mind, in such a hurry'. The aggression of her report, though hardly unexpected, is still shockingly unconcealed. The 'dispossession of Orson Welles, moon-faced boy wonder,' she says, was because 'the space was urgently needed for those engaged on current productions' (*Tarzan Triumphs*, as it happens, a Sol B. Lesser production); the order was made by 'the able Charles Koerner'. Her report only mirrored the brutal urgency of RKO itself. The day after Schaefer's resignation, senior executive Ross Hastings wrote a brisk and chilling little document to the able Koerner, describing 'what is necessary to terminate further operations by Mercury Productions'; most employees, he noted, had no contracts and could be *terminated* immediately. Twenty-four hours after Hastings's memo was written, Jack Moss, Herbert Drake and five secretaries left the lot, taking with them, according to the *New York Times*, 'the Mercury files, a mimeograph machine and a few other "meager" possessions'. 'Like Leonardo da Vinci evicted from a draughty garret,' said Herb Drake a little unconvincingly. They moved to an embattled position in the Hollywood Hills north of the Trocadero nightclub, 'to await the return of their leader from Brazil' late that month. 'A telephone with a long cord was brought out into the back garden,' the *New York Times* informed its readers, 'so that a faithful hench-woman can sit on the grass and answer Mercury Productions whenever it rings.' Cocking a parting snook at their former bosses, Jack Moss took the bronze fittings ('material no longer available because of the war') from the famous steam-bath installed when Mercury first arrived on the lot, thus rendering it useless, as a hapless RKO-Pathé executive, intent on a little soothing rehydration, discovered. Spirits were schoolboyishly high among the evicted Mercurians. JUST TURNING A BAD KOERNER, someone wrote up on the wall of their temporary office: ALL'S WELL THAT ENDS WELLES, riposted RKO. The whole thing had the feeling of a prank. Meanwhile, the fate of three films remained in the balance.

On 1 July, all remaining Mercury Productions staff were thrown off the lot; the same day, the able (and infinitely crafty) Charles Koerner gave a dinner for the main *It's All True* crew on their return from Brazil: 'I agree with Phil that on the whole they are an exceptionally fine group of capable men. I am positive that in the final analysis they will be able to do a very fine salvage job.' Welles was now history as far as Koerner was concerned, and he was already busy trying to make the best of what he considered to be a bad job. His strategy was to separate Welles's collaborators from him. 'Meltzer is on his way home and I understand he in turn had a falling out with Welles and we should have no trouble in putting him to work for us.' Meltzer had produced a memorandum for the front office that was uncharacteristic almost to the point of parody, doing a hard Hollywood sell on the Urca sequence, listing the performers:

GRANDE OTELO: He is a natural actor, natural comic and all in all spells 'Sure-fire' at the Box Office.

LINDA BATISTA: Best 'sambista' in the world. Better singer than Carmen Miranda, but she eats too much, is therefore fat. Spell 'Sock!' at the Box Office.

PERY MARTINS: Biggest child discovery since Jackie Coogan. If he could speak English he would be worth millions to any studio, and is clever enough to pick up a Shakespearean vocabulary within 20 or 30 minutes. Spells 'Wow!' at the Box Office.

EMILINHA BORBA. Urca star . . . white brunette, sells herself and her song competently, spells 'Wowser!' at the Box Office.

ELADYR PORTO: A buxom *morena*. Works on radio and makes records. Her figure spells 'Socko!' at the Box Office.

HORACINA CORRÊA: Flashy Negro wench. Now featured at the Urca in a number with Otelo. Turns in for us probably the best performance of any of the singers. Has a tremendous personality. Best described as a young Ethel Waters.

Phil Reismann, it appears, had a plan, too: perhaps, he suggests, they could bring over some of the Brazilian writers who had worked on the picture and get them working on the material. Anyone, in fact, other than Welles.

The man thus being exiled from his own work was, meanwhile, in a place that might have seemed to belong to a different planet, or maybe a different universe, from that of Melrose Avenue and the palace revolutions of RKO, the schoolboyish hijinks of the Mercurians and the spitefulness of the press. He was suddenly perfectly focused – perhaps for the first time in five months – pursuing a vision of extraordinary purity.

CHAPTER NINE

Look Who's Laughing

WELLES HAD not left Rio de Janeiro in an atmosphere of serenity. WELLES GROUP LEFT NORTH OKAY WITH FINAL GESTURE THROWING FURNITURE ETC OUT APARTMENT WINDOW TO AVENIDA CAUSING NEWSPAPER SCANDAL, Lynn Shores wired Phil Reismann. The scandal was real enough: on 14 June *A Noite*, under the headline ORSON WELLES ANGRY, reported that 'it was about 5 o'clock in the p.m. when disinterested passers-by on avenida Atlantica noticed that from the sixth floor from the window were coming chairs, clothes, empty bottles and other objects that were breaking up on the public street. It looked like a quarrel of a badly behaving couple.' The incident immediately became notorious, widely and increasingly imaginatively reported; cartoons were legion. Welles, trail-blazer that he always was, seems here to be anticipating rock stars of more recent times. Various explanations for his behaviour have been advanced, not least by himself, some of which are marvellously inventive; he told Peter Bogdanovich that it was a protest against the wear-and-tear charge for the apartment. The Mexican ambassador had visited him and urged him to give them something to really charge for. 'And he threw a small coffee table out of the window. So I took a chair and threw that, and we started throwing everything out . . . it was a great joke, we were howling with laughter.' In another version, Welles claimed that he suddenly noticed that the crockery in the apartment was Japanese, so out of the window it went, 'while an increasing crowd of *cariocas* gathered round to cheer'. Such incidents lose something in the retelling, and the humorous conceit does not survive the impact of the furniture on the heads of passers-by, as proved to be the case here. The aftermath rumbled on unpleasantly for some time, providing ample grist for Lynn Shores's mill. By then, the tiny Welles group was in Fortaleza, and the serious work of shooting was under way.

Welles seems to have been oblivious of what was happening in Hollywood. If communications were poor in Rio, they were primitive in Fortaleza, though an occasional telegram could be got through. From time to time he fired off telegrams to Phil Reismann denouncing Lynn Shores and denying the damage to the apartment: SHORES AGAIN SERIOUSLY SABOTAGING ME DELIBERATELY COMPLICATING CONFUSING EXAGGERATING SITUATION REGARDS MY APARTMENT STOP TERRIBLY CONCERNED MUST INSIST YOU COME MUCH LOVE. Again he asked for more money to shoot in Fortaleza. But he was pissing in the wind: no one in Hollywood was listening to him any more. Reismann was explicit: ABSOLUTELY NO MORE MONEY AVAILABLE FROM THIS END STOP SHORES HANDLING THIS UNDER INSTRUCTIONS FROM STUDIO BEST REGARDS YOURSELF AND GANG. On the day Schaefer resigned, Welles telegrammed Reismann: SHORES NOW SUCCEEDED GETTING PROCESS SERVED ON ME RIO STOP THIS CRIMINAL SABOTAGE SINCE I COMPLETELY WILLING PAY RENT DAMAGES STOP PLEASE HELP STOP PICTURE HERE REALLY WONDERFUL. He had no idea how completely he had queered his pitch with virtually anyone of the slightest influence; he clearly still thought that someone cared about what he was doing. In fact they were simply waiting more or less impatiently for his return, so that they could finally get rid of him, while salvaging something – anything – from the material he had shot. In his despatches to Reg Armour, Shores continued relentlessly detailing the problems he had inherited from Welles and Dick Wilson (who was in Fortaleza): the rights to the songs, thirty-six by more than a dozen authors, were a mess; the apartment required an expenditure of $1,100 damages, $1,000 back rent and a fee to break the lease; the Urca claims were mountainous: 'The office is haunted daily by various members of the Urca – musicians, principals and so forth – looking for the elaborate bonuses that Welles had promised them . . . there are so many promissory deals engineered by Welles hanging fire here that I may have to get measured for a bullet-proof vest if things get any tougher.'

Shores had managed to get the equipment out of the country:

As no one has particularly thanked me for it, I want to say that I think I did a masterful job . . . in pushing them out as fast as I did I had two ideas in mind, one to get them back for you to use and save expense, but the major thought was to get everything to hell out of here before Welles figured out another idea of prolonging the agony and shooting more stuff. I can safely say the only way we stopped him was that we ran out of film. Before he could think up a good proposition in black and white we had everything broken down and sealed in the customs house where he couldn't touch it.

The crew – or most of them – couldn't wait to get home. Even Shores, reporting everything to his Hollywood masters, had to admit that the revulsion and the weariness were not universal: '70% of them were very happy on going home, the other 30% tried to figure out a way of staying as long as possible'. The appearance at precisely this moment of an article by Frank Daugherty in the *Christian Science Monitor*, quoting Herb Drake as saying, 'Orson is making this picture without anyone from Hollywood around to watch,' could not have been more ironic. 'Mr Welles's picture will at least border on the documentary,' the *Monitor* continues. 'It should mark a new and interesting phase of Hollywood development.' And so it might have done, had there been a limitless supply of time and money from some kindly benefactor. RKO, after the aberrant indulgences of George Schaefer, had made it clear that it was not in the business of philanthropy; both time and money had run out, to say nothing of goodwill.

As it happens, the risky strategy of simply shooting until the nature of the film eventually declared itself – a strategy followed by certain more recent documentary film-makers – was finally about to pay off. In Fortaleza, wind-whipped and sun-scorched, Welles was gravely welcomed back into the community of the *jangadeiros* without reproach and with the active participation and support not only of the three survivors of the disaster at Barra Da Tijuca, but also of members of Jacaré's own family. There, denied the fleshly distractions to which he was so susceptible, with no lectures to give or awards to receive, with neither recalcitrant Technicolor cameramen, nor pesky production managers, nor feckless urban extras coming and going at will, Welles – supported by his own tiny group of friends, who pitched in whenever necessary, and one very inventive professional cameraman picked up in Brazil – worked with undeviating singleness of purpose to realise a vision of the lives of the fishermen unlike anything else in his output. Had he shot nothing else in his life, the surviving fragments would have marked him out as a supreme artist in film. The story was simplicity itself, a record of the diurnal round of the community: the fishermen prepare their craft, they arrange their nets, a wedding takes place. What is exceptional is the grave beauty that Welles and his cameraman achieve, recalling the work of his hero, Robert Flaherty, though in its epic sky-filled framings, with its tiny human figures and occasional extreme close-ups, it evokes even more strongly the manner of Sergei Mikhailovich Eisenstein, whose work Welles at that time claimed not to have seen (which is perfectly possible). Particularly striking is the resemblance to Eisenstein's abandoned masterpiece, *Que Viva Mexico!*, of exactly ten years before, which Welles had almost certainly never seen.

There is a superficial parallel between the two adventures: both brilliant directors seeming to come adrift in South America; both sponsored by a man (Upton Sinclair in Eisenstein's case, Schaefer in Welles's) absolutely convinced of their genius; both accused of monstrous over-shooting and reckless disregard for finance; both prevented from completing their work. The differences are, notwithstanding, considerably more significant, starting with an essential disparity of temperament – Eisenstein cerebral and sanguine, Welles sensuous and moodily capricious – and continuing with their fundamentally contrasted approaches. *Que Viva Mexico!* was a carefully constructed, fully conceived screenplay, consisting of a series of carefully wrought episodes designed to cover the whole span of Mexican history, relating the heroic past to the dynamic present; Eisenstein knew exactly what he wanted, and was prepared to wait for it (they filmed for more than a year). *It's All True* was an improvised compendium, a 'magazine', as Welles said, loosely related sections evoking the feel and texture of life on the sub-continent. Both films, as it happened, came to a climax at Carnival, but the Mexican Day of the Dead offers a very different image from the sensuous seduction of the samba. Welles's purpose, as we have seen, was in a sense to lament the transformation of the Carnival into something respectable; Eisenstein's sequence, in which a small boy removes his death-mask and smiles cheekily, celebrated the vitality of reborn Mexican society.

In Fortaleza, however, the two films (and perhaps the two men) came to resemble each other. Welles's response to the simple life of the *jangadeiros* was one of respect, exhilaration, envy. George Fanto, the remarkable lone cameraman, with his single camera, was a Hungarian who, as a result of various upheavals, found himself in Rio, and he formed an intimate and intense friendship with Welles. It reveals him in an unaccustomed light. It is always well to remember that aspect of Welles's disposition to which he so strikingly confessed in an interview with Kathleen Tynan: 'I'm a total chameleon and a hypocrite, and if I like somebody, I pretend to be what I think they want me to be. I have no integrity in that respect . . . I don't stand on my opinion, unless somebody's arrogant,

who isn't a close friend of mine. I only argue with negative opinion.'
But here in the north, he spoke to Fanto about the earth, about
the rhythms of nature and, above all, about God and Christ, in
whom, he told Fanto, he had absolute faith. That he seems never
to have spoken to anyone else in these terms proves nothing: his
was an inclusive nature, but also a curiously shy one. He would
scarcely have spoken in these terms to someone who he felt might
mock him. Here in Fortaleza, too, Welles seems to have lost his
natural impatience. He hired a young local photographer called
Chico Albuquerque who, nearly fifty years later, remembered
Welles's generosity: 'he taught me everything I know about framing'.
Albuquerque became one of the greatest South American photo-
graphers; his photographs of the *jangadeiros* immortalise a
now-vanished world. In the extant rushes, Welles works with his
amateur and uneducated cast with the greatest tenderness; in some
unedited sequences, his long tapered fingers can be seen gently
adjusting the actors in the frame. In Rio he had learned, for the
first time since he made *Hearts of Age* as a schoolboy, to work with
non-professional actors on film, and here in Fortaleza he encour-
ages them to give performances like no other in any of his movies:
still, intense, natural, the very opposite of the sort of high-spirited,
adrenalin-fuelled, verbally exuberant inventiveness that characterises
the acting in the rest of his output. It does not, in fact, seem to
be acting at all.

Seen in the context of the rest of the *Four Men on a Raft* material
assembled in the released reconstruction of *It's All True* by Richard
Wilson and his colleagues, the impact of this material is redoubled, in deliberate contrast to the material shot in Rio of the
jangadeiros arriving at the end of their heroic voyage. Fortaleza is
presented as a world of work rituals, of crosses and processions,
of lean, muscular men and modest, vibrant women. The fishermen
take to the sea with canny watchfulness, the epic wide-shots of
the ocean emphasising the simplicity and vulnerability of the tiny
jangadas. Even when conditions are inclement, they maintain a
steady focus; the film unflinchingly shows them in relation to the
empty vastness all around them. Then, when they reach their desti-
nation, the whole energy of the movie changes: bravura shots
introduce Rio in all its cosmopolitan diversity, the smooth Carioca
beach-lizards reacting to the arrival of the primitive barques
manned by the four fishermen with their little white helmet-like
hats, interlopers from another age, another world. Power-boats cut
a swathe through the water around the *jangadeiros*. Suddenly the

formerly sky-filled frame becomes crowded. Aeroplanes swoosh about overhead. The effect is almost as shocking to the audience as it must have been to the *jangadeiros* when they first sailed into the great port. The style of the film changes with the kind of society shown.

What is remarkable in the development of Welles's work is that he deals here for the first time with an open-air world, a natural world a million miles away from the largely interior worlds of *Citizen Kane*, *The Magnificent Ambersons* and *Journey into Fear*, and that he does it with absolute confidence and authority – an authority, however, that does not proclaim the identity of the director; it is, in so far as such a thing is ever possible, an objective world. His discovery of this manner of film-making arose because of circumstances – adverse circumstances, in fact. The lack of money and equipment, the unavailability of Technicolor (which he insisted right up to the last minute was essential to *Four Men on a Raft*) and the relative simplicity of his surroundings taught him a new approach to filming, which he rapidly mastered; no one ever learned faster than Welles. His constant protests at not being allowed to experiment are the cry of the autodidact who has some catching up to do. His education – both as a film-maker and as a man – was always conducted in public. To some extent this was inevitable. The luxury of self-discovery readily available to the artist in most other spheres – painting, writing and even, to a lesser extent, the theatre – is unavailable to the film-maker, except on the smallest scale, and Welles was never going to function in that way. Even when his films are short, they are big.

After he and the rest of the crew left Fortaleza, they returned to Rio via Recife and Bahia, where they shot various sequences. Welles then planned to take in various other Central American countries on his way back to Hollywood. Lynn Shores, naturally, was against both of these ideas, claiming that 'the Co-ordinator's office bluntly told me over the telephone that they did not relish the idea of Welles coming back to Rio at all and the sooner he got out of here the happier they would be'. The detour to Recife and Bahia inflamed Shores even more. He wired Phil Reismann: PROMPT ACTION NECESSARY YOUR END RECALL WELLES TO STATES IF IN ACCORD PLEASE APPLY ALL PRESSURE AND ADVISE COORD OFFICE OR MYSELF; Reismann refused because it would have established contact with Welles. The situation could scarcely have been uglier, until, that is, Lynn Shores decided unilaterally to take out an advertisement in *Aviso* stating that RKO refused to accept responsibility for 'any act done by Mr Welles in Brazil'; for this he was reproved, somewhat half-heartedly, by Walter Daniels at RKO, but not before the local newspapers – no doubt tipped off by Shores – reproduced a *Hollywood Reporter* article revealing that Mercury Productions had been expelled from the RKO lot.

Welles arrived in Rio on 22 July, spending five days there before embarking on his South American Grand Tour, conquering adoring and wondering new communities in, among other places, Argentina, Bolivia, Mexico, Peru, Chile, Ecuador, Colombia and Venezuela, leaving Lynn Shores behind to carry on the mopping-up operation. The Welles team had no doubts about Shores's malign intentions. 'Shores and gang,' George Fanto, still in Fortaleza, wrote to Dick Wilson in his as-yet-imperfect English, 'prepared a last dirty trick very unpleasant for Orson while friends and press appeared to show their appreciation for Orson. From Shores injustified actions against Orson it is quite clear that he did every-thing as to make our expedition a failure.' He describes an incident in which his assistant had an accident with the camera, after Welles had left, damaging the camera a little. 'But Shores already tried to make the allusions that Orson gave orders to brake it. So don't let anybody be wise on you.' Despite Shores's vilifications and the newspaper reports he engendered, Welles was as well received as ever by the intellectual community, who continued to view the Giant Boy – a Rio journalist's phrase for him – as a fabulous curiosity, an improbable phenomenon, both physically and mentally.

He found a particularly fervent admirer in Ray Joseph, RKO's man in Buenos Aires, to whom he gave a blow-by-blow account of the whole *It's All True* saga, firing the first salvoes in a war of justification. Shocked by what Welles told him, Joseph agreed to write Welles's side of the story. The project was 'hazed with more rumours than a senatorial cloakroom,' wrote Joseph. Welles explained away 'some of the fancy yarns brewed up'. He didn't deny, said Joseph, that there had been 'harsh cablese Western Union between Rio and RKO's office in Radio City', but insisted that reports had been exaggerated. There was never any question of his going there for four weeks. Nine months was always the intended period; he was to take as long as he needed. The budget was left open. He did not over-stay his time; such budget over-shoot as there might have been, he maintained, was because the budget for 'a film called *It's All True*' was tacked onto 'the Brazilian film'. The film itself, Welles roundly declared, was in splendid shape. 'He believes one more sequence will be necessary for the film, which he describes as not just one picture but as an evening at the movies.'

It is curious that Welles should have chosen to mount a long-distance propaganda counter-offensive, rather than simply going to Hollywood to defend himself. It is even more difficult to understand how it was that Welles felt able to mosey back to Hollywood by means of this huge cultural and geographical detour. Possibly he truly believed that the quality of the material he had shot would be acclaimed – once he returned and it could be put into context – as masterly, and that all would be forgiven. In the case of *Four Men on a Raft*, it is just possible that some such sequence of events might have occurred. But by now the head of the studio for which he worked had been ousted, specifically on account of his activities; his production unit had been very publicly ejected from the lot, under ignominious circumstances; and his current activities were a laughing stock in the press: 'the movie that Welles, the incredible, has been shooting all over South America,' reported the *Daily News*, 'is entitled *It's All True*. One man was killed in its filming, while Welles tore out the wall of the State Theatre in Rio for one scene, and shanghaied startled passers-by as extras for others. Some of it is in color, some in black and white and only a small portion of it is in Hollywood.' Yet, despite Herb Drake's good advice to come home 'with trumpets and banners', Welles chose not to take the first available flight back to Miami and thence to Los Angeles, but to cool his heels in Rio for a few days, then spend nearly a month roaming South America as a self-appointed goodwill ambassador. This is one of the most remarkable of Welles's absences, which were increasingly to characterise the pattern of his life, withdrawal at a critical moment. The definition of the psychiatric term 'fugue' or, more technically, 'psychogenic fugue', seems appropriate here: 'a sudden and unexpected leaving of home with the person assuming a new identity elsewhere'. Of course, Welles was not, strictly speaking, adopting a new personality, but retreating into an old one, one in which he was not required to deliver results, but simply to emanate charisma, for which he would be warmly acclaimed. In this environment, simply being Orson Welles was more than enough. In Hollywood, it no longer sufficed.

Typically, he turned the story of his missing month into a comic escapade, a deliciously absurd anecdote. He had 'a marvellous three-week trip among head-hunters', he told Peter Bogdanovich, many years later; he was pretending to be a leprosy doctor because there was only one free seat on the plane, and a young Jesuit priest had congratulated him on the release of *The Magnificent Ambersons* – 'and that was the first word I'd heard of it'. There are enough little smatterings of truth in this account to give it an aura of authenticity – and no doubt Welles did take a brief trip up the Amazon at some time during those three weeks of sub-continental peregrinations, and no doubt he was mistaken for a doctor at one point (as he told a friend at the time), but his acquaintances in the intellectual communities of Buenos Aires, Lima, Santiago and Bogotá, where he spent most of his time, might have been surprised and a little hurt to find themselves described as 'head-hunters'. The detail of his three-week *Wandermonat*, though amusing, is scarcely the point. What is extraordinary is that he should even have contemplated going up the Amazon to look at head-hunters or sipping cocktails and munching canapés with the gilded intellects of South American café society when his life was falling apart. It is inconceivable that no one in the Mercury office had thought to tell him that *The Magnificent Ambersons* had been released, or that his colleagues had been ejected from their suite at RKO. He knew very well that he and *It's All True* were in deep trouble. Instead of facing it, he chose to play truant.

A week before Welles's return to North America, *The Magnificent Ambersons* – the film Welles and all his associates believed would eclipse *Citizen Kane* – had been released to an incurious world, mutilated, on a double bill with the Lupe Velez vehicle *Mexican Spitfire Sees a Ghost*. There was no fanfare of any sort: '[RKO] didn't even hold a cocktail party for the critics,' said Herb Drake. The symbolism was not lost on the press. 'A spanking is an inspiriting thing,' said *Time*. 'Last week [RKO] rubbed it in by premiering *The Magnificent Ambersons* at two local movie houses with a Lupe Velez screechie. From a studio where good pictures have been even scarcer than United Nations victories, these goings on were high low comedy.' The reviews themselves, as it happens, were for the most part good, though Bosley Crowther in the *New York Times* (not yet the only opinion-forming newspaper in the city, but highly influential) wrote the words RKO had, since Pomona, dreaded seeing in print: 'Welles has a picture that's distinctly not attuned to the times . . . the focal point of the emotion is so inconsequential as to be ludicrous. With a world inflamed, nations shattered, populations in rags, with massacres and bombings, Welles devotes 9,000 feet of film to a spoiled brat who grows up as a spoiled spiteful young man.' The film's underlying theme, the development of the automobile and the mixed blessings that it brought – the critique of Fordism, potentially a great American theme – must indeed have seemed bizarrely irrelevant at a time when the United States was gearing itself up for massive production of mechanised transportation of every kind. The *Herald Tribune* had its reservations about the film, but nonetheless insisted that it was 'packed with cinematic power . . . *The Magnificent Ambersons* is a lot of motion picture. It is only a pity that it is always going off at loose ends.' The *Times* returned to the picture the following week, again noting the unhappy timing: 'In a world brimful of momentous drama beggaring serious screen treatment, it does seem that Mr Welles is imposing when he asks moviegoers to become emotionally disturbed over the decline of such minor league American aristocracy as the Ambersons represented in the late Eighteen Seventies.'

The review in Henry Luce's *Time* magazine, by contrast, was a Mercury dream come true, on every count; indeed, Jack Moss wired Welles – still in South America – to that effect: TIME THE MAGNIFICENT REVIEW FOR AMBERSONS WONDERFULLY ALSO BEAUTIFULLY SPANK RKO FOR RECENT ACTION. It was in fact less a review than an assault on RKO:

> *The Magnificent Ambersons* is a magnificent movie. It is also
> Round Two of the Orson Welles v Hollywood set-to. The
> upstart young producer-director-author-actor won Round One in
> a walk with his first picture, *Citizen Kane. Ambersons* is not
> another *Citizen Kane* but it is good enough to remove Director
> Welles for keeps from the one-picture-prodigy class. Despite . . .
> faults, *Ambersons* is a great motion picture, adult and demanding.
> Artistically, it is a textbook of advanced cinema technique . . .
> side-lighting creates a visual suspense in the very act of
> clarification . . . 350 [*sic*] degree turn-around in the ballroom . . .
> gives the narrative subtle, succinct meaning.

The anonymous reviewer, noting that Hollywood 'fears and hates the heavy-faced, heavily talented youngster', declared him vindicated. Hollywood 'gave much of the credit for *Kane* to cameraman Gregg Toland who photographed it. Stanley Cortez photographed *Ambersons* and it has all of *Kane*'s rich technique. Hollywood is now confronted with the painful necessity of admitting that Outsider Orson Welles is its most important and exciting cine-maestro.' The article continued with a precisely accurate account of Welles's ousting from RKO, quoting in definitive form what Welles purportedly said when told that Mercury had been thrown out: 'Don't get excited. We're just passing a rough Koerner on our way to immortality.'

All of this press coverage took place while Welles was in Fortaleza. His bust-up with RKO was still hot news. The *New York Times* article headlined WELLES VERSUS HOLLYWOOD AGAIN, telling its readers that there have been measured statements on both sides, added that 'Hollywood is hopefully awaiting the fireworks which are regarded as inevitable when Welles himself gets home.' He did not return direct to Hollywood, instead preferring to head for New York and his old chums after his pan-American detour. When he did, he was profiled by Theodore Strauss in the *New York Times*. ROLLING UP FROM RIO, the headline stated, DESPITE A SEA OF TROUBLES, ORSON WELLES REMAINS HIS IRREPRESSIBLE SELF. Strauss found him in his old stamping ground, '21', with his drinking pal Burgess Meredith; from time to time during the conversation various distinguished figures came up to make cameo appearances: the critic George Jean Nathan and the maverick Anglo-Hungarian producer, the newly knighted Alexander Korda, among them. Welles, says Strauss, was chortling 'like a Katzenjammer kid'. He was in expansive mood. 'New York? Why, in Rio they told me in New York people are fighting over sugar. Imagine! I had visions of people storming warehouses, riots in the streets, a whole epidemic of tabloid sugar murders,' he tells Strauss, whereupon 'the young gargantuan broke into explosive laughter . . . Orson Welles, after half a year below the Equator, was back, healthy, hulking and at the moment hilarious.' Strauss recapitulates the story of Welles's falling-out with RKO: *The Magnificent Ambersons*, Welles says, was completed 'without too frequent recourse to his advice as producer'; ditto *Journey into Fear*. He expresses some uncertainty over what he'll do with the Brazilian material: maybe complete it with *Bonito the Bull* and a North American sequence. 'Mr Welles was back and come hell or high water, he was enjoying his homecoming. Even the most casual onlooker could see that, despite the slings and arrows of outrageous fortune, Mr Welles was, happily, intact.'

So this was Welles's tactic: no tidal wave of wire stories, as Herb Drake had recommended, no party before the studio issued its own story. Just a good-natured shrug and then back to business as usual. Life would resume, he seemed to be saying, as if the whole RKO interlude had never happened. He had already – almost from the moment he stepped off the plane – started making various appearances, including one in the radio propaganda feature *Men, Machines and Victory*, and was the guest of honour at a meeting to raise money for Russian War Relief. These two activities – political activism within the framework of the war, and serious public-service broadcasting – would dominate his professional life for some time. For the moment, as a film director, he had burnt the one bridge he had.

In fact, *It's All True* gnawed at his brain throughout the coming period, and indeed for many, many years after that. Welles knew that there was the seed of something exceptional in that material, and he was no doubt right. It had long outgrown its original purpose of fostering hemispheric unity – Brazil had now joined the war on the side of the Allies, anyway, in the very month of August in which Welles returned to the United States – but in his work on the origins of the Carnival and the controversial filming in the *favelas*, in the Urca Casino sequence, and above all in the *jangadeiros* section, which had brought forth from him such epic visual poetry, he glimpsed something wonderful and utterly original. He came to believe that in some ways the work was cursed, and often told a story about the *macumbas* who had come to him on one of the many occasions when filming was suspended for lack of money; Welles was fascinated by their voodoo-like sect, and used them in several sequences. During his discussion with them, he had been called away to talk to head office, and when he came back, the *macumbas* had gone, leaving only the screenplay on the table, impaled by a needle to which a piece of wool was attached. 'That was the end of the film,' Welles said. 'We were never allowed to complete it.' (The events of the story in fact happened to Richard Wilson, but Welles annexed them to himself as somehow expressing a deep truth.) Nonetheless, both he, and, to a lesser extent, RKO, attempted for some time to find a way to convert the huge amount of footage into a viable film. The Office of Inter-American Affairs issued a statement in September referring to the dispute between Welles and RKO and claiming that everything possible was being done to resolve it; they hoped to accomplish this within thirty days. 'If RKO does not wish to continue the production, which may require additional expenditure of upward to a half a million dollars,' the statement continued, 'it is our hope that another major studio will assume responsibility for the completion of the picture under Mr Welles's supervision. It is the government's wish that the picture be completed with all possible speed and that its production be of a quality that will accomplish the Co-ordinator's purpose and be satisfactory to the Brazilian government and its people.'

RKO quite clearly did not want to continue with the production, though in view of the authority and prestige of the I-AA they gave an appearance of attempting to do so. Privately, their position was unchanged: 'It appears that the indiscriminate mingling of blacks and whites in the Welles Brazilian film will be found objectionable south of the Mason-Dixon line in the United States and in a good many countries of Latin America,' wrote William Gordon to Charles Koerner, noting that in a recent film Samuel Goldwyn had on these grounds deleted close-ups of the two coloured members of Gene Krupa's band. Gordon, the self-described expert on South American affairs, also notes that although Latin American countries are on the whole free of racial prejudice, they don't want the world to think they are preponderantly black. 'It is my studied opinion that the carnival film will propagate a contrary view which is apt to be greatly resented by those other countries.' Having drawn a blank with RKO, the I-AA next moved on to Twentieth Century Fox, who were interested in the film, but Welles was not interested in them. In an exceptionally revealing letter, he wrote to Nelson Rockefeller, 'it is my definite feeling that any deal of the kind 20th can offer represents a serious mortgage on the coming years' – that is, they would be offering him much less than his accustomed fee as director. 'Money, for me,' he added, 'is no object as regards *It's All True* and never has been any object.' This was a frank admission of exactly what Schaefer and pretty well everybody else at RKO had been saying from the beginning. Rockefeller replied with a steely letter:

I naturally hesitate to encourage you to accept any contract that your lawyers advise against and which, as you state, may mortgage your future. However, if you want my candid opinion, the collective future of the American people is in danger of being mortgaged, and individual or personal sacrifices that any of us can make today that will contribute even in a small way to the preservation of the freedom and human dignity of the people of this country seem to me to be a privilege. Few people have the great talent that you have to offer and, knowing you as I do, I am confident that, in the last analysis, your own decision in this matter will not be influenced by anything but your true desire to serve your country in this time of need.

This letter clearly indicates why Rockefeller was Rockefeller, and Welles was Welles, and confirms the truth of former Vice-President Wallace's wisecrack about him: 'Nelson Rockefeller's definition of a co-ordinator is someone who can keep all the balls in the air without losing his own.' Back Welles went to RKO, where the new executive president, Peter Rathvon, in schoolmasterly vein, told him the conditions under which they might be interested: 'If on your own responsibility you are willing to spend time on the picture I should think the proper procedure should be the preparation of a complete layout of the work to be done on the Brazilian section . . . not an off-hand stab but a complete study and layout.'

Three days later Welles was telling the *New York Times* that he didn't understand RKO's refusal to spend the extra $200,000 needed to complete the film, because once it was completed they could invoke the co-ordinator of Inter-American Affairs' guarantee of $300,000 payable on completion and release. To his friend Ferdinand Pinto, the owner of the Jangada Clube in Rio, he wrote that his quarrel with RKO was assuming 'Homeric proportions'. As he also wrote that they were refusing to release the film, though it had been completed in August, this letter cannot be regarded as a strictly factual document. In December, Welles held a screening of a selection of the footage to various producers and studios; there were no takers. There was a screening early in 1943 for the I-AA; vague plans were advanced for a collaboration with Fox. A few months later Welles applied to Rathvon for a greatly reduced budget of $75,000 to complete *My Friend Bonito* and a further $25,000 to knock the Carnival material into shape. To this end, he finally produced, in a sixty-five page document, the unifying structure for which everyone had so long been clamouring.

The format was not excessively ingenious: Welles himself – fancy! – was to be at the centre of the film with his real-life secretary Shifra Haran and the cameraman Harry Wild, pooling their brains about how to make a film concerning Latin America that is not a documentary, or a travelogue, or an illustrated lecture. 'He's ready to leave elaborate historical pageants to other movie-makers,' Welles writes of himself. 'The way he looks at it, people are interested in people, and he's going to use his camera to show American people to each other.' The various already filmed sequences are linked by newly filmed passages: 'Since the focus of the main part of our picture is on simple people, the incidental characters in the linking sequence are, wherever possible, presented as cultivated and well-to-do. The purposes of this tactic are, I am sure, self-evident.'

Several of the linking scenes involve Welles, Wild and Haran discussing the movie they want to make, reviewing on a projector the footage they've already got; the film thus becomes a film about filming. The *jangadeiros'* story is shown in fragments, while Welles reads Jacaré's own testimonial: 'We are part of another land. We belong to a great nation – Brazil. There is a President in a capital city. He is just. If he knew of these things, he would never permit them. We will go to him and he will help us.' They determine to interview Vargas, who now appears being humbly questioned by Welles. 'The producer's relations with the President of Brazil were of the very warmest,' says the treatment. 'No possible official objection need be expected.' The sycophantic portrayal of Vargas ends on his 'sly, warm smile'.

In places, the treatment aims for whimsical charm and even has elements of a romantic caper about it, specifically in the relationship between Welles and Shifra, with a hint of amorous expectations on Welles's part. It presents Welles in an unaccustomed role – one with which he would occasionally flirt in the years to come – that of dashing leading man. Baulked of a date with Shifra, he mediates between Dorothea, a Chilean girl, and a young Brazilian waiter, who have no common language. Welles now becomes fascinated by Dorothea himself and woos her by taking her to the *favelas* to listen to the music. They encounter Grande Otelo: 'From here we will come upon him often as a type among carnival celebrants, a personalisation of many popular aspects of the institution. This we think has been managed in the completed film in terms of truly uproarious entertainment.' Sitting in his car with Dorothea, Welles produces the instruments used in the Carnival, and plays them 'expertly but glumly'. Next day, he brings her to the location as they shoot the Carnival sequence. Sweeping across the vast numbers of revellers, Welles notes, 'Here we demonstrate another of the amazing truths about carnival: the unpoliced good behaviour of carnival's mobs.' This sequence is intercut with the Urca Casino footage: 'When it seems that everything has been shown, the star enters to top everything. In our case, the star is the Americas. Rio's carnival becomes Pan-America's carnival . . . the Americas, all the Americas together, are joined in fact as well as in idea, today rather than in the future.' The Carnival sequence ends with Otelo snoozing, then waking and wandering through the debris, singing 'Farewell Praça Onze'.

The scene changes to Welles interviewing a government representative, Donna Maria, extolling the beauties of the changes that have been wrought in Rio, including the demolition of the Praça Onze and its replacement with the Avenida Getúlio Vargas. Welles allows himself an uncharacteristic panegyric for the new versus the old: 'Rio's one of the only beautiful old towns where new things are even more beautiful than the old ones.' And he gives Donna Maria a speech in which, bright-eyed, like the heroine of a Soviet propaganda movie, she tells him, 'the hills up there, for instance, where the poor people live, where the Schools of the samba come from – you were up there photographing one of them, Senhor Orson – do you know we've got new housing projects for all those places – model homes? They're going up right now.' 'That's fine,' says Welles. The film ends with the return of the *jangadeiros* to Ceará. As their plane soars into the sky, Welles's narration tells the story of the success of their petition:

> The flight back really happened. This picture is all true. Bonito was pardoned; carnival was just as you've seen it; the four men from the North really sailed all those long miles to Rio in five logs of wood with only the stars to guide them, so they could talk to the President of their country. Naturally our cameras weren't always on the spot. Some of the action we had to reconstruct. Here – for instance – before we'd finished our work, Jacaré, the leader of the *jangadeiros*, had died in the sea. But this is still the end of our picture. Because this is the best place we know to stop. Also, it's true. Jacaré did go back to Ceará, of course, he's still there – alive in the love of his fellows; still with us, like the Dragon of the Sea who told the slave traders he'd carry no more slaves. For Jacaré lives now in American history. This picture is his: a humble, solid declaration. To Jacaré, then! To his sixty days on the open sea, and the eight hours it took a plane to fly him back through the air, over fields and mountains and jungles to his family on Ipacema Beach; to the hours less it's going to take to fly there tomorrow; to all brave flights and voyages; to his dream of the future.

This treatment was handed over to William Gordon for his comments: they were not kind. 'Possibly this outline can be brought in at a nominal, acceptable cost. However, in light of our previous experiences with the producer, the cost could reach exorbitant, even fantastic proportions, especially since it is so loosely drawn and none too well particularised.' Suspicion of Welles runs through the report, which is worth examining as the only existing detailed contemporary account of the footage, however predisposed against it the attitude may be. 'This newest version of *It's All True* makes nice reading, but I don't think it's a practical motion picture. To me, this outline appears to be full of fast, smooth, evasive double talk – another example of Welles's charming, persuasive, impractical self. No matter how you slice it, all in the world you have here is a bullfight in Mexico and a carnival in Rio. There is no sustaining story, no romance, no nothing, except what undoubtedly are well-photographed travelogue scenes.' Gordon had little faith in the impact of Welles's personality on the public: 'Audiences (composed of what audiences are composed of) will be indifferent to seeing him enjoying the beauties of the countries he visits.' *Bonito* is dismissed: 'I doubt whether in a picture advertised as tending to better inter-American relations, it is fair to Mexico to set up the promise to audiences to show them Mexico at its best – including the culture and the fineness of the people – and then restrict this demonstration to a bullfight, no matter how noble the bull or how many little boys are crying over the beast's imminent departure from this life.' He adds that 'North American audiences do not like bullfights and will pay you not to show them.' The Rio sections are impressive as shots of 'the great pageant that is Rio', but nothing more. There is no story. Gordon intimates that it's Welles's home movie, 'which will not mean much to the guys who whistle in the gallery . . . it still looks like a hodgepodge . . . we will not keep a typical movie audience in its seats if all we've brought them is a nicely photographed scene of dancing in the streets, interspersed with that high and mighty attitude of Welles'.

It becomes clearer and clearer how insufferable these RKO executives – not all of them money-obsessed philistines – find Welles: they *really* don't like him. Professing himself worried by comparisons with *Saludos Amigos*, Disney's wildly successful contribution to hemispheric unity, in which Donald Duck teams up with a parrot called Joe Carioca (and which, surprisingly, Welles himself proposed putting on a double bill with *It's All True*), Gordon scorns Welles's 'constant and continuous showing off . . . the use of Portuguese and Spanish reaches ridiculous heights when he acts as a Brazilian interpreter for the Chilean girl. Any Spanish-speaking person can follow Portuguese intelligently – certainly better than one who learned the language in six easy lessons.' He gravely doubts whether Welles will get Carlos Chávez and Heitor Villa-Lobos to write the score, as he seemed to believe; repeating the conventional wisdom that the *jangadeiros* – described in the report as 'Indians' – will be quite unsellable in the South, he also observes that it is impossible to understand from the film why they travelled down-country to present their petition, which is a reasonable comment in the light of the extant *Four Men on a Raft* material.

Gordon was not necessarily wrong about the probability of Welles spending a great deal more on this version of *It's All True* than he suggested he would. Whenever Welles started work on something, he saw a better, a richer, a bolder – and almost certainly a more expensive – way of doing it. The treatment itself is a curious mix of straightforward Popular Front politics (surprisingly enthusiastic about the deeply undemocratic Vargas, with whom, it was rumoured, Welles had liked to have contrast-and-compare conversations about their respective sexual achievements), rather corny and coy boy-meets-girl guff, and the core material at the Urca Casino, in the *favelas* and on the ocean. It is an uncomfortable mix as described, but any film is only as good as its realisation, as Welles knew better than most. What is surprising is that the finest material – *Four Men on a Raft* – only appears in fragmentary form in the treatment; Welles clearly believed that it was the entertainment value of the film that was its best claim to public attention, and maybe he was right. But it is the footage shot on Ipacema Beach, in Recife and in Bahia that justifies the whole of the rest of the film.

This would not be the last attempt to salvage the material, nor was it the last elaborate recasting of the structure. Welles's career was full of magnificent obsessions, starting with *Five Kings* (to which he returned twice, the second time in triumph), continuing with *Macbeth* (four versions) and culminating in *Don Quixote*, a twenty-five-year fixation without ultimate issue. He never ceased to regret the potential of *It's All True*, with the complex love one bears for something that has come close to destroying one. He wrote to Ferdinand Pinto early in 1943, when he was still busily trying to reclaim the material, 'I have a degree of faith in it which amounts to fanaticism, and you can believe that if *It's All True* goes down into limbo I'll go with it.' The film did go into limbo, from which it only partially emerged in the early nineteen-nineties. Welles occupied a more productive place, but it is true to say that had he never received the invitation from the Office of Inter-American Affairs to make a film in Brazil, his life would have been radically different. It is doubtful whether *Journey into Fear* at its best would ever have been anything other than an entertaining *jeu d'ésprit*, but *The*

Magnificent Ambersons – though it would never have been in tune with the times – would at least have been a complete work, unified in its vision, the work of one artist.

We shall never know, since in December of 1942, Charles Koerner, utterly disregarding George Schaefer's parting injunction to spare the film for posterity as Welles shot it, 'now agrees', as an anonymous internal memorandum put it, 'that we may now junk all positive and negative trims and out-takes which you have been holding on *The Magnificent Ambersons*'. The nameless functionary chooses his verb with particular relish. *Ambersons* was an emblem of exactly the thing that Koerner knew had to be rooted out of RKO: art for art's sake. The mood both in the country and in the movie business was dead against everything that had led to Welles's arrival in Hollywood: specifically the New Deal, with its extension of the subject matter of both theatre and film, its belief in the centrality of the arts to human life and the appropriateness of subsidy for its activities, its sense of collaborative activity in every sphere and its wide social embrace. Roosevelt had been slowly withdrawing from his social revolutionary programme; by the time war was declared, he had shifted his priorities, and Welles was among those who denounced him for it.

Charles Koerner enunciated his new-broom policy to Peter Rathvon with crystal clarity: 'I believe that probably the greatest attribute we can bring to the Organisation is one of good common sense, and frankly that seems to be at something of a premium in Hollywood. It is going to take us a solid six to eight months to get rid of the choking commitments we have at this time.' His arrival at the studio was hailed by the trade press. 'This new set-up looks like the best RKO ever had,' exulted the *Hollywood Reporter*. Charles W. Koerner had operated a small movie house in Montana in 1914, and had been in the theatre-management business ever since. 'There's no "genius" stuff about Mr Koerner,' said a spokesman for RKO, pointedly referring not only to Welles but to Gabriel Pascal and Jed Harris, who had also been summarily *junked* by the studio, in their case without shooting so much as a frame; Pare Lorentz managed to shoot most of his epic *Name, Age and Occupation*, which, though never released, survives. 'Our production forces will be levelling off at only one major target, the exhibitor, and through the exhibitor, the public.' Koerner declared war on what he sneeringly described as 'interesting film events', like Gloria Swanson's come-back and various recently acquired theatre properties. He put his faith in specially developed stories answering the need of the moment: in this case, war and service features 'with direct appeal to servicemen on leave and war workers with fat pay envelopes'. In other words, it was down with the movies as art.

The first great box-office smash of Koerner's regime, starring the radio comedian Fibber McGee and his assistant, the ever-faithful Molly, bore the triumphant title *Look Who's Laughing*. 'Showmanship in place of genius' was Koerner's much-vaunted watchword, and in terms of fiscal probity, he was entirely successful, wiping out the studio's debts (though the phrase is a little misleading: it was poor showmanship, rather than wasteful genius, that had lost the most money – as in the case of the star-packed flops *Sing Your Worries Away* and *Valley of the Sun*). The importance of Koernerism was as much a question of image as of finances: wartime America needed to be amused and enthused; there was no place for subtleties, experiment or, God forbid, questioning. What were suddenly perceived to be eternal American values had not only to be maintained, but seen to be maintained. 'Welles was offering Americans an unfamiliar and uncomfortable view of their world,' as Laura Pells observes, 'at precisely the time when they hungered for whatever seemed tranquil and routine.' He also embodied in conspicuously flamboyant form the notion of wayward individualism, an idea equally profoundly out of sympathy with the times. In a sense, the Second World War was another part of Welles's bad luck: unlike his fellow director-producers, Noël Coward, Charlie Chaplin and Preston Sturges, he was temperamentally unable to join the mainstream when it seemed appropriate.

No doubt the existence of the Welles Unit at RKO had been something of an anomaly from the start, and it was only a matter of time before it would have been disbanded. From Welles's personal point of view, however, what happened was profoundly regrettable. The association had offered him unparalleled opportunities and a degree of support that would never again come his way. Henceforward, every film that Welles made was a massive struggle against the odds. Even when he worked for a studio, he was employed from the outside and had to fight for what he needed. Circumstances conspired to end his relationship with RKO in the worst possible way, with maximum damage. Given those circumstances and Welles's own temperamental vagaries, it remains something of a miracle that at least one completely achieved masterpiece saw the light of day: *Citizen Kane*. For the one and only time in his life, he was able to work within a structure that allowed full play to his prodigious gifts, neither oppressing nor inhibiting him, and causing no compulsion to flight on his part. He had been given unexampled latitude by RKO, provoking profound resentment both inside and outside the film industry. He left it with a reputation for unreliable brilliance, still regarded as a peerlessly promising film-maker, but for the time being, at any rate, too hot to handle.

For his part, Welles felt frustrated by the limiting demands of commercial production: when he insisted on the artist's right to experiment, he was not speaking idealistically; he was very precisely stating the only conditions under which he could work. He made his films, as he had made his theatre, on the floor, in the heat of the moment. As he worked, the full possibilities of what he was making revealed themselves, and only then; *It's All True* was the ultimate instance of this. Nothing could be more inimical to an industry operating within the confines of the studio system. For some film-makers this system was a perfect set-up, allowing them the stability to pursue their own dreams. A Hollywood film-maker who had exactly the same idea as Welles was Charles Chaplin, who set no limit on the amount of time and money he would spend on a film. But he owned his own studio, and was – at least at this point in his career; it would not always be so – guaranteed huge ticket sales on the strength of his name alone. Welles was in no such position, and never would be. The balance sheet was still formidable: *Kane* an acknowledged work of inspirational brilliance; *The Magnificent Ambersons*, even in mutilated form, recognised as an astonishing achievement for such a young film-maker ('Although *The Magnificent Ambersons* seems to lack pertinence now,' said the *New York Times*, 'it has integrity and sincerity of purpose. Mr Welles has grown much in a short while; he may yet assume the full stature that can be his'). *It's All True* remained a mystery, and *Journey into Fear* was yet to be seen. Nobody was underestimating Welles, but he was already thought of as somebody who might not be his own best friend.

A curious postscript to the Brazilian adventure is a persistent rumour that the copy of *The Magnificent Ambersons* – the answer print that RKO had shipped out to him in Rio – is still there. David Kamp in the magazine *Vanity Fair* traced its progress through the man who was the head of Cinedia, Adhemar Gonzaga, a film collector 'before it was common to be so'. Gonzaga got to know Welles, of course, in 1942. When Welles left, Gonzaga wired RKO to ask what he should do with the copy. They telegraphed him, telling him to destroy it; he duly replied: PRINT DESTROYED. But was it? Gonzaga's daughter, now head of Cinedia, has searched for it but found nothing, though she points out that it may be in there somewhere, mis-filed. Josh Greenberg went to Brazil in 1994 and 1996 and found nothing, but he did meet a man who claimed to have seen it in the nineteen-sixties, after which it disappeared. 'We pursued some leads, even talking about tracking it through gypsies,' says Greenberg, 'but after that we kind of ran out of leads.' In 1984 Fred Chandler broke the news to Welles that all the cut footage was gone. 'He broke down and cried in front of me. He said it was the worst thing that had happened to him in his life.' Welles did no such thing at the time, but his life was before him then, and he may not have grasped what he was losing when he broke with RKO.

Part Two

PLAIN TALK BY
THE MAN
FROM MARS

CHAPTER TEN

Ceiling Unlimited

To ALL intents and purposes, Welles the director withdrew from Hollywood in August of 1942. He had many plans for films; none of them would fall within Hollywood's remit. He was now, in effect, an independent film-maker, a very exposed position in 1942. His passion to communicate was undimmed; he was brimming with ideas about society and about life. In particular, he was full of what he had seen and understood of South America, and was as eager as ever to make his contribution to hemispheric unity. But first there was the small matter of making a living. For this he naturally turned to his first big source of income, radio – the medium of which he had unquestioned mastery and for which he commanded substantial fees. Although he was under financial pressure, his idealism as usual came to the fore. He had made two highly praised broadcasts from Brazil, the first called *Pan-American Day*, the second a celebration of President Vargas's birthday, both of which had been enthusiastically received in North America. This was the vein – informative, celebratory, progressive – that he sought to mine in the work on which he embarked on his return, although the very first programme was a somewhat uninspired remake of *The Hitch-Hiker*, one of his big successes on the *Lady Esther* programme. He also participated in a number of shows in the *Cavalcade of America* series, 'radio's class act', as Arthur Miller put it in his memoir *Timebends*, a cut above the regular patriotic broadcasts, which he dismisses as 'more like yelling than writing'.

Miller was one of *Cavalcade*'s regular writers, and had been given sufficient latitude by CBS to write a play about the Mexican revolutionary Benito Juárez – in verse. Arriving at Studio 8-A with his script, 'I heard a tremendous but vaguely familiar baritone-basso voice,' he recollected. 'I saw that the cast wore expressions of real anxiety, some with eyes lowered to avoid looking at the giant orator, who, I now realised, was Orson Welles.' Welles was railing at the programme's historical advisor. 'It is a TRAVESTY, I tell you,' he raged, 'a LIE, a purposeful and contemptible distortion of KNOWN

FACTS in order to justify the unforgivable!' The hapless advisor was either drunk, Welles roared, or corrupt; the historical incident in question had been dramatised as a great American success in Latin America, 'when in reality it had been a catastrophe and a disgrace'. The rehearsal collapsed, which is when Miller entered, Juaréz script in hand. Welles demanded to see it. Finding that it was in verse, he immediately became fascinated, and started to read it out loud with other Mercury stalwarts, 'ringing out the syllables like a rebuke to the professor'. Miller slipped into the booth and listened 'amazed at Welles's genius with the microphone; he seemed to climb into it, his word-carving voice winding into one's brain. No actor had such intimacy and sheer presence in a loudspeaker.' The earlier fracas was by now quite forgotten. 'After the reading I came out of the booth and he pulled me to him in a loving embrace, and I went home on the IRT in triumph.'

The impression Miller gives of a king returning to reclaim his empire − 'he already had his loose and wicked belly laugh and the noble air of a lord' − is not inappropriate: here was a realm in which Welles was absolute monarch. With *Cavalcade of America*, he vigorously imposed himself on a series that, as Miller points out, was already well established. He brought his characteristic energy and intelligence to the presentation, creating a surprising narratorial presence, both impatient and easily wrong-footed and far from omniscient. In *Admiral of the Ocean Sea* (about Columbus, later published as *Columbus Day*) his slightly pompous narrator has his dignity punctured by the interventions of a sassy young girl who turns out to be rather smarter than he is; Welles's experiments with narration would never cease throughout his career. Here, too, his passion for dramatising information, and his commitment to an enlivened educational process, is demonstrated in the way the historical facts are personalised, made vivid and accessible. The episode was partly written by his old chum, Bob Meltzer, but Welles's influence is everywhere.

As usual, the programme was very much made on the floor. William S. Paley, powerful head of CBS, the company that broadcast *Cavalcade of America*, writing to Welles to tell him that he had been 'magnificent' in the broadcast, added, 'You probably heard from my secretary that I was very upset when I learned you had not appeared for the dress rehearsal. I probably also made some impetuous remarks to her. Little did I know how easy it was for you to do a superb job with so little preparation.' The sheer aliveness of the show in question is remarkable even now. A few months after making it, Welles gave a speech on education in which he affirmed the strength of his enthusiasm for the medium: 'The radio is realising its potency as a teacher,' he announced, adding a sly dig at Hollywood, 'and the movies are so good nothing can stop them, not even the movie makers, who have certainly tried.' He praises radio for imparting information 'in these war times . . . clearly and loudly and effectively'. He asks his audience to contemplate the extension of this idea into all phases of education, which, he says, 'would be like asking you to look upon the limits of the universe . . . there will be no more frontiers. We'll most of us live to see the last of the frontiers – and they'll be frontiers of the mind.' He reiterates the time-honoured 'efforts of education', as he puts it: instructing, enlightening, acquainting, informing, enthusing, inspiring, elevating. He insists that new means for transmitting the spoken word 'bring education's ultimate aims within the limits of human possibility. Yes, I'm talking about the millennium,' he concludes. 'If we don't reach now for its approximation, we shall certainly be faced with the facts of chaos. It's our fight – education's fight – and the time is now.' Welles's insistence on the primacy of education (he who had had so little of it) is striking.

Bob Meltzer was producing radio programmes now, and he roped Welles into a new show sponsored by the aviation giant, Lockheed. Its purpose, one of simple propaganda, was to boost morale within the industry in order to underpin the vast increase in productivity that war demanded. Arthur Miller was again to be the writer. In preparing his outline, he paid unforced tribute to Welles's unrivalled authority at the microphone: 'I didn't know until Jack told me over the phone last night that I was to draw up a format,' he wrote to Welles. 'I've been thinking about it today, however, and I feel sure of one thing: we don't need one. Your voice is a format. The only two things that must be heard at the beginning of the show every week are your voice and Lockheed Vega . . . your voice, if I may say so, portends much. It and Lockheed Vega identify the show, along with the title. That's all a format can do, portend and identify.' Welles had named the programme Ceiling Unlimited, a perfectly Wellesian concept, although one not without a certain irony, coming from the man notorious (if inaccurately so) for introducing ceilings into movies. The sponsors had not been keen on the title at first, noted one magazine, 'then genius won'.

At the same time as Welles was working on the Lockheed show, he was planning his pan-American series, Hello Americans; the first programme of each series was broadcast on consecutive nights. This pattern persisted over the thirteen weeks of the season: it was Welles wall-to-wall on the airwaves, and the press was all over him again, if with an appreciably greater level of gentle mockery than in the past. 'It is the first time a major airplane manufacturer has bought network time for weekly coast-to-coast broadcasts. Even the producer is unique – Orson Welles who at 27 has been in the Boy Wonder class since his broadcast of an imaginary invasion from Mars threw large chunks of the populace into a panic.' There were, *Newsweek* reported, problems in pinning Welles down to work on scripts. 'Harried angry executives complained they couldn't get in touch with him; he offered to talk business any midnight at "21", Hollywood's favourite New York night-spot.' With a touch of unkind glee, the article notes that he may not be free to do the programme for very long: he might be drafted, despite his obsolete classification 1B for 'a combination of spinal displacement, heart murmur, and flat feet'. Everything was known about Welles, absolutely everything; the smallest embarrassing physical shortcoming was not allowed to remain private.

As far as *Ceiling Unlimited* was concerned, Welles's involvement in it had certainly brought up the temperature on what might otherwise have been a worthy, though scarcely exciting, show. Before broadcasting had begun, Welles and entourage had swooped down on the Lockheed plant, where he told the startled workers (perhaps a little to their alarm) that if the show wasn't a triumph, it would be his fault; he then swept off again. The first programme, *Newsweek* opined – not without a certain smirking superiority – was 'all Welles and a yard wide'. In his preparation for the shows, he had immersed himself in the history and literature of aviation, reading, among others, Saint-Exupéry, and over the programmes he returns again and again to a bracingly lyrical celebration of flight, often with a touch of fierceness, quite fitting to wartime. Interviewing Leonardo da Vinci, he tells him, 'We've given your bird a great heart and we've given her claws too, machine guns and cannons.' There was, as *Newsweek* observed, 'plenty of opportunity for the booming Welles voice to declaim'. 'O Flying Fortress,' he addresses the aeroplane, in his most inspirational manner, 'O living answer to the eyes of nations, the free people wait and watch the sky for your coming: the people enslaved pray for your coming. Fly well!' It wasn't all uplift, though. All the facets of his radio persona are there to be heard: the sonorous, the skittish, the flatteringly charming, the sternly hortatory. He presents himself as the listener's intelligent, playful, modest friend, nonetheless able and willing to state great and important truths – a self-amused patriot who happens to have a silver tongue, an aristocratic Everyman. The oxymoron is part of the piquancy of the Wellesian persona, the grandee with a racily popular touch.

An extraordinary amount was packed into the fifteen minutes of *Ceiling Unlimited*. For *Hello Americans* (twice the length), he had a ready use for the huge volume of research that he and his fellow-workers had done in Brazil. He wrote to Nelson Rockefeller, whose Office of Inter-American Affairs was involved in sponsoring the programmes, describing his many-pronged assault on the airwaves: 'The best good-will propaganda is to sell South America to North America.' The pan-American cause, with its inclusiveness, its celebration of diversity and its challenge to the values of white Anglo-Saxon Protestantism, was something to which Welles felt deeply attracted. His enthusiasm for it impressed his colleagues: 'Orson is working harder on this series than anything he's ever done before,' Jack Moss wrote to the I-AA, clearly struck by the focus and commitment of his often wayward boss. 'I would like to say,' wrote Jackson Leighter of the Motion Picture Society for the Americas, for whom Welles had narrated a film about Mexico, 'that in all my dealings with artists, I have never found anyone who lends so willingly his time and talents as you do, and surely I can say without being fulsome, that no other artist has so much to offer in the work we are endeavouring to do.'

Each week *Hello Americans* profiled another country. The Americans of the series' title were roundly pronounced to be the inhabitants of both North and South. Welles constantly sought the most vivacious method of presentation, not dissimilar to the *Ceiling Unlimited* formula, interviewing the great dead as if they were alive, evoking the country in question in sounds and atmospheres, dramatising the historical while never forgetting the present reality: *conquistadores* rub shoulders with civil engineers. The first episode was devoted to Brazil and was, naturally, among the richest of the programmes, drawing particularly on the samba material so prodigally amassed for *It's All True*. Welles brings a certain wildness – more than a touch of the spirit of the Carnival – to his approach. This exuberance is vividly conveyed by Bret Wood in his description of an early sequence in the first episode. It sounds a little quaint now, and it is to be feared that it may have sounded somewhat quaint even then; Welles's populism, though entirely genuine, never altogether loses its self-consciousness. But there is no denying its charm. 'One first hears the rhythmic beat of jungle drums,' writes Wood. 'This is soon joined by other instruments, polished and allowed to flourish in a lively orchestral rendition of the samba. Welles calls out, "Dig that rhythm, you cats, that's the Amazon and the Conga talking!"'

Both series continued till the end of January 1943, and both were solid successes for Welles, much appreciated by his sponsors and fellow-broadcasters, though they scarcely answered the pressing questions concerning his future or his financial security. Worse, they failed to attract the audiences that had been hoped for, and at the beginning of 1943, he was dropped from them. NATURALLY WE ARE UPSET, cabled the I-AA's representative. WE FEEL THAT THE SERIES HAS DONE A GREAT AMOUNT OF GOOD. And no doubt it had. They – and other ventures like them – are representative of a vital and now largely submerged aspect of Welles, what might be called the Todd legacy, dinned into him (as it would continue to be for the rest of his life) by Skipper Hill, but also so clearly a part of his mother's heritage: the belief that an enlightened approach to education was the linchpin of life, and that without it there could be no democracy, no progress and, ultimately, no happiness. Perhaps only an autodidact could feel these things quite so passionately. Perhaps, too, only an autodidact could quite so shamelessly show off as he did on *Information Please*, a radio quiz in which Welles not only answered every single one of his own (rather difficult) questions, but was also audibly champing at the bit to answer everyone else's.

Another persistent facet of Welles's cornucopian nature was his longing to be funny, and his perfect willingness to undermine his own dignity in order to do so. Shortly after his return from Brazil, his dismissal from RKO and the ruin of all his dreams, he was to be found on a comedy half-hour shrieking away at the microphone in a riotous send-up of *Les Misérables*, one of his earliest, finest and most serious achievements on radio. It was as if he been oppressed by the seriousness all along, and needed to let off steam. Or perhaps he felt that if he were too serious, he would not be loved. The symptoms of the latter syndrome were to be seen throughout the rest of his career, in many bizarre manifestations.

As for film, *Journey into Fear* was still, as far as Welles was concerned, unfinished. He had secured RKO's agreement to allow him to do a final cut on the film. The letter authorising this was cold and not without a certain grim satisfaction: 'You will go to Hollywood to arrive there not later than October 23rd 1942 to do re-editing on *Journey into Fear*,' wrote Peter Rathvon, the new head

of the studio. Welles must finish within fourteen days; there would
be no retakes except one additional scene, to be shot in one day,
using only Joseph Cotten and an extra. Then came the really bitter
medicine: 'Your work at the studio shall be under the supervision
of Mr Charles Koerner. The cutters, cameraman and others whose
services shall be used shall be people assigned by Mr Koerner.'
Welles was thus answerable directly to the man who had destroyed
George Schaefer, who had determinedly extirpated Mercury from
RKO, and who had declared personal war on Welles himself. In
a sense, it was. better than nothing: had he had even that amount
of time and those meagre facilities with which to work on *The
Magnificent Ambersons*, it might have been a very different film.

Welles devoted his allotted fortnight to cleaning up the final reels
of *Journey into Fear*; this cliff-hanging sequence, as Banat pursues
his quarry across the rain-spattered façade of the hotel, remains the
most successful in the film. It is impossible to tell what Welles might
have achieved with the movie had he been given a proper post-
production period: again, with the dissolution of his team, he was
effectively working with one hand tied behind his back. The contribution that might have been made by special effects and an
interesting (as opposed to merely generic) score was potentially
enormous: had Bernard Herrmann, for example, an absolute master
of suspense and exotic effects, written it rather than poor old Roy
Webb, he might have taken the film to a different level of finish
and wit. As it is, Webb. did a decent workmanlike job; it is
honourably competent, the last thing one expects or wants from a
Welles film. At least one executive at RKO had faith in it: Al
Galston of the sales department sent a telegram to Welles saying:
WE BELIEVE YOUR REVISED JOURNEY INTO FEAR WILL BE ONE OF
THE BIG BOX OFFICE GROSSERS OF THE YEAR. Alas, it was not to
be.

*

Whatever the ill will between Welles and RKO, Hollywood at
large had not dismissed him; he was still a huge figure in the
landscape. But what to do with him? In 1942, the producer David
O. Selznick was planning another of his grandiose literary adaptations; unlike his recent triumphs, *Gone with the Wind* (1939)
and *Rebecca* (1940), this one was to be drawn from a truly great
source, *Jane Eyre*. He decided that Welles should play Jane's moody
employer, Edward Rochester. Welles had known the producer
since they had dined together after a performance of *Doctor*

Faustus in 1936, when Selznick had offered him the job of head of his story department (Welles slyly suggested that his then business partner, John Houseman, might be better at it). As was his wont, Selznick sought to throw every particle of talent he could muster at the project. *Jane Eyre* was the dream of the English-born director Robert Stevenson, who had been under contract to Selznick for some time without actually making a film for him. His biggest success in America had been *Tom Brown's Schooldays*; he had just completed a decent and financially productive French Resistance movie, *Joan of Paris*, for RKO, and was preparing to join the Forces himself as soon as *Jane Eyre* was shot. Selznick had equipped him with an army of writers, including Aldous Huxley and John Houseman, now indeed (just as Welles had suggested he should be seven years before) part of Selznick's permanent staff.

Selznick was not, in fact, technically speaking, the producer of *Jane Eyre*: having packaged the film, he had sold it to Twentieth Century Fox, who appointed William 'Bill' Goetz – another son-in-law, like Selznick himself, of Louis B. Mayer – as producer, but Selznick kept a sharp eye on the production from beginning to end. It was Selznick's idea to cast Orson Welles as Edward Rochester to Joan Fontaine's Jane; he may have hoped that some of Welles's genius would rub off on Stevenson. Such was his regard for Welles's work as a director that he had begged RKO to deposit a copy of Welles's original cut of *The Magnificent Ambersons* with the Museum of Modern Art in New York, a tantalising prospect that, needless to say, never materialised. Selznick had long admired him as an actor and thought him, with some reason, peerless as a director of dramatised novels on radio; he had vexed Alfred Hitchcock during preparations for *Rebecca* by constantly referring to the version of the novel that Welles had just made for *The Campbell Playhouse*: 'if we do in motion pictures as astute a job as Welles did on the radio,' he had told Hitch in one of his celebrated memos, 'we are likely to have the same success the book had and the same success that Welles had.'

From Welles's point of view, *Jane Eyre* was from the start a questionable enterprise, compromising as it did his status as a so-called quadruple-threat. His profile as producer-director-writer-actor had been perceived by his advisors (and to an extent by him) as being the *sine qua non* of his reputation. In the end, financial considerations – the money he owed RKO, his alimony, his tax arrears, the extravagance of his lifestyle – demanded that he accept the job, but he and his representatives did everything they could to protect his position. Anxious that Welles might be mistaken for a mere actor, Herb Drake told *Look* magazine that Welles was only doing *Jane Eyre* 'in the interest of Uncle Sam's tax department', demonstrating a dangerous contempt for acting on Welles's part. Perhaps Welles thought that by affecting to despise his job, he would win public sympathy; the opposite is invariably true, as in the case of Marlon Brando's similar statements of some twenty years later. Why should anybody want to pay money to see someone do something for which they have contempt? Welles's attorney Loyd Wright took issue with Twentieth Century Fox's proposed contract, insisting that 'he must not deviate from his well-earned position, that of a recognised independent producer', even if he was only to act in the film, and had nothing whatsoever to do with its physical realisation. Wright suggested a credit for him: PRODUCTION DESIGNED BY ORSON WELLES. Merely acting in a film was clearly regarded by Welles and his team as a dire demotion: how could he, who had done every job on a movie, simply take direction from some lesser mortal?

Selznick was aware of the anomaly and, when he wrote to Goetz telling him that he'd like to be present at a forthcoming casting meeting for *Jane Eyre*, he added, 'I should like also to urge you to have Orson there, because I know few people in the history of the business who have shown such talent for exact casting, and for digging up new people.' There was from the beginning some confusion about exactly what Welles would be doing on the film, a confusion that Welles did nothing to dispel. This was a pattern that would be repeated many times throughout his career: the creation of a suspicion that he might have had something of a guiding hand in the realisation of another director's film. In the case of *Jane Eyre*, the impression is even more insistent because, in addition to the casting of three of Welles's actors – Erskine Sanford, Eustace Wyatt and the great Agnes Moorehead – two of his key collaborators worked on the film: Bernard Herrmann (a great deal of the music, as it happens, is recycled from Herrmann's score for Welles's radio version of *Rebecca*); and, no doubt to Welles's considerable displeasure, John Houseman. In the event, Houseman – to the relief of both himself and Welles – was not present at any point during either filming or the pre-production period.

There was an active move on Welles's part, or that of his representatives, to secure a formal credit for him as producer of *Jane*

Eyre, a move that Selznick equally actively resisted. 'I don't believe Orson himself would any more think of taking this credit, once he had all the facts and understood what he might be doing to Stevenson, than he would think of taking directing or co-directing credit,' he wrote to Goetz. 'Actually, direction or co-direction credit would be no more damaging to Stevenson in this case than production credit for Orson, for the latter places Stevenson in the position of simply having carried out Orson's plans, than which nothing could be more inaccurate.' Selznick had already conceded Welles first billing over Joan Fontaine (an undisputed star since *Rebecca*), because an acting-only credit would 'reduce' him from his status as a producer-director-actor-writer. For him to have associate producer status would thus be 'a double injustice – to Stevenson, and to Joan's status as a star of the first magnitude . . . I do not think that he will want anything that is not his due, at the expense of another man for whom he has professed – very sincerely, I am sure – great admiration.' Interestingly, only a few weeks after sending this to Goetz, Selznick wrote to Joe Schenck of Twentieth Century in very different terms, agreeing to Welles receiving credit as producer, while Fontaine gets first billing. Among the various practical reasons he cites, there is, he says, 'general disbelief' that they would not give first billing to Fontaine, ceding second billing 'to a man who, whatever his prestige, is clearly not in the same category as a star'. Conversely, it was thought absurd to lose the prestige of Welles's name as producer in the credits; in their eyes, his stature was clearly unaffected by the RKO debacle. Stevenson, Selznick continued, was going into the army, so Welles's credit would not damage him; the publicity department, meanwhile, had reported that 'there can be no wide-spread belief that Mr Stevenson is not the director of the film in every sense of the word'. So much for appearances. More significantly from Welles's perspective, Selznick reports that they have just learned that 'Welles did a great more producing on the picture than we had previously known. We have been informed by people from your studio that Mr Welles worked on the sets, changes in the script, in casting, among other things, *and that he had charge of the editing*.'

All of this is extraordinary, but what is conveyed by the last phrase (my italics) is simply sensational. To edit another man's movie is to cut his balls off, as Welles had better reason than most to know – to edit creatively, that is, rather than merely functionally. In the technical sense, moreover, at this point Welles was scarcely the master of editing that he later became, having only directed

Citizen Kane (largely edited in the camera) and *The Magnificent Ambersons* (on which Welles's editing contribution amounted to precisely three days – and nights – in Miami). And yet: *he had charge of the editing.* The letter ends: 'please understand that we are in no sense pressing this [the suggestion that Welles should receive a credit as producer], and are extending it purely as a courtesy to 20th Century-Fox'. For whatever reasons, it never happened: Welles received no producer credit, and he had to settle for second billing to the star.

On the set, however, he hardly comported himself as a mere actor, according to Joan Fontaine's perhaps not entirely objective account. 'Orson Welles was a huge man in 1943. Everything about him was oversize, including his ego,' she wrote in her autobiography, *No Bed of Roses*. 'Orson's concern was entirely for Orson: *Jane Eyre* was simply a medium to show off his talents.' She describes how, on the first day of filming, the cast and crew were assembled at one o'clock; at about four, the stage door suddenly burst open and Welles whirled in, accompanied by his doctor, his manager, his secretary and his valet. 'Orson strode up to a lectern . . . placing his script on it and standing before our astonished group, he announced to the director and cast, "Now we'll begin on page four!"' Stevenson – 'slight, timid, gentlemanly' – was 'suddenly demoted to director-in-name-only'. The journalist Sheilah Graham wrote a profile of Welles during the making of the film, in the course of which she reported that 'Welles has four secretaries, two offices, and is making a government "short" in between takes of *Jane Eyre*. At the same time he is scripting one broadcast a week and cutting *Journey into Fear*. Also,' she added, with casual savagery, 'he is directing the director of *Jane Eyre* on how to direct.'

It is worth noting that at this stage Welles had never been directed by anyone else on film – indeed, he had hardly been directed by anyone else in any medium, at least since his youthful days at the Gate and the slightly later period with Katharine Cornell and Guthrie McClintic. It must have been a hard adjustment for him, one that he did not handle with grace. It signals the beginning of his essentially awkward relationship with the film community: if you hired him as an actor, you got so much more – more perhaps than you wanted. It is fair to observe that, in this particular case (perhaps unbeknown to Fontaine), he had been involved in both the screenplay and the casting, so it is hardly surprising that he expected to be treated differently from everyone else. But this behaviour (no doubt exaggerated by Fontaine, though there are plenty of comparable reports, then and later) suggests a childish determination to demonstrate his importance. It also marks the beginning of the long sulk that so often coloured his work in other men's films: they won't let him make his own movies, so he's damned if anyone else is going to enjoy making theirs.

This attitude was not, however, inflexibly maintained: 'Orson couldn't keep up to the position he assumed,' wrote Fontaine. 'He was undisciplined, always late, indulged in melodrama on and off the set.' On one occasion he failed to show up on time for a photo-shoot: 'He'd been lying in the bath sulking because I didn't trust him to show up on time.' This aspect of Welles – the infantile tyrant – is widely attested, and coexists with the passionate and high-flown broadcaster, the political writer, the master-craftsman and the inspiring leader. They were all Welles, and the different personae could succeed each other with bewildering speed, or could indeed be on display simultaneously. At the time, Welles was having an affair with Lena Horne, who was singing in a nightclub on Sunset Strip, and he liked to report his wilder activities to Fontaine while they were shooting. (Shorty Chirello, Welles's chauffeur-valet, confided in her that in fact Welles sat in bed every night with a tray, 'which didn't jibe at all with Orson's version of his nocturnal exploits'. For once, Welles's version of his own life may be more reliable than his chauffeur's.) Despite everything, Fontaine realised, he wanted to be liked. Eventually she warmed to him. Moreover, she noted that, despite all Welles's peacock displays, Stevenson quietly and slowly regained the directorial reins. With filming completed, however, he joined the army and Welles was presum-ably able to assert his authority in the editing suite.

Whatever the truth of this, the film – though certainly domi-nated by Welles's startling interpretation of the character of Edward Rochester – is not especially Wellesian in style; indeed, to a large extent it is actually opposed to his aesthetic. The very opening of the film, showing a bookshelf laden with great tomes of the past, proudly declares itself a literary adaptation, which might be thought to have been anathema to the radical educationalist in Welles. The film ends with a photograph of a bound copy of the novel with the slogan 'Buy yours in the theatre'. The cinema as a route to literature, not an art form in its own right. If Welles stood against anything as a movie-maker, that was it. The cinematography, by the distinguished cameraman George Barnes (who had just shot *Rebecca* for Hitchcock), is of great refinement of tone, softly focused, evocative and painterly in a way that Welles and Toland – formerly

Barnes's assistant – had utterly set themselves against in *Citizen Kane*; *The Magnificent Ambersons*, too, though aspiring to a period look, uses depth of focus and a kind of energy in the camera movements to engage the viewer critically with the way in which the story is being told. Barnes's work in *Jane Eyre*, by contrast, contrives to create a world in which the viewer can forget that he or she is watching a film and simply marvel at the expressive beauty of the pictures. In his own films, Welles did everything he could to prevent this. It is not a style ideally suited to Welles's talents as a performer. Indeed, it may be argued that Welles's acting is always at its best with the cinematographic style that came to be associated with his name – one of unexpected angles, sudden distortions, epic perspectives (the style Carol Reed adopted for *The Third Man*, in which Welles gives arguably his finest performance). The performance he chooses to give in *Jane Eyre* is on the brink of the grotesque, in much the same manner as his aged Kane: curiously doll-like, strapped into corsets, a great beak of a nose imposed on his own, his facial skin pulled back by the gum of his wig. Interestingly, the image he creates is not unlike the one he invented for himself as a thirteen-year-old playing Richard III. He wears the make-up, which reproduces Brontë's 'stern features and a heavy brow . . . gathered eyebrows', like a mask, affecting a highly theatrical, consciously stentorian vocal delivery; his British accent is not that of an English squire, but of an English actor (sometimes tipping over into the lordly Anglo-Irish tones of his youth in the Dublin theatre); it is part of a theatrical gesture. His Rochester is an impersonation, not an interpretation; with Welles, the outside never goes in.

This is by no means to say that the performance is uninteresting: on the contrary, Welles sees the character as a kind of tortured monster, physically strange, clumsy, only half-human. It is exactly the sort of line on the character that another actor, Charles Laughton, might have taken. Had Laughton done so, he might well have created an equally extreme physical life, but he would (at his best) have transfigured the portrait, touching some universal chord, provoking pity as well as terror, giving us the man within. With Welles, the interpretation is an idea, put on (like a suit of armour), very striking, very powerful, but merely a thing manipulated by the actor, and thus incapable of moving us. It betrays, as much of his acting does, the influence of German Expressionism, the most theatrical of all filmic styles. This, his first conscious bid for movie stardom, was not a promising calling card; the gesture is so extreme that he only suffers by comparison with the rest of the acting in the film, which in its straightforwardly realistic manner is excellent, ranging from the childish charms of Elizabeth Taylor and the remarkable skill of the teenage Peggy Ann Garner (as the young Jane), through the stalwart and strikingly accurate character work of Henry Daniell and the human warmth of the Abbey Theatre veteran Sarah Allgood, to the uptight vulnerability of Joan Fontaine in one of her best roles. In this company Welles seems distinctly out of place. So, it might be argued, is Edward Rochester, but Welles's massive presence and anguished histrionics have a distinctly unbalancing effect on the film. *Jane Eyre* was not released till 1944, a long year after *Journey into Fear* finally hit the screen in February of 1943; as far as the public was concerned, they scarcely knew what to make of him as an actor. Up to that point Orson Welles's performances on film had consisted of the many-faceted but not necessarily many-layered Charles Foster Kane, and the preposterously corny Colonel Haki. The release of *Jane Eyre* was something of a moment of truth for him as an actor.

Welles moodily told Robert Stevenson that the notices he received for the performance had been 'the worst accorded to an American actor since John Wilkes Booth'. On the whole, in fact, the reviews were baffled, as well they might have been, though respectfully so. The *Hollywood Reporter* detected 'certain overemphases that are occasionally offensively flamboyant and approximate', while *Variety* noted Welles's 'declamatory delivery'. Only James Agee in the *Nation* really took the gloves off, describing Welles's 'road-operatic sculpturings of body, cloak and diction, his eyes glinting in the Rembrandt gloom, at every chance, like side-orders of jelly. It is possible to enjoy his performance as dead-pan parody; I imagine he did.' Unkindly, Agee adds that he might have enjoyed it himself, 'if I hadn't wanted, instead, to see a good performance'.

Friends were not much more supportive. Welles was not encouraged by receipt of a telegram from Micheál macLiammóir praising him for his performance of Mr Rochester as Count Dracula, though that sharp little sally has a bit more in it than pure malice: Welles's performance is indeed in his line of tortured monsters, of which his radio Dracula is the most remarkable. The problem is that his desire to provoke pity is a notion, an intellectual ambition: he does not take the steps necessary to effect it in the viewer, such as connecting with his own experience or allowing his imagination to engage at a deep (as opposed to a merely pictorial) level. Welles defended himself on curious grounds: 'There are about eight or nine parts that every individual actor can really play and the Rochester role is one of my eight or nine,' he told an interviewer. 'I don't agree with those sedulous character actors who study and "live" a role for seven months in advance of playing it. If they have to work at it that long, it's a sure thing they aren't fitted for it. They can only . . . detract from the true possibilities of the role . . . if the role doesn't fit the actor then he's false no matter if he lived it 100 hours a day, and no matter how great his talent for mimicry. I'm striking a blow for realism.' Realism was not a characteristic that either the press or the public were much inclined then – or ever – to associate with the name of Orson Welles, and his comment suggests that self-knowledge continued to elude him.

As Welles had admitted, acting in film was a minor element in his life, which was stirring in all sorts of other directions. Many of these departures had considerable significance for his immediate and not-so-immediate future. Whatever his success or failure in any one arena, the scale of Welles's celebrity was such that new ventures were always easy to come by, new spheres always waiting to be conquered. Leonard Lyons, his old admirer on the *New York Post*, asked him to write a guest column for the paper, and Welles obliged with gauche charm. 'This may be the last time I write a column, but it isn't the first.' In the piece he recounts the – largely true – story of his infant journalism, when he was the eight-year-old opera critic for the *Highland Park News*. Then he tells a sweet, if slightly less convincing, story about his time as ghost writer for a drunken movie critic 'in a city which shall be nameless – and a newspaper which should be'. He wrote the reviews, he says, never having seen the movies in question. Then one day the movie didn't show up, but his review came out nonetheless. He claims, too, to have written pulp fiction in Ireland – 'I never was much good at it; it's a great art' – and rounds the piece off with a long and somewhat inconclusive story about Edgar Wallace, which feels like padding, adding, as a final tag, a teary compliment to Leonard Lyons for writing about him 'when I needed it'. Pleasant enough stuff, but not promising for a future as a columnist. The tone of voice is archly orotund, like a well-oiled after-dinner speaker ('Memory's treasure trove yields up another wistful bauble in the episode of . . .'). No doubt the piece served its purpose – a stopgap while the resident columnist was on holiday – but it scarcely suggested a future in column writing. Before long, however, that is exactly what Welles pursued with almost desperate fervour.

For the present, he was immersed in another novel enterprise, substituting for an indisposed Jack Benny on his eponymous show. Welles's passion for vaudeville in general, and comedians in particular, was one of the great constants of his life: in the late 1960s he was to be found happily fooling around in front of a camera with some of the bright young things of British comedy of the day, Graeme Garden and Tim Brooke-Taylor. It was a taste he had acquired in childhood as he trailed around the vaudeville houses of Chicago with his stage-door Johnny father. To his unconcealed delight, in March of 1940 – a full year before *Citizen Kane* was released – Welles had been invited to be the guest star on Benny's show. He plunges into the proceedings like a great big dog jumping into a river and emerging, dripping but triumphant, with a stick between its jaws. He is hugely game and quite fearless, cracking himself up shamelessly and stumbling charmingly over his script. He is not especially funny, but he is utterly engaging. The persona created for him in the show is an exact reflection of the public's perception of him at the time: precocious (he left high school at five, Benny says: even his diapers had cuffs) and extravagant, a sort of deranged actor-managerial-megalomaniac. He runs three careers simultaneously, and sounds veddy, veddy British, dictating notes on several topics to his various secretaries – a private one and another who is 'right out in the open' – speaking to London on the phone while being measured by his fussy tailor. Benny and the rest of the team constantly refer to the Welles legend ('scared anyone today, Orson?'). The plot of the episode concerns Benny's dream of being a great actor, to realise which he takes lessons from Welles ('with his technique and my feeling for the finer things, I could really go places'). Welles duly rehearses Benny in a scene from *The Hunchback of Notre Dame* – in the film of which, as it happens, Charles Laughton had recently had an overwhelming success, playing the part originally offered to Welles – and this gives Welles a chance to do his brilliantly observed and extremely funny impersonation of the very grand Sir Cedric Hardwicke (Frollo in the movie). It's all high-spirited and droll, with Welles bearing the brunt of most of the jokes.

Since this romp, three years earlier, Welles's career had experienced spectacular vicissitudes; Benny, meanwhile, remained (as he had been for nearly a decade) the biggest radio star in America, and probably the world. His show was built around the minutely detailed character he had invented for himself – musically incompetent, curmudgeonly, prissy verging on camp – and he played his live audience like the violin he was supposedly incapable of mastering, with freedom, elegance and hair's-breadth timing. (The most famous and best-loved of his exchanges involved Benny being held up by a robber. 'Your money or your life,' the robber demands. Long silence from Benny, which provokes a huge laugh from the audience. When it eventually subsides, the robber repeats his demand. Another even longer laughter-filled pause from Benny, who finally says, 'I'm thinking it over.') Every part of the exchange depends on the audience's familiarity with the Benny persona, whose very facial expressions the listeners could vividly imagine. The idea of actually standing in for this comic genius, as opposed to simply making a guest appearance on his show, would have been nerve-rackingly daunting to anyone with an iota of self-doubt. It is a considerable tribute to Welles that Benny was prepared to entrust the show to him (with the sponsor, Grapenuts, clearly being equally confident in his abilities), and a measure of Welles's fearlessness and supreme self-confidence that he accepted the invitation at all.

In the five shows in which he deputes for Benny, Welles acquires Benny's entourage, including the outrageous black manservant Rochester, but of course plays himself – or rather, as before, the public perception of himself. It is startling how much older he seems than in his earlier incarnation of only three years earlier. The crisp, brisk, flamboyance of the 1940 'Orson Welles', precocious actor-manager, has been replaced by a rather sombre, moody figure, pompous and tyrannical: The Genius. 'Quiet on the set!' one of the characters regularly exclaims, 'Mr Welles is about to Direct!' – or Explain! – or Emote! Benny's normally frisky entourage is cowed into servility, swiftly silenced if they make a suggestion of any sort, and reduced to monosyllables in the sections when they act in the film that 'Mr Welles' is purportedly making. 'I call my film quite simply *The March of Destiny*,' 'Mr Welles' says, 'and it deals with everything that ever happened.' There is immense emphasis on his genius: 'Phil,' he tells one of his henchmen, 'you're a genius, and I ought to know.' But genius evidently has its disadvantages. 'Sometimes,' he muses gloomily, 'I wish I weren't perfect, so people could differ with me.' He performs a striking and elaborate send-up of the standard commercial plug for Grapenuts with epic grandiosity, but whichever way you slice it, it's still a plug. The studio audience is obediently appreciative, though naturally there are none of the huge extended laughs that Benny regularly coaxed out of his audiences. Part of the problem is that, unlike the Jack Benny character, which is preposterous and bears no relation to the real man or his career, this 'Orson Welles' is uncomfortably close to the real one: are we laughing at or with him? It sometimes feels self-serving. At least one person of considerable influence, however, was very impressed. After the first show in which Welles deputised for Benny, William S. Paley (boss of CBS) telegrammed him to say: NOW THAT YOU HAVE QUALIFIED AS A COMEDIAN OF NO MEAN STATURE WOULD YOU BE INTERESTED IN DOING YOUR OWN COMEDY SHOW ON A REGULAR WEEKLY BASIS. It was some time before this new idea came to fruition, but the seed was sown.

While edging towards comedy, Welles had by no means abandoned his more serious ambitions for radio, and did not hesitate to advance his radical political views. 'I know that you agree with me that radio has a very definite responsibility in the matter of the current race riots,' he wrote, as a member of a committee of Writers' Mobilisation, to Davidson Taylor at CBS, 'and the growing tension in many of the industrial communities between black and white, whites and Mexicans and other minority groups.' He was trying to persuade the company to produce a script called *Snowball*, written, as it happens, by Howard Koch, with whom he was now back in partnership, despite the rupture of their relationship over Welles's claims to have written the script for *The War of the Worlds* broadcast, though Koch was unquestionably its author. For *Snowball*, Welles had assembled the talented cast of Gary Cooper, Jo Cotten, Canada Lee, Walter Huston 'and your obt. servt.'. Taylor's reply presaged a long and ultimately frustrated struggle on Welles's part to put race relations at the centre of public debate. CBS had broadcast an Open Letter on 'the Negro Problem', which had been very successful. But, Taylor tells Welles, 'You may not know the difficulties it caused.'

The issue of race, despite the extraordinary advances achieved by the National Association for the Promotion of Colored Peoples, was still, in America in 1943 and for many years to come, an explosive one; courage and tenacity were called for even to raise the matter. Welles had both qualities in overplus, and no lack of candour – not always of the most diplomatic variety. Taylor says that he'll consult their educational advisor, Lyman Bryson, to which Welles replies:

> Mr Bryson and I are not strangers. We keep bumping into each other on the platforms of women's clubs, and for your friendly ear I can't help but remark that this 'Director of Education Department' speaks, like Gratiano, 'an infinite deal of nothing'.

He is persuasive in Lyman Bryson's behalf, and cosily certain of the success of his moral crusade within CBS. He has mastered the fashionable idioms of the intellectual caste and exhibits everywhere that sort of sprightly serenity so often confused with open-mindedness. I shudder to think that this dollar-book scholar, this luncheon sage, is the man to decide whether the negro problem is to get another half hour on the network. But then this is a world to shudder in – Burn this. Fond regards.

The object of Welles's contempt wrote a letter to him shortly afterwards, saying, not unreasonably, that 'We cannot with much hope of success do two smashes on the same question so close together if we hope to carry the network along with us.' They are anxious, he insists, 'above all to use broadcasting to the very limit of its social value', but explains that they simply cannot get the affiliated stations to carry the programmes. 'We are hoping to attack other social questions dramatically and to increase the willingness on the part of the general public to face these difficult and violent matters with reasonableness.' The solution is time and patience. This would not do for Welles, whose admirable passion in the matter – in any matter about which he felt strongly – could not tolerate a softly-softly approach: his gut inclination was to storm the citadel. In the end, this would prove to be his undoing as a political figure, resulting in fireworks, certainly, but not the general conflagration he so ardently desired.

Welles was accepting more and more invitations to speak publicly. The war was the inevitable theme, often within the context of broadcasting or the movies. He spoke loftily and passionately, using all the skills of rhetoric that were central to his own acting, allowing his extraordinary vocal instrument free rein, and his audiences were greatly stirred. At first, he spoke as any committed actor might have spoken, with more ardour than analysis, appealing principally to the emotions: 'I am sorry to have been advertised as a speaker,' he said when he appeared with Charles Chaplin at a meeting billed 'Artists' Front to Win the War'. 'I have nothing to say to you which you don't know . . . but I am here on this platform and I'm speaking to you because I must: because even if I'm not the best man for the job, there isn't anyone in these United States who hasn't the right to speak up about the war.' This is Orson as Everyman, a favourite manifestation of his. 'As it happens we approve of our leadership. We endorse it . . . this isn't a protest meeting . . . finally this is a people's war – on all fronts – a people's war and we're all in it. Just that.' Later, he spoke more articulately and with more precision, addressing the Adult Education Conference on the subject of 'New Techniques in Mass Education': 'All educators, whether they like it or not, are in the amusement business, and all movie makers and radio broadcasters are educators,' he told the conference. 'In this shrinking new world of ours, adult education must first enlist in the war against provincialism. Exactly as long as the proposition that all men are created equal is a faith real enough for men to die for it, educators, which means every one of us in possession of the instruments of education, are sworn to the tremendous task of telling people about each other – about their works which are called wisdom and culture.' His commitment to pan-Americanism was undiluted. It was, he insisted, 'a requisite for our victory . . . and making the dream of inter-American unity come true is less a job for diplomatists than it is for educators. The United Nations are fighting for a united mankind . . .' Narrowing his scope, he describes, as an example of the educational value of celluloid, the possibility of filming – for the benefit of medical students – great surgeons performing operations; then he expands again into a resounding peroration: 'with the present development of communications, I don't think there will be a spot on the globe that will long be what we now call remote. There will be no more frontiers. The new elements of mass education will be to the dark places of the human mind as bright sunlight is to the crawling things under a lifted stone. The vermin and bacteria of intolerance cannot survive in the bright gleaming light of understanding.' He knows, he says, that he sounds as though he is talking about the millennium: 'I am, and I believe that it has a very good chance of happening in your lifetime or mine.'

The speech was a great success, and there were many requests for a transcript. One letter told him that 'We admired tremendously your broad views and *complete* understanding of the problems of adult education and your very practical theories for solving them.' He was clearly possessed by the idea that fundamental change in society was a real possibility; the thinking of the Popular Front informs his every phrase. Welles had been radicalised; politicisation was not far behind. It is worth noting here that if it is a little unusual for a movie director or actor of his stature to have appeared in radio comedies, or to have written popular columns for tabloids, it is virtually unheard of for one to have become an orator of a decidedly political bent while remaining a practising artist. The political community was delighted: his celebrity would be a tremendous boost to their appeal. Both his endorsement and his oratory were widely sought by the many committees and councils, anti-fascist, pro-second front, pro-labour, pro-education, to which the war had given a new sense of relevance. He was so much in demand that he sometimes felt hounded. On one occasion he wrote to a certain Helen Bryan, who had reproached him for cancelling an appearance, that 'stage and screen performers of progressive persuasion are so frequently exploited that many of them have been forced into retreat or at least political seclusion. I hope I am made of somewhat sterner stuff, but I understand the attitude of these men and women and after our "misunderstanding" I must confess it is a temptation to sympathise with them.'

In reality, retreat or political seclusion was not an option for Welles in 1943. On the contrary, the scope of his public utterances was getting wider. At a rally at the Lewisohn Stadium in Upper Manhattan, his fellow-speakers were Paul Robeson and Roosevelt's Vice-President, Henry Wallace, no less. Welles gave an address with the resonant title 'Moral Indebtedness'.

My part in this free meeting is just this: it is to say that to be born free is to be born in debt; to live in freedom without fighting slavery is to profiteer. By plane last night I flew over some parts of our republic where American citizenship is a luxury beyond the means of a majority. I rode comfortably in my plane above a sovereign state or two where fellow countrymen of ours can't vote without the privilege of cash. Today I bought my lunch where Negroes may not come, except to serve their white brothers, and there I overheard a member of some master race or other tell those who listened that something must be done to suppress the Jews. I have met Southerners who expect and fear a Negro insurrection. I see no purpose in withholding this from general discussion. There may be those within that outcast 10 per cent of the American people who someday will strike back at their oppressors. To put down the mob, a mob would rise. Who will put down that mob?

He was careful to identify his political position, which was a sensible precaution. The FBI and its informers, now hot on his trail, had no doubt as to where Welles's sympathies lay, even though they could never quite pin anything on him. 'The scaly dinosaurs of reaction,' Welles said, 'will print it in their papers that I am a Communist. Communists know otherwise. I am an overpaid movie producer with pleasant reasons to rejoice – and I do – in the whole-some practicability of the profit system . . . surely my right to having more than enough is cancelled if I don't use that more to help those who have less. This sense of humanity's interdepend-ence ante-dates Karl Marx.' Describing the war as 'the current plot against liberty', he avers, in classic Popular Front phraseology, that 'when all the fascist armies have formally surrendered, the end of fascism will still be out of sight'. As so often in his speeches, he consciously used the references of his profession – 'This world fight is no melodrama. An armistice is no happy ending' – and concluded with some ringing curtain lines: 'The people well know that Peace is harder won than war . . . none of us will live to see a blame-less peace. Our children's children are the ancestors of a free people. We send our greetings ahead of us to them. To history yet unmade, our greetings. To the generations sleeping in our loins, be of good heart, our children! The fight is worth it.'

The response to this speech was enormous, both from individ-uals and from organisations. Identifying herself as a black woman, Muriel Miller wrote to say that she honestly felt 'that it was one of the most tremendous talks of all time and regret that it was not broadcast for the nation'; another member of the audience testi-fied to Welles's perhaps unexpected seriousness: 'You were confronted by almost insuperable conditions. The audience· had been exhausted by an intolerably long program. What they had been led to expect from you was more entertainment and they were not in a mood for more entertainment. The manner in which you were introduced was no help. – And yet you prevailed, and delivered an address that was a masterpiece of génuine eloquence, intensely and convincingly personal, but with the speaker standing behind rather than in front of his message.' Someone else told him that, as a political speaker, 'you're a red-hot potato'. The Packinghouse Workers, perhaps surprised to find such a glamorous figure so wholeheartedly àdopting a radical line, praised him for his 'liberal and courageous remarks', adding that 'we wish you to know that we deeply appreciate your comments and your position regarding the common men and women in America'. His words had redoubled their enthusiasm 'in their fight for a free and liberal labor movement in America'. Polly, of the United Automobile Aircraft and Agricultural Implement Workers, obviously had her doubts: 'I'd give anything to know if you really believe what you so convincingly said – please tell me and the big fraudulent "ego" bubble of the paltry press will be burst in the hearts of all your

avid followers who will see you in a true light for the first time.'
Nevertheless, she still signed off 'Fraternally yours'. The *Trade Union
Press* headed its report: PLAIN TALK BY THE MAN FROM MARS. There
were many requests for copies of the speech, not least from the
Vice-President; before long it was printed as a pamphlet by the
Chicago United Nations Committee to Win the Peace.

It seemed as if Welles's entry into the arena of political speech-
making was to be every bit as spectacular and precocious as his
entries into the professional theatre and film-making. His speech
to the Overseas Press Club was printed in Elsa Maxwell's widely
syndicated column: something of a harangue, it first dwells on the
word 'fascism' and its interpretation. Then he pauses to consider
the nature of the enemy. 'The armies of our united nations seem
pretty sure by now that they're going to lick the hell out of the
fascists. It seems the only question is: how soon? Here's another
question: are we fighting all the fascists?' He notes that the Allies
are doing business with fascists, and the fascist view has its spokesmen
both in the press and in the government:

> I hope no one will understand me to have said that we have a
> fascist administration or a proto-fascist journalism. I merely repeat
> an opinion widely held, that our free press is sometimes and in
> some places in the hands of freedom's enemies. If you ask me
> the names of the enemies of freedom, I will answer that this is
> your job and thank you for doing so much of that job so very
> well. The freedom to take away freedom is the fifth freedom, and
> the hope of the fifth column. Against this assault on freedom
> stands the free press. I am here in the name of your readers to
> celebrate that stand.

He speaks with real urgency, even if it is a little difficult to
imagine what the assembled hardened journalists can have made of
it. 'The advocates of defeat – the isolationists, the counter-
isolationists – are preparing for [democratic man] a terrible burden
of despair. You can lighten that burden.' Again, education is his
central theme. 'You are the scouts – mark his path for him, and
mark it well. Name his enemies. Teach him the value of his vote
– believe in him as he believes in you.'

Welles's inclination to speak on behalf of mankind was even
more strikingly indulged when he addressed the Soviet-American
Congress. In a memo, he had promised that he would acknowledge 'the debt our theatre and motion pictures, our writing and

our music owe to the genius of the Soviet generation', reassuring the organisers that 'the speech will be very short and will be wholly uncontroversial politically'. In the event, it was uncontroversial to the extent that it endorsed the new-found rapprochement between the two governments, but in the course of doing so Welles smuggled in a number of somewhat contentious statements about the relationship between art and society. Entitled to speak, he says, only by 'my own small work', he identifies the artist's duty: 'he speaks for his nation to all the nations. He goes before the diplomat into far lands, interprets for the races of man, translates for the generations, declares for the people.' Then, in the strangely archaic prose considered de rigueur at such gatherings, he roundly declares that 'who speaks for an interest but not the peoples' – he is no artist. He is a hack and a whore' – a phrase that would surely have made Stalin's cultural commissar Zhdanov positively beam. He insists that 'the men and women of Russia could not fight as they fight now for freedom without owning it'. America and Russia are friends, he says, 'because we are free'.

Welles was hardly alone on the radical Left in his idealisation of the Soviet Union; his friend Marc Blitzstein, in particular, had inculcated in him a deep respect for the Stalinist experiment. But something oddly thuggish and menacing enters his tone as he denounces the lawyers – 'the gangster lawyers' – who, he predicts, will filibuster at the peace. 'The people will remember them,' he says, ominously. 'They have good cause who would divide us. They are the enemy. The people will remember them and have their way with them.' This has the feeling of a speech from *Danton's Death*, the Büchner play he had directed in 1937 (whose production, ironically enough, the Communist Party had tried to prevent); it is quite unlike the urbane and persuasive Welles of some of his other political utterances, but it exemplifies a tone that surfaces in his speeches from time to time – hectoring, bullying, threatening. He was a natural chameleon, setting out, as his revealing remarks to Kathleen Tynan indicate, to please his audience: if this was his aim, his Soviet–American speech was a triumph.

For all his emotional enthusiasm for the USSR, the goons of the FBI were quite wrong to suspect Welles of communism (though reading this speech, they may be forgiven their error). His radicalism had nothing to do with Marxist-Leninism, whose authoritarian prescriptions were personally insufferable to him, and everything to do with classical prescriptions of liberty, equality and fraternity, modified by a peculiarly American sense of justice and an instinctive internationalism. Thus racism, imperialism and corporate tyranny were all anathema to him. He was moved by the idealism of Blitzstein and Co., and inspired by what he took to be Russia's collective endeavour to eliminate ancestral injustice. But his intellectual models were closer to home. As his mind became increasingly engaged by politics, he moved rapidly away from the non-aligned position of his early twenties, via a brief flirtation with communism, to a stance that was non-doctrinaire but highly consistent, and passionately – almost obsessively – held. 'Elsa,' Welles told Elsa Maxwell over supper one night, as she reported to her readers in the *New York Post*, 'having a theatre and putting on plays is FUN. But working for the cause of human liberty against reactionism and retrogression is the most serious job I can do today, and I know you agree with me for you are fighting for the same thing yourself. The theatre must wait for a few months until I see what part I have to play in this greater drama, no matter how small the part may be.'

The part Welles had in mind was not small at all, in fact. 'I thought I was going to be King of the World, you know,' he told Kathleen Tynan. 'No: I thought I would be President.' He had acquired, at around the same time, both a political hero and a political mentor; their joint influence amounted to a political conversion of sorts. The example of these two radically different men helped him, in the one case to crystallise his views, and in the other to learn to think politically. Between them – one unconsciously and at a distance, the other by direct instruction – his hero and his mentor led him far away from his former haunts of Hollywood and Broadway, so far that it seemed that he might forsake them permanently for a political life.

CHAPTER ELEVEN

It All Comes Out of the Tent of Wonder

THE HERO was Henry A. Wallace, since 1940 Roosevelt's unlikely Vice-President — that uncommon figure, a politician who genuinely disliked politics. A visionary, both politically and scientifically, Wallace was acknowledged even by his enemies, of whom there were a great many, to have been the greatest Secretary of Agriculture of the century. As an agronomist he had pioneered hybrid corn, transforming the production of food and guaranteeing the prosperity of the farming industry — and thus of America itself — for generations to come. Privately, he was a searching philosopher of a somewhat mystical religious bent, and chronically indifferent to political manoeuvring, a weakness that would ultimately unseat him. In 1942, however, when Welles and he first met, he was — as controller of the wartime Economic Defense Board — almost as powerful as the increasingly unwell President himself; the *New York Times* dubbed him the 'Assistant President'.

Welles's initial contact with Wallace seems to have been fleeting; but by 1943 he was in regular contact with him, advising him, for example, on the use of slides in visual propaganda. But more significant than any personal contact the two men may have had was Welles's response to the vision adumbrated by Wallace in his speeches. Despite his private reclusiveness, Wallace was an exceptionally charismatic figure and a compelling public speaker, never more so than in the speech he had delivered in 1942 as a riposte to 'The American Century', Henry Luce's influential and consciously provocative *Life* magazine editorial of the same year. In the piece, Luce had laid out in the most unqualified terms a view of America's place in the world. 'America must undertake now to be the Good Samaritan of the entire world,' he had asserted. 'America as the dynamic center of ever-widening spheres of enterprise, America as the training center of the skilful servants of mankind, America as the Good Samaritan, really believing again that it is more blessed to give than to receive, and America as the powerhouse of the ideals of Freedom and Justice – out of these elements surely can be fashioned a vision of the 20th century to which we can and will devote ourselves in joy and gladness and vigor and enthusiasm.' But that was only the beginning. 'The vision of America as the principal guarantor of the freedom of the seas,' he continued, 'the vision of America as the dynamic leader of world trade, has within it the possibilities of such enormous human progress as to stagger the imagination. Let us rise to its tremendous possibilities.' Luce's apparently idealistic world-view was in its essence steeped in a realpolitik profoundly inimical to the radical Left. It offered a scenario that contained all the Left's worst fears – a continuation of the old dispensation based on latent antagonism of interests, which would and could only be resolved on the battlefield – 'nor need we assume that war can be abolished . . . large sections of the human family may be effectively organised into opposition to each other'. Luce's peroration was an unashamed paean to American supremacy: 'we must accept whole-heartedly our duty and our opportunity as the most powerful and vital nation in the world and in consequence to exert upon the world the full impact of our influence, for such purposes as we see fit and by such means as we see fit'.

Luce's intemperate and vainglorious assertion of the values of capitalism, red in tooth and claw, caused widespread repugnance (to the publisher's wounded surprise); but it provoked a speech from Wallace that provided the battle-cry for Welles and his generation of radicals, their Gettysburg Address. Wallace's speech was entitled 'The Price of Free World Victory', but it soon came to be known by another title. 'This is a fight between a slave world and a free world,' Wallace said of the war in progress:

Just as the United States in 1862 could not remain half slave and half free, so in 1942 the world must make its decision for a complete victory one way or another . . . everywhere the common people are on the march. When the freedom-loving people march – when the farmers have an opportunity to buy land at reasonable prices and to sell the produce of the land through their own organisations, when workers have the opportunity to form unions and bargain through them collectively, and when the children of all the people have an opportunity to attend schools which teach them truths of the real world in which they live – when these opportunities are

open to everyone, then the world moves ahead . . . some have
spoken of the American Century. I say that the century on
which we are entering – the century which will come out of
this war – can be and must be the century of the common man.

This last potent phrase immediately became the radicals' slogan;
Welles would return to it again and again. 'Everywhere,' Wallace
continued, 'the common man must learn to build his own industries with his own hands in a practical fashion. Everywhere the
common man must learn to increase his productivity so that he
and his children can eventually pay to the world community all
that they have so far received. No nation will have the God-given
right to exploit other nations. Older nations will have the privilege to help younger nations get started on the path to
industrialisation, but there must be neither military nor economic
imperialism.' With precise eloquence, he repudiated Luce's national
Darwinism: 'There can be no privileged peoples. We ourselves in
the US are no more a master race than the Nazis.' His global vision
was essentially inclusive: 'Those who write the peace must think
of the whole world.' It was a crusade, one in which Welles enlisted
unhesitatingly. 'There can be no half measures . . . no compromise with Satan is possible. We shall not rest until all the victims
under the Nazi yoke are freed. We shall fight for a complete peace
as well as a complete victory. The people's revolution is on the
march, and the devil and all his angels cannot prevail against it.
They cannot prevail, for on the side of the people is the Lord.'
Wallace was no more a Marxist than Welles, as might be inferred
from the strongly religious tenor of his Common Man speech, but
(somewhat gulled by his visits to carefully stage-managed model
villages on one of his many fact-finding tours of the world) he
enthusiastically embraced the positive aspects of Soviet communism. 'Russia, perceiving some of the abuses of excessive political
democracy, has placed strong emphasis on economic democracy,'
he wrote, somewhat ingenuously, in his *Tribute to Russia*. 'This,
carried to an extreme, demands that all power be centred in one
man and his bureaucratic helpers. Somewhere there is a practical
balance between economic and political democracy. Russia and the
US both have been working towards this practical middle ground.
The new democracy by definition abhors imperialism.'

It is striking that both Luce and Wallace were thinking, even at
this early stage of the war (early, that is, from America's point of
view), about the post-war period. Between them, the terms of the

opposing views of America's future place in the world were now defined, the battle-lines drawn. Both acknowledged, as did Welles, with increasing desperation in his speech-making and his political writing, that the world was at a crossroads; it was a matter of some urgency to lay plans for the peace. Wallace's thinking, and indeed his rhetoric, shaped and informed Welles's whole political being, and for some years, that was the centre of his life. Wallace, born and raised in the agricultural communities of Iowa, a world away from Welles's cosmopolitan and theatrical world, spoke with the particular passion and precision of a man who had devoted himself to ensuring that those who worked the land – farmers and labourers alike – should receive their honest due; but what he said represented everything that the twenty-seven-year-old Welles believed, and he was everything that Welles hoped for from his politicians. Like many of his generation, Welles had a complex attitude towards Roosevelt, admiring and sharing the vision that had given birth to the New Deal, but deploring the degree to which he was prepared to compromise it in the interests of an achievable result. Wallace was untarred by this brush. For Welles, Roosevelt was King Arthur, old and sick and cunning; Wallace was Lancelot, incorruptible, shining bright in his service to the people. There was no doubt as to which of them was Welles's model. His ambition was never, strictly speaking, to become a politician: what he wanted to be was the Tribune of the People, a role that, in the American system, could perhaps lead to the ultimate prize.

Nonetheless, he well understood that virtue, commitment and a good heart alone would not suffice. He needed a mentor in the rigours of political analysis, and in 1943 he found him. Welles, messianic on the subject of education, was always willing to submit to a teacher. He had done so with Hilton Edwards, he had done so with Marc Blitzstein, he had done so with Gregg Toland. Authority was a different matter: at that he always bridled ferociously, consumed with haughty rage and insensate stubbornness. But when he needed or wanted to learn something, he was an apt and voracious student. The moment he met Louis Dolivet at the house of the actress (and heiress) Beatrice Straight, whom Dolivet was shortly to marry, Welles knew that this man was altogether his superior as a political thinker and willingly became his apprentice. Dolivet, enormously tall, commanding, newly arrived from France with all the prestige of his work with the Free French clinging to him, had reached America in a manner worthy of a sub-plot in *Casablanca*. Having joined the French Air Force, he was forced to surrender with his unit; somehow he got to Marseilles, where the American consul put him on board ship for the United States. On the voyage he had broken his hip; limping off the boat, he was immediately put in touch with Michael Straight (Beatrice's brother, lately of the State Department and now editor of the journal his parents had founded, the *New Republic*). Straight put him up, and it was through him that he met Beatrice.

Dolivet's credentials were extraordinary and impeccable: since 1930 he had been the director of the Rassemblement Universel Pour la Paix in France; in 1937 he had been the leading orator at a huge anti-Hitler rally at the Peace Pavilion in Paris. His analysis of events was sophisticated and subtle; his internationalism highly articulate. If he preferred to remain silent about his earlier years – a subject, he claimed, too painful for discussion – what of it? The important thing was the coming political battle to be fought. In 1942, no one, of course, knew that Michael Straight had been (and probably still was) a key member of the communist cell at Cambridge that also comprised Anthony Blunt, Guy Burgess and Kim Philby (which was how Dolivet had been given Straight's name as a contact), nor that Dolivet himself was in fact Ludovicu Brecher, born in Polish Galicia and brought up in Romania. These things were only discovered in 1947, by a private detective hired by the family when the marriage to Beatrice had collapsed and he refused to divorce her. That same year, Dolivet would be denounced in the *Washington Evening Star* as an agent of the Communist International (along, of course, with many others, some rightly and some wrongly). In 1949, he left the United States for France, having finally agreed to a divorce; the same month he was denounced by Representative Jenison at the House Un-American Activities Committee. These revelations then took a turn for the tragic when his and Beatrice's young son drowned (they were by then already divorced). He tried frantically to get back to America but failed, as did his distraught attempts to instigate an autopsy, whereupon he disappeared from sight for some years, only to turn up, seemingly out of the blue, as producer of Welles's film *Mr Arkadin*. His own story is as Wellesian as anything in that movie, but of course, in 1942, when Dolivet and Welles fell into conversation about the subject that excited Welles more than any other, he seemed exactly the right man at the right time. Dolivet assumed, in fact, something of the character of a father-figure for him.

From the moment of his arrival in America, Dolivet had been busy creating the International Free World Association, in the name of which he mounted rallies, staged conferences and published the magazine *Free World*, 'A Monthly Magazine devoted to Democracy and World Affairs: under the aegis of the International Free World Association for Victory – for World Organisation'. The honorary board included Einstein, Mme Chiang Kai-shek and Count Sforza; the editorial board Michael Straight and Dolivet; and the first number had an introduction by Cordell Hull, Roosevelt's Secretary of State. It contained pieces by, among others, Welles's old mentor, Archibald MacLeish. Michael Straight was a remarkably well-chosen connection: recently employed in Roosevelt's office, and now Washington editor of the *New Republic*. Dolivet was very persuasive, and the most distinguished names vied to contribute both to the magazine and the conferences. The writers Ernest Hemingway, Theodore Dreiser, Thomas Mann and Bertrand Russell all wrote pieces for *Free World*; as did the politicians Jan Masaryk, Tito and de Gaulle. As its formal title, 'The Price of Free World Victory', indicates, Wallace's speech hailing the century of the common man had been delivered at a Free World Conference. Whatever complex transactions may have occurred between Dolivet and his supposed Soviet masters, the programme of the Free World Association, with its four key phrases – international democracy, political democracy, economic democracy, association of nations – was straightforwardly social democratic with a particularly international bias.

In one edition, Dolivet offers an apologia for Soviet Russia. 'Despite being a political dictatorship [it] cannot be compared in any way to the totalitarian regimes in the Axis countries.' The Soviet Union, he insists, views aggression or domination of other countries as being counter-revolutionary. It has achieved economic democracy and is determined to pass 'from a temporary period of dictatorship to democratic socialism and Communism'. It was helping to win the war and had behaved well except for Finland, which it only invaded because of Hitler. This analysis may have come from a somewhat roseate perspective, but it was one shared broadly by the Left; it is scarcely insidiously propagandistic. It would have been familiar to Welles and indeed essentially reflected his own view. In fact, Dolivet's contribution to Welles's political education was less concerned with his intellectual position than with his polemical skills. This meant, above all, being prepared in argument. Welles's natural instinct was rhetorical: engendering emotion through cumulative oratorical effects. Dolivet taught him how to debate, in print and on his feet. The habit of research was not alien to Welles, but had hitherto been pressed into service in the process of creating radio programmes or as background to a film. Dolivet, no mean dialectician, taught Welles to provide himself with the ammunition required to advance his case. Barbara Leaming recounts a somewhat brutal example of this teaching, when Dolivet and Welles went together to Washington. The older man was to deliver a speech to a group of Roosevelt's aides. At the last moment Dolivet asked Welles to deliver the speech for him, which he did, of course, with effortless brilliance. Dolivet then abandoned him to answer questions from the assembled aides. Welles floundered badly. Leaming reports him returning to his hotel room weeping tears of humiliation. The lesson was well, almost too well, learned.

In due course Dolivet appointed Welles one of the team of editors of *Free World*, and the articles he filed were often fact-filled to a fault, though the rhetorical instinct died hard. Many of them were adapted from his speeches, and his oratorical flourishes can still be detected. Most often, though, the tone is the familiar energetic banality of political journalistic discourse everywhere, in every age: the heavy irony, the sententious summaries, the triumphant pile-up of facts. The effect is somewhat numbing. Welles's first piece was, naturally enough, about inter-American affairs:

> The Good Neighbor policy is not a sales campaign for the
> United States. There has been too much of 'selling' the purity
> and warmth of our friendship. It was an easy mistake for us to
> fall into since the force of Axis propaganda has attacked that
> friendship . . . in spite of all the dictators supporting it, in spite
> of its stumbling caution, its blind snobbishness, in spite of itself,
> the Good Neighbor policy is an anti-fascist alliance, a community
> of nations bound together in the name of democracy. As such it
> is a preliminary sketch for world organisation. A good start, full
> of meaning for the future, was made the day our guns
> underwrote democracy in Uruguay. The big stick is a weapon of
> international thuggery. Our friends have reminded us that it is
> also the tool of the policeman's trade.

Inevitably, these vigorous and heroically certain pronouncements – perfectly sound in themselves – turn Welles into a soap-box sophist. There is no question whatsoever that Welles was utterly sincere in this manifestation. His political position was consistent, passionately expressed and (thanks, no doubt, to Dolivet's instruction) factually accurate. He was also astonishingly industrious in pursuit of his mission, employing (at considerable personal expense) a small army of researchers, chief among them the uncommonly well-informed Miss Geneva Cranston (Lamont's smarter younger sister perhaps). What is perplexing is how lacking in individuality his utterances are: perhaps inevitably, since he seeks to speak on behalf of The People, and consciously seeks to spell out the issues involved.

Impatient, perhaps, with the constraints imposed upon him, Welles sometimes breaks loose from this straitjacket, and then the rhetoric pours out in unstoppable torrents. An article entitled 'The Unknown Soldier', for example, which had its origins in an earlier speech about winning the peace, finds him in full flood. Someone, Welles reports, has put a cigar into the mouth of a statue to the Unknown Soldier. What sort of man could do such a thing, he asks?

> Very probably the man with the cigar was one of those prefabricated pagans who rode the joyless carousel of the twenties and thirties. One of those, you know, who doubted if anything is ever really bad, or really good. If he's alive he may have changed his mind. It's possible he's found something bad enough to fight. He may even think that something good is real enough to defend . . . we have this to be glad of: those who are of little faith, the blasphemers, experts in chaos, or the sick in spirit, those who can't, who won't affirm the plain magnificent decency of human folk, all such as in this brightening world are rallied in the shadows now under the banners of despair. Defeat is their profession and their destination.

In purely personal terms, there is something almost desperate about this hymn to decency and to the light, from a man whose work depicts – even celebrates – the exact opposite. Is it an ache to be normal? To be freed of the inky fluid always threatening to engulf him? Or is it simply a part that he's playing: the orator of the people? His longing to be Henry Wallace? 'Even when the world is free, we'll know we've just begun. "Here it is. Here is the peace," we'll say, standing in the midst of it like ploughmen content with the good order of their fields: standing together, since Mankind will be every man's family when the tools of war are put away for good . . . then the abundance of the human spirit will be ready for harvest and the children will see that even final peace is merely history's first date.' This odd kind of prose-poetry, pastoral-historical, like a Soviet-realist canvas backed with appropriately uplifting music, seems incongruous coming from the mouth of Orson Welles, the familiar denizen of the bars and the clubs, the brothels and the dives, the cosmopolitan sophisticate, the rumbustious actor-manager; it is without equivalent anywhere else in his output, although the *jangadeiros* sequence of *It's All True* contains an element of it: the yearning for the simple life of community, of decency, of neighbourliness, that Edenic ache again, which he had carried with him since those boyhood days in Grand Detour, Illinois. It was, too, very important for Welles to feel that what he did mattered, that he was part of the big world, that he had some influence.

Perhaps somewhere behind this slightly strained emotion was embarrassment concerning the fact that he was still a civilian. In the early 1940s he had done everything he could to get out of fighting in a war in which he did not then believe. Now it was a rather different story. It is uncertain if he actually wanted to enlist or not, but it was unquestionably the case that here he was, very conspicuously still at home and in civvies while most of his contemporaries – Dick Wilson and Bob Meltzer among them – were in uniform and directly involved in fighting the war. The press delighted in making merry of him, and he regularly rose to the bait. In May of 1943, when he was summoned for a medical, he was met at the clinic by a gaggle of curious newsmen. He testily informed them that in the same post he had received one letter summoning him for induction and another telling him that he was 'an essential worker in an essential industry' and thus exempt from conscription. He had decided to destroy the second letter, and here he was, ready to be examined. He further informed the assembled pressmen that he had taken off the back brace that he had worn for the previous six months, and then disappeared into the consulting room. Emerging shortly afterwards, he told them that he'd got a 4-F rating, declared unfit to serve (as on his earlier exemption) on the basis of bronchial asthma, flat feet and a scoliotic spine. 'I got a tip,' he said, frankly enough. 'There was a smear campaign in the making against the motion picture industry in conjunction with its men in the draft. It came to me that I'd better not louse up myself and the movie industry itself by taking advantage of that deferment . . . I went down there to get in the army, of my own free will, and they threw me out.' He wrote to Robert Stevenson, *Jane Eyre*'s director, briefly on leave in London, that he envied him tremendously: 'the fool who makes a deliberate choice of the cozy life in these times is a damned fool. When it isn't a choice, you're damned anyway, as I am, and I'm not too sure about the fool part of it either.' He compensated for his frustration by hurling himself ever more energetically into the war effort at home.

With one charming exception, this did not involve film. His career in celluloid was, to say the least, desultory. MGM was trying to push him into playing the tiny part of the Prince of Wales in *Mrs Parkington* opposite Greer Garson, which he successfully (and wisely) resisted; Darryl Zanuck was similarly rebuffed when he tried to persuade Welles to appear in *The Keys of the Kingdom*. Welles was planning an educational 16mm colour film, but this, like most of his educational projects, came to nothing. Mercury Productions continued essentially as his private office, engendering projects and acquiring rights. One of the more promising of the projects was Saint-Exupéry's just-published *The Little Prince*, which Welles, seeking to maintain the book's enchanting relationship between word and image, envisaged as part live action, part cartoon. This was not a new genre: Walt Disney had mixed forms several times, and indeed Welles approached him with a view to collaboration on *The Little Prince*, only to have his overtures rebuffed. Disney is said to have smilingly observed that there was only room for one genius in his studio – no doubt a reference to the widely publicised RKO debacle. This is to be regretted, because Welles's was a witty and playful approach to a masterpiece whose later filmic incarnation as a plodding, over-reverential musical was something of a catastrophe. Welles's interest was serious: he paid the substantial sum of $12,500 for the rights after reading the American translation in proof, plus an option advance of $1,250, and actually wrote a first draft screenplay (later he tried to buy the stage rights too, another enticing prospect that came to nothing). The extant screenplay is one of the innumerable discarded torsos that constitute such a large invisible proportion of Welles's output; even at times of apparent inactivity, his industriousness was never less than prodigious. Welles was many things, but he was no slouch.

The most significant project on which he worked, the most properly Wellesian in its scope and the one that came surprisingly close to being made, was Tolstoy's vast epic *War and Peace*. There is a certain magnificence about attempting to film a novel of such density, with its complex and challenging analysis of war, in the midst of the greatest embroilment in human history. The idea was the result of the exuberant encounter between two fearlessly ambitious figures, Welles himself and Sir Alexander Korda. Korda (born Sandór Laszlo Kellner in a Hungarian *shtetl*) had renamed himself after the Latin phrase that headed his film reviews when he was a young journalist in Vienna: *Sursum Corda* – Lift Up Your Hearts – which was pretty much the effect he had had on the British film industry. Denied continental outlets during the war, he was starting to spread his net wider, concentrating in particular, very successfully, on co-productions with American companies. *Lady Hamilton* and the Lubitsch masterpiece *To Be or Not To Be* were among the results. Korda had met Welles on the celebrity circuit; the two showmen instantly took to each other. Korda liked his artists flamboyant, a quality in which Charles Laughton – with whom he had worked on three films, two completed and one abandoned – had been disappointingly deficient. Welles's contagious breadth of enthusiasm was far more congenial to him than Laughton's intense searching and agonising.

Building on the meeting he and Welles had had after Welles's return from Brazil, Korda sent the temporarily fallen hero a telegram suggesting that they work together: *War and Peace* was the outcome. Welles was off like a greyhound out of a trap: he would produce, direct, write and play the central character. Korda announced the film as part of his ten-year, £35m package to secure the future of British film. The prospect of working for an independent producer, especially one who was not based in Hollywood, was exhilarating for Welles, and he set to with a will. Or at least he intended to: by mid-1943 he was apologising to Korda for being so heavily involved in radio work, but was still raring to go, he insisted: WOULD LIKE START WORK WITH WRITERS HERE OR MAKE SHORT TRIP LONDON THEN POSSIBLY MOSCOW. Clearly his experience in Brazil had done nothing to discourage Welles from impossible trips in wartime conditions; naturally he was eager to make a personal demonstration of the Soviet–American friendship that he had so often endorsed from the conference platform. Korda, with his incomparably wide circle of international acquaintances, had mentioned the project to his friend Sergei Mikhailovich Eisenstein, then rather busy himself – 'personally, I am up to my neck in very difficult and serious work, filming two series about the life of *Ivan the Terrible*'. Eisenstein had already, with Vsevolod Pudovkin, offered Korda some thoughts (now lost, alas) on how to shoot the great novel. But the great film-maker encouraged Korda's project, revealing his own remarkable ability to be au fait with gossip on the other side of the world, as it must have appeared: 'It seems that from the very start you have insured the success of your undertaking by engaging Orson Welles for the production and for the role of Pierre Bezhukov. I think that here your brilliant intuition will bring excellent results,' he wrote in his very good English. 'Curiously enough, Orson Welles seems to me as one of the most interesting and promising figures of the Western Cinema, although I know almost nothing about him (two or three comments about *Citizen Kane*, two or three stories about radio activity and I believe a photograph of him with a beard, sitting at table in "Brown Derby"). Would like to learn more of him in order to check up on my own intuition.'

Welles continued to work on *War and Peace*, or at least to plan for it (no portion of a screenplay exists); in interviews, he claimed to have asked Shostakovich, then very much the outstanding Russian composer of the day – his 'Leningrad' symphony recently rushed out of Russia on microfilm to be played in every concert hall in the free world – to write the score. But somehow, nothing happened with the film. Partly this was to do with a liver complaint, which had felled Welles for some weeks over Christmas and the New Year; partly to do with the sheer difficulty of accomplishing such a vast project in wartime. His energies meanwhile had been diverted into a project very dear to his heart, scarcely on the scale of *War and Peace*, but rather easier to realise.

Seeking to make a personal contribution to the war effort, he turned to the theatre, and to his first love – vaudeville preceding even his passion for Shakespeare. He had lately given some expression to this love in his radio comedy shows, but had already indulged it as far back as 1936 with *Horse Eats Hat*, his surreal take on *An Italian Straw Hat* at Project 891, its cast crammed full with out-of-work music-hall entertainers; and, in the same year, with *The Great McCoy: His Wonder Show of 1936*, a gala *jeu d'esprit* staged to raise money for the theatre. Central to Welles's feeling for vaudeville was his passion for illusion, and specifically for magic, which he loved immoderately, both as spectator and as practitioner. Like Charles Dickens, he was obsessed by mastering its skills; he subscribed to all the trade magazines and was a dedicated member of, among other organisations, the Los Angeles Society of Magicians, the International Brotherhood of Magicians, the Society of Amateur Magicians, the Pacific Coast Association of Magicians and Bert Wheeler's Circle of Magic. This was no passing enthusiasm, but a lifelong commitment: in his first production for Unit 891, *Doctor Faustus*, he had made extensive and startling use of magic, but that was just the beginning. Over the years he disbursed sizeable sums on tricks; his correspondence of the early forties reveals him putting in large orders at least once a month, often more: within five weeks in May/June of 1944 he submitted urgent demands for *The Art of Illusion*, *U-Namit-I-Find-It*, *Something Borrowed, Something New* and complete courses in stage hypnotism, the *Hypnotic Rigid Test*, *Hypnotic Influence* and *Hypnotism on Animals*; to his considerable, and somewhat petulantly expressed, chagrin he was unable to get hold of the Edwards Magnetic Wand and the Frank Kelly Gimmic Cup, which, he insisted, should match the Petrie Lewis shell wand. On the other hand, he was able to acquire the Squirmy Worm rope, whose tricky wrigglings he managed, in the fullness of time, to master. But it was not as a technician that he shone: his personality was the real magic. For him, there was poetry in the very names of these ingeniously devised tricks, and it is touching to find him poring over the instruction leaflets, like any child with his magic set.

In fact, childhood – the scene of his first exposure to magic, on his father's trawls through the vaudeville theatres of Chicago, often dropping in on Harry Houdini backstage, he claimed – is the key to Welles's understanding of magic. At a highly impressionable age he had seen Howard Thurston perform the Levitation of Princess Karnac. Thurston had passed the hoop around the floating princess in question to prove the absence of wires, rods or sheets of glass. He then came down to the footlights and implored the audience to be as quiet as possible, because 'the slightest noise might have a dangerous effect on the princess'. They all knew, he says, that Thurston was lying, because they knew that the machinery wouldn't budge. 'But we couldn't see the machinery – Thurston had shown it couldn't be there so we gave up. It wasn't a puzzle any more – it was magic. In the precise meaning of the words it was marvellous and wonderful. Nobody made a sound.' Like Dickens, Welles longed to reproduce in his audiences the innocent awe of his own first infant experiences in the theatre. 'Magic is pure theatre and a good magician does more than he pretends – not less,' he said. 'The transformation of an audience of grown-ups into as many little children is the best trick there is and no one's explained how it's done.' In a phrase that resonates with profound echoes across the whole of his career, he wrote of the conjuror, in his introduction to Bruce Elliot's book *Magic as a Hobby*, that 'he'll fail to amuse if he doesn't amaze'. A real magician's task, he continues, is 'to abolish the solution, the very possibility of *any* solution in the minds of those he seeks to amuse'. In magic's Golden Age, he adds (there is always a Golden Age with Welles), 'magicians offered laughter as part of the show but never permitted disenchantment.

For a marvellous hour or two they elevated their most adult audiences to the status of delighted children.' Lamenting the decline of magic into entertainment for jaded sophisticates – 'Wizards of today . . . work their wonders in the frowsty hubbub of the cabaret, competing with bad whisky for control of the beholder's mind' – he notes that 'the children are all home asleep, and of course the children are magic's source and meaning, magic being, after all, no more than a formal and serious approach to the serious business of playing with toys'.

It is striking to find a man who saw childhood as a prison from which he longed to escape so warmly extolling the condition. The truth is that Welles had indeed bypassed his own childhood, but had immediately begun to wonder whether he had not forsaken Eden for something far less precious: mere adulthood, the world of knowing and understanding, the sphere of will. Magic – proper magic, as he saw it – represented that blissful lost kingdom. It is noteworthy, too, that, proclaiming himself 'one of that dwindling and gloomy body of cranks who wishes magic could have been kept a mystery', he stresses that there should be no possibility of the audience analysing the tricks, just as he hated any analysis of himself or his work: mysteries that must not be probed, like the mysteries of his own life – the mysteries of personality, of talent, of creation. He sought to purvey astonishment and delight, unquestioned as to methods or motives: making himself omnipotent – like the child-conjuror who seeks to strike his audience of family and friends dumb with awe – he requires a trusting public, who will not merely suspend but altogether banish disbelief. 'If astonishment and delight won't bring an audience into a playhouse any more, then of course something is rotten in the state of the Union, and it isn't only magic that is doomed.' In truth, Welles was never a very skilled magician, mainly because (as his magic supplier in the nineteen-seventies, Richard Bloch, observed) he was unable to stop himself trying to improve the tricks, but also because – which is perhaps only to say the same thing from another angle – his personality overwhelmed the magic, as it overwhelmed everything else to which he turned his hand. Richard Himber (the Richard Bloch of the early forties) had written Welles a note accompanying a trick he was supplying: 'with my lousy presentation, the audience used to gasp, but with the way you present tricks, you will probably have to have a doctor round to revive the fainting women when they see how you crush this bag into your pocket'. It didn't quite work out that way.

Welles had made his first tentative appearance in the guise of conjuror in 1941, with his then girlfriend Dolores del Rio as his lovely assistant (he sawed her in half); but now, in 1943, he felt ready to offer himself in that guise to a wider public in a show specifically staged for servicemen under a circus tent on the MGM lot on Cahuenga Boulevard; such members of the general public who came along would have to chip in with a few dollars. 'It's taken me a lot longer than I hoped to grow up to be a magician,' he wrote in the exuberant publicity blurb for *The Mercury Wonder Show for Service Men*, as he called his entertainment. 'Many things have interfered with my career. This week it really started though.' Despite the adjacent red-and-gold circus ticket wagon, the purpose of the presentation was by no means to make money (merely not to lose any would have been an unforeseen bonus; it had cost $40,000 – $26,000 of which was contributed by Welles personally). During the day, to promote the show he talked on local radio programmes, visited women's clubs, addressed shipyard workers and wrote guest newspaper columns; there was some competition for audiences even when the seats were free.

Welles approached the *Wonder Show*, as he approached everything he cared about, with lavish inventiveness and imagination and very little preparation. It had taken seventeen weeks 'and several dollars' to get the show together; friends and colleagues, regardless of experience or qualification, were summarily roped in. They included, among the cast of twenty, Joseph Cotten (Jo-Jo the Great, the Weird Wizard of the South), Agnes Moorehead (as Calliope Aggie), Gus Schilling, Shorty Chirello (his valet, in charge of Hortense the Goose), Lolita Leighter (his general manager's sister) and an unidentified individual known as Death Valley Mack; Phil Silvers, Rags Ragland and Paul Stewart roared away as barkers out front on the bally walk; while among the backstage workers were Jackson Leighter; Welles's guardian, Dr Bernstein; and his secretary Shifra Haran. The show was on a stupendous scale: 'The tent,' reported *Collier's Magazine*, 'which has a picturesque midway, replete with lurid and wondrous posters and a calliope which gets its notion of noise from Orson himself, seats 1,100 servicemen and 400 suckers . . . the carnival spirit is everywhere evident.' How delighted with that comment Welles must have been. 'Cursed with the ambition that has been the despair of himself and everybody around him,' the reporter acutely noted, 'Welles has improved on the old magic-show formula and has streamlined it to the point where it combines the features of a three-ring circus and a phantasmagoria.' It was a favourite formula of Welles's: *Horse Eats Hat*, albeit on a slightly less extravagant scale, had been just such a combination; *The Mercury Wonder Show* would not be his last essay in the form. 'From the moment the show opens,' the magazine reported, 'the stage is a-flutter with chickens, geese, ducks, rabbits, and bare-legged chorus girls and it remains in more or less that state during the entire evening.' Now and then Welles would dive into the audience to pull a watch out of someone's collar or a serviceman up onto the stage, 'and altogether the art of mystification is splendidly embroiled with the patter of little feet'.

Welles had twenty-three changes of costume over the course of the evening, covering his head with turbans, shawls, silk hats, tricornes and – somewhat alarmingly – surgical masks, 'all in the cause of thaumaturgy and total war'. Mostly he was to be found, cigar in mouth, wearing a striped, tent-like garment and fez and 'a bewildered, slightly bitter expression', reported *Vogue*, noting that 'though he does the magic, the pulling of white chickens out of a hat, the coin and the handkerchief and the string tricks . . . he hasn't got the Merlin's spiel that the true magicians use who know that every trick will work. He doesn't know positively.' It all adds to the charm of his performance, remarks the unnamed reporter, adding, with throwaway perceptiveness, 'there is always something unpolished about the Welles performance, as though he were groping, pugnaciously, through to new paths with his own peculiar energy, his own extravagant way of messing up the slick, the precious, carefully thought-out and spinsterish'. This remarkable analysis of the curiously unfinished feel of all of Welles's work – not merely as a performer – is a key to everything he ever did; the adverb 'pugnaciously' is particularly well noted. *The Mercury Wonder Show* was a classic example of his determination to unsettle expectation, an unrelenting bombardment of the audience with an absolute indifference to polish or decorum. Under the headline 'Welles's Wonderland' *Collier's Magazine* broke down one of the show's items into its component parts: 'The Witches' Farmyard, an incredible mixture of *sortilège* not to be duplicated in the history of thaumaturgy, presents: Bovine Obedience; At the Shooting Gallery (including Marksmanship reward); Evaporation in the Mystic Dairy; The Dalai's Milk Pail (direct from Tibetan lamas); The Flight of the Hare; Fowl Elusive; *La Rapière du Diable*; A Voice from the Dead; Faster than Light or the World Famous Balsamo's Secret; and the Casket of Count Cagliostro.' Free or not, it was certainly value for money: in addition to The Witches' Farmyard, the playbill announced The Haunted Aviary, The Miraculous Chicken Farm, Dr Welles Presents His Experiments in Animal Magnetism (All Nature Freezes at His Glance), Pekin Service, The Secrets of the Sphinx, Chained in Space and Scenes from a Hindoo Marketplace; during the intermission there was a wild animal show, in which the big cats Jackie the Lion, Satan the Tiger and Dynamite the Black Leopard – more accustomed to appearing on sound stages than under a tent – were put through their paces; and the climax was provided by the Grand Finale Voodoo ('A re-enactment of Mr Cotten's interesting experiences with witch doctors in Africa').

Most sensational of all, perhaps, was the appearance of Rita Hayworth as the Girl with the X-Ray Eyes, and who, in The Flight of Time, was made by Welles to disappear from the Death Casket after he had sawn her in half. Hayworth was the new woman in Welles's life. His relationship with Dolores del Rio, whom he was set to marry until her divorce had been temporarily held up, had inevitably deteriorated during his Brazilian sojourn; swept away by the erotic possibilities of Rio de Janeiro, he had stopped returning her calls. On his way back to the United States he had met up with her in Mexico City, where they had something of a reconciliation. With characteristic magnificence, she had thrown a party for him to which she invited the ambassador of every South American country, plus, for good measure, Pablo Neruda and Diego Rivera. But even this formidable love offering, appealing equally to Welles's political passion for Good Neighborhood and his personal enthusiasm for South American art, was to no avail. He had already fallen in love with another Latin American beauty (born Margaret Cansino and renamed by her first husband, who also shrewdly encouraged her to dye her hair auburn), whose picture Welles had seen on the cover of *Life* magazine – upon which, it is reported, he had immediately decided that he would marry her. The same decision had no doubt been taken by millions of young men all over the world, but Welles was in a position to do something about it. The first step in this direction, as we have seen, had been to invite her to appear with him on radio just before he left the country to start shooting *It's All True*; on his return from Brazil he had engineered another meeting, and another, and, in the fullness of time, he had become her lover (to the considerable chagrin but with the gentlemanly acquiescence of Victor Mature, Welles's predecessor in this capacity). Now here he was, sawing her in half on Cahuenga Boulevard: being publicly bisected was clearly something of an occupational hazard for Welles's mistresses. The press already knew all about their relationship, swiftly dubbing them Beauty and the Brains. Hayworth was by now deeply in love with Welles – the first man, she said, ever to take her mind seriously – and happily participated in the high-spirited romp he had devised. Less happy was Harry Cohn, the flint-hearted head of Columbia Studios to whom Rita Hayworth was exclusively contracted, and whom she had neglected to notify of her involvement in the show. After the heavily publicised first night, he threatened to sue her for breach of contract (she was filming *Cover Girl* with Gene Kelly during the run of *The Mercury Wonder Show*) unless she withdrew, so she bitterly pulled out, though she watched the show from the wings every night of its run. Marlene Dietrich gamely stepped into her shoes for the rest of the season; her current beau, Jean Gabin – to add to the starry hugger-mugger – helped out backstage on props.

Welles was scarcely going to take Cohn's behaviour lying down. The night after the opening, at the point at which Rita Hayworth should have been sawn in half, Welles made a speech that ('in the continued absence of Miss Hayworth') he made every night thereafter. Rita Hayworth, he said, had rehearsed for sixteen weeks, but 'Miss Hayworth also works for motion-picture studios, and motion-picture studios are very odd. Columbia Pictures in the person of Harry Cohn – and I feel it is only fair to name names – has exercised its prerogative by insisting that Miss Hayworth withdraw from the show. This is trebly unfortunate, and I want to tell you that if any one of you feels that the absence of Miss Hayworth in any way spoils your evening, you have only to go to the Box Office and your money will be refunded and we hope you will remain as our guest for the rest of the evening. We had hoped that reason might prevail, but Mr Cohn is adamant, a chronic condition with that gentleman.' He then added, in an aside, 'Needless to say, I shall never appear in a Columbia Picture.' In terms of a career, these are not wise sentiments to be airing publicly (though as it happens, in accord with the rest of his complex relationship with Hollywood, Welles's prediction turned out to be false, and within three years he was not only appearing in a Columbia Picture, but writing and directing it too).

As may be imagined, *The Mercury Wonder Show* attracted wide publicity, and the anomaly of the director of *Citizen Kane* metamorphosing into the Ringling Brothers and Barnum and Bailey rolled into one was lost on no one. Nor did anyone, least of all the trade press, think that it was an entirely innocent gesture. 'The case of Orson Welles versus Hollywood (or vice versa) is still going on,' said the *Hollywood Reporter*, 'whatever beliefs to the contrary might have been induced by the apparent calm which followed Mr Welles's dissolution as a one-man band and his subsequent reduction to the status of actor and general handyman on *Jane Eyre* at Twentieth Century Fox. It now develops that the canny Orson was biding his time.' *Collier's Magazine* told its readers that he had forgotten the success of *Citizen Kane* 'and the harrowing and beautiful experience in Brazil where he took eighteen billion feet of film and came out (not at his request) without a picture', and was now taking simple delight in the large and rowdy crowds. 'The applause is tremendous and the great Orson . . . beams gratefully and trembles with gratitude. But as he is bowing, he is also thinking. In his mind he is turning over an idea that will revolutionise magic and pretty much everything else. "I haven't quite got it," he reports, "but if I do get it, it'll be *big*." He lowers his voice and looks round apprehensively. "It's a disappearance act," he says, "and when I perfect it, I'll just give one wave" – he makes a vicious swipe with his hand – "and there goes Hollywood."'

As a final slap in the face to Cohn (and Hollywood in general), on 7 September 1943, in a highly co-ordinated operation, he snatched Rita Hayworth away from the Columbia lot between scenes of *Cover Girl*, to get married in a local church. It was a tiny and very private ceremony. Dadda Bernstein and his wife Hazel were there; Joseph Cotten was best man; and the second Mrs Welles was back at Columbia before anyone had noticed her absence. When he did find out, Harry Cohn's rage was terrible, but there was nothing he could do. He exacted some petty revenge some years later, when he, Welles and Hayworth worked together; he had, just this once, been outsmarted, but in the end he held all the power and he knew it. Welles's high-spirited defiance made little impact on him, nor indeed on Hollywood in general. Welles was still the resident *enfant terrible*, from whom bad behaviour was positively expected; he was a colourful part of the landscape, but no longer a significant figure.

His profile in Hollywood at the time is perfectly embodied in the only film in which he was involved in more than eighteen months, which captures something of the charm of *The Mercury Wonder Show*, though little of its anarchy. *Follow the Boys*, directed by Eddie Sutherland, was a wartime morale-raiser whose gung-ho working title had been *Three Cheers for the Boys*. Patriotic it may have been, but it was scarcely a charitable venture: Welles earned $30,000 for his five days' work; George Raft, the link-man, earned $100,000 dollars, a cool sum for 1944. The film's framework must have been highly congenial to Welles: it starts on the very last night of big-time vaudeville on the stage of the about-to-be demolished Palace Theatre in New York, and traces the determined effort of a member of one of the acts (George Raft), rejected on physical grounds from enlisting, to make his contribution to the war. Welles is first seen at a mass-meeting of film-workers, sitting among his fellow-actors and entertainers, patiently waiting to learn how they can help the war effort. 'I'm an amateur magician,' Welles pipes up, modestly, 'perhaps I can help.' He is next seen on a film set in Hollywood being called on the phone by George Raft. The call goes through to a man working on top of a telegraph pole. A bravura, comically over-the-top Wellesian overhead shot shows Welles himself and his many bustling assistants from the phone's point of view; the instrument is then tossed down to him; he takes the call with modest and witty charm and we cut to the theatre where the performance takes place. First a rabbit appears, then a puff of smoke, then Welles, dapper in tails, cigar in mouth: 'That's the first time you've ever seen a rabbit produce a magician,' he says. There is much play with the cigar, which appears to be floating; a flock of pigeons is produced from behind a paper screen. At this point, Marlene Dietrich appears in silhouette behind the screen, smoking a cigarette. As she emerges, Welles announces that she'll be sawn in half and asks for volunteers to do the sawing; half the audience of GIs rushes forward. 'Orson,' says Dietrich with every indication of barely suppressed panic, 'we haven't rehearsed this. How does it work?' Welles: 'Don't worry, it'll kill you.' He hums extravagantly as the men saw away at her; he produces a cigar from behind a volunteer's ear, then lights it from a light bulb, which he tosses over his shoulder. He seems unnaturally energised. Finally, the men finish sawing. To her alarm, Miss Dietrich's legs stand up and walk away from the rest of her; she then gets them back again. 'How do I know they're mine?' she asks. 'Don't worry,' says Welles, 'I'll hypnotise them.' He and she lock eyeballs; he faints. End of sequence.

It is an episode of great appeal, Welles in particular being at his most elegant and droll; it is almost as if the young Charles Foster Kane were performing the act. Of course, it bears little resemblance to what was done on stage in *The Mercury Wonder Show* itself – quite rightly. The possibilities of the medium are used in a way that would have gladdened Jean Cocteau's heart, satisfying the fascination with vaudeville, magic and illusion that the Frenchman shared with Welles. It is to be presumed that Eddie Sutherland, a man of unpretentious expertise, would at the very least have consulted Welles as to how best to realise the scene, which has an elegance and a wit not be found in the rest of a solidly enjoyable film, which seamlessly weaves together what seems to be an irreconcilably diverse array of talents including Dinah Shore and W. C. Fields, Artur Rubinstein and Leonard Gautier's Bricklayers. The film displays towards Welles an affectionate sense of his youthful extravagance and absurdity, a wry enjoyment of his roguish, boyish ways. It is scarcely a portrait of the director of the most explosively original film ever to have come out of Hollywood, the central figure in a fight to the death between himself and a studio. *Follow the Boys* shows a well-loved Hollywood character, with Welles playing the part of a swashbuckling director-laddie.

There was at present no prospect of his actually directing anything. He continued in a fairly desultory way to pursue *War and Peace*, wiring Korda: AS YOU KNOW I HAVE BEEN SERIOUSLY ILL SO IT'S JUST AS WELL I DIDN'T SPEND THE LAST THREE MONTHS IN WARTIME LONDON BUT AM VERY MUCH ON THE MEND THOUGH DOING RADIO TO PAY THE BILLS WAR AND PEACE REMAINS MY CHIEF, INDEED, MY ONLY AMBITION. He urges Korda to help Rita Hayworth with her permit to travel with him to London and Moscow; but when that was not forthcoming, he finally gave up on the project, as he publicly announced to Hedda Hopper in a rare interview with her around the time of his birthday (his twenty-ninth). Years later he told his biographer Barbara Leaming that he had written a full screenplay of the novel, but that Korda was not serious about it: he simply wanted to have an office at Metro. For neither of these propositions is there any evidence. Meanwhile he was, as he had told Korda, working in radio again, again pursuing the ignis fatuus of a popular show that was also capable of seriousness, embarking yet one more time on the difficult project of integrating the diverse and seemingly contradictory aspects of his nature.

CHAPTER TWELVE

Unrehearsed Realities

W HEN HE started work on his new programme, Welles had
barely recovered from a sharp bout of hepatitis, which had
in turn provoked his chronic back problems, forcing him to resort
to the somewhat medieval corrective device that had been so
commented on at the time of his recent army medical. As may be
readily imagined, Welles was not a placid invalid, modelling himself
instead on Sheridan Whiteside in Kaufman and Hart's play *The Man
Who Came to Dinner* (a part Welles always claimed had been written
for him, and in which he did eventually appear on television in
the mid-sixties): demanding, cantankerous, domineering. He and
Rita Hayworth spent Christmas of 1943 at the Straights' family
home in Old Westbury in Long Island, with Beatrice Straight and
her husband Louis Dolivet. Beatrice's young half-brother and sister
William and Ruth Elmhirst were deeply impressed that Welles,
alone of all the guests, was fed a diet of steaks, a luxury known
to few at the height of wartime rationing. Dadda Bernstein had
sent a note insisting that Welles must have large quantities of meat,
which he was prepared to back up with an order form to the Food
Rationing Board. It proved unnecessary at that time, but he had
occasion to issue the order more than once during the remaining
two years of the war. The Welleses moved on to Miami for New
Year, but soon went back to Los Angeles to be nearer Dadda and
medical care; they stayed in the Beverly Hills Hotel. Welles's depend-
ence on Dadda is very striking; at times of physical stress he became
a big, needy baby.

He had sufficiently recovered by early January 1944 to apply
himself to his new radio programme, *The Orson Welles Almanac*.
There was a new sponsor – the Socony-Vacuum Company – and
he was dealing with a new agency, Compton's. The form of the
programme was original, loosely based on the magazine format that
Welles had striven for in *It's All True*, with a nod towards annual
predictive publications, like *Old Moore's Almanac*. It threw together
cod astrology, knockabout comedy with guest stars, a 'No, but

seriously, folks' spot with great poetry or prose or a scene from a play, plus topical comment. Welles was not the same person he had been in 1941 when he had produced his last series, *The Lady Esther Show*. In particular, he was much more politically aware. Almost immediately he ran into trouble with his sponsors, who attempted to censor a satirical item about Generalissimo Franco. The intervention made Welles anxiously question his future relationship with them. In fact, he was hoping surreptitiously to increase the political content of the show, while at the same time seeking to establish himself as a mainstream comedian. These are not irreconcilable ambitions, though radical political comedy, of a sort practised in the second half of the twentieth century by the great Italian clown Dario Fo, or in the first half by the German political cabaret artist Karl Valentin, for example, has never been part of the central English-speaking tradition; and indeed, Welles made no attempt to integrate his comedy and his politics: they were to coexist side-by-side.

The history of the *Almanac* was the history of his attempts to pursue these two separate strands, the comic and the political, in the face of resistance on both counts. With the serious stuff – the extracts from great plays and the poetry readings – there was no quarrel. Welles had no desire to experiment with form, pushing the radiophonic boundaries as he had in the thirties; his aim with the *Almanac* was to create a free-wheeling half hour of fun and stimulation imbued with Popular Front sentiments. He was as inventive and exuberant as ever, but only in point of content, not form. 'February 2nd is Ground Hog day,' he wrote to the writers of the show, 'so please give me some jokes on the ground hog. I have an idea for this and if you gentlemen say you don't "feel it" I'll stuff you with red rocks, sew up your lips and throw you in the Amazon. Here's the idea – an interview with a ground hog himself.' He also hoped to introduce ('sneak', as he put it) some real jazz into the programme, convinced as he was that jazz, being both popular and radical, had been deliberately sidelined into becoming an esoteric delight for buffs. He was, in fact, quite a buff himself, and had the researchers seek out the veteran clarinet player Jimmie Noone, 'who, I believe, is still playing at the "Streets of Paris"'. This element, too, was an immediate success.

It was the comedy that proved difficult. Welles found himself under attack in an area where it is painful to have to defend oneself. The network tried to push him towards broader humour. 'You say that people are slow to accept me as a comedian,' he wrote awkwardly to Bob Presnell of CBS shortly after the programme had begun transmission, to poor responses, 'but I think we are breaking down their resistance pretty quickly.' Propounding his theory of comedy, Welles cites Jack Benny and Fred Allen, the leading radio comedians of the day: 'the one is comic in himself, the other isn't. Benny is a butt, Allen a butt-er'. He (Welles) he says, must be the latter, a butt-er, because he is the producer of the show, and identified as such. He must be in control, in charge. 'I don't intend you to think that I imagine myself to be another Fred Allen — but I do think of myself as Orson Welles and I do believe that my personality is sufficient to carry a half hour of fun and jokes without the imposition of such farce devices as your letter proposes.' It would spoil the 'serious spot' at the end, making it a dramatic situation — that is, not real. 'What I am trying to say is that unless I am clearly the master of the show I am presenting, everything that transpires on it may partake of a sort of spurious suspense — Maybe I don't make myself clear. The hell with you! — Fond regards.'

He may have made himself all too clear: mastery was a very big issue with Welles; it was impossible for him to be subordinate. His entire personality was constructed on being masterful, and to acknowledge that he might be genuinely vulnerable — that he might be wrong-footed, thrown off course, not know what to do at any moment — was something he could not contemplate. Alas for his future as a comedian, this is the essential predicate of comedy. Even the blustering Fred Allen is taken aback; things don't turn out the way he expects them to. Welles's contrast of Benny and Allen echoes Georges Feydeau's famous analysis (of farce, as it happens, but it applies equally well to all comedy): in comedy there is one who is kicked, and one who does the kicking. But the kicker is only funny when his kick misfires, or when he falls down afterwards. Welles thought that to offer himself up for mockery was a guarantee of mirth; it wasn't, unless somewhere behind it was an admission of genuine vulnerability. Behind Benny's vanity is real aspiration; behind Allen's ferocity is dim-wittedness. There is thus tension, and the possibility of surprise. Welles as a comedian is monolithic and one-dimensional, because he himself is trapped in the very thing he seeks to use as his comic persona. He cannot, dare not, let us see anything behind it.

Shortly afterwards, John McMillan from Compton's Agency sent a telegram to Presnell gently criticising the show's repetitiveness, adding: YOU ALSO HAVE TENDENCY TOWARDS UNPLEASANT

ANATOMICAL HUMOUR. He urged them to improve on the Serious Spot. LAST WEEK'S SHOW . . . SEEMED CONFUSED AND PREACHY. It appeared, he said, TO BE GILDING THE LILY OF DEMOCRACY. He apologised for his toughness, was with them 100 per cent, AND APPRECIATE YOURS AND ORSON'S PROBLEMS. In fact, Presnell never got this wire; Welles intercepted it, 'rashly put into my hands by CBS who said they thought I might be interested in it. How right they were. It held my attention from beginning to end. I think it would be a good policy if you would wire your thoughts about the show directly to me from now on instead of forcing me to steam open Presnell's correspondence . . .' He responds ferociously to the criticism it contains: 'it would be helpful if you would specify exactly what is meant by quote unpleasant unquote quote anatomical unquote and I am tempted to say quote humour unquote'. An attempt at irony tumbles over into sarcasm of the heaviest kind: 'Your closing expressions of sympathy are what caused me the most serious concern. You say quote appreciate yours and Orson's problems unquote. I didn't have any problems until I read your wire and Presnell hasn't any problems until you read this wire. In closing may I warn you against using invisible ink in your inter-office memos and besides I think you ought to know that our counterespionage experts can break down any code in twenty four hours.' He was deeply hurt, feeling himself under attack from all sides. He wrote to his old supporter Leonard Lyons of the *New York Post* to apologise for having sent a grumpy wire about Lyons's quotation of a rather inspired Noël Coward witticism about Welles's jaundice ('When Orson gets sick it would be in Technicolor'): 'the main intention was comic and as a rueful acknowledgement of the bad press I have been getting everywhere in the last few weeks'. At moments like these, Welles's genuine hurt can be glimpsed. 'I very much want you to know,' he told the columnist, 'that you can publish anything you want about me any time. And that even if, god forbid, you never mention me again, I love you . . . now please write to me again.' The storm passed, though the sun never really came out for the *Almanac*.

A show in early March with Lucille Ball is characteristic: it opens with a sketch concerning the Orson Welles Fan Club; cue for much squealing from the audience. Most of the jokes are about his girth (then of course a fraction of what it was to become): Welles attempts to dictate letters to his secretary Miss Grimace, who tells him, 'That'll be all.' 'That'll be all *who*?' he demands, testily. 'That'll be all, Fatso.' The horoscope gags at the beginning are dismally poor: 'The Moon is in Sagittarius, which rules the thighs and hips, so it should be a great night at the Palladium.' There is a lot of breaking up by the actors, some of it real, some faked; Welles himself stumbles over the script beyond the acceptable point of charming human error. Regular characters – Dr Snakeoil and Prudence Pratt – make dutiful appearances, and the audience laughs at the standard wartime jokes in Pavlovian fashion. An air of frankly amateurish chaos prevails until a sudden gearchange for the Serious Spot, which this week illustrates what Welles calls 'the immense proposition that every man belongs to all men': he intones Donne's mighty sermon on that theme – 'never send to know for whom the bell tolls; it tolls for thee' – sonorously enough but without making it fresh.

The following week Charles Laughton is the guest star, which naturally provokes a further orgy of fat jokes, plus some about how ugly they both are. There is a passably funny scene with the man from the Reducing Studio, then a sequence – richly appreciated by the audience – about filling in government forms, amortisation, et cetera. He and Laughton perform the tent scene from *Julius Caesar*, with Welles as Brutus very close to the microphone, emoting nobly as in his earlier radio version. By no means typecasting for 'lean and hungry Cassius' – but it is radio, after all – Laughton, with his much wider range, is very arresting. The applause is polite. Then Welles suddenly comes alive in a verbal rhapsody about jazz: 'many of you listening have never heard it before. What you've heard are jazz ideas slicked up by commercial musicians.' There always has to be a villain with Welles, but in this case it adds real punch to what he says. 'The whole thing started in the wide-open good time carnival city that was New Orleans before the last war. From that it spread to Chicago and all over the world and influenced all popular music. This is Art for Art's sake if anything ever was – music musicians play for themselves for their own satisfaction, just because they like it.' He introduces what he calls 'the only existing jazz band' made up of Mutt Carey, Kid Ory, Jimmie Noone, Buster Wilson, Ed Scott, Zutty Singleton – called The All Star New Orleans Band, but renamed for the occasion the Mercury All Stars. The trombonist Ory holds himself somewhat aloof from Welles; when introduced he says, 'What's that name again?' Welles, unfazed, embraces him, rattling off the names of all his albums. It is infectious and genuine and full of love, alive with his electric powers of communication, and it feels as if Welles is relieved to be able to throw off the burden of comedy.

The band worked well with him; their spot became a weekly feature. There was some dissension within the band as to who was the leader. Then, on the morning of the show of 19 April, Jimmie Noone dropped dead of a heart attack. Welles, again at his inspired best, ad-libbed a tribute. For once he seems genuinely moved. 'Jimmy died suddenly last night,' he continues, 'and now, in his honour, his friends are going to play one of his works.' The band, tearful, plays 'Blues for Jimmie Noone' or 'Jimmie's Blues', Noone's latest opus; the audience is palpably moved. After Noone's death, the jazz spot continued with Wade Whaley and then others, including Zutty Singleton's Swing Combo. Welles was quite right; no one else on radio was giving space to this kind of music, and many in his audience knew nothing of it. His enthusiasm, boyish but deeply informed, his eloquence and generous sympathy are all as infectious when listened to today as they must have been at the time. If he could have found a structure that accommodated that, then he would have been onto an absolute winner.

John McMillan understood this. He was leaving Compton's and, in his parting letter to Welles – after telling him that he had wired New York to 'relax and leave us be on this show' – McMillan urged him to use himself, 'the warmth of your personality', rather than rely on formulas. The show, he says, has improved enormously, but still has a long way to go. 'I know that you can do anything in the world with this show,' he tells Welles, 'if you only have the courage to believe in yourself' – on the face of it an extraordinary thing to say to Orson Welles, who seemed to embody the concept of self-assurance. McMillan continues in a vein somewhat surprising in the executive of an advertising agency: 'Very frankly, Orson, the idea and ideal of the programme as we discussed it and planned it – the deep, almost religious belief, which I am sure you share, that there can be a synthesis between what is good and what is popular – that millions of people like good things if they are only made free of their fear of liking' – everything, in fact, that the jazz sections of the show had so brilliantly evinced – 'all this goes far deeper with me than any business considerations . . .' It is clear from the quiet, regretful tone of McMillan's letter that he feels in some measure disappointed, that he has believed what Welles told him about his hopes for the programme, and that Welles has let them both down. 'You have come a long, long way from the first broadcast,' he concludes. 'But I am absolutely certain that the best programme we have had in this series to date represents only a fraction of the potential of which this programme is capable.'

If McMillan's tone was that of a wise housemaster, a sterner, sharper report was to come. A month later, Dick Compton himself wrote a letter to Welles's agent William Collier of the William Morris agency, bluntly stating its theme: 'To renew or not renew?' Both the agency and the client, Socony-Vacuum, were wholly in agreement that the gas and oil business peculiarly required 'big-time, night-time, highly legible, highly visible radio', they had accordingly been willing to experiment, to spend money. What had been the results? Poor, from the beginning, with the Hooper rating over ten weeks showing no improvement whatsoever. To be fair, the Serious Spot had been highly successful – the John Donne sermon and a scene from *Cyrano de Bergerac* had been 'inspiring in their rendition'. Compton was not alone in feeling this: Eddie Cantor, then close to the height of his fame, had written to the embattled Welles that his dramatic reading of 'The Ballad of Bataan' was 'the finest thing I have heard since the advent of radio'. But the rest of the show, insists Compton, was a disappointment – above all, the comedy. Welles had told Compton over lunch one day that he still felt he had to achieve greater familiarity with 'the comedy form'. He had stated 'most frankly'·that he felt 'nowhere near the mastery of the comedy form that he felt with the dramatic form'. This was Welles's first venture in 'the comedy form', says Compton, and then he fires off a series of highly pertinent questions:

Does he like to work in that form? Does he feel that he can express himself adequately to the public in that form? Does he feel that he wishes deeply to study that form and put against it the same time and kind of effort which he has put against his undoubted mastery of other forms? Does he feel that because the comedy form, when successful, more consistently than any other form tends to draw a large audience; that he, over the years, wishes to use that vehicle as a means of reaching and influencing larger numbers of the public?

The architecture of the show had not been well planned, Compton says. It needed clearer direction – that is to say, control. Welles's appearances outside the studio must be controlled, too. More time needed to be spent. In the end, it was a question of Welles's attitude:

Now, we realise that this is quite an extraordinary letter to write about a package show. It contravenes every article in the constitution of package show producing . . . we and our client hope that you will receive it in the spirit in which it is written and we wish to state that spirit explicitly. It is this: we believe that we have the essential ingredients of a highly successful show. We hope to achieve a highly successful show, and having achieved it, to stay with it for years and years. We do feel, however, that the success for which we are reaching can only be achieved by more detailed and effective supervision and by a closer spirit of co-operation between everybody connected with the show.

It is entirely characteristic of the extremes so often simultaneously present in Welles's life – one foot in heaven and the other in hell – that on the very day that he received this chastening tutorial from the head of an advertising agency on the obligations of being the host of a comedy show, a letter arrived from Henry Morgenthau, Secretary of the Treasury, one of the two or three most powerful men in the country, to confirm that they wanted Welles to spearhead the radio campaign to launch the desperately needed Fifth War Loan Drive. 'I am sure you will be very helpful to us,' wrote Morgenthau, adding words that must have been music to Welles's ears: 'this will give you an opportunity to put your talents to better use in the war effort than you have been able to do thus far. The job that lies ahead of us is tremendous.' Official confirmation arrived by the same post: 'You are hereby appointed a consulting expert in the office of the secretary, War Finance division, with compensation at the rate of $1.00 per annum.'

Welles immediately hurled himself, as only he could, into the task of producing the broadcast, which would come first from Texarkana, in Texas, and would then be repeated in Los Angeles and Chicago. Whipping up a storm of energy and excitement, he contacted the participants personally: included in an impressive group were the composer Aaron Copland, the poet Carl Sandburg, the man of the theatre Oscar Hammerstein II and the conductor Leopold Stokowski. WON'T YOU PLEASE WRITE US A PRAYER OR A DEDICATION? he wrote to Sandburg. I DON'T NEED TO TELL YOU WHAT ABOUT. Old colleagues were roped in: I WOULD LIKE MUSIC FOR THIS TO BE NOT INCIDENTAL BUT OF EQUAL IMPORTANCE, Welles wired Bernard Herrmann. I WILL BE VERY UNHAPPY IF YOU CAN'T TAKE PART IN IT. MY DEAREST LOVE TO YOU AS ALWAYS. Naturally Herrmann replied by return: DELIGHTED . . . ARRIVING HOLLYWOOD JUNE 5. It was just like the old days: adrenalin overriding everything. But despite the exhilaration, there was no doubt in

Welles's mind of the seriousness of the undertaking, or of the gravity of the hour. Suddenly he was at the heart of great events: Fred Smith of the Treasury Department, who had been instrumental in approaching Welles, warned him to eschew levity in the broadcast: it might be the second or third day of invasion, or perhaps its eve. BE SURE TO KEEP TEXARKANA SHOW POINTED TO JUSTIFYING COSTS OF INVASION, Smith wired him, ESPECIALLY IN BLOOD, signing himself off somewhat incongruously LOVE AND KISSES FRED; even the politicians started talking showbiz under the influence of Welles's expansiveness.

Within days, Welles had a request for Smith: NOW HERE'S A JOB FOR YOU AND I MEAN A JOB. WE NEED A TWO-LINE MESSAGE FROM EISENHOWER AS FOLLOWS: QUOTE WE KNOW WHAT WE ARE FIGHTING. OUR TERMS ARE ON THE RECORD — UNCONDITIONAL SURRENDER. WE WON T TAKE ANYTHING LESS AND THAT'S WHAT WE'RE GOING TO GET UNQUOTE. THE MESSAGE NEEDN'T BE LONGER THAN THIS AND MAYBE EISENHOWER WILL AGREE TO THOSE EXACT WORDS. A week into the job, and Welles is writing dialogue for the Supreme Commander of Allied Expeditionary Forces; ten days earlier he had been enduring lectures from Dick Compton about 'the comedy form'. And the day before he was ordering conjuring tricks, including a real skull for a talking-skull act. Such was the helter-skelter of Welles's life. 'Today we talk of the sacrifices we are called upon to make,' he wrote to the War Finance Committee, giving a sample of his script. 'Sacrifices? Hardly! The real sacrifices were made at the birth of our nation more than 160 years ago. More truly we are permitted great privileges. Living in a democracy is truly a great privilege, and the opportunity to help perpetuate and extend that privilege is a far greater privilege.' Fred Smith, with his better informed view of the realities of the war, suggested that Welles add a description of the desperation and determination of the enemy, and the probable deaths that America would endure during the invasion. Emphasise the need for support from behind, he said, from the home country; and of course that is what Welles did. In its own small way, producing the broadcast was like waging war: getting all the participants into the studio at the same time was a massive physical operation, which then had to be repeated twice. Welles and everyone involved was aware that it mattered; the broadcast — though perhaps somewhat hampered by over-solemnity — is impressive for its sense of urgency and sincere patriotic commitment, no doubt connected to the fact that the massive D-Day operation had taken place a mere six days before, on 6 June. The broadcasts succeeded beyond all expectation in the task of raising money, and it was understood that Welles was more responsible than anyone for that result. His particular gifts for shaping and synthesis were well noted. 'I want you to know,' Morgenthau wrote to him, 'how much I appreciate your help in Texarkana, Los Angeles and Chicago. The material you prepared for me is by far the best I have ever had. I am particularly impressed by the way you caught what I was trying to say and brought it back to me in a way that could not have been improved on.' There was a slightly ugly moment when the War Finance Committee quibbled over payments for the Texarkana broadcast, despite Fred Smith's clear statement to Welles that they had lots of money and it was his to command, but the moment soon passed.

In all the excitement, the demise of *The Orson Welles Almanac* went almost unnoticed. The grapevine knew of it before the participants. 'It was a business decision,' wrote Dick Compton, 'and as you know business decisions are often tinged with personal regret.' There was ugliness there, too: NBC raised an invoice to Welles, charging him for 'repainting dressing room defaced by you'. Asked for clarification, NBC cited 'drawings or caricatures on the walls of the dressing room occupied by Mr Welles, and from the evidence unearthed it is our conclusion that they were drawn by Mr Welles himself'. Orson the bad boy had evidently not quite got it all out of his system in Brazil; he finally coughed up the $250 demanded. Despite ending on this curiously silly note, the whole *Almanac* episode is not without significance. Compton had, in his tight-lipped way, spoken the truth – what he quaintly insists on calling 'the comedy form' on radio did, 'when successful', tend more consistently than any other form to draw a large audience. Did Welles want that audience? Compton and his client wanted to achieve a highly successful show 'and having achieved it, to stay with it for years and years'. Did Welles, or did he not, wish to use that successful vehicle 'as a means of reaching and influencing larger numbers of the public'? The answer had, of course, to be: 'not in that form'. His dreams of establishing himself as a comedian had proved hopeless – humiliatingly so; his educational aspirations were confined to the Serious Spot, which, though he knew he could certainly pull it off, he must also have known inevitably ended up as a mere plummy interlude between the gags; while his hopes of introducing genuinely political elements would never get past the sponsor.

He therefore abandoned his attempt to reach a mass audience.

In doing so, he also abandoned the vast bulk of his income: in 1944, his radio earnings amounted to the enormous sum of $170,000 (he earned an additional $10,000 for the Texarkana broadcast, so patriotism did not go unrewarded). Thus liberated, Welles turned increasingly to his consuming interest of the period – politics – which he pursued on twin tracks: his growing contribution to Dolivet's Free World Association as speaker, writer and editor; and his increasing involvement with the campaign to re-elect Roosevelt. The two activities were not necessarily wholly compatible; *Free World* maintained a healthily critical attitude to the President. Welles's new commitment to Roosevelt was something of a conversion, partly brought on by his contact with government at the highest levels, partly by his conviction of the danger of anyone other than Roosevelt being elected, but above all by the intoxicating sense that he might actually be involved in the great task of remaking the world when the war was won. Increasingly, he embraced the role of spokesman, effortlessly commanding the appropriately stentorian tones: 'To the fighting armies of the united nations, and to the courageous underground, We, the Free World Association of Hollywood,' he said at the Association's rally, 'offer this solemn pledge: We will exert ourselves to the utmost in the support of this war and toward the fulfilment of its high purpose. All attempts at betraying the American democratic system we will rigorously expose – and we will combat unflinchingly every effort to weaken the authority of the people by divisions of race or of sect or of class . . . we the Free World Association of Hollywood invite all men and women enlisted in the cause of freedom to join with us now.'

This relatively new manifestation of Welles's persona naturally attracted ironic comment: earlier in the year, *Time* magazine had mocked one of his speeches, and he had wired them a dignified defence of his right to be taken seriously:

We filmmakers realise our community is a gorgeous subject for satire. We grant, or anyway most of us do, that we are the world's funniest people. You can write more jokes about us than you can about plumbers, undertakers or Fuller brush salesmen. Hollywood is guilty of deliberate withdrawal from the world. It seeks to entertain and we suspect that the success of that withdrawal is what makes Hollywood funny. But let *Time* magazine view with alarm or point with pride but not laugh off Hollywood's growing recognition that every movie expresses or at least affects political opinion. Moviegoers live all over the world, come from all classes, and add up to the biggest section of human beings ever addressed by any means of communication. The politics of moviemakers therefore is just exactly what isn't funny about Hollywood. *Time* mentions room temperature burgundy and chopped chicken liver as though these luxuries invalidate political opinion. *Time*, whose editors eat chopped chicken liver and whose publishers drink room temperature burgundy, knows better.

Meanwhile, his absence from screen and stage had not gone unnoticed. While *The Orson Welles Almanac* was still running, Hedda Hopper had written a 'Whither Welles?' piece; it well expresses the general bafflement about his career. Welles had sent her one of his comically blustering letters of complaint concerning something she had written about Rita Hayworth earlier in the year: 'I send you herewith a number of ancient Irish Curses, all unprintable, even under the audacious banner of your own by-line. You were my family's only syndicated friend and now you are publicly on the side of the Savage of Gower Gulch [Harry Cohn]. This is to remind you that the good God sees everything that we do, and that it is never too late to repent. I'm still a watery-kneed invalid, but I'm just strong enough to raise a palsied fist and shake it in your direction . . . I remain, wounded but adoring, yours always' – a remarkably playful letter to have written to a woman who, with her co-harpy, Louella Parsons, had done everything she could to have *Citizen Kane* not merely suppressed, but physically destroyed.

Under the heading GENUS GENIUS, Hopper reports on Welles's present situation, his abandonment of *War and Peace* and his radio show. Helpfully, she tells him that he's not a comedian and should give it up and attempt another *War of the Worlds*. New laws introduced after that show, he solemnly tells her, mean that no such thing could ever be done again. What about his proposed reading of the Bible with symphony orchestra? 'Those who were interested in the Bible before,' says Welles, who must have been enjoying himself enormously, 'think it's too slow now.' He recounts yet again the legend of his career, with the usual imaginative touches, and, specially for her, adds a brilliant new detail: he bumped into Gordon Craig when he was fifteen, he tells her, in the American Express office in Paris, and immediately fainted at his feet, whereupon he was taken home by Craig, who taught him stage design and took him to Florence to meet all the great artists (Michelangelo, Piero della Francesca and Benvenuto Cellini, one presumes). Daringly, Hopper mentions *Citizen Kane* and, even more daringly, acclaims it: he got more praise for it, she asserts, than people who had been producing for years; then – more and more daring – she mentions the great beauty of the footage from *It's All True*, which she has evidently seen. 'If by some miracle he can get hold of it and make it a successful picture,' she says, risking the displeasure of some powerful figures in the industry, 'he will have justified himself and made liars of those who defamed him. I don't think Orson is the greatest actor we've ever had. In fact,' she goes on, in her artless way, 'I don't think he's a great actor. There's very little warmth in him on screen. He doesn't stir you the way Frank Sinatra does. But I do think he's a great producer.' She trails his lack of a producing credit on *Jane Eyre*, but he won't be drawn on that subject, and describes his domestic contentment. It is a curious, elegiac piece, almost compassionate, halfway between an obituary and a doctor's report. 'How many folks do you know who, at the age of thirty' – he had actually just turned twenty-nine – 'have done so many things? All the ingredients for greatness are there, but will he ever reach the goal he's striving for? Only time will tell. But to me, Orson Welles has only scratched the surface of Orson Welles.' It is an unexpectedly interesting summary, all the more so for its naivety; in fact, like virtually everybody else, including some very sophisticated people, Hopper quite genuinely didn't know what to make of him. His new-found political activities, increasingly high in profile, only further confused the picture.

*

Welles was now becoming sharply focused on the election campaign. Roosevelt, having won an unprecedented third term, was, in November 1944, offering himself for a fourth. His re-election was by no means a sure thing: the maverick Republican Thomas E. Dewey, governor of New York, was making some headway; and there were still large sections of the electorate who distrusted Roosevelt, including some on the Left. Welles had squarely reposed his faith in Vice-President Wallace and his visionary, radical policies: he had introduced Wallace, with due metaphoric reference to his distinction as an agrarian reformer, at a meeting of the Independent Voters' Committee for Arts and Sciences for Roosevelt (a fact duly noted by the FBI). 'Henry Wallace,' Welles said, 'has counted up our debt to the complex past of nations and continents. His life is a celebration of that debt . . .

the American spirit is not the love of possession. It is the love of growth. It is the sense of tomorrow. It builds against the wind. It plants against the winter. There are lessons for democracy in the art of farming and Henry Wallace has learned those lessons and taught them.' Welles's idealism, unforced and admirable, was entirely genuine. 'The speaker you'll hear now has always denied the necessity of hunger. He shares with Lincoln and Jefferson and Franklin Roosevelt a perfect confidence in the capacity of the earth as a provider for all men and in the capacity of man to provide for man in a just abundancy. These are great days and there are great men for these days. Here is one of them. Ladies and gentlemen, the vice-president of the United States, Mr Henry A. Wallace.'

For Welles, Wallace's presence at Roosevelt's side was democracy's finest hope. It was therefore something of a shattering blow for him when, at the pre-election Democratic Convention in September, Wallace failed to secure renomination, being passed over in favour of the little-known senator for Missouri, Harry S. Truman. Roosevelt (not in good health) had played one of his inscrutable poker-games, endorsing neither man, though giving both reason to hope; in the end Wallace, who despised political trafficking, lost out to the greater master of the Democratic machine. Welles rushed to print in his *Free World* editorial to say as much: his emotionally charged analysis was explicitly critical of Roosevelt. 'There is something to thank God for in the spirit of Henry Wallace. We can only regret that each of these great men has not a little of the other's greatness. They were a wonderful team. If Roosevelt were even braver in pursuit of principle, and if Wallace had mastered a little more of the tricky craft of politics, perhaps the team would not have broken up.' Welles's identification with a man who couldn't work within the system of his own party is striking; he makes this even clearer in comparing Wallace's Chicago speech to one given in Wisconsin by Wendell Wilkie, the dissident Republican for whose One World Internationalist policy Welles had the highest regard. 'Both men functioned within the framework of their political parties, both were at war with their party machines and party bosses, and both were disastrously reckless in that warfare.' The system, as always with Welles, is the enemy. He contemplates Roosevelt's reluctance to distance himself from the Democrats' party machine in order to found the great liberal party 'whose emergence is generally expected after his retirement', a curious misreading of the American political scene. '*Free World* is certain that if liberal opinion remains a minority vote, democracy is doomed. Henry Wallace is the particular prophet of that opinion . . . his thoughts are often expressed with poetic intensity, but his common sense is the full measure of his sensitivity.' In conclusion, he reaffirms his support for Roosevelt (as had Wallace): 'the President remains, in spite of everything, the beloved liberal of the world, but his popularity at home seems to be all that holds together the left and the right wing of the democracy party, and his liberalism is in strategic hibernation . . . most progressives remain Roosevelt partisans even though few among them have forgotten his cheerful scuttling of Dr New Deal, just as few have forgotten that he was their most effective champion'. Like his colleagues at *Free World* and many others on the Left, Welles had an apocalyptic sense of the forthcoming struggle for the world's soul, one with which Roosevelt would presumably not be involved; for the time being, 'the beloved liberal of the world' must be supported; there could be no more important task. But he was warming to the task personally. The creation of heroes and villains, in art as in life, was an essential part of Welles's way of approaching the world; now, at Democracy's critical hour, he did not have far to look to find them.

He took to the campaign stumps, rolling up his sleeves and weighing in with fists flying. He was, he told the Hollywood Democratic Association, suspicious that if the war were to end earlier than expected, 'they' would try to get Roosevelt out. 'You understand what I mean by "they",' he says. 'You know who they are. They are not essentially Republicans, but they have seized the Republican party as a vehicle for their ambitions. They are the partisans of privilege – the champions of monopoly – the opponents of liberty – the adversaries of the small business man and the small farmer. They have been here a long time. They used to own the earth and run the world of men, but – just now – they're losing out . . . they are the internationalists but their pacts and treaties are as secret as crime. Theirs,' he says, in a striking anticipation of globalist theory, 'is the internationalism of the cartel.' He does not hesitate to get personal. 'The background of Thomas Dewey is colourful – as spuriously colourful as the plot of a "B" movie. What of his backers? Well, here are some real names – Pugh, Raskob, Sloan, Hearst, Patterson, McCormack.' In other words, industrialists, financiers, press barons.

As the election drew closer, Welles became rougher and tougher: at a registration-week luncheon he spoke at length against those who claimed the war could not be won. 'What happened to the men who raised that question? Our freedom here is such a perfect thing that even today – even those wicked men – are free! What happened to them, the doubters and the dissenters . . . the men who thought we couldn't win, and the men who said we couldn't produce to win . . . what are they up to now? One of them's running for President. Thomas Dewey, you'll remember, told us it was silly to even think of producing fifty thousand airplanes for the war effort.' He starts to hector, making wild accusations. 'Do I hear someone say that Dewey should not be smeared by associating his name with treachery? Even this late in the war, even in the course of an American Presidential campaign, it is a matter of proof and record that Dewey associates with traitors.' His oratory becomes a little hair-raising, as if he were not entirely in command of his emotions. 'I know that Dewey stands everyday before the cameras smiling in the company of the wicked men . . . Wendell Wilkie would not smile with them and would not stand with them . . . we know what happened when he found out what Thomas Dewey well knows – when he found out what forces had seized power in the Republican party – I cannot guess what Dewey's men have contrived for him to say about a man whose presence in the world was an embarrassment to him and a rebuke. It may be possible that Dewey is even greedy enough to electioneer at that funeral. But I know,' he says, blustering, 'I tell you that I *know* . . . what Wendell Wilkie thought of him. It is for Wilkie's closest friends to decide when and in what manner they will make that public. Meanwhile the Dewey forces would be well advised to hold their silence.' This is the voice of Charles Foster Kane denouncing Boss Jim Gettys. 'I have used strong words here today. I am using them in this election. Strong words are called for. I say that dangerous, woefully, terribly dangerous forces foisted this present candidate on the Republican Party. I say that those forces are the consecrated enemies of American progress and the professional wreckers of world peace.' The speech was a great success and was repeated frequently; at the same time he was making broadcasts – 'This is Orson Welles speaking' – on behalf of the American Labor Party, defending Labor's record against Dewey's accusations, quoting General Marshall to that effect, listing Labor's programme and urging all to register and to vote for Roosevelt, 'the man who saved the country in 1933'.

On the subject of Roosevelt he became more and more eloquent, particularly after he had been invited to meet him on board the presidential train. 'I cannot believe that there are many serious people who privately deny the greatness of Roosevelt,' he told the *Herald Tribune* Forum on False Issues and the American Presidency.

'I think that even most Republicans are resigned to it, that when the elections are over and the history books are written, our President will emerge as one of the great names in one of Democracy's great centuries.' Welles had exhausted himself in the first weeks of the campaign, and had to take to his bed; Dadda Bernstein had rushed out a note to the Food Rationing Board certifying that Mr and Mrs Orson Welles were under his care and that they required additional supplementary meat. 'They are both suffering from malnutrition and low metabolism,' he stated. 'They require at least six pounds of lamb and beef per week for a period of eight weeks.' Roosevelt, notified of Welles's increasingly strenuous efforts on his behalf, had wired him: I HAVE JUST LEARNED THAT YOU ARE ILL AND I HOPE MUCH YOU WILL FOLLOW YOUR DOCTORS ORDERS AND TAKE CARE OF YOURSELF. THE MOST IMPORT-ANT THING IS FOR YOU TO GET WELL AND BE AROUND FOR THE LAST DAYS OF THE CAMPAIGN. This intimation of the value of his contribution had an understandably galvanising effect on Welles. 'Dear Mr President,' he replied:

This illness was the blackest of misfortunes for me because it stole away so many days from the campaign. I cannot think I have accomplished a great deal but I well know that this is the most important work I could ever engage in. Your wonderfully thoughtful and generous message reached me at exactly the moment when the doctors and I had decided that I couldn't do anything but get worse. Your wire changed my mind.

Welles was up and on his feet for the final week of the campaign, and on the eve of the election he spoke of Roosevelt more person-ally than usual, in strikingly emotional terms: this is the vocabulary, not of politics, but of hero-worship:

At such a time as this none of us, however he intends to vote, can fail to think of our President without some feeling of tenderness and affection. In days of darkness and in nights of doubt he has borne heavy burdens – he has borne them without murmur or complaint. Abused as none but the great are abused, reviled and rejected by many of the rich and powerful in his own land, he has never faltered in his faith – his faith in the limitless capacity of the people, in the ultimate and perfect justice of the people's will. I'm sure that tomorrow the people he believes in will show their confidence in him.

Meanwhile, Welles's attacks on Dewey became wilder:

Some years ago, I put on a show of acts of magic and prestidigitation for the amusement of the armed forces stationed in southern California. The public was very kind to my few acts . . . but within the past few months, the starch has been taken out of me. A show has been making the rounds of the country, headed by a far greater illusionist, trickster and conjuror than I can ever hope to be: I admit it: I yield the palm to the master illusionist, the Republican candidate for president, Thomas E. Dewey. There has been nothing like it before. The acts are stupendous; the deceptions colossal; the cast takes in some of our biggest industrialists, our most unyielding politicians. To the old tricks of the trade a new repertory has been added. The illusions are almost (but not quite) convincing.

The press followed him closely. At another meeting of the Independent Voters' Committee for Arts and Sciences for Roosevelt, when Welles happened to scowl, a news photographer obligingly caught it on camera. 'You can sell that to the Hearst press at a premium,' Welles quipped. 'It shows me in my angry Communist mood. And this' – he said, smiling – 'is my *benevolent* Communist mood.' He told the newsmen how happy he was that writers and artists were becoming increasingly interested in politics. He had persuaded the independent producer, Walter Wanger, he told them, to buy Howard Fast's biography, *Citizen Thomas Paine*, for him to turn into a movie, but didn't yet know how; otherwise he was engaged in 'educational stuff' and editing *Free World*. 'I'm doing a lot of research,' he said. 'I spent a deal of last year learning, not doing.' He'd done nothing to earn a living, except occasional guest appearances, since the *Almanac* went off the air a month or two before. 'Pictures? I've done nothing but turn them down. They don't do very good pictures today, I find.' The question arises: did Welles never want to work again as an actor – or, indeed, director? For the time being, a certain part of his nature – the articulator, the teacher, the spokesman – was satisfied. His passionately held convictions mattered more to him than any mere film, part or play. He had made a desultory attempt for the producer Billy Rose to mount a play, *Emily Brady* by the humorist and screenwriter Donald Ogden Stewart. Rose had rather wittily created the Rosebud production company to present it, but Welles – having offered a key role to his old colleague Walter Huston and been turned down

– immediately concluded that the play was impossible to cast, and sent a telegram to Stewart withdrawing from the production. Stewart replied with a sharp dig at Welles's magical activities: I AM AFRAID I DON'T UNDERSTAND. ONE DOESN'T SAW A WRITER IN TWO SO CONVENIENTLY, ON ANY BASIS OF RESPECT FOR EITHER ME OR MY PLAY I THINK YOU OWE ME SOMETHING MORE THAN A TELEGRAM. But with the world on the brink of *Götterdämmerung*, Welles really had no interest in the theatre.

He was very clear about what concerned him. Addressing a group of journalists, the surprised recipients of a weightily considered summary of his political philosophy, he assured them that he was not running for office and expected no special or personal rewards for his efforts. 'It is precisely for this reason that I think you may respect me enough to want to hear me out. I am a serious student of world affairs and the editor of a serious magazine on that subject.' He insisted that he was nobody's lobbyist, simply democracy's friend. 'Communism,' he says, 'has never been an issue in this country. Liberalism, on the other hand, has been an issue in every American election since the days of Jefferson. The Republican strategy makes it important to say again that liberalism and Communism are not partners. They are competitors. I am an American liberal and I am jealous of the prestige of Communism as a world idea.' His view of the relationship between communism and what he calls liberalism is possibly a little rose-tinted, but is the result of mature reflection: 'We need not fight Communism; our duty is to compete with it and so live to see Communism out-rivalled by our democratic achievements. As to foreign policy, I believe that it must remain in essence an extension of the policies of Franklin Roosevelt, who believes that America with England and Russia and all other freedom-loving governments are entered upon a wholesome rivalry to do good.' He concludes with a quite unexpected goal: 'To realise peace on earth, to ease the burdens of man and to secure for him a free and friendly world where he may finally realise his divinity'. This exalted vision seems to echo back to the intense conversations he and George Fanto had had on the beach at Fortaleza in the far north of Brazil, with their intimations of numinosity. It was rare for Welles to express himself in this manner, but a Blake-like sense of the perfectibility of man is consonant with everything else we know of Welles's world-view, closely associated with his frequently demonstrated sense of paradise lost, of a vanished realm of natural decency, generosity, benevolence. The reverse of this, of course, is a sharp sense of the malign and poisonous forces of the post-lapsarian world. He never expressed himself less than lovingly about his fellow-human-beings – in general. Individuals were another matter.

He shared in the general jubilation at the largely favourable outcome of the presidential election, and was swift to analyse the significance of the result in *Free World*; for him – perhaps a little surprisingly – the crucial issue had been race. 'The racist and all the other liars failed. Their argument may have been heard by ears that never heard such arguments before, but the arguments have been answered by ballot. The people have discredited the racist advertisements. The lies of reactionaries were blown to bits on November 7th.' The other great success of the campaign, he claims, was the Labor movement, with its 'new capacity for politics and vitality which leaves no doubt of labor's future as an influence in the largest affairs of the government'. And he notes that the Republican campaign has been a failure in spite of the fact that at least six times more was spent on it than the Democrats could afford. This, he insists, proves beyond doubt that 'the majority of our people are in the broadest and best sense of the word, progressive'. He allows himself a personal reminiscence:

> Among the politically unsophisticated, your Editor discovered
> the most wholesome, whole-hearted understanding of
> Roosevelt's contribution to the beauty and security of American
> life, and an equal understanding of the basic assumptions of
> Roosevelt's liberalism. Your editor comes out of this campaign
> convinced that liberalism is no longer a small voice. It is loud
> and sure. In 1944 it can be heard above all other voices in our
> nation. We are sure that the next four years are going to be
> great years . . . as world citizens we march into the first days
> with the most perfect pride.

The rhetoric betrays the influence of his mentor Dolivet, whose idiom it closely resembles. Welles's general enthusiasm for the election result was enhanced by the receipt of a drolly phrased letter from Roosevelt himself (which appears to have been the standard letter of thanks to his supporters in the entertainment world, but which Welles took very personally): 'Dear Mr Welles, I may be a prejudiced spectator who had a special interest in the action but I want to thank you for the splendid role you played in the recent campaign. I cannot recall any campaign in which actors and artists were so effective in the unrehearsed realities of the drama of the

WELLESCHMERZ

Left: Isaac Woodard (second left, standing) with other members of the Blind Veterans' Association.

Above: Woodard (centre) with Walter White (right), head of the NAACP.

Left: Woodard at a press conference, July 1946.

WE MUST ESTABLISH
BEYOND ANY DOUBT
THE
EQUALITY
OF MAN.

Above: The newly-blonde Rita Hayworth with her Svengali
behind her.

Below: Welles shooting *The Lady from Shanghai* in Catalina.

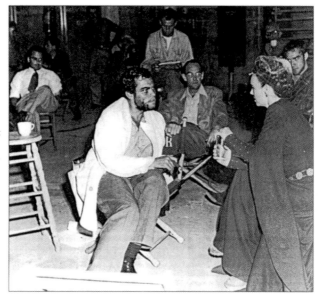

Facing page
Above: Michael O'Hara takes a tumble: the fun-house sequence in *The Lady from Shanghai.*

Below: The famous climax of *The Lady from Shanghai.*

Above: Welles and Jeanette Nolan in intense conference on the Republic lot for *Macbeth.*

Below: Welles surveys *Macbeth.*

To speed filming and swell extras on *Macbeth*, some camera-men wore masks on the backs of their heads while shooting.

Soldiers behind Macbeth
Misty
Silhouettes
in
Thick
FoG

HEATH

Welles's sketch for the film of *Macbeth*.

Macbeth on stage: Salt Lake City.

Welles with masks at a rehearsal of *Macbeth* on stage: a gasp-inducing moment
for the audience in Salt Lake City.

American future. It was a great show in which you played a great part. Very sincerely yours Franklin D. Roosevelt.' 'Dear Mr President,' replied Welles, 'You cannot know how your marvellously thoughtful and very kind letter was appreciated. I count my small part in this last campaign as the highest privilege of my life, and our visit on the train as the richest experience. Rita joins me in wishing you the compliments of the season.' He signs himself with a rather striking adverb: 'Yours truthfully, Orson Welles.'

Altogether, 1944 ended on a cheerful note for him. He had been engaged on extremely favourable terms by the *New York Post* as a syndicated daily columnist, and on 17 December, Rita Hayworth had given birth to a daughter whom they named Rebecca (not after the Daphne du Maurier book that Welles had twice performed on radio, but after the Jewish heroine of Walter Scott's *Ivanhoe*, which Hayworth – always desperate to catch up on her husband's omnivorous reading habits – had rather impressively just finished). Welles drew a sketch with stars to celebrate the baby's arrival and put it on that year's Christmas card. It was the most personal endorsement Rebecca Welles would ever receive from her father, although the event elicited telegrams of congratulation from Mrs Roosevelt and Harry S. Truman, which most certainly endorsed *him*; not many actor-directors might have expected their baby's birth to be welcomed by both the President's wife and the Vice-President. In his message, Truman said, 'I know she can't help having a grand career with the support she will have from her parents' – a prediction that proved sadly untrue at any level.

CHAPTER THIRTEEN

Actor Turns Columnist

WELLES SHOWED as little interest in the birth of his new baby as he had in the birth of Christopher Welles six years earlier. In fact, Christopher's principal significance in his life was as an occasion for acrimonious disputes over alimony, which finally ended up in court; his pleas of poverty got him off the hook. (In a piquant turn of events, Virginia Welles's new husband was the screenwriter Charles Lederer, who happened to be the nephew of Marion Davies, William Randolph Hearst's mistress; Christopher accordingly spent occasional weekends in San Simeon under the roof of the man who had done everything in his power to destroy her father and his precocious masterpiece.)

Meanwhile Welles's relationship with Rita Hayworth had reached a watershed of sorts. They had been together for nearly eighteen months, during which time the exhilaration of Welles's initial triumphant conquest of one of the supreme sexual icons of the day – one who proved, if anything, more passionate in the bedroom than his fantasies had imagined – had inevitably been tempered by day-to-day reality. He discovered that the sultry goddess of the screen was in person sweet-natured and homely, which was delightful and touching, but that she was also immensely needy, which was less so. It was something of a novelty in a relationship for Welles, who had hitherto been the one requiring attention, consideration and support – all of which Dolores del Rio had provided in abundance. Not that Hayworth was ungiving emotionally: on the contrary, she idolised Welles, which was by no means the thing he most wanted; indeed, it was perhaps the thing he least wanted. The feeling of being looked to for everything, of being looked at to the exclusion of all else – in extreme close-up, so to speak – was displeasing to Welles. The inherent feeling of responsibility oppressed him and made him feel exposed; his shiftiness under that all-loving, all-needing gaze was immense. Educating Rita soon lost its charm for him; she was not an apt pupil, and he longed for the conversation of his intellectual equals.

It soon dawned on Welles that there was something beyond mere common insecurity in his wife's incessant demands for attention; he swiftly apprehended the degree to which she had been damaged by the two successive evil geniuses in her life, her sexually abusing father and her pimping first husband, to whom might be added, on a non-sexual level, the obsessive control exercised over her by Harry Cohn, who was still her unrelenting employer. She wanted above all to find a man whom she could trust; the one she chose was as far from the ideal in that regard as could be imagined. From the very beginning of their time together, her jealous suspiciousness of Welles was overwhelming, which inevitably impelled him to justify her suspicions; before long – particularly after she had become pregnant – he was vigorously playing the field, leaving her alone with the baby he thought would satisfy both her domestic and her loving impulses. In fact, Hayworth had two rivals for his attention: other women (sometimes lovers, like Judy Garland, but most often prostitutes); and his work, which now comprised writing a daily newspaper column, starting two new radio series in quick succession, pursuing a political career as a prominent supporter of the newly re-elected Roosevelt, editing *Free World* magazine, working under Dolivet for the organisation, planning theatre productions and, finally, acting in the one film a year he was prepared to make to earn some serious money.

In fact, Rita Hayworth was the principal bread-winner in the family, and had, early in their relationship, lent Welles some $30,000 to stabilise his finances. His sense of humiliation in having a wife who was not only immensely more famous than he was, but also richer, is not to be underestimated in explaining his compulsive absenteeism from her side. Interestingly, she shared his political views, broadly speaking, and was indeed a considerable asset to him in his capacity as Free World activist. When he organised a conference in early 1945, shortly after the birth of Rebecca, she was the guest of honour; there was great anxiety when she feared that she might not be able to attend, and it was clear that in that context, of the two of them, Welles was the more dispensable. But when they went to stay (as they frequently did) with the Dolivets at the Whitney mansion in upstate New York, she was expected to be quiet while the two men discussed the higher questions of strategy and philosophy; Hayworth and Dolivet's wife, the brilliant actress – and no mean intellect – Beatrice Straight, were encouraged to repair to the verandah and take afternoon tea together, which they did, uncomfortably. It was understood that Welles was being groomed for political office: Dolivet had plans for him as a possible secretary-general of the soon-to-be constituted United Nations Organisation, while Roosevelt – in whose court he had become, he said to Kathleen Tynan, 'a kind of licensed jester' – encouraged him to think that he might one day be President.

In so far as this meant that he would be leaving Hollywood (and taking her with him), Rita Hayworth was all for it; her loathing of the studios and everything that they represented was even greater than Welles's, and perhaps with better reason. Somewhat to her surprise and entirely to her displeasure, at the beginning of 1945 he decided to act opposite Claudette Colbert in the film *Tomorrow Is Forever*. It was a second stab, after *Jane Eyre*, at conventional Hollywood stardom. The film's producer, Bill Goetz (who had produced *Jane Eyre*) announced that casting Welles in it was one of the most important casting assignments in the history of his company, which may have been so, but his excitement was not widely duplicated beyond the company. It is one of many wartime films that deals with the loss of loved ones: the somewhat strained plot here has Welles being disfigured in action, having reconstructive surgery and returning to his wife under a pseudonym and with a foreign accent some twenty years later. It is a performance like none other in Welles's career as an actor, interestingly pitched (once the somehow awkward opening sequence with him as the young American is over): very softly, very quietly, the impeccable German accent used to striking effect, and with an undertow of real feeling, as if Welles was moved by what was happening inside him. The make-up (by Maurice Seidermann, whom Welles had discovered sweeping up the floor at RKO and had promoted to chief make-up artist on *Citizen Kane*) is curious: it is quite obviously artificial, as so often with Welles, although for once he uses his own nose, which sits a little strangely with the bearded face, creating an uncommon feeling of vulnerability.

The performance itself – as distinct from the make-up – is as close to a full transformation as Welles ever comes on film, restrained and sensitive. It is his misfortune that his co-star gives one of her very finest performances, living wholly in the minute, going with pinpoint precision from emotion to emotion, from the early dreaminess of her anticipation of her young husband's return from war, through numb grief, to growing happiness in her new family, anxiety about her son's desire to enlist and intuitive disturbance at the bearded stranger's arrival. By comparison, Welles is somehow static – nothing moves within his conception of the character;

statement of character follows statement of character: intelligent, varied, feeling, sensitive, but without any of the involuntary surges of impulse to which the camera so eagerly responds. Welles is always *doing* the performance; it's never simply happening, never out of his control, and his great climactic emotional moment, when he is called upon to speak the title line, is simply stagy. It is a very different kind of theatrical performance, to be sure, from those he gives in *Kane*, *Jane Eyre* and *Journey into Fear*, but it remains essentially projected: the camera (and hence the audience) is never allowed to be make its own discoveries; it is always told what to feel, what to think. After *Tomorrow Is Forever*, Welles's status as a film actor remained what it was before: he was thought of as a formidable presence who always seemed somehow too big for whatever film he chose to appear in.

For Rita Hayworth, the period of shooting was a sort of nightmare. Convinced (quite rightly) that Welles was seizing the opportunity when he wasn't actually on the set to have assignations with young women, she would appear at the studio in a frenzy of jealous rage; but he was well protected by his colleagues, and she would disappear again in an anguish of frustration and humiliation. Meanwhile, and throughout the period of filming, Welles was writing his column for Ted Thackrey's *New York Post*. It was Thackrey's idea: he told Welles's manager Jackson Leighter that they were 'as excited as hell' about it, and were looking forward eagerly to the first of them. Tempting fate, Welles called the column 'The Orson Welles Almanac', preserving the pot-pourri character of the failed radio show as well as its strained conceit of guyed fortune-telling in the manner of *Old Moore's Almanac* or the *Farmers Almanac*. He was desperate to succeed in this latest incarnation, not only from financial motives – and if the column was successfully syndicated, he stood to make a very great deal of money – or even because he saw it as another platform for his political causes, but because he genuinely wanted to do it well. He was as touchingly eager to make a go of it as he had been to be a radio comedian. In a sort of trailer for the column, he had filled in again for his old chum Leonard Lyons, the *Post*'s much-loved regular showbiz columnist. 'What is it that makes a man want to write for the newspapers?' he asks, confessing to his early pulp writing again, name-dropping furiously – Thornton Wilder and Alexander Woollcott (he calls him Alec) begged him to stop, he says. He repeats the tale of his 'Inklings' column in *Highland Park News* and his Dublin escapades. 'All too often my public appearances have had more to thank presumption than equipment, so don't ask me why I think I can write a column.' In fact, his public appearances had more to do with equipment than with preparation. 'Compare me, if you will,' he ended, with one of those after-dinner-speech flourishes to which he sometimes succumbed, 'to my foolish and finny cousin the salmon, who toils and labours upstream against the most fearful odds, only to lay his little eggs.'

He started jauntily and with great industriousness, which is just as well: six columns a week is a very serious undertaking. Declaring himself as nervous as a kitten, Welles promised Thackrey two solid weeks of columns in advance, asking for twenty-four more hours 'to fuss'. Thackrey was delighted with what he read: ALMANAC VERY LUSTY FROM BIRTH, he cabled. SURE TO HAVE LONG USEFUL HAPPY EXISTENCE WITH NO ARTIFICIAL RESPIRATION NECESSARY. Financial indicators from the syndicate were encouraging, promising a return of at least $15,000–20,000 a year, though Thackrey believed that the minimum would be $40,000 'up to eighty' – a huge sum for 1945. Welles retained his researcher Geneva Cranston from the radio *Almanac*; working from Washington, she supplied him with regular analytical reports and insider gossip – 'It looks as if the administration is going to have another hot potato on its hands very shortly, possibly within the next few days. I refer to the proposed senate investigation into violations of the mails by the Office of Censorship' – which would form the substance of the political element of the columns, in which anniversaries, astrology, hard-hitting political analysis and Little Known Facts ('The onion and the asparagus are members of the lily family') jostled for the reader's attention.

The very first column, at the end of January, was particularly well stuffed. It started: 'Our Astrology department says that this is a good day for all born under all signs, and for planting all things that grow above the ground'; then Welles told his readers that Byron was born on this day, as was D. W. Griffith. He furnishes a quote from Woodrow Wilson about the purpose of war; then he launches into the main matter, an account of Roosevelt's fourth inauguration. 'The whole affair was as simple as anybody can remember. If you've been married more than twice, you like your wedding to be small and quiet. I think that's how the President felt about this inauguration. He played his part in the ritual like a veteran bridegroom. I was there and I got the impression that this fourth term was his favourite wife. The inauguration of a President really is a kind of a betrothal – with promises to love, honour and obey. I

always feel like crying at a wedding, and that's how I felt Saturday.'
Quoting Roosevelt's famous rallying cry, 'we have nothing to fear
but fear itself', he ends: 'I think the man who said that is man
enough for America's biggest job, which is the biggest job in history.'
The tone is overtly political and treats his readers as if they are
grown-ups with political opinions of their own. The big success
of the column, of course, is his eye-witness account of the inauguration, which he wrote, as it happens, three days before the event.

In fact, this column is unlike almost all its successors, which
suggests that Welles may have decided at the last moment to scrap
what he had written and go for a big story. This is a little dangerous,
since it is crucial in a column to establish a voice and a format that
becomes habit-forming for the reader. The second column ('the
Feast of St Ildephonsus and a good day for fishing') is indeed much
more heterogeneous, though not lacking in political content,
including a rather dry account of world reaction to the Dumbarton
Oaks Conference, another news item about France's frustration with
Big Three diplomacy, a scoop about the Teheran Conference and
a report, under the heading JAPANESE INVENTIONS DEPARTMENT,
that they have invented a chemical antidote to B-29s. Welles signs
off: 'The sting of a bee does not make a muskmelon sweet.' It is
an awkward mixture of elements; the tone seems misjudged.

Before he really had time to get into his stride as a commentator, the rest of the press was already providing its own commentary
on him. No matter how brilliant the column might have been, he
was not going to be allowed to get away with it: journalists are
understandably unenthusiastic about amateurs muscling in on their
patch. Under the heading ACTOR TURNS COLUMNIST, *Time*
magazine reported that 'Orson Welles, 29, precocious Master of a
number of trades – and jack of several more – apprenticed himself
to a new one: newspaper columning.' Readers, the piece amiably
continues, got: '1) excerpts from Welles's favourite reading, the
Farmers Almanac; 2) handy hints about cooking; 3) cocksure remarks
about foreign affairs; 4) personal chitchat'. Then the writer swiftly
and proficiently goes for the jugular, casually revealing that Welles's
account of Roosevelt's inauguration had been pure invention. Poor
Welles, always being caught out! The *Time* writer expresses further
scepticism about Welles's 'cocksure remarks about foreign affairs',
specifically his pretence of insider knowledge of events at Teheran.
However, Welles was not to be daunted. In the same article, he is
quoted as dismissing such quibbles, staunchly informing the *Time*
reporter that 'right now I'm much more interested in politics and

foreign affairs than I am in the theatre. I have set up my life in such a way that I can spend more than occasional time on these interests.' Statements of that sort always enrage journalists.

He offered an even greater hostage to fortune to the *New Yorker*: 'The column is so important,' he said, 'that I plan to devote all my time to it as soon as I can. I've given up all my Hollywood work except to act in one picture each year.' He had already vexed the journalistic community with his anti-fascist lecture tour, which started in New York. 'Until the other day,' the magazine reported under the headline DEDICATED WUNDERKIND, 'we regarded Orson Welles as simply an actor, producer, writer, costumer, magician, Shakespearean editor, and leading prodigy of our generation, and then out of our mail fluttered an announcement that he was . . . delivering an oration called *The Nature of the Enemy* at the City Centre.' The writer quoted the publicity leaflet verbatim and without comment: 'Mr Welles's understanding of international happenings,' the leaflet stated, 'has been widely acknowledged. Not only has he the ability of analysis, but of prophecy, and he also has the master's art of making his statements felt by everybody.' His gift for prophecy had obviously been invaluable in his account of the presidential inauguration. The anonymous *New Yorker* journalist cornered Welles during a publicity-shot session to promote his lecture tour, and found him looking 'the same as the last time we saw him – moon-faced, girthy, bland and authoritative', noting 'a considerable resemblance to the Boy Orator of the Platte'. Welles was still on the defensive. 'Naturally,' he says, 'a lot of people are going to ask, "What's a ham actor think he's doing as an expert on international affairs?"' His participation in public affairs, he argues, will prove that 'international matters are not as mysterious as Rosicrucianism or something. We've got to outgrow our Toy Tinker stage of anti-fascism and use a sophisticated approach.' Welles is so intense about fighting fascism, the *New Yorker* snidely continues, 'that he's not only going to orate against it but also will give it hell in the newspaper column he's launching this week in the *Post*.' Welles is swift with his riposte: 'The editor of this *Almanac* has been concerning himself with matters of state and the hope of a permanent peace for just about as long as the editors of the *New Yorker*. Indeed, he already has a big scrapbook full of indignant newsprint demanding his immediate return to the seclusion of the playhouse.' He claims misreporting. 'By inventing a queer string of surrealist sentences and attributing them to him, this current issue manages to imply that his hatred of fascism is nothing but a rather silly fad. The *New Yorker* ought to be ashamed of itself. It knows as well as you do that anti-fascism is never silly, even when a movie director or a comic newspaper work in its behalf.' A very understandable reaction, but his reply was not, perhaps, the best move; inevitably he ended up sounding pompous.

In his columns Welles was absolutely consistent in his themes as he strove to find the column's voice, hitting on a curious persona, a blend of sophisticated insider and People's Tribune: the Shadow on a Popular Front ticket. Urging faith in the forthcoming Big Three meeting at Yalta, he writes, 'I visited our State Department the other day – that former citadel of cynicism – and they told me that hopes were high'; he finds the same, he says, in his visits to the British and Soviet embassies, implying casual familiarity. He confirms his allegiance to Henry Wallace, now, of course, out of government; Welles was unmistakably flagging him up as a possible successor to Roosevelt, when the time should come. He appeals to Wallace's constituency, imagining it to be identical with the readership of the paper. 'In the Post Office on Pennsylvania Avenue you'll hear the people's voice speaking out from frayed scraps of paper, from simple neat sheets of stationery, from penny post cards. The little grocery man, the fellow who runs the hardware store, the farmer who's getting ready to start ploughing – he has no time to call Washington, he can't afford a telegram, but he's for Henry Wallace.' Welles cannot write exclusively for the customers of the Post Office on Pennsylvania Avenue for long. He is too restless. He cannot be confined. The key to a successful column is the reader's identification of the columnist: he or she comes to recognise the writer, to know his views, his style, the area of life about which he writes. They do not need to agree with his opinions, simply to know what they are. But who is Orson Welles the columnist? For whom is he writing? He seems to be everywhere, and to know everyone: one day he reports from a conference in Mexico, which he is attending on behalf of *Free World*. He finds Henry Wallace, his temporarily eclipsed hero, there: 'This war is not all destruction, it is also hope – faith in the destiny of the common man. Henry Wallace's political body lies mouldering for the moment in the grave, but his statesmanship goes marching on.' Welles's passion for pan-Americanism naturally finds rich matter in the activities of the conference, which brings out his hemispheric omniscience. He appears to have first-hand information about everyone present, and even some who are absent. Writing of the overthrow of Colonel Jorge Ubico, the Guatemalan dictator, he says, 'we still make jokes about those revolutions down in Central America. We used to be right because they used to be funny, or at least, futile. What happened down in Guatemala wasn't a bit funny. Almost nobody except the Reader's Digest ever had a good word for Ubico, who was one of the worst despots of our time. What's worse, he was clever. It wasn't easy to get rid of him.' He seems to have everyone's ear: 'one of the most exuberant of Guatemala's young officials – speaking in a tone of the most genial sincerity – said this to me: "The Leader of our government is a fine man. We love him but we keep a gun at his head. If he betrays our revolution we will shoot him."'

This is good, vivid foreign-correspondent writing of a school that even in Welles's day was vanishing, and might have come out of a novel by Ambler or Greene; it seems not quite to belong in a column like the 'Almanac'. In the same vein, writing of the death of the Mexican General Maximo Avila Camacho, Welles says:

> The general was the finest example of his kind I've known. Wonderfully generous to his friends I know he was, and I've heard wonderfully dangerous to beautiful ladies and to his enemies. He had authentic glamour, and he muted the gaudiness of his position with a certain sleek elegance. The fans adored him. It's too bad he had to die, said my fellow turista, and just then a turista came up to read the news board. The general is dead, I said to him. Gracias a dios, said the Mexican. I climbed in a cab to go back to the hotel. The driver was weeping.

This is quintessential Welles, and could have gone straight into a narration from one of his own films – one in which he would, of course, have played the general himself. Welles's love of the colourful detail, of the panache of bravura personality, sits interestingly with his espousal of homespun American values. Reporting on Ezequiel Padilla's speech at the conference, he says, star-struck, 'Mexico's Foreign Minister fought in the revolution. He rode beside Pancho Villa wearing a natty black suit. And a stiff white collar.' But he constantly and diligently reverts to the issues. Regardless of prejudice or personalities, Welles says, this conference is getting down to brass tacks. He solemnly reads his notes on Padilla's speech to a fellow-conference member who missed it. 'This war is above all a social revolution, the greatest in history.' It is an extraordinary and improbable vision: Welles sitting at his desk, notepad in hand, like a good student in class. It is yet another Welles, an entirely authentic one: a natural radical, but drawn to power like a moth to the flame, and willing to earn his place in its orbit.

This must have been heady stuff for the readers of the *New York Post*, drawn to the column, perhaps, by having heard Welles on the *Jack Benny Show*, or having seen him in *Jane Eyre*. To find him hobnobbing with the revolutionary cadres of Latin America must have been quite a surprise. Just when they were getting used to that Welles, readers were introduced to another – Welles the would-be revolutionary artist. In the column he writes passionately but precisely about the Mexican painters David Siqueiros, Diego Rivera and José Clemente Orozco, drawings by the last-named having just been seized and destroyed by US Customs. He laments the descent into banality of Rivera and Orozco, coming out in favour of Siqueiros as a true artist of the revolution. 'Bursting up out of the bloody crust of the earth complete with ball and chain,' he says of the mural entitled *Democracy*, 'even the torch of liberty and the clenched fist of Communism salute. Its lack of sophistication would have been vulgar and even silly if it were not great painting. And it is.' He compares this piece by the committed communist with the trivialisations of his politically neutral fellow-artists: 'It would be easy to denounce Siqueiros as the blind servant of the party line, but he is doing the most adventurous and independent work in the world of art. As for his unshackled comrades, Rivera is decorating night clubs, and Orozco is depicting democracy as a rattled and bedizened whore.' Everywhere in this piece is Welles's longing for real revolutionary art, art that matters, that expresses something more important than mere personal relations, mere personality: the sort of work he had touched on so briefly and so frustratingly in the *jangadeiros* section of *It's All True*. There is too the sense that this antinomian, this born foe of authority, longs to have some parameters, to be contained, especially by strongly held convictions.

The political arena is clearly the one that he wants to inhabit in the column, but from time to time he comments on the world of theatre and film, name-dropping genially. John Barrymore is a frequent guest star, so to speak, a sort of recurring character: 'we loved the man this side idolatry . . . we knew Jack since we were five. He was our foster uncle and our foster brother and our foster child.' The great actor, it appears, had the curious and rather suggestive notion that if Hamlet had stayed in England ('and avoided ghosts and graveyards') he would have lived to be old and fat and become Falstaff. 'The good life is about to be the death of him.

He's ruined himself, and it's been fun. Hamlet or Mad Jack – Falstaff or Barrymore (call him what you will) only regretted his sins because there weren't more of them . . . Barrymore, who was the last Hamlet of our theatre, lived to be a lean lascivious Falstaff.' A few days later, he describes how Barrymore hit true genius at the dress rehearsal of his first *Hamlet*, but this particular column seems to tell us more about Welles than about its ostensible subject:

> the rest of his life was anti-climax. There wasn't anything left
> to do except go on imitating, as accurately as possible, that one
> great evening . . . the truth is that after that dress rehearsal,
> Jack began to fear that he couldn't do anything else as good
> again. I think he was afraid to find out for certain, so he set
> about destroying himself, as publicly and as entertainingly as
> possible . . . he used to tell me that he hated theatre. But he
> couldn't kid either one of us. We spent hundreds of hours
> together, planning the production of a dozen plays. And I
> began to guess that what he hated was the responsibility of his
> own genius. Jack wanted to keep it a secret from both of us.

(Barrymore held a kind of emblematic significance for Welles, as a sort of alter ego, a spiritual *Doppelgänger*, and he always writes very touchingly about him. It has soberly to be noted, however, that there is no evidence whatsoever for the level of intimacy that Welles suggests existed between them; no biography of Barrymore – and there have been many – even mentions Welles.)

In another column, Welles casually observes: 'Chaliapin used to hold me on his knee when I was very little.' In Kenosha, Wisconsin? 'He made such an impression that I finally confused him with God and directed all my prayers at him . . .' (From time to time in later life, Welles would claim that Chaliapin was his real father. Or it might be Edward VII.) Then there is more general comment on the entertainment business. One striking column is devoted to an attack on the monopolising tendencies of the studios as they move in on the nascent medium of television: 'The me-only boys are trying to sew up television and they will, too, unless we stop them. Receiving sets in New York are so adjusted that you can only get ten television broadcasting studios . . .' Television, he says, has long been considered potential competition to the movies. The big studios are now applying for licences; Warner Bros have bought a site for a television studio. Welles brings the subject a little closer to home. The studios had been prohibited by law from owning movie theatres.

'[Jack Warner] says he can't see why his company shouldn't be allowed to own the theatres that play his pictures. I say that sort of ownership is what makes independent productions so perilously close to the impossible.' Welles clearly now sees himself as separate from the studios. 'Jack claims that one of his theatres will play one of my pictures as quickly and cheerfully as it will give the time to one of his. I say that's spinach and I say the hell with it.' This six-foot-three David simply can't help aiming his pebbles at Goliath. And of course he was right; the studios were so constituted that there was never a chance for him to work the only way he knew how on film or in television. His confidence in the power of free speech is touching, though he undoubtedly knew that his crusade was doomed.

Nor was his combativeness confined to potential employers. On another occasion, he breaks a taboo on attacking the work of a colleague; the general view is that artists get enough distress from critics without adding to it themselves. Welles lines his sights up against the Shakespeare productions of Margaret Webster, the English-born doyenne of classical directors in America, particularly noted for her work with Welles's arch-enemy, Maurice Evans: 'Every season for quite some time now Margaret Webster has presented our theatre with at least one Shakespeare revival. None of these productions has been very original or remarkable in any way, but all of them have met with unqualified success. Indeed, I think Miss Webster has avoided bad notices too long for her own good. She's a director and so am I, so maybe I'm not the one to break her luck. I'm going to anyway. She's a lady but I'm no gentleman.' He describes her as a skilled and careful craftsman who has never presented anything to the public that is perfectly terrible. 'As a producer who has offered something perfectly terrible to the public even more frequently than he's been panned by the press, I regard that infallibility with envy.' He quietly savages her pleasant and widely acclaimed production of *The Tempest* ('intensely theatrical', according to the critic of the paper in which Welles was writing), offering instead his own view that the play 'should be something between a magic show and a ballet'. This again is a curious use of the column: the attack on Webster seems mean-spirited, as it always does when anyone attacks their own kind. (It is to be regretted en passant that Welles never directed or acted in *The Tempest*, which would have suited his gifts perfectly, with Shakespeare's great magician bang at the centre of the action.) Similarly, in praising William Castle's B-movie *When Strangers Marry*, he says, 'It isn't as slick as *Double Indemnity* or as glossy as *Laura*, but it's better acted and better directed . . . than either.' This was presumably Welles's attempt to be more showbizzy, but it was dangerous stuff, and likely to do him no good – not that that was ever a great concern of his.

Perhaps he had been told to stir things up. Looking round for targets, he next attacks a fellow-columnist, Westbrook Pegler, whom Frank Sinatra, having allegedly come from a meeting with union organisers, had punched on the nose. 'If it was his plan to celebrate the Roosevelt victory by punching Pegler, Frank did not confide it to us, although that notion is one that might have occurred to any one of 25 million people . . . I can't speak for his intentions regarding the man who has repeatedly defended lynching as an American institution, but I'm very sure that if Sinatra ever felt like hitting him, it wasn't merely because Mrs Roosevelt's husband was re-elected.' This interesting glimpse of Popular Front solidarity – at this early stage of his life Sinatra was very publicly associated with left-wing politics – also contains a note of violence that appears from time to time in Welles's public statements, an ugly tone that carries intimations of personal menace. Denouncing the painter Orozco's latest work, for instance, he says: 'The villainous customs official who destroyed the one of José Clemente's best years, might redeem himself now by smuggling an axe and a blow-torch into Mexico's Mecca for the international white trash. A few minutes of honest vandalism could undo a great wrong.'

Welles was absolutely fearless in taking the opposing view to that of the majority of his readers. Noting the anniversary of Emmeline Pankhurst's imprisonment, he even dares to suggest that being a law-abiding citizen might be a relative concept: 'Mrs Pankhurst and her lady friends broke the law as well as the windows, but the millions of women who now enjoy the vote are grateful for that little insurrection, and it would be difficult to show that the suffragettes displayed any subsequent criminal tendencies . . . I say hooray for Mrs Pankhurst.' This must have been particularly striking in a mildly Democratic but distinctly mainstream newspaper, and in a column that continued to offer its readers homely advice on how best to cook roast potatoes ('Rub bacon fat on before baking. For mashed potatoes add a small amount of baking powder'). Most startling, writing about Richard Wright's autobiography *Black Boy*, which had just appeared, Welles says that 'it should be sent in a plain wrapper to every living soul who ever claimed to "understand" the Negro . . . the Negro isn't somebody to be studied, he's somebody to be saved . . . most of those who "understand the Negro" will also tell you that you don't "understand conditions in the south". These citizens,' he goes on, 'should be tied down with banjo strings, gagged with bandannas, their eyes propped open with melon seeds, and made to read *Black Boy*, word for word.' The underlying sentiments are unexceptionable, but the strain of violence is disturbing, somehow in excess of his own experience of the iniquities he denounces. Some personal, irrational rage of Welles's own seems to have attached itself to the cause. In fact the column (as columns will) was revealing rather a lot about their author. The burden of filling the space day-to-day compels the writer to dip rather deeper than he may intend into the bran-tub of his own psyche. The *Orson Welles Almanac* provides an almost stream-of-consciousness account of his preoccupations, prejudices and passions – as well as, it may be added, an entirely fascinating and unexpectedly comprehensive account of the preoccupations, prejudices and passions of the time in which he was writing.

His colleagues and employers watched his evolving self-invention with anxiety. 'I know that Orson can do this job as he can do anything else he sets out to do,' a manager from the New York Post syndicate wrote, 'and we have to give him a sufficient period in which to find himself.' The questions 'Who Is Orson?' and 'What to Do with Him?' remained as pressing as ever. Even his researcher, Geneva Cranston, was on hand with advice: Welles, she says, should avoid giving the impression that he even contemplates competing with Leonard Lyons. Welles is 'the fantastic Mars genius who did such a wonderfully dynamic and intense job on the [Roosevelt re-election] campaign . . . being this phenomenally intelligent and versatile young chap he should have causes, give sharp views, get on a limb occasionally, cause controversy, making it imperative that everybody read him before going on to the cocktail party – in order to argue violently about his clearly stated position on things'. Cranston was responsible for a great deal of the material in the column, and its tone was largely set by her and others. 'People have heard Hitler mention plans to erect a Statue of Liberty as his number one post-war aim,' runs one of her submissions to him (not, in fact, used). 'But there's much more to it than choosing a site, Adolph. To begin with, France may not suggest helping you with your little project.' This is the characteristic tone of many of the 'Almanac' columns; it would be hard to say whether the writer was Welles or Cranston. The FBI was, of course, convinced that Welles's ghost-writers were communists: 'Ghost writer . . . is a member of the CP . . . *Almanac* is written by Communist who also wrote *This Is My Best*.' The fascination of the FBI with Welles's authorship of his own work, long before the critics started asking questions about it, is richly ironic.

In truth, things were not going well with the column. Jackson Leighter, Welles's manager, valiantly assured Ted Thackrey of the constantly improving response to the column, as Welles moved away from reporting and editorialising towards a more personal style. Then, in a little bit of a giveaway, he suggested that Thackrey might like to buy a small magazine for Welles along the lines of *I. F. Stone's Weekly* or – in England – Claud Cockburn's *The Week* – which of course would have been the perfect medium for his purposes, though financially rewarding neither for Welles nor for his proprietor; it would also have forfeited the mass audience that had always been Welles's target. The figures were inarguable, however: subscribers to the syndicate were cancelling left, right and centre. The vision of riches beyond the dreams of avarice vanished: from now on, Welles would earn only his $300 per week for writing the column, a derisory reward for the time and labour involved – time during which he could have been earning large sums in either radio or film. But the column mattered deeply to him. It was an article of faith that it was possible to reach the general public with progressive views that essentially, he believed, reflected their own values. He had simply not found the right approach: the medium, not the message, was at fault.

To whip up interest, he started to look for controversial subjects, and found one in an unexpected place: the numerous German-language newspapers that proliferated, particularly in Welles's own Mid-West. He found that they continued to take a broadly pro-Nazi line. The column he wrote about them provoked angry responses, as had his earlier assertion that the Founding Fathers of the United States had been torn between adopting German and English as the official language. He quoted the official Soviet newspaper, *Izvestia*: 'These German newspapers which live on the hospitality of the American people are being given active support by the reactionary trio of Hearst, Patterson and McCormick.' His contempt for the two newspaper proprietors was well established; Patterson was a right-wing columnist who had declared the newly instituted midnight curfew a curtailment of Americans' liberty. 'I guess I don't get around enough because I don't happen to know that kind of people,' writes Welles, disingenuously. 'If you're acquainted with somebody like that, please tell him that while he's pouting about being properly entertained after midnight, tell them . . .', and Welles lists the heroic and selfless activists of the war effort, children, blinded veterans and so on. It is a little surprising to find him claiming not to know anybody who demands to be entertained after midnight. Everything anyone knew about him might have suggested that he might have been exactly such a person himself. Sometimes he literally seems to forget who he is.

After three months the column itself underwent a change of identity, scrapping the tenuously maintained pretence of the 'Almanac' format, and becoming *Orson Welles Today*, a straightforward political commentary. The first column under the new name was a fairly opportunistic response to a brouhaha that Noël Coward had brought on himself with publication of his war journal *Middle East Diary*, in which he had singled out a young Brooklyn serviceman for showing outward signs of discomfort when all around were being bravely stoical. Welles was stung into action by reports that Coward had been visiting hospitals, introducing himself to the patients and leaving then with the regal words, 'All right – go ahead.' Welles bridled angrily at this, creating an imaginary GI called Brooklyn Joe:

> I've read most of Noël's book *Dear Middle East Diary* (or whatever it's called) and some of Joe's letters back home. Both want the whole damn mess finished up as soon as possible. But Joe wants to get back to Brooklyn and Noël wants to get back to 1928. There's another important difference. Joe's been spending a lot of time where it's muddy and unpleasant and Noël . . . well, Noël's done everything Noël could do in this war – everything except the easiest thing which was to be a little generous to some very gallant gentlemen who happened to be foreigners . . . but Noël is a small town boy, and there is no provincialism like that of the international set . . . between Joe and Noël looking at each other in the hospital is a difference greater than race or class, graver than any insult or injury, real or imagined. Joe and Noël belong in two different worlds, all right, but they also belong in different wars.

It's pretty nasty, a reflection of Welles's anti-imperialist views (which frequently surfaced in the columns in attacks on Churchill's Toryism), but a curiously cheap way of whipping up sentiment; for the most part, liberated from the obligation to be ingratiating, Welles pursued an increasingly hectoring manner in the column, often falling into the conventional rhetoric of the Left.

Perhaps this was not unconnected to developments in his own political life, which had now taken a more practical turn. Louis Dolivet had laboured long and hard to identify his Free World Association with the idea of a United Nations Organisation; at the end of April, the San Francisco Conference was convened to progress the work of the Dumbarton Oaks Conference and bring the Organisation into existence. *Free World* – and Welles in particular – insisted that the UNO was the world's only, and last, chance for a better world. 'Remember that there is no choice between Plan "A" and Plan "B",' he wrote in a column. 'There is only the choice between Security Organisation Number One . . . and World War Three.' In *Shaping Tomorrow's World* Dolivet had defined *Free World*'s position, acknowledging America's inevitable pre-eminence in the post-war world. Warning his readers of the dangers of world control or world domination through financial or economic means, he observes, 'there is no doubt that this leadership idea could degenerate later into imperialistic tendencies, or could be considered such by other nations'. Dolivet sharply states the difficulty with American liberalism: 'whenever one injustice is committed, the American liberals stand up as one man in defence of the victim. They have, by doing this, written glorious pages in the history of freedom. But once this particular fight is over, they disappear – nobody knows where. The man in the street who was moved and convinced by their arguments writes letter after letter. He offers to join, but nobody is there to reply. They are organising committees for the best causes in the world, but the committees disappear as rapidly as they come.' Dolivet organised a pre-conference forum in Washington, spread over several Sundays, with further sessions in Hollywood.

Welles, whom Dolivet had been diligently preparing for the event, was installed as 'Moderator of broadcasts and mass meetings'; he duly wrote to Roosevelt on behalf of *Free World* (on behalf, in fact, of the world, he said) to ask, a little fawningly, for a message for the forum: 'Personally it would make me most happy and I know of nothing that would make me more grateful than a direct message from the President to the people of the world.' Roosevelt, in response to this impassioned appeal, wrote back (with due approval from the State Department):

April will be a critical month in the history of human freedom. It will see the meeting in San Francisco of a great conference of the United Nations – the nations united in this war against tyranny and militarism. At that conference, the peoples of the world will decide, through their representatives, and in response to their will, whether or not the best hope for peace the world has ever had will be realised. Discussions by the people of this country, and by the peoples of the freedom-loving world, of the proposals which will be considered at San Francisco, are necessary, are indeed essential, if the purpose of the people to make peace and to keep peace is to be expressed in action.

This was exactly what Welles believed and what he wanted Roosevelt to say. The forum duly took place; the participants in the broadcasts he chaired included the US Secretary of State Edward Stettinius, the prominent Soviet apologist Ilya Ehrenburg, the British Deputy Prime Minister Clement Atlee, former Soviet ambassador Maxim Litvinov (his analysis of the German threat now amply verified), the war journalist William L. Shirer and the liberal columnist Sam Grafton. Blue Network claimed a listenership of 500 million. Welles's sense of being, if not centre of the stage of history, at the very least in the wings, was overpowering; he grew a beard as a mark of his seriousness, and maintained a relatively low-key presence, stage-managing the event rather than producing it. He was also editor of the daily newspaper published by Free World at the San Francisco United Nations Conference. 'This newsletter,' he wrote in the first edition, 'is particularly important because, unfortunately, the daily newspapers in San Francisco which will be the first contact every morning of the foreign delegates with American public opinion will be largely unfree, if not hostile, to the idea of true world co-operation . . . the San Francisco conference is without doubt the major political event of our time. All those who are not engaged in direct fighting or war work must give the fullest amount of their time to facilitate a successful conclusion of the United Nations.' It is the familiar voice of political activism; Welles deeply felt the importance of the Conference, with reason, poised as the world was between the possibility – the tenuous possibility – of a more hopeful future and a past in which global nightmare had been so narrowly averted. The war was not yet over, but the outcome was a fairly safe bet.

At the Conference, as he reported to the readers of *Orson Welles Today*, he had seen the footage of gas chambers and concentration camps, and struggled to give a calm account of it: 'The heaped-up dead in evidence. The burdened ovens. The ingenious machinery for the gift of pain. The eyeball blinking in the open grave . . . Patton and Bradley, their eyes choked full of this. Eisenhower, moving slowly, with immense dignity, through the long tableau. A huge black anger knocking with heavy blows on the commander's heart.' He cannot pretend to any objectivity about the Germans, 'the solid citizens. They are dressed like people. You recognise the costumes . . . these creatures are less alive than the dead they have been called to view and bury.' In the film, they are required to go and look at the evidence of the horrors that their fellow-countrymen have perpetrated:

> The Military Police are gentle with the *herrenvolk*. You realise that they need to be or they would strike them down, each with a single blow . . . one place of torture, you will learn, was camouflaged as a madhouse. Here the most grisly of all Grand Guignol conceits was realised: here the wardens were the lunatics. You watch the chief of these being interviewed in the newsreel. The subject is poison. He is very businesslike. Between phrases he touches his upper lip with a fat lizard's tongue. The frown is professional. He is the man of science called for expert consultation, only the poison gives him away. And his chin. It is wet with drool . . . the newsreels testify to the fact of quite another sort of death, quite another level of decay. This is a putrefaction of the soul, a perfect spiritual garbage. For some years now we have been calling it Fascism. The stench is unendurable.

Welles was a gifted reporter, as these and other despatches make clear, a better (or at any rate more compelling) reporter, perhaps, than he was an analyst. He saw the world around him, and he dramatised it. When he was unable to do so, his writing became conventional, his more politically tendentious reports from the Conference – on Japan, on unemployment – lacking the vividness of his personal reportage.

Then quite suddenly he was knocked sideways by an event that devastated him, both personally and politically. On 12 April 1945, during a short recuperative break in Warm Springs, Georgia, Franklin Roosevelt died of a massive cerebral haemorrhage. America – and indeed the world – was aware that the President was in poor health, though Welles had given a broadcast a few weeks earlier reporting him to have been in fine fettle: 'Mr Roosevelt isn't 29 years old, but he's tougher than I am.' The President's sudden demise so soon after re-election and his recent highly publicised participation in the Yalta Conference was nonetheless a considerable shock: military victory, of which he was widely felt to be the principal architect, was within sight; and those like Welles and his political allies who dreamed of a new dispensation once hostilities ended were terrified that Harry Truman, the conservative backwoodsman and political fixer with no discernible radical tendencies who now became President, would allow the golden chance to slip through his fingers, squandering Roosevelt's hard-won achievements. In the slogan of the time, the winning of the peace was every bit as important as the winning of the war, and Welles had the darkest suspicions of the forces of reaction within his own country and in the world at large. On a personal level, he had been profoundly impressed by his contact with the elegantly charismatic Roosevelt and flattered by the great man's playful suggestion that Welles himself should run for the highest office. When Kathleen Tynan asked him if he regretted not becoming President, Welles said, 'No, not for a moment. It's no fun. Roosevelt was the last one to have fun – but to do that, you'd have to be Roosevelt.' Welles responded to a kind of gallantry, a certain patrician insouciance in Roosevelt that fully activated, as few men did, his considerable capacity for hero-worship. He gave free rein to his feelings when, remarkably, he was called on by CBS to record an immediate response to the President's death.

His eulogy begins with an account of Moses bringing his people to the Promised Land. 'Today another servant of the Lord and of his people entered history. He's gone. We can't believe it but he's gone. The dark words throw their shadow on the human race; Franklin Roosevelt is dead. His, the Mosaic tragedy of looking upon a land to which he's led a hopeful people – even to its borders – and which he may not enter. The land is neither Canaan nor Utopia. It is called Democracy.' Using quotations from Roosevelt himself as headings for his subsequent paragraphs, Welles continues: 'Only a little while ago he wrote this to me: "April will be a critical month in the history of human freedom."' Welles recalls 'the tremendous labours of an American president, of a commander-in-chief, of the master architect for an abundant world'. The speech ends: 'Two days before he was elected for his last term of office, he asked me to read these words by the Apostle Paul: "My brethren, be strong in the Lord and in the power of his Might . . . take the helmet of salvation, and the sword of the spirit, which is the word of God."' Welles's address was simply phrased, simply delivered, dignified by biblical echoes and cadences, and it moved America.

He does not overstate his personal relationship with Roosevelt, but it is striking evidence of the unique position he occupied in American public life, despite his current lack of professional profile. Which other actor/director could possibly have discharged such a task? And who could have done it with such distinction? He may have been in the wilderness, but his presence there was highly conspicuous; when the occasion demanded it, as here, he was able and qualified to speak for America.

The following night, he was called on to pay more formal tribute: his speech on that occasion was both more considered and more overwrought. 'Something is on its way on a slow train from Georgia . . . tonight we do it reverence, this lifeless relic of our living history, this dear memento. Tomorrow these tears should celebrate the thing, the great and nameless thing which gives it meaning. This thing is the American truth which Franklin Roosevelt stood for – truth – you'll remember – held to be self-evident. We dare not lag behind, you and I – we must keep up with it – for it goes marching on. Franklin Roosevelt needs everything you have to give him but your tears.' With some audacity Welles managed a plug for his organisation. 'We must move on beyond mere death to that free world which was the hope and labour of his life. Something is on its way from Georgia to the Capitol, but Franklin Roosevelt never left your home.'

After this emotional climax, life, as Welles had said, went on. The Free World Forum continued, as did *Orson Welles Today*. But his radio career – ironically, in view of his recent universally regarded broadcast tributes to Roosevelt – almost immediately suffered a humiliating setback. His relationship with the medium of which he was acknowledged to be supreme master, and which was also his most dependable source of income, had rapidly declined since the unhappy experience of *The Orson Welles Almanac*. Early in 1945, he had recorded a series of eight programmes of political commentary under the sponsorship of Eversharp razors, but they had never been broadcast. He then embarked on a series called *This Is My Best*, sponsored by Cresta Blanca wines, a return to the format of his glory days, the Mercury Theatre on the Air and *The Campbell Playhouse*, though significantly, at thirty minutes, half the length of either of those programmes. As before, they consisted of literary adaptations, with a couple of original scripts thrown in: the classics were *The Master of Ballantrae* and *The Diamond as Big as the Ritz*; there were two new pieces of no great account and a very mild satire on Hollywood bureaucracy and, finally, Walt Disney's

Snow White. In fact, none of it was of any great account, not even the opening show, *The Heart of Darkness*, which had had such a key place in Welles's development, and of which he had already made a striking version. He incorporated various elements of his unfilmed screenplay into the new version, but in radiophonic form they are somewhat limp, Welles's own performances as both Marlow and Kurtz (a double that would have featured in the film as well) were sleepy.

The impression throughout the programmes is that Welles was essentially uninterested in making them – not least, no doubt, because he was not officially their director. There had been difficulties during the planning stages: Wayne Tiss from the advertising agency wrote to Jackson Leighter that there had been constant tension between Don Clark, the nominal director, and Welles, culminating in a flare-up. 'I am going to ask that you be as co-operative with Don Clark as you can,' wrote Tiss lamely ('never otherwise,' Welles had scrawled in the margin, 'even when Clark was *very* drunk'), proposing the very awkward (and clearly inaccurate) billing '*This Is My Best* produced in co-operation with Orson Welles'; cooperation was the one thing not on offer. Welles had tried to change the format agreed with the client and failed, not perhaps the best state of mind in which to embark on a series. The end came swiftly and without ceremony. Welles wrote to a friend at the advertising agency lamenting that he had been sacked from *This Is My Best* – which was '*my best* in every sense of the word' (an egregious piece of self-delusion). He claims that there had never been an ugly word, and yet now he's fired. 'When an office boy is fired, he gets a note about it. I have yet to receive any sort of note. When a stenographer is let go, she's called in by regular custom, and given some sort of explanation. I've been given no explanation, and after calling repeatedly to ask for one, at least by phone, Wayne Tiss told my agent to request me not to ring him any more, because he wouldn't be at home to me.' Welles describes the incident that precipitated the sacking: after reading through *Don't Catch Me*, a version of the novel by Richard Powell to which he had the screen rights and of which he had already co-authored a screenplay, he realised that it wouldn't work, arguing with 'X' who was drunk (presumably Don Clark) that they should substitute Ferenc Molnár's *The Guardsman*, with himself and Rita Hayworth. Rather surprisingly the client refused to accept this dream package, even though the agency agreed with Welles. 'Three hours later Bob Braun' – from Welles's agency William Morris –

'came on the set and told me I was fired.' He had tried to address rumours – since '*even my agent has been given no reason why I'm fired*' – on the question of music, of casting, and so on:

> You must understand that words have been put into my mouth I never spoke. Lies have been told. Somebody, for his own purposes – in the interests of his own career – has treated me very, very shabbily. There may be two sides to every argument – but there wasn't an argument – I was sentenced without trial. Speaking of trials, my lawyers assure me I'd win a suit if I brought it against your people, but I think you know that I'm not that kind of a person. I think you know, too, what this affair has cost me in the radio business. The cost to my own feelings is the most painful part of it all.

The incident was humiliating. How could the noble orator who had moved the nation to tears at the time of Roosevelt's death only weeks earlier be thus summarily executed, dismissed from a rather unremarkable series and reduced to nearly incoherent pleading with the agency? Clearly there is more to the story than Welles repeats; but equally clearly the company had had enough of him and felt it was simplest to release him. The supreme master was easily dispensable.

The *New York Post* was kinder and more patient with him, but here too Welles was perceived as a problem, and the terms in which the problem was posed pierced him to the core. Robert Hall from the *New York Post* syndicates division wrote to him pointing out the relative failure of the column with the general reader, even after revamping it as *Orson Welles Today*. 'Editors did not expect that your column would be regularly on politics and international affairs, for frankly in the public consciousness you are not known as a political writer. The average reader knows Orson Welles as one of the leading actors and producers of this century. Why don't we, as a new lead, attempt to capitalise on this? If you gave us more Orson Welles reporting of contacts in Hollywood, radio, theatre etc. – with an occasional political piece – I believe we could go to town.' It is extraordinary that the paper had allowed him his head to such a degree on political matters; but the alternative notion that Welles might like to provide an insider's gossip column was humiliating and repugnant to him. 'Frankly I haven't recovered from the shock of your letter,' Welles replied to Hall. 'I haven't found it easy to adjust to the fact that the column is a flop. Strangely,

I hadn't suspected it.' He offers to give up the column. 'Under any circumstances the column costs me many times as much money as you pay me for it. I've thrown over really big financial opportunities in order to serve it loyally and with my best efforts. It takes a huge daily toll, it calls for enthusiasm and love and energy, all of which (no matter how disappointing you find the results) it's had from me in full measure. Since your letter, those necessary qualities have been very hard to come by.' He is shaken by the lack of confidence in him that Hall expresses: 'it was generally believed when we commenced this undertaking that if it failed, it would be because I lost interest in the job. An assumption very flattering to me, as it turns out, since I've lost no interest, only readers. From here on in, getting that piece off is the toughest, most thankless day's work I've ever been faced with.' Above all, he resents the insult to his readers. 'You say that you want me to write about political matters no more than once a week, and to spend the rest of my wordage on Hollywood and personalities. Of course this would build an audience, but Bob, it wouldn't be the audience I want to address. There is a serious public. I believe that time could teach that public to take me seriously. You don't agree. – Where do we go from here?'

Halls's proposition was impossible. Welles doesn't point out the obvious contradiction: an insider who attempts to write a column about his colleagues very swiftly becomes an outsider, shunned by those colleagues and therefore bereft of stories. Moreover, Welles didn't care to move in those sort of Hollywood circles. His interests at this stage were divided between the political and the sexual: he spent his time on *Free World*, at the pan-American conferences and in the house of the producer Sam Spiegel, where there was always a ready supply of call-girls of every shape, size and hue. Otherwise, you might find him in a jazz club or at a magic show. But he was not to be found in the habitual purlieus of the movie community; to all intents and purposes, though he continued to live in Los Angeles, he was scarcely part of Hollywood at all and had no gossip to report.

His columns had occasionally touched on artistic matters, as distinct from showbiz gossip: he reports an almost surreal occasion in Los Angeles when a young woman had leaped up and danced at the side of the stage when Toscanini and the NBC Symphony Orchestra played Mendelssohn's Overture to *A Midsummer Night's Dream*; elsewhere he writes about Eisenstein's *Ivan the Terrible*, just released in America – 'it's the darnedest thing you ever saw' – and ventures some rather searching observations on film in general. He imagines that critics and audiences in the English-speaking world – 'accustomed as they are to the pallid stylessness of the "realistic" school' – are likely to be impatient, even moved to giggles by the antics of Ivan and his friends. 'This is because the arts and artists of our theatre have been so busy for so long now teaching their public to reject anything larger than life unless it be stated in the specific language of glamour and charm.' He offers a very surprising analysis of what is wrong with the film: it is 'what goes sour with the work of any artist whose bent is for eloquence. Eisenstein's uninhibited preoccupation with pictorial effect sometimes leads him, as it has led others who work with the camera, into sterile exercises, empty demonstrations of the merely picturesque.' The striking similarities between Eisenstein's work and Welles's own, both in framings and in montage, had clearly not occurred to him. 'The Russians go out for the effect itself – and when they find what they're after – they manage moments of an exclamatory and resonant beauty on a level of eloquence to which our school cannot aspire. When the Russian method fails it is funny; it falls flat on its bottom and we laugh. When Hollywood fails, it falls flat, the result is merely dull and we yawn. The star in a Russian studio,' he continues, still apparently blissfully unaware of any concordance between his subject and himself, 'is the director. When his camera performs as a principal actor, we are offered great cinema. But when that camera dominates the action at the expense of the rest of the performers, it's as tiresome as any star hogging close-ups or taking pleasure in the sound of his own voice.' Because of inferior equipment, the Russian camera must assert itself by what it selects and the manner of selection. 'The Hollywood camera spends its time lovingly evaluating texture, the screen being filled as a window is dressed in a swank department store.' So often in the years to come, Welles was to be working with inferior equipment; his cinema became entirely one of selection. He makes another observation of some profundity: 'When the American movie-maker becomes aware of a discrepancy between his film and the appearance of life, he corrects the difference in favour of "realism". The search for the direct and the literal produces some of our best effects' – a path that Welles was rarely to follow.

In one of the columns, seeking to combine his political and show-business interests, he writes about Jack Benny's black side-kick, his butler Rochester, a much-loved feature of the radio show. Benny is on tour, doing public performances of the show in variety houses around the country. But he has not taken one of the show's most popular characters with him, for the simple reason that Rochester is black. Welles writes an open letter to his old chum Benny, urging him to take Rochester with him on the road and defy the racists. The column must have been cleared with Benny, with whom Welles had always been (and remained) on the very best of terms. But it is a superb peg on which to hang Welles's indictment of American attitudes on race; it is exceptionally vivid; he speaks in his own voice, always a good idea in a column. In fact, it feels as if it really might be a letter: direct and personal. From the *Post*'s point of view it was also about show business and roped in one of the most famous names in America. And it pleased Welles's bosses.

Replying to Welles's letter, Bob Hall of the *Post*, obviously shaken by Welles's genuine dismay at his proposal, assures him that he doesn't want a gossip column from him, but believes that Welles should use the fields 'in which you are a recognised authority', citing the column about Jack Benny as the perfect way to deal with a political point: 'through reference to situations and people with which you are thoroughly familiar and – what is more important from a columnar viewpoint – with which readers know you are thoroughly familiar. That gives you prestige from the first word you write, and it puts you in a columning position which few can touch.' It is not a bad point. Hall's letter was soon followed by one from Ted Thackrey stressing the importance of the column being personal, and not a mere mouthpiece for political positions. He takes it very seriously. 'Without question, the daily task of poking into one's own subconscious and dragging out the mass of inter-twined thought and emotion, and setting it forth for public gaze, is for most of us the most severe possible drain upon energy and psyche,' Thackrey writes. 'The material which pours from you instantly, apparently almost instinctively, will be likely to be truer, warmer and more convincing than anything gathered in your behalf by others.' He urges Welles to dismiss any organising and fact-collecting staff he might have, and inverts Welles's argument about not patronising his readers:

Only one sentence in your letter proved really disturbing to me . . . this was the suggestion that you prefer to write for the small, select, few 'serious' thinkers possessed of very special knowledge and by implication of some special kind of brains. If this were really so, you could not possibly think of a newspaper,

or any other general, means of communicating in a democracy as
your medium . . . if by any chance you do feel that there is a
gulf between you and the average man who walks the streets
which cannot be breached by common words, then, and only
then, I should urge you by all means to abandon writing.

The question of Welles's relationship to his audience – whether
readers, listeners or film-goers – is a central one in his career: his
lifelong belief that he had something to say to the broad mass of
mankind. The common touch was always to elude him, but by no
means for want of trying.

Also central to his life was the question of his relationship with
his fellow-workers. Thackrey touches astutely on that, too. 'When
you do resume your daily writing,' he ends his letter, 'I would
counsel only one constant, patience, patience, and above all, patience
with your fellow-craftsmen . . . whose opinions are, by the very
nature of things, certain to be representative and therefore a clue
to the unfinished business always ahead of us all.' He ends 'with
all our affection and confidence', which clearly he genuinely feels.
This remarkable letter – a lesson from an older man advising a
younger who is clearly overwrought and has misjudged the whole
situation, but who is not to be punished for it – must have been
a shocking one for Welles to receive. In the gentlest possible terms,
Thackrey is saying to Welles: if you're going to come and do our
job with us, then do it properly. It's not a game, a hobby, an indulgence; nor do you have any God-given right to do it: it's a job,
one you have to work at, like any other, despite your – as he says
elsewhere in the letter – 'unusual talents'. It has a certain family
resemblance to letters that Welles received from time to time from
his guardian Dadda Bernstein and his old headmaster, Skipper Hill.

Something in the now thirty-year-old Welles still inspired a
certain kind of paternal concern in older men, and by contrast
with his violently rejecting attitude towards authority figures, he
received the letter with a sort of gratitude. 'For three weeks,' he
replied to Thackrey, 'I've been trying to find some answers to your
letter – it was a very kind and wise letter.' He attempts to redefine
his position about his readers. 'All I meant was I wanted to write
a column for the people who read editorials; that I didn't care
about the fans . . . but the sum of my breast-beating letter was
simply this: you are unhappy with my work and I think it's the
best I can do. Therefore why not drop me quietly overboard? I still
think you ought to. Maybe,' he ponders, stating what to someone

else might have been an obvious truth, 'the only way to do a good column is to do nothing else.' But of course he can't afford to do that. 'Maybe if I spent half of five days on a single Saturday piece, the result would better deserve your confidence and your news space. I do so much value your friendship and Dolly's [Dorothy Schiff, Thackrey's wife, and owner of the *Post*], I so much wanted to do everything you believed I could do . . . maybe if I do quite well I'm not letting you down as much as if I continue poorly – please tell me how I can be fairest to you.' Here is yet another Welles, boyish and rather touching. A week later he wires Thackrey: HOW WAS LAST COLUMN? DID IT HAVE ENOUGH PERSONALITY? IS IT IN THE DIRECTION YOU HAVE INDICATED? MUCH LOVE. The column had indeed changed somewhat; Welles's own voice became clearer and more confident, without losing its political edge. He ranged further than he had: from time to time he managed a mention of Hollywood, though in far from gossipy vein.

One of the best of his *Post* columns, 'His Gorgeousness, the Bey of Beverly Hills', in which he invents a producer who sums up everything he despises, is a devastatingly frank attack on the system Welles so hated and to which he was nonetheless still somehow indivisibly attached. 'The sleep of the great man is guarded by private police, he has worn only a small percentage of his shirts, his race horses are happier than his lady friends and almost as numerous. Yet he is a man of simple tastes. Look at his movies and you'll see what I mean.' One day a female tourist asks Gorgeous George, 'Why don't you make better movies? Why are they getting worse and worse instead of better and better?' He murmurs, 'Unions,' but she continues unstoppably, 'I think it's because you make too much money, or rather, because you don't lose enough to learn anything.' A fascinating complaint from Welles, who knew all about losing money for studios. 'Silence followed this, only broken by the tiny patter of dropping options all over the valley.' The female tourist resumes, 'I'm tired of your telling us that we have 12-year-old minds. America is now the strongest nation the world has ever known, and the movies are a greater power than the atomic bomb. If you deserve exclusive rights to this whole empire of ideas, why don't you prove it by growing up a little? The army is not supposed to be a place you join for artistic freedom, but your people have produced better pictures in uniform than you ever let them make on your lot.' Welles then advances an argument very familiar in the late twentieth century, but an outrageous one for 1945: 'Every other big business spends lots of income on research. You make your artists experiment on the job. If what they try doesn't work, you ground them. And they don't get to try much. The old stuff still sells, because there isn't anything else on the market. That's why I think you need a few more flops, even a little competition.' The right to fail, a phrase coined by George Devine at the Royal Court Theatre in London in the mid-nineteen-fifties, was an idea whose time had most certainly not yet come in Hollywood, 1945; would indeed never come to Hollywood in any period. In Welles's column, the tourist woman, disappointed, leaves. Gorgeous George, the Bey of Hollywood, changes the subject. 'I have it on the best authority,' he says, chillingly, 'that there never was in Europe during the occupation – what you'd call a real underground.' The piece is powerful, precise and of course quite suicidal – the last line above all.

Considered as journalism, however (especially by the criteria of Ted Thackrey and Bob Hall), it was exactly what was wanted: intelligent, trenchant criticism, on a subject on which Welles could easily be counted an expert; it was controversial, but not hectoring. Subsequent pieces, if not so directly personal, were similarly individual: a strong pro-union piece, rather clumsily dramatised, contained a charming (and accurate) description of Clifton's Cafeteria in downtown Los Angeles, which suggests a hitherto unsuspected power of observation in Welles, though his evocation of this working-class playground teeters dangerously on the brink of contempt: this is not precisely the popular culture that Welles wished to endorse:

> Clifton's. A marvellous place where birds sing over chronic organ music as homey and dreary as the complaint of a vacuum sweeper. There is a tame waterfall and free birthday cakes. The food is free, too, if you can't afford to pay, and you may take your tray into a place called Tropical Hut, where, the sign says, it rains every fifteen minutes. The customers are mostly farm folks, visiting or moved out to California with just enough for their old age. When they're finished eating they walk round under the neon trees and read the poetry and philosophical maxims, bronze samplers studding the bright plaster walls. The ladies are given leis of paper flowers to wear around their necks, and at five o'clock there is community singing. I don't imagine they expect much more from Heaven.

Prelapsarianism, so central to Welles's world-view if it concerns elderly vaudevillians or holiday hotels in Illinois villages, does not necessarily embrace other people's innocent delights.

In another column, he invents a supposedly anti-union Aunt Lou, disturbed by the rash of strikes that preceded the general peace. 'It's always "Labor trouble",' writes Welles, 'never "management trouble". Aunt Lou, the men and the women on the picket lines aren't deliberately conspiring against our personal comfort. Because they want a better livelihood doesn't mean at all that they're plotting the overthrow of prosperity . . . but keep your hat on, Aunt Lou. It's been worse before, and it's bound to get better.' But his primary concern is with foreign policy. Again and again he comes back to the question of America's power in the world; in an Open Letter to Jimmy Byrnes, now Secretary of State, whom he has consistently attacked, Welles attributes Russia's current anxieties to the failure of America and Britain to impose a tough peace on Germany, leading the Russians to believe that 'we're figuring on the possibility of going to war again – and not with Germany'. It is the first frost presaging the start of the Cold War, and Welles contemplates the loss of all the hopes of which he and his colleagues in the Popular Front had dreamed: 'From where I sit, Mr Secretary, it looks to me like Russia is wrong about a lot of things, but I do think – and most of my neighbours agree with me – that since we carry the biggest stick in the world, we could afford to speak a trifle softly. You don't have to shout, Mr Secretary, you can lower your voice for a minute. Our back isn't against the wall. We're big and strong and rich but we can afford to make a few more friends in the world if we want to influence people.'

There is chilling prescience in Welles's analysis of the situation: some months earlier, reporting from Bretton Woods, he had written: 'We are the world's greatest production plant and the largest creditor nation. Without sensible economic agreements between England and the US, Mr Luce's prediction of the American century will come true and God help us all. We'll make Germany's bid for world supremacy look like amateur night. And the inevitable retribution will be on a comparable scale.'

CHAPTER FOURTEEN

An Occasional Soapbox

IN ADDITION to the newspaper column, Welles had continued throughout 1945 to pursue his political interests, preparing for a new radio programme in which he was actively encouraged to address current affairs, making speeches across the country, and editing *Free World* magazine; for a while he was authorised correspondent for the Rio newspaper *Oglobo*. In fact, Welles was one of a number of contributing editors to *Free World* under the general supervision of Dolivet, and could be relied upon to run up a piece on pretty well any subject of current concern. A typical wire from Dolivet requesting an editorial reads: EITHER LATIN AMERICA OR PALESTINE WITH EMPHASIS BRITISH OR OTHER MANDATES NO LONGER CAN BE KEPT AS EXCLUSIVE PRIVILEGE OF RULING NATION; Welles chose Latin America. The cover of the Special Peace Issue of the magazine, devoted to fears about the bomb and other chemical means of warfare, carried the headline FROM MARTIAN BROADCAST TO ATOM BOMB and focused specifically on Welles's own history, recalling the *War of the Worlds* panic. 'Among the closing lines of Mr Welles's broadcast was this one: "We annihilated the world before your very ears." By now the gigantic hoax can become a terrible reality and the author is writing in deadly seriousness about the important decisions humanity has to make since the mastery of atomic energy.' Welles's piece itself ends with a curious rhetorical flourish, which might have worked as oratory, but whose grandiloquence seems rather overwrought on the page:

> The alternative to Chaos is grander than all dreams, and we are greater than our dreams. We, the living, are the ancestors of a people who will be, truly, men like Gods. We will not fail them. Among all creatures, the human has the marvellous bent for the art of survival. The universe is none too big for him. Man is no puny thing. He is greater than all his tools. He burned himself with the first fire, but there came a day when he built a forge

and he made a plow. Today man turns the key in the last padlock of power. Tomorrow he will be worthy of his freedom.

Elsewhere he takes a slightly more pugnacious tone. 'We know that for some ears even the word "action" has a revolutionary twang, and it won't surprise us if in some quarters we're accused of inciting them. *Free World* is very interested in riots. *Free World* is interested in avoiding them. We call for action against the cause of riots. Law is the best action, the most decisive.' His conclusion reverts to the cause that he espoused above all others throughout his career as a commentator, and indeed throughout his life, with truly admirable tenacity, lending his name and his authority to it whenever he could, often at considerable danger to himself. 'This is our proposition: that the sin of race hate be solemnly declared a crime.' He was something of a beacon to his fellow-liberals, and his presence on various progressive platforms was perpetually in demand. At the beginning of 1944, Will Rogers Jr had written to Welles asking him to be the narrator for *We Will Never Die*, a concert protesting against Nazi slaughter of the Jews, assuring him: YOUR APPEARANCE WILL MAKE PROFOUND IMPRESSION. In similar vein, though with a slightly different catchment area in mind, Ray Pierre of *Glamour* magazine asked Welles to write a piece on tolerance in society. 'We are in complete sympathy with everything you have been saying in your lectures and your column in the *New York Post* . . . we feel that your name as well as your point of view would strike home with our young women readers – a pretty wide audience that sadly needs your message.'

The piece that Welles wrote for Pierre, 'Mrs Wentworth,' is one of his most extended pieces of political journalism; read by him, in a voice of sweet reason, its impact would have been overwhelming, though it is powerful enough on the page. 'Mr Thomas Martin Wentworth is a popular member of his country club. Mrs Wentworth is perfectly charming, and so are the children. Dinner at the Wentworths if not exactly an event is a delightful way to spend an evening as you probably know. The wines are pleasant, the food excellent, the conversation sufficiently diverting to stave off bridge and home movies. But you must be careful what you say to Mrs Wentworth: she comes from the south . . .' Welles then reveals that she has a black half-brother. 'The difference in skin pigmentation will surely seem to the students of this era in centuries to come the quaintest of all possible reasons why a sister should expect her brother to step off the sidewalk and avert his eyes when she appears before him . . . our textbooks and our teachers are careful not to give "offence" to Mrs Wentworth. Our movies and our radios religiously avoid the very stuff which alone can save the Wentworth young . . .' The husband is tolerant:

> What in God's name does Mr Wentworth have to tolerate? The fact there are people different from himself alive in the world . . . no, in Mr Wentworth's little world, there isn't anybody to 'tolerate' except Mrs Wentworth. If she has read these words to this bitter end, I know she will be screaming now that I'm one of those Communist Yankee agitators who doesn't know 'conditions'. Dear Mrs Wentworth, I'm half a southerner and despite the fact that I *do* know 'conditions', I'm not even a quarter Communist. I believe our American system can work. But it won't until you, Mr Wentworth, and you, Mrs Wentworth, sit down and shut up long enough to let our educators teach your children how wrong their parents are.

The curious touch of menace, of a veiled threat, is characteristic. (His casual claim to be half-Southern is another charming piece of self-fabulism. There are so many halves to Welles that by this stage he must have added up to several people – a whole family, perhaps.) His anti-racism led him to become spokesman for the Citizens' Committee for the Defense of Mexican-American Youth, to combat anti-Mexican agitation stirred up in, among other places, the Hearst press, which had been instrumental in drawing attention to the celebrated Sleepy Lagoon incident in August 1942, when seventeen young Mexican-Americans had been arrested for murder. Two of the defendants were beaten up by the police; they and the others were convicted. Welles wrote a simple but eloquent preface to a pamphlet published by the otherwise unknown Mercury Printing Press; in October 1944, thanks in large part to Welles's agitation, the court overturned the convictions. He was, in this as in so many other areas of his life, apparently fearless; everything he did or wrote was duly recorded by the FBI, which was scandalised to note that Welles was going to make three short films for the Mercury Theatre, to be shown throughout the country in public schools, 'on the contribution of the Negroes to American music and letters'.

He pursued a heavy programme of public speaking. This was not a purely idealistic enterprise: his highly successful anti-fascist lecture tour at the beginning of the year had earned him 70 per cent of the gross over $300, so financial necessity and political progressiveness were not mutually exclusive. But welcome though the emolument undoubtedly had been, it was not the driving motive: he derived great personal satisfaction from addressing large numbers of people on what he rightly regarded as urgent themes, relishing the directness of communication and the chance to sway people's opinions; naturally he was powerfully thrilled by the contact with large crowds, sometimes as many as 5,000 strong. He was Charles Foster Kane, but on the right side. The impact he made was immense. The celebrated educationalist, Helen Keller, both deaf and blind, had written to Welles that her assistant 'had your speech put into Braille for me and I have read it over and over. It startles me with the thunder of a waking social conscience . . . your spirit of prophecy inspires working faith.' Welles had been introduced to her and displayed the courteousness that was habitual to him when dealing with older people. 'It is delightful to recall the knightly gallantry with which you guided me through the surging crowd at the stage entrance. And there was in me an emotion too deep for words as I sensed their huge love pressing round us and hands touching us lightly but eloquent in their dumbness.' She sensed in him a kindred spirit. 'There is nothing like the affection of a great crowd, and I know neither you nor I would change it for any earthly treasure – except their increased welfare and happiness.'

This continuing absorption in political life had at one point seemed a bond uniting Welles and Rita Hayworth (their Christmas Card for 1944 read 'To the Spanish Republicans and other anti-Fascist refugees, my wife and I send greetings. Will you join us? Just fill out the enclosed check and mail it to the joint anti-Fascist Refugee Committee immediately. Your donation will mean relief and rehabilitation for those first fighters against fascism. Thank you and the season's greetings to all of you. Signed Rita Hayworth and Orson Welles'). But now it only served to widen the rift between them, taking him away from her both emotionally and geographically. The FBI, which maintained a lively interest in Welles's sex life, reported that when he was in San Francisco for the United Nations Conference he spent 'considerable evenings engaged in extra-marital duties with [name deleted], former Main Street burlesque striptease artist, who recently promoted herself to a higher type of night club appearances in the city. Also sometime ago when Welles appeared in San Diego in connection with a bond tour, he took some girl other than his wife, to be with him there.' He absent-mindedly abandoned his elaborate considerateness for his wife. When her mother Volga Cansino, with whom Hayworth had such a dangerously complex and unresolved relationship, suddenly died, Welles failed to return to Los Angeles for the funeral. His indifference to his new daughter was absolute, and when Hayworth occasionally joined him in New York or Washington, she found him wholly absorbed in conferences with his advisors. To remind him of her existence, she would throw explosive tantrums, which had the desired effect in the short term – he would disappear into the bedroom to comfort her while his collaborators tiptoed embarrassedly away – but which in the only slightly longer term drove him further and further away from her.

The paradoxes of their unlikely relationship had started to manifest themselves very early: the more he embraced needy mankind, the less able he seemed to extend his concern to the individuals for whom he was personally responsible. Welles had been drawn to Hayworth because of her sexually iconic quality; conquering her had boosted his image and his ego. He had courted her by gently penetrating beyond the goddess and the star and by urging her to reveal her private hopes, disappointments and dreams. She was attracted to him because he was the first man who seemed willing to listen to her and treat her as something other than a sex-object. Having won her, Welles rapidly lost interest in the *Pygmalion* aspect of their relationship. Initially fascinated with the disparity between the potency of her image and her utter lack of inner confidence, between her public glamour and her private homeliness, he soon found the complexities of her character distinctly anaphrodisiac, her urgent demand for affirmation through sex the opposite of enticing. Welles wanted to pursue, not to be pursued – least of all by his own wife. She thus found herself married to possibly the only heterosexual man in the Western world who did not want to go to bed with her. Hayworth's former husband had encouraged her to advance her career – and thus their joint bank balance – by sleeping with other men as well as himself, a profoundly disturbing and damaging proposition; Welles's contribution to her battered psyche was that – having discovered, to his surprise, that she was at heart a housewife and a mother – he felt that providing her with a daughter had discharged his marital responsibilities. Being constitutionally incapable of doing anything that didn't interest him, he largely absented himself from the relationship, which of course compounded her already advanced feelings of abandonment. A further, and perhaps crucial, complication in their situation was that in business terms she was worth a great deal more than he was, and was infinitely more famous and popular. All the more reason to absent himself from her ambit, though he was not above borrowing large sums of money from her. As her cronies from the studios reported more and more of Welles's infidelities to her (including the semi-public liaison with Judy Garland, a surprising choice if it was complexity and emotional neediness that he was running away from), Hayworth began to drink heavily; often, inebriated, she would drive around the Hollywood Hills at reckless speeds, once with Welles (on one of his rare visits home) as her terrified passenger.

His real life was elsewhere, in the bars and clubs, on the stump or editorialising. The new radio programme, frankly entitled *Orson Welles's Commentary*, was his final attempt to find the radiophonic pulpit he had been seeking for some years now. Lear Radios, his new sponsor, had taken the precaution of having him record a sample programme, with which they were well pleased: '[an] expert blending of the humorous and the dramatic with abundance of human interest,' wrote William Lear, which gave promise of 'something that radio sadly needs, namely, a new type of entertainment. I don't know of anyone in the country better suited to supply such a need than you.' Clearly Lear and the agency had the highest hopes for the programme: they were paying Welles the startling sum of $1,200 a week, rising to $1,700, for his 'commentary on affairs of national interest, books, plays, films, and relative subjects and personalities involved therein'. The programme precisely fulfilled this brief, and was something quite new in Welles's use of the medium, his first solo broadcast, an exercise in minimalism alongside his ramshackle attempts at variety shows and his ambitious and sometimes radical literary dramatisations. This is radio pared down to its bare essentials, designed as a nearly abstract exercise in his exceptional ability (in Arthur Miller's words quoted earlier) 'to seem to climb into' the microphone.

The first show opens with great directness, but the sudden intimacy – instead of being engaging – is almost oppressive, a far cry from the infectious actor-managerial introductions to the Mercury Theatre on the Air riding on the adrenalin of Bernard Herrmann's souped-up version of the opening bars of the Tchaikovsky First Piano Concerto, or the bright and breezy welcomes to *The Orson Welles Almanac*. 'Hello,' he says, 'this is Orson Welles,' and it is as if he has phoned you personally. 'I've come to call, I've come to visit with you at this time for a few minutes and, with your permission, every week have a little conversation and talk about this and that. I'm going to speak my mind about the news. And, you know, we don't have to agree on everything to be friends. This is a free country after all. I'm no more of an expert than you are, I haven't got a stable of spies working for me in Washington or Hollywood, though I've got a whole lot of interesting friends and I meet a lot of people.' As a point of fact, he did, as it happens, have a network of informants in Washington (though not in Hollywood); Geneva Cranston and her associates had been hired again to keep Welles *au courant* with events. He defends the right of actors to have a voice of their own, adding that he personally broadcasts because 'a few people are doing a lot of harm to the things I believe in and love and want to serve. I don't believe I speak for a minority.' He speaks, of course, of a Free World. 'You may find me on an occasional soap-box but you may be sure that I'll be speaking in behalf of those notions drafted into our constitution and our Bill of Rights. I'll try to have a story for you each week, I'll tell you about a new film, and then I'll say something about the trouble in Korea.' The sponsor says 'a few interesting words'. The new film he plugs is Robert Siodmak's *The Strange Affair of Uncle Harry*, featuring Geraldine Fitzgerald whom he first met, he reveals, when they made their debut in the same theatre in Dublin. She may not have the starring role, he says, because 'the people who push the buttons and push people around in Hollywood may not have decided that she is a star yet, but she's a real actress'. The film is a mystery story, he tells us, a better one than the week's other mystery story: 'Frankly,' he asks, 'who cares whether Herr Schikelgruber is dead or alive?' He reports that he's off to see a bull-fight across the border, in Mexico, 'with Jo and Lenore Cotten and my wife'. There is much mention of Rita Hayworth, though their relationship, as we have seen, was by now in rapid free-fall. He speaks of bull-fighting uncomfortably and defensively, knowing that most of his fellow-Americans find it repugnant, admitting that he's tried it out in Mexico and Spain – 'pre-Franco, of course' – and recounting a long and unamusing story about a legendary bull-fighter of his acquaintance, who was locked out of his hotel room in downtown LA wearing only his towel.

One senses that all this is an obligatory prelude, a mere hors d'oeuvre to the political meat. The moment Welles reaches this section, his tone changes into one of rising emotionalism containing more than a hint of hysteria; we have already heard a touch of it in his references to Hitler and to Hollywood; indeed, it would be hard to say which of the two he regarded as posing the greater threat to mankind. Speaking of Korea, he analyses American policy lucidly enough, comparing it to its approach to Italy: 'suppressing Communism by suppressing Democracy'. This, he says, his voice beginning to strangle with outrage, is 'Simon-pure baloney. We are using Japan to protect Korea from the Koreans. We cannot fight Communism, we can only compete with it.' By now he is standing four-square on the soapbox that he prophesied at the beginning of the programme. America, he continues, 'is committed to moral as well as economic leadership. We are the bearers of man's brightest torch. This is a great moment, the greatest moment in history.' After this grand peroration, he signs off, hoping ingratiatingly that the audience will want to make hearing the programme a weekly arrangement, and ending with the time-honoured and always faintly improbable formula, 'I remain Obediently Yours, Orson Welles.'

The agency was surprisingly delighted with this rather curious show, as was Lear, who wrote to congratulate them on it, at the same time congratulating himself: 'I'll bet it is an interesting experience for Welles to have a sponsor who isn't messing with his show.' It must have been, but it didn't last long. By the third programme it was already thought advisable to preface the show with a disclaimer to the effect that 'Mr Welles brings his views and opinions which are not necessarily those of Lear Radios.' Welles was now broadcasting from his home in Brentwood, an unprecedented arrangement, and apologised in advance for possible irruptions from the cocker spaniel or the eight-month-old Rebecca. His tone is somewhat less intense and somewhat more unguarded than in the first programme: he tells his listeners that the London conference of prime ministers was 'a wash-out'; that 'the honeymoon is over for Truman'; and that the movement towards independence in India is too slow. Palestine, he says, is not accepting enough of the Jews of Europe, while the British are starving more than they did in the Blitz. In the story slot, he provides a long and reverent retelling of *Bonito the Bull* as a peace-offering to those of his listeners whose sensibilities were offended by his earlier mention of bull-fighting. The Flaherty story makes for a very sweet bedtime story, but the general tone of the show is even less clear than that of the launch programme. Welles now does something that he had never done before at the microphone: he dictates to the listener, instead of inviting him or her in. He does to the microphone, in fact, exactly what he later accused Laurence Olivier of doing to the camera: he tries to dominate it.

Something was clearly not working; from the beginning, listener

figures were poor. Welles's political analyses were those of his newspaper column (which was still running) and, in slightly simplified
form, of his editorials in *Free World*; they were clear and, with
hindsight, more often than not accurate. But whatever he might
like to think, they were not those of the majority, and the queru-
lousness that crept into his expression of them was an unconscious
acknowledgement of this. He sought in his tone to imitate a hoped-
for sense of outraged radicalism that was alien to most of his
listeners, who might perhaps have responded to a more calmly
reasoned discourse. The soapbox was not, as he had promised, occasional; it was his permanent base, and the snippets of movie reviews
and anecdotes of the famous were ill-concealed attempts to sugar
the pill of hard political lessons.

Even more problematic, the programmes were not engaging in
radio terms; they made uncomfortable listening. By November of
1945, two months into the series, William Lear was writing to
Welles that he and his colleagues were deeply distressed at the
ratings remaining so low 'despite the arrival of the good listening
season'. He was glad to note less political commentary and more
entertainment, but remained disappointed with the show by
comparison with 'the audition record'. He had, he said, been hoping
that 'somewhere along the line you would come up with a whop-
ping new idea – an unorthodox experiment perhaps – or a unique
story technique'. He begs Welles to 'strike a new and unusual radio
chord'. What he (and no one) fully grasped was that, in both radio
and newspaper journalism, Welles had ceased to be interested in
form and was concerned only with content. He felt the eternal
passion of the newly converted (whether religiously or politically)
that these matters were too important for subtleties of expression:
they were self-evident truths, which needed only to be clearly stated
to secure the conversion of the listener or reader. Lear and Thackrey
of the *Post* were still thinking of Welles as the Boy Wonder, and
were surprised and disappointed when he wasn't able to come up
with dazzling tricks. They required him to create special excitement; they did not expect or want him to be a political guru, but
nor did they expect him simply to be efficient, like everyone else.
His job was to startle, to amaze. '*Étonne-nous*, Orson!' was their
constant cry. They would not, in fact, let him grow up.

That it was perfectly possible to combine mature liberal views
with experimentation was proved by the work of Welles's great
contemporary, Norman Corwin, but in his own radio work Welles,
it seems, was now impatient with artistry: what he wanted were

facts and analysis, leading to action. He wanted politics, but he lacked the stamina for the democratic process: when Senator Hiram Warren Johnson died in August 1945, leaving a vacancy, Welles – who had been privately assured that he would be the next senatorial candidate from California – decided against running, promising that he would do nothing to oppose the Democratic candidate's senatorial ambition 'inasmuch as [he] felt that Carlson would be far the better candidate'. What Welles wanted was direct access to the people, whether through the press or on radio. He pursued the radiophonic path for nearly another year, rising to extraordinary heights of demagoguery, before finally admitting defeat. Meanwhile – mostly from sheer financial necessity – he picked up the pieces of the God-given career he seemed almost completely to have abandoned: that of actor-director.

Part Three

WELLESCHMERZ

CHAPTER FIFTEEN

The S. T. Ranger

DURING THE fifteen months of his absence from film, Welles had tried wherever possible to put his talents at the service of his ideals – recording, for example, a series of great democratic speeches for Decca. His attempt to record the Bible (the Mercury Bible, it would have been) never quite got off the ground. His proposal was scorned as both intellectually unstimulating – 'its attempt to tie in with present history was nothing more than the average minister does every day of the year' – and formally conventional: 'with Welles's great flair for the imaginative, and his undisputed originality . . . he might have done a more inspiring job'. What finally scuppered him was that the project needed the approval of the clergy, but 'reservations have been expressed about Orson's personal life'. He was damned both ways: too shocking in life, not shocking enough in art.

As for the stage, he was still in demand, particularly on what would now be known as the fringe, or off-Broadway: the Theatre Guild offered him the part of jealousy-maddened Leontes in *The Winter's Tale*, while James Light of Readers' Theatre suggested that he do *Tamburlaine the Great* for them, an inspired idea that would have provided a fine sequel to his *Dr Faustus*, a play in which his rhetorical gifts – indispensable in Marlowe, if of limited value in Shakespeare – would have found their perfect fulfilment; had they also wanted Welles to direct it, he would surely have done that particularly well, too. He was, both as artist and as man, perfectly Marlovian, a born over-reacher. Shakespeare was on offer, too. The designer Oliver Smith and his partner Paul Feigay, who had just produced the Bernstein-Robbins smash hit *On the Town*, were keen for Welles to direct and star in *King Lear*. He turned them all down, but his mind was clearly turning towards the stage again, nearly four years after his sensational production of *Native Son*. 'No matter how bad the Broadway stage gets,' he told the *New York Times*, with an implicit dig at Hollywood, 'it will always represent a great art form.' He wanted to write a book about the theatre, he said, but when a potential publisher asked for some advance material, none was forthcoming and negotiations petered out.

Meanwhile, Welles's unique position in the profession was being acknowledged from an illustrious and wholly unexpected quarter: the curator of film at the Museum of Modern Art, the formidable Iris Barry, had written to him to say that 'we should like to organise a one-man exhibition here on the work of a living American artist who has been active both in the theatre and in film . . . and we would like that one man to be yourself'. By that definition, he was indeed the ideal and – until the rise of Elia Kazan and the Method directors – perhaps the only serious candidate for such an accolade. But it is still worth remembering that Iris Barry's letter arrived just four days after his thirtieth birthday, on 6 May 1945; and that he had been inactive both in theatre and in film for some three years – as a director, at any rate, the capacity in which he was being fêted. He responded to the Museum's demand for material with swift excitement, immediately assembling and despatching a substantial batch. Then there was no more. A year later they were still asking him if he had anything else. The prospect of such concentrated exposure and analysis may have seemed rather daunting; perhaps it was best to leave the aura of retrospective glory unexamined. The sense of Welles's limitless but somewhat undefined promise persisted: the *Writer's Yearbook 1946*, at any rate, was confident of the future: 'He is a potential master and will make the greatest contribution to society.'

So far as film was concerned, Welles was scarcely Hollywood's forgotten man – his public profile had never been higher – but he seemed to make strenuous efforts actively to distance himself from it. In every interview, and in every medium at his disposal, he had fearlessly and even recklessly criticised it and its product, attacking both producers and directors, demanding a new dispensation. 'Pictures are in a bad way. They need revitalising,' he had written in a formal statement in the *New York Times*. 'They have no Toscaninis. We should have theatres financed by the Government for private film experimentation and a chain of adult theatres free from Hays Office Code censorship. Films dealing with serious and important subjects should be produced even if the big boys have to be taxed for them.' His proposals, eminently attractive though they might have been from a utopian perspective, were scarcely likely to find any direct practical response, at the same time alienating anyone who might be in a position to employ him; it often seemed to be more important to him to be right than to be employed. In fact, short of financing a movie himself (which, given his track record, was a rank impossibility), his only hope was to find an independent producer, a breed that did not exist in the Hollywood of the mid-forties (with the exception of Capra and Chaplin, both of whom produced only their own work). Korda would seem to have been an ideal partner, but since the demise of their plan to shoot *War and Peace*, their relationship had drifted somewhat. But then Welles fell in with a man – a bargain-basement version of Korda, in many ways – who was embarking on a career that would in the fullness of time result in his being first a pioneer and finally the prince of independent production. Sam Spiegel, like Korda, had been born in a *shtetl*. After various continental adventures, a brief sojourn in Hollywood and a spell in Palestine, he had served – somewhat to his own surprise – as head of Universal's European operation in Berlin until Hitler's assumption of power, at which point he moved to Vienna. In 1939 he returned to Hollywood, where he had earlier worked as a story translator in the nineteen-twenties. His first film as a producer, using the transparent alias of S. P. Eagle, had been the enjoyably European *Tales from Manhattan*.

Now, in 1945, he was developing a film with a rather elaborate provenance: based on a story by Victor Trivas, drawn from original material by Decla Dunning and Philip MacDonald, it had been written for the screen, under the title *Date with Destiny*, by Anthony Veiller and John Huston. Huston, like Welles, had regularly availed himself of the facilities of Spiegel's fun palace on Hollywood Boulevard, and had already collaborated with him on an unrealised version of the play *Russian Life*; as a serving officer at the front, he could neither direct *The Stranger* (as *Date with Destiny* had become) nor even accept a writing credit. Spiegel had already cast Welles in the central role of Charles Rankin and now – when Welles asked him point-blank – invited him to direct the film too, under certain very stringent conditions, the most critical of which was that the final cut rested with Spiegel. In fact, Welles was quite familiar with this condition; only on *Citizen Kane* had he had final cut. The financial deal was reasonable, even generous, in itself ($2,000 for each of the eight weeks of the shoot, plus $100,000), but it came with a requirement to indemnify any losses in case of failure to complete the film; in any dispute, Welles agreed to submit to the studio's will. Moreover, Spiegel also demanded a guarantee to that effect from Rita Hayworth, which she duly gave. These conditions were imposed by William Goetz and Leo Spitz, who created the Haig Corporation specifically to finance 70 per cent of the negative cost of the film. It is reasonable to assume that Bill Goetz, who had produced *Jane Eyre* and had regarded casting Welles in *Tomorrow Is Forever* as an enormous coup, was instrumental in his appointment as director, but neither he nor Spiegel was going to allow Welles the slightest opportunity for self-indulgence.

But Welles had no intention of indulging himself. In later life he dismissed *The Stranger* as his attempt to prove to Hollywood that he could make a mainstream film under budget and on time, which was no doubt true, but at first he was genuinely enthusiastic about the project. The subject matter had much to recommend it to him, from both a political and an emotional point of view. Rankin, the central character, is not what he seems – always a favourite figure in Welles's work: he is in fact the disguised mastermind of Hitler's concentration camps, Franz Kindler, biding his time in a small town in Connecticut before resuming the struggle for world-domination or total annihilation. Nazi resurgence was something of a preoccupation of Welles's for many years to come, and his newspaper columns were frequently devoted to the danger it represented. The degree of his input into the script has never been clearly determined, though it seems almost certain that he must have been responsible for the speeches in which Rankin/Kindler analyses the nature of the Nazi quest, so familiar are they in theme and cadence to Welles's own speeches, articles and columns.

In fact, as with every film Welles made in Hollywood after *Citizen Kane*, it is difficult to judge his contribution to *The Stranger* with absolute precision, since none of them was released, or indeed exists today, in exactly the form in which he made them. The screenplay lost thirty-two pages – over an hour of screen time on the usual calculation of two minutes per page – even before filming began, this service being helpfully provided by Spiegel's nominated editor, the veteran Ernest Nims. Welles managed to assemble a couple of his old associates behind the camera: Perry Ferguson, who had been responsible for *Kane*'s sets (though they are credited to Van Nest Polglase), was the designer; and the cinematographer was Russell Metty, who had shot *Kane*'s very witty trailer (and, incidentally, and rather less wittily, some of the reshoots on *The Magnificent Ambersons*). Welles tried to get Bernard Herrmann to write the music for him, but he and his wife had just had a second child and were reluctant to come out west; instead Bronislaw Kaper churned out an all-purpose high-romantic suspense score (though he must be forgiven much for invariably referring to the film as *The S. T. Ranger*, in a droll reference to the producer's alias).

In front of the camera was a group of actors with none of whom Welles had ever worked before, which was not his ideal situation. Not one of them was his first choice. Wholesome, naive Loretta Young, playing Rankin's wife Mary, was under contract to Goetz's Universal Studios and came with the deal; Edward G. Robinson as the Nazi-hunter Wilson was Spiegel's idea. Welles argued bootlessly to persuade the producer that it would be much more interesting to turn the character into a woman, to be played by Agnes Moorehead, but Spiegel never took this suggestion seriously. Welles satisfied his taste for Edwardian acting by asking Philip Merivale (the original Colonel Pickering in *Pygmalion*, and the first actor to play the part of Higgins in America) to play Judge Longstreet, Mary's father, meanwhile indulging his passion for vaudevillians by creating a role for the comedian Billy House as Potter, the owner of the town's soda fountain, the hub of its communal life. Despite the relatively poor opportunities for the high spirits in which he preferred to work, Welles set about making the film with a will, and despite the physical problems involved in erecting a 124-foot tower (claimed at the time to be the tallest set ever made for a film, though surely *Ben-Hur* and *Intolerance* must have been larger) and re-creating a Connecticut town on the Universal lot, the film was comfortably completed in its allotted thirty-five days over eight weeks. The discipline he brought to the process is symbolised by his personal discipline in losing some twenty pounds in weight, though this owed more to regular amphetamine injections than to abstemiousness.

The film as we have it is unlike anything Welles had made so far, though as a narrative it has something in common with *Journey into Fear*. But where that odd gallimaufry, with its cast of Mercury regulars and its striking textures and quirky camera moves, was all Wellesian style and no substance, *The Stranger* is more formally melodramatic, building through an increasingly tense action to a bravura climax that owes a great deal to the Victorian theatre. The acting, particularly in the cases of Robinson and Young, is mainstream Hollywood: linear, text-bound, existing within a narrow compass emotionally and expressively; this was perhaps inevitable in view of the uncommonly stilted dialogue (realising that her newly wed husband is indeed a Nazi psychopath who has just nearly murdered her brother, Young screams, 'It was I you intended to kill!' 'No!' roars Welles. 'Why wasn't it I?' she ripostes, stamping her foot, '*Franz Kindler!!!*'). Welles himself gives a performance in a very different vein, one of great intensity (his unaccustomed slimness adds to the neurotic charge), but without the psychological verisimilitude that might have lent credibility to what, as written, is essentially an operatic figure, tormented, hysterical, deceitful, visionary, murderous. He goes hell for leather for a characterisation which, set to music by Verdi or even Wagner, would have brought the house down, but in a film designed to give troubling reality to the still-present threat of Nazism, it stretches belief: a child of three would spot that something was seriously untoward. Every potential threat to his cover is indicated by heavy breathing, whitened knuckles, popped eyes; whenever he goes into the forest to kill a man or to commune with his dog's corpse, he sheds his suave exterior, his hair becomes not so much dishevelled as longer, rougher, sweatier as he hunkers down to breathe heavily and Hunnishly. This sort of behaviour, de rigueur in Nibelheim and its environs, seems disproportionate in Harper, Connecticut, or indeed anywhere else in the wider world in 1946. It offers an interesting preview of Welles's performance in *Macbeth*, and is, needless to say, utterly compelling, but it is neither convincing nor in any way affecting – one is not touched, or scared, or appalled by the man. One just watches a performance desperately in search of a context. His expressive repertoire is essentially formulaic, a sequence of coded gestures, like kabuki or what we know of the Elizabethan theatre: in the realistic universe provided for the film by Welles the director, Welles the actor seems simply stylised. As for the movie itself, it is (as it now stands) curiously unsatisfying as a narrative, largely because of lacunae in both story and relationships caused by the cuts imposed by the producers; the effect is immensely plotty, both complicated and illogical.

After opening titles over a sixteenth-century German Gothic clock at the top of the bell tower in Harper, Connecticut (how it got there is never explained), and a first scene in which Edward G. Robinson is established as a Nazi-hunter (Wilson), there is a highly evocative sequence in which a character called Meineke (Konstantin Shayne, a very Wellesian actor both in nervous energy and expressiveness of physiognomy) is released from prison in the hope that he will lead them to his old boss, Franz Kindler. This is exactly what he does, travelling between the continents by ship to find him, while Wilson, at a discreet distance, tracks him. The cinematography of this sequence is composed in shadows and sudden lights, not unlike Struss's approach to *Journey into Fear*, but even more like Metty's own inspired work for Welles on *Touch of Evil* more than ten years later. As soon as we – and Meineke, with

Wilson in hot pursuit – arrive in Harper (a beautifully designed set, little used, apart from the gigantic bell tower, which compulsively draws the eye to itself, presaging the climax that inevitably ensues), the camerawork becomes as conventional as the acting. Mary Longstreet (Loretta Young) is casually introduced into the action – on the day of her wedding to Rankin/Kindler – when Meineke comes to her house in quest of her fiancé. He's not there, so Meineke swiftly goes off to find him, stopping Welles in his tracks to eye-popping effect shortly after we have seen him chatting to the schoolboys he teaches (Welles introduces a few charming *hommages* to Todd, his old school; even the notice on the gym door is signed 'Coach Roskie', Welles's – rather under-employed, one imagines – sports master when he was there). Meineke comes to him, he says, with a message from the All-Highest, who turns out to be, not der Führer, but God, so Rankin/Kindler takes him to the forest and kills him, then rushes back home to get married. Shortly after the wedding, Wilson is invited to supper; during a discussion about the future of Germany, Rankin, after cowering a bit like a cornered dog, makes an eloquent, purportedly critical, speech about how Germans will never give up till they have found their new Messiah – who will be, he says, another Barbarossa. 'All Germans aren't like that,' pipes up Mary's young brother, Noah. 'What about Karl Marx?' 'Marx wasn't a German, he was a Jew,' – says Rankin quickly, too quickly, and this remark lodges in Wilson's mind, convincing him that Rankin must be Kindler.

Thereafter Wilson slowly stalks him, enlisting the help of Noah, while making enquiries about town, trying to locate the missing Meineke. Rankin meanwhile confesses to Mary that he saw Meineke on the day of their wedding: Meineke was trying to blackmail him over an accidental homicide from his old student days. Rankin gave him all the money he had, he tells her, and the blackmailer disappeared. Soon afterwards Meineke's body is discovered, and Rankin now admits to Mary that he killed him: what else could he do? Mary, terrified, stays loyal to him, even after Wilson and her father (old Judge Longstreet) have shown her footage of the death-camps, and told her that her husband is in fact Franz Kindler. Rankin knows that he must now get rid of Mary, too, and devises a plot to kill her, sawing through the rungs of the ladder to the bell tower and sending for her, while he creates an alibi – and gives the film some tension – by playing checkers with Billy House in the soda fountain. Rankin returns home and is shocked to find Mary there: her old maid, told not to let her leave the house under any circumstances, has feigned a heart attack, and so Mary has asked Noah to go to the tower for her, which he does, accompanied by Wilson; both have a narrow escape. When Rankin realises what has happened, and that he has probably been responsible for Noah's death, he screams at Mary, smashing his grandfather clock in a sequence that recalls Charles Foster Kane's impotent fury when Susan Alexander leaves: there is real danger and rage here, an emotion that Welles seemed effortlessly able to summon up. Quite why he should be so remorse-stricken at the thought that he might have killed Noah, when he unequivocally intended to kill Mary, is unexplained.

By now, Wilson and the family are knocking the door down, and Rankin makes a swift retreat. Night falls, and Mary sleeps. She is troubled, however, and rises somnambulistically from her bed, picking up a box and throwing a coat over her nightgown, and heads through the cemetery for the bell tower. She climbs to the top, where she finds Rankin in full Hunnish mode: shaggy, long-haired, unshaven, pointing a gun at her. She tells him that she's come to kill him. Soon they're joined by Wilson, who confronts him with his past. 'I followed orders, I did my duty,' he says, wild-eyed, as Mary shoots him in the shoulder. Finally he staggers out onto the parapet; the mechanism of the clock springs to life as he scampers round to safety; suddenly turning, he is impaled on the sword of the Teutonic knight who is circling Satan round the clock, and he and the knight fall 124 feet to the ground. The breath-taking brilliance of the staging of this piece of Grand Guignol is bizarrely undercut by Wilson's jaunty last line to Mary as she descends the stairs leading from the tower: 'Sweet dreams!' he chortles. Kaper's music – strings, horns, piano arpeggios – swells headily: THE END, says the final caption. Indeed.

Kaper's music is blatantly incongruous, purveying a curiously inappropriate swirling romanticism in flat contradiction to the theme and tone of the film. The question of tone is one that hovers over a great many of Welles's films, always excepting *Citizen Kane* and largely excepting *The Magnificent Ambersons*. It is not co-incidental that those two films were scored by Bernard Herrmann, whose music (as well as having uniquely atmospheric properties) was always solidly based in formal structure, integrating the elements and lending the film a powerful sense of unity. It is easy to mock Kaper's workman-like score; the problem is that its excitable lyricism spreads a layer of monosodium glutamate over the whole film, and Welles's genius for detail, for tension, for atmosphere, is diffused and diluted. The use of sound, so potent in both *Kane* and *Ambersons* – where Herrmann so well understood when to shut up, recognising the power of silence punctuated, perhaps, by a clock or a sleigh-bell or the whirr of an engine – is negligible here. A question almost impossible to answer at this distance, and in the absence of letters or memoranda, is whether Welles willingly acceded to the corny music and the absence of a sound score, or whether he was overruled. Whichever it was, it shows a tragic indifference to his great strengths as a film-maker. Not that either score, musical or sonic, represents the greatest problem with *The Stranger* as it stands, but they do administer the *coup de grâce*. The truth, once again, is that the film Welles actually shot was infinitely more interesting and ambitious than the one posing under the same name and now widely available in a spanking new print. Whether it would have been, in the last analysis, a better film we can never know, but it is almost a relief to know that Welles's originality and imagination had not deserted him completely, which is the inevitable conclusion after a viewing of *The Stranger* as it was released. Thanks to the diligent labours of that tireless Welles sleuth, Bret Wood, it is now possible to discern the film that might have been; what he has uncovered reveals a framework that not only enhances the narrative, but suggests the mind of an artist at work.

The finished film as edited by Welles lasted 115 minutes; the presently available version is a full twenty minutes shorter. The single greatest cut, imposed by Spiegel and Goetz before shooting began, removed what would have been two complete reels depicting Meineke's tortuous quest for Kindler in Latin America. But much more damaging are cuts removing the entire framework of the film. In the director's cut, the film opens with the sound of a bell tolling, under the image of a demon silhouetted against a white screen. The camera pulls back and we see that it is in fact nothing but the shadow of a tree in Mary Longstreet's bedroom. She is asleep on the bed; a man's voice tells her to get up and walk through fields, through the cemetery. She obeys, while the voice recites the names of members of her family who have died for their country. She goes trance-like to the bell tower, climbs up into the belfry, looks down and sees an angry mob below. The mob looks up and sees two people fighting on a ledge of the belfry; they finally fall and die. Then, and only then, do we get the titles, followed, as in the present cut, by the scene in which Wilson tells his colleagues to 'leave the cell door open', and the scene of Meineke at customs entering an unspecified Latin American country. Then the two-reel cut followed: in these scenes Meineke was shown going to a kennels, where he is given a truth serum under whose influence he says he believes that God delivered him from prison. He has, he tells them, a message from the All-Highest. They send him on his way, watched by a young woman working for Wilson. Meineke goes to the morgue, where he gets a new passport and a new identity; shortly afterwards Wilson's young female agent is brought in, dead, savaged by dogs. Meineke next visits a photographer, as in the released version, but a sequence is cut that explains Kindler's new name – F(*Ran*)z (*kin*)dler. (Representative John Rankin, incidentally, was chairman of the House Un-American Activities Committee – a sly touch, though whether it was Welles's or that of one of the other screenwriters is hard to know.)

Whether the two cut reels, and even the cut explanation of Rankin's name, are a tremendous loss is hard to judge – everything depends on how they were done (and, as already noted, the scenes on board ship and at customs are among the most visually tony sections of the film). But from a narrative point of view, the opening dream sequence not only makes sense of a number of baffling elements in the released version – Mary's final-reel sleepwalk to the bell tower; Wilson's constant reference to her unconscious ('we have only one ally: her subconscious'); his otherwise incongruous final line – but also seems to turn the whole film into her night-mare. What could be more appalling for a pretty, nicely brought-up young woman in Harper, Connecticut than to find out that her fiancé is not at all who he seems to be, but the monster of the death-camps, whose existence had only recently been revealed to the general public, and the horror of which may well have entered into the subconscious of many a suggestible individual. This is a curious and far-fetched premise, but it has a certain poetry about it, and it takes Welles into a territory where he was very comfort-able as an artist: the dream- or nightmare-world in which Expressionism resides. It also makes perfect sense of his own performance of Rankin as a baffled ogre, the stuff both of fairy tales and of nightmares.

There are further cuts that explain some of the narrative hiccups. Another seriously damaging one is the scene in which Mary and Rankin meet each other for the first time under the bell tower. Rankin says, 'You know my first impression of your town was the incongruity of a Gothic clock in a Connecticut church tower,' dealing with that question, and also establishing him as a connois-seur of clocks, which is the only lead Wilson has on him. Rankin then speaks the lines first heard in voice-over at the beginning of the film, telling her to get up. Mary is frightened of heights, but he persuades her to cross a bridge; the screenplay then intercuts Meineke on board ship for America with Mary announcing her engagement to Rankin. After this the screenplay continues substantially as in the released version, until after the scene between Noah and Wilson. The next scene between Mary and Rankin is another significant cut and a real loss: in it Rankin describes the ideal social system in terms of chronometry. 'The force that runs the clock, the spring or the weight, or whatever it is, is the head of the State. The pendulum is his government which transforms his inspirations into law. The train of gears are the working masses . . . formed into economic units which engage each other without friction . . . the teeth are individuals, just as these are of flawless metal, well ground and polished, so must the individual be of good blood, trained and fit physically.' It is a perfect example of Popular Front writing, and could almost have come out of Geoffrey Household's *Rogue Male*; Welles must have done it superbly and it might have had the same impact in the film as Harry Lime's amoral little aria in *The Third Man*. When Rankin finishes speaking, a spring breaks in the clock. Then the screenplay continues as in the released version until after the screening of the death-camp films to Mary.

In the subsequent sequence, another cut, Rankin gives Mary a sleeping draught; she 'brings her hands together in the immemorial gesture of blood guilt. Now her subconscious is in control and thus she acknowledges her complicity in the crimes of [Kindler].' When she sends Noah to the bell tower in her stead, she realises he's going to his death and faints. Then comes the second most damaging cut, another more impressionistic dream sequence in which Noah climbs to the belfry: a rung breaks and he falls; rung after rung breaks; at last one stays intact. 'Beneath it the two shafts of the ladder stretch down into space like a pair of cosmic stilts.' Red, the dog (poisoned by Rankin), is at 'the base of this lunatic machine', howling and barking. His barks merge with the music. Then Rankin is on the ladder. The camera dollies in on his eye until it fills the screen. Rankin says, 'Failing to speak, you become part of the crime . . . with these hands. The same hands that have held you close to me.' The pupil of his eye fills the screen, then turns into the face of the clock. After this the film would have proceeded as released until the final dialogue, which was to have been between Wilson and old Potter of the soda fountain (Billy House), who says he's had enough trouble, but 'they say accidents come in threes'. 'In threes?' asks Wilson. 'What about World Wars? Mr Potter, I devoutly hope and pray you're wrong. Good night, Mary. Pleasant dreams.'

The dream sequences – which so strikingly anticipate the Hitchcock of *Spellbound* – are obviously tricky to bring off and may or may not have worked, though on the page they certainly add much-needed depth to the character of Mary Rankin. They also suggest an allegoric quality to the whole film. The film in the shooting script is a perfectly accurate reflection of two of Welles's most pressing political concerns: the survival of fascism and the threat of a Third World War. The film Welles wanted to make was in the nature of a warning: the evil that Hitler represented had by no means been expunged. The introduction of the element of the subconscious, and the revelation through it of Mary's guilt at her innocent collaboration with Rankin, exemplifies another preoccupation of Welles's: the complicity of the silent majority; it is another of his wake-up calls to America. All these are potent themes. The question is whether the essentially melodramatic plot device could ever have made them serious points. (It is almost the mirror image of the plot of *Tomorrow Is Forever*, Welles's most recent appearance as a film actor, where a war hero returns to his unsuspecting wife in disguise, instead of, as in *The Stranger*, a war criminal disguising himself in order to insinuate himself into the heart of an innocent woman.) It is of course true that from the time the film was shot up to the present day, covert Nazis have been unmasked, and Nazi-hunters such as Simon Wiesenthal have pursued them to the ends of the earth. Many of them have changed their names, married and had children. To be credible, however, the approach to such material would have to be rigorously realistic, an approach that was never to be that of Welles. It underlines the difficulty Welles had in dramatising his ideas – his natural inclination was to melodramatise them, except (one can only monotonously repeat) in *Citizen Kane*, where of course he had the services of a remarkable writer at his disposal. However, *The Stranger* was clearly – at least potentially – a much better film than the one released to modified rapture (but healthy sales) in 1946, and the missing reels are almost as great a loss as the original end of *The Magnificent Ambersons*.

The actual shooting of the film was, as indicated above, straightforward. Welles and Robinson, though political allies, seem not to have hit it off particularly well; Robinson's performance is solid and clear, but not vividly engaged, containing – for him – a rather high proportion of 'ers' and 'ums'. The running business of his pipe, which breaks in the first scene and then reappears taped, is lumberingly done. For his part, Robinson found Welles (or at least the film) uninspiring. In his memoirs he writes: 'Orson has genius but in this film it seems to have run out.' Loretta Young, that skittish young Catholic miss, simply found Welles fun, laughing so hard with him in the make-up van that the make-up artists had to get stern with her; she may have had something of a crush on him.

Welles himself, to judge from a grumpy interview he gave to Hedda Hopper on the set, was not wholly engaged by the work in hand. 'Tell me, Orson,' she asked, vexingly, 'what is it you really want to do? First it's one thing, then another – radio, movies, painting, the stage, dabbling –' 'No,' he barked, 'not dabbling. I'm no dabbler. Sometimes I wish I were. Dabblers have all the fun. But I'm constitutionally unable to do anything but take my jobs seriously.' Alexander Woollcott, he tells her, had asked him, 'I wonder if you really want to go places in show business?' Welles had replied, 'I don't think I do.' 'My real interest in life is in education,' he told Hopper. 'I want to be a teacher. All this experience I've been piling up is equipping me for that future . . . I shall know how to dramatise the Art of imparting knowledge.' Welles told Barbara Leaming that he had approached the foundations and offered himself to spearhead an education drive. He had no takers. 'And will you be leading the people to a way of thinking?' continued Hedda Hopper, smelling a political rat. 'No. The people can be trusted to do their own thinking . . . masses of people are never wrong. They're always right. The public's judgement on a play is always right, though the critics may be wrong. I shall try only to help people to the knowledge that will aid them in forming correct conclusions.' Abandoning this slightly dubious line of thought, he speaks of Todd School, in which he says he has a personal and a financial interest. 'One day I shall leave all this behind me, go back there, and give full rein to my ideas. That's when life will really begin for me.' It is an unlikely vision – Welles as a prep-school master – but a charming one. 'Rita thinks my idea is swell.' No doubt she would have done, had she believed it for a second – had she indeed had any recent conversation at all with Welles. Bringing the interview to an end, he puts his finger precisely on his problem. 'The truth is, I'm a sweat guy. I hear that Noël Coward can write a play in a week. Not me. If I can write a play at all, or a radio script, or a scenario, a newspaper column or anything, it's only by virtue of sweating it out. I will fight to the last drop of sweat – but believe me, I do everything the hard way.' It was true enough.

All the early work was achieved by audacity and adrenalin, sheer exuberance and delight in the work of his colleagues. Now, at the age of thirty, adrenalin was harder to command, and audacity not enough. The magic touch that had so sustained Welles in his twenties had disappeared: now it was just hard, hard work, and he was no longer sure that he enjoyed the job. But what to do instead? It is a question that many a performer has asked himself or herself when the honeymoon of their early career is over – can it really only be this, over and over again? Actors and directors are not, generally speaking, well qualified for any other job; most hit on their vocations precisely because they seemed no good for anything else. This is the moment at which character and power of endurance – what the Victorians' used to call 'bottom' – becomes almost as important as talent, and much more important than luck.

There was still politics, of course, but Welles appeared quite reconciled to never entering that arena full time. He couldn't afford it, for a start. And he felt he had missed his moment; had he stood in 1944, he told Barbara Leaming, instead of '45 or '46, he might have been elected. He was discouraged from standing in California by his doughty research assistant Geneva Cranston, who told him that he'd never carry Los Angeles because of the communist opposition to him. How bewildered the FBI – still busily monitoring his every move – would have been to hear that. 'There were a lot of card-carrying fellows,' he told Leaming, 'never forget that – and I was very much not of their group.' He contemplated standing in New York and then in his home state of Wisconsin, but the Republican candidate had the support of the dairy workers, so Welles did not bother to challenge him. The man's name was Joseph McCarthy. 'And that's how there was a McCarthy. That's a terrible thing to have on your conscience.'

Welles was, in fact, somewhat depressed politically. Truman had been a bitter disappointment to him, both as a man and in terms of what he stood for. He was loyal at first. Shortly after Truman succeeded Roosevelt, Welles had written a column in which he said, 'Our new President has taken over the biggest job there ever was in the world. For our sake, let's make it a little easier for him than we did for the great man who died for us last week.' This moratorium did not last long. While shooting *The Stranger*, he wrote a column (one of his last) in which he described a nation-wide presidential broadcast: everyone on the set stopped filming to listen. No one was impressed, Welles says, and they were from all points on the political compass. One of the grips was called

'Missouri' because – like Truman – he came from there: 'He says he's the only registered Democrat from his state who hasn't got a job in Washington. This is, of course, bitter and unfair . . . maybe Roosevelt's heir is as good a man as he looked for a while there. A lot of good Americans who voted for him are saying they've got to be shown.'

The very particular political melancholy that is engendered by disappointment in the leader of the party you support had descended on Welles. A subsequent *New York Post* column, also written during the shoot of *The Stranger*, describes lessons he is taking to learn to drive, but his intention is not purely anecdotal. He reveals an unexpected longing for some kind of meaning to life. He has been for a drive with 'some daredevil instructor' who gave him his licence, 'laughing heartily as he filled it out. He must have thought I was kidding, or else the man was floundering in hysteria . . . all I know is that it's now perfectly legal for me to drive. I only wish I could.' (This is no columnist's invention: Welles was wholly ignorant of the art of driving a car, but was nonetheless so impatient behind the wheel that the smallest journey was a threat to pedestrians, passengers, fellow-drivers and above all himself. Shifra Haran recollected that he was so eager to arrive that he would quite unconsciously put his foot over hers on the accelerator when she was driving.) After he received his licence, he continues, the car broke down. 'I did whatever it is I do to a car to make it stall.' He didn't know where he was, then spotted the spire of the set for *The Stranger*. He asked a passing child if the church belonged to the movies, but she didn't know. 'I figure that the child and I, and maybe you, need something we can rely on,' he ends on an unaccustomed note. 'Something that won't be torn down to make room for a new movie, but it had better be something as good as churches have been when they were good.'

CHAPTER SIXTEEN

Full, Complete and Unrestricted Authority

THE TRUTH is that Welles's mind was already turned away from Hollywood, even before he had completed shooting *The Stranger*. He had determined on a return, in the grandest possible style, to the stage: the old standby. It was like a parental home to him, where he could always be sure of a welcome. And if he was returning to the theatre, let it be to the theatre theatrical – that, it seems, was his thinking when he decided to do a version of the much-adapted Jules Verne novel *Around the World in Eighty Days*. He himself had already adapted it twice, once on radio and once as a screenplay for George Schaefer in 1941, when they were still thrashing around for a film with which to follow *Citizen Kane*. The novel had the advantage, apart from anything else, of being out of copyright; moreover, the two previous film versions had been as long ago as 1914 and 1916, so he would be in a good position to transfer his efforts (if successful) to the screen.

The new stage show would be a love-letter to the almost forgotten genre of Musical Extravaganza, a form of theatre of which Welles can have had only the most slender personal experience. Perhaps in Chicago in the early nineteen-twenties there may have been some residual traces of it, but essentially it was a species of entertainment that had died out by the end of the First World War, due to its extraordinary demands in terms of backstage crew, of which large armies were required, and whole acres of painted scenery, which were heavily dependent on intensive skilled labour. In theory, it was a form of theatre that should have been anathema to Welles the Expressionist and Welles the master of agit-prop. But the theatre of Orson Welles was a broad church. A not insignificant side of him longed, as we have so often seen, for sheer escapism in the theatre, not of the romantic variety, but of the thrills and spills, gasps and 'oohs' and 'aahs' kind: he required his timbers to be shivered, his withers to be wrung, his heart to be lodged more or less permanently in his mouth: he wanted, in short, to become a child again. 'If astonishment and delight won't bring an audience into a playhouse any more,' he had written in his introduction to Bruce Elliot's *Magic*, 'then of course something is rotten in the state of the Union, and it isn't only magic that is doomed.' The genre of extravaganza embraced many theatrical delights: vaude-villian comedy, romantic interest, lovely leggy girls, spectacle, livestock, costumes, scenery, special effects. He would have it all, and more.

So to make it happen, in August of 1945 – just before the commencement of principal photography for *The Stranger* – he formed a partnership with a properly old-style impresario, Mike Todd (born Avrom Hirsch Goldbogen), then only in his mid-thirties, but already a byword for flamboyance and reckless enterprise, fresh from his triumphs with *Hot Mikado* (Gilbert and Sullivan jazzed), Cole Porter's *Something for the Boys* and *Mexican Hayride*. Todd enlisted the composer of the last-named only modestly successful musical to provide songs and incidental music for *Around the World* and, after agreeing to pay Welles $2,500 a week to write the show during the first few months of 1946, with a view to putting it on in the autumn of that year, left the co-authors to block out the plan for the script and music. His contract with Welles gave the author-director – there was no plan for him to appear in the show – 'full, complete and unrestricted authority'; there had never been a contract like it since his first contract with RKO. Porter, at a rather low point both in his career and his life, was cheerfully stimulated, excited to be associating himself with 'the crazy and unusual production of the theatre – the kind of thing one dreams about but never quite dares to attempt . . . it's because I'm bored. I want to do something "different".' He saw *Around the World* as 'a drama with music, too', though as the programme note for the show pointed out, there is more music in *Around the World* than in most musicals. As well as a set of four songs, Porter had provided music for the filmed sequences, the chase, the circus, the magic show and other non-song sequences. After the initial meetings, Welles plunged into shooting *The Stranger*, taking occasional trips to New York to continue his work with Porter.

At the same time – a sure sign that his adrenalin was begin-ning to flow again, bringing with it a renewal of his former intemperate appetite for work – Welles was becoming intrigued by the prospect of directing a play by the exiled German dramatist

Bertolt Brecht, whom he had met in Los Angeles, where Brecht was part of the expatriate circle centred on Berthold and Saskia Viertel's salon in Santa Monica. It was there that Charles Laughton had met the playwright; they had taken a remarkable shine to each other, finding common ground in their love of Japanese art and a sense of the social purpose of the theatre – Brecht from a thoroughgoing Marxist perspective, Laughton from a passionate faith in the power of art to change people and, as he said to an approving Brecht, a conviction that 'I know what people are like, and I want to show them'. Welles and Laughton were acquainted too, and had circled round each other admiringly but suspiciously for some time. Laughton had been at the Los Angeles premiere of *Citizen Kane*, and had twice appeared as the guest on *The Orson Welles Almanac*; both had hurled themselves into wartime fund-raising activities on the radio and on countless platforms. But where Welles was politically fearless and highly public, Laughton was furtive and private, partly because he was terrified of being exposed as a homosexual, but also out of a deep instinct to protect his inner life. As artists, they were polar opposites, Welles functioning on adrenalin and great sweeping gestures, Laughton toiling away on his inner processes before gradually committing himself to the heroically ambitious performances for which he was widely admired as one of the greatest living actors – if not, perhaps, the greatest of them all. But just as Welles had passed through a period in the wilderness, artistically speaking, so Laughton had suffered a recent decline in his reputation as an actor since the sensational climax of his Quasimodo in *The Hunchback of Notre Dame* some seven years earlier. After a run of undistinguished films, he was now universally referred to – sometimes approvingly, sometimes not – as 'a ham'. His slowly deepening relationship with Brecht had restored his joy in acting and his self-respect; they had been working together for some years on an English version of Brecht's work-in-progress, *The Life of Galileo*, a fruit of his exile. The play had already been done in Zurich, but Brecht was still developing what he wanted to say about the founder of modern physics and his vexed relationship with the Church of Rome. The unique praxis evolved by actor and author working together on the play, a method celebrated by Brecht in some beautifully personal poems, was all the more extraordinary in that they had no common language: Laughton spoke no German, and Brecht could barely understand English. Nonetheless, Brecht felt able to judge the merits of the translation that Laughton, working from a literal version of the text, was offering him, and together, by some osmotical-dialectical process, they arrived at a play that satisfied them both.

The Augsburger Brecht and the Yorkshireman Laughton were both shrewd and deep-thinking men, so when they decided to ask Orson Welles to direct *Galileo*, it was not done lightly. In December of 1945, Brecht noted in his diary that Laughton had read the play to Welles: 'His attitude is pleasant; his remarks intelligent.' Laughton – who had checked out various possible directors, including, unimaginably, that epitome of Broadway elegance Alfred Lunt – wanted a sounding board for his acting, feeling, as he said, that the nearer he got to rehearsals 'the more scared I become of being directed by anyone but an actor'. Welles immediately knew that he was being offered something remarkable, quite unlike anything else he had ever done: the play, suffused with Brecht's premonitory anxieties about the development of nuclear weaponry, which Welles urgently shared, and dealing profoundly with the question – so pertinent to Welles's own experience – of the radical's relationship with society, instantly inflamed his imagination. He started to think of staging solutions that would serve the play's revolutionary nature.

Barbara Leaming claims that Welles had absorbed Brecht's theories, and that they profoundly influenced all of his subsequent work. There seems to be little evidence for this, though he was what might be called a spontaneous Brechtian. The famous and much-misunderstood *Verfremdungseffekt* was second nature to Welles: he too wanted to make the audience assess what they saw on stage in a critical spirit, rather than encouraging them to empathise with the characters; his work, too, was designed to appeal to the brain rather than the heart. And he shared Brecht's faith in The People. Equally passionately, he longed to break the mould theatrically, and *Galileo* was clearly the play with which to do it, demanding the kind of anti-theatrical theatricality he had stumbled on when he was forced to stage Marc Blitzstein's *The Cradle Will Rock* without decor, lights or a normal theatrical environment. 'Dear Charlie,' he wrote to Laughton, 'I'm much encouraged to note from your thoughts about scaffolding etc that we're thinking along identical lines. My God how I wish there were some kind of brand new place for us to play our play in!! . . . lacking it, of course, we'll have to work a little magic and somehow make the Shubert rat-traps *seem* new . . . with something that makes it clear we're only pitching our tents.' He was reaching out for something new in his own work. But though he loved the play, Welles was by no means overawed by the playwright. 'Brecht was very very tiresome today,' he told Laughton, 'until (I'm sorry to say) I was stern and a trifle shitty. I hate working like that.' Welles was unaccustomed to dealing with living authors in the theatre, especially ones who happened to be superb directors themselves. Nor was he prepared to succumb to the alternation of ruthless high-handedness and manipulative charm by which Brecht enslaved his collaborators, and he was determined to make that clear from the beginning. He was more than capable of matching Brecht's ruthlessness, going straight for the jugular. 'I said to him one day, while we were talking about *Galileo*,' Welles told Peter Bogdanovich, 'that he had written a perfect anti-Communist work [and] he almost became aggressive. I said, "But this church you describe has to be Stalin and not the Pope. You have made something resolutely anti-Communist."' Welles relished this sort of intellectual rough-house, and suspected that Brecht did too. 'Brecht had an extraordinary brain. You could tell he'd been educated by the Jesuits – he had the kind of disciplined brain characterised by Jesuit education. Instinctively, he was more of an anarchist than a Marxist, but he believed himself a perfect Marxist.' Welles dealt equally breezily with that other product of a Jesuit education, Charles Laughton: 'So you find my confidence in my own charm overbearing, do you?' he wrote to Laughton. 'Then go fuck yourself! Love Orson' – leaving Laughton, no doubt, blinking and speechless, though perhaps just slightly exhilarated, too.

Laughton was free in the autumn, not the spring, so Welles and Dick Wilson, now returned from the military and enthusiastically reviving the long-dormant Mercury Productions, agreed – against the better judgement of both Mike Todd and Cole Porter – to advance *Around the World* (as the show was to be called) to an April out-of-town opening, and both shows were duly announced. This meant a great deal of intensive work at a time when Welles was heavily involved in the thankless task of editing *The Stranger*, while still making his weekly broadcast, writing the last of the newspaper columns and contributing weighty articles to *Free World*. Dolivet never ceased pressing Welles to do more work for the organisation, and to take the idea of himself as a potential candidate more seriously. Welles was by no means inactive politically – in November he had fired off a telegram in support of a World Peace Rally, in celebration of the twenty-eighth anniversary of the establishment of the Soviet Union, again unhesitatingly allying himself with a dangerously unpopular cause: OUR CHOICE IS SIMPLE. THE END OF

WAR OR THE END OF THE WORLD. THE PEOPLES OF THE UNITED STATES AND OF THE SOVIET UNION OF RUSSIA ARE MEANT TO BE FRIENDS. IT IS UP TO THEM TO CRUSH ALL CONSPIRACIES AGAINST THAT FRIENDSHIP.

But by the end of the year Welles needed to take stock. His marriage to Rita Hayworth had broken down completely and he spent Christmas of 1945 in the Mexican jungle, as far from family and friends as he could manage. On Christmas Day he found himself, he told Barbara Leaming, on top of a pyramid that he had climbed and sat there 'all alone . . . all alone in the ruins of the Mayans. I've never been so happy in my life.' Despite the shades of Rider Haggard, so familiar from his Moroccan yarns (he even killed a bull, he says: 'they made a great stew of that'), there is a ring of truth to the claim that Welles wanted to be alone for a moment. His habitual craving for stimulation occasionally (as it had done a couple of years before, in Fortaleza) gave way to a need for self-communion – nothing analytical, nothing, strictly speaking, religious: just stillness. The second he returned to the United States, Rita Hayworth started divorce proceedings against him; among other things she wanted repayment of the $30,000 he owed her. All he could offer was a half-share in *Around the World*. The lawyers duly set to work, though Hayworth betrayed no very great urgency in the matter.

Welles quit Los Angeles, returning to New York to live, moving to East End Avenue and working on *Around the World*. All through the first months of that year he was also active again on the speech-making circuit, generally on the Free World platform, passionately analysing the Yugoslavian situation, unemployment, world peace, on a tide of ringing phrases: 'Peace is possible without appeasement . . . if the United Nations fulfil the purposes which brought them into partnership, war as a threat or a fact will be outlawed. Outlawed as a crime by the courts and councils of a militant peace. And more effectively outlawed as a possibility by the logic of history.' His standing at these gatherings was enormous, in sharp contrast with the slightly humiliating status of his career. Here he was needed; here he could make a difference. NATIONAL COMMITTEE TO ABOLISH THE POLL TAX IS EAGER TO HONOR YOU AT THE FESTIVAL OF FREEDOM, said a telegram early in the New Year. THE PEOPLE OF CHICAGO ARE EAGER TO ACCLAIM YOU. Another telegram, this one from Tacoma, read: CITY BEING VERY BACKWARD NEEDS OUTSTANDING NATIONAL FIGURE TO BE AWAKENED TO A SPIRIT OF BROTHERHOOD BETWEEN RACES AND CREEDS. They wanted him to address the local people, no fewer than 150,000 of them, at a Brotherhood Rally. YOUR APPEARANCE WOULD TREMENDOUSLY STRENGTHEN DEMOCRATIC SPIRIT IN A COMMUNITY WHICH NEEDS IT BADLY. Welles scrawled YES on the telegram and a week later he was giving the people of Tacoma a talk entitled 'Brotherhood or the New Hell'. The subject was one by which he became increasingly obsessed: the atomic bomb.

Citizen Welles, he has been dubbed by more than one writer. No doubt the sobriquet is ironically intended, a droll reference to his most famous film, but among the many matters on which Welles can be faulted, at this period of his life his commitment to the well-being of his fellow-human beings shines brightly. He no longer sought election (IMPOSSIBLE TO CONSIDER ENTERING ACTIVE POLITICAL LIFE THIS YEAR, he had replied to Lloyd F. Saunders's suggestion that he stand as a Congressional candidate); he was no longer being paid to speak. He simply wanted to rally his fellow-Americans. In later life he was inclined to suggest that politics was his hobby, something he pursued as others may follow the horses or their football team, but the record is indisputable: for many years Orson Welles unstintingly and tirelessly gave himself to the cause of radicalism; few actors or directors – certainly in the English-speaking world – have given more practical proof of their profound belief in democracy. In some curious way he had a greater clarity about politics than he did about his work, although he never understood the strategies of power, any more than he did in his own industry. That the causes for which he fought – anti-racism, international cooperation, trade unionism – were under siege through much of that time is a mark of his courage and prescience. The gap between his public compassion and his private carelessness did not go unnoticed, however. 'Dear Orson,' wrote the photographer Brent Gallagher:

> I listen with interest as you defend the people's interest against abusers or unscrupulous wielders of power. I'm not complaining about being paid nothing for photographing *Caesar* . . . I'm not complaining about non-payment for the *Five Kings* series . . . but when in my absence during the war, you borrow these negatives to dress up your movie studio, you fail to pay even the token charge of $10 each for the five used that I suggested, you fail to return the negatives, and you refrain from answering letters from me or my counsellor, well, I just wonder from what source you draw all that righteous indignation. Respects.

More cheering was a letter from Marc Blitzstein, in the world premiere of whose ambitious Airborne Symphony Welles had taken the spoken role of The Monitor. 'I can't say it any better than I did; you've grown up; and I seem to be grateful and proud about it, as well as pleased. The way you rubbed yourself out in behalf of the work, and the way your stuff came shining through, made me realise it. The wrong people will, as before, hate us both, have already evidenced their hatred; and that makes us both happy. – The voice would have been something by itself. But the spirit! Thanks, baby – Marc.' Welles recorded the piece some twenty years later under its original conductor, Leonard Bernstein, and it is Welles at his incomparable best, superbly spoken, perfectly phrased, informed with genuine passion (the recording was made at the height of the Vietnam War, an event Blitzstein was happily spared). The narration is in the vein of *Ceiling Unlimited* and no one will ever fulfil its aviation rhetoric more inspiringly than Welles:

> Laugh it off.
> This little thought knocks out a mountain range,
> Tears up the jungle. This notion eats oceans,
> Puts the desert in its vest pocket,
> Has geography for tea.
> The barriers to the other side of the world –
> They can pack it up now and call it a day

He continued to apply himself to his theatrical extravaganza. His previous adaptations of the Verne novel gave him something of a head-start, though he knew that whatever he put down on paper would be the merest discussion document. With Mike Todd and the $40,000 in cash that he had put up behind him, Welles stinted nothing; spectacle was the name of the game. He had his model before him: the original Paris production, only two years after publication of the novel, had transferred to New York the following year, in 1875; it employed more than 275 people and cost more than $50,000. 'The scenery and mechanical effects are ingenious on a grand scale of magnificence. Europe has been ransacked for novelties.' Welles intended to match that show, thrill for thrill, spill for spill.

Following Verne fairly systematically, Welles's script took Phileas Fogg and his man Passepartout from London via the English Channel, Paris, the Spanish border, Barcelona and the Mediterranean to Suez, thence to the Great Indian Forest, the

Pagoda of Pilagi, a jungle encampment in the Himalayas, a street of evil repute in Hong Kong, an Opium Hell in the same city, the China coast, Yokohama, and the Oka Saka (sic) circus. That was Act One. Act Two took place largely in America: San Francisco, the Rocky Mountains, Medicine Bow, the peak of Bald Mountain, the Frozen Plains of the West, New York Harbour and then jail again, before ending up where they had begun, in the 'London Whist Club', a substitute for Verne's Reform Club. Many of the transitions would be shown on film on a huge movie screen that would be flying in and out, but there were still at least fifteen entirely different locations. To design this terrifying 'behemoth of a spectacle', Welles engaged a very young Robert Davison, whose previous stage experience had been confined to doing the sets and costumes for *Comedia Balletica* for the Ballets Russes de Monte Carlo; before that he had worked in Hollywood on large-scale projects for, among others, Vicente Minnelli, but had never had sole charge of any of them. Alvin Colt, equally young, though very much taller (six feet six inches), whose job as costume designer was hardly less demanding (there were more than 300 of them, almost all involved in very quick changes), had also come from the world of ballet. His mentor, the visionary Russian émigré painter Pavel Tchelitchew, had been close to Welles at the time of the Mercury's first seasons. Nelson Barclift, 'a young hopeful' (ex-leading dancer in *Lady in the Dark*; assistant choreographer on the GI show *This Is the Army* during his five years' military service), was responsible for what *Variety* referred to as the 'terp staging'; he had been Cole Porter's suggestion. It was not a heavyweight team; none of them, indeed, had been responsible for a major musical show, any more than Welles had. But that was his way. Experience was not a priority as far as he was concerned: he valued enthusiasm, eagerness, invention. He also had a taste for old pros, and to stage the Oka Saka ballet at the end of Act One, he engaged one of the most exotic and in his time idolised performers of the twentieth century, the man known as Barbette.

Born Vander Clyde at Round Rock, a few miles from Austin, Texas, this highly original *travésti* high-wire artist had turned himself into a severely androgynous figure, beautiful but forbidding, who became the star turn of the Casino de Paris, courted by high society, photographed iconically by Man Ray, hauntingly filmed by Cocteau in *Le Sang d'un Poète*. 'He walked the tightrope high above the audiences without falling,' Cocteau wrote of him, 'above incongruity, death, bad taste, indecency, indignation.' In 1929, he momentarily lost his foothold and fell to earth, smashing his teeth and scarring his face. Appearing in his own country at Loew's State, he caught a chill, and woke one morning to find himself physically locked. Operations followed; he had to learn to walk from scratch. Apart from a brief appearance in Billy Rose's prodigious *Jumbo*, his career as a performer was over; thereafter he trained circus performers, and when Welles found him, he had been arranging the aerial ballet in John Ringling North's Circus. Barbette was rather different from the sort of old vaudevillians and broken-down thespians whom Welles usually liked to cultivate, but he appealed to Welles's sense of the exotic; the aristocratic *froideur* that only a Texan drag-artist could muster certainly added a touch of class to the proceedings: at the height of his fame he travelled with twenty-eight trunks, a maid, 'and a maid to help the maid'.

As for the performers, Welles knew that it was his own presence as director – and the show *qua* show – that would sell it, not the actors, and the group he assembled accordingly lacked any great names or, it would appear, talents. Among them were a couple of old chums (Brainerd Duffield, who had done some radio writing for Welles, and Stefan Schnabel, the great pianist's son, a real Mercury veteran from the first theatre season and innumerable broadcasts); a boyfriend of Cole Porter's (Jack Cassidy); two more or less winsome juveniles as Princess Aouda and Passepartout – Pat Passepartout in this version (Mary Healy and Larry Laurence, a young Italian crooner who, under his original name of Enzo Stuarti, later had a brief moment of glory in the charts); seasoned character man Alan Reed as Detective Inspector Fix; and the dependable Anglo-American actor Guy Spaull in a variety of roles. Most of them doubled, trebled, even quadrupled parts. For the rest, there was a very large ensemble of singers, dancers and acrobats: a total cast of well over fifty. Welles left his key piece of casting till remarkably late in the day: three days before rehearsals were due to begin he went to the first night of *Little Brown Jug* at the Martin Beck; liking the work of one of the leading actors, Arthur Margetson, he went backstage and on the spot offered him the role of Phileas Fogg, which Margetson was pleased to accept, since the play in which he was appearing proved a distinctly flawed vessel, running for only three more performances. A dry, witty performer, with a background in revue and high comedy (his great success in his native London had been *Let Us Be Gay*), Margetson had exactly the qualities Welles needed from his leading man, even if in life he was inclined to be tiresomely fussy; at an early point in rehearsals Welles renamed him Shirley, and Shirley he remained to the end.

The lateness with which casting was completed may have been due to a shock that Welles had just received. His old-style producer had just done a very old-fashioned thing: he pulled out at the last moment. Todd claimed that it was because Welles insisted on having an actual derrick on stage from which at a certain climactic moment he would spray the entire cast with oil. 'I've decided I simply can't afford you,' said Todd. 'The show is yours from this moment on.' On another occasion he claimed that he withdrew because 'part of luck is a pet superstition: I have to have a script, even a bad one. Here it was, two weeks before rehearsals and Orson was still ad-libbing the script.' Welles replied to these accusations with some dignity: 'It became apparent that, among other things [Mr Mike Todd] was in no position to provide finances [so] I was forced to take over the responsibility of this myself.' Any, and probably all, of the above explanations seem perfectly feasible: no doubt Welles did want a cast-spraying derrick, no doubt his script was in a permanent state of flux, and no doubt Mike Todd did run out of cash; he shelved several shows at about the same time: 'the Todd casualties of '46' as Welles called them. Todd did not seem to require his investment back, but Welles somehow had to find the rest.

For a brief moment, to judge from a press release early in March, Welles's friends Paul Feigay and Oliver Smith stepped into the breach, but Dick Wilson seems to have persuaded Welles to go it alone as 'a Mercury offering', in Dick's words. But where would the money come from? Needless to say, neither Mercury nor Dick himself had any money themselves. Welles was heavily in debt to the woman who was about to be his ex-wife, and Lear Radios had just withdrawn their sponsorship of *Orson Welles's Commentary*. ABC, the radio network, agreed to keep the show on the air, but Welles's salary was reduced from $1,700 a week to $50. He had only one thing to sell: his soul. So he swiftly put in a few calls, the first of them to Alexander Korda, who gallantly bought the movie rights to *Around the World* for $100,000, which would tide them over for a little while. The asking price was a gentlemen's agreement for Welles to direct four films for him. It still wasn't enough; the costume houses were demanding advance payment for fabrics to the tune of $25,000, so Welles made a second and infinitely less agreeable call, this time to the man whom he had only recently referred to as the Savage of Gower Gulch, the man who prevented Rita Hayworth from appearing in *The Mercury Wonder Show*, the man he said would never employ him: Harry Cohn, head of Columbia Pictures. Again, all Welles could offer him was the promise of a film – to star, needless to say, Rita Hayworth, who had just come to the end of her exclusive contract with Cohn. Welles offered him his treatment of *Carmen*, which was also one of the movies that he was discussing with Korda, but not quite in the same terms. 'The theme of this picture is sex in the raw and this is the major opportunity . . . at this point we interpose the sexiest footage of the entire picture . . . *Flesh and the Devil*, purple passion, every attitude of amorous dalliance, the longest kisses the censors will allow.' It was not Welles's accustomed language, and it would not have been Welles's accustomed film. That was not the point. The point was to get Cohn to cough up the dough: and he did. The show could go on.

By now, of course, they were in rehearsal for *Around the World*. To Margetson's surprise, Welles turned out to be highly liberal as a director. On the first day the cast had been called at ten; the whole vast company were there on the dot. 'Orson made his entrance about ten-twenty,' Margetson wrote in his unpublished memoir, *Orson and I*. 'We timidly told him we didn't care too much about 10 a.m. calls. And to our amazement, the Ogre replied, "Tell me whatever time you would like to be called and providing we get in eight hours a day (which is Equity maximum time of rehearsal) I will endeavour to oblige you."' Whenever they started, rehearsals were wild, exuberant, laughter-driven affairs; Welles was, in Margetson's spinsterish phrase, 'on the water-wagon', and full of energy and invention. 'Orson made the whole thing seem so entertaining and effortless.' The show contained a little over thirty minutes worth of film (Hyde Park, the Bank, a Hong Kong den, Fogg's flat, the Whist Club, and on the boat), and Welles shot the footage in the rehearsal room. Just before they were to do the storm scenes aboard ship, at around eleven o'clock that evening, Margetson reported, a crate of whisky mysteriously entered the studio. Welles urged the three actors to drink heartily. 'Alcohol!' he cried, 'Inside and out! I beseech you to take plenty of alcohol. Arthur, dear boy, please take another shot before your next shot.' 'Let's face it,' says Margetson, 'he was being just a trifle Machiavellian as well as kind (he *has* a definite sadistic trait, anyway – though only in mild form).' One of the actors, Larry Laurence, was, it turned out, unused to liquor; Mary Healy, from New Orleans, wasn't; and Margetson had been drinking whisky all his life. The liquor was being ladled out in such bulk, however, that before long even he became very unsteady. Suddenly Welles threw a huge hogshead of water in his face. 'It is a matter of record I took it all without so much as dislodging my monocle. Was it great acting? Or was I simply feeling no pain?' To Welles all this was wildly entertaining: the fun and togetherness of the theatre; this is where he reclaimed the childhood he never knew.

The final run in the rehearsal room lasted three hours and forty-five minutes, with Welles leaping up to fill in for any absentees. He was clearly enjoying himself more than he had for some time – certainly more than on any movie set, where such romps can never happen. However, he must have got on the train for Boston with some anxiety: three and three-quarter hours is simply too long for any show, except perhaps *King Lear* or Eugene O'Neill, and even O'Neill is questionable. *Around the World* was, moreover, bound to get longer. When actors are first exposed to a set, a show invariably puts on time, at any rate until they get used to it and cuts can be instituted. And this set was a completely unknown quantity. The actors were due at the theatre for an 8 p.m. dress rehearsal. There were no costumes; no lights had yet been focused. Livestock ran loose backstage, pieces of set smashed into each other, actors concussed themselves on swinging bars. 'We are the prey of drunken stage hands and drunken electricians,' Cole Porter wrote to a friend. 'Even when they are sober most of them are ninety years old. They all hate the show because there are so many lights and scene changes. They are used to nice comfortable operas where there are two sets and no lighting changes whatsoever.'

The predictable chaos ensued: expensive chaos. The run of Act One ended at nine o'clock the following morning; it had taken thirteen hours. The fifty-four stage hands and orchestra of more than thirty players were on double and finally triple pay. Eventually everyone was sent home to sleep. The opening performance, due that night, was cancelled while they attempted the dress rehearsal of Act Two. Again, they started at 8 p.m., this time finishing at 6 a.m., after which Welles and the circus continued to rehearse. Welles, who had very wisely declared from the beginning that he would not be appearing in the show, had impulsively decided that 'honouring Boston', as he put it, he would after all make an appearance, as Fu San, a Japanese conjuror, causing doves to materialise in an empty net, skewering a dancing girl with his rapier, producing aces of spades from unlikely ears. On those few occasions when he wasn't needed at the dress rehearsal, he would slope across to Al and Jack's bar across the street to practise the act, which he had never performed in public before. Perhaps it was a way – a highly unusual, entirely Wellesian way – of calming his nerves. Had he allowed himself a moment to contemplate the mayhem he had unleashed, he might simply have taken the next train back to New York.

The world premiere of *Around the World* took place at the Boston Opera House on 27 April 1946, at 8.45 p.m., precisely twenty-four hours late. No single mechanical element of the show – the scenery, the turntable, the props or the lighting – worked as planned. The stagehands were as audible as they had been during the dress rehearsal the night before. 'The prop eagle which was supposed to sweep me off the stage in a flash from its nest, on which I was perilously standing almost as high as the top of the proscenium,' wrote Margetson, 'came on late and very slowly; then receded and returned backwards to drag me offstage.' The scene immediately following was supposed to be a backdrop obviously depicting London, and as an actress entered saying, 'Is this London?' practically all the drops for the entire show were lowered and raised alternately at lightning speed – all, that is, except the London one. The audience was, of course, enchanted. The final backdrop to fall showed a minor train-stop somewhere in the snow-clad Rocky Mountains. At this, an actor sticking doggedly to his script and looking at the scene, replied, 'Yes, this is London, all right!' By now the audience was in seventh heaven. The show ended at 11.45, 'several scenes having been totally amputated', according to Margetson, which at least had the advantage of reducing the running time.

The *Boston Daily Globe*, drily observing that 'the Orson Welles genius – if that is what it is – is expressed in many ways', sensibly refrained from commenting on the 'grandiose musical extravaganza' until the stage was working better and at least forty-five minutes of the show had been cut. 'Nonetheless,' it continued, 'it is easy to see that there is more production than show . . . the actors are pretty well lost in the forest of gadgets.' Margetson came out of it well enough, as did Alan Reed ('a marathon of quick changes and dialect comedy'). The reviewer, though admiring the circus interlude, was anxious about a spectacular slide done over the audience without a net: the performer, Ray Good, walked a tightrope from the stage to a second balcony box, then slid backwards onto the stage. In fact this last proved too much for the censor, who ordered it cut on the grounds that 'the slider, though imperturbed, might fall and demolish some of the people in the seats below'. The veteran critic Eliot Norton was very taken by the Japanese circus, and particularly the eagle rescue (the bird was shot at and feathers fluttered down into the auditorium). But the general sense was of overkill. Production, the *Globe* acknowledged, is important to a show, but here it was emphasised 'with a smothering ferocity'. The inevitable verdict was that *Around the World* needed a lot of work. Norton put it with precision: 'A good theatrical plot has to be so devised that you are not only curious but also eager to see and hear what happens to the principal characters. In this show it is silly to guess at what is coming next. Mr Welles has crammed in everything which he liked in the theatre as a child.'

In the circumstances, it seems little short of a miracle that the piece held the stage at all. But this was how Welles preferred to work in the theatre: making the show on the hoof. Even he, however, the veteran of the massive *Five Kings* – where he had tried to put *Henry IV Parts One* and *Two* on stage in one three-hour sweep – had never dealt with anything as vast and diffuse as this. The only strategy for this sort of epic mayhem is, paradoxically enough, to plan meticulously, down to the last tiny detail, but that was quite alien to Welles's temperament and his habitual modus operandi. Film-making, particularly with films made by or in a studio, to a large extent provides a built-in planning framework; the work is by its nature tightly structured. Welles found this assumption suffocating and uncreative, and his whole drive during the rest of his film-making career was to combat it, restoring as much as he could the slap-dash, adrenalin-fuelled improvisatory abandon of earlier film-makers. At the pre-war Mercury Theatre, where he was able to call all the shots within a relatively small organisation, he could make it up as he went along, seeking inspiration in the materials before him. But here, in Boston, with fifty bewildered people backstage, and another fifty bewildered people on stage, and thirty people on triple time in the orchestra pit, he had no such luxury.

He maintained the highest of spirits in the face of what would have caused a nervous breakdown in virtually anyone else. 'Orson has been a tower of strength,' wrote Porter. 'The whole company loves him and rightly so because he never loses his temper or his power to surmount almost impossible difficulties, so if the show flops, I shall at least have had a great experience with a wonderful guy.' Porter had been enchanted to hear Welles say to a particularly burly stagehand, 'please, sweetheart, get that scenery up'. The first chaotic performance had done nothing to dent Welles's optimism. The following morning, reports Margetson, 'there was Orson smilingly greeting us with "Rise and Shine – now we've opened and read the roasts, we can *really* go to work"' – which they did. By the time of the performance that night, Margetson, who carried the weight of the show, and who had been more than a little shaken by the experience of the last three days, fell ill (and one may be sure that with an actor of Margetson's generation and temperament, nothing short of total collapse would have kept him off the stage). There was of course no understudy, so – it goes without saying – Welles went on for him, 'in a fashion typical of his past feats that won him the title of Boy Wonder of the American theatre', as the *Globe* reported. 'Welles not only ran through the long lead of the show letter perfect but also played the part of the magician which was his original role. And to make his one-man-gang performance complete, he sang two songs that he had hurriedly learned half an hour before curtain time.' This was bliss for Welles. The tedious struggles of the past few years, wrestling with editors, both in print and in film, studios, sponsors, wives, lawyers, children, were all – however temporarily – dissolved in the sheer joy of the physical act of theatre, and he was able to rejoice in an image of himself with which he was entirely happy: actor-manager of the old school, a father-figure who is at the same time reckless and untrammelled, the Vincent Crummles of the Mid-West. On *Around the World*, he was both in charge of his company – and quite a fierce disciplinarian when he needed to be – and the chief reprobate, gloriously indulging himself, breaking up on stage, making his lines up as he went along.

For the most part, the audience adored it. Margetson, seeing Welles's triumph in his role, made a swift recovery, as may be imagined, but a few days later Larry Laurence, his tenorial tonsils in tatters, retired from the fray, so Welles went on for him. Throughout rehearsals and the opening, and even as Phileas Fogg, he had still worn his moustache from *The Stranger*, now, playing the juvenile, he shaved it off without a moment's hesitation, struggled into something more or less appropriate from the wardrobe and positively bounced on stage. Naturally, he improvised the role, as, inevitably, did Margetson. 'On one occasion I was forced to say, "Passepartout, you don't know what you're talking about", whereupon Orson replied, "You never said a truer word" . . . whether he was good or not in either part, matters little. He was exciting and unpredictable at all times, both on the audience and the actors.'

Despite all these high-jink enjoyments, he was constantly working on the show, and beginning to get somewhere, he felt. The Boston press monitored his progress. According to Eliot Norton, Welles tried to negotiate an extension with the management of the theatre, offering the incoming company, the Ballets Russes de Monte Carlo ('a miniature extravaganza, which requires for transportation a mere half dozen cars'), a large financial inducement to find another venue; *Around the World* was intricate scenically, so cumbersome and involved to operate that it would not work at all 'until the stage-hands have had a course of training equivalent to that which the army gives to P-38 pilots,' wrote Norton. 'He might well have taken over the ballet intact and made it part of his own show. A ballet of a hundred or so would have been easy to absorb. Where there's a Welles there's a way.' Welles, he claims, was on the verge of hysteria at least once on the first night. ('A less cautious observer went so far as to say he went off the deep end and over the verge, backstage.') Noting Welles's propensity for stepping into the roles of missing actors, Norton observes that 'he did not take part in the nautch dancing nor did he conduct the orchestra, perhaps through an oversight'. Suddenly, the gentle mockery over, the schoolmaster's hand is revealed. 'If he wants to rescue the show in time for the New York opening, I suggest that he give up, for three or four weeks, the role of director. Bring in George Abbott, George S. Kaufman, or possibly Rouben Mamoulian to integrate, co-ordinate and speed up the show. *Around the World* needs the sure hand of such an expert and the fresh, objective point of view which such a one will bring to it.' Of course Norton's prescription would have been anathema to Welles: it may be a terrible show, he might have countered, but at least it's mine. Equally, Norton is absolutely right, and *Around the World* would no doubt have been a triumph of a particularly delightful kind had his advice been followed. Interestingly, one member of the audience in Boston had no criticism of the show at all. 'This is the greatest thing I have seen in American theatre,' he said when he went backstage. 'This is wonderful. This is what theatre should be.' It was Bertolt Brecht, and he was now more than ever delighted that Welles would be directing *Galileo*.

New Haven was the next stop. Here the dress rehearsal was over in its entirety by 1 a.m. It was Welles's thirty-first birthday, and he was persuaded to get off the wagon and have a drink or two with the actors, doing conjuring tricks for them till 3 a.m. Later that same day, the show opened at the Shubert Theatre. At the first performance the movie projector broke down almost immediately. Welles walked on stage to say, 'With your kind indulgence, we will now begin the show again,' which they did. The projector broke down again. Welles returned: 'Cut the movies! – Ladies and gentlemen, I shall try to explain how this play – or whatever you want to call it – begins.' The movies suddenly started up again. Welles left the stage. The movies broke down again. 'It is obvious,' Welles, returning, told the audience, 'as most of us stage actors have always believed for some time now, that the movies are not here to stay.' As if mechanical problems with the physical production were not enough, one of the actors began to be troublesome. Alan Reed, playing Detective Inspector Fix, complained that his role had been transformed into that of a villain; he wanted to be funny. Margetson reports Welles muttering at one show as he stood in the wings, gloomily watching Reed, 'I've written the part wrongly – this is not a comedian's role – it should be a heavy – he or the part or both must be changed.' 'You mean you're thinking of replacing him in New York?' 'In New York? – nothing. He must be replaced tomorrow at the matinée . . . by me, until I can find someone else, and I hope that will be damned soon.' Welles the serial pinch-hitter duly took over and was very funny, and hardly villainous at all. As Dynamite Gus, one of Fix's aliases, he walked into a bar and demanded a drink of 'straight formaldehyde with a black widow spider riding the olive'. He knocked it back, at which point his moustache fell off: 'Mighty powerful stuff, that liquor.' 'Since he had just written the part for himself, it was rather difficult to know whether he was improvising or not,' said Margetson. 'But I assure you, it gave us a tremendous up-lift and drew much laughter from both sides of the footlights.' This was the antic spirit that Welles so prized – though it is worth pointing out that the people he admired so much, the real vaudevillians, would never have indulged in it. Every giggle would have been carefully rehearsed. But nothing could show more clearly quite how much he longed to get up there on stage. How good, one wonders, was Alan Reed? Was it his carping that Welles took against? Or was Welles's need to perform simply overwhelming? It is all a little murky and not entirely creditable.

Meanwhile, the bandwagon rolled on. The Chestnut Street Theatre in Philadelphia was the next and last stop, a place that held no very happy memories for Welles: here, eight years earlier, *Five Kings* had foundered, victim of the erratic electrical supply, which caused the turntable alternately to whizz and to crawl. Welles, expecting the worst, appeared before the curtain on the first night of *Around the World* to apologise in advance. Everything went perfectly, causing him to apologise retrospectively at the curtain call for the slur on Philadelphia. Despite this graciousness, the indulgent Boston and New Haven press was not duplicated in Pennsylvania. '*Around the World* bears the eccentric hallmark of its producer,' said the *Daily News*. 'It is an off-the-beaten-path musical as musicals go. Our guess,' the paper added, helpfully, 'is that most playgoers will balk at what it has to offer. Personally we found much that was rewarding, plenty that was funny and even more that was downright stupefying.' There was mystification that Welles – '"Orson the Amazing . . . one of the biggest masters of self-exploitation of our times"' – was not staying in the show. 'Welles is one of the prime reasons for most of the customers flocking into the Shubert . . . they want to see him IN PERSON. Welles is very funny, whether he is making a curtain speech apologising for the lights and the defective sound system, playing the part of a comedy detective, or just doing a magician act and pulling ducks out of conductor Harry Levant's dress shirt . . . whatever he does has his personal ingeniousness stamped on it, and is certainly in character.' Cole Porter, well past the initial euphoria of his first encounter with Welles, was darkly suspicious that the more he worked on his new role, the more Welles cut the musical score. He had changed the character from Verne's Detective Inspector Fix to Dick Fix, the detective's nark, and this seems to have given him unlimited freedom to do pretty well whatever he wanted. The *Record* made an observation that would become the running gag of all subsequent reviews: 'The show has about everything in it – except the proverbial kitchen sink. But when that is brought to Mr Welles's attention, he will probably order one installed. And when he does it will be a large and handsome one with hot and cold running surprises.'

No sooner had these reviews been printed than there was a newspaper strike, which meant that the Mercury's marketing campaign went for nothing; and then, immediately after that, there was a train strike. They struggled on for the two weeks of the run to exiguous audiences, with tensions rising in the number-one dressing room, which Welles shared with Margetson, five other principals, three chorus boys, two circus clowns, three Japanese actresses and Barbette. Margetson describes the atmosphere in the dressing room, with Barbette ironing the white streamers used by the girls in the circus, while the rest of the company rushes in and out, screaming and demanding things. Barbette announces petulantly, expertly plying his iron:

'Hardly my job, but if I don't do it who in the hell will, I'd like to know . . . some of these little bitches have the audacity to cut the ends off because they find them too unwieldy, I suppose – how do they know which streamer they'll get back tomorrow night? There won't be anything left of them at this rate . . . and furthermore that property man positively hates me and the whole circus. He ruined the girls' trapeze act by using one of *my* ropes for Orson Welles's bloody magic act. Mon Dieu! In Paris I was respected.'

'Oh shut up!'

'Taisez-vous yourself. Le style c'est l'homme même.'

'Where were you born, Barbette?'

'Texas, why?'

Finally the behemoth rumbled into New York. The financial situation was worse than ever, and again Welles went begging to Korda, who formalised the relationship by offering him another $30,000 for *Around the World*, effectively an inducement for the film deal that followed three months later, by the terms of which Welles was to get $75,000 per picture for a three-picture deal in which he would appear as 'artist and/or director and/or producer'. It is possible to imagine worse penalties. Welles never seemed to take Korda's proposals entirely seriously; not that he was focusing on anything much beyond the immediate all-consuming needs of the theatrical monster he had bred. The sympathetic left-wing magazine *PM* sent its reporter along to talk to him; Welles was uncommonly candid about its misfortunes, but mindful as ever of the particular audience he was addressing. 'I never heard of a show which had so much bad luck. If all the money, time, effort and heartbreak we've put into it could be spent changing Truman's anti-strike bill it might be worthwhile. The cast has gone through real misery. I'm mortgaged and bleeding. If the show does well, it will deserve it on its pain alone.' He insists that he's trying to get someone to replace him in the show, since he's due in Hollywood on 7 June for what he calls a 'film chore' (an as-yet-unannounced film for Harry Cohn). His expectations of personal success are low: he's never had a good notice in the New York theatre as an actor, he says (which was not entirely untrue). 'The average newspaper writer always seems to think it's time to take me down a peg. Why, I could show you eight floors with clippings that are nothing but wild roasts.' He allows himself to show a little vulnerability. 'I wouldn't mind being taken down if they'd let me climb up once

in a while. Actually I don't like publicity. I don't like to be interviewed or photographed. I'm afraid of being misquoted. I'm just
a tired sort of male Katharine Hepburn,' he added, coquettishly.
In 1937, he says, wistfully, *Time* thought he was great. 'I was the
Laurence Olivier of that year.'

Olivier was much on Welles's mind at that moment. The Old
Vic Company, under the aegis of the Theatre Guild, was playing
in New York and had just taken the town (or most of it) by storm,
presenting the cream of their repertory from the legendary season
that included *Henry IV* Parts One and Two, the audacious double
bill of *The Critic* and *Oedipus*, and finally *Richard III*, in the title
role of which Olivier had repeated and magnified the ecstatic
response he had received in London. Olivier (and to a lesser extent
the rest of the company, Ralph Richardson, Joyce Redman, George
Relph among them) was used by the American critics as a stick
with which to beat American classical acting, generally held to be
far inferior to its British equivalent. Nothing could have been better
calculated to upset Welles, who had very little enthusiasm for the
sort of solid, somewhat fustian acting that, leading actors aside, the
majority of the Old Vic Company of the time represented
('anything but a noteworthy group', opined George Jean Nathan).
Moreover, and even more threateningly, Olivier's film of *Henry V*
had been attracting ecstatic encomia: another actor-director-
producer – and in Shakespeare, too. Welles bit his lip on this
occasion, but after describing the circumstances of Alan Reed's
dismissal in a nice fresh version specially minted for the interview
– Welles played the part one night to show him how it should be
done, and Reed replied, 'You're absolutely right, that's the way it
should be played. But I can't do it that way' – he adds, 'maybe we
can get Olivier to play it. He'll be out of work in two weeks.'

The New York press was agog at the sheer scale of the promised entertainment about to open at the Adelphi Theatre. The
venue, on 54th Street, was something of a *théâtre maudit* – or, to
put it a little differently, 'the dump of all dumps', in William
Craxton's eloquent phrase – with its unprepossessing brownstone
exterior, behind which the auditorium and stage-house were located
in a large warehouse-like structure. 'Finished in rough stucco and
Tudor-inspired panelling around the proscenium, the auditorium
might easily have been mistaken for a high-school assembly hall,'
according to *Lost Theatres of Broadway*; evidently the theatre was lost
long before it stopped putting on plays. After opening its doors –
as the Craig Theatre – flop had followed flop until the WPA took

it over in the nineteen-thirties for the Federal Theatre Project; it was then occupied by an esoteric religious group until the Shuberts bought it. The first show under their ownership was *On the Town*, a triumph that almost immediately moved to a better theatre. The Adelphi was finally demolished in 1970 and is now the site of the New York Hilton. Dick Wilson had obviously secured a good cheap deal from the Shuberts, but being at the Adelphi was not something to crow about. It was a lively enough scene backstage, however, when the *New York Times* visited the technical rehearsals: HOW WELLES'S 'WORLD' GOES ROUND, the piece was headed, and it was clearly a bit of a mystery that it went round at all. 'Backstage at the Adelphi looks like Cain's warehouse brought to life by a madman who added a circus and a barnyard . . . out front this is a musical extravaganza, backstage it is raucous bedlam in chiaroscuro, born of a Salvador Dali–Mack Sennett merger.' (Favourable or unfavourable, Welles and his work always inspired – *demanded* – that journalists strut their stuff; it was almost a point of honour.) The reporter boggled over the forty-five tons of sets, the 1,600-pound mechanised elephant and the fifty-four stage hands (they obviously hadn't managed to cut back on any). 'Sets are dropped six deep; the stage director sets up his script and cue sheet – which look more imposing that the score for the Verdi Requiem. The lighting operator scrutinises six portable boards – twice the number for most musicals – which pull 2,300 amperes.'

Not only reporters were inspired to heights of prose-writing by Welles: the cartoonists went to town, too. The great Al Hirschfeld produced one of his small masterpieces, which suggested something of the impact of the movie screen in conjunction with the live action, turning the Indian rope trick into an odd, embryo-like profile of Welles. Don Freeman's view of the backstage area in the *New York Herald Tribune* was even more vivid, with Welles as Dick Fix somewhere in amongst all the livestock, the elephant, the eagle, the nautch girls, the stagehands, the moon, the boat and the drums, with Margetson and Mary Healy high up on a platform, their backs to us, facing the audience. The cartoon appeared the day of the only two previews, matinée and evening. The press night, the next day, was Friday 31 May, Memorial Day. It was the last show of an exhausting season to open. That morning, Cole Porter took a plane to California. No such luxury was available to Welles. He had to sweat it out, quite literally: there was no air-conditioning in the Adelphi. 'In hot weather,' *Fanfare* reported, the theatre was 'an approximation of a Methodist Hell'. Despite the heat, the show went as well as it had ever gone, mechanically, musically, dramatically, comically; there were fourteen curtain calls. Holding his hands up for silence, Welles made a speech: 'Ladies and gentlemen, I can't tell you how wonderful it is to be *asked* to make a speech. Hitherto I've only *had* to make one to apologise for the performance.'

CHAPTER SEVENTEEN

Wellesafloppin'

As so often in the theatre, that first night was the best of it. The following day brought the sort of notices that, while not totally dismissive, nonetheless failed to make the theatre-goer, weary after a long season, reach for the telephone and make a booking. Welles had a following – there was a modest advance – but the huge show required a capacity audience merely to break even; in these situations, it is the floating voter who needs to be persuaded, and nothing in the notices suggested that you would be unable to face your grandchildren if you missed it. While acknowledging this or that item of merit, an impression of enervating incoherence was conveyed. It was all, of course, very personal: it was Welles (and not his show) that was being judged, although, oddly enough, he was thought to be the best thing about it.

'There is hardly a word to fit this musical fare,' said Vernon Rice of the *Post*. 'It is mammoth, it is gigantic, it is lavish. It is also dull.' Irving Cahn found it 'as amorphous as a splash of mud and as pedestrian as its title . . . if *Around the World in Eighty Days* lasts that long, I'll be surprised.' Robert Garland – 'only eighty days? you ask yourself. Surely it must be more' – added: 'Orson, disguised as a magician, makes ducks, geese and chicken disappear. He is good at this disappearing stuff, is Mr Welles. So good is he that, halfway through *Around the World*, he has made the plot disappear as well. No plot, no show!' *Time*, which gave the show its most quotable quote – '*Around the World* is Orson Welles with his foot on the loud pedal which is roughly the equivalent of a lunatic asylum at the height of an electrical storm' – brutally observed that 'there is something pretty empty and amateurish about the show. It falls down as burlesque, displaying far too little wit, far too much Welles.' The problem, *Time* said, was that 'unwisely Welles's extravaganza pauses from time to time for identification as a musical comedy. But the love interest, the exotic dances and Cole Porter's tired score merely check the pace without livening the party.' Welles the leading actor seemed out of step, again, with Welles the director.

The elements of his multiply-split personality stubbornly resisted integration. The *Times* made the same point: 'When the guffawing Mr Welles goes off stage, the show goes with him . . . the production numbers have an inclination to take themselves seriously . . . miles removed from Mr Welles's vast burlesque.'

If Welles felt he had never had good reviews from the New York press, he could no longer maintain that, though admittedly his performance was praised only in order to denigrate the rest of the show. 'Orson in casting himself temporarily as Mr Fix has made a grave error. For when he has to quit to report to Columbia, he is robbing the show of the only personality to support it. It is his tongue-in-cheek playing – his versatility – his vitality that set the pace and dominate the entire company. If once again he wanted to prove himself the Welles of Onlyness, he's accomplished his purpose. For without him, *Around the World* will be the Welles of Loneliness.' It is probably unnecessary to identify the quote as coming from the trade paper, *Variety*. There were more amiable reviews that relished the quirkiness of the show, notably an appreciation by Wolcott Gibbs in the *New Yorker*, who, describing the show as 'a fine musical cheese dream conceivably suggested to him by something once written by a man called Jules Verne', hoped that 'Mr Welles will be able to keep it open for the entertainment of other happy adolescents at least until another spring'. The child-like quality of the entertainment was identified by a number of reviewers: 'Out of the same mould as the British pantomimes, traditional Christmas entertainments for children,' said William Hawkins of the *World-Telegram*, accurately identifying what was clearly an essential problem of the show: 'The material is too often imitative of the period it is depicting . . . rather than being amusingly satirical.' Welles was obviously dangerously torn between affection for the genre and the desire to send it up. 'It's all done in a let's-put-on-a-play spirit . . . children will probably love this show. But the guns in your ears and feathers in your hair are not mature substitutions for a contagious sense of humour.' Nichols of the *Times*, half admiring, half critical, wrote: 'These products of showmanship are put forward with great gestures and an air that is half burlesque, half small boy. Mr Welles and his associates are enjoying themselves and make no secret of that fact . . .'

John Chapman came to the rescue in the *Daily News*: 'I, on the other hand, had a wonderful time. To me *Around the World* was grand, gorgeous and goofy.' Obviously the evening was bursting with high spirits and goodwill. Equally obviously it was seriously lacking in the sort of skill that is not merely the *sine qua non* of vaudeville, but its *raison d'être*. 'Mr Welles's own magic act,' said the sweetly benevolent Gibbs, 'has an air of being a genial, off-hand parody of all such performances, and it must be somewhat irritating to professional workers in the field . . . not even Mr Welles is quite up to two-and-a-half hours of sustained comic improvisation.' Lewis Nichols, returning to the show, pronounced it 'the latest example of the good and bad qualities of Orson Welles the showman'. Falling into the tut-tut school of criticism that Welles so readily provoked, he said, like a caring but anxious schoolteacher, '[the show] needs discipline. It needs some higher editorial authority to say "no" loudly and frequently. Through carelessness, inertia or just the guardian angel's being away for the moment, it slows down into failure.' He was not necessarily wrong. The one aspect of the show that was universally praised was the Japanese circus, staged by Barbette with iron discipline, no doubt: circus has no alternative; in its absence the result is death or disfigurement. 'This fills the stage,' said Nichols. 'This is what the whole should be.'

The physical beauty of the circus scene – all pink and white – is clear from the production photographs, and owed much to Welles's vivid appreciation of Japanese art. The physical production in general was clearly remarkable. 'Mr Davison has been prodigal with his talents.' Cole Porter's wife Linda claimed, no doubt rightly, that the sets were inspired by illustrations for a very rare first edition of the Verne, which she bought her husband when they were embarking on the project. Davison reproduced Victorian theatre techniques with some thoroughness, and the result was impressive in very much the way the eighteen-seventies production must have been; there can scarcely have been so much painted scenery on the American stage for fifty years. No doubt there was a danger of over-kill in the sheer profligacy of the design, but it was still a remarkable achievement. It was Alvin Colt's conceit to have the girls wearing exaggerated bustles wherever they were, 'and as the world tour progresses it is fun to wonder where those Victorian rears will pop out next'. John Chapman was one of the few reviewers to have anything good to say about the score: 'Cole Porter's tunes have a way of sneaking up on one . . . like Begin the Beguine which I and everyone else failed to notice when it first appeared.' But Wolcott Gibbs remarked, 'if God will forgive me, Cole Porter's music and lyrics are hardly memorable at all'. Chapman tried to suggest that Welles had created a new genre. 'It is part musical show . . . part circus, part vaudeville, part Olsen and Johnson, part movies.'

Nobody thought the show was perfect, not even its greatest partisans; in the end, judgement came down to whether you were in sympathy with Welles's underlying impulse in staging it. 'The production at the Adelphi is shot through with the personality, imagination and drive of Mr Welles,' said Chapman, 'and for my money he is . . . the ablest and most versatile in the American entertainment business.' There was something, many people felt, that Welles had that no one else in the modern theatre did. Lewis Nichols, observing almost wearily that 'the recent arrival of *Around the World* brings up the matter of Orson Welles again', suggested that 'the State legislature should pass a bill prohibiting Mr Welles from leaving the theatre . . . excitement is needed on Broadway and he is the one that can give it. Even in the case of a show as far removed from the superior as is *Around the World*, there are a good many original qualities. They are qualities only known to a showman and their appearance in the neighbourhood of Times Square is too rare.'

Alas, he did not also say: go and see the show. It was absolutely imperative and a matter of some urgency that tickets should be sold: the show had cost, according to Suskin in *Show Tunes*, $300,000 at a time when a big musical could be produced for $100,000. *Kiss Me, Kate*, two years later, cost $180,000. Even the critics were worried – Wolcott Gibbs said:

> There are mischievous rumours that the thirty-four scene changes
> (requiring the presence and this time, it may even be, the actual
> services of fifty-five stagehands), the incredible profusion of
> mechanical devices, and the employment of a cast that must
> include every fascinating character that Mr Welles has ever met
> make the cost of *Around the World* literally prohibitive – the idea
> of conducting an enterprise that can't possibly make money
> would, of course, have an almost irresistible charm for that rich,
> unusual mind.

Broadway was suddenly aware of the dangerously escalating cost of putting on shows; Burns Mantle, writing in that same season of 1946, laid the blame at the door of the unions: 'Unless some means are found to check the mounting demands, which in the case of the stagehands' union have gone to the absurd limit of threatening action on plays with a single set of scenery unless extra hands are employed for a second imaginary set, the future may see an unavoidable, drastic curtailment of production.' The gargantuan cost of

Around the World was as much attributable to reckless planning and lack of forethought as it was to union demands, but simply to keep the show running on Broadway was a vast expense: the show needed to take a thumping $28,000 a week to break even.

To whip up business, Welles wheeled into action: his first stop was the all-powerful broadcaster and *New York Daily Mirror* columnist Walter Winchell. Welles sent him a telegram telling him that he had made a curtain speech quoting Winchell's remark that they had everything in their show but the kitchen sink, and saying that they'd fixed that, bringing out a real kitchen sink for the bow. HATE TO KEEP HECKLING YOU BUT IT'S LIFE OR DEATH FOR ME. PRAY YOU CAN FIND A WORD ON YOUR AIR SHOW TONIGHT. I KNOW I HAVE NO RIGHT TO ASK YOU THIS, BUT HONESTLY SHOW DOESN'T DESERVE TO CLOSE, AND YOU'RE THE ONLY HOPE. Then Welles asked the great composer-producer Billy Rose, for whom he had tried and failed to mount the play *Emily Brady* two years earlier, to put in a word, and Rose duly wrote a column addressed to Welles, to whom he referred as 'this wild-and-woolly wunderkind'. 'Listen, Thunder-In-The-Mountains, isn't it about time you made up your mind whether you're Senator Pepper, D. W. Griffith, or Kupperman the quiz kid?' Rose wants to reclaim Welles for the theatre. 'I'd like to see you go back to being Just Plain Orson, the toy tornado, who tore the town apart a few seasons ago. You've been away too long, Doubledome. I knew it when I saw your show the other night. To this paying customer *Around the World* is the doodles – a small boy's dream of show business come true.' Again and again, the references are to toys and small boys. 'When it comes to high-jinks – you're Belasco shooting Roman candles! Anyone who'd like to be in a toyshop at midnight when the toys come to life will adore your show . . . this is your town . . . as far as I'm concerned you've got more rabbits in your hat than anybody who has hit the theatre since George M. Cohan.'

(It's worth noting, by way of a brief parenthesis, that Billy Rose was responsible for *Jumbo*, his own 1935 musical extravaganza, to which *Around the World* was sometimes compared. It starred Jimmy Durante, with Paul Whiteman and band, a Rodgers and Hart score, a Hecht and MacArthur book, bareback riders – one of whom was seventy-five years old – a troupe of acrobats all aged sixty-plus (among them Barbette), midgets, clowns, death-defying aerialists, jugglers, fire-eaters, tightrope specialists, lion tamers, and close on 500 live animals, including Big Rosie in the title role. The clown A. Robins kept pulling everything from chairs to endless bananas out of his pockets, while he changed costume with a flick of a handkerchief 'and never for one moment lost a beat from the rhythm of cacophony he emits'. Beside this, *Around the World* and Orson Welles were rather small beer. *Jumbo* cost $340,000 and lost $160,000, so perhaps an encomium from its producer and creator was not the ideal endorsement.)

Welles obviously buttonholed John Chapman of the *Daily News*, who wrote in his piece that 'Orson tells me that if necessary he will act Hamlet and do a roller-skating act if these would seem helpful.' Elsa Maxwell was wheeled in next: 'I was thrilled, entranced, goggle-eyed, bewitched and bewildered by my trip *Around the World*,' she wrote in her influential column in the *New York Post*. 'Mr Welles inadvertently dominates every part of the stage, scene and play whenever he appears . . . his magnetic, amazing, opulent rich personality makes out of a tiny insignificant part something so gigantic as completely to overwhelm and in fact wipe out the rest of the cast.' She reports that Welles is making a curtain speech in which he reminds critics of the demise of Percy Hammond after *Macbeth*. 'He does it in such a funny manner, with a Welles-ian tongue-in-cheek-ism, that is quite delightful and Mr (George Jean) Nathan and Mr Garland need not worry too much about their summer colds.' None of it made any discernible difference at the box office.

In fact Welles had a splendid platform from which to promote himself and the show. Just before he had started rehearsals for *Around the World*, he had revived the Mercury Summer Theatre of the Air, which was transmitted on Friday nights (meaning that there could be no Friday performances of the stage show, another blow to the chances of financial recoupment: his suggestion that the show could be broadcast from the theatre during an extended intermission was scorned by the unions). On the first Friday of the run at the Adelphi, *Around the World*, naturally, was the chosen classic, and the broadcast is a potted version of what was happening on the stage every other night of the week. If the show was chaotic, the radio programme is bedlam. The narrative – a fairly simple one, after all – is virtually incomprehensible. Margetson soldiers valiantly on, giving a reasonably clear account of himself and the role; Welles roars around, indulging in the radiophonic equivalent of pulling faces (pulling voices, perhaps). 'I'll get your man, Inspector, if I 'ave to search the 'ole of London from Tooting Bec to Putney Green,' he says as Dick Fix. 'I'll join you later, Chief. It's time for me to go to church and write blasphemies all

over the 'Oly books.' The pallid songs, including 'Snagtooth Gurtie'
and 'Flow, music, flow', make little impression, except for Elsa
Maxwell's favourite, which is moderately amusing in a sub-
Cowardian manner:

> Alas if you'd only been
> Born on British land
> Ruled by our gracious Queen
> The more readily you'd understand
> Wherever they fly the flag of old England
> Wherever they wear the old school tie
> Wherever a fox would never chase a fox-hound
> Wherever a steak and kidney make a pie
> Wherever they're certain that
> The Derby's not a hat
> Wherever to ice your drink is still a sin
> Wherever the air is full
> Of old John Bull
> Whatever is not cricket can't win.

Welles is breathless and charmless as narrator, a role in which he
had never before failed. No doubt it was all done in a frantic rush,
but it was a sad waste of an opportunity, firstly, to create a record
of the show, and secondly, to sell tickets for it. (The comparison
with the first, 1938, *Mercury Theatre of the Air* version is painful: in
that Welles had played Fogg simultaneously clipped and suave, rather
like his Lamont Cranston (The Shadow's soigné alter ego), and
none the worse for that; while the Mercury stalwarts – Ray Collins,
Edgar Barrier and indeed Stefan Schnabel among them – gave
masterclasses in radio acting.)

Continuing to promote the show in a slightly lower key, Welles
used his other radio slot – the *Commentary*, still broadcast under
the aegis of ABC on sustaining radio, and reaching a relatively
small listenership – to muse on the show and its fate:

I think the theatre is suffering from a galloping lack of dignity.
The theatre has never been so poor in my lifetime. But this is
always true right after a war. Not that there aren't many deserved
hits on Broadway right now. Nor is *Around the World* the
antidote. On the contrary, *Around the World* is made up of very
old stuff – things that have enchanted me from the time I saw
them under canvas, in a one-ring circus, in the theatre or a

Carnival. It's like hanging around the toy displays at a department store around Christmas time. Or going out and buying a whole store.

It is curious how frequently in moments of great enthusiasm this self-confessed hater of childhood refers to the delights of infancy: directing a film, famously, was 'the best train set a boy ever had'. He lists the delights on display at the Adelphi: 'There's a train wreck, an attack by Indians, old-fashioned movies, low comedy and a score by Cole Porter. Actually I would go and see the show myself many times,' he says, 'perhaps once a week . . . if somebody else were putting it on.' He continues in that vein of aggressive nostalgia to which he is prone in moments of depression, with the sense that there are no standards any more. 'I haven't liked a musical since the old Ziegfeld days when they had really funny men and lush women. Not that *Around the World* is a musical comedy – it's an extravaganza. Musicals today are too smart, too chic.' All alone at the microphone, he becomes unexpectedly emotional and personal. 'Let me tell you something of what it's like at a Broadway opening . . . any Broadway opening has much in common with a bull-fight . . . it's a question of life or death. Kill or the bull kills you . . . and with a show it's kill the people – or – or else the audience just walks away and leaves the show to die of loneliness.' There is, for Welles, an unusually strong unarticulated emotion here; a real feeling of rejection. 'Our show is getting ovations from its audiences. So,' he claims, not entirely accurately, 'we have been successful in building it into an authentic hit . . . in spite of the real killers of the theatre . . . the dramatic critics who deliver the swift justice of an oriental court. Because of the power they wield, the critics have retarded the theatre these past years.' He rehearses complaints familiar to actors, directors and writers from time immemorial: 'because they must see each new play that is presented they are too easily bored and too readily lose sight of the fact that the theatre is primarily intended to entertain'. This is scarcely the position Welles had occupied in his assaults on Hollywood, which he had ruthlessly attacked for its vacuousness, so at this point, perhaps wisely, he moves on to another topic. In any case, the argument with critics can never be won: a critic criticised suddenly becomes the champion of free speech, the aggrieved artist someone who 'cannot take criticism'.

In the case of *Around the World*, it is clear that critics were, on the whole, broadly unsympathetic to what Welles was attempting, and that they felt, moreover, that he had failed in what he set out to do. To that there is no answer. A quick look at what was going on in the theatre that season suggests that Welles's taste for extravaganza was not in tune with the times; nor was his acting likely to win the palm: Broadway had taken to its bosom Laurence Olivier (at his classical zenith) and the very young Marlon Brando, two actors of exceptional individuality, in their different ways both single-minded artists, next to whom Welles was bound to seem generalised and outmoded. In that year's *Variety* poll, Olivier was elected Best Actor, Brando Best Supporting Actor and Most Promising Young Actor. As for the shows, the musicals were all book musicals with immensely strong scores: *Call Me Mister, Three to Make Ready* and *Annie Get Your Gun*, with *Oklahoma!, Show Boat, Song of Norway* and *Carousel* from the previous season still playing. There was a strong dramatic showing, apart from the Old Vic's contribution: new plays included the Lunts in *O Mistress Mine* and Judy Holliday in *Born Yesterday*, and from the year before Laurette Taylor in *The Glass Menagerie* and *State of the Union* (the Lindsay and Crouse play about the search for a Republican candidate for President, the sort of thing Welles might profitably have turned his hand to); there was in addition a slew of 'Negro problem' plays. *Nellie Bly* – another tale about a trans-global traveller who sets out, in fact, to beat Fogg's record – had opened and closed ignominiously in January at the Adelphi; not, perhaps, a great omen for *Around the World*.

In this context, from the perspective of 'profile', Welles's show could only seem a bizarre anachronism. To be sure, there were those who loved it: Joshua Logan, director of that season's hit, *Annie Get Your Gun*, wrote to Welles: 'your production is fresh, witty, magical, exciting and all the other words I can't think of now. I was thrilled to hear the audience response at the end and I'm sure you were.' He added some generous and practical observations about the excessive speed of the first scene and attendant narrative unclarity, ending: 'at any rate your work is like oxygen to the theatre and I hope you keep at it forever'. There was in many quarters a nagging feeling expressed by a few sympathetic critics that Welles brought to the theatre something unique, rare and in danger of disappearance. 'I have been to see the show three times and I might say I am enchanted with it,' wrote Oliver Smith. 'I really felt it was the most exciting show of the year for me, and all I can say is – I love it. It really gives me a certain excitement about working in the theatre.'

And yet, against these expressions of admiration, it is worth remembering that a mere ten years earlier Welles had been not merely the object of a few connoisseurs' enthusiasm, but the white hope of the theatre, and the Mercury – now a mere commercial producer – had seemed to contain the seeds of the longed-for National Theatre. The visit of the Old Vic, and the sense of continuity that it represented, had stirred up the slumbering idealism of the American profession. The visit had been sponsored by what Burns Mantle called 'that . . . altruistically minded non-profit organisation, Theatre Incorporated', which had also just presented *Pygmalion* with Gertrude Lawrence. Theatre Incorporated was a non-profit, tax-exempt corporation committed to 'a sustained programme of great plays of the past and outstanding plays of the present'. Its income was devoted to 'the continuation of such a programme on a permanent basis; to the encouragement of young playwrights, directors and actors through a subsidiary experimental theatre; to the utilisation of the stage as an educational force, to the ultimate development of a true people's theatre'. Welles and *Around the World* must have seemed quite irrelevant to such a serious-minded policy, though it was almost exactly the Mercury's programme and closely describes Welles's declared aims. It appears to have been some kind of collective with no designated leader or artistic director; Welles, of course, could only have functioned at the head, and as the mascot, of any such organisation, but he had long ago abdicated that possibility.

In fact, *Around the World* is an extraordinary episode in Welles's career, though not without precedent. There is a clear line in Welles's work from *The Drunkard*, his first semi-professional production when he was a teenager, at Woodstock, Illinois, to *Horse Eats Hat* at Project 891, through *Too Much Johnson* and on to his variety circuit tour of *The Green Goddess*, *hommages* all to the broad and flamboyant popular theatre of the mythical theatrical past, a passion that amounts almost to an obsession. None of it, though, had been remotely on the scale of *Around the World*, which is best understood as a last heroic attempt to re-create the theatre of his childhood, in order, perhaps, to do something for the father who introduced him to it, who believed that life should above all be *fun*, and towards whom he carried a heavy burden of guilt throughout his life, feeling that he had abandoned him to a lonely, squalid death. Welles had so often honoured the memory of his socially conscious mother in all the improving, avant-garde, politically progressive projects he had undertaken; *Around the World* was a counterbalance to all that worthiness. It is perhaps worth observing that someone innocent of Welles's work outside his filmography would find it almost impossible to believe that *Around the World* was the work of the same man who created *Citizen Kane*, *The Magnificent Ambersons* or even *The Stranger*. It seems somehow so utterly devoid of the shadows that are so intrinsic to those films. The films all have clear, strong themes, even a pot-boiler like *Journey into Fear*, and common preoccupations. *Around the World* has no connection, however tenuous, with any of them. It is a *jeu d'esprit*, pure carnival, Welles's subconscious on holiday, the bridge between his forays into radio comedy and the films. One is inevitably also struck by the extraordinary discrepancy between the expenditure of time, effort, ingenuity and money on the show and the amount of pleasure it engendered – modest, even in the eyes of its fans. Welles's films (contrary to what was generally believed) went relatively little over budget. With *Around the World* he seemed to have no sense of budget whatsoever: he spent money on the show the way he spent his own money in real life. There is something fundamentally disproportionate about the whole venture that is utterly characteristic.

Meanwhile, there was the show to do. Arthur 'Shirley' Margetson shared a dressing room with Welles and his valet Shorty Chirello, who functioned as his dresser. The Japanese acrobats, Barbette and the other principals had been relegated to their own quarters at the Adelphi. The life of the dressing room was obviously very congenial to Welles. He had had a primitive show-relay system – unknown in Broadway theatres for at least another decade – rigged up so that he could listen to the parts of the show that he wasn't in and make notes on them. He was inundated with letters from the public and liked to read them out to Margetson. ('My husband has been anti-Christ all his life until he heard you read from the Bible on air the other Sunday,' said one of the more memorable ones. 'He has been going to church with me every Sunday since; but it isn't doing him any good. Dear Mr Welles what shall I do about it?') Margetson reports the nightly charade whereby the house manager Hugo Schaaf would slip $20 to Shorty, who would then slip it to Welles. One night Dick Wilson caught them at it; all denied it. Welles was thrilled with the deception. 'He'd gotten away with something! Twenty dollars.' Welles was in fact on the Equity minimum of $50.50 throughout the run.

Margetson reports Welles's little naughtinesses: his delight in trying to make Mary Healy or Margetson dry up on stage; his late arrival at the theatre (he was seldom there before 8.45, with a first entrance at 8.50). Three minutes before going on as Fu San, he would call Shorty over to give him a shave. 'You might think this was a pose of his – and who am I to say it wasn't?' Welles was clearly very fond of the old fusspot he called Shirley. Margetson reports some of his kindnesses: out of the blue one day, for example, he said, 'Watch the papers next week.' Margetson found that Welles had given him prominent billing: now the posters and the papers said: 'Orson Welles and Arthur Margetson in *Around the World*'. He never failed to mention the older man in his nightly curtain speech. 'Now that an air-conditioning machine has been installed via the Shuberts at great expense,' he would say, 'the very latest thing, mind you, not just Mr Lee Shubert blowing through a block of ice – I do so hope, if you liked our *little* show, you'll tell your friends – don't wait until you bump into them, telegraph them. After all, it's only the presence of an audience that distinguishes a theatre from an icebox – although you may find a ham in both.' 'Whereupon,' Margetson writes, 'he would look at me and say, "I am referring, of course, to Broadway's newest star."' And of course Margetson was hopelessly in love with him for ever after.

Despite the steadily declining attendance figures – not helped by a particularly hot summer – Welles was clearly enjoying himself, and, using his dressing room as a base, he spread himself in ever more directions. Under the headline YOU COULDN'T KILL HIM WITH A CLUB, *Daily News* reporter Robert Sylvester described the movement order of a typical professional week. After detailing Operations A–E, he continues:

> F: preparations for his September night-club debut at the Copacabana for which he'll have to write himself out of the early scenes of *Around the World*, run to the Adelphi then hustle back to the Copa for his two late shows; G: plan to do *King Lear* matinées when *Around the World* isn't playing; H: plan to revive *Five Kings*. His week actually starts Friday night after the half-hour broadcast. As soon as this is over, he chooses the script for the next week, begins trimming it in time and casting for the finished script. He works on things through Saturday morning. His dressing room off-time is spent Saturday afternoon and evenings dictating the script for his Sunday radio lecture.

The previous week he had recorded Oscar Wilde's *The Happy Prince* with Bing Crosby. But his more visionary activities were not ignored, either. 'The other day he accepted a directorship with a new theatre arts foundation which is going to do everything from educating actors to getting them jobs. He has no further plans at the moment, he says. "I'm just sort of dawdling."' Of course Welles encouraged the image. But it was more than just self-promotion; he hardly felt alive unless he was operating on every imaginable front. At some point during the run his current secretary, Jackson Leighter's sister Lolita Herbert (who had taken to distilling his letters into a question requiring a Yes/No choice at the bottom of the page), sent him an itemised memo with running commentary; among the items are:

4): am enclosing a letter from S. Eisenstein of Moscow . . .
6): am enclosing a letter from a typical Welles fan in England to whom I have sent your photograph. You are deeply loved & admired there and I have yet to find a letter from the British Isles that is filled with anything but the highest praise for you personally & for your varied activities . . . 11): as a result of the wonderful plug you gave the new matchmaking course at Birmingham Hospital a couple of weeks ago on the Pabst show, I was asked to visit the various depts the other day.

*

Amidst so much activity, there was one notable absence: *Galileo*. In early May, while he was still on the road with *Around the World*, Welles had had Sunday lunch with Brecht; Ferdinand Reyher, Brecht's close collaborator, had recorded in his diary: 'Welles now ready to direct *Galileo*.' But in the interim, while Welles was wrestling with his behemothian extravaganza, Laughton and Brecht – mere amateurs at theatrical production – had begun to worry about finance. Eventually they decided to approach Mike Todd (the same Mike Todd with whom Welles had just fallen out to such disastrous effect on his personal finances), and Todd had enthusiastically agreed to produce the show. He was not, after all, averse to a bit of culture, having just successfully revived Major Maurice Evans's *Hamlet* – the *G.I. Hamlet* (Todd's title, needless to say) – at the City Center, to Welles's great chagrin, the dapper, dry, polished Evans being everything that he loathed in an actor. Todd's accession to the producing team of *Galileo* was casually announced to Dick Wilson towards the end of June at a meeting with Bert Allenberg, part of Laughton's agency, Berg-Allenberg; Welles and Wilson immediately withdrew from the project. The timing was poor: *Around the World* was desperately struggling to cover its costs, precisely because, as Dick Wilson insisted in a letter to Laughton, they had opened it in the spring instead of the autumn, to allow Laughton to fulfil his filming schedule. If they had waited, *Around the World* 'would have been a big and substantial hit'. He continues: 'We don't like to put the blame on anyone for what apparently is happening, but we can't escape the conclusion that we've been treated very badly.' Brecht, meanwhile, having heard rumours in Los Angeles that Welles was unavailable, had sent Mercury Productions a telegram asking if the *Galileo* team could quote their enthusiastic endorsement of the play to other directors. Smarting from these two slaps in the face, Wilson wrote a somewhat rash letter of reproach to Laughton, informing him that:

> directing *Galileo* is only half of what Orson can do or intended
> to do with the play. The idea of the production, the
> contribution to the work of scenic and costume designers, the
> casting values – all these count as fully as the direction. When
> Orson does a play . . . he really does it. Not a detail of the
> production-in-plan escaped him. That's the only way he can
> function right. The productions show it. As a result, he has no
> equal in the theatre. On a play like *Galileo*, with a great actor
> like yourself, and with a great author, direction is only a job, and
> one which might so easily be at odds with the production.

It is quite impossible, he says, for Mercury to work with Todd, whose words and actions since their falling out 'are certainly not conducive to another affiliation'. He ends by expressing how disappointed he is 'to lose the opportunity to do (and be associated with you in) one of the greatest productions of the contemporary theatre'.

One way and another it is a very provocative letter, though it is quite clear that Laughton and Brecht were in the wrong in the matter of Todd. It is also clear that they were worried, not unreasonably, that Mercury would not be able to hold up financially under the impact of the widely perceived disaster of *Around the World*, and that they could help by securing some sort of underpinning. Wilson's frustration that 'the terms offered to Todd were basically ones that were refused to us' is wholly understandable. It is, however, a little hard to know exactly what he is getting at in his paragraph about Welles the director – that he's worth the money and the trouble; that he will do it better than anyone else could;

or that they should just let him get on with it. Whatever the case, it seems a little bizarre that Wilson should be writing to these two world-class *hommes du théâtre* as if they had never done a show before. Laughton replied not to Wilson, but to Welles himself – 'I do not appreciate your habit of using a third party to do the calling' – in a letter of which the draft is clearly much rewritten in anger, full of false starts and rubbings-out. His rage and frustration are palpable. 'I will answer two points only. First, my contract with Todd is not at all the same as yours. All the points I protested are eliminated. Second, I might have called you and told you immediately when Brecht and I had decided on Todd, if we could get him. I just plain was not going to put up with the inevitable procrastination. Either the play was going on the earliest possible day or I had to do some movies. Time at my age is dear.' (He was forty-seven.) Unsurprisingly, he picks up on Wilson's odd panegyric on the scope of Welles's directing activities. 'The rest of Dick's letter seems to me to be nonsense, including a passage which says "When Orson does a play . . . he really does it." I was under the impression that we were all three to collaborate on "the idea of the production" and so on (now it would be four of course) for this new and difficult play – otherwise how could I also "function right". You are an extraordinary man of the theatre and therefore I flatly do not believe that you cannot function as a member of a team.'

Here Laughton had completely misjudged his man. Welles was not interested in the sort of collaboration that Laughton and Brecht had in mind, a kind of triumvirate – or, horror of horrors, quadrumvirate with Todd. Welles simply did not understand the idea of democracy in the theatre, or this sort of creative pool. Laughton and Brecht had blurred the lines between author and actor, and now they wanted to blur the lines between director, actor and author. That would not suit Welles. He led; that was it. 'You are the best man in the world,' Laughton continued, 'to put the Church of Rome on the stage, to mention only one aspect of the play. This appears to me to matter. Cannot this unimportant thing between you and Todd be worked out. Todd has never spoken ill of you to either of us. The strongest word he has used is "afraid". That also is nonsense when there is this play to be told. Brecht greets you. Charles.' Laughton puts the whole matter in perspective with his fine phrase 'there is this play to be told', a phrase of which Brecht would certainly have approved. The telling of the play was Laughton's whole ambition, to which everything else was subservient. To Welles it may have seemed exciting, fun, a challenge, 'one of the greatest productions of the contemporary theatre' – in other words, more glory; but to Laughton it was a way forward for the future – the future of the theatre, but equally, perhaps, the future of mankind. 'It seems that Brecht is our man and is launching the theatre back to us on the old Elizabethan terms,' he had written to Alfred Lunt. 'This is a new play, and it is of such stature! It is as important as, if not more important than, reviving the classics.'

Welles replied to Laughton's passionate letter with some dignity, but without making any concessions. He was prepared to let the play go rather than deal with Mike Todd. He reviews the history of the venture, starting with Todd's withdrawal from *Around the World* after finding himself to be 'fresh out of dough': 'Believe me, Charlie, we had no desire to produce this dam costly behemoth of a spectacle.' He describes their negotiations with Brecht and Laughton, holding out for a decent deal, then proposing to forgo any stake in the show. 'According to our understanding, we were to start rehearsals about a week from now in Los Angeles. *Nothing short of the news of your deal with Todd would have kept us from fulfilling this commitment.*' It is hard to accept this argument, since *Around the World* was still running at the Adelphi, and there was no talk of the show closing. Welles challenges Laughton's claim that he needs to make a movie – he's had five months since they agreed to do *Galileo* in August. As for Dick Wilson's phrase about Orson really doing a play, 'he was just trying to reassure you that once I start in on the actual job of rehearsal it would be the hard work of dedication, with no other concerns or projects to interfere'. He thanks Laughton for 'thinking I'm "the best man in the world to put the Church of Rome on the stage". I think I'm the best man in the world to put *Galileo* on the stage. My love for it as a director, if not as intimate, is quite as warm as yours: the actor–author's. This is my particular equipment for the work and I terribly regret that this equipment can't be put humbly and industriously – as it would have been – to the service of a noble and important theatre work.' He says that Todd's abandonment of *Around the World*, plus giving *Galileo* the good autumn slot:

has combined to cost me more money than I'll be able to make for quite some time. This is absolutely no concern of yours, but it does have its little place in the crushing weight of my disappointment. You say Todd 'has never spoken ill' of me. And I'm thankful to learn that the 'strongest word he has used is *afraid*'. Well, it's sure Todd has nothing to fear from me now. I'll never cost him a cent. And if he manages to get together enough money for the play, I fervently hope he'll never cost you an hour of unhappiness. I don't honestly think he will. He can be generous, and is utterly incapable of pretentiousness. You don't, of course expect him to inspire you, but I do believe you'll find him stimulating. He is touched with that particular grandeur which belongs to all the best circus showmen. You will enjoy this, for he has plenty of accompanying charm; and you will know how to translate it into terms useful to Broadway success.

He ends on a note of genuine personal disappointment. 'He could take nothing from *Galileo* but me. This, for whatever it matters, he most assuredly has done. I'm the best man to stage the play, but I'm far – very far – from indispensable. I cannot but acknowledge that I need *Galileo* far more than *Galileo* needs me. For my last word, take my oath that while I look forward to its production with all the bitter jealousy a thwarted producer can suffer, it is also with the highest hopes a most admiring friend can enjoy.'

Game, set and match to Welles in the epistolary tournament. His restrained irony and eloquence and dignity make the other two look rather shabby, his generosity both sincere and nobly expressed. But he ended up not directing *Galileo*, so he was in fact the loser. It is impossible to calculate how his life might have changed had he created for the play the sort of astonishing production that – as he and Dick Wilson both said – he was peculiarly equipped to do, especially if it had had at its centre a great performance by Laughton. Brecht's American reputation, too, might have been transformed, as might Laughton's somewhat faltering standing as an actor. In contemplating what might have been, however, one has to wonder about the degree to which Welles would have been able or willing to deal successfully with either Laughton or Brecht, with their very particular and very different demands, however 'shitty' he might have forced himself to be. Laughton's attitude to Welles was always uneasy. Powerful, rich and famous though he might have become, his cautiousness, intellectual inferiority complex and slow-moving cussedness remained intact. He was daunted and a little panicked by the whirlwind that was Welles. What position could Laughton adopt in relation to him? He could be neither teacher nor pupil, his preferred relationships. Welles would simply make him feel dull and old, leaving him blinking foolishly as Welles performed his verbal, artistic and actual conjuring tricks, not knowing quite how he did it but vaguely suspecting a fraud somewhere. Moreover, Laughton demanded patience and empathy from a director, qualities of which Welles had rather short supplies. Welles had never directed a major actor, with all the profound sense of self-protection proper to them; and Laughton was not only profound, but fathomlessly subtle. In sharp contrast to Welles, adrenalin was the least of the elements of his work process; small wonder that when he came to direct his own first film, *The Night of the Hunter*, he had as happy an experience with the meditative, art-loving cinematographer Stanley Cortez as Welles had had a miserable and frustrating one. Laughton's stubbornness would no doubt have set in at an early stage, and he was not easily to be railroaded; more than one distinguished director in his past had been reduced to impotent despair.

As for Brecht, he was to be messed with at one's peril, although the two men did have something in common: a relaxed attitude to authorship. Both understood the word in the spirit of a Renaissance painter's workshop: the name on the title page represented the joint labours of a team of contributors under the general guidance of the designated author. Whether Welles would have allowed the boot to be on the other foot for once, and would have been happy to have subsumed his contributions under Brecht's name, is an interesting question. Certainly Brecht would have tolerated no co-credit. In conversations with Barbara Leaming and Peter Bogdanovich, Welles describes Chaplin and Olivier, two of the biggest beasts in the jungle (and with both of whom he had damaging encounters from which he emerged the loser), as possessing at their core a kind of peasant cunning; and to some extent, and in different ways, both Laughton and Brecht had this quality: it was the thing that had brought them together and kept them together – a certain caution, a shrewdness, a cogitating tenacity. Welles entirely lacked this quality, preferring to throw himself at a problem – to throw his resources at it – personal, financial, energetic. He rarely emerged the winner in his dealings with skilful operators, especially those who played a long game.

In the event, after much toing and froing, during which both Elia Kazan and Harold Clurman were considered and dismissed as potential directors, Joseph Losey was given the job on the clear understanding that he was very much the lesser of the triumvirate – triumvirate because Todd, too, had fallen out with Brecht and

Laughton when they refused to countenance his notion of hiring the furniture and costumes from MGM. It was another year before the play reached the stage, and when it did, it was at the Coronet Theatre in Los Angeles, and the producer – to Welles's infinite vexation – was his old adversary and former colleague, John Houseman, whose path he seemed inevitably to cross. The play was a *succès d'estime*, albeit of a rather sober kind, which left its audiences thoughtful rather than excited – not at all the sort of experience Brecht must have had in mind when he decided that the director of *Around the World* was the ideal man to stage his play.

That monstrously money-consuming spectacle was now coming to the end of its rackety life. The notice to close went up on 27 July. DEAR ORSON, Cole Porter, who was present at neither the first nor the last night of the show, wired Welles a couple of days later: YOUR TRAGIC NEWS ARRIVED THIS MORNING STOP ALL MY SYMPATHY GOES OUT TO YOU FOR HAVING MADE MORE THAN HUMAN EFFORTS TO KEEP OUR POOR LITTLE SHOW RUNNING SO LONG YOUR DEVOTED COLE. For him there were no hard feelings, only pleasant memories; unlike Welles, Porter had lost little in the venture, and – perhaps reinvigorated by his exhilarating contact with the young master at his most exuberant – shortly afterwards started work on the show generally considered to be his masterpiece, *Kiss Me, Kate*. For Welles, of course, *Around the World* had been nothing less than a financial catastrophe, causing him to mortgage his future, at the same time creating tax problems for himself that would not be resolved for many years, and then only partially. The running costs were a staggering $27,000 a week: the best weekly figure – and there were few other weeks as good – had been $24,000. The show finally closed on 3 August, having lasted, as maliciously predicted by Irving Cahn, quite a few days less than Phileas Fogg's little trip. Welles was left with nothing to show for it but the 10,000 specially printed souvenir programme books, a mere handful of which had been sold; the publisher gave them to him for nothing, and later that year he sent them out as Christmas cards.

Over the next few months there were desperate attempts to take the show elsewhere: enlisting first Alexander Korda (with whom Welles was currently trying to set up a number of films), then the great showman Charles B. Cochran – who had so ardently desired to transfer the Mercury *Julius Caesar* to the Royal Albert Hall, no less – but he was unable to convince them that London, or indeed Australia, would take to the show that Broadway had so expensively rejected. Dick Wilson wired Cochran with the suggestion that *Around the World* might be suitable for the pantomime season, offering him costumes and scenery valued at $130,000 (which would cost $10,000 to transport) and Welles, who could stay in the show till 15 January. Cochran replied: REGRET IMPOSSIBLE SECURE ANY LONDON THEATRE FOR AROUND THE WORLD AT CHRISTMAS. FURTHERMORE, he added, a little tartly, CANNOT AROUSE ANY INTEREST IN PROPOSITION WHICH HAS ALREADY BEEN OFFERED FOR SOME TIME BY KORDA. That same Korda – who shared Welles's belief that if you said a thing often enough it was bound to happen – had been making some rather large promises: 'I thought,' Dick Wilson wrote plaintively to Korda's number two at London Films, 'he said he would have the necessary permits and have the theatre lined up in a couple of days.' Through Korda, Welles had attempted to meet Rex Harrison, with a view to inveigling him into playing Fogg; but it all came to naught.

A month later the set was still languishing at the Adelphi Theatre; finally, at considerable expense, it was moved out and into storage, where it stayed until it was eventually scrapped. The same fate had befallen the set of an earlier beloved behemoth of Welles's, *Five Kings*, of a revival of which Welles continued to dream, until one distant day it mutated – the idea, if not the set – into *Chimes at Midnight*, first, unhappily, on stage, and finally and gloriously on film. No such apotheosis lay in store for *Around the World*, although the memory of a gallant folly lingered. 'The show flopped,' wrote Stanley Kauffmann in his *New Republic* obituary of Welles, 'but sometimes I meet someone who saw it. Immediately we start to bore everyone in the room by reminiscing about it.' But nostalgia was the last thing Welles was feeling by the time the curtain finally fell on *Around the World*. In its last days he had embarked on a crusade that engaged him as passionately as anything in his life ever had – or ever would.

CHAPTER EIGHTEEN

Officer X

TWO DAYS before Welles put up the sign backstage at the Adelphi Theatre giving his *Around the World* company a week's notice, he received a letter from Walter White of the National Association for the Advancement of Colored People; they had an urgent matter on which they wanted to communicate with him. The following day White, the executive secretary of the organisation, visited him in his dressing room with Oliver Harrington, famous in the black community as creator of the radical cartoon Bootsie in the *Pittsburgh Courier*, but now starting his new job as publicity director for the NAACP. The story they brought Welles cannot have been unknown to him, because a fortnight earlier Harrington had secured head-lines for it in the left-wing press to which Welles subscribed, and which – not least because of the incessant search to find material for his weekly *Commentary* programme – he studied assiduously. His old rag the populist *New York Post* had carried a front-page story, but it was the *Daily Worker*'s headline that put the story as succinctly and as shockingly as possible: SOUTH CAROLINA COP GOUGED OUT EYES OF NEGRO VET WHO FOUGHT IN PACIFIC; in a boxed inset was the phrase GET THAT COP!

The story had first broken in the *Lighthouse and Informer*, South Carolina's leading black paper, after which the NAACP had taken it up, approaching the War Office for redress. It was the rejection of responsibility by the War Office's legal department on the grounds that Sergeant Isaac Woodard Junior, the veteran in question, had been officially discharged (albeit only five hours earlier) that provoked the NAACP's release of the material to the major news-papers; and it was the determination of White and Harrington to secure not only justice for Woodard, but also maximum publicity for the cause, that led them to Welles. Welles's access to the airwaves, however relatively small his listenership, meant the possibility of a nationwide campaign. They, like everyone else, never ceased to think of him as the man who brought America to a standstill with *The War of the Worlds* – radio's Barnum and Bailey, its unparalleled showman. They also knew him and profoundly respected him for his absolutely consistent and unwavering support for racial equality, not merely as an ideal, but in professional and personal practice, from as early as the Harlem *Macbeth* ten years before, through his constant sponsorship of black jazz musicians, his plan to film the life of Duke Ellington, and the rumours of how he had intended in *It's All True* to feature the black population in the Rio de Janeiro *favelas*. He was, in a way that few of even his most liberal colleagues were, genuinely 'colour-blind'.

Welles had long anticipated the growing demand among black people for equal opportunities and rights and constantly – in speeches, in articles and on radio – warned of the lurking dangers of the continuing privation and humiliation of a large section of the populace. The war, as he frequently observed, had changed everything; black servicemen had seen a world in which racial prejudice was not institutionalised, and had fought side by side with their white companions-in-arms, experiencing a proximity and a parity, almost a camaraderie, that they would never have known at home, especially if they came from the South. Moreover, the particular circumstances of war had given black activists at home a lever with which to extract concessions; the establishment in 1941, under threat of a mass protest in Washington, of the first all-black flying squadron, the 99th Pursuit Squadron, at Tuskegee in Alabama (lyrically celebrated on the Broadway stage the following year in 'Flying Man' from Oscar Hammerstein's *Carmen Jones*), was a giant first step towards self-respect. Similarly, but more sombrely, the return from war of veterans accustomed to being treated at the very least as human beings – and no longer prepared to tolerate their former servility – had given rise to a series of incidents of which the Isaac Woodard story was not necessarily the worst, but was certainly the most poignant. The NAACP, keenly aware of the historical moment, was understandably eager to make the very most of it, and looked to Welles to fan the flames.

They knew that he was fearless. After a recent *Commentary* (7 July 1946) in which he had mildly suggested that, on the face of it, there was no reason why a black man and a white woman might not get married – a broadcast for which he had received the enthusiastic support of Negro organisations – he had received a letter from a young woman in Los Angeles, Mrs Edna Fraser, which showed something of what he was up against; what they were all up against.

My dear Mr Welles

You are not advocating inter-racial marriages between the Whites and Negroes, are you, Mr Welles? Your commentary last Sunday, July 7th, would lead one to believe that perhaps you are. It is very difficult for me, who have believed in you so much, to believe that a man possessing the intelligence that I have credited you with possessing, could be swayed by a trend of insidious propaganda, or would lend his time and talents to championing such an unworthy cause. – No, Mr Welles, I am not prejudiced against the Negroes . . . but the Negro, as a race, is mentally incapable of taking a place alongside the white man. He is not competent to make intelligent decisions for himself . . .

I do not expect you to understand the humiliating experiences that young women of today are being forced to endure from Negro men. *But* – your young daughters are growing up, Mr Welles – your own lovely little daughters – Christopher and Rebecca – and it will not be many years before they too shall be attractive young women, like myself. How will you feel then, if Negro men whistle at them? Undress their slim bodies, join their eyes? Try to pick them up in cars? . . . It is something to think about, Mr Welles. Think about it, Mr Welles, think about it a long, long time. Would you consent to your lovely daughters being touched by Negroes? God knows, surely, you couldn't! And yet, Mr Welles, by your very words of last Sunday you are helping to contribute to a condition that is already subjecting other men's daughters to that very thing. Think about it, Mr Welles – take a long walk in the park, and think about it – while there is still time! You are not advocating that, are you, Mr Welles? – If you *are* advocating that, Mr Welles, then as I have loved and admired, so I should despise and loathe the very sound of your name and voice. I should never want to see you again, nor to hear you, nor to hear of you. And I should ask God to forgive me for ever believing in you as I have believed. Will you please save my belief in you, Mr Welles. It is very important to me. I wait your word.

Ever sincerely

Edna Fraser.

It is the world of the Wentworths, the nice, suburban Americans, the depth of whose prejudice is all the more dismaying for being expressed in tones of reason. 'Dear Mr Welles,' wrote the staunch Democrat Miss Mary Houston of Chicago, a bookkeeper of a somewhat pious bent:

loving the memory of our beloved President Roosevelt so much
I certainly resent the way you conduct yourself on the radio. You
make believe you are a lover of right and fair dealing, yet you
incite a bitter hatred in the minds of those of us who want
REFINEMENT in all things. I called up the radio station and they
tell me you are a Jew, which doubtless accounts for quite a bit in
your broadcast. You and that half-wit, half-breed Ben Grauer, the
other announcer over at ABC . . . now believe me, formerly I
have loved you so very much for your *so-called loyalty* to my
happy and deeply-missed PRESIDENT ROOSEVELT . . . PLEASE don't
right off say 'Oh, she hates the Jews too', that is most certainly
not true, for my LOVING SAVIOR was a Jew when He trod this
earth more than nineteen hundred years ago, but HE was refined
. . . ask any REAL SOUTHERN NEGRO and they will tell you they
are proud of their race, they will open your eyes, and will most
certainly tell you they are mighty proud of their white friends
and as for this, right here in the slums where I work, the
worthwhile negroes will say the low type are simply IGNORANT
NIGGERS. You are doing more harm for your own race as well as
for the Negroes and I simply detest you for dragging down my
beloved Democratic Party . . . I can associate with whom I want
and still I will know that my HEAVENLY FATHER loves me . . . if
you and other Jews of your class and the Negroes want us to
love you and be friends with you, why not better yourself . . .
please pardon if you think I am not a Christian for I am and
love our HEAVENLY FATHER much and want always to follow in
HIS STEPS, that is why I want to LIFT UP the low standards and
not pull down the high standards, and excuse errors in type, but
I want to send this right off, sincerely your friend.

Welles received literally hundreds of letters of this sort, repre-
senting a deep, pervasive and widespread racism among what would
properly be described as ordinary people. The letters cannot have
been pleasant to read, and are almost inconceivable a mere few
months after the end of a world war waged against a dictator whose
genocidal activities had only just been revealed in their full horror,
but they were scarcely threatening.

The emotions inspired by the case that White and Harrington
brought to Welles in his dressing room at the Adelphi were of an
entirely different order – both in quality and in intensity – from
the petty racism of Mrs Fraser and Miss Houston: for one thing,
it happened in the South, which was presently in a state of uproar,

bellowing and lashing out wildly like some cornered animal. The profound sense that something had indefinably changed, and that the tide of history was, however gradually, flowing irreversibly away from it, its entrenched world-view dissolving in the wake, sent a wave of terror through the Southern states. It was a time of extraordinary ferment: in February of 1946 the riots in Columbia, Tennessee, had rapidly descended into what the black writer and activist, Langston Hughes, described as 'a hate-filled orgy'; twenty-eight Negroes were charged with attempted murder in the first degree, and although (thanks to the NAACP) they were all finally acquitted, it was, as Hughes wrote, 'a dangerous, costly and heart-breaking process – one hardly calculated to bolster a returning veteran's faith in democracy'.

The very day before the NAACP delegation's visit to Welles at the theatre, there had been a particularly brutal quadruple lynching of two men and their wives in Walton County, Georgia, where the governor-elect, Eugene Talmadge, had called for mob action to 'keep negroes in their place'. Walter White, that heroically tire-less campaigner against lynching, had issued a statement to the Associated Press denouncing the deaths as 'the inevitable, inescapable result of Talmadge's and the Ku Klux Klan's advocacy of outright violation of the laws of the Federal Government and human decency'. Describing Talmadge as 'a man as brazen as Hitler in his racial theories', White observed that his election made 'other such dastardly crimes' inevitable, calling on the Federal government and public opinion to halt it. 'Negroes were the victims yesterday,' he said. 'Other minorities and eventually democracy itself will be the victims tomorrow.' The Federal government had failed to stop mob violence. 'What other alternative is left to these citizens, many of whom are veterans?' Other NAACP officials linked the outrage in Walton with what they called 'the bestial gouging out of the eyes of veteran Isaac Woodard in South Carolina'; while White forwarded a telegram to the Attorney General, Tom Clark, pointing to suspected police complicity in the lynchings and, by implication, sympathy with the Klan. 'At a time when our statesmen are demanding democracy and a restoration of morality in Iran, Germany, China, Japan, Yugoslavia and Bulgaria, it seems ironic that Americans are dying because of a lack of this same demo-cracy in Georgia, Mississippi, South Carolina (the home of our Secretary of State) and other parts of the South.' Welles had been saying the same thing for years: there were atrocities in America's own back yard that ranked with the atrocities of the Axis powers.

The NAACP was an organisation after Welles's own heart: radical without being doctrinaire. Few of its members belonged to any other left-wing grouping, and virtually none was communist (though Oliver Harrington was eventually to leave America in disgust, first for Paris and finally East Berlin, as he recounts in his autobiography, *Why I Left America*). Welles scarcely needed persuading to take up cudgels on Isaac Woodard's behalf.

When he heard the full story, and read Woodard's affidavit describing precisely what had happened to him, Welles knew that he could do full justice to it; moreover, he knew it was exactly what he was looking for. 'It was on Friday night. When I and my associates read it in my backstage dressing room, we knew we must begin the fight immediately.' Just as the NAACP knew that it was an ideal story to make their case, both human and particular – who cannot respond to a story about a blinding? and the blinding of a soldier returning victorious from war at that – so Welles was aware that it would give sharp focus to his radio programme, which was in danger of becoming a catalogue of complaints against non-right-thinking people; a couple of weeks before he had taken on A-bomb tests and the ending of rent and price controls, and had struggled to make the programme cohere. Woodard's affidavit (no doubt composed with a little help from his friends at the NAACP) was a clear and credible statement of events, but was shot through with a sense of bitter irony and injustice, its opening paragraph setting the tone: 'I, Isaac Woodard Jr, being duly sworn, do depose and state as follows – that I'm 27 years old and a veteran of the United States Army, having served 15 months in the South Pacific and earned one battle star . . . when they discharged me from Camp Gordon, I'd given four years of my life to my country. I had survived the war and come home to "the land of the free". I became a casualty five hours later.'

As he described it, on the afternoon of 12 February 1946, Sergeant Woodard had been discharged from the army at Camp Gordon, near Augusta, Georgia. That evening he boarded a bus for Winnsboro, South Carolina, where his wife lived. At Aiken, South Carolina, the bus stopped and he asked to be allowed to disembark and use the toilet; the driver was aggressive, accused him of being drunk (which he was not) and told him to sit down. Woodard persisted in asking to use the toilet, which he was finally allowed to do, but when the bus next stopped, he was taken off it by police and arrested. When he protested, he was viciously beaten around the head with a blackjack, a lead-weighted bludgeon, and taken to jail. Next morning, his eyes red and swollen, he found that he was unable to see. Brought to the mayor's court, he pleaded guilty to being drunk and disorderly, for which he was fined $50; he only had $40 in his wallet, plus another $4 in his watch pocket, which the court accepted. At first they wanted him to cash in the cheque for his army discharge payment, but gave up after ascertaining that he was unable to countersign the cheque because he could no longer see it. From court he was taken to the Veterans' Hospital in Columbia, South Carolina; three months later, in May, he was discharged, totally blind, the bulb of both eyes having been irremediably ruptured. On leaving the hospital, he was helpfully advised by the doctor to enrol at blind school. After that, he went to New York to be looked after by his sisters. His wife stayed behind; and that was the end of his marriage.

Once in New York, Woodard went to the NAACP, where he met Thurgood Marshall, the chief legal counsel, and his assistants. They approached the War Office which, as we have seen, denied responsibility because Woodard had been discharged – even if only for five hours. After the NAACP broke the story in the *Daily Worker*, the *Post* and *PM*, the FBI finally sent someone to Aiken to investigate, while Woodard himself started to talk publicly about his story, with extraordinary calm and modesty. 'Down South they think we are worse than dogs,' he said. 'Nobody would treat a dog like they treated me. But the harm's done now and I'm not near as bitter as my mother and father.' It was the NAACP's offer of $1,000 for the arrest and conviction of the policeman who beat and blinded Woodard that finally resulted in headlines in the *New York Times* and the *Herald Tribune* as well as the *Post*, which in turn stirred the War Office and the Department of Justice into action at last.

The crucial thing Welles seized on was the fact that no one had yet identified the policeman responsible for the crime. GET THAT COP! the *Daily Worker* had declared, and that is what Welles set out to do. Working closely with Oliver Harrington, who spent each Saturday night after the show working with him on the broadcasts, and using the latest unpublished on-the-spot reports from the *Lighthouse and Informer*, Welles wrote what were in effect a series of dramatic monologues, which are among the most deeply felt, revealing and personal utterances he ever made, recklessly outspoken on a subject that, as we have seen, was a matter of deep ambivalence for many (if not most) Americans in 1946. In the broadcasts he plays the role of a kind of omniscient avenger determined to track down the perpetrator of the assault. It is a role – pitched somewhere between The Shadow and Inspector Javert from *Les Misérables*, with maybe a touch of Captain Ahab thrown in – and yet it is Welles, too, recognisably the same commentator who had been engaged in intense, urgent dialogue with the American public for nearly a year now – passionate, rhetorical, now angry, now lyrical. These weekly fifteen-minute Sunday afternoon programmes had developed a distinct identity, building on the telephonic intimacy of the early programmes (still sponsored by Lear) to become almost confessional in tone, expounding Welles's deepest political feelings, communicating his hopes for democracy and his frequent disappointments with it.

From his first words, there can be no question that Welles is deeply and genuinely scandalised by what has happened to Woodard the man, and to Woodard the unwitting representative of his race. Welles starts quietly, evenly, with the affidavit: 'I, Isaac Woodard Jr, being duly sworn, do depose and state as follows . . .' He reads it quickly, almost casually, slowing down only for the doctor's advice to Woodard to enrol in a school for the blind. Then, leaving Woodard's statement hanging in the air, he segues, in a characteristic device, into a story – almost a parable – told to him, he says, early that morning when he went for a coffee with Woodard's affidavit burning a hole in his pocket. The story, told to him as a joke by someone in the coffee shop, concerns a commercial traveller, a white man who stays in a black hotel, sharing his room with a black man. The next day he goes to get on the train, but is refused admission and told to go to the Jim Crow part of the train. He protests, but as he reaches out his hand he realises that he's turned black, and realises why: 'They woke the wrong man!' Welles then comes back to Woodard:

> Now it seems that the officer of the law who blinded the young negro boy has not been named. The boy saw him while he could still see, but of course he had no way of knowing which particular policeman it was who brought the justice of Dachau and Oswiecim to Aiken, South Carolina. He was just another white man with a stick, who wanted to teach him a lesson – to show him where he belonged: in the darkness. Until we know more about him, for just now, we'll call the policeman Officer X. He might just be listening to this. I hope so.

Now Welles's tone changes: he becomes almost seductive. 'Officer X, I'm talking to you. They woke up the wrong man. They woke up the wrong you – the you that God brought into the world all innocent of hate, a paid-up member of the brotherhood of man. That you could have been anything – it could have gone to the White House, it could have gone to heaven when it died. They woke up the wrong man!' The other Officer X, he says, the servant of the feudal South, blinded Woodard. 'Wash your hands, Officer X! You'll never wash away that leprous lack of pigment, the guilty pallor of the white man.' He dwells on the question of payment in this life: 'Nothing is ever paid back. Everything has a price.' He considers the price of things. 'You want love?' he asks, and gives an answer it is impossible not to take autobiographically. 'The cost of love is independence. You want to be independent? Then pay the price and know what it is to be alone. Your mother paid for you in pain.' He continues, 'What does it cost to be a negro? In Aiken, South Carolina, it cost a man his eyes. What does it cost to wear over your skeleton the pinkish tint officially described as white? In Aiken, South Carolina, it cost a man his soul.'

He returns to the question of price. 'What are they quoting for one eye? An eye for an eye? You had eyes to see, but you have never seen. You were born in a pit.' Then suddenly, passionately, he asks: 'Where stands the sun of common fellowship? When will it rise in your dark country? When will it be noon in Georgia? I must know, Officer X, because I must know where the rest of us are going with our American experiment.' In this phrase, Welles articulates the despairing, underlying quest of his past few years. He returns to Officer X:

We invite you to luxuriate in secrecy. It will be brief. Go on, suckle your anonymous moment while it lasts. You're going to be uncovered. We will blast out your name, your so-called Christian name. We will give the world your given name, Officer X. If he's listening to this, let him listen well: Officer X, after I have found you out, I'll never lose you. If they try you, I'm going to watch the trial. If they jail you, I'm going to wait for your first day of freedom. You won't be free of me. I want to see who's waiting for you at the prison gates. I want to know who will acknowledge that they know you. I'm interested in your future. I will take note of all your destinations. Assume another name and I will be careful that the name you would forget is not forgotten. I will find means to remove from you all refuge, Officer X. You can't get rid of me. We have an appointment, you and I – and only death can cancel it.

The effect is rousing, certainly, but also somewhat disturbing. Who exactly is speaking, one wonders? The tone is personal, vengeful, obsessive, but also melodramatic, stagy. As if to answer the unspoken question – and to puncture the theatricality – Welles asks: 'Who am I? A masked avenger from the comic books? No sir. Merely an inquisitive Citizen of America. I admit that nothing on this inhabited earth is capable of your chastisement. I am simply, but quite actively, curious to know what will become of you. Your fate cannot affect the boy in the county hospital for the blind. We want a word to lighten his darkness. You're sorry for him? He rejects your pity. You are ashamed? He doesn't care. We want to tell him soon that all America is ashamed of you.' The rhetoric resumes, mounts; the sentences become shorter. There is endless play on the idea of eyes and seeing. Woodard will never see, but the lids are merely closed on Officer X's eyes. One day, Welles hopes, he will learn 'to try the wild adventure of looking . . . then there will be a shouting of trumpets to raise the dead at Gettysburg. A thunder of cannon will declare the tidings of peace and all the bells of liberty will laugh out loud in the streets to celebrate the good will towards all men. The new blind can hear. It would be very good if they could hear the news that the new blind can finally see. Then, Officer X, you'll find you can wash off what should be washed, and it will be said of you – yes, even you – that they awakened the right man.' He pants, seems to be shaking with emotion. The programme ends with him broken-voiced as he signs off 'Obediently yours'. There is nothing obedient about it: the commentator is no one's servant, except perhaps blind justice's.

It is a remarkable performance, both in conception and execution, a passionately eloquent affirmation of human values; but – certainly at this distance – there is a quality of hysteria about it that seems curiously solipsistic. In dramatising the events, the feelings of the pursuer come to seem as important as those of the victim, while the perpetrator of the crime – however loathsome he might be – is elevated under the weight of this onslaught to an almost sacrificial status. As has been noted elsewhere in these pages, it is characteristic of Welles to identify an enemy, a villain (whether the Hollywood studios or Governor Dewey or John Houseman), and to denounce them relentlessly. Equally characteristic is his sense of Evil: Officer X has become Satan. It is Welles's natural tendency as a dramatist, from as far back as *Bright Lucifer*, his fifteen-year-old exercise in Manichaeism.

The impact of the broadcast on his listeners was understandably electric. 'Orson,' Les Lear, his former sponsor, wrote in a letter after the first Woodard programme, 'I can't begin to express the profound admiration you have won on the part of thinking America for the magnificent manner in which you are championing every-thing and anything that has to do with the American way of life. I am confident that, should you ever elect to head a world-wide movement to further tolerance, your followers would outnumber all other mankind-benefiting societies a million to one.' Another letter of support, more personal, came from the all-Negro Santa Fe Waiters'Union: 'as soon as your broadcast message were reported to all the waiters and bartenders on the Santa Fe Railroad from LA to Chicago, at union meeting we suggested someone should send our appreciation to such a loyal an liberal white person . . . the young negro appreciates people like yourself, Mrs Roosevelt and other liberals in America for fighting pieceful for we believe the pen is mightier than the sword. – We thank you very very much for ever your loyal friendship from over 1,500 people we remain yours, Al Laster.' The children's writer Sol Stein wrote, 'Yes, Mr Welles, you spoiled my week that's coming up – and pray god you keep right on the microphone, continuing to spoil it, and the weeks ahead. – There's so damn much work to be done. You're doing a swell job.' It was not all roses: someone signing himself A FORMER FAN wrote to Welles that Woodard was trying to get away from the policeman, and anyway he had already been blinded in an earlier fight with another Negro; and the flagrantly reactionary Congressman John Rankin sent a copy of the broadcast to J. Edgar Hoover at the Federal Bureau of Investigation.

More disturbingly, at the urging of Police Chief Sprawls, Aiken mayor Odell Weeks wrote to Welles: 'Since your Sunday night broadcast went out to the nation, and the locale of the story was wholly untrue, I urge that you have the courage and forthright-ness to retract the wrong you have done this city in your broadcast next Sunday night, giving to your retraction the same emphasis that you placed upon your original broadcast of the story.' The city of Aiken, a former health resort, prided itself on its southern charm; once a winter colony for the wealthy, it had become an equestrian sporting centre, and its population included a number of well-heeled socialites. Mayor Weeks was genuinely affronted by the slur on the city's good name, although the county of which it was the seat was rather less fastidious, boasting as it did a sign on its borders that stated: NIGGER, DON'T LET THE SUN GO DOWN ON YOU IN

AIKEN COUNTY. But the mayor had a point. No one had been able to trace either the policeman who had assaulted Woodard, or the incident itself: there was no record of it in Aiken's jail or its courtroom. In fact, both the FBI and the NAACP had good reason to believe that Woodard had mistaken the place where the bus had stopped, but both were biding their time until they had made thorough investigations; they did not let Welles into their suspicions.

He took to the air again the following Sunday (the day after the closing night of *Around the World*, which may have somewhat affected his mood). It was a typical *Commentary*, starting with Welles musing on the betrayal of Yalta and the Peace. He denounces all the Allies: Stalin, who has reneged on the terms of the treaty a mere week later in Bucharest; Roosevelt's party, which follows a Republican programme; the Labour Party in Britain, which is dancing the Dance of Death of Tory ignorance and Tory cowardice; it is the eleventh hour for mankind, as people prepare for a Third World War. He brings to his bitter reflections a tone of scathing despair at the post-war world: is this, he asks, what we fought for? The feeling is very personal and hurt – above all, weary – but it is something of a harangue, and listening to it is like being trapped in a bar with a very gloomy fellow on New Year's Eve; it is almost impossible to believe that the speaker is only thirty years old. After a general survey of the world and the state of democracy, delivered in a listless monotone (even the jokes are weary: 'some people feel Mr Truman should stay out of local politics; some people think he should never have left it'), he introduces Woodard, and suddenly becomes very lively.

Quoting from Mayor Weeks's letter, Welles turns the tables on him, inviting him to join in the manhunt. He hopes, he says, to be able to retract the story and be able to apologise to Aiken. 'There are thousands of cities where negro soldiers have not been blinded. I hope that it will be my privilege to announce that your city is one of these . . . I've sent investigators to your city who should bring out the truth, unless it is too skilfully hidden . . . there is an American soldier who believes that it did happen in your city. And I cannot forget that. It is to him, Mr Weeks, that you should address your first and most indignant letters. They will of course have to be transcribed in Braille.' He is on curious ground here, arguing that there are more important things in life than Aiken's *amour-propre*; but if you pose as the champion of truth, it doesn't do to get your facts wrong – far less to hurl around false accusations. The tone is, again, worrying: 'I've sent investigators to

your city.' Who does he think he is? Aiken was certainly not molli-
fied, and duly delivered to the *New York Times* a packet of evidence
exonerating itself from the indictment, securing itself a front-page
headline the day after the broadcast: AIKEN IS ANGERED AT WELLES
CHARGE. Welles's answer was to broaden the terms of the debate
in the following week's broadcast. His text was drawn largely from
the speech he gave at the great Peace Rally in Chicago in 1943,
subsequently published in pamphlet form under the title *Moral
Indebtedness*, as he acknowledged: 'I've said this before: to be born
free is to be born in debt; to live in freedom without fighting
slavery is to profiteer.'

In the broadcast he dilates on the idea of progress, dwelling
particularly on racism. 'Race hate isn't human nature; it is the abandonment of human nature . . . the Indian is on our conscience,
the Negro is on our conscience, the Chinese and the Mexican-
American are on our conscience. The Jew is on the conscience of
Europe, but the neglect gives us communion in that guilt, so that
there dances even here the lunatic spectre of anti-Semitism.
This is deplored; it must be fought, and the fight must be won.
The lynching must be stopped. What business of mine is it?' he
asks. 'God judge me if it isn't the most pressing business I have.
The blind soldier fought for me during this war. The least I can
do now is to fight for him. I have eyes. He hasn't. I have a voice
on the radio. He hasn't. I was born a white man . . . and so I
come here not as a radio dramatist (although it pays better), not as
a commentator (although it's safer to be simply that). I come in
the boy's name, and in the name of all who in this land of ours
have no voice of their own. I come in the name of justice.' He
extends the case to embrace all racism, in the United States, in the
world. Now quoting from his article for *Free World*, he says: 'I come
with a call for action . . . I know that the word action has a revolutionary twang in some quarters – it wouldn't surprise me if I
was accused of inciting to riot. I'm very interested in riots: I'm
interested in avoiding them.' Exhorting his listeners – 'we, the
people – black, brown and red' – to 'rise to the occasion of our
brotherhood', he declares race hate a disease. 'Anything very big
is very simple. If there's a big race question, there's a big answer
to it, and a big answer is simple like the word "no". Our children's
children are the ancestors of a free people. We send our greetings
ahead of us, to them. To history yet unmade our greetings, to the
generations sleeping in our loins. Be of good heart! The fight is
worth it.'

It is fine, rousing stuff, delivered with the sweeping rhetorical power that was uniquely his, and it produced a passionate response. 'Keep up the marvellous work,' said an anonymous correspondent. 'We're all behind you 100%. Too bad you're not in politics . . . we need such men as you.' Another note said: 'I wonder if anywhere in the world today [a Sunday, of course] was preached a sermon that was comparable to your expression.' Yet another listener wrote: 'I can think of nothing nobler expressed by anyone at any time in world history. You deserve the deep gratitude of everyone that has a spark of nobility and I hope you continue to devote your great ability to the same noble purpose.' Quite separately from his work as actor, writer, director, Welles's impact as an inspirational non-party-political figure was immense; for many people, he was a beacon.

The momentum in the Woodard case was building inexorably. The NAACP arranged a huge rally in the vast Lewisohn Stadium in New York under the sponsorship of the black newspaper *Amsterdam News* and the Isaac Woodard Benefit Committee; the singer Carol Brice and the great boxer Joe Louis were prominent members. Thirty thousand people heard Louis read a statement by Welles, who was by now in Los Angeles, preparing the film he was to direct for Harry Cohn:

Isaac Woodard is on the conscience of America. – The sin which was committed against him is the sin committed every day against his race – which is the human race. We cannot give him back his eyes. But we can make tough new laws – laws to drive the concentration camps out of our country – we can make laws to stop lynch law. – We can make prejudice illegal, and see to it that our American Nazis are punished for their crimes. – If Isaac Woodard had to lose his sight to show us that we need those laws, the least that we can do for him is to make those laws and make them now and make them stick. – If we don't, we are more blind than he. – The only defence against the mob is the people.

Woodard himself spoke with his characteristic simplicity and dignity, and then – to what he later said was the most tumultuous reception he ever received, Woody Guthrie sang the specially written 'The Blinding of Isaac Woodard', sung to the tune of 'The Great Dust Storm'.

It's now you've heard my story, there's one thing I can't see
How you could treat a human being like they have treated me;
I thought I fought on the islands to get rid of their kind;
But I can see the fight lots plainer now that I am blind.

That afternoon from California Welles broadcast the fourth of his programmes devoted to Woodard, armed with a telegram from the NAACP saying that the attack probably took place in Batesburg, South Carolina, nineteen miles away from Aiken. HOSPITAL RECORDS AMAZINGLY BRIEF NO MENTION NAMES POLICEMEN WHO DELIVERED VET TO HOSPITAL NOR PLACE WHERE ATTACK OCCURRED THIS EXTREMELY UNUSUAL FBI REPORTS CONFIRM OUR INVESTIGATORS.

Welles starts the broadcast with Aiken. He notes that the film he had made a couple of years before – *Tomorrow Is Forever*, with Claudette Colbert – had been scheduled to play in the local movie house; it was banned, 'the actual celluloid driven out of the city as with a fiery sword'. Under the direction of the city council, a detachment of police officers solemnly tore down the posters advertising the film and burnt all printed matter having reference to it, in a formal bonfire in the public streets, 'to protect the impressionable and youth of Aiken from the shock of my name and likeness'. Later, Welles himself was hanged in effigy. 'That's nothing. I'm used to being banned,' he says, with a certain playful modesty. 'I've been banned by whole governments. The Nazis in Germany have banned me. Here at home, the merest mention of my name is forbidden by Mr Hearst to all his subject newspapers. But to be outlawed by an American city is a new experience. The movie in question is neither controversial nor obscene but I'm in it, and for the taste of Aiken that makes any movie too offensive to be endured.' Without undue anguish, he apologises to Aiken, and reveals that the work of 'my investigators', and those of the NAACP and the FBI, has revealed that the place Woodard thought was Aiken appears to have been the town of Batesburg in South Carolina and – he seems to be reading from Associated and United Press reports as they come in – claims that 'we're getting close to the truth': the chief of police of Batesburg, a Mr Shaw or Shawl or Shull, is almost certainly Officer X, the man who blinded Isaac Woodard. He recollects that he promised Woodard that he would find his assailant. 'Well, we have. And now that we've found you out, we will never lose you.' He repeats another promise, in the identical words with which he ended the first programme: 'If Chief Shaw or Shawl or Shull is listening – and I have good reason to think that he is – I say: if they try you, I'm going to watch the trial . . . we have an appointment, you and I – and only death can cancel it.' And then he moves on to deal with the Texan gubernatorial election.

Chief Lynwood Shull (as opposed to Shaw or Shawl) had indeed been found, and admitted to having struck Woodard with his blackjack when he became unruly, taking the stick from him. 'I grabbed it away from him and cracked him across the head. It may have hit his eyes.' Thus vindicated, the NAACP took the case to the Department of Justice, which – purely because it was an election year, in the view of the judge who finally tried the case – finally intervened, filing federal charges. Oliver Harrington had no doubt about Welles's influence on this outcome: YOUR TRULY GREAT COMMENTARIES IN BEHALF OF ISAAC WOODARD ARE RESPONSIBLE MORE THAN ANYTHING ELSE FOR THE APPREHENSION OF THE POLICE TORTURER IN BATESBURG COUNTLESS THOUSANDS OF AMERICANS ARE BETTER HUMAN BEINGS FROM HEARING YOUR BROADCASTS AGAINST FASCIST SADISM NOW SWEEPING A LARGE SECTION OF OUR COUNTRY. Samuel Procter, a black man who fought in the Second World War, wrote: 'The crying need of the minorities, particularly the coloured man, is a spokesman. I believe you can fill that job, even though it means being a martyr . . . I hope you will accept the enclosed check to help defray expenses involved in making America conscious of its duty and its opportunity' – a phrase that must have moved Welles, because that is exactly what he hoped and believed he was doing. Someone else wrote to say that he had fought in the war, but 'it seems that I was fighting in the wrong place', a common reaction. A nameless fan was even more enthusiastic: 'Thousands of years ago/ God gave to the world Moses – the great teacher/ Then Jesus the Saviour/ Then Abraham Lincoln the Emancipator/ Then Franklin Delano Roosevelt the great Humanitarian/ and Now Orson Welles – the most wonderful fighter for the rights and freedom of all mankind.'

Aiken felt a little differently. 'Please don't come to Georgia,' said one sinister little note, 'we don't think it would be very healthy for you down this way.' The Republican county chairman John Willingham had issued a ghoulish invitation – COME OVER HERE SOMETIME WE ARE ANXIOUS TO ENTERTAIN YOU – followed by a more explicit threat of a libel suit: YOU MUST REALISE THAT AN IRRESPONSIBLE PERSON OF YOUR CHARACTER CANNOT MERELY HAVE ACCESS TO THE WAVE FREQUENCIES AND DEFAME A WHOLE COMMUNITY WITHOUT PROVOCATION. No doubt it was this that put the wind up Adrian Samish, vice-president of ABC, and his colleagues: OUR NEWS DEPARTMENT HAS BROUGHT TO MY ATTENTION, he wired Welles, THE PROBLEMS THEY HAVE BEEN HAVING LATELY ABOUT TRYING TO GET YOU TO WRITE A SCRIPT AND TRYING TO GET YOU TO SUBMIT IT IN SUFFICIENT TIME FOR THEIR REGULAR REVIEW OF ALL COMMENTATORS FOR LIBEL, GOOD TASTE AND APPROPRIATE NEWS AUTHORITY. His script, Samish continued, must be submitted at least two hours before broadcast time. Welles will not be permitted to ad lib; if he persists, they will be forced to cut him off the air, explaining that he is broadcasting material he has refused to submit to ABC. WE ARE HAPPY TO GIVE YOU THE OPPORTUNITY OF UTILISING YOUR GREAT TALENT BUT UNDER THE FCC LAW THE RESPONSIBILITIES OF BROADCASTS ARE ABC'S I AM SURE YOU WILL UNDERSTAND OUR POSITION AND I AM TELLING OUR NEWS DEPARTMENT THAT I PERSONALLY KNOW YOU WILL CO-OPERATE. And he added, a little desperately, PLEASE DON'T LET ME DOWN. It was scarcely to be imagined that Welles would be allowed to get away with it for much longer.

Ignoring Samish and with only the merest nod in the direction of Aiken's offended civic pride, he returned to the fray the following week. 'The place was Batesburg,' he says firmly, then recapitulates what happened the week before in Aiken: the banning of the movie, the stripping down and burning of the posters, the hanging in effigy. 'They've even threatened to sue me for $2m for goodness' sake.' He reviews the case in the light of the new evidence, describing how Woodard was witnessed in the street by a minister and a workman, having his face washed over and over again by a policeman, who asked him repeatedly: 'Can you see yet?' Everything, he says, points to chief of police Shull. 'Mr Shull is not going to forget me. I will haunt him.' Then he quotes the letter from his Former Fan who claims that Woodard was blinded by another Negro. 'It seems the Yankees always have to pick on someone about something, especially from the South.' Southerners respect blacks, he says, it's just that the two races shouldn't live together. Welles is trying to engineer some kind of mulatto nation, an abomination to the gallant men and women of the South who have 'certain well-founded beliefs'. Welles wants to give the Negro a better chance than they would the white man. 'Dear Former Fan,' replies Welles, 'Batesburg is not a battle in the civil war.' He eloquently rebuffs his ex-fan's specious arguments, mocking the suggestion that Woodard wanted to spawn a mulatto nation: 'he went to see a woman of his own race bearing his own name, but he never did see her. He'll never see her. Even Chief Shull, he says, doesn't pretend that he was preventing Woodard from marrying his sister.' Welles sums up his own contribution to the story, returning to his Shadow mode:

> When I stumbled upon this story several weeks ago . . . the name of the guilty policeman was unknown and it looked as though it always would be. I promised to get that name. I have it now . . . we won't let him go. I promised I'd hunt him down. I have. I gave my word I'd see him unmasked. I have unmasked him. I'm going to haunt Police Chief Shull for the rest of his natural life. Mr Shull is not going to forget me. And what's more important, I'm not going to let you forget Mr Shull. Well, that's enough of that for now. We'll come back to Mr Shull next week. And the week after that. And the week after that.

He moves on to a retelling of the story of the Unknown Soldier, one he had already written up for *Free World*, to which he brings exactly the same degree of emotion as he brought to Woodard's story. 'The people want world government,' he cries, 'standing side by side, when the tools of war are put down forever.'

There is no contradiction in this, no insincerity: but in the end it is rather like being at Hyde Park Corner, with Welles, the radical gun for hire, on his soapbox, ready to sound off on the good causes of the week. In fact, he didn't return to Woodard, or Chief Shull, until the penultimate *Commentary* some weeks later; after which Samish, true to his word, cut him off the air, selling his space instead to *Chimney Sweep*, the latest in a long line of ignominious substitutions that had started with *Tarzan* at RKO. Samish offered him a lifeline: if Welles was interested in doing a *Commentary* that completely ignored politics, Samish believed he had 'a commercial spot where he can be sold'. It was not a proposition Welles cared to entertain. Significantly, just before Samish made his new offer, Dick Wilson had asked ABC whether they might like to use Welles as roving reporter from Europe: Welles was of course planning a number of films in London with Korda, but there is a sense that his patience with America was running out. In that penultimate *Commentary*, he says, wryly, 'I'm being sued for $2 million, and I've been burned and hanged in effigy because of the things I've said on this program. I'd like to thank ABC for giving me the chance to say those things . . . and I'd like to say that if I ever got the chance to say those things again . . . I'll say them again.' Then, with justified pride, he quotes the telegram Oliver Harrington had sent him, informing him that Lynwood Shull had been made the target of a criminal information charge by the Department of Justice for violating the Civil Rights Statute, a seldom-used statute passed by Congress in 1870 giving civil rights to black people: ACTION OF JUSTICE DEPT IS HISTORIC MOVE PROFOUND IMPLICATIONS I PERSONALLY FEEL YOU MORE THAN ANY OTHER RESPONSIBLE PLEASE ACCEPT DEEP GRATITUDE OF THE NAACPS 700,000 MEMBERS.

In a letter to radical Congresswoman Helen Gahagan Douglas, Welles said that he had had thousands of letters, almost all of which were commendatory, and hundreds of requests for the script. 'You will all be disappointed to know,' he said, alluding to the 1870 statute, 'that the penalty is only one year and the fine an extremely nominal one . . . Attorney General Clark has stated that he will ask for an amplification of the penalties . . . we must hold him to it . . . and use the publicity generated by this case to guarantee other minorities' rights.' It was the single most effective political action of his life, though not in its immediate outcome, because, as the trial judge J. Waties Waring feared, Truman and his Attorney General – 'alarmed at the increased racial feeling in the country' – were more interested in being seen to have done something about the situation than in actually doing it. Waring was none too impressed by Welles's involvement, either, directing the jury not to be influenced by 'publicity seekers on the radio agitating for the prosecution of this case, or by politicians, mindful of the ballot box'. To his wife he wrote, 'I do not believe that this poor blinded creature should be a football in the contest between box office and ballot box.' The prosecution case was at best half-hearted, crucial witnesses were not called, defence witnesses were indulged, and despite Waring's instruction to the jury that they were trying 'only one white police officer, not the South's racial customs', the defence attorney declared: 'If delivering a verdict against the federal government means that South Carolina will have to secede again, then let's secede.' The judge had to force the jury to discuss their verdict for at least twenty minutes. The instant they re-entered the courtroom, they returned a 'not guilty' verdict. Chief of police Lynwood Lanier Shull resumed his job, ending his days, covered in respect and affection, in a retirement home in Batesburg, South Carolina.

The event nevertheless had a considerable long-term effect. Among other things, it politicised Judge Waring, who became a close associate of the NAACP; he lived to be the first judge of modern times formally to declare segregated schooling unequal.

The path to racial integration, the bare minimum for civilised inter-racial relations, was a long and stony one, and one that has perhaps not ended, but the Woodard case was a valuable step along it. His testimony illustrated as vividly as anything could have done that the issue was, above all, one of the right to respect. The whole incident had begun in the bus when the driver had cursed him for making him stop so that Woodard could use the toilet. 'Talk to me like I'm talking to you,' the mild Woodard had said. 'I'm a man just like you.' It was for this outrage that the driver reported him to the police. And when he got off the bus at Batesburg to meet 'someone I want you to see', and Shull had hit him on the head with his blackjack, Woodard answered the question as to whether he'd been discharged from the army with the single word 'Yes'. 'Don't say yes to me,' Shull had said, 'say yes sir.' And then, enraged by Woodard's impertinence, he laid about him again with renewed vigour.

Welles did not often speak of his involvement in the case, but some years later, in London in 1955, he recounted the story on his television programme *Orson Wellès's Sketch Book*. And having recounted it, he observed:

> We're told that we should co-operate with the authorities. I'm not an anarchist. I don't want to overthrow the rule of law, on the contrary, I want to bring the policeman *to* law. Obviously individual effort won't do any good. There's nothing an individual can do about protecting the individual in society. I'd like it very much if somebody would make a great big international organisation for the protection of the individual. It would be very nice to have that sort of an organisation, be nice to have that sort of card. I see the card as fitting into the passport, a little larger than the passport, with a border around it in bright colours, so that it would catch the eyes of the police. And they'd know who they were dealing with . . . and it might read something as follows. 'This is to certify that the bearer is a member of the human race.'

This mellow and rueful tone was not available to Welles in the forties. Too much was still at stake.

His last *Commentary* for ABC was on 1 September; a few days before saw the beginning of a campaign to keep him on the air. The Hollywood Independent Citizens' Committee of the Arts, Sciences, and Professions, whose board included Olivia De

Havilland, Lena Horne, Linus Pauling, Dore Schary, Frank Sinatra (the vice-chairman) and F. Y. Harburg, took an advertisement saying, 'ORSON WELLES NEEDS HELP! He's doing a terrific job in the matters of minorities and race relations . . . HE'S DOING THAT JOB FOR US! But – because of his strong & fearless attack – the enemies of freedom are attacking *him*! YOU NEED ORSON WELLES AND HE NEEDS YOUR HELP!' Not everyone was sad to see him go. Yet another lost radio listener and his family wrote to him: 'We, the People, have been listening to him "tell us off" for some time now. Now it's time for we, the people, to tell Orson Welles off and set him down a peg or two and get him down off his high horse. He's been needing someone to give him a piece of our minds and now I think he's getting it as he deserves.' But there was support, some of it in verse: 'You mustn't quit – don't quit, fight one more round/When things go wrong, as they sometimes will/When the road you're trudging seems all uphill/When the funds are low and the debts are high/And you want to smile but you have to sigh/When care is pressing you down a bit/Rest, if you must – but never quit' – words he might well have taken heart from over the next forty years of his life.

The *Commentary* of 1 September was not only Welles's last appearance in the series, but very nearly his last appearance on American radio, the medium in which he had earned a living for most of his professional life, and which he had loved in so many and various ways – some admittedly not wisely, but too well. He had understood its possibilities from the moment he started to work in it; he had brought what he learned there to the theatre and to film. Latterly, he had seemed to lose his youthful interest in it as a medium *per se*; he had become captivated rather by its possibilities as the most direct means of conveying his ideas, unmediated by production of any sort, to the American people. It was a very pure form: just his voice and the listener's ear.

While he was giving his *Commentaries* – indeed, while he was still doing *Around the World* seven times a week until it closed – he was also producing, directing and acting in weekly instalments of the Mercury Summer Theatre of the Air, but any resemblance to its great namesake of the late thirties was largely coincidental. Many of the shows were reprises of former programmes. *Around the World* was, as we have seen, a shambolic ghost of the previous incarnations of the same story; *Abednego* a much less vivacious version of the original in the *Hello Americans* series. Significantly, the most distinguished of them – *The Moat Farm Murder*, about a murder in rural England – was not written by Welles, but by Norman Corwin, the other most vital force in American radio, who (unlike Welles) had continued to explore its potential, creating some of the most remarkable wartime programmes. The music to *Moat Farm* and to several other of the shows was by Bernard Herrmann, who continued to bring his very particular sense of the contribution of music to the dramatic soundscape. But there is no question that Welles's heart was no longer in it. There was an entire absence of the electricity of the original Mercury Theatre on the Air and *Campbell Playhouse* shows, where the narrative was brilliantly framed, every scene illuminated by some startling detail, each performance freshly imagined and the whole event welded together at white heat by the inexhaustible energy and imagination of Welles himself, throwing himself into the leading role with reckless bravura.

His Summer Theatre version of *Moby-Dick* – again not by him, but by his friend Brainerd Duffield, and originally intended (as Welles rather oddly informs us) for performance by Charles Laughton on disc – is adequate as an adaptation, but utterly without imagination in conception. Welles adopts a voice at once rough and tremulous and has a number of mighty outbursts, but the listener is never taken inside his head or inside Melville's world; the narration by Ishmael is perfunctory and the eponymous whale is barely evoked at all. Only Herrmann's music, full of strange harmonics and intimations of majestic movements of the ocean, brings tension or exerts any kind of spell, which is all the more surprising since *Moby-Dick* – 'certainly the greatest novel written on American soil', as Welles describes it – was a lifelong obsession of his, which would finally result in a play on the London stage widely considered, by himself among others, the finest piece of theatre he ever created. The last in the Mercury Summer Theatre series sponsored by Pabst (which nobly confined its plugs to the beginning and end of the programmes) was *King Lear*, but again inspiration runs low, and Welles's own performance is a preview of the sonorously sleepy performance of the part he was to give on television in 1953, itself replicated by all accounts in his stage production of three years later. No, radio was no longer his playground: he had moved on. Or rather, back – back to film.

Welles's cinematic plans were plentiful and ambitious, especially his plans with Alexander Korda. For those, Welles was looking to his three-picture contract with Korda which was to start in January of 1947, with a film of Robert Louis Stevenson's *The Master of Ballantrae*, of which he had not so long ago done a spirited radio adaptation in the *This Is My Best* series. As we have seen, for Welles adapting something on radio had often been the first step on the path to a future film; Stevenson was a favourite author, another of his enduring boyhood tastes. On this occasion, alas, it was not to be, the difficulties proving insuperable, but his plans for a version of Oscar Wilde's *Salomé* were, by September of 1946, very well advanced. His adaptation was predicated on the extraordinary notion of merging that quintessentially decadent play with Wilde's great children's story, *The Happy Prince*; Wilde himself was to be a character in the film, in a framing sequence set in a Paris café. Vivien Leigh was Welles's ideal for the psychotic princess; he was keen to cast her partner (and his rival) Laurence Olivier as Herod. 'If Larry wishes to play Herod,' wrote Dick Wilson to Korda, 'Welles will play anything that Larry doesn't want to play.' Cocteau's designer Christian (Bébé) Bérard was to design the sets and costumes. Korda, asking for preliminary sketches and designs, wired back that Bérard might not be available; would Cecil Beaton, who was under contract to him, do? No, wired back Welles, he wouldn't: if Bébé was busy, what about Tchelitchew, Welles's old sparring partner from the early days of the Mercury, a major and still some- what shocking figure in contemporary art? And so they bubbled on, everything seeming possible. They planned to film *Cyrano de Bergerac* (something of an *idée fixe* with Korda, who had already tried to set it up once with Charles Laughton in the title role), but it fell through, at which Welles declared himself COMPLETELY HEARTBROKEN. But there was always *Carmen*, in Welles's own version, which retained Merimée's original framing device of a report on the death of Don José by a representative of the central government, and whose theme would be, in Welles's words, 'sex in the raw'. No wonder the devoutly Roman Catholic Joseph Breen, Welles's old boss at RKO and present head of the Hays Office, would not extend his approval, any more than he had accepted *Salomé* ('We regret having to report unfavourably on this well-known play'). Welles's preferred Carmen was Paulette Goddard, but the film, he warned, would only work if they could shoot in Spain and the South of France; this was fine by Korda. Neither *Carmen* nor *Salomé* was filmed.

It is a cause of great sadness that not a single one of the many projects that Welles and Korda so enthusiastically planned together – most of all, perhaps, *War and Peace* – should have come to fruition. With Welles's imagination and Korda's contacts, their combined temperaments might have led to remarkable work. Korda was the sort of producer – mercurial but effective – with whom Welles might conceivably have worked harmoniously. It was clearly not for want of trying, as their voluminous correspondence and Korda's considerable outlay of funds testify, though for a man like Korda who thrived on constant contact and exchange of ideas, Welles's elusiveness, which increased with every passing year, was a serious obstacle to a relationship. MY TIME IS GETTING SHORT, the older man wired Welles. I WAS UNSUCCESSFUL IN CONTACTING EITHER YOU OR WILSON NEITHER DID HE CALL ME AS AGREED STOP ALL THIS IS EXCEEDINGLY ODD AND QUITE A NOVEL EXPERIENCE FOR ME. By the time of that telegram, however, Welles was fully immersed in a very different sort of film from any he was planning with Korda.

CHAPTER NINETEEN

If I Die Before I Wake

THE IMPULSE to make *The Lady from Shanghai* was by no means purely artistic. Pressing financial demands were the motor for Welles's involvement in the film: he had received a substantial advance from Harry Cohn, who (unlike Korda) expected something concrete and immediate in return for it. He also owed money to Rita Hayworth, to whom he was still married, though they had led separate lives for nearly a year (she had been involved with the singer Tony Martin) – to say nothing of the maintenance for their daughter Rebecca that he had consistently failed to pay. In fact, in late 1946 his financial affairs were in a state of near-collapse, due to a combination of reckless expenditure and absolute indifference to bookkeeping. Messrs Nichols and Phillips, who had the unenviable task of supervising Welles's financial affairs, wrote to him in the hope of getting a signature for a Treasury form for $10,191.29, which would absolve his IRS debt, and are eloquent on the subject:

> May I direct your attention to a number of detrimental factors
> encountered: 1. you did not keep books for three years;
> 2. inability of your office staff to locate and deliver me the
> working appeals and other details relative to 1941 and 1942
> returns; 3. tens of thousands of dollars of deductions claimed are
> based upon amounts listed in loose-leaf single entry accounts,
> many items being in round hundred and thousand dollar amounts
> bearing no relation to any specific thing . . . many of the
> accounts apparently represented the commingling of expenditures
> for personal and business purposes.

There follow six more points of equal severity. Then, in the final paragraph, a *cri de coeur*: 'an undue amount of time has been expended by the Bureau of Internal Revenue and the writer in the examination of your income returns for the three years . . .' The letter ends with the recommendation that Welles should pay the $10,000 and run. How he must have loathed that wagging finger, but it must have been borne in even on him that his self-induced financial chaos was forcing him to do things that he did not really want to do. His radio work had come to an end; his newspaper work had never made him any money (indeed, had cost him a great deal in researchers), and his final withdrawal from it – or its from him – had been gently confirmed by an elegant letter to Dick Wilson from Welles's old publisher on the *New York Post*, Ted Thackrey, stopping the weekly $100 which, through an oversight, they had been paying: 'I have written to Orson that, as nearly as I can figure it, he owes the *Post* approximately 54 columns, advance payment having already been made, and that we will be happy to receive them some time in the next century.'

Otherwise, Welles was maintaining establishments in New York and – on and off – Los Angeles, paying alimony to his first wife Virginia and maintenance for their daughter Christopher. His losses on *Around the World* dragged heavily on him; making cash was now a matter of primary urgency, and Harry Cohn of Columbia was offering rather a lot of it: $2,000 a week for a twelve-week shoot and $100,000 if Columbia's expenses were covered, plus 15 per cent of the producer's profit. It is perfectly understandable that Welles would work for Cohn; as he was to remark some years later, the cherry-pickers go where the cherries are. What is more surprising is that that graceless and unforgiving mogul, with whom Welles had fallen out so comprehensively and so publicly – the man he still referred to as the Beast of Gower Gulch – should want to employ him.

From a purely commercial point of view, Welles – despite the respectable showing of *The Stranger* at the box office, largely thanks to the presence in it of Loretta Young and Edward G. Robinson – had fallen drastically in critical standing: the film had been released during the last month of the run of *Around the World* without fanfare, without interest and for the most part without honour, suffering from being released in the same week as the British compendium movie, *Dead of Night*. Contrasting the two films, Hermine Rich Isaacs in *Theatre Arts* commented that *Dead of Night* started leisurely, until the plot closes in 'as the audience is caught in the grip of a series of horror tales each one more terrifying than the one which precedes it'. Michael Redgrave's ventriloquist was praised as 'an almost unbearable performance' (exactly what Welles's Rankin should have been). The first half of *The Stranger*, by comparison, 'pursues its ominous course with the tension of a taut rubber band', but, 'its mystery solved in mid-passage', it works its way home by a tortuous route of none too surely contrived melodramatic and psychological devices which make demands of the players 'far beyond their capacities'. Not a triumph, then. For his part, Cohn had recently had a string of successes, not least with the films that Rita Hayworth made for him, *Gilda* being the most recent and the most successful. His output had been distinctly classy by comparison with that of many other studios; he was not, however, noted for his enthusiasm for experiment. *The Stranger* was Welles at his most mainstream, but the reputation of being a whizz-kid, a wunderkind and so on still clung to him, and no sensible producer would have expected the expected from him. Possibly the failure of his marriage with Rita Hayworth had reduced the jealous hostility that Cohn had felt towards Welles at the time of the wedding. He had extended the advance to Welles with the encouragement of Hayworth, and saw some publicity value in a reunion – on screen, at any rate – of the couple whose private shenanigans had provided so many column inches over the years.

Welles's first suggestion was his version of *Carmen*, but 'raw sex' was not the image Cohn wanted for his star. Welles was at something of a loss until he came across R. Sherwood King's 1938 thriller *If I Die Before I Wake*. Welles later spun various fables about how he came to choose the material that became his film for Rita, all of them expertly exploded by Charles Higham. It was scarcely as fortuitous as Welles suggested: the book was not unknown. Indeed, the actor Franchot Tone seems to have had an interest in it: when Welles urgently needed a copy, it was to Tone that he applied. But long before that, before Welles and Hayworth were married, William Castle, a B-movie director whose film *When Strangers Marry* Welles had once praised in his *New York Post Almanac*, had given a copy of the novel to Welles, thinking that it would make a good movie, and Welles had shown immediate interest in appearing in it. 'Dear Bill,' he wrote to Castle, 'about *If I Should Die* – I love it. It occurs to me that maybe by saying I had ideas for it, you'd think my ideas are creative. Nothing of the sort. What I'm thinking of is a practical use Mercury could find for the property. I have been searching for an idea for a film, but none presented itself until *If I Should Die*. I could play the lead and Rita Hayworth could play the girl. I won't present it to anybody without your OK. The script should be written immediately. Can you start working on it nights?' Welles adds a postscript to the letter that is not only instructive about his relationship with Hayworth at the time, but also gives a vivid impression of the way in which he bound to him with hoops of steel those whom he wished to use. 'Give Rita a big hug and kiss and say it's from somebody who loves her very much. The same guy is crazy about you and you won't ever get away from him.' It would be a strong man who could resist such force-nine charm.

As is so often the case in these matters, Castle heard no more about it. And then one day, some three years later, when he was working at Columbia preparing his next B-movie, he was suddenly summoned to Harry Cohn's office. 'In an unusually expansive mood, Cohn announced he was taking me off *The Crime Doctor's Warning*,' wrote Castle in his autobiography, *Step Right Up*. Cohn told his secretary to hold all calls:

and, all charm and smiles, called me by my first name. I started to worry. Cohn crossed the room and sat down beside me. 'I just made a deal with Orson Welles to do a picture for us at Columbia. That boy's a genius.' He handed me a treatment and asked me to read it immediately. Glancing at the cover, I read, *If I Die Before I Wake*. 'You know, Bill,' Cohn continued, 'it takes a genius like Orson Welles to find material like this. The dame being a murderess is a brilliant and original idea.' Shocked, I sat frozen while Cohn informed me that he had given Orson the choice of anybody in Hollywood to be his associate producer and he had picked me. Furious, I reached Orson in New York. He excitedly told me how he had sold *If I Die Before I Wake* to Harry Cohn for $150,000. It was a package deal – Orson would produce, direct, write and co-star. I had paid $200 and Columbia had turned it down. 'We'll be working together, Bill. Isn't that what we planned? Get to New York as quickly as possible so we can begin preparations.'

Trying to rationalise that working with Welles in any capacity would be a great learning experience, Castle endeavoured to push aside his disappointment at not being able to direct. Welles told him that Cohn had agreed to let Rita Hayworth play the girl and that *If I Die* was to be one of the big pictures of the year. 'If I had directed, it would have been an inexpensive $70,000–budget whistler. After a sleepless night, I decided to see what would become of *If I Die Before I Wake* in the talented hands of Orson Welles, the boy genius.'

In fact, no explanation for the way Welles came across the book was required, since he was an insatiable consumer of thrillers;

indeed, he always used to travel with a couple of trunkfuls of the stuff to get him through the sleepless nights. He often claimed that as a youth in Chicago he had written pulp fiction and been paid for it, so R. Sherwood King would have been a man after his own heart: 'when Sherwood King had reached the mature age of 12,' his publicity said, 'he found a book, cover and all, which he had written so long before that he had already forgotten it: on the title page was *The Adventurer* by Sherwood King, author of *The Island of Death*.' At fifteen, he wrote *The Outlaws of the Air*, in two volumes, 480 pages of closely packed text; he also supplied the advertisements for the book, one of which read: 'Absolutely the most thrilling story ever published . . . you will read it over and over again. Sherwood King says of this novel: "I sincerely believe this is by far my best novel."' A Mid-Westerner, he had attended Chicago Heights Police School, got a diploma and become a fingerprint expert; his first published book was *Between Murders*. *If I Die Before I Wake* is often dismissed (generally by those who have never read it), but this is unjust: though no masterpiece, it is a crisply written and not unintelligent piece of work. King worked on it for more than a year, he reported, doing his writing in a cheap Chicago boarding house – the sort of place 'where the landlady gave literary teas each week to step up her income'. Like Scheherazade, King had to read out a chapter of *If I Die Before I Wake* each week in lieu of rent: if the results were liked, the rent continued to be waived; if not . . . 'Needless to say,' in the words of the blurb, 'King stayed for the year.'

*

The novel has substantially the same plot as the film, but it is worth describing it in a little detail, since Welles's departures from it and his inventions around it are significant. His changes are in structure, in location and above all in the two central characters. In addition, the book has what might be called, even in such an essentially unpretentious work, a metaphysical undertow that deeply influenced the film Welles made, and which is contained in the title, drawn from the child's prayer 'Now I lay me down to sleep/ I pray the Lord my soul to keep;/If I should die before I wake . . .' Sleep is the book's central image. As in innumerable thrillers of the forties and fifties, the central character is in a state of increasingly perplexed bewilderment as events seem to entangle him in thickets of incomprehension. King goes one step further: his hero, Larry Planter, is perceived to be (and perceives himself to be) in a state of slumber; the plot administers a series of shocks to him, but it is not until the end of the novel that he feels himself to be fully awake. 'Bannister was right,' he tells Elsa, quoting her husband. 'I'd been asleep before. You woke me up. Now I'm living. Now I'm *alive*!' *The Lady from Shanghai* is similarly permeated with a sense of somnambulism, the hero walking dream-like through his life as if in complete ignorance of the forces that shape it, passing through nightmare into some kind of freedom, the freedom of being awake.

The novel plunges the reader straight into the plot without preparation: '"Sure," I said. "I would commit murder. If I had to, of course, or if it was worth my while."' Handsome young Larry Planter, after years as a sailor on tramps and an unsuccessful spell as a writer, has become chauffeur to the crippled lawyer Mark Bannister, whose wife, the lovely Elsa, is fifteen years his junior and deeply unhappy. Larry also drives Bannister's partner, Lee Grisby, and it is Grisby who in the opening chapters makes the shocking proposal to the young man that for $5,000 he should allow himself to be framed for apparently murdering him: Grisby wants to leave his wife and escape to the South Seas. He also wants, he tells Larry, to kill Bannister to claim the insurance. All of this, which is transferred directly to the film, is held back in Welles's screenplay until nearly halfway through. This was no doubt a wise decision: in the novel the crime has been committed and Larry is arrested and imprisoned by the end of the second of the book's five parts; for the rest of the novel he is either in court or in prison, which would make for very static cinema. In his screenplay, Welles adds a prologue in which his hero – transformed into Michael 'Black Irish' O'Hara and endowed with a line in Irish philosophical whimsicality – picks up a young woman (Elsa Bannister) in a buggy in Central Park at night. After they travel together for a while, Elsa goes off alone and is chased by muggers. Michael rescues her and delivers her back to her car, but refuses her suggestion that he should come and work for her and her husband on their yacht, *Circe*. The following day, Bannister seeks him at the Seamen's Hall and, after much alcohol, passes out, obliging O'Hara to take him on board the yacht, where Elsa and others persuade him (against all his instincts) that he should take the job. In the novel, Larry's recruitment is much simpler. He simply swims up by accident onto Bannister's beach: the crippled lawyer, impressed by his youth, good looks and 'such a marvellous physique', offers him a job as his chauffeur. It is one of several more or less explicitly homoerotic passages in the book ('I looked at him; he was taking me in. "Man, but you've got a build," he said') that have no counterpart in the film.

Needless to say, Welles's decision to make Michael O'Hara captain of the Bannisters' yacht opens up the action in many ways. While *If I Die* is set entirely on Long Island, where the Bannisters live, the *Circe* is able to travel, and she does – to Acapulco, for a picnic, enabling Welles to introduce the South American flavour he so loved; it also offers all the visual delights of a ship at sea and the fascinations of life on board ship, cabins and decks and steering wheels. In *The Lady from Shanghai* the Bannisters actually live in San Francisco, the most photogenic of cities, and one that credibly and naturally provides the film's two huge visual climaxes, one after another: the Chinese Opera and the Crazy House. Welles's geographical scheme is immensely ambitious, from the New York of the beginning to the jungles and the beaches of Acapulco, and to San Francisco and its exotic amusements, which include an aquarium. In narrative terms, Welles chooses to speed up O'Hara's arrest – he runs straight from the pretend murder of Grisby into the police's arms – and allows him, by somewhat improbable means, to escape from the courtroom, where he has just been found guilty, into the Chinese Opera, and from there to the Crazy House, which he then walks away from. In *If I Die Before I Wake* all the main twists of the plot are conveyed to Michael in his cell – the last cliff-hanging sequence actually takes place in the condemned cell, where Bannister taunts him with a detailed description of what will happen when they administer the electrodes before going away. At the fifty-ninth minute of the eleventh hour, just before he goes to the electric chair, Elsa breaks into the cell to tell him that Bannister has killed himself, and therefore can never admit that he killed Grisby; but hard on her heels is the kindly detective who has always believed in Larry, who arrests Elsa for all three murders: Grisby, Bannister and the butler Broome. In *The Lady from Shanghai* Elsa, abandoned by O'Hara, famously dies in the Hall of Mirrors; in the novel she takes her chance with a jury. At the end, Larry (like Welles's O'Hara) can make no sense of what has happened to him, and withdraws, in his case to Tahiti.

Though so much of the plot and most of the characters derive directly from the novel, virtually none of the dialogue has been used. King's dialogue is perfectly workable, but Welles prefers a more highly charged note of eloquence; in the novel, when people start to talk in that way, King undercuts them ('we were talking like high-school kids and we knew it'). Michael O'Hara, as we have seen, is Irish and of a meditative bent; Welles has added to this a romantic politico-criminal past (he killed a Franco spy during the Civil War) and a disgust with the idly destructive rich, giving him a highly characteristic Wellesian fable about sharks tearing each other to pieces. He is also – a vague memory, no doubt, of Larry Planter's literary ambitions in *If I Die* – seen briefly at a typewriter, though no reference is made to him having any writerly aspirations. In the novel, Larry the would-be novelist is aware that when he makes love to Elsa, he is simply quoting: 'I gave it everything I had, all the things I remembered out of books.' Interestingly, in *The Lady from Shanghai*, in their most intimate scene together, after Michael has hit the spy Broome, Elsa and Michael speak in similarly self-consciously high-flown terms: 'I'm the Princess in the Fairy book,' says Elsa. 'So you hit him and make a pretty speech to me and we ride off together into the sunset.' 'Well,' says Michael, 'why don't we? . . . it's been known before you know, with real life people. That's where they get the ideas for the books.' 'Books aren't like people,' says Elsa. 'People try to act like books.' 'Oh no, Rosaleen,' says Michael, using his nickname for her. 'People are much better than books.'

The most important quality Welles adds to King's Larry Planter is innocence – 'stupid[ity] more like it' as he says at the end of the film – and a certain chivalric gallantry. In this, he is deeply contrasted with Elsa Bannister (in the novel, oddly enough, a red-headed ex-chorus girl), who is shown to be a woman of extraordinary calculation and deceitfulness. The Chinese background indicated in the title may or may not be the source of her inscrutability and ultimately her ruthlessness, but the screenplay takes away from her the fierce outbursts against Bannister she is occasionally allowed in the novel – 'has it honestly never occurred to you,' she screams at the crippled Bannister, 'that you might be better off dead?' – replacing all her feelings with a perfect mask. Welles also endows her with a profound sense of what she calls 'badness': 'Everything is bad, Michael, everything. You can't escape it or fight it. You've got to get along with it – deal with it – make terms.' King's Elsa may well have felt that, but she doesn't say it. In virtually every other regard, the film's Elsa is the novel's, as are the film's Grisby and Bannister. Needless to say, vitally important though it is, a screenplay is the merest maquette for a film, providing structure and dialogue (though both can be changed); the visual realisation – in conjunction with the actors' contribution – is the crucial process, giving the film so much of its meaning, its identity. But it is fascinating to observe how thoroughly Welles responded to his raw material, changing the balance here, altering the stress there, subtly transforming character, translating implicit ideas into statements. This was his first screenplay since *The Magnificent Ambersons*, which was scrupulously faithful to Tarkington, both in action and in dialogue. *Journey into Fear* was Jo Cotten's, with help from Welles, and departed substantially from Ambler, as much due to wartime internal pressure as any other consideration; *The Stranger* was not Welles's, though he certainly added dialogue to it and influenced structure. *The Lady from Shanghai* is more personal, more private almost, than any of his other films to date, and might have been even more so, had it been shot as he wrote it.

The first stumbling block was the censor. Welles completed the initial draft of the screenplay that was then called *Take This Woman* (and had earlier been called *Black Irish*, before finally settling into *The Lady from Shanghai*) in September 1946, shortly after the last of the Isaac Woodard broadcasts, and submitted it to Breen's office, only to have it immediately rejected: 'this basic story is unacceptable under the provisions of the Production Code in that a murderess escapes justice by committing suicide. Any such basic story could not be approved.' There were countless other objections: there must be no drunkenness, no illicit sex and, above all, the censor refused to allow a scene in which a judge was shown to have a racing form with him on the bench. As usual, these obstacles were negotiated away without excessive losses; Elsa's suicide was not a critical element and her death at Bannister's hand served exactly the same function. The next hurdle was Harry Cohn, who required the deletion from the screenplay of a number of scenes on the grounds of excessive complication; in so doing he seems to have added to the confusion rather than alleviating it. It is hard to judge – given that it is in the nature of *noir* thrillers for the audience to be as confused as the protagonists – whether Cohn's input on this matter was positive or negative. For the most part, and for the time being, that was the extent of the interference; for better or for worse, Welles was left to himself for the duration of the shoot.

He was, of course, working for a studio, and the team assembled for him was not one with which he had ever worked before: the cinematographer was Charles 'Buddy' Lawton Junior, who had shot, among other things, *The Thrill of Brazil*, something that he could share with Welles; the editor, Viola Lawrence, was one of Cohn's key personnel, and something of a famous dragon; the composer, Heinz Roemheld, was another of those musical journeymen who ran the studio music departments. It was not an especially congenial group from Welles's point of view. Dick Wilson and the somewhat erratic William Castle were associate producers, under Welles. To cheer himself up, he cast a number of Mercurians – Everett Sloane as Bannister (whom he rechristened Arthur instead of Mark), Erskine Sanford as the judge and Gus Schilling as Goldie – with a couple of old hands thrown in playing walk-on parts: Bill 'Vakhtangov' Alland (Thomson in *Citizen Kane*) and Dick Wilson himself. In the sort of jovial actor-managerial what's-the-play-and-where-is-the-stage style that few actors failed to respond to, he called the Broadway actor Glenn Anders to ask him to play the part of Grisby (rechristened George instead of Lee): 'Glennie darling, get on the next plane to Los Angeles,' he told him. 'Never mind what the picture is. It's a great part. You'll get the Academy Award. Just bring spring clothing.'

Welles put himself on one of his fierce, amphetamine-led diets to get trim; and he cut Rita Hayworth's hair and dyed it blonde. This last decision, which made Harry Cohn's jaw drop and the rest of Hollywood gasp, was provocative on several levels: it transformed one of the great cinematic icons of the day, gambled with the public's devotion to one of the most bankable of celluloid stars, and asserted Welles's potency, both as a director and as a man. He was doing to Rita Hayworth what men had always done to her: making her in the image they desired. What made it all the more startling was that it was done with her complete consent. She was as eager as he to be liberated from a self with which she did not identify, that of the sultry charmer. 'Men go to bed with Gilda and wake up with me,' she famously remarked. She also wanted to challenge her limits as an actress, and there was no one she trusted more to help her with that than Welles, the only man who – initially, anyway – had taken her mind seriously. She was, too, on quite a simple level, blissfully happy to be in daily contact with the man she still obviously loved, despite his unmistakable signals of indifference to her as a woman; he genuinely admired her as an actress and was determined to extend her range. Indeed, she suggested that he might like to move in with her again, and he did, as if nothing untoward had happened during the nine months they had been apart.

Before they all left Hollywood for location shooting in Acapulco, Welles screened that quintessential cinematic nightmare, *The Cabinet of Dr Caligari*, for everyone, a very logical thing to do in view of the nightmare that Welles had envisaged in the screenplay, and they set off in high spirits. As Welles had told Castle, *The Lady from Shanghai* was no whistler: it was a big picture, with the substantial budget of $2.3m. Welles and Lawton scouted for locations in Mexico and Sausalito near San Francisco; it is suggested that Welles seized the opportunity to do pick-up shots for *It's All True*, but that project seemed to have finally slipped away from him when – thanks to his haemorrhaging losses on *Around the World* – he was unable to meet the deadline that RKO had given him for paying the first instalment to buy the rushes. Besides, *The Lady from Shanghai* was quite demanding enough: it was as if Welles's cinematic imagination, shackled on *The Stranger* and unused during his long fallow period of political commentating, had run riot, encompassing exotic location work in Mexico and San Francisco, long sequences at sea (always difficult to shoot because of constant and ungovernable motion), the creation of a massive fun-house and a shoot-out in a Hall of Mirrors; the last posing as complex a logistical challenge as could be imagined. Moreover, Welles was interested in creating an especially demanding cinematic language, one that eschewed conventional close-ups and two- and three-shots, using instead the sort of width and depth of shot that he had deployed in *Citizen Kane* – but on location, which created major problems for lighting and for the camera itself, particularly in the matter of tracks. As it happens, the shoot, which was embarked on in such high spirits, was no fun at all. Despite the relatively luxurious twelve weeks allowed for principal photography, it turned out to be a punishing schedule, given the frequent shifts of location and the attendant difficulties of each.

Welles had shot on location only once before, in Brazil for *It's All True*, and though the world was no longer at war and communications were generally functioning, the hazards of shooting on the spot remained considerable. Surprisingly, Columbia seemed no better organised than RKO four years earlier. Dick Wilson insisted that they had sent too large a crew, which would only hamper them, and so it proved. They started shooting in mid-October, in Acapulco, at the worst possible time of the year, the height of the hot, humid rainy season. Both Welles and Hayworth succumbed straight away to his old bugbear, sinusitis, a nearly incapacitating condition for an actor. More alarmingly, they were shooting in shark-infested waters; the Mexican swimming champion was hired to swim near Hayworth when she was shooting in the water, in order to ward off marauding barracudas. Hurricanes threatened and storms constantly blew up, impossible conditions in which to shoot and record sound; being on board was bad enough. On more than one occasion they managed to get no more than one or two shots a day.

William Castle had been sent ahead to arrange the yacht. 'Orson, an insomniac, refused to believe that anyone required sleep and picked the wee hours of the morning to call with any new idea he had at the moment. "This is Orson," his voice would boom. "I hope I didn't wake you." "No, Orson," I yawned. "I'm always up at four a.m." "You're leaving for Mexico," he said. "Acapulco, at noon today." I was now wide awake. He continued, "I want the *Zaca.*" "What's a zaca?" I asked. "Not a – *the Zaca,*" he replied, "Errol Flynn's yacht. I want you to make a deal with him." "Yes, Orson, but how do I find the *Zaca* and Errol Flynn?" "That's your worry."' Presumably Welles thought they could save money by hiring the yacht from Flynn, but before long it was clear that any savings were more than counterbalanced by the sheer obnoxiousness of the man – drunken, lascivious, racist, potentially violent – and by his preciousness with regard to the *Zaca.* 'Flynn joked, cajoled, needled, threatened, blackmailed us about his boat,' reported Dick Wilson in an official report on the shoot. 'He never stopped expressing his misery about the fast deal he claims we put over on him.' Inevitably repairs were needed; Flynn had them done by his own people at vast expense, at which point, catastrophically, it was discovered that the company had forgotten to take out insurance. Flynn himself had lied about his third-party insurance. Over and above the nefariousness of Errol Flynn, the impression given by Dick Wilson – who, admittedly, was trying to shift blame for a massive budget over-run – is that 'the organisation of the studio is inefficient for the Class "A" pictures'. The set dresser was 'a 90% incompetent'; the production manager 'reacted on our production in a manner which slowed it down rather than speeded it up'; the unit manager proved 'disastrous rather than helpful'. The schedule started slipping from the first day, and it only slipped further and further.

Very early on, actual disaster had struck when Don Corey, the assistant camera operator, suddenly keeled over and died. The production closed down out of respect, and deep gloom set in. Illness was rife throughout the company almost from the beginning: the crew were constantly going down with dysentery, which attacked both Welles and Hayworth, losing precious days of shooting; on another occasion Buddy Lawton was struck with the virus, but somehow carried on working, albeit at half-pace; Welles, multi-allergic, succumbed to histamine poisoning. He was never fully well throughout the shoot, chronically lacking sleep. Hayworth's ailments were more persistent and more severe; from early on in Mexico, Dick Wilson reported her 'general condition of fatigue . . . which made possible only about a half day's results no matter whether she worked a full day or not'. Eventually, he says, it became a serious problem for scheduling and completing important scenes in the film. The second location, in San Francisco, cold and damp, was no more satisfactory; they had to cancel shooting twice on account of adverse conditions. All of this created more pressure on Hayworth, and on 27 December she collapsed on the set and had to stay away for ten days. Welles, too, was seriously ill at the same time, as well as spraining his ankle on more than one occasion and sustaining some unspecified injury to his face.

In San Francisco they had in addition to contend with the continuing strike of Hollywood technicians, which had been mooted before shooting started, but had not been expected to last; budgets had been drawn up on the assumption that it would soon be over and had to be revised drastically. Despite a large and in some instances retroactive pay rise, labour troubles persisted throughout the shoot. As a result of the strike, painting costs increased, Dick Wilson calculated, by 1000 per cent. To the disapproval of the union, Welles had personally designed the hair-raising murals on the interior of the Crazy House, and decided to paint them himself, his tiny chauffeur/butler/odd-job man Shorty Chirello at his side, holding the paint pot for him like a medieval apprentice. When Welles, dissatisfied, wanted the walls to be repainted, the production co-ordinator (Columbia's man, Jack Fier) refused to authorise it, so Welles and a couple of chums broke into the studio and did it overnight. As a result they were picketed by the paint unions, who thereby won triple time to redo it. The construction of the Crazy House, which was done from scratch, was a massive job, with its 125-foot zigzag slide, which the cameraman had to ride to give O'Hara's point of view. It was forty feet wide and twenty feet deep. The dragon's mouth (itself thirty feet wide) ended in an eighty-foot pit. The maze of mirrors used 2,912 square feet of glass and eighty plate-glass one-sided mirrors; it cost $60,000 to build – at least $15,000–20,000 more than it should have done because the prop shop insisted on building it. Throughout the shoot on American soil, the camera crew were working an unofficial go-slow: 'the guys walking up and down on the outside,' as Wilson said, 'radically affected the work of the guys walking back and forth on the inside'. Welles raged at them ('there's too much stalling around here . . . someone go put pressure on those men. Go rub up against them the wrong way'), but to little effect. For a while the great Rudolph Maté (Dreyer's cinematographer on *Vampyr* and *Joan of Arc*) relieved Lawton and, according to Dick Wilson, things speeded up immeasurably, so clearly some of the slowness came from the cinematographer himself, always a nightmare for the mercurial Welles.

Somehow he maintained his exuberance. Thomas A. Brady found him on the set in Hollywood in December of 1946, chivvying the crew, indefatigably energetic, 'followed by 23 assistants and technicians in a queue . . . when the queue had dwindled to three people, Welles turned and spoke charmingly to a minor actor who thanked him for his engagement on the picture'. In answer to another reporter's question, Welles very sensibly replied that Columbia had treated him with 'the utmost generosity up to that time in matters of fiscal and artistic autonomy'. And it was true: up to that time. Brady reports that he went off to get some sleep. 'Have the doctor meet me in the car,' said Welles to some assistant. 'He can attend to my needs on the way home. I am to be called at 6:30 tomorrow morning: I must go to the baths.' At which, says Brady, he wrapped his coat around him 'after the fashion of a black cape' and strode out into the mists of the Hollywood night. The following morning, he directed the first scene of the day while a barber shaved him and cut his hair – a feat, says Brady, 'which even Cecil B. DeMille has never equalled'. Welles's instinct for publicity was clearly unimpaired. Despite what he had said, and in addition to what he clearly perceived as an obstreperous attitude from the crew, he was dealing with constant long-distance input from Harry Cohn, who was concerned to feature his star as prominently and as attractively as possible. To this end he encouraged Welles to create a sequence in which she sang (providing, as it happens, a musical equivalent of the scene in the novel in which Elsa somewhat unexpectedly recites a poem: 'Deep on the couch of night a siren star/Steeping cold earth in swooning loveliness . . .'); this added a couple of days to the schedule. Another two and a half days were required to shoot a sailing montage decreed by Cohn. The fight in the judge's chamber was another unscheduled extra, though this appears to have been Welles's own idea.

The result of all these delays and additions was that a film scheduled to take sixty-five days to shoot took ninety-eight, at a cost of nearly half a million dollars more than budgeted. Dick Wilson wrote a lengthy memo to Welles to support him in his arguments with Columbia, rebutting many of the charges of wastefulness and extravagance of which Cohn accused him. There is no question that they faced trying circumstances, not of their own making; it also appears to be true that the studio's accounting practices were somewhat dubious. Once again, it seems, Welles and his partners (in this case, Wilson) had been oppressed by a rapacious and inflexible organisation; once again, they can have expected nothing else. It seems that Welles had underestimated his opponent, not for the first time. 'He snarled at you as you came in the door,' he told Barbara Leaming of Harry Cohn, 'and you could gradually throw him little goodies and he would quiet down and start lashing his tail.' Wrong. Cohn had bugged the portrait of him that hung in Welles's office at Columbia; Welles cheerily greeted it, every morning and night, with the words 'Well, that winds up another day at the Mercury. Tune in tomorrow.' This devil-may-care attitude is endearing, but it was no defence against the ruthless man for whom they were working, who wanted nothing more or less from them than a profitable movie. He was clearly no George Schaefer, supporting and sustaining Welles, aiding and abetting him in his artistic dreams, as became immediately evident in his responses to the rushes.

From the beginning, Cohn and Jack Fier (about whom Welles quipped, perhaps somewhat desperately, 'we have nothing to fear but Fier himself') were convinced that the film would never work, their opinion being confirmed by the veteran editor and feared termagant Viola Lawrence, who reported that the footage was 'a jumbled mess'. Welles had no approval of the final cut; indeed, he seems not to have been involved in the editing process at all. At no point did they accept or acknowledge Welles's stated intention of giving the film 'something off-centre, queer, strange', which had a 'bad dream' aspect, as he put it. They refused to understand that he wanted the film to be satirical in feel. In fact, their whole purpose was to introduce coherence and logic – and give Rita Hayworth her proper quota of close-ups. Where Welles had evolved a subtle and complex critique of her glamour – first showing Grisby, for example, studying her voyeuristically through his telescope, and then making the audience into voyeurs by letting us see her through the telescope, too – Lawrence and Cohn steamrollered him into shooting a large number of pick-up close-ups of Hayworth, which, though undeniably lovely in themselves, destroy the film's visual and imagistic coherence; the film's eye, as it were, stops being beady and cynical, and suddenly mists up. The result is yet another Welles movie that must be discussed in terms of what might have been, rather than what is: another mutilated torso. Welles reckoned that

Cohn lost about 20 per cent of the footage – a substantial amount – cutting a number of important details; worse than that, he imposed on the film a dreary score by Heinz Roemheld, which Welles wittily and appositely demolishes in a memo that is one of the most useful surviving accounts of his complex understanding of sound, the precision of his requirements and, en passant, the fineness of his taste. It also confirms just how significant a contribution he expected music to make to his work.

The memo to Cohn was written after the unsuccessful first preview, for which (as is not uncommon) a temporary soundtrack had been provided, music written by the distinguished film composer and former avant-gardist, George Antheil, for something quite different. Antheil's score had, says Welles, 'an atmosphere of darkness and menace, combined with something lush and romantic', whereas the title music as it stood was 'atrocious'. The score as a whole depends to the point of exasperation on a constant recycling of the Roberts and Fisher song 'Please Don't Kiss Me' sung by Elsa (in fact sung by Anita Ellis on the soundtrack), but 'there simply isn't enough musical content in [it] to support its use throughout a serious melodrama'. Moreover, 'Mr Heinzman' – at all times Welles refers to Roemheld as Heinzman – 'is an ardent devotee of an old-fashioned type of scoring now referred to as "Disney". In other words, if somebody falls down, he makes a falling down sound in the orchestra.' This is precisely the practice Bernard Herrmann abolished in his scores for Welles, creating instead constant interplay between the music, the image and the text – and silence. Of Roemheld's inanely associative and compulsively voluble music, Welles notes: 'If the lab had scratched initials and phone numbers all over the negative, I couldn't have been unhappier with the music.' In the sailing montage, 'he seems to have gone out of his way to create an effect totally different from the one I indicated . . . the temporary track . . . had *variety, movement, romance*. It conveyed the feeling of a journey – a journey – a journey taken into a picturesque and highly-coloured world. It had besides this, a quality of *satire*.' He cites the musical response to Hayworth's second dive: 'the dive itself has no plot importance. What does matter is Rita's beauty, the beauty of the scene, the evil overtones suggested by Grisby's character, and Michael's bewilderment. Any or all of these might have inspired the music. Instead the dive is treated as though it were a major climax, or some antic moment in a Silly Symphony; a pratfall by Pluto the Pup, or a wild jump into space by Donald Duck.' The entrance to the bay at Acapulco had, in the preview version, 'a very curious and sexy South-American strain', which established the 'rather sinister sort of glamour' the scene required. What Roemhold provided is corny, 'second-rate Germanic filler'. It is all a matter, he says, 'of taste and dramatic intelligence'. Again Welles stresses the deliberate oddness he is aiming for: 'Our story escapes the cliché only if the performances and the production are *original* or at the least, some-what *oblique*. This sort of music cue destroys that quality of *freshness* and *strangeness* which is exactly what might have saved *The Lady from Shanghai* from being just another whodunit.'

Welles implies that he wants this disorientation simply to take the curse off drearily familiar material; almost all of his work, in theatre, on radio and in film, administers shocks to the audience. This is to some extent congruous with Brecht's *Verfremdungseffekt*: making things strange, unexpected, therefore puzzling and arresting (the opposite, in Brecht's formulation, of the narcotic and lulling); but in his use of this procedure, Welles speaks simply as a smart showman, a knowing manipulator of audience responses, an enter-tainer. Where he and Brecht coincide perfectly, though, is in wanting an active, not a passive, audience. 'The strongest mediums are those which ask the most from the public,' Welles said in an interview, and this notion was of course anathema to the Harry Cohns of this world, who delighted in Roemheld's music – 'the poorest and the purest corn', as Welles says, and thus perfectly undemanding. Sequence after sequence is rendered ordinary, banal, stagy, phoney or just dull. 'The audience should feel at this point [in the Chinese Theatre], along with Michael, that maybe they are going crazy. The new dubbing job can only make them feel that maybe they're going to sleep.' The music for the Crazy House 'is an insult to the material . . . this is a chance for the score to tie together the whole "bad dream" aspect of the production and resolve it – to deliver the story to its climax *on a new dimension*. Given the faintest premonition of what sort of music was going to be imposed on this difficult and costly sequence, I would never have gone to the trouble or expense of shooting it.' The end of the picture, he says, is done incalculable injury by a particularly swoony and meaningless reprise of 'Please Don't Kiss Me'. His comments on the sound are equally trenchant: he discerns a process of 'smoothing-out' in both the effects and the voices. Tracks are frequently dead; vocal tracks lack 'peaks and accents'. In the song sequence, 'Grisby's voice is no longer intrusive and nagging . . . all the "levels" are so precisely balanced that the sequence achieves, for the first time since I started work on it, an overall quality of flatness and banality.' The courtroom scene is deprived of 'the vitality and punch it previously possessed', with the echo effect that Welles wanted dropped entirely. The tension created by an over-amplified recording of heavily and deliberately corny Hawaiian music has been lost. Michael's run from the pier, in which 'a careful pattern of voices had been built up with the expenditure of much time and effort by me' – has been 'junked in favour of a vague hullabaloo'. The interesting sound pattern they developed for the Crazy House has been dropped.

This eloquent and precise document is a vivid record of the amount of detailed and conscious thought that Welles brought to every aspect of his films. It is one of a long line of similar memoranda to the powers-that-be – stretching from *The Magnificent Ambersons* to *A Touch of Evil* – railing against bad and insensitive decisions that have wrecked, or will wreck, his work. They always concern the post-production on the film, editing, music, sound; and they are always too late. This particular memo is an expansion of notes given to Welles by Dick Wilson; it evidently took Welles some time to gather his thoughts and express them with force. Even as he writes, he seems to know that nothing is going to happen, and indeed, in this case (as in the others) it didn't. Its only purpose seems to be to set the record straight, an understandable impulse, but an ineffective one. The question arises: how did such a talented, bright, powerful – indeed formidable – man allow himself to be constantly worsted by less intelligent, less talented, altogether less remarkable men than himself? Knowing how critical post-production was to his work – more, perhaps, than to that of any other major director – how did he allow this to happen, again and again?

No doubt the answer lies in the condition of the film industry: its cost-intensiveness means that it is in the hands of those who can best raise and make money. Occasionally, a George Schaefer or a David O. Selznick will emerge who is responsive to the idea of art; in the case of Selznick, this brought with it massive interference. Welles had a further difficulty, which was that for all his appreciation of popular culture, he was at heart an experimentalist: to keep him interested, each film had to be a challenge. The point of genre was to play with it, invert its conventions, challenge it from within. This has never been the route to popularity. In *The Lady from Shanghai* he had, because of a personal connection, access to one of the greatest icons of the screen. To expect that he would

PLAIN TALK
BY THE MAN
FROM MARS

Left: Welles learning from a master. Co-starring with Jack Benny.

Below: GIs queuing for *The Mercury Wonder Show.*

Bill of fare for *The Mercury Wonder Show*.

Above: Orson the Magnificent in *The Mercury Wonder Show.*

Below: Rita Hayworth emerges unscathed, supported by Orson Welles and George 'Shorty' Chirello.

Shooting *The Stranger*: Orson Welles, Loretta Young and hound.
Behind the camera: Russell Metty.

Another moment of barely controlled pandemonium from *Around the World*.

Left: Orson Welles as Dick Fix, scandalising Julie Warren as Mary Muggins.

Below: Al Hirschfeld's multi-media depiction of *Around the World* in which Welles has become his own Indian rope trick.

be allowed to deconstruct and reinvent her at the expense of her owner (because that is what, in effect, Harry Cohn was) was an unrealistic notion. To assume that the machine of Columbia Studios would put itself behind him and attempt to realise his highly idiosyncratic vision was to surrender to fantasy. It is fascinating to find, then, that the central character of *The Lady from Shanghai* is just such a figure, a dreamer, a romantic, who explicitly associates himself (or did before Harry Cohn made his cuts) with the figure of Don Quixote — whose bony profile was to cast such a long shadow over Welles's life and work.

The film that we have — compromised, butchered, coarsened, cheapened — is still a remarkable and a highly personal work. *The Lady from Shanghai* is the story of Michael O'Hara, just as *Carmen* is the story of Don José. Welles had done some intensive work on his version of the Prosper Mérimée story while preparing *The Lady from Shanghai*; James Naremore persuasively suggests that he may have used it as his model. Something happens to both Don José and Mike O'Hara; by the end of their respective stories, both are changed, whereas Carmen and Elsa Bannister remain what they always have been: spiderwomen, catching men in their webs. They both die, but unlike poor love-maddened José, Michael O'Hara lives; to that extent it is an optimistic tale. The opening of the narration, over a mysterious shot of the Brooklyn Bridge at night, might well have some autobiographical resonance for Welles (and more than one review eagerly seized on it as such): 'When I start out to make a fool of myself, there's very little that can stop me. Once I'd seen her, I was not in my right mind for some time.' We are thus immediately introduced to Welles's Irish brogue, a thing much mocked, though in fact it is a more-than-halfway decent west of Ireland accent such as he may well have heard fifteen years before, in Galway, at the start of the mad adventure that was his career. It is perhaps rather relentlessly deployed, however, the same cadence repeated over and over again, and ultimately becomes something of a straitjacket, stiffening his phrasing and inhibiting his natural expressiveness; its authentic softness lends a certain sleepiness to Michael's utterances, too. No sooner have we heard our hero than we see him, in Central Park, in the dark, catching sight of a beautiful young blonde in a carriage, and setting out to pick her up. The first glimpse of Hayworth transmogrified into a short-haired platinum blonde must have been a real shock, and perhaps a thrill, for the film's initial audiences; it again turns us into voyeurs, goggling at Elsa rather than simply looking at her.

Welles himself – for the first time on film *sans* beard, false nose or other facial make-up – might have been quite a surprise, too. It is a remarkable face, astonishingly protean, seeming to change with every changing angle: now puffy, now angular; huge eyes and small retroussé nose surmounting heavy and seemingly boneless jowls; often, in repose, seeming sullen, only to blaze with anim-ation in action. Dick Wilson noted in his memo, 'Rudolph [Maté] took a whole day to learn how to photograph you', and one can see that it might have been a challenge. The best solution was to contrive shadows along the jawline and light deep into the eyes, inevitably a somewhat stylised effect. As often, Welles had chosen to play one essential trait of the character, in this case chivalry, and though it is not without charm, it is an unassimilated assumption, put on like the jaunty cap he sports, an indication of a type. It is a good sketch of something, but it is scarcely a performance, let alone a characterisation. The transformation (such as it is) is entirely superficial; there is never a point at which the character seems to have autonomous life, and never a moment at which – in David Hare's admirable formulation – his gestures cease to be about one thing and become about everything. The particular is so impre-cisely expressed that it can never become general. In an interview Welles gave during the shoot, he expressed his impatience with acting:

> I have a small public now whose interest in me is sufficient at the box office to make my appearance on the screen a necessary adjunct to my writing and directing. But no critic has ever liked my acting. I can show you, frame for frame, that my eyebrows move less than Ray Milland's in *The Lost Weekend*. If I permitted myself a tenth of his expressions in that excellent performance, I would be howled out of the theatre. I have only to walk into camera range and the critics are convinced that I am a ham-bone. I am an actor of the old school. That is the only way I can explain it.

The explanation won't wash: there are plenty of actors of 'the old school' – Pierre Brasseur, Michel Simon, Nikolai Cherkassov, Laurence Olivier, George C. Scott – who made searing and profoundly moving impressions on the screen. The truth is that on screen Welles was an extraordinary presence, but rarely an engaged actor. It is hardly to be wondered at that his mind was elsewhere when he was standing in front of the camera during *The Lady from*

Shanghai: he was working sleeplessly round the clock on a film that was in danger of spinning out of control, with a leading lady who was exhausted and ailing, while rewriting on a daily and some-times hourly basis. But the fact has to be faced that on this exceptionally ambitious film of his, playing a role that was so very close to his heart, Welles gives a limp, rather absent performance, and it damages the film.

The opening sequence in Central Park suffers from this, despite some witty camera work during the first flirtatious dialogue between Michael and Elsa, whom he dubs his Rosaleen; when she sets out on her own, he finds her handbag and its concealed gun, then hears her being pursued by muggers in the park. Welles's fist-fight with her assailants is just a little half-hearted; Central Park itself makes a slightly stagy impact, too. Once Elsa and Michael go to the car park, reality kicks in. Michael refuses her offer of a job and, as she drives off, various low-lifers emerge to ask about the classy blonde dame; at which point the unforgettably sweaty and drunken features of Glenn Anders as George Grisby loom up like a death's head and then slide speechlessly away. In the loose reper-tory company that acts Welles's films, there is often a glamorous star (Rita Hayworth, Jo Cotten, Anthony Perkins), a number of first-rate character actors (Ray Collins, George Coulouris) and an actor of profound inner life. Anders is one of the last-named; Agnes Moorehead was another, Michael Redgrave (in *Mr Arkadin*) a third. Anders's Grisby is a recklessly brave but perfectly centred perform-ance, exuding a sense of fathomless corruption and self-disgust that is deeply disturbing, and it electrifies every scene in which he appears.

After Grisby has slithered out of the frame, the scene changes to the following day, at the Hiring Hall, where Bannister comes to look for Michael. Everett Sloane brilliantly and audaciously char-acterises what Sherwood King calls the crippled lawyer's 'comic, jerky walk', swaying backwards and forwards on his two cane sticks like some curious bird, an impression enhanced by the beakiness of his nose – a nose the actor so hated, having operation after operation to have it reduced, until finally (according to Welles) he knew there was no further he could go and he killed himself. Although the nose does indeed limit the amount of physical trans-formation possible, Sloane's Bannister – sharp, demanding, anguished – is a far cry from the actor's kindly, pixie-like Mr Bernstein in *Citizen Kane*. Welles contrives a good atmosphere for the Hiring Hall, with a monkey for exotic effect, and the scene in which Bannister gets drunk, or appears to get drunk, is a classic piece of Wellesian overlapping and repeated phrases, the faces crammed tight into the frame as they huddle round the table and a barely audible Frank Sinatra croons on the juke-box.

When O'Hara brings the drunken Bannister back to the yacht, he meets Elsa for the second time and is forgivably smitten by her all over again. Hayworth wears the shortest of skirts, a captain's blue jacket and a nautical cap at the most provocative angle. Everyone, including the black maid, begs him to come to work for the Bannisters; he succumbs, and over the following deftly shot sequence of yacht life, the sense of sexual tension between Michael and Elsa grows, in its strange way: Hayworth provocative but withdrawn, Welles looking mournful, his great panda's eyes filled with doomed yearning. Finally they are in each other's arms, only to be interrupted by Grisby who has rowed up on a boat, leering and cackling and rather queeny. Elsa goes off to swim, and Grisby follows her with his telescope, as eventually so do we, witnessing her dive to the accompaniment of poor Heinz Roemheld's misplaced orchestral orgasm.

The song sequence, dropped in to please Harry Cohn, suggests that perhaps the old monster knew a bit about film after all. As shot by Welles, it has extraordinary tension, and is clear proof (if any were needed) of his exceptional sensitivity to music. Michael is in the cabin with other crew members as Elsa starts to sing; one of the guys picks up the tune on his guitar and Michael is drawn upwards, the music leading him forward like a snake charm, up, up onto the deck where Elsa, exquisitely passive in her swimsuit, purrs her anti-love song, holding three rapt men in thrall: Michael moonstruck, Bannister watching like a hawk, Grisby entertaining who knows what dark designs. The next scene, the following day, takes us away from this tense triangle of admirers into a sunlit world, with Michael joined at the wheel by Elsa, in her cheeky captain's uniform: a radio commercial creeps up. It is advertising Glosso Lusto, a shampoo that restores natural sheen – an ironic comment, perhaps, on Elsa's impossible perfection. Against the sparkling freshness of the sky and sea, she and Michael flirt ever more intensely, and Elsa delivers herself of two highly characteristic Wellesian proverbs (Chinese, emphasising her unfathomable background in fact from him: Yutang's *The Wisdom of China*): 'It is difficult for love to last long. Therefore one who loves passionately is cured of love, in the end.' The second, even more typical and if anything more fatalistic, says: 'Human nature is eternal.

Therefore one who follows his nature keeps his original nature, in the end.' Michael is understandably baffled and frustrated by these cryptic injunctions to action, but is increasingly ensnared by Elsa.

The next sequence thrusts us out of the enclosed world of the yacht with its games-playing passengers and into a teeming, swarming world of celebratory life. Bannister has impulsively decided to have a picnic at Acapulco Bay, and his party is borne along by the waves of energy created by the Mexican populace, canoeing, dancing, singing, and later floating by with flaming torches. It is a sequence of outstanding bravura, the sudden irruption of a whole culture, absorbed in its own rituals, moving to its own exhilarating rhythm. A few bearers and porters struggle through the jungle and guide the party up to their clearing, while all around them, below them, above them, the great celebration goes on into the night. Welles's feeling for South American life and music pre-dated his trip to Brazil with *It's All True*, and continued beyond it; but a great part of the spirit of what he saw and filmed in Rio de Janeiro and Fortaleza informs this section of *The Lady from Shanghai*, framing and highlighting the emotional dance of death of a small and over-privileged group of another, decidedly less healthy culture. 'When you give a picnic, it's a picnic. Time for another?' squeals Grisby, his tiny eyes glistening with malice and greed, oblivious to the joyful splendour all around him. For him, it's just background to the fascinating drama being played out in what he takes to be the foreground, and in which he is of course a principal figure. But the film contradicts him, and the shooting style evolved by Welles and Lawton – in which the sweating, savage, smirking figures of Grisby and Bannister, the anguished figure of O'Hara, and Elsa's cool, unperspiring beauty are held within a frame that also includes the constantly moving, rhythmically chanting, torch-bearing Mexicans – results in an epic canvas that seems to owe something to Welles's deep encounter with the paintings of Rivera and Siqueiros. And then no sooner is the power of this established than the dreary taste of Viola Lawrence and Harry Cohn dully thrusts itself into our faces, and the scene resolves itself into a series of conventional set-ups, including, most damagingly, Welles in a particularly puddingy medium close-shot, backed by some blurred and generalised process footage, for his chilling story about the sharks and their feeding frenzy. As if in homage to his great doomed dream, *It's All True*, he has O'Hara tell us that the story took place in Fortaleza, 'on the hump of Brazil', where Welles shot *Four Men on a Raft*. 'They eat themselves,' O'Hara tells the Bannisters and Grisby. 'There wasn't one of them crazy sharks that survived.'

The following day they travel further up the Acapulco coast, and in the dazzling sunshine – 'which can't hide the hunger and the guilt: it's a bright, guilty world,' as Michael says – Grisby makes his proposition. Higher and higher they climb, for Michael's temptation on the mount, as Grisby speaks of the impending end of the world. The camera rises vertiginously over them as Anders, white-faced and almost deranged, barks out his challenge: 'I want you to kill me.' Over the shoulder of the appalled Michael we see, a thousand feet below, the sea and the rocks. The same sea twinkles benevolently beyond the balcony of the hotel where, that night, Bannister is sitting tensely with Elsa, who abruptly gets up and leaves him and the dancing couples and runs down the side of the hill – another shot demanded by Cohn, but in fact rather beautiful – to join Michael in the street. They walk along, speaking of life and death and Grisby. She, looking especially perfect in white, talks of the pain of her life; they become more and more intimate, until they are interrupted by Broome, who insolently wonders whether Bannister knows where they are, a line of thought cut short by Michael's fist. The punch sends Elsa flying down the street from which they've just come; the camera races ahead on the dolly and the soundtrack suddenly erupts into vigorous Mexican music – 'Hey-ho, hey-ho!' – exactly as Welles intended it to. Bret Wood quotes the appropriate direction from the screenplay, and it is revealing to see how closely detailed his requirements are, and, when they are left untampered with, how effective:

The Whorehouse piano plays through until Mike has punched Broome in the nose and Rita starts to run away. On the first cut of her crossing the street, there is a strong backlight on this. There is a cross-fade on this in which we hear Fading OUT the sound of the Whorehouse piano and Fading in over this Shot a very fast rumba which is probably going to be the one from the Astaire picture. It isn't important – a lot of drums and action . . . this goes through from the Quick travelling shot of Rita running and just as we come to the shot of the band as she runs: a quick QUICK cross-fade which takes us into 'Palabras du Mohair' which plays through until we cut outside and the line 'What's the name for a drunken bum' is repeated.

(It is striking that in this version of the screenplay, Welles refers to all the other characters by their story names, but Elsa is only ever 'Rita'.)

At the end of the chase, Michael and Rita find themselves in a secluded room. He asks her to dance, and immediately the music police (having let Welles get away with a whole sequence as he wanted it to be) assert themselves by imposing a backing that is both rhythmically and atmospherically meaningless. It is in this scene – all shadows and shafts of illumination – that Elsa scoffs at Michael's dreams for their life together, telling him that he must come to terms with all-pervading badness. 'You don't know how to take care of yourself,' she tells him, 'so how could you take care of me?' Here it is distinctly moot as to whether it is 'Elsa' or Rita talking. The next scene at the jetty brings more doubts on Elsa's part: how will they live? Will she take in washing? As she parts from him, that wretched pop song, which has wound its way into every scene like ivy, wells up into a ghastly mutated Irish rhapsody for viola and strings; in his memo to Cohn, Welles says, '*I think that damn tune is in every scene!*' It very nearly is.

Now it is imperative for Mike to earn the $5,000 for appearing to murder Grisby, and he agrees to Grisby's plan. Through the window of the bar in which they're drinking, they see Bannister and converse with him; again and again in *The Lady from Shanghai* people are glimpsed through glass, sometimes shattered, often at an odd angle. The intention is, naturally, to create visual variety (to take the curse off the cliché, in Welles's own words), but it also seems increasingly to predict the film's penultimate sequence in the Hall of Mirrors, where it is impossible to tell what is real, what merely reflected. O'Hara, though apparently living in the real world, is already being swept along by events and people that seem to change every minute. After being given secret instructions by the Chinese chauffeur to meet Elsa at the aquarium, Mike goes to meet Grisby, who gives him the money and dictates a statement for him, confessing to the murder. This section of the plot is not, it must be said, an improvement on the relative simplicity of Sherwood King's narrative, but it is a scene superbly played by Anders and Welles; the latter is seated throughout, as Anders (shot from below) circles him, prattling about his new life in the South Seas. None of it makes sense to O'Hara, who is starkly lit to emphasise his panic and confusion, as if caught in headlights; he becomes curiously boyish, staring up at Grisby in terror.

Welles had asked for the corniest Hawaiian music imaginable in this sequence, to be played at a high level; as it is, it is a vaguely Polynesian, virtually inaudible murmur behind the scene, thus depriving it of a level of edginess that is central to Welles's technique, both in the theatre and on radio. *Citizen Kane* is inconceivable without those heightened moments, in which sound – including, of course, dialogue – creates a hectic intensity, ratcheting up the nervous tension, inducing instability and thus unpredictability. Where another director creates energy by the linear pursuit of action, or by focusing on the psychology of the characters, Welles seeks to shock, alarm, almost to ambush the audience with dynamic contrasts and skewed perspectives. The desired effect is, so to speak, in-your-face, a super-realism in acting, in image and above all in sound. Remove any of these elements and the result is less impressive. Harry Cohn and his team worked hard and long to eliminate as many of them as they could, especially visually and sonically. The fact that a scene like the one between Grisby and O'Hara succeeds as well as it does, deprived of a critical factor in the scene – the intensified sound score – is a tribute to the force of Welles's imagination and the actors' flair, but is not quite what he intended.

Michael is next seen in the aquarium, where Elsa comes to him, dressed in black. Against a background of monstrously magnified fish, he tells her what he's agreed to; reading the statement he's signed, she is troubled. They kiss; some schoolchildren (a slightly clumsy touch) giggle at them; she tells him he must be careful. As the scene progresses, the lighting on their two figures becomes more and more stylised: it picks out her perfect profile as he speaks of his passion; then they become pure silhouettes, with the shadowy, watery shapes pulsing gently behind them.

The reality of what he has agreed to hits Michael in the next scene. He drives Grisby back to the Bannisters' house; Grisby goes through the garden but is intercepted by Broome, who lewdly suggests that he knows about Grisby and Elsa. The scene is shot in a heightened way to show the battle for domination between the two men. Crossed, Grisby shoots the insolent butler and returns to the car. When questioned by Michael as to the gunshot he replies, his leering sweaty face filling the frame, 'It was *taar*get practice, just as you were *suppoosed* to have been doing when you threw my *coorpse* into the bay!' These extreme exaggerations are brilliantly handled by Anders, the perfect Wellesian actor, making huge shapes and filling them with wit and danger. Grisby can barely suppress snickering as he contemplates his own feigned demise, almost whimpering with suppressed delight and anticipation. The effect is not melodramatic or hammy, because it is so precise and so convincing. In a nutshell, it is brilliant acting. Grisby's bubbling excitement continues through the subsequent car ride to the beach; suddenly another vehicle looms up and they smash into the back of it – Michael confused and worried; Grisby blithely accepting the card of the other man, hardly waiting till he has gone to tell O'Hara that this will confirm their story; both of them are bleeding. This whole plot mechanism is derived more or less without alteration from *If I Die Before I Wake*; and Welles's O'Hara, like King's Larry Planter, is by now in a positively trance-like state. The heavy shadows from the smashed windscreen – which Welles shoots head-on at the time of the crash, giving us the passengers' point of view – sit across their faces in parallel bars, a strange and dream-like vision.

Back at the Bannisters', we see the dying Broome telling Elsa that Bannister is to be shot. O'Hara and Grisby arrive at the jetty; after snatching Michael's cap, Grisby makes off in the speedboat and O'Hara nervously lets off his three shots. Immediately people throng out to see what's happened; in a brilliantly organised sequence, he stumbles off, waving his gun, saying that he's been doing 'taarget practice' as the crowd· pushes around him. We cut to a shadowy shot of Grisby at the San Francisco landing jetty, cocking his gun. O'Hara gets away from the crowd and makes a phone call to the Bannisters' house: Broome answers, telling him that he's been framed and that he must get to the office in Montgomery Street, which he does, arriving to find a throng of policemen, into whose arms Michael runs just as Bannister sways into view, shortly followed by Grisby's corpse and then Elsa. Bret Wood reports a cut scene (whether actually filmed or deleted from the script is unclear) in which Grisby is seen from the partners' office, high above the street; a bullet rings out and he is dead. Whether this would have added a great deal is also unclear.

Elsa has promised Mike that Bannister will defend him, and she and Bannister are sitting on a bench in the judge's chambers discussing how they will proceed; Elsa lights up under a very prominent 'No Smoking' sign. They are in shadow, and now the shadow of the judge looms over them; Bannister exchanges knowing banter with him: we only ever see the judge's shadow. Bannister tensely conveys to Elsa how hopeless Michael's case is: his story about Grisby makes no sense, and he has been found with $5,000 on him. He tries to touch her; she recoils. Later, she visits Michael in jail: he is behind a metal mesh. He knows how bad his case is.

The scene is highly striking visually: the narrowness of the room Elsa is in is underlined; Michael's face is only ever seen with the metal mesh in front of it, at the end squaring him up like graph paper. She tells him she loves him, but can offer little hope. Welles had intended them to be barely audible; here they boom away with, needless to say, 'Please Don't Kiss Me' chundering mournfully away on solo cello.

The following trial scene is presented as circus or something out of *Alice in Wonderland* – or perhaps Kafka – with red-faced Erskine Sandford battily presiding over the strutting attorneys while the public chatters, eats, sneezes, snoozes, 'oohs', 'aahs' and gasps on cue; two young women discuss the case in Chinese; 'You're not kidding,' the first says at the end of the conversation. At one point the prosecution suddenly calls defence counsel – Bannister – as a witness; Bannister gets into the box, but harangues the judge from it, then insists on his right to cross-examine himself (both of these developments, surprisingly, suggested by the novel, which conveys an equally farcical aspect to the proceedings). The camera keeps changing its position restlessly, now at the back of the courtroom, now at the side, now above, now in the judge's lap. Welles's own cutaways, shot much later than the main scene, belong to a wholly different world visually, and indeed seem – in technical jargon – to cross the line: that is, he appears to be looking in the opposite direction from the one he should be. Elsa Bannister is suddenly called to the witness box; she cannot deny that she kissed him. The judge adjourns the case while the jury deliberates; we cut to a Chinese family, high up, looking over San Francisco and listening to reports of it; we see the judge, reflected in the window, looking over another part of San Francisco, playing chess with himself; we see Bannister, Elsa and O'Hara in the empty courtroom, waiting. Bannister tells O'Hara with vicious relish that he'll go to the electric chair. Outside, the judge, summoned to return to court, sprays his throat and starts to make his entrance; as the court files back, O'Hara eyes the tablets that Bannister is taking and suddenly swallows a few. There are screams; he must be kept moving, someone shouts, or he's done for, and so he is escorted upright out of the courtroom into an adjacent room, where he suddenly slugs the young policeman who has been helping him on the jaw, knocks over furniture and bookcases, empties cabinets and hurls a statuette at the camera, narrowly missing it and smashing a sheet of glass, just where you would expect the camera's lens to have been. He then makes a run for it, using as decoy a jury deliberating another case, and slips away into Chinatown.

The courtroom scene is a classic piece of Wellesian staging and – apart from the strangely disorientating dropped-in single shots of Welles and Hayworth – works brilliantly. Here again, Welles complained bitterly about the elimination during editing of the raucousness of the public, the nearly permanent sense of hubbub present on the original soundtrack, and it is clear that the more grotesque the scene could have been, the better. The three scenes while the court is in recess are effective contrasts in stillness; but the plot device of swallowing the tablets – obviously not drawn from the novel, where Larry is found guilty and spends the rest of the book in jail – is a little desperate, and the subsequent getaway straight out of a Boy's Own adventure book. Welles is not at his most convincing as a dashing escapee, and the undoubted virtuosity of the staging, with police and judiciary rushing about left and right, seems to belong to another film: it ceases to be a nightmare and briefly (and unconvincingly) becomes a caper movie. Once Michael hits Chinatown – we see him scurrying down the streets, through a series of shop windows painted with Chinese characters – the film regains its stylistic coherence; plunging into a performance of the Chinese Opera, O'Hara takes us with him into a deeply exotic world, wonderfully and evocatively filmed in wide-shot and close-up, from on stage and backstage and from the auditorium. For Michael, it is a sort of beautiful nightmare, at once incomprehensible and compelling. This sequence, like the scenes at Acapulco, transcends mere background. Welles had been in Shanghai with his father as a boy and had written a vivid account of Chinese theatre in his local newspaper; he had followed it knowledgeably ever since. His sense of its integrity gives the scene a depth and power it would lack in the hands of someone else: paradoxically, however theatrical, it is a wholly real world into which he has stumbled, not something devised for passing effect.

Michael slips into a seat at the theatre, where Elsa soon joins him. We have seen her running down the same streets of Chinatown, asking passers-by – in Chinese – whether they've seen him, finding the theatre, going to the dressing room and finally (eyed by an actor about to put his wig on) making a phone call to Lee, an elderly Chinese man whom we saw earlier listening to reports of the trial on the radio. Infuriatingly, Viola Lawrence cut an exchange between Elsa and O'Hara, in which she recounts to him what she pretends is the story of the play: 'I'll tell you the plot. The lady loves a man . . . a poor sailor . . . the poor sailor's accused of murder, but the lady's jealous . . .' O'Hara takes the story over, ending with the words: 'With the partner dead, who is it gets the benefit of the insurance? Who stands to gain by killing him?' To which Elsa replies: 'One person – only one.' In the film as released, she simply sits beside Mike as the police enter the auditorium; she whispers to him to sit still, and suddenly kisses him to make sure of it. The shot of the two of them is wittily fringed by an ancient Chinaman in the row in front, a half-smoked cigarette jutting out of his mouth, three inches of ash threatening to fall at any moment, which produces its own comic tension. The police prowl around the auditorium, the camera picking up eyes everywhere: Mike's, Elsa's, those of the police, above all the actors', their huge and stylised orbs swivelling from side to side in terrified curiosity. Mike starts to free himself from Elsa, telling her that he knows who the murderer is: 'You're the killer.' He finds her gun – the gun with which she must have killed Grisby – in her handbag, but even as he threatens her with it, the tablets take effect and he slumps to the floor. Elsa's friend Lee has been standing by the light switch and now abruptly plunges the theatre into darkness. Out in the street, we see Lee and his friends taking O'Hara to a nearby out-of-season Crazy House, where he wakes up.

Here the nightmare becomes explicit. Michael stumbles through horrors presumably devised to scare children, though some of them would be quite disturbing enough for adults. Stumbling past Caligarian abstract projections, he moves on through flapping hands and dangling arms, through elaborate webbing at the centre of which is a slogan telling him to STAND UP OR GIVE UP (which might have been Welles's motto in life, but also of course recalls Michael's drugged near-collapse in the courtroom), past skeletons and upturned mannequins. As he does so, in a great rush of enlightenment, he pieces together the baffling events of his recent life and finally understands them. 'I was the fall-guy,' he says, and duly tumbles down the vast twisting slide and into the jaws of the dragon, at the bottom of which he finds himself walking rubber-legged into a room of distorting mirrors. Once out of there, he finds himself in the Hall of Mirrors, where it is impossible to know what is real and what is merely reflected; there he discovers Elsa, endlessly replicated, and the final phase of the nightmare begins. This is the most celebrated sequence in the film, which alone would have earned Welles a place in the Hollywood pantheon; however, the Crazy House sequence that precedes it is less satisfying, spectacular but somehow perfunctory. The reason for this is predictable: Cohn and Lawrence cut a great deal of it. It was, according to Welles, the most interesting sequence in the film: 'I was up every night from ten-thirty till five in the morning for a week painting that funhouse . . . this was THE big tour-de-force scene.' Harry Cohn had neither liked nor understood it: 'What's all that about?' he said and, in Welles's phrase, 'yanked it out'. There remain a few stills – all later withdrawn – from the sequence, and it is clear that the nightmare was much darker than the one we see in the commercially available version of the film, containing mutilated faces of clowns and mannequins, bisected women, ghoulishly contorted skeletons. There is an unmistakable element of violence, especially violence to women.

If this is Michael's nightmare, it is a strange one for him to be having, bearing little connection to the gentle dreamer and chivalrous champion we have seen throughout the picture. It is, rather, a curious but very direct emanation from Welles's obviously frenzied imagination, and has led to some fairly feverish speculation about his possible involvement in a murder that took place in Hollywood in January of 1947, the notorious Black Dahlia case, in which a young woman, Elizabeth Short, was found cut up and mutilated in a very distinctive, highly skilled way. According to Mary Pacios, childhood friend of the murdered woman turned amateur sleuth, writing in 1998, the mutilations on the faces and torsos, the way in which the limbs on the mannequins are arranged and the skeletons severed at the waist in Welles's scenery are all uncannily like those on Bette Short's corpse. It seems that the production shut down on 15 January, the day of the murder, and the following day; that Welles took out a passport a few days later; and that, most bizarrely of all, a few days before he had made a formal written application to register as an assistant with the local mortuary (this application is to be found in the Mercury archive at the Lilly Library). In the way of these things, Miss Pacios kept on finding more clues: that Bette Short was seeing a man called George (Welles's first name, used by certain of his intimates) and ate in a restaurant that Welles frequented, Brittingham's near the Columbia studios; that the body was left, carefully arranged, on the former site of *The Mercury Wonder Show* on Cahuenga Boulevard – where, of course, Welles had so famously sawn a woman in half; and a collage message from the murderer sent to the police with the girl's address book and birth certificate, which heavily features the letters O and W. Miss Pacios rather overplays her hand by triumphantly revealing that the next play Welles did was *Macbeth*, in which . . . More appositely, she cites an oration given by Welles at the funeral of Darryl F. Zanuck in 1976, in which Welles said, 'If I did something really outrageous, that if I committed some abominable crime, which I believe it is in most of us to do, that if I were guilty of something unspeakable, and if all the police in the world were after me, there was one man, and only one man I could come to, and that was Darryl. He would not have made me a speech about the good of the industry, the good of the studio. He would not have been mealy-mouthed or put me aside. He would have hid me under the bed. Very simply he was a friend.' The speech has a curious resonance in that when Welles left America at the end of 1947, not to return for ten years, it was to play a part hastily rustled up for him by Darryl Zanuck.

As it happens, a book appeared in 2002 (*Black Dahlia Avenger*) which definitively and beyond reasonable doubt identified the Black Dahlia murderer − it turned out to be the father of the book's author − so Welles is off the hook; it is irresistible to reflect how he would have loved the story. It had all the elements of a perfect Wellesian film, à la *A Touch of Evil*, with crooked cops, seedy club-owners, girls on the brink of prostitution, and an innocent who, determined to prove that her murdered friend was not a whore, finds herself blocked at every turn, finally stumbling on a terrible truth, to which everything points but which it is now impossible to prove. Miss Pacios is right, however, to suggest that during the making of *The Lady from Shanghai* Welles was in a dangerously driven state, physically and mentally − those night-long painting sessions, followed by even longer days of shooting both behind and in front of the camera, can scarcely have created a calm state of mind, and no doubt when he let his fantasy run, the images that swam into his consciousness were not especially wholesome; they were clearly too much for Harry Cohn. Perhaps they expressed something of the self-disgust that Welles so often felt; without question they reveal some complexity in his dealings with women, as does *The Lady from Shanghai* in general.

Curiously enough, only weeks after the Black Dahlia murders, Rita Hayworth was sent a disturbing letter: 'The Scar never fails. This I assure you sis is no crank letter, unless $2,000 in cash is sent to me by the 10th of this month, then I assure you that your baby will be snatched from your home, and that your beautiful face will be ruined by having lye thrown into those beautiful eyes of yours.' The sender tells her to mail the money in $5, $10 and $20 bills.

'Rest assured, the Scar gets what he wants you don't want to look like the Blue Dahlia do you, nor do you want your child to be disturbed from your arms, this is your final warning RITA, ORSON WELLS cannot help you nor the FBI, for they have been wanting me for some time no one can help you only the money can talk.' In fact, the Scar was apprehended before Hayworth ever saw the letter, but *The Lady from Shanghai* is informed throughout with the violence that seems to have surrounded its making like a sinister force-field.

The climactic sequence in the Hall of Mirrors is a triumph of organisation, a brilliant embodiment of the multiphrenia of the central characters: who are they, really? Michael has never known. Idle rich? Homicidal monsters? Romantics in the grip of obsessive passion? It is a brilliantly achieved *coup de théâtre*, a piece of high romantic stagecraft that would many years later be echoed by Roger Planchon in his masterful production of Racine's *Britannicus* at the Théâtre National Populaire, where, as in Welles's cinematic *mise-en-scène*, the mirrors' revelation of the heightened isolation and duplication of the obsessed characters reveals the fundamental narcissism of their fragmented selves. The sequence in the Hall of Mirrors is rightly held to be one of Welles's most remarkable achievements, a passage of uncommon filmic bravura. It is no diminution of that achievement to trace its antecedents – both in other films (most notably Chaplin's *The Circus*, in which the chase climaxes brilliantly in a Hall of Mirrors, though there of course the intention is purely comic), but also in two other screenplays on which Welles had worked. The first was John Fante's *Love Story* – intended as part of *It's All True* – which contained a Crystal Maze sequence that Fante's biographer Stephen Cooper, quoting the Welles scholar Catherine Benamou, claimed Welles had 'cannibalised' for the Hall of Mirrors sequence in *The Lady from Shanghai*. Equally, Brett Wood has drawn attention to a sequence in the unfilmed screenplay *Don't Catch Me* – the project Welles had worked on with Bud Pearson and Les White a couple of years earlier. As always, it is necessary to point out that in film, ideas for scenes are mere starting points; the realisation is all. Moreover, Welles worked actively with Pearson and White on the screenplay, and no doubt encouraged the development of a sequence with such obvious visual potential. The point is not about plagiarism, but about Welles's remarkable ability – an ability he shared with the greatest artists in every medium – to remember and recycle material from one project to another, and to perceive potential in a notion, a technical concept.

It is hard to imagine the idea of a shoot-out in a Hall of Mirrors being more perfectly adapted to its context than this scene in this film. It had found its perfect place. Looming lopsidedly into view with his cane, Sloane's Arthur Bannister (multiplied by five) flourishes his gun at Hayworth's Elsa, crying, 'Killing you is killing myself.' But which self? There are so many. Welles's O'Hara, trapped in this ontological nightmare, has the appearance of a rabbit caught in headlights. As the guns start to speak and the mirrors shatter, first Bannister and then Elsa collapse to the floor; he is dead, she is quickly dying. Welles's camera films her, wincing and straining on the floor, in extremely unflattering close-up – an even more shocking destruction of her image, perhaps, than the one wrought by the coiffeurs' peroxide. From her semi-supine position, she rasps out her philosophy, so richly justified by the turn of events: 'the world's bad but we can't run away from the badness . . . we can't fight it. We must deal with the badness . . . make its own terms. We can't win.'

This is a world-view not dissimilar from that of Welles the artist, though Welles the political writer – another of the many fragments that made up the multi-faceted creature that was Orson Welles – continued to espouse his belief in the perfectibility of man and the triumph of the forces of light over those of darkness. 'Give my love to the sunrise,' she gasps, before a sudden access of terror at the thought of death. 'Come back here. Please. I don't want to die.' But O'Hara is all through with her, as we understand from the shot of him standing at the wicket of the Hall of Mirrors, its slatted shadow falling on Michael, and behind him the sign with its unnegotiable message: CLOSED. In voice-over, Michael tells us that he went to call the cops. He broods on the word 'innocent' – 'a big word', he says. 'Stupid's more like it. Everybody's somebody's fool.'

Michael walks away from the Hall of Mirrors, back towards the sea he so foolishly renounced for the love of a woman. On the soundtrack, the strains of 'Please Don't Kiss Me', which have been murmuring away under this on a fairly tight leash, now abandon any attempt at self-control and burst out in a sentimental ecstasy as Welles speaks the last lines of the film, which have so often (on no evidence whatsoever) been assumed to refer to his own relationship with Rita Hayworth: 'Maybe I'll live so long that I forget her – maybe I'll die trying.' In fact, the end of the film was the end of their relationship, although from time to time in the next years she attempted, according to Welles, to revive it. No, if the film allegorised any relationship in Welles's life, it was the one with Hollywood, the treacherous beauty whose intentions could never be fathomed and whom it was impossible to know on an equal basis. Michael's walk away from Elsa and the Crazy House towards the ocean and its implied lands beyond symbolised an exile that Welles was shortly to embrace. But before that, there was one last stab at creating a new sort of structure by which to make films, a fusion of his worlds of art, a possible matrix for a way in which he might function effectively in a universe whose workings he either did not, or would not, understand.

CHAPTER TWENTY

The Forces of Darkness

IT WAS in the midst of filming *The Lady from Shanghai*, in late January 1947, when Harry Cohn and Viola Lawrence were starting to tamper with his footage, when both he and Rita Hayworth were ill, and when lunatics were sending them threatening letters, that Welles received a telegram from Vinton Freedley of the American National Theatre and Academy: RE POSSIBILITY OF YOUR APPEARING IN KING LEAR OR A NEW PLAY FOR ONE WEEK IN SALT LAKE CITY. The lure of the great roles was one that persisted with Welles to the end of his life, as was his determination to bring them to the screen; he died with his plans for a film of *King Lear* at an advanced stage. He seems immediately to have seen the possibilities in ANTA's suggestion of using the brief week in Salt Lake City as a cheap and efficient way of preparing for a film version of a classical play; he correctly calculated that if the subsequent film was shot very quickly and on a relatively low budget, he would have more control over the production. Now all he needed was a studio to take up the challenge. Almost immediately, one fortuitously presented itself.

When shooting on *The Lady from Shanghai* came to an end, he and Rita Hayworth – no longer held together by work – parted again, this time for good. Welles moved into a large house, which he shared with Charles K. Feldman. The former agent, whose Famous Artists agency had managed some of the biggest Hollywood names, had been active since the early nineteen-forties as a producer of some class. He and Welles had worked together on *Follow the Boys*; his subsequent body of work included *To Have and Have Not* and *The Big Sleep*, and in the years to come he would produce such elegant fare as *Walk on the Wild Side*, *The Group* and *The Honey Pot*. Feldman was witty, shrewd and literate, and in 1947 he had a five-picture deal with Herbert J. Yates, head of Republic Studios. He and Welles took Yates the idea of filming a Shakespeare play that had previously been done on stage. The small studio was principally noted for its cowboy quickies, many of them starring

Roy Rogers, but Yates, a hard-headed businessman (whose precociously developed business instincts had led him to become an executive in a tobacco company at the age of nineteen), was at the same time quietly pursuing a more artistically enterprising line of work. There is a certain pleasing congruousness in the fact that the reason Republic was interested in making quality films at all was due to Yates's infatuation with his lovely wife, the ex-skating champion Vera Hruba Ralston, who had artistic ambitions, and for whom he created many unsuccessful vehicles to which the public stubbornly refused to flock – a relationship strangely echoing that of Marion Davies and William Randolph Hearst; moreover, most of Miss Ralston's films were directed by a man named Kane. Not all the art films starred Miss Ralston, though. The year before Yates signed the deal with Feldman, he had released the exotic *Specter of the Rose*, Ben Hecht's ambitious and slightly bizarre fantasy about a murderous schizophrenic ballet dancer; the visionary director Frank Borzage had signed a three-picture deal with them, which would result in the film widely considered to be his masterpiece, *Moonrise*; and in years to come Republic would produce two major John Ford movies, *Rio Grande* and *The Quiet Man*.

Yates readily signed up for the Welles project, agreeing a budget of $880,000 – not large by contemporary standards, but adequate for the planned twenty-three-day shoot. Welles's own salary for directing and acting in the film was $100,000; as with his contract for *The Stranger*, any overspend was to be deducted directly from his salary. Feldman would be the executive producer, while Dick Wilson – good, solid, long-suffering Dick – would be the associate producer. It was not, at that stage, to be billed as a Mercury Production, though there would be many Mercury players in it; the company that Welles and Feldman had formed had the somewhat deadly title of Literary Classics, Inc., a name that would surely have made the younger Orson Welles shudder.

The project turned out not to be *King Lear*, or a new play, but *Macbeth*, a play with which Welles was exceptionally familiar. It had been one of the texts in the *Everybody's Shakespeare* series, which – at the age of eighteen – he had edited and illustrated in conjunction with his former headmaster and loving mentor, Roger Hill; in 1947 his edition was still in print and in regular use in the classroom. *Macbeth* had also been his first collaboration, at the age of twenty-one, with John Houseman, then head of the Negro Theatre Project; his all-black, voodoo-haunted version of the play, a kind of barbaric cabaret set in the eighteenth-century Haiti of

Jean-Christophe and performed in Harlem, had electrified New York; on the road, when Jack Carter, Welles's brilliant but erratic Macbeth, had failed to show up for a performance, Welles had taken over the leading role at a moment's notice. More recently, again playing the title role, he had recorded a seventy-five-minute version for CBS Records, which had enjoyed some success.

The play's dark world, a vortex in which unnatural forces weigh in on the characters from outside and violent and destructive impulses well up from within them, had compelling attraction for Welles, with his almost Manichaean view of human life. As early as in his play *Bright Lucifer* (written when he was sixteen) he had shown a keen sense of the presence, not to say the omnipresence, of evil: 'There's evil on this earth!' cries the central character, Eldred, the self-described 'bitch-boy', filled with malevolent hatreds and fully conscious of his occult powers, a transparent and more than slightly disturbing self-portrait of its young author. 'In holy days, men fought it – there were charms and chants and bells and books and candles, and good men fought for good. But now they don't believe! Vampires fatten, werewolves range and witches go unburnt . . . thicker and quicker flows the force and tide of evil. Strong with a million years' momentum, since the great flaming fall when all the hosts of Lucifer showered down out of the sky like comets . . . they are – everywhere . . . there – there, behind you!' Welles liked to claim that his hated grandmother had dabbled in black magic, and he was conscious of having certain intuitive powers himself, telling Peter Brook in the nineteen-fifties that as a young actor on the road, trying to make a few pennies, he had set up as a fortune-teller, employing all the usual corny devices to trick people into revealing themselves. He achieved some success at it, until one day he started to experience accurate intimations of the past (often of a tragic nature), at which point he swiftly decided to pack the whole thing in; it was too hot, he felt, to handle.

For Welles, the supernatural was not an imaginative conceit; he was powerfully and alarmingly aware of its reality. In his Harlem *Macbeth* he employed African drummers to play the witches, encouraging them to use authentic voodoo chants; these sections of the production were genuinely disturbing. Famously, when the critic Percy Hammond gave the production a tepidly condescending review, the drummers, egged on by Welles, chanted against him through the night; the next day he was taken ill and within days he was dead. Welles returned to this area in his first production for

Unit 891, Christopher Marlowe's *Dr Faustus*, where he gave full rein to his sense both of black magic and of illusion. In *Bright Lucifer* the ravings of Eldred – who, by the end of the play, has become a devil – seem to echo Marlowe, rendering his exalted rhetoric grotesque. Immature and jejune though it is, *Bright Lucifer* has the power to disturb; the horrors have a certain force. The adolescent Welles knew something about guilt, about despair and about evil: '*The whole world will be your haunted house,*' Eldred screams at his guardian, 'devils don't [die] – *I won't. The evil that we do lives after us . . . my demon will never die.*' The malign and uncanny aspect of *Macbeth*, which has made it a universally known byword for ill luck in the theatre, had great weight for Welles. He told Peter Bogdanovich that 'when you do that play it has a really oppressive effect on everybody. Really, it's terrifying – stays with you all day. The atmosphere it generates is so horrendous and awful that it's easy to see how the old superstition lives on.' This sense of dread, added to the play's profound study of power's corrupting attraction, is strongly present in the Mercury recording for CBS.

The one aspect of the central character with which Welles fails to engage, either as adapter or actor, is perhaps the most famous: Macbeth's poetic imagination, which almost prevents him from killing Duncan in the first place, and which subsequently robs him of any satisfaction from his attainment of the throne. Welles has consciously cut much of the most sublime, almost free-associating verse that expresses the falling apart of Macbeth's mind, the whole of human life passing before him. His performance, in truth, is fairly rudimentary; recorded in 1940, just weeks before many of the actors (including, of course, Welles) went into the studios to start shooting *Citizen Kane*, it presents a straightforward approach, from a radiophonic point of view very far from the audacious experimentalism of the Mercury Theatre on the Air. It was intended as a teaching tool, and the scene numbers and stage directions are helpfully read out by William Alland. Some of the acting is arrestingly old-fashioned (mostly from the non-Mercurians Fay Bainter, the now fifty-year-old Edwardian ingénue who plays Lady Macbeth, and Richard Warrick, the plump-toned actor engaged for Banquo, who sounds more like Macbeth's grandfather than his companion-in-arms). The narrative is swiftly handled; the witches (men, by the sound of it, though they are uncredited) have a certain power, and Welles himself is vigorous, vocally refulgent and at times emotionally hysterical. Of the noted complexity of the man, there is little; nor, inevitably, is it possible to care for him, because we are not admitted into his inner life. What transforms the production is the remarkable and economic score of Bernard Herrmann, composed largely of fanfares and drum tattoos – the fanfares some-times in slow motion, sometimes urgent, sometimes blaringly barbaric; the tattoos now on timpani, now on snare drums, now on woodblocks. Under almost the whole action they run, instilling foreboding, but also seeming to be the issue of Macbeth's brain, alternately spectral and overpoweringly insistent. At certain moments of great intensity an almost abstract passage is heard, less a melody than a monstrous texture, a tense swelling of strings backed by woodwinds, suggesting the building pressure within the play and inside Macbeth himself. There is nothing specifically Scottish about the music, nor indeed about the performances.

Now, seven years later, Welles was returning to the play. While he continued to do battle with Harry Cohn and Viola Lawrence over *The Lady from Shanghai*, Welles prepared the Salt Lake City text using this adaptation as a basis, with some reference to his *Everybody's Shakespeare* cut. A great deal of the new arrangement of the text, however, was conditioned by a view of the play he had developed since making the recording, and which he best expresses in the prologue he wrote for the 1950 recut of the film:

> Our story is laid in Scotland – ancient Scotland, savage, half-lost
> in the mist that hangs between recorded history and the time of
> legends . . . the cross itself is newly arrived here. Plotting against
> Christian law and order are the agents of Chaos, priests of hell
> and magic – sorcerers and witches. Their tools are ambitious
> men. This is the story of such a man, and of his wife. A brave
> soldier, he hears from witches a prophecy of future greatness and
> on this cue murders his way up to a tyrant's throne, only to go
> down hated and in blood at the end of all.

It is an interesting view of the play, though one for which there is scant evidence in the text. That by no means invalidates it: Shakespeare would not need to spell out what was commonly known or assumed by his audience; in fact, Welles was supplying a context for the play. It is derived from a perception of Shakespeare that strikingly anticipates some of the radical criticism of the nineteen-eighties, inspired by the work of the great Russian anthro-pologist, Mikhail Bakhtin. 'Shakespeare was very close to the origins of his own culture,' Welles told the critics of *Cahiers du Cinéma*. 'The language he wrote had just been formed; the old England, the old Europe of the Middle Ages, still lived in the memory of the people of Stratford. He was very close . . . to quite another epoch, and yet he stood in the doorway of our "modern" world.' Welles would have embraced Bakhtin's revelation of the persistence of the medieval into the early Renaissance period, his awareness of the pagan, the animistic and the ritual lurking only just beneath the surface of the seemingly rational world of the sixteenth century. 'The main point of the production,' he told Peter Bogdanovich, 'is the struggle between the old and the new religion. These people are holding off not just the forces of darkness but the old religion, which has been forced underground.' In order to clarify this interpretation, Welles created a character whom he called, on stage, the Friar, and on film the Holy Father; he pilfered the text of this figure from various other characters, including occasionally Macbeth himself.

Welles's approach represents a continuation of his work on *Five Kings*, and is a very significant departure from his approach either to his first *Macbeth* or to *Julius Caesar*. There he used the texts to release the relevance of the plays – in the case of the earlier *Macbeth* by transplanting the play into an exotic and sensational context, which provided a credible environment for the ideas of witchcraft and of tyranny; in *Caesar* by creating specific modern parallels (in that case to fascism). With *Five Kings*, he started to talk about the author's world and how best to convey a sense of it to a modern audience: stressing, in other words, not in what way the characters and their lives resemble our own, but how they differ from them. He showed no interest (now or at any point in the future) in Elizabethan stage conventions, but was increasingly gripped by the Elizabethan life-experience. Paradoxically, this radical approach made the productions inspired by it, including the Utah *Macbeth*, look more old-fashioned than his earlier productions had. The Utah settings – attributed to a local designer, but entirely according to Welles's own conception – were essentially modelled on the spatial dynamics of the Harlem *Macbeth*, though they were their exact opposite in imagery: stark where the earlier production was lush, severe in line where the other had been turreted, battlemented and machicolated; the costumes belonged to the period of the eleventh century in which the historical Macbeth had his reign.

A further, apparently authentic touch was the decision to speak the play in Scottish accents, a notion that, Bret Wood suggests, had come to Welles as a result of his experience on his 1945 radio production of Robert Louis Stevenson's *The Master of Ballantrae*,

where all the actors had gamely pitched in with their approxima-
tions of that accent. As far as *Macbeth* is concerned, it would, of
course, be impossible to reconstruct an eleventh-century Scottish
accent and, if it were possible, it would be completely incomprehensible. Welles's purpose in proposing its use was other: conscious
of the difficulties experienced by most American actors, especially
young ones, with Elizabethan verse, he convinced himself that a
Scottish burr would compel them to speak more slowly and thus
more intelligibly, while at the same time avoiding the twin curses
of either a posh English accent – BBC, as Welles called it – or the
actors' own American accents, jarringly betraying their local origins.
He himself, as it happens, had cultivated an accent for Shakespearean
purposes that was perhaps an ideal medium for the language –
neither locally American nor imitatively English; if anything, it had
a touch of Irish in it, presumably acquired from his exposure to
macLiammóir and his other colleagues at the Gate Theatre in
Dublin, where he made his professional debut at the age of fifteen.
If there seemed a touch of the old school about it, that was scarcely
surprising: in addition to Welles's natural archaism – his courtly
mode of address, his flamboyance as of another era – the diction
and vocal manners that he had learned from macLiammóir were
themselves a throwback to an earlier period, acquired by the Irish
actor during his years as a child star in Beerbohm Tree's company
before the First World War (gramophone records of Tree clearly
reveal the source of macLiammóir's phrasing and vocal music).
Naturally, for uniformity, Welles would himself be adopting a
Scottish accent – or his idea of one. English actors have recently
become much better at American accents, and American actors
now regularly adopt flawless and geographically particular British
accents, but 1947 was still the dark ages as far as transatlantic mimicry
was concerned; Welles's notion was a recipe for complete phonetic
mayhem.

The cast he assembled for the stage show in Utah was very much
the usual Mercury cocktail: stalwarts like Erskine Sanford and
Edgar Barrier, radio colleagues like John McIntire and his wife
Jeanette Nolan (the voice of, among many other contemporaries,
Eleanor Roosevelt on *The March of Time*), some new blood (in this
case the Dublin actor Donal O'Herlihy from the recently released
Carol Reed movie *Odd Man Out*) and the young English-born
actor, Roddy McDowall, late of *Just William*, *How Green Was My
Valley* and *Lassie Come Home*). In addition there were a couple of
semi-actor-factotums, like Bill Alland, who also stage-managed, and

Brainerd Duffield, who had helped Welles with the adaptation, plus – as in the Harlem *Macbeth* – a large number of local actors and supernumeraries. The chances of any of them being able to achieve credible Scottish accents was slight, though it is also reasonable to observe that there would probably be few in a Salt Lake City audience whose ears were so acutely attuned to the nuances of British dialect that they would find any inaccuracies jarring.

In the event, most of the reviewers of the stage production were charmed by the accent; it added colour and, they felt, aided comprehension. The whole production, in fact, was acclaimed to the very rafters. Welles had rehearsed most of his leading actors in Hollywood (only the Lady Macduff, Joyce Barlow, was from Utah), spending the last few days of the three-week rehearsal period integrating the local actors and staging the show in the massive Kingsbury Hall of the University of Utah. As usual, in these circumstances, his ability to galvanise a group of people, his sense of showmanship and his instinctive response to a particular space and to the specific individuals at his disposal resulted in a semi-improvised piece of spectacular theatre, here given special excitement because he was working with the community. It was the sort of thing – less considered, less detailed, but equally electric in its impact – that Max Reinhardt had done in Salzburg: a kind of sophisticated folk theatre, attended by the whole town (or as near as dammit). It was, said Governor Herbert Maw, 'the greatest thing that ever happened to Utah', which certainly puts Brigham Young in his place.

Salt Lake City was ablaze with the particular excitement that only Welles could engender. 'His sense of theatre,' Jeanette Nolan told the distinguished Welles scholar, François Thomas, 'exceeded our wildest dreams. And the first night in Salt Lake City was a magical event from the first minute.' At the beginning of the show the auditorium was plunged into darkness. Even the EXIT signs were extinguished 'against the regulations, but there were plenty of things against the regulations'. Welles had covered the doors completely so that no one knew how to get out, which reinforced the feeling of mystery. Then, from the very back of the theatre, almost inaudibly at first, the sound of bagpipes was heard. There were six of them, hired locally. 'They came down the steps, then out of the theatre, reaching the road still playing, and it was the only thing the audience heard until they stopped,' Miss Nolan continued. 'A mood of menace was established, adding to the thrill. And just as they finished playing, when they came down to the battlements again, there was a huge explosion in the orchestra pit, and a great green phosphorescent flame leaped out of it, out of which ran the witches. The audience roared. It was a truly terrifying entrance.' Above the witches were masks, designed and indeed painted by Welles, atop fifteen-foot-high poles, painted black. Later in the play, when the witches came down to the heath again, 'the auditorium was plunged into blackest darkness again and the masks suddenly lit up above the spectators' heads. People went mad and screamed.'

Gladys Goodall, the critic of the local rag, reported that 'last night's show was about as much as the normal emotions can take'. *Variety*, present at the 'preem' (*Variety*-speak for first night) of what it called 'Shakespearian stand-by *Macbeth*', described it as 'Welles from curtain to curtain – and good Welles. It's a Welles production, a Welles adaptation, a Welles directing job – and a Welles interpretation of the title role. It's pretty hard to find anything wrong with any of them.' The paper added: 'the audience . . . notorious for its ability to sit on its hands . . . did everything but cheer at the final curtain, and gave the cast six curtain calls, almost unheard of here'. They had been held rapt for the just over ninety minutes to which Welles had cut the play, twenty minutes longer than the gramophone version, but nearly an hour shorter than most productions. In addition to the cuts and arrangements, Welles had ensured maximum fluidity by minimising scenery and effecting transitions with light changes; the lighting plot was confined to side light and front spots, with no footlights or general wash. 'The Wellesian stage settings and lighting effects,' said the *New York Times*, 'were impressively eerie, though at times the darkness was slightly overdone.' Miss Goodall describes the setting: a dynamic line of stairs that swept from extreme right upstage, ending in a circular spread at left centre; the stage built out over the footlights; stairs going down into the orchestra pit. The six bagpipers were augmented by trumpets and drums playing uncredited fanfares and marches. This style of production – swift, spare, epic – became something of a norm in the nineteen-seventies and eighties; its contrast with contemporary productions must have been great. 'No lily-wristed, well-combed Shakespearean players paraded through endless scenes of sweet impressionism in this version,' wrote Goodall. Lady Macbeth's entrance in her first scene, she reports, descending the grey-black cloth-covered stairway, was 'hair-raising'.

This was Jeanette Nolan's theatrical debut: despite nearly twenty years in front of the microphone, she had never ventured onto a stage, or indeed in front of a camera. She seems to have taken to it like a duck to water. 'Jeanette Nolan "of the radio",' said the *New York Times*, was an 'excellent' Lady Macbeth. 'Her lines are delivered with intensity and intelligence,' said *Variety*, 'and her good looks enhance her interpretation.' The rest of the cast was admired: Donal O'Herlihy was 'swashbuckling', 'ex-screen moppet' Roddy McDowall 'sensitive', the Mercurians, Sanford and Barrier, 'strong'; 'the local fillins', however, were found 'not to rate more than adequate'. Welles himself was held by the *New York Times* to have given 'an unexpectedly conservative reading, indulging neither in melodrama or exaggerated moralising . . . his was an outstanding job of restrained and sustained acting' – phrases not often used to describe Welles's performances. By contrast *Variety* spoke, approvingly, of his 'flamboyant touch', and had special praise for his audibility – no mean feat in that vast auditorium. Gladys Goodall, equally approving, was a little more sensuously responsive: 'Mr Welles appeared not only to have been without sleep for months, he looked as though he needed a bath. He was unkempt, bedraggled in a gross manner, and thoroughly haunted.' The whole event was evidently a triumph of organisation, energy, goodwill and theatrical audacity, carried along on a thrilling wave of adrenalin. The fact that it was all preliminary to a 'Republic picturization', in *Variety*'s words, simply added to the excitement. 'While Welles's *Macbeth* production will never have the beauty of Mr Olivier's *Henry V*,' that sharp observer Gladys Goodall commented, 'it promises to be a parallel in effectiveness when it is made into a movie. The ghoulish effects,' she added with sweet innocence, 'will be intensified in motion pictures.' The name of Laurence Olivier was to loom ever larger in the months and years to come in consideration of Welles's film of *Macbeth*.

That was to come. The production in Salt Lake City was a triumph for ANTA, exactly what their brief indicated. This noble organisation, whose board boasted such sovereign names as Brooks Atkinson, Rosamond Gilder, Raymond Massey, Guthrie McClintic, Gilbert Miller, Oscar Serlin, Robert E. Sherwood, Lee Simonson and Margaret Webster, had been convened, by Act of Congress, in 1935, as a tax-exempt, self-supporting People's Theatre, yet another outcrop of the New Deal, with the explicit remit of spreading theatre of quality across the classes and through the land. Due to various political machinations, ANTA had been dormant until 1945, and the new president of the organisation, the Broadway producer Vinton Freedley, was vigorously seeking to reactivate it. None of the board members, it must be said, were particular enthusiasts of

Welles or his approach, but all of them were aware that he was as big a figure as the American theatre had ever thrown up. The Utah press acclaimed the Welles *Macbeth* in this light, roundly asserting that 'ANTA has completed a project that typifies the type of work it is set to do for other university and community theatres.' Helen Hayes, a prominent ANTA board member and current First Lady of the American theatre, sent Welles a first-night telegram underlining the production's significance for the organisation: OUR APPRECIATION FOR ACCEPTING THE CHALLENGE AND PAVING THE WAY WITH MACBETH FOR A NEW AND IMPORTANT PHASE OF THEATRE. She continued in terms that were exactly calculated to gratify Welles: IF WE ARE SUCCESSFUL IN ENLISTING MORE ADVENTURERS SUCH AS YOU FOR THIS SORT OF ACTIVITY ANTA'S PROGRAM OF ELEVATING THE THEATRE TO THE STATUS OF A NATIONAL FORCE IN THE LIVES OF ALL OUR PEOPLE WILL BE UNDER WAY BLESSINGS.

Welles saw the venture in much the same light; a programme note stated that Utah Centennial's invitation to stage *Macbeth* in Salt Lake City 'offered an opportunity to test the effectiveness of the professional and the highly skilled amateur theatre working as a unit'. The dividing line between professional and amateur was one that Welles was always willing to smudge, as seen in the casting of all his films after *Citizen Kane*; more significantly, it expressed his genuine – though somewhat fickle – commitment to direct contact, on an educational basis, between the theatre and the community. He was also delighted to find a new framework with which to assert the radical nature of his work; with the single unhappy exception of *Around the World*, he had only ever, after all, worked in what would later be called the alternative theatre. 'While tonight's production of *Macbeth* is not truly or entirely a Mercury production,' the programme note continued, Welles revelled in the strict limitation of time imposed on the production, and the necessity of conducting rehearsals both in Hollywood and Salt Lake City for an extremely short period and then fusing the two companies. 'So pleased are Mr Welles and Richard Wilson his co-producer and partner in the Mercury,' the note ends, 'that they hope to make this a yearly venture.' It might, indeed, have offered Welles a perfect opportunity for the continuation of his theatrical project; so confident was he that he even announced the next production, 'another great classic, seldom seen in the American theatre, *King Lear*'. The day after the first night of *Macbeth*, Bob Breen, ANTA's executive secretary, eager to cement the relationship, wired Welles to suggest that he might like to take an ANTA-promoted show to the second

Edinburgh International Festival the following year. Breen pursued Welles with ever-increasing desperation for four more years, but the dream of Orson Welles at the head of an American National Theatre – an idea extant at least since his work with the Federal Theatre Project in 1936 – was doomed to remain just that.

*

The production ran for four days, with two matinées for schools thrown in. At the end of the week the company returned to Hollywood, and Welles and Dick Wilson began the task of preparing for the film version. They had three weeks in which to make themselves ready for shooting. Whether the theatre run had bought them any real gains, apart from a certain familiarity for the leading actors with their roles, is to be doubted. Certainly the physical production was very different. The film's epic sets, some of them monumentally high, were already under construction at Republic during the short Utah run. Welles told Peter Bogdanovich that his own designs were scrapped at the last moment before shooting began; on screen they are credited to Republic's regular art director, Fred Ritter, but there is little doubt of Welles's influence on them. They share with the stage production the sweeping staircase that had been so effective in Salt Lake City; inevitably the interiors and the heath had no counterpart in the open-stage theatre design. A few surviving sketches in Welles's hand show elements that were to become very prominent in the design: the leafless tree on the crag where the Weird Sisters are to be found, and which so evocatively hangs over the exterior sequences; and a costume sketch of the strongly characteristic Viking/Tartar helmets ('soldiers behind Macbeth/Misty silhouettes in thick FOG,' the sketch says). Most of the stage costumes had been hired from the Hollywood costume house, Western Costumes, and they were planning to retain many of them for the film. Welles paid a great deal of attention to revisions to the Utah costumes, and his typically witty and lucid memorandum to Dick Wilson on the subject is usefully revealing of his general intentions, as well as being indicative of his close attention to detail and his practicality.

What is altogether unexpected is his concern for authenticity. Far from attempting to create, as he is generally held to have done, a kind of imaginary world, Welles attends scrupulously to specifics of period and location, relying heavily on a capitalised entity that he calls 'Research'. Writing of Duncan's outfit – King Duncan, as he refers to him – he says, 'Again I urge that we examine the old pictures of the fully-draped tartans that almost cover the body. It is a very noble effect.' Lamenting the fact that in Salt Lake City, Roddy McDowall's Malcolm looked like 'the third page boy from the left', Welles suggests that he should wear tartan of the House of Duncan. 'Research should check on this and we should be sure that the tartan we select will photograph near enough so as not to disturb the 422,000,000 Tartan-wearing Scotsmen.' McDowall's wig as it appeared in Salt Lake City is a disgrace, says Welles, 'one of the most comical ever presented by any wig-maker to any actor . . . the bushiest hair since the House of Solomon or the House of David played baseball in the '20s. Mr McDowall is to be given a Prince Valiant Wig (for Prince Valiant see the Hearst Sunday papers).' The costume for 'Lord Banquo' passes muster, though he too should be wearing tartan, but Macduff's – all of them – have to be redesigned. 'Mr O'Herlihy's figure is an extraordinary one in that the man has a "pot belly" – no muscles whatever. Therefore his legs must not under any account be bared. He must be heavily corseted, and his upper chest must be padded along with his shoulders.' Welles knew whereof he spoke, since this was very much the procedure applied to his own body in *Citizen Kane*. He continues with brutal frankness:

> He is to be made as attractive as the art of Hollywood can do it, and since he looks very well in a modern suit there is no reason why he should look so god-awful in costume. Nothing at the front must be opened. There is something about the way Mr O'Herlihy stands and comports himself that makes it essential that his entire front, from the chin down to the knees, present a flat aspect so that he can't bulge or sag. There is a way of coming apart which we've got to guard against. After one step he starts to crack at the seams.

This tone of affectionate exasperation, of despairing encouragement, is entirely characteristic of Welles's tone with his actors; there is more than a little of the actor-managerial style about it. Brainerd Duffield as First Murderer wore lifts in Utah: 'he is to be denied this privilege'. Welles becomes positively Wildean in his comments on Duffield's wig: 'his being the cheapest wig that was given out is by far the best since it was a true theatrical wig made of inferior hair, and inferior hair is the only hair which makes up into a good wig . . . neither his [nor Bill Alland's] wigs are to be tampered with or dressed by any man between now and the last day of the picture. They are to be kept in an old box and no attention is to be paid to them in the line of dressing. Otherwise they will be ruined.' The Friar's costume 'is not wild and woolly enough' – he should resemble 'an early Evangelical Christian preacher rather than like a member of the brotherhood of hopovers, which this resembles'. There are doubts about his wig, too. In Utah the Friar had worn a bright-red helmet 'suitable for a high school operetta version of "The Mikado"'. It may be, Welles says, that 'Research will show us some interesting early bishops', though on the whole he prefers the idea of a bare-footed itinerant preacher. He was not dissatisfied with Ross's costume. 'I do, however, have this notion. If it is true that there were reindeer in Scotland as there are now, then I would like to see Ross with antlers attached to a helmet. It might be very stylish. Ross is one of those who should have, in my view, braids. And if he is played by a very large man, very long heavy braids. One of our characters ought to have one of those long knee-reaching Brunnhilde jobs.' Welles has a conception of a division of the characters into what he calls 'Tartan or Scots' and 'Viking', though the guiding principle by which they would be one or the other is unclear. In Salt Lake City, he says, 'we were at our best when we were naked or fur-bearing, so I suggest Ross should be the big Viking-looking guy, with antler trusses and furs, with naked knees'. Neither this role nor those of Lennox, the Doctor, the Porter, Seyton or Fleance were cast at this point; no doubt the tightness of the budget made it hard to get actors of high quality.

In contrast to the Research-determined costumes for the men, Welles feels that Lady Macbeth's first dress should have 'a rather modern evening dress look to it'. This aspect of the costume was much commented on in the reviews: it is hard to grasp his rationale for it. Later in the same memorandum he tells Wilson that they should try to 'work against a sort of young lady dressed to give a recital of songs', an obviously commendable aim, but to do so by introducing a distinctly anachronistic note – while all those around are wearing costumes of almost slavish period accuracy – seems odd. It is clear, however, that this is exactly what Welles intended. He was unhappy about Nolan's Salt Lake City coiffure, and sought 'a new method of doing her hair'; there is no reference to Research in this matter, either. He was concerned that the Gentlewomen's dresses looked like Grand Opera, too dressy, 'a little more civilised than we want'. His comments on the Siwards, junior and senior, again betray his obsession with historical accuracy. 'They were fine up in Salt Lake City, except that the period was too late, I'm afraid

. . . I would be happy if Research would justify our keeping the costume the way it is.' He is very concerned about the correct distribution of the Celtic crosses; and positively pedantic about heraldry. 'It is my hope that Research will justify our taking the license and giving to Duncan the Celtic Cross. So it is first intro-duced with Duncan and Malcolm and later re-introduced with a vengeance at the end of the play.' He is equally precise about social detail. Seyton, though 'a virtual slave', must not be wildly dressed: 'we need to sense that he is a Castle servant, an indoor servant . . . a steward' and is 'in charge of others, poorer than himself'. He will be surrounded by 'a little pack of people who will be care-fully chosen. They will be messengers and hangers-on around Seyton, who will have a special personality and character.' This singling out of an otherwise unremarkable character to create a centre of interest around which to form a structure of subordinate relationships was always a hallmark of Welles's theatre productions, a technique he shared with the great Irish director Tyrone Guthrie, a director with whom he had much in common – an avoidance of psychology, a gift for engendering dynamic stage action, an eye for startling detail. All of these elements are, of course, strongly present in his films.

As is clear from the costume memorandum, a considerable number of parts had to be recast in a very short space of time; it is curious to find this important task being left so late. Lady Macduff was the largest of them, and for a while, too, Welles seriously considered replacing Jeanette Nolan, presumably for box-office reasons, since he otherwise expressed complete satisfaction with her performance. They offered the part to 'everyone', Welles said, among them Tallulah Bankhead and Vivien Leigh. (He only stopped short, he said, at Dame Judith Anderson, the Australian actress who had committed the unpardonable sin of playing the part not only opposite Olivier in London, but more pertinently in New York with Welles's *bête noire*, the mild-mannered Maurice Evans. Evans's performance in the title role, like all of his Shakespearean performances, had, to Welles's rage, been acclaimed as definitive and a histrionic triumph. Welles's barbaric conception of the part owes something to his violent antipathy towards the Evans school of acting.)

As for the rest of the parts, he followed his usual eclectic policy of casting. Some actors came from within his personal circle: the not insignificant role of Seyton he gave at a late stage to his chauffeur and general dogsbody, George 'Shorty' Chirello, a dwarf, whom he had already used on stage in *The Mercury Wonder Show*; as Macduff's son, again a substantial speaking role, he cast his daughter from his first marriage, Christopher, while – to keep it all nicely incestuous – the Third Witch was to be the screenwriter Charles Lederer, Welles's first wife's second husband (who, as previously noted, also happened to be Marion Davies's nephew and thus a regular guest at William Randolph Hearst's table). There were Mercury veterans: Gus Schilling (*Five Kings, Citizen Kane, The Lady from Shanghai*) was the Porter, his role sadly truncated; Lady Macbeth's doctor was Morgan Farley (from *Heartbreak House* and *Danton's Death* nearly ten years earlier). John McIntire withdrew from the role of the Friar, and the English leading man Alan Napier, distinguished of voice and demeanour – and with whom Welles had worked in the broadcast *Master of Ballantrae* – took over the part, now renamed the Holy Father. The pretty but inexperienced Peggy Webber was to play Lady Macduff and double as a witch, alongside a couple of Goldwyn Girls, Brainerd Duffield and, as we have seen, Charlie Lederer. The extras were mostly supplied by Republic, a refreshing change for them, no doubt, from playing cowboys; Welles took great care over selecting the most gnarled and wild-looking faces.

Apart from these preparations, the principal activity of the three-week gap between stage run and shooting was pre-recording the dialogue. Welles justified this obsession of his, already attempted on *The Magnificent Ambersons* and then to universal relief abandoned, in various ways at various times: it was designed, he sometimes said, to eliminate the tiresome recording boom, which can have a cramping effect on camera movement (especially since he proposed using three cameras simultaneously, the cameramen to be disguised with costumed dummies on their backs, thus swelling the ranks of extras); he would also be able to do long takes without worrying about sound. At other times he said that the technique liberated the actors: they could concentrate on acting without worrying about diction. On yet another occasion he suggested that it meant that he and the cameramen could shout out instructions over the action, since the soundtrack already existed. During the preparatory period, he coached the actors untiringly, making take after take. 'Orson explained to me,' Jeanette Nolan told François Thomas, 'that partly because I was a novice in film . . . it would help if we recorded the whole film beforehand. Like that, when we came to act in front of the camera, we wouldn't get muddled up in the dialogue. And he didn't want the public to be put off by the facial expressions we'd pull if we felt too much emotion.' It suited her very well:

not only because of my radio background but also because of Orson's magnificence as a director. He could focus on a single passage for five hours. The speech, 'Come, spirits, unsex me here', we recorded and recorded again and again, finding first one way then another, and then he, like the stimulating director he was, would have yet more ideas. All of us who had worked in radio took special pleasure in our different ways of going about things; with pre-recording you could do the same. We spent days and days having fun recording what we'd already done in the theatre, breaking down each line.

Fun it might have been, but perhaps not entirely helpful. 'True, the result was a little disconcerting: hearing the playback was a shock, your brain went back in time. You heard a line you'd recorded in a particular way, which seemed the opposite of what one hoped one had done. Having done it that way, one wanted all the rest to be the same. But it was Orson's prerogative as director, and he could have gone on playing with the sound forever.' It is an altogether bizarre procedure; whatever the potential gains, the losses – above all of any kind of spontaneity – would be huge. Apart from anything else, a recording made in a recording studio would have an entirely different feel from the piece performed on the set, with physical actions. Film acting is an unnatural experience under the most propitious of circumstances: the requirements of camera and light are such that actors are called upon to perform every manner of acrobatics (mental and physical) to accommodate them, but generally speaking there is at least a certain freedom of verbal expression – the rhythm, the tempo, the overall shape of a phrase can vary, as the actor in take after take is able to make deeper and better contact with his or her fellow-actors and with the script. If all that has been decided in advance, the performance is wholly pre-determined. It is ironic that Welles, who so loved actors and acting, should have devised such an inhibiting procedure. It meant, of course, that his authority over the performance was absolute: by rehearsing and re-rehearsing the actors' vocal performances until they were perfectly to his satisfaction, and then recording them, he could ensure complete conformity to his intentions. Not even Hitchcock at his most domineering ever imposed such rigid control over his actors.

Shooting began on 23 June. As he would do again on later films, Welles deliberately chose an apparently impossible schedule for his first day's filming to make a clear and readily understood statement of his mastery. At the beginning, the atmosphere on the set was not good, the crew surly and uncooperative. 'They were really hateful,' Nolan told François Thomas:

They wouldn't cooperate in any way, they resented him so much that they seemed to have only one purpose in life, to show him he had no right to be there. When we started, we got nothing but sarcasm, resistance and negativity. The first day of the shoot, we began at 9 in the morning. It was a long take, several minutes, the murder of Duncan. There were dozens of camera positions. Everyone insisted that Orson had no chance whatever of doing it. And at five past midnight, when he'd got exactly what he always knew he'd get, everyone was eating out of his hand – they gave him a round of applause. And the next day, they were very grateful to be under the same roof as him. For me, that was the high point of the film.

The cinematographer, one of Republic's house team, was John L. Russell, but he too, like Fred Ritter, was more of an executant than a collaborator, and needed to be galvanised. To accomplish everything that was needed in the three and a half weeks of the shoot, enormous energy was required, and Welles supplied it in overplus. Shooting took place on two sets; while one was being prepared, they would shoot on the other. With the cameramen using hand-held camera operators darting among the warriors in the battle sequences, wearing masks on the backs of their heads to blend with the throng, the soundtrack blaring away, and Welles and the crew roaring over it – even when Welles was in a scene, but not actually in shot – the atmosphere bordered on the hysterical. As they moved from one set to another, Welles cheerily shouted to Alan Napier, 'RUN, don't walk! Remember, this is a B-movie. Time is money!' Roddy McDowall, frankly unenthusiastic about Welles in general, found acting with him unnerving: 'One eye was on you, the other was sort of mad . . . as if he had two completely separate eyes.' Once Welles gave the young actor an observation about some unsatisfactory aspect of his performance: McDowall, partly by way of explanation, muttered: 'I'm so hot.' Welles, thinking he'd said: 'So what?' raged at him so long and so extravagantly that McDowall, young as he was, understood that Welles was operating at a level of adrenalin that rendered him almost out of control. During one take, a high, keening noise was heard – one of the cameramen, an epileptic, was in the throes of a seizure. Welles, still in the scene though not on camera, shouted above the unnerving wail: 'Let the fucker have his fit. Keep shooting.' To McDowall, 'there was a streak of contempt running right through that man . . . he was too talented to behave that way continually'. Nolan, on the contrary, adored every moment of it, with one exception: the famous soundtrack. 'God, I've never experienced fear like the first time I heard that huge sound, wiping everything else out, that thunderous, unrecognisable voice – mine, no doubt about it – filling the whole of the vast sound stage at Republic. And I was supposed to act with that voice booming in my ear! I could only see one way out, to run away into the night and forget it all. Later, they turned the volume down and we adjusted to the technique.' But even a willing accomplice like Nolan finally drew the line. 'Actually, we did the sleepwalking scene without playback. I asked Orson to let me do it exactly the way I had in the theatre and he did.'

The actors were willing if bewildered, but the somewhat jaded extras, by now no doubt longing for their chaps and Stetsons, needed serious galvanising. This was a different sort of challenge, to which Welles rose with accustomed resourcefulness. At the end of one long morning, requiring a sudden rush of energy towards the castle from Macduff's soldiers, he had trestle tables laden with food set out on the other side of the mound; instead of calling 'Action', he roared 'LUNCH!' The resulting sequence is visibly more animated than elsewhere. Welles was winning. The hard-boiled writer-producer Jerry Wald and his colleague John Windust of Warner Bros visited the shoot. Wald wrote to Welles: 'The important thing to me was the excitement that you generated on the set. Everybody seems to be pitching for the picture.' Wald had seen some of a rough assemblage of the material and proclaimed himself impressed. 'From what we saw on the screen, the extra work is certainly justified. Both Windust and I came away tremendously enthusiastic about what you are getting.'

Shooting ended a couple of days after Wald's visit; Herbert Yates celebrated the event with a ringing letter of acclaim. 'From the human side, once again you have made history in Hollywood. The job you have done has not only served as an inspiration to your own cast and crew, but to every other company on the Republic lot – in fact, in every studio in Hollywood.' He particularly praised Welles for his good husbandry:

> In this day of rising costs and sky-rocketing budgets, it has become mandatory to all of us involved in the business of

making motion pictures to do everything in our power to make it possible for us to stay in business. You have demonstrated beyond a doubt that superior product can still be made within reasonable cost and with assurance of a justifiable return. – Again I salute you and congratulate you on the greatest individual jobs of acting, directing, adapting and producing that to my knowledge Hollywood has ever seen.

CHAPTER TWENTY-ONE

The Welles of Onlyness

A T THIS point Welles disappeared to Europe for a twenty-five-year exile from which he would only return briefly and occasionally, leaving behind him a soundtrack and three weeks of loosely assembled footage. It was three years before the finished film would achieve anything like a general release, and when it did it was in such truncated and refashioned form that it was scarcely the film he had shot. Once again, his work had been confiscated from him. It is hard not to detect a pattern of sorts. Had he learned nothing from his absence from the post-production process on *The Magnificent Ambersons*? He knew from bitter experience that long-distance, remote-control editing was all but impossible, to say nothing of absence from the increasingly important preview period at which studio executives were prone to panic. With *The Stranger* he had ceded final cut in his contract; *The Lady from Shanghai* was always in Harry Cohn's ruthless hands. But with *Macbeth* he was dealing with very different people: Yates was no monster in the Cohn/Spiegel mode, and Republic was not a palace of the Borgias, like RKO and Columbia, rife with schemers and counter-schemers. At Republic Welles was admired, even revered, as Herbert Yates's letter to him makes clear. He would certainly have been allowed and encouraged to make the cut he wanted. And yet he went. The student of Welles's life feels like the audience at a melodrama: 'Don't go!' one wants to cry, 'Finish the film!' But off our hero canters, oblivious to the destruction of all his dreams.

The immediate motive for Welles to leave America was a financial one. The exotic actor-writer-director Gregory Ratoff had invited him to play the leading role of the eighteenth-century heretic, magician, conjuror and Freemason, Count Cagliostro, in a screen-play derived from Dumas's *Diary of a Doctor*. Shooting was to take place in Italy; Ratoff, the movie's executive producer Edward Small and Welles's agent all besought him to accept the role, but Welles made himself hard to get, though it was obviously a part (and an author) after his own heart. (One of the many projects he had canvassed as a possible follow-up to *Citizen Kane* had been the life of Dumas.) DEAR ORSON, Ratoff wired him only weeks before shooting was due to begin, YES OR NO PLEASE CALL ME. Welles replied: IF I MUST GIVE YOU A DEFINITE ANSWER TODAY, THEN THAT ANSWER IS NO. At this point the agent weighed in. BELIEVE ME AS YOUR FRIEND I BEG YOU NOT TO TURN THIS DEAL DOWN.

Welles was now in some demand as an actor; a little earlier, Michael Curtiz, director of *Casablanca*, and still riding the crest of the wave created by his recent hit *Mildred Pierce*, had written to ask Welles in the most flattering terms to appear in *The Unsuspected*: 'You will readily see that the character of Grandy was written with you specifically in mind. The man is an unusual, charming, suave, hypnotic individual with a touch of the genius about him, and all of us feel that no one could bring him to the screen with the same finesse and understanding which you could give to the characterisation.' Welles was in the midst of shooting *The Lady from Shanghai* at the time of the offer, so he could not have played the part if he had wanted to (eventually it went to Claude Rains, which suggests that the role must have been rather flexible), but it is indicative of his new reputation as an actor – or at any rate as a commanding presence on screen – that his agent seriously advised him to give up directing movies and stick to appearing in them. There was also persistent demand for his services in the theatre: Gertrude Lawrence asked for him to star opposite her in an adaptation of Thomas Wolfe's posthumously published novel *The Web and the Rock*; Welles didn't do it, nor was it ever apparently done, but the story would not have been without resonance for him, concerning as it does a love affair of Wolfe's autobiographical alter ego, George Webber, so traumatic that he abandons America to seek in an older culture the stability he could not find in his native land (though it is to be doubted whether stability was ever part of Welles's quest).

ANTA was desperate for his services and pursued him unrelentingly, though by far the most intriguing offer came, perhaps significantly, from Europe – from Britain, to be precise. John Perry of the West End management H. M. Tennent wired Welles to ask whether he'd be interested in playing the part of Titus Andronicus under the direction of the twenty-two-year-old Peter Brook at the Shakespeare Memorial Theatre at Stratford-upon-Avon, in settings by Jacob Epstein. It would then transfer to the Lyric Theatre in Hammersmith. This preceded by some seven years Brook's famous and sensational production (not designed by Epstein, and starring Laurence Olivier), which ushered in Olivier's greatest period of classical performances, in a role hitherto thought unplayable, and indeed hardly worth playing. SORRY, Welles replied, COMMITMENTS MAKE IT IMPOSSIBLE CONSIDER YOUR INTERESTING OFFER. BEST WISHES. Another spurned call from destiny; or maybe not. Perhaps it just seemed like an interesting but irrelevant possibility.

Much more in the forefront of Welles's mind was a theatre production that he planned to stage, an 'oratorio' version, as he called it, of *Moby-Dick*, the text to be written by Brainerd Duffield. Duffield had written the 1946 radio version of *Moby-Dick*, itself a spin-off, as we have seen, of yet another project originally conceived for Charles Laughton. (Welles, incidentally, had sent a very comradely, if perhaps ever so slightly ambiguous, telegram to Brecht, Laughton and John Houseman on the first night of *Galileo*: I HOPE GALILEO IS EVERY BIT THE SUCCESS YOU WANT IT TO BE). The 'oratorio' version of *Moby-Dick* had been commissioned by the San Francisco Theatre Association, which was waiting impatiently for it, as was C. B. Cochran in London (ARRIVING SEPTEMBER 15TH, wired Welles to Alexander Korda, FEAR CAN'T GIVE MOBY-DICK SUFFICIENT PRE-CHRISTMAS PREPARATION THEREFORE ADVISING COCHRAN SEEK THEATRE FOR SPRING); so too, according to Welles's French supporter Maurice Bessy, was the Comédie-Française. 'Please answer, urgently, when you will produce your oratorio in London,' wrote Bessy, 'and when, eventually, the show can start in Paris.' Welles replied that he'd do it in London in April 1948, in Paris the following month.

Thus, cheerily, he disposed of his time, little thinking of the languishing reels of *Macbeth* (or, indeed, whether or not he had a script for *Moby-Dick*). It obviously made sense for Welles to be in Europe, since he was committed to making a film with Korda, though exactly which one was still unclear. They had worked intensively on *Salomé*; the actor-writer Fletcher Markle had been with Welles in Acapulco working on it while he filmed *The Lady from Shanghai*. They had planned to be in production with the film, possibly even in America, in the summer of 1947. IT IS ALMOST CERTAIN I WILL HAVE FOR SALOME THE PERSON I TOLD YOU ABOUT ON TELEPHONE, Korda wired Welles in January of that year. SHE IS AVAILABLE ONLY BETWEEN FIFTEENTH OF APRIL AND END OF JUNE THEREFORE IT IS IMPERATIVE YOU SHOULD NOT TAKE ON ANOTHER JOB HERE. Two months later he was complaining: YOU TOLD ME YOU COULD START IN AMERICA EARLY. Clearly, though, Korda had not raised the finance required. WHO WOULD YOU DO IT WITH QUERY WHAT SORT OF ASSOCIATION COULD WE HAVE WITH AMERICAN

PRODUCTION COMPANY FROM THIS SIDE. Meanwhile Korda pressed hard for the Scottish actress Eileen Herlie (the 'person' referred to in his telegram) to play the title role, which Welles had earmarked for his current girlfriend, the French nightclub star Barbara Laage, twenty-one years old and, on the face of things, a much more likely candidate to play Wilde's barely pubescent anti-heroine; Miss Herlie had just filmed the role of Gertrude for Laurence Olivier, which would certainly have constituted a most unusual double. Their divergent views on this issue proved to be an insuperable obstacle, and so when, early in 1947, José Ferrer postponed the film he was planning to make of Rostand's great play *Cyrano de Bergerac*, Welles and Korda, who had toyed with the idea a year earlier, eagerly turned their attention back to it.

The prospect of Welles as the proboscially-challenged Gascon is a fascinating one, the apotheosis of all those nasal appendages of which he was so fond; but Cyrano is at core a swordsman, and it is a little difficult to imagine Welles finding the dexterity to time his hexameters to his duelling strokes, as Cyrano must. Korda had already spent a frustrating year, a full decade earlier, trying to make a film from the play. In that case the leading part was to be played by Charles Laughton – also not, perhaps, nature's idea of a nimble swordsman, though no doubt Laughton's unhappy relationship with his own appearance would have led to remarkable insights. It is particularly hard to imagine Welles in the capacity of a vulnerable lover. Interestingly, he told Peter Bogdanovich that he had intended to change the plot so that Cyrano – instead of nobly aiding Roxane's handsome but tongue-tied young suitor Christian, by lending his own eloquence to the young man – intended to betray him, revealing that the eloquent voice to which she had surrendered her heart had been his (Cyrano's), and not Christian's at all, but that he was prevented from doing so because Christian dies in battle, and honour obliged him to do the noble thing. Welles said that he believed Cyrano should be a short man, so they were going to make all the furniture larger. He said he would have made his nose get smaller and smaller as the film went on, till at the end you hardly noticed it. He said an awful lot of wonderful and witty things about it, but this project, too, foundered before long, partly because Welles had agreed to do *Cagliostro* (or *Black Magic* as it was to become).

The money ($100,000) was certainly welcome. His financial affairs were as chaotic as ever, scarcely aided by the loss of several boxes of records on a train journey between White Plains and Grand

Central; and a lawsuit doggedly pursued since 1941 by Franchot Tone, still determined to secure money promised to him by Welles at the time of the unfilmed Dolores del Rio project *Mexican Melodrama*, came to court again, producing this agreeable exchange:

Q: Mr Welles, have you ever had your deposition taken before?
A: No, not deposition. I have been sued. No such ceremony similar to this has occurred in my memory. That is all I can answer in truth.
Q: Was it in the year 1943?
A: I have answered that I don't have a good recollection in this matter.
Q: Was it in the spring, the summer, the fall or the winter?
A: We live in California. It is hard to determine the seasons.

Witty and nonchalant Welles might remain, but his sources of income were drying up; radio in particular was now a no-go area for him. There were various offers, all of them with intolerable limitations attached; and from time to time someone would come up with some trivial novelty formula that seemed to suit him, such as Frederick Ziv's notion of a programme featuring a 'climax scene' three minutes into the show, the kind of *wonder idea* that advertising agencies were always trying to urge on him. Curiously, even his radio prospects were better abroad: the young English producer Harry Alan Towers, hearing that Welles was planning to come to Europe, offered him $1,500 a week to do a radio transcription programme. But in his own country he was essentially *persona non grata*.

Before shooting on *Macbeth* began, in the middle of June 1947, Welles (unable to attend in person) had contributed a recorded speech to be played at a *Voice of Freedom* lecture: there had been a phenomenal rush on tickets, 'largely because your name topped our list of speakers, even though we most honestly noted that it was Orson Welles in transcription'. It is a remarkable theatrical image, a paradigm of the medium itself: a recording about the threat to radio played to an audience listening to him, not in the flesh, but exactly as they would listen to the radio. It is also a historical moment, a last testament to the importance and seriousness of radio on the very brink of the television age. It must have made then – and makes today – remarkable listening. The speech is obviously improvised, freely associating and more than a little overwrought, signalling that what Welles has lost is far more than a secondary career. Beyond that, it tells us a great deal about Welles's state of mind in the months before he left America. 'The people is heroic and suicidal,' he says. 'The people is everybody. This grand, mind-staggering "we" – yes! It is all of ūs – all and every one of us.' A highly charged emotional vibrato informs his voice. 'A government dedicated to the sanctity of the unpopular, a reputation thoughtfully attuned to the unimportant vote. Which guards as national treasures the minorities.' He senses that everything in which he and his fellow-radicals believed – the old Popular Front, Roosevelt – is falling apart while they look on powerlessly:

> We the people, where are we headed now? Backwards. We have become the pilots of suicide. Fearful, perversely fearful of our scheduled but rejected greatness: when the ideal dies so dies the civilisation which was supported by it. It may be that this ideal of ours is only hibernating. But there are no signs of a spring. The Roosevelt Democratic Party was not a political party – it was a way of life for most of us who work for a living – the good cheer for most Americans born into darkness . . . that way has become a conspiracy: we stand accused of every black brand of disloyalty. We are no longer spokesmen because we cannot speak. Not one of us is small or casual enough to escape attention.

It is strange, almost moving, to hear Welles speak of himself as small. 'Ours was an argument which carried its own eloquence. They kicked us off the air, the old, old interests of aggregated wealth. It is radio and this strange new medium of radio silence that is the subject. The Truman doctrine was not handed down from some tablets of the law. FDR won his campaigns – all of them – on the air. Freedom of assembly – airtime was our meeting hall and we are now denied its use – a killing censorship or else collaborate or else it was all very pleasant and urbane.' He becomes less controlled; the suspicion grows that he may be in his cups, as he tells his audience:

> Free speech has been politely and unobtrusively murdered – we had nothing to lose but our microphones. Your obedient servant as a result of his efforts as a radio commentator has been successfully muffled now even in his old profession of radio actor. Not that he hasn't had some offers. The radio you know is always available if you'll promise never to use the radio to say anything. A big, big manufacturer of breakfast food, for instance,

sent out a feeler lately. Five broadcasts a week at big, big money might be mine if I would undertake to deal exclusively with (what I must take to be unconscious irony) the 'human interest side' of the news. There was an even longer string than that attached to it. The proposed contract covered not only air-time, but all my waking time. Every public utterance was to be checked for content with a special board of advertising agency ideologists. In a word, they were putting up a heap of dough to buy outright a man's long-term opinion . . . it's more than possible that radio is happier without me, but I *can* speak for my fellow spokesmen and I do. They were most necessary debaters. The debate was most necessary. Now the debate is closed. It must be opened. And now thank you and until the next time – until our American radio is free again . . .

He ends, particularly poignantly, with his customary valediction: 'I remain as always – obediently yours.'

Political despair is a powerful emotion. Perhaps most bitter to endure is the sense that the party that one would naturally support is betraying its own ideals. It is a kind of stalemate: there is nowhere to go. Truman, with his shady antecedents deep in the bowels of the southern Democratic machine, seemed to be betraying every aspect of his legacy from Roosevelt, alienating many of his own supporters to such a degree that an overwhelmingly Republican Congress had just been voted in. Welles's favoured candidate, Henry Wallace, Vice-President before Truman outmanoeuvred him for the job, was regrouping; his cause was as yet a somewhat unpopular one, though he spoke with peerless eloquence for the radical Left, even talking of founding a new party 'to let the people of the world know that those who believe in peace and understanding still have some means of expression. It would provide the evidence that the United States had not gone completely imperialistic and psychopathic.' But Welles was not at his side. It fell to Katharine Hepburn to speak on Wallace's behalf, seizing the opportunity to denounce the House Un-American Activities Committee, presently investigating the communist influence in Hollywood; in the words of Gordon Kahn, she 'literally seared the ears off the [right-wing] Motion Pictures Alliance for the Preservation of American Ideals'. The temperature of the Cold War was plummeting, exactly as predicted in Welles's *Almanac* and in the pages of *Free World*, the threat of nuclear war an ever-growing possibility, but Welles was silent. His response to the idea of involvement in political activity, once unquestioned, seemed to falter. He told the Citizens Committee on Displaced Persons (whose members included Eleanor Roosevelt): TERRIBLY SORRY BUT MY MONEY IS ALL SPENT IS THERE ANY OTHER WAY I CAN HELP BEST WISHES. And when he was asked to speak against a proposed broadcasting bill in terms he would have been unable to resist not so very long ago – THE MIGHTY 'WE' LIKE YOU WOULD FOCUS ATTENTION OF NATION ON EVILS OF BILL REACTIONARIES TRYING TO RUSH THROUGH QUIETLY SINGULAR CONTRIBUTION TOWARD RETAINING AT LEAST SEMBLANCE OF FREEDOM OF AIR BILL WOULD COMPLETELY WIPE OUT – he replied that he was in the midst of filming *Macbeth* and could not write anything new. For most people, this would have been a perfectly straightforward response, but it was quite out of character for the Welles of the early nineteen-forties. Something had died in him. That thing was hope.

As far as film was concerned, his confidence that he could persuade anyone to let him make the films he wanted to make – the films that were needed for the coming dark hours – had disappeared. He wrote to Louis Dolivet at the end of 1946 to inform him that 'after weeks of haggling begging bargaining and generally busting my neck', he was unable to get their 'atomic bomb picture' off the ground. 'I must report that this industry is even worse than I thought it was.' Perhaps Europe – the Europe of Ophüls, de Sica, Renoir – would have a more sophisticated response (both political and literary) to his cinematic vision; it would also be considerably cheaper to film there. In America, even the films he had managed to get made were released without fanfare, or sometimes not released at all. Harry Cohn had inexplicably held up distribution of even the mutilated and musically bastardised version of *The Lady from Shanghai* for at least six months; it would be another six months before it was seen. Almost equally significant for Welles was the industrial unrest in Hollywood, from which he had suffered personally during the shooting of the Crazy House sequence: he, one of Labor's most outspoken supporters, had been picketed, hectored, denounced by union members. This was a strictly personal matter: Welles had taken it upon himself to do the job of qualified men. Like many of us, he was something of a political nimby, an enthusiastic proponent of the right to strike if it was in factories in Delaware or railroads in the south-west; not so welcome if it interfered with one's own work.

More threateningly, he had also suffered sharply from the growing power of the right wing within the film craft unions: in September of 1946, before shooting on *The Lady from Shanghai* had begun, the *Hollywood Reporter* approvingly noted – under the headline HOLLYWOOD STARS ARE BLASTED AS 'REDS' BY AFL OFFICIAL – that Matthew Woll, a vice-president of the American Federation of Labor, the dominant force in American unionism, had threatened the motion-picture industry in his union's paper, *American Photo Engraver*, with a 'league for political decency' and a nationwide picketing of movie-houses 'unless the movie industry takes steps at once against many high-salaried stars and script-writers who are part of a Communist fifth column in America. Hollywood today,' wrote Woll, 'is the third largest Communist centre in the United States.' As an egregious example, he singled out Welles alongside Edward G. Robinson, Myrna Loy, Burgess Meredith, James Cagney and Lionel Stander, among several others. In a comprehensive and not unsophisticated denunciation of the creative community, he continued:

Ashamed of the meaningless roles in which they are cast, oppressed by a sense of guilt because of their swollen incomes, smarting under the taunts of superior but non-Hollywood intellectuals, these world-savers in greasepaint find refuge in the Communist Party or its peripheral organisations. Somehow, playing at revolution seems to justify the possession of a swimming-pool and improves the taste of Astrakhan caviar and the feel of Russian sables. Ill-equipped either by experience or learning, these light-minded mimes imagine they are doing something for the oppressed of the world. Actually they are permitting themselves to be used as window-dressers for the most tyrannical political system in the world today, a system which crushed all human liberty and all human dignity.

The mixture of panic and contempt perfectly expresses the temper of the times, to which is added a naked loathing of the acting profession. 'The sharpening conflict between loyal American patriots and the subversive members of Stalin's fifth column in this country makes a show-down imperative. This conflict is well under way in the American Labor movement.' Woll's attack is a vintage and chilling example of early Cold War rhetoric, confirming everything Welles had ever said about the right-wing influences in Hollywood. Woll's clinching argument was exactly the point, from a diametrically opposed position, that Welles and his fellow Popular

Front affiliates had been making for years: 'The movies are not only a means of entertainment, they are also an important instrument by means of which our youngsters are unconsciously influenced in their social and political thinking. If stars like Orson Welles,' Woll ended, menacingly, 'continue to flout American patriotism, then loyal Americans will stage a protest which these sponsors of totalitarianism will not soon forget.'

Three of the light-minded mimes in question responded to the article. Myrna Loy – just months earlier acclaimed for her superb performance in *The Best Years of Our Lives*, a tireless worker during the war for the Red Cross, voted 'Queen of the Movies' a decade before and undentably popular ever since – denied everything. Edward G. Robinson responded with a magnificent philippic starting, 'I shall continue in the future as I have in the past to contribute as much of my time and energy as possible to the American democratic way of life' and ending, 'if you think I am guilty of treason, or engaging in subversive activities, then it is your duty, as an American, to report the matter to the authorities to take action against me. In other words, PUT UP OR SHUT UP.' Welles denied nothing, and averred nothing, maintaining a position of legal formality. 'I definitely intend to take some action as a result of the libellous statements made concerning me. I am today consulting with my attorneys to decide exactly what form this action will take. I intend to protect my legal rights and protect my name against scurrilous attack by whatever legal means my attorneys advise, probably by lawsuit.' A month later, the *Hollywood Reporter* withdrew its endorsement of Woll's statement; the following week it carried a front-page apology: after investigations by its own reporters, it declared that 'a grave injustice has been done to Mr Welles', Welles was again silent.

By curious chance, the same edition of the paper in which Woll's denunciation had first appeared carried a report in which Alexander Korda announced that Welles would start shooting *Salomé* in England in January of 1947; he already appeared to be distancing himself from Hollywood. The whole period in Hollywood was one of savage industrial conflict – union against studio, and union against union. The crafts unions were at war with each other, the right-wing IASTE (International Alliance of Theatrical Stage Employees and Moving Picture Operators) being violently opposed to the ultra-radical CSU (Conference of Studio Unions), which was behind the jurisdictional strike by 400 AFL members that was bringing Hollywood close to a standstill – the same strike that Dick

Wilson identified as holding up shooting on *The Lady from Shanghai*. 'Shall the studios remain open or shall they be forced to close their doors?' asked the *Hollywood Reporter*. In October 1946, Roach, Goldwyn and Republic summarily dismissed all their CSU members. There was intimidation and hysteria; in November of the same year, IATSE took out a box-ad in the paper, offering a reward of $5,000 for information leading to the conviction and arrest of the parties responsible for the bombing of the home of one of its members. The SAG (Screen Actors' Guild) was uncertain as to whether its members should cross the picket lines; eventually – urged on by keynote speaker Ronald Reagan – it was decided that they should. Under the influence of the dapper reactionary Adolphe Menjou, SAG was moving rapidly rightwards; it took out a large advertisement claiming that a small percentage of the CSU did not want the strike settled and were simply trying to destroy the system. Things were moving away from the realm of the idealistic politics that Welles had so eagerly embraced.

He was one of 339 motion-picture celebrities who had protested against the investigation of the motion-picture industry by the House Un-American Activities Committee, but he made no individual statement. Henry Wallace was again fiercely eloquent in denunciation, attacking 'the group of bigots first known as the Dies Committee, then the Rankin Committee, now the Thomas Committee – three names for fascists the world over to roll on their tongues with pride'. But Welles, who had spoken with such courage on the most incendiary of topics, said nothing. And yet he was in the forefront of the attacks. Melvyn Douglas sent him a clipping from the *Denver Post* of 10 August 1947 describing how the vaudevillian, revue artist and character actor Frank Fay had launched an attack on communists in Hollywood: 'Orson Welles – red as a firecracker/Charles Chaplin – oh boy, probably one of the reddest Reds I ever saw/Melvyn Douglas – his real name is Hesselberg. He holds meetings in his house.' And he ended with a call to arms: 'Don't let the reds get a hold anywhere – not even a little hold.'

Welles said nothing, nor is there any record of any response of his to the telegram sent to him (and many others) by John Huston, William Wyler and Billy Wilder: THIS INDUSTRY IS NOW DIVIDING AGAINST ITSELF UNITY MUST BE RECAPTURED OR ALL OF US WILL SUFFER FOR YEARS TO COME YOUR AID IS REQUIRED IN THIS CRITICAL MOMENT . . . THIS IS MORE IMPORTANT THAN ANY PICTURE YOU EVER MADE. Perhaps he was only interested if he initiated the activity; perhaps his lawyers had advised him to keep quiet, though, as we have seen, he was not particularly vulnerable. The FBI, for all its vigilance, had never managed to establish him as a member of the Communist Party (and even had they been able to do so, of course, such membership was not a crime). But in the words of Eric Barnouw, historian of American radio, 'the year 1947 was dominated by monomania. The concern of the nation was a search for traitors, who might be anyone, including your neighbour – especially your neighbour.' John Cromwell, the director, described it as being like a small Terror, 'with a small-town Robespierre and a committee doling out the future of a great many people'. In September of that year, the screenwriters and directors who came to be known as the Hollywood Ten were subpoenaed; a month later they were brought before the committee, and a month after that, having refused to answer the sixty-four-dollar question (as Parnell Thomas called it) as to whether they were then, or ever had been, members of the Communist Party, they were in prison, for contempt of Congress. And still Welles was silent. The point is not to lay blame: Welles was perfectly within his rights to keep his own counsel. It is simply that it was so unlike him. It would appear that he had given up on America.

His mood, in general, was not good, nor indeed was his health; he had been plagued by an ear infection throughout the early autumn, not throwing it off until October. Writing to Arthur Margetson, he observed that 'even my few remaining friends like you have joined the majority opinion on the Welles question. If you plan therefore to spit upon me in the streets be advised there is a considerable waiting list . . . my dearest love goes with this in case you care about that.' FROM THE WAY YOU SOUND, Bruce Elliott, author of *Magic as a Hobby*, wired him in response to a letter signed 'your ever-erring chum', apologising for non-delivery of a promised preface, YOU SHOULD CHANGE YOUR NAME TO WELLESCHMERZ THESE DAYS. THE ATOM BOMB GOT YOU? OR IS IT JUST YOUR MANIC DEPRESSIVE CYCLE?

CHAPTER TWENTY-TWO

The Charm's
Wound Up

BEFORE HE left for Europe, Welles had done a certain very limited amount of work on *Macbeth*. In fact, much of it was being done by Dick Wilson, with occasional visits from Welles to the editing suite. After one of these visits, he wrote to Wilson, apropos a particular sequence, an interesting note: 'All of this stuff of lighting candles should occur either before Macbeth's soliloquy or Lady M's lines, or after my soliloquy and before Lady M starts to talk to me or both. Don't let the fact that I have a candle in my hand after I have risen and don't before I rise bother you one bit because by cutting away from the full shot I think I can get away with it.' This is illuminating concerning Welles's indifference to rules of continuity, and also betrays a certain general pragmatism. Unlike Hitchcock, he by no means had the precise sequence of the whole film in his mind as he shot; he was not the slave of the storyboard in the least. When he saw what he had filmed, he may have been surprised by the result. After the euphoria of shooting and the immediate excitement of the daily review of what has been shot (they don't call them rushes for nothing), one is faced with the reality of the material one actually has, viewed in sequence. If only this shot had been different, if only that performance had been faster/slower/louder/quieter/better! Some sort of compromise is then arrived at, given the available material; sometimes one has a chance to reshoot certain sequences.

At about this time Welles had written in the usual affectionate terms ('My Beamish Beanie') to Bernard Herrmann, who was going to write the score, that he had hoped the rough-cut would be ready sooner, but alas it would not be. 'Good news is that picture looks wonderful,' he added. Passing through London a couple of months later, however, he told Alexander Korda: 'Some of the individual scenes are the best things I've done, but when they are stuck together, the picture may be a complete flop.' Any film-maker might have said the same about his work at the beginning of the post-production period. It is perfectly possible, though, that when Welles spoke to Korda he meant what he said: that he was genuinely disappointed with what he had, and that he had indeed lost conviction in the film. This would certainly explain his lack of drive in the matter of achieving a final cut, which had bewildered his colleagues at Republic, exhilarated as they were by what they had seen, both on the set and in rushes. The news that Welles was decamping to Rome and would continue to work on the film there was greeted at the studio with dumbfounded disbelief: their first, not unreasonable reaction was to want to charge him for the cost of transporting the rushes and an editor to Italy, a demand that Wilson was reluctantly obliged to accept.

Welles meanwhile was established on location, lording it over *Cagliostro*, a troubled production. The usually shrewd producer Edward Small was experiencing difficulties with a film that, thanks to a lethal combination of logistical and temperamental factors, had run into innumerable problems. The delightfully incomprehensible Gregory Ratoff, who was directing, was under such huge pressure that he was genuinely grateful for a strike in the middle of filming: it meant that he could at last catch up on his sleep. To some of his colleagues, he seemed close to a nervous breakdown. Welles was by far the most powerful personality on the set; his co-star Nancy Guild, already something of a film noir favourite, was at the beginning of a brief career whose subsequent highlight was *Abbott and Costello Meet the Invisible Man*; for the rest he was surrounded by Russian actors from Ratoff's stable, one of whom, Akim Tamiroff, thereafter became part of Welles's stable. Language problems were one of the many difficulties facing the film. Welles was not shy of offering helpful input. 'Being a director at heart,' reported the studio apparatchik, Warren Doane, to his superiors, 'he does bother Gregory by his suggestions. At the same time,' Doane continued, 'Gregory is the first to admit that many of his suggestions are good. They do result in delay, since Gregory likes to lay his work out and then follow through. All in all,' he concluded, 'the delays are not losses in all cases.' Understandably, though, Welles's 'input' – and he would not be the man to offer his suggestions modestly, in private, but in full view of the crew at top volume in that uniquely carrying voice – had not endeared him to his fellow-workers. 'He is adequately cooperative, and friendly enough – at least to our faces,' continued Doane. 'He is, as you know, most unpredictable and thoroughly disliked by all and sundry.' He had been ill: 'we are having some trouble with colds but no one has been really sick abed but Welles. We don't know how sick he actually was, but undoubtedly he was sick.'

Welles was clearly not wholly engaged by his work on *Cagliostro*, whether as actor or backseat driver. He had already been studying the *Macbeth* footage and sent his responses to Dick Wilson via a Dictaphone-like device called a SoundScriber (sales pitch: 'Winston Churchill used it'); both he and Dick were rather boyishly excited to be among the first to have one. 'There is too much footage of Banquo in the opening scene unrelieved by shots of me,' says Welles. 'I think the feeling of moving in will help it . . . and I also think I will look better moving down there without my gut sticking out. Go to closer shot. That doesn't mean going to closer shot we made. It wasn't very good, was it?' He offers detailed suggestions as to how Herrmann's music will function in specific scenes. The dubbing of certain performances displeases him. 'Doctor too theatrical, much too theatrical. Much too theatrical. I begged, begged you not to let him get that way and he is. Much too theatrical! It should be clinical. He is trying to get like the third witch, he's, you know, bitchy.' There was much more of the same.

Meanwhile, back at the ranch, Wilson was dealing with a very angry front office (as well as with Welles's domestic requirements, such as buying sweaters for Dr Bernstein). 'Several sections of Republic Pix expressed a certain unhappiness that there remains more to do on the picture. I might even say that questions were raised in the strongest language, and displeasure might be spoken of as the common denominator in the entire production organisation.' Wilson was doing some pick-up shots, and had been hoping to get the sound looping done before the return of Herbert J. Yates. He was trying to get it finished 'before I'm presented with some hideous fait accompli'. He was taking the brunt of Republic's anxiety. 'Yesterday I had a two-hour meeting (or inquiry) in Chairman Newman's office. I felt like the 19 hostile witnesses rolled into one.' The tone was ugly. Bob Newman said that if Louis Lindsay, the editor, didn't have it done in a couple of days, 'then Lindsay will be fired and a cutter will replace him who will!' Wilson reports an explosive conversation with an apoplectic Bernard Herrmann (the phrase is no doubt tautological) who would not consider doing the picture until it was completed. 'A series of irrational statements were made. Bernard, on this occasion, blew his top,' saying that he'd been lured to Hollywood under false pretences, and refusing to be involved unless Welles was there 'to back him up on every argument'. In this he showed a shrewd knowledge both of Welles and of the studio system. *Citizen Kane*, his first film as a composer, set a standard for his contribution to the process of film-making, which he refused to compromise. He had told Robert Newman that he simply would not be involved 'if Welles runs out on the picture, which,' Wilson reminded Welles, 'demands that you be there while he scores and dubs'. And that was impossible. Newman had no patience with Herrmann, saying that Ernst Toch should score it. (It is worth noting that Republic had a certain class: Toch was no hack like Roy Webb or Heinz Roemheld, but a hugely distinguished teacher and composer of excellent scores for *Catherine the Great* and *The Cat and the Canary*; they could have done worse.) The upshot was that Herrmann, who had come to Hollywood on the understanding that he would be shown a completed cut, and broke his holiday to do so, had taken the first flight back to New York. Even the ever-optimistic Wilson realised that Herrmann perhaps meant it this time and would not be returning, so they started to think of alternatives. The name of Marc Blitzstein was brought up and summarily dismissed, while Newman raged about the need to meet deadlines for trailers, main titles, and so forth. Wilson was in an impossible position; he had no answer to any of these perfectly sensible objections to Welles's behaviour. There had been some talk of Wilson going over to Italy, but he was of the firm opinion that 'somebody from our side should be here practically all the time until you return, if only to watch and to reason over unwise action'.

A couple of days later Herbert Yates, now back from his travels, stopped Wilson on the lot, and had a nice, moderate conversation with him. He was anxious about Bernard Herrmann, but seemed satisfied with the work in progress, although, says Wilson, 'the whole lot — executives and artisans — are buzzing and making with the jokes about any little thing that has to be done'. Yates's biggest problem, he told Wilson, was promoting the film. 'His most ominous sentence was in this section of the conversation, in which he said, "Anything that we might be doing to the picture now, really isn't going to make a big difference. It's either there or it isn't."' Yates added, mildly, that he thought Welles was making a big mistake by not completing it swiftly, and what a shame the whole thing was. Wilson's letters over the next month continue in the same vein, explaining the situation at Republic, charting the resentment and the rage of the studio, the despair and confusion of their collaborators, his own loyalty and attempted good cheer, and Welles's non-communication – 'for Christ's sake write!' Meanwhile, at the end of November, Louis Lindsay had flown out to Rome with the sound-effects and the footage, and Welles worked directly on the material. Slowly. He had started to think about *Cyrano* again, talking to Alexandre Trauner, Carné's great art director, about possible designs; he fitted in *Macbeth* between shooting *Cagliostro* and the infinitely more agreeable sessions with Trauner. He had discovered that the distinguished French composer Jacques Ibert was in Rome as director of the Académie de France, and accordingly – to the considerable pique of Republic – hired him to write the score for *Macbeth*. It was, he felt, a bit of luck that such a distinguished and experienced composer was there: Ibert had written a great deal of incidental music for the Paris stage (*Antony and Cleopatra* and *A Midsummer's Night's Dream* among them) and a number of film scores, including two particularly fine ones, for Pabst's *Don Quixote* starring Chaliapin and for Julien Duvivier's *Golgotha*, as well as a score for a radio production of *Dr Faustus*, which must have delighted Welles. They spent four very pleasant hours together, watching the film together, discussing it after every two reels, after which Welles disappeared and Ibert, under the guidelines they had established, worked alone.

Welles remained in Rome with Lou Lindsay after shooting on *Cagliostro* was over in the spring of 1948; as they worked on *Macbeth*, they discussed *Cyrano* (of which Korda had now finally washed his hands) and Welles's production of *Othello* for the Edinburgh Festival, which he planned to film. *Cagliostro*'s producer, Edward Small, was keen for him to do it in Hollywood, with the same speed with which he shot *Macbeth*, and in Technicolor. Small's principal anxiety was that Welles wanted to play Othello as a black man: Joseph Breen of the Hays Office had advised him that they would refuse to pass any such picture. How deeply that must have confirmed Welles's resolve to remain out of his native country. Wilson, meanwhile, was in financial trouble. He had not been paid himself, and it was increasingly difficult to fund the office. Yet his affection for Welles never falters. 'Dearest Chuck,' he calls him in Macbeth's own words, and signs off 'With much, much, much love'.

By early March, Lou Lindsay was back with the picture, more or less finished. Wilson, had been 'low and generally confused'; he was much cheered by what he saw. 'I love what you did. It has a simplicity and a beauty unexcelled in the motion picture cinema.' But it was still unfinished. Now not only Republic but Charles Feldman (Welles's chum and partner in Literary Classics) was beginning to

urge that the film be completed, with or without Welles. Soon afterwards, with various changes proposed by Welles, the film was run
for Feldman and Robert Newman. 'When I talked to Feldman,'
wrote Wilson, 'he said that he had always liked the picture, and that
he liked it even better on seeing it last night.' At this stage, there
was no score; it had not yet been recorded. Ibert refused to work
until he was paid. Republic, ever eager to get things moving,
proposed that work on the sound should be abandoned because
music would cover it – a shocking proposition on a Welles movie;
Dick Wilson successfully resisted it. In the fullness of time, serious
contractual quibbles having finally been resolved, Ibert duly wrote
the score and, because of the limitations of international travel in
1948 and Ibert's refusal to travel by air, it was recorded not in
Hollywood but in Rome, under the skilful baton of the Russian-
American conductor Efrem Kurtz. Having received a copy of the
recording, Welles advised on how best it should be used, asking for
some ancillary bagpipes, which Ibert had neglected to include in
his instrumentation. The composer was professional, intelligent and
imaginative, and his score is everything that any similarly endowed
musician might have hoped to produce in the time. But it bears no
comparison with the texturally detailed and profoundly subtle work
of Bernard Herrmann. It is, in fact, incidental music of very high
quality, playing while the film runs, but not an integral part of it.
How could it have been otherwise? Losing Herrmann was a disaster
for *Macbeth*, but no one seems to have felt it at the time. No
composer, at any point in Welles's career, ever worked with him
the way Herrmann did. And the films are accordingly diminished.

Dick Wilson held Republic's music department at bay while the
question of where and by whom the score would be recorded was
being thrashed out. It is impossible not to feel pity for the man as
he wrestles with problems not of his making, endlessly prodding
Welles (who was still swanning around in Rome) to provide photographic stills, this or that loop for the dialogue track, and a dozen
decisions about crucial matters; Italy's forthcoming elections were
rendering the country increasingly unstable. Not only was Wilson
attempting to get *Macbeth* into releasable form, he was trying to
keep Welles's American operation afloat, as well as set up *Othello*,
which was to play a two-week season in Edinburgh a mere three
months hence and then go straight into shooting – but when?
Where? How? The Salzburg Festival was eager to have *Othello*, too,
a testament to Welles's growing European reputation. 'Please send
some generalisations at least about the script version, cast, etc, etc

of *Othello*,' Wilson wrote. 'The most general and the roughest sort of lira budget would also be very helpful, and I'm sure you know how valuable it would be to have the script as soon as possible. I once sent you word of some of the equipment needed for the sound system (here is another copy). I'm still anxious to find out whether they can be procured in Italy. As you know, this can save a tremendous shipping expense and trouble. Love.' Throughout the exchange, he maintains his good humour and his affection for Welles. 'Dear Old Hank Cinq: it was quite a boost to hear your voice and to find that you really hadn't dissolved into air or got lost behind the "Iron Curtain" or any of the other imaginary alternatives.' But Welles simply would not make the decisions. 'For Christ's sake let me know!'

As must inevitably happen in a vacuum of leadership, Republic started to make decisions themselves. Wilson felt entirely unsupported. 'For your information, Charles K. Feldman is a shit! And not one bit of help in anything . . . Newman quotes Charles K. Feldman as the strongest proponent of finishing the picture immediately with or without you. I must say that Feldman to me on this latter point is still interested in your finishing it.' Uncertain of its own judgement, Republic had asked Welles's distinguished radio colleague, Norman Corwin, for his advice, which he gave with characteristic incisiveness: 'There's no reason why the witches who open the film should sound as if they come from *Li'l Abner*.' His suggestions were extensive, affecting not just the now universally acknowledged problem of the accents, but matters of tone and dynamics; he even suggested cutting Lady Macbeth's death-leap, one of Welles's most audacious interpolations. The extent to which others were dabbling in his work behind his back is extraordinary, but hardly surprising – except perhaps to Welles himself, whose innocence or ignorance of the world's way is sometimes baffling. It is almost incomprehensible that Welles would have let things come to this pass, had he cared in the least for the integrity of his film. Instead he moved on to his next European film, while Wilson was left to deal with everything, not least the break-up of Welles's personal entourage: Shorty Chirello was cutting up rough about certain sums owed to him, and was hanging on to the money raised from the sale of Welles's car.

Eventually a version of *Macbeth* was ready to be shown to a preview audience: Wilson reports great restlessness at various points. He suggests remedies, but doubts whether he has the shots to implement them. Perhaps revoicing would help? If only they had asked for music for the exile scene . . . sound might help. Or maybe not. There was more tinkering. Then, in a curious and still-murky episode, in September 1948 the film was entered for and then withdrawn from competition in the Venice Festival, because, it is said, Welles felt that Laurence Olivier's newly released film of *Hamlet* was bound to win. This was the first hint of the eventually all-engulfing shadow that Olivier's movie would cast over *Macbeth*. Though *hors concours*, *Macbeth* was widely reviewed. The London *Daily Telegraph*'s man Campbell Dixon, who had seen both films, was in Venice to report: '[Welles's] own opinion of his work is no secret. He considers it infinitely superior to Olivier's *Hamlet* which for some reason strikes him as "Wagnerian". An odd adjective, you might think for a production of so much taste and disciplined beauty but one not wholly inapplicable to Mr Welles's *Macbeth*.' Dixon's comments on the film adumbrate the derisive tone of virtually every review of the film in the English-speaking world thereafter. 'The problem of creating a Scottish castle in Hollywood was solved by making the Macbeths a tribe of troglodytes inhabiting caves . . . surely a queer background for characters pouring out the rich and subtle poetry of the English Renaissance. For past delights one can forgive Mr Welles a good deal, and if faults were only in the setting – but alas the whole conception of the play seems to me mistaken to a degree I should have supposed impossible to a man of so much talent.' Here, too, the criticisms of the Scottish accents appear for the first time. 'The three witches become Glasgow washerwomen clacking round the tub, Lady Macbeth is a wee body sair set in her opinions.' Dixon was generally contemptuous, too, of the use of the verse. 'Lady Macbeth says "Gentle! My lord", rather than "Gentle my lord". I suggest that if Shakespeare had meant "Wait a minute, honey", or "Hold your horses, handsome", he would have said so.' And this was to become a common theme in subsequent responses to the film.

The European press was naturally less interested in the matter of language and accent, and reacted on the whole warmly to it: '[It] grabs the audience by the throat,' reported *Il Tempo*, 'and does not let go of it until the very end.' The audience applauded four times during the showing, reported *Il Tempo*, declaring the film Welles's best since *Citizen Kane*. Jean Cocteau, who had seen and reported on Welles's 1936 *Voodoo Macbeth* with a sort of fascinated repulsion, immediately acclaimed this new version as a *film maudit*, a somewhat complex accolade, though he did not enter the movie for his festival of similarly cursed films held in Biarritz later that year. Cocteau later wrote his impressions of Welles's film. 'Coiffed with horns and crowns of cardboard, clad in animal skins like the first motorists, the heroes of the drama move in the corridors of a kind of dream underground, in devastated caves leaking water, in an abandoned coal-mine . . . at times we ask ourselves in what age this nightmare is taking place, and when we encounter Lady Macbeth for the first time before the camera moves back and places her, we almost see a lady in modern dress lying on a fur couch next to the telephone.' This engaging account suggests that the film is somehow Coctelian, which is misleading, to put it mildly. It is, if nothing else – for better or for worse – perfectly Wellesian, a notion that continental (especially French) cinéastes were beginning to embrace. Marcel Carné pronounced it superior to Olivier's film from a cinematographic point of view; Bresson loved its 'fake light and cardboard settings'.

These plaudits were of little use in selling the film to the American market. The home-grown preview reviews were generally tepid, and any tiny peep of praise contained in them seemed inaudibly faint beside the deafening fanfares that greeted Olivier's *Hamlet*. Republic, expecting to be showered with praise for their bold foray into Shakespearean drama, were suddenly anxious. They were up against an unstoppable and ever-expanding tidal wave of praise for *Hamlet*. 'It may come as something of a rude shock to the theatre's traditionalists to discover that the tragedies of Shakespeare can be eloquently presented on the screen,' wrote Bosley Crowther in the *New York Times*, 'but now the matter is settled; the filmed *Hamlet* of Laurence Olivier gives absolute proof that these classics are magnificently suited to the screen.' This was exactly what Welles believed, of course, but his understanding of the word 'film' was quite different from Olivier's. If *Hamlet* was what they wanted, then they were not going to like *Macbeth*. Crowther shrewdly notes that what Olivier does in his film is to bring the audience closer to the stage. 'A quietly-moving camera which wanders intently around the vast and gloomy palace of Elsinore . . . gives the exciting impression of a silent observer of great events, aware that big things are impending and anxious not to miss any of them.' By contrast, Welles's camera is always highly active, almost assaulting and battering the viewer. Crowther says the acting in Olivier's film is 'beautiful', the articulation 'perfect', the interpretations 'inspired', the cutting 'judicious', the music 'intriguing', the design 'rich'; the dark and haunted palace is 'the grim and majestic setting' for 'an uncommonly galvanic film'. The sort of aesthetic nobility implied in all these adjectives is the exact opposite of what Welles was striving for. If *Hamlet* was to be the yardstick – and it was, almost universally – then *Macbeth* could only fail.

By a process first analysed by Theodor Adorno, Laurence Olivier had been informally elected the representative of theatrical culture, just as Toscanini had been appointed the greatest conductor in the world, beside whom all others were somehow inauthentic, while Jascha Heifetz had become *the* violinist. Now Olivier *was* acting, anointed and sanctified. To dare to criticise him was to reveal one's ignorance. His recent knighthood had added a heraldic shine to his beatification, especially perhaps in America; even to those who would not naturally be drawn to his films, he was a byword for acting, the epitome of High Thespian Art. That this elevation bore little relation to the man or his approach to his work is neither here nor there; now there was a Gold Standard (somehow confirmed by the blond locks Olivier had acquired for Hamlet) by which all others must be judged. *Life* magazine, an important arbiter in these matters, was not slow to confirm his new status: a four-page spread sang the glories of the new film. But just as light is only light because of the existence of dark, so a Shakespearean failure was needed to endorse Olivier's reign as monarch of culture. Here to hand, so very conveniently, was Orson Welles's *Macbeth*.

According Welles's film a three-page spread, *Life* came not to praise it but to bury it. 'The scene opposite is not, as you might think, from a musical comedy skit set in an alcoholics' ward,' said the anonymous piece, with fine courage. 'It is Orson Welles's movie version of Act III, Sc i of Shakespeare's *Macbeth*. Mr Welles has had the idea that 11th century Scotsmen appearing in a 17th century play should express themselves in the accents of Sir Harry Lauder on the vaudeville stage of the 20th. Thus we have . . . Lady Macbeth sweeping down an endless stone staircase shrieking "Oot, damn'd spot, oot, I say."' The reporter condemns the reordering of the play – 'scenes have been ruthlessly juggled, characters interchange their lines freely' – and though he acknowledges that Olivier and his text editor, Alan Dent, did much the same, 'Olivier did [it] to make a consistent and harmonious movie . . . Welles on the other hand has gone back to the senseless violence of all the hams who have hacked and gesticulated their way through *Macbeth* for out-of-town audiences.' He or she seizes on Welles's use of the witches' line 'The charm's wound up' to end the film – the line with which he had brought the curtain down on the *Voodoo Macbeth* – berating him for failing to understand its meaning: 'despite what Mr Welles may think, not "over and done with" but "ready to work"'. But that is precisely what Welles intends: that we're in for more of the same trouble – spuriously, perhaps, in terms of the play, but accurately in terms of the line. Pitying Welles, 'who, a few sad years ago, was the Boy Wonder of Hollywood', the piece ends: 'confusion hath now made his masterpiece'. And *Life* was not alone. 'If Welles has failed utterly to live up to the standard set by Laurence Olivier's *Hamlet*, he has at least failed honestly,' said *Newsweek*. 'In both acting and directing, Welles's limitations are strongly, sometimes offensively, apparent.' 'There is no doubt,' said *Fortnight*, 'that Orson Welles is gifted with colossal ingenuity and resourcefulness. It would take colossal ingenuity to make so great a bore of Shakespeare as he has done in this outrageously poor production of *Macbeth*.'

The edition of *Life* magazine in which its hatchet job appears was on sale in Boston at the time of the film's premiere, which, much against Dick Wilson's advice, had been arranged by Republic in conjunction with ANTA. Emerson University sponsored it, and in order to obliterate largely inaccurate reports of a fiasco in Venice, it was billed as a 'world premiere', which meant that the review from *Il Tempo* and others equally glowing could not be quoted. The film's reputation as a stinker was growing; anyway, Boston's critics, as Wilson pointed out, 'had exhausted themselves with writing superlatives about *Hamlet*', which had been running there for ten sold-out weeks. The audience that *Macbeth* got was largely a young one, 'because they admire you for your courage and liberal attitudes'; the financially lucrative carriage trade was slow to build. Most woundingly, ANTA (whose idea it had been in the first place to translate a stage production of a classical play into a movie) had dissociated itself from the picture; board members who had seen it filed bleakly negative reports.

Under the pressure of all this negative reaction to a film over which he had, in Welles's absence, personally laboured for months and months, fighting his wayward boss's corner in a studio where he was a barely tolerated outsider, Wilson allowed himself a rare outburst against Welles, a real *cri de coeur*. 'Of course I think the whole thing cries out for a fight – a fight on the order of the one you waged for *Around the World*. I think it's tragic that you're not here personally to lead it because I'm absolutely and sincerely convinced that if you were around for the next three or four openings to lecture, meet the critics, women's clubs and all that, you could put this over the top and turn it into a controversy such as the industry has seldom seen.' As far as he knew, there was no reason why Welles couldn't be there; he wasn't filming at the time of writing. As far as Wilson knew, Welles was doing nothing at all. He cannot bring himself to criticise Welles's behaviour during post-production, but he does dare to raise the question of Welles's 'industry and general public relations', which, he says, 'are in a period and state of crisis'. He reveals that Newman of Republic has told him that he doesn't think Welles will get a penny of bank financing for any picture he ever tries to produce again; Edward Small (*Cagliostro*'s producer, and their potential partner on *Othello*) has been quite explicit about Welles's position in the industry, in Hollywood 'and all over the country with exhibitors'.

Pushing on fearlessly – 'I know that this usually bores or infuriates you' – Wilson brings up the question of 'the unhealthy press we have right now'. Leonard Lyons of the *Post* manages the occasional warm (albeit pointless) anecdote, but the rest of the columnists 'take nothing but digs at you'. He begs Welles 'to get again directly before the people and directly to the people'. He would have 'tremendous popular sympathy and understanding' if he went on the road on *Macbeth*'s behalf. 'The deterioration that has gone on since you left the air on the *Commentary* series can hardly be overestimated.' He implores Welles at least to pen a fighting piece for the *New York Times*, and to write round to his chums on the various newspapers. Hedda Hopper, surely, could be co-opted, 'if you would extend yourself personally to cope with the situation'. Welles behaves as if it is nothing to do with him. 'Please write me a letter so that I know what the hell is going on with you and I really want, need and hope to get the material I've asked for in this letter. I promise to put it to good use because I intend to follow this as closely as Republic allows me – anyway, you know I'll be in there punching. Much much love and affection.' The whole letter is a mark of the force of Welles's personality and the often exasperated loyalty that he inspired. But Dick Wilson had no power within Republic or within the industry in general. Welles himself, at the head of a massive charm offensive, might just have been able to swing things in his favour; in his absence, events would inevitably take their own course. Republic – above all Robert Newman, the chairman – had started to form an opinion that *Macbeth* needed radical reworking.

This is perhaps the moment to look at the film as it stood in 1948, the film acclaimed in Venice, the one derided in Boston. This film disappeared from view shortly afterwards, presumed lost or destroyed. Then, in 1985, the film as originally issued – which was anyway thirty-five minutes shorter than the first rough-cut – was discovered in nearly pristine form, and reissued; for the first time it was possible for a general audience to see the film in which, as Welles himself said at the Venice Festival, 'for the first time in my life I got what I aimed for'.

The opening credits proudly proclaim 'A Mercury Production' – not since *The Magnificent Ambersons* had a Welles film been able to claim as much – while Ibert's rackety, hectic overture, filled with fanfares, plays; it ends with a sly quotation from Herrmann's Xanadu theme from *Citizen Kane*. The first image of the film is swirling fog. It is striking that this is exactly how Olivier's film of *Hamlet* begins, as does Kurosawa's 1956 *Macbeth* film, *Throne of Blood*. As in those two films, fog remains the essential element: everything looms up out of it and dissolves back into it. In Welles's film, the camera pushes deep in to reveal three hags toiling over a cauldron. In an arresting montage they seem to be brewing a constantly metamorphosing stew, which is now viscous, now fluid, now opaque, now mere mist. The witches – seemingly possessing many more than three voices, some male, others female, some young, others old – work on a doll made of clay. On cue – 'something wicked this way comes' – two warriors in seemingly Tartar garb appear, Macbeth and Banquo on horseback, galloping across the mist-obscured heath. They are immediately engaged by the witches, who make their predictions: as they tell Macbeth that he will be king hereafter, their voices rise to a chilling shriek. The rest of the army draws up, headed by a strange, rugged, unshaven figure, with plaits – apparently Anglo-Saxon, carrying a banner with a Celtic cross; this is the Holy Father, who, somewhat unexpectedly, doesn't seem upset by the Weird Sisters. Macbeth steps aside for his first soliloquy, which is spoken – just as in the contemporaneously filmed *Hamlet* – in voice-over as we study the actor's face. Welles's make-up emphasises his huge eyes with great smudges of kohl; his nose is the one he was born with, small and retroussé, unencumbered with the habitual putty; he has a light, stubbly beard shaped into mustachios, which follows the line of the chin.

Since childhood, Welles had been described as looking slightly oriental, or sometimes even Mongolian, and his physiognomy here seems to have something of the steppes of Central Asia about it. Almost from the moment we see him, this Macbeth appears haunted and dismayed; with one striking exception, we never see the seductive charm that is such a large part of Welles's appeal as an actor.

His conception of the role seems to be of a man tranced, somnambulistically obeying a destiny over which he has no sway. This is very much how he had played Franz Kindler in *The Stranger*. The danger of such an interpretation, which Welles does not entirely avoid, is that it will rob the part of any dramatic progression and will fall into an unchanging rhythm. But, like Olivier in his *Hamlet* (with which *Macbeth* has very much more in common than either its detractors or admirers would like to admit), Welles wants to take us into his leading character's head: harking all the way back to his early radio work and his planned film of *The Heart of Darkness*, he seeks to explore the subjective viewpoint. 'What I am trying to do,' he told *Cahiers du Cinéma*, 'is to see the outside, real world through the same eyes as the inside, fabricated one. To create a kind of unity.' His *Macbeth* has an oneiric quality throughout, and – which is perhaps to say the same thing from a different viewpoint – the quality of a particularly harsh and frightening fairy tale. This aspect of the film is manifest in the constant metamorphoses of elements – the Macbeths' castle, for example, seems to be made of the same clay as the witches' voodoo doll – but also in a certain pictorial naivety and occasional oddly anachronistic touches; the condensation of the action, telescoping and eliding events, enhances this sense of temporal and geographical unreality. Macbeth himself, shot from on high or from far below, often appears as an ogre, while Lady Macbeth is played and filmed like a wicked stepmother. (Welles was much exercised by the idea of kingship – he told Kenneth Tynan that as an actor he fell into the category of 'he that plays the king' and lamented to Peter Bogdanovich that 'we can't have a great Shakespearean theatre in America anymore because it's impossible for today's American actors to comprehend what Shakespeare meant by "king": they think a king is just a gentleman who finds himself wearing a crown and sitting on a throne'; but, despite his physical stature and vocal refulgence, he chose to present both the monarchs he impersonated – the other is King Lear – as unstable and lacking in natural authority.)

Welles's purported approach to *Macbeth*, his attempt to evoke a time poised between the pagan and the Christian – where pagan is equated with evil – is more in the nature of a design concept than of an examination of the play. From his stated intentions, it seems that what he had in mind was the creation of an early medieval world in the manner of Tarkovsky's *Andrei Rublev*, but the text scarcely gives him the opportunities to achieve this; nor could he possibly have done so on his schedule and with his budget.

From a theological or a social-anthropological point of view, there is a certain incoherence to the idea. Perhaps, as André Bazin, with his habitual elegance, suggested, Welles had created 'a prehistoric universe – not that of our ancestors, the Gauls or the Celts, but a pre-history of the conscience at the birth of time and sin, when sky and earth, water and fire, good and evil, still aren't distinctly separate'. Whether this is remotely what Shakespeare had in mind is neither here nor there. But some of the uses to which Welles puts the Holy Father – the key figure in the working out of his idea – are a little perplexing. He displays surprising equanimity when he sees Macbeth and Banquo talking to the Weird Sisters, surely the enemy incarnate. He is next found taking dictation from Macbeth; quietly and efficiently he writes down a very nearly seditious letter to Lady Macbeth. Banquo comes in, and he and Macbeth amiably jest about the witches' prophecies – prophecies that, in the case of Macbeth, can only mean the death of King Duncan and his immediate heirs. Yet the Holy Father, who seems at the very least to be Duncan's chaplain, goes on diligently practising his stenography in the background.

The dissolve to Lady Macbeth reading the letter brings us a first touch of anachronism – exactly as Welles requested (apparently, as Cocteau so wittily noted, on the point of making a phone call). She lies on her bearskin bedspread, and her first soliloquy is heard in voice-over, accompanied by Ibert's wistful, seductively skirling strings, as she voluptuously, tremulously enjoins the spirits to unsex her, gazing out into the encircling mist. It is a striking realisation of the scene. Though Jeanette Nolan is unimposing physically, she conveys an intense inner life, revealed less as a terrifying ruthlessness, than as a rather complicated sexuality.

It is when she first appears that the vexed question of the Scottish accent forces itself to the forefront. Miss Nolan was a skilled mimic and, technically speaking, the accent, consonant for consonant, vowel for vowel, is more or less accurate (more so than that of many in the cast – Dan O'Herlihy lapsing frequently into Irish, as sometimes Welles himself does). What she is unable to do is to transcend the accent so that it is a natural, breathing instrument of her thoughts and feelings. The Olivier film, with which *Macbeth* was so unfavourably compared in this regard, is not flawless: the accents – even Olivier's – have a slightly clipped, cut-glass character that sets them in their own period. But in *Hamlet* the actors are, of course, absolutely at ease with what they are saying, and able to play effortlessly with each other. Welles's actors are in a constant

double struggle, with the accent and with the demands of synchron-
isation: the result is stiff and inexpressive. It is not entirely surprising
that the most favourable responses to the film have been from non-
anglophone countries: if the film were in Latvian or Swahili, it
would be much more enjoyable. Welles's core problem is that he
is dealing with a text that – almost by definition – lives in its
language. Moreover, in this particular play (more than many others
of Shakespeare), the level of poetic inspiration in the writing of
the central character is integral to an understanding of the man. It
is one of the commonplaces of dramatic criticism that Macbeth is
a great poet – is, to some extent, undone by the power of his
imagination, which comes between him and his capacity to act
sufficiently ruthlessly in pursuit of his ambition. A great amount
of his text is, inevitably, cut; but in addition Welles, as has been
observed before, lacks a poetic sensibility, excelling instead in
rhetoric – making a fine sound for the sake of effect, rather than
inhabiting the metaphorical landscape of the verse. His sense of
music is oratorical rather than personal, and tends to the hypnotic
(and sometimes, frankly, soporific) rather than the mercurially
responsive.

Interestingly, Welles's great rival in putting Shakespeare on film,
Laurence Olivier, was also lacking in the sort of instinctive poetic
sensibility possessed by a Gielgud or an Irene Worth, but he had
made of his voice such an extraordinarily flexible instrument that
he was able to orchestrate the language to constantly arresting effect;
his sharp response to imagery would lead him to draw attention
unexpectedly to subordinate phrases, suddenly illuminating a passage
unforgettably (if sometimes irrelevantly). His goal was immediacy
of comprehension; he always sought to root his work in the
perceived world. Ideas scarcely engaged him at all. Welles's approach
to verse-speaking, and indeed to acting in classical plays in general,
was very different. He was in some ways a throwback. Michael
Anderegg in his masterly study *Orson Welles: Shakespeare and Popular
Culture* draws attention to a tradition of 'wildness' in nineteenth-
century Shakespearean performers, associating Welles with this
tradition. Certainly, he consciously dissociates himself from the
contemporary tradition of Shakespearean acting, sometimes hurling
himself at a scene with huge energy and indeed wildness, although
this never affects his performance of the text, which hurtles on –
where formerly it had rolled on – with perfect fluency, but without
real individuation. He finds a cadence, quick or slow, and he sticks
to it, and the result is sometimes impressive, but very often simply

monotonous. Physically, he handles himself like a silent-movie actor (or an opera singer), putting enormous emphasis on his eyes; as director, he uses his own face – often filling the frame with it – as a kind of emotional landscape; the effect is static: a painting, as it were, of feeling, which is often impressive in the photographic stills deriving from the shoot, but dramatically inert in the film itself. It is impossible to separate the movie from its leading actor, because he has naturally thrust himself to the forefront of the frame, but his performance is not, needless to say, the whole story: the physical realisation of the action and the overall visual language are quite strikingly separate from it. Welles the *metteur-en-scène*, and indeed Welles the director of other actors, is a very different creature from Welles the actor. The central paradox of his film of *Macbeth* is that he deploys a radical shooting style to film a conventional and generally rather limited performance of the piece.

In terms of staging and shooting, he is frequently brilliant, particularly considering the constraints of budget and time. The frankly painted image of the Macbeths' castle is pure fairy tale, at the same time – whether intentionally or not – irresistibly recalling the distant view of Charles Foster Kane's Xanadu. The arrival of Duncan at the Macbeths' dank and dismal fortress is an especially stunning sequence, with Kodo drummers thundering, their shadows dancing over the walls, as the army, with flickering torches and Celtic crosses, processes into the dank and gloomy courtyard; unseen pigs squeal frantically – in preparation, presumably, for a coming banquet. Ibert provides a suitably impressive, swaggering, swelling march. The royal entourage having arrived, the Macbeths withdraw to an area somewhere between a rock and a hard place, to which the cyclorama with its projected but static clouds lends a highly unreal background; during the course of the film, much more will be seen of this essentially theatrical feature. When they rejoin the crowd, which is praying and singing hymns, Lady Macbeth whispers her plot into her husband's ear, his haunted face registering the baffled doom that he clearly lives with all the time, as if the voice were coming, not from his wife, but from inside his head. In a scene that has no equivalent in Shakespeare's play, the Holy Father then calls on the assembled company to renounce Satan; the subsequent scene with Duncan (Erskine Sanford, dressed up as Santa Claus or an elderly crofter who has wandered into the castle) is impossibly stilted, and the troops wander off in desultory fashion. The celebrated lines referring to the castle in Inverness having a pleasant seat, the air sweetly and gently recommending itself unto their gentle senses, are very wisely cut, though Shakespeare's martlet still makes an appearance (in the score, too); for a while after Duncan retires to sleep, the film seems to lose power. Welles makes little of the deliberately riddling nature of 'If 'twere done when 'tis done, 'twere best 'twere done quickly'; Nolan seems suddenly very domestic; the courtyard in all its papier-mâché vastness has the feeling of a stage set, and a rather empty one.

Left alone, Macbeth hallucinates a dagger, which in his mind's eye merges with the witches' voodoo doll of himself, slicing its head off; the subsequent scene of the murder is well enough played, with Welles slumped in disbelieving horror at what he has done. The hammering at the gates duly electrifies him and he speeds away. The Porter's sexually quibbling speech is of course cut; it is Banquo at the door arriving with his son Fleance (Jerry Farber) – the young actor gives real urgency and lucidity to his speech, something of a lesson to his elders. The scene of the discovery of the murder using the extreme height of the castle set is urgently done, extensive use in particular being made of the great sweep of the staircase (as, again, in Olivier's film of *Hamlet*, though Welles favours more vertiginous angles than the English director); the uproar is excitingly managed, the universal suspicion of Macbeth – every eye narrowed as he blusters unconvincingly – belonging again to the fairy-tale world of expression, with a nod in the direction of the court of Ivan the Terrible. The sudden cut to the Weird Sisters' cauldron as they crown their clay doll is another typically bold and disturbing image, significantly a realisation of an incident not in the text – indeed, without text – thrillingly dissolving into Macbeth's distorted face, crowned with what came to be known as his Statue of Liberty crown, as he gazes balefully into a metal mirror.

Macbeth sets off for what is presumably his coronation banquet, past line after line of soldiers holding their high flags aloft, moving somewhat uncertainly down the staircases: he is clearly drunk. Ibert underpins this with a Tubby the Tuba march, pompous, ludicrous. Welles's Absurdist view of the reign of King Macbeth is unmistakably spelt out when he finally ascends his throne, which is impossibly high, separating him from his subjects by a wide gap, but devoid of majesty or power. He – even he – simply looks and feels small and lonely in it. Welles's essentially Expressionist approach (imbibed as a boy from theatre magazines excitedly reporting developments in the German and the Soviet theatre, and more formatively still impressed on him by Hilton Edwards at the Gate Theatre in Dublin when he first worked on the professional stage at the age of sixteen) leads him constantly to externalise the internal: subtext and the gradual revelation of character or situation are alien to his method. Everything must be stated; nightmare is the essential framework, wherein fears and longings are played out in magnified form. In this context, Welles's use of space and of his camera (and it is to be presumed that John L. Russell was his obedient servant) constantly seeks to convey Macbeth's disturbed inner life. When the play itself cannot follow him there, he is often content to shoot very simply and conventionally.

One of the most remarkable sequences in the film starts with Macbeth's briefing of the murderers (Brainerd Duffield and Bill Alland – Thompson from *Citizen Kane* – covering themselves in professional disgrace, vocally, physically, emotionally) in which Welles, looming above them in his high-chair/throne, allows himself one of his few human touches in the role, smiling seductively like the young Kane to persuade them to their murderous task. This leads straight on to his encounter with Lady Macbeth ('Be innocent of the deed') and his sudden plunge into guilt and an awareness of the absurdity of it all, finally leading to a dissolve into mist, revealing the murderers magically perched in a fairy-tale tree, their coats of animal hide seeming to metamorphose them into forest creatures: pure Brothers Grimm. The score's urgent, tragic cellos over muted strings evoke the pity and terror of what is to follow in a sequence of what might be termed pure cinema: picture and sound create an image that is both unforgettably haunting and pregnant with dramatic tension. The sharp plunge back into horror after the murderers reveal to Macbeth that Banquo is dead, but that Fleance has escaped (in the fullness of time to breed a line of kings), drives him – roaring and raging like a bull – into the nightmarish banquet, but not before he has, in a striking moment, washed his hands in the waterfall that rather strangely runs down the inside walls of the castle. Welles, playing drunk for rather more than the text's hints to that effect might suggest, shows Macbeth stupefied as he sees sitting round his table, first Banquo and then (an effective innovation of Welles's) Duncan. He throws the table over as the guests look appropriately mortified. The sequence is conceived almost balletically, the full horror of the appearance of the undead curiously muted. Macbeth's subsequent speech to Lady Macbeth – 'It will have blood, they say: blood will have blood' – is, however, filled with that atmosphere that Welles told Peter Bogdanovich makes doing the play so oppressive: 'Really – it's terrifying – stays with you all day . . . so horrendous and awful that it's easy to see how the old superstition [about the play's unlucky nature] lives on.'

Revolted by what he has done, Macbeth strides off into a space that is nowhere at all, smoke clinging to the ground, a storm raging, shadows playing over what is very clearly a cyclorama. Above the roar, in voice-over, the witches give him their deceptive reassuring prediction that only when 'great Birnam Wood to high Dunsinane hill/Shall come against him' will he be vanquished. As the camera swoops in, the light focuses down to a single spot on Macbeth's tortured face, and then there is a blackout. Now this is pure theatre, from beginning to end. On stage it would be conventional, but on film it is radical, pure expression, referring to no observable reality. Some of Welles's most drastic compressions of the text and action follow: extraordinarily, Lady Macbeth is present at the beginning of the scene of the murder of Lady Macduff and her children, as is the Holy Father, who pokes his head through the window to offer some dubious comfort. Macduff's son is played by Welles's daughter Christopher, giving a bright if not especially talented performance, and she hurls herself at her father with some passion when Macbeth (in a radical departure from the play) arrives to despatch the whole family personally. This direct involvement of both of the Macbeths in one of the most savage of all Shakespearean murder scenes ensures that any vestige of sympathy for them that one might have harboured is wiped out, making of Macbeth an unredeemed hell-hound (as Macduff later describes him). Its effectiveness is undeniable, a steep descent into the abyss.

The subsequent scene – what is left of the so-called England scene, in which the self-exiled Malcolm takes the lead against the usurping tyrant – is wretchedly acted, shot and conceived. Roddy McDowall as Malcolm is pallid and bleating, and though Edgar Barrier's Macduff is strong and soldierly enough, he is unable to rise to Shakespeare's terrible demands of the actor, hearing that his wife and children have been slaughtered ('All my pretty ones?/Did you say all? – Oh hell-kite! – All?/What, all my pretty chickens, and their dam,/At one fell swoop?'). The scene is also burdened with the defection of the Holy Father – whom Alan Napier plays with gravelly solemnity, but who is unable in the end to do anything but hover about in his plaits looking Hugely Significant – and with an odd Falstaffian figure who stands amiably by, his occasional utterances quite audibly dubbed by Welles. The gathering of the troops under Malcolm and Macduff is a more vital affair, their forest of banners topped with Celtic crosses making a striking effect, though McDowall remains feeble at their head. This liberation army makes its way across a land oddly reminiscent of Arizona with its parched plains, its ravines and gulches; no doubt many a posse of Republic extras had covered the same terrain.

In the castle, Macbeth's endgame has begun. He himself is found in a large empty courtyard in his shirt sleeves, looking curiously boyish and vulnerable despite his deep-sunken kohl-rimmed eyes. He is attended by a couple of lords and by Seyton (rather strangely, and one can only hope fortuitously, pronounced Satan by Welles), played – as we have seen – by Welles's chauffeur, Shorty Chirello, who, when he is not scuttling about the castle on errands, stands quizzically in the frame like a Domenichino dwarf, just looking; it is an exotic touch, which, though it could conceivably be justified historically, brings to the proceedings a Renaissance colour that seems quite alien to Macbeth's world. After dismissing the cream-fac'd loon, Macbeth, calling for his armour, moves in a single remarkably free shot from his courtyard through to Lady Macbeth's bedroom, where she is lying wide-eyed and staring on her bed; Macbeth and the doctor discuss her condition over her prone form, giving grim vividness to Macbeth's profound questions about mental illness ('Canst thou not minister to a mind diseas'd,/Pluck from the memory a rooted sorrow'?). The rebel army has meanwhile reached Birnam Wood, an unexpectedly beautiful vision of leafy trees rising out of the mist; Malcolm enjoins his men to cut them down, but before we see them do so, Welles interpolates Lady Macbeth's great sleep-walking scene. Nolan plays this with great range – it was, as we have seen, the one scene where she was permitted to speak without use of pre-recorded sound; the result is noticeably freer than the rest of her performance. She actually sings some of the lines as she moves across the battlements, ending up in her husband's arms; she recoils. 'Needless to say,' Nolan recalled, 'I wasn't delighted when he decided to put himself as Macbeth into the sleep-walking scene, but he was the director, it was his version of the play.' In fact, his attempt to embrace her, in the context of the rest of the film, is a powerful image of his inability to control the outcome of his actions; an even more audacious extension of this idea is his decision to show Lady Macbeth's death – merely reported in the play, and presumed to be the outcome of her distemper – as a suicide leap from the castle walls. Her body's twirling descent to the gorge is an archetypally dream-like moment which, sandwiched as it is between the impressionistic, almost surrealistic advance of Birnam Wood, filmed in a slight haze, and the shifting clouds over which Welles speaks the lines 'Tomorrow and tomorrow and tomorrow', shifts the film decisively into a non-realistic idiom. The outer becomes inner. As it happens, Welles disappointingly chooses to intone Macbeth's most famous speech in his Great Verse throb, courting sentimentality, laminating the stark phrases with baritonal plushness, nobly intoning them but never touching their unsparing confrontation of life's terrible truths.

The last phase of the story is hectically enacted, a fine montage of medieval castle-storming techniques (which includes the famous 'Lunch!' shot). Macbeth's first action is to spear the Holy Father through the heart, an event that carries less weight than it seems to demand. Welles is filmed over the shoulder facing the massing troops below, while Ibert sounds high-pitched fanfares; Macduff appears, heavily backlit, in silhouette, and when he tells Macbeth that he was untimely ripp'd from out his mother's womb, the phrase is echoed, high-pitched, on the soundtrack by the Weird Sisters. Macbeth is mocked on all sides. The end comes swiftly: as Macduff's sword slices off his head, so is the clay doll decapitated. The banners and torches of the victorious rebels proclaim their triumph. In a fine closing sequence, the mysterious Xanadu-like castle, so frankly painted and unreal, is established; then, in a billow of cloud, we see the outline of the Weird Sisters, and one of them says – so suddenly that it is almost over before we have heard it – 'The charm's wound up', and the story is at an end – until, Welles implies, the next time.

Seen in this, its original form, *Macbeth* is an extraordinary piece of work, by turns daring and imaginative, then clumsy and conventional, breathtakingly fresh, then suddenly dull and ponderous. Welles's overpowering presence is at odds with his capacities as an actor; the performances in general are at best interesting, at worst risible; the visual world is crudely created, but often potent; the interpretation of the play jejune, but the cinematic concept often thrilling. Welles himself dismissed it in various ways at various times, but the best description of it is his remark to Barbara Leaming that it was 'a bold charcoal sketch', a sort of maquette for a possible approach to putting Shakespeare on the screen. As such it is highly stimulating, and contains within it the seeds of much of Welles's subsequent work. Above all it identifies him as what he was: an experimental artist, deeply unconcerned with commercial success or indeed with the idea of a finished art-work – finished either in the sense of being completed or of having a smooth veneer. Apart from *Citizen Kane* and parts of *The Magnificent Ambersons*, all Welles's films lack finish. He may be compared to a painter who prefers to leave some of the canvas unfilled, or a sculptor who seeks to remind you of the marble from which the image has been fashioned. This notion of film-making has nothing to do with Hollywood, or with making profitable films, so it is perhaps not surprising that Republic began to feel that they had been taken for a ride. Speaking of *Macbeth*, Welles said in London the following year: 'I don't think films made on a small budget and in a short time are any answer for an industry which is doomed anyway.' As shown briefly in 1948, the film's credits are followed by Republic's picture card: an eagle sits on top of a massy (but not particularly pointed) mountain, rather like the ones we have just been watching; like them, it is surrounded by clouds – a nice image of solidarity and continuity, it might have seemed: Welles and his studio at one. But Republic was now increasingly eager to get its hands on the film before releasing it generally, hoping – under the guidance of the reviews that had appeared – to knock it into some kind of commercially acceptable shape.

There were various screenings of the film 'as a basis for discussion', with Wilson fighting the film's corner not only against Republic executives but, to his fury, against Charles Feldman, who had brokered the original deal with Republic and whose name was on the film as producer. Wilson had been hoping to show at the screenings how ridiculous the proposed cuts were, but, he wrote to Welles, 'I have had the considerable disillusionment of hearing Charlie request some of the god-damnedest things it's possible to imagine. I've had the odd experience of being supported by Newman against the suggestions of your good friend and partner, Mr Feldman.' Wilson tells Welles that he had better resign himself to the fact that 'there is going to be editing on the picture'. He has persuaded Republic to send a list of their cuts. They include – Feldman's suggestion, this – Lady Macbeth's first soliloquy and the first murderers' scene. Feldman was also obsessed with certain details of costume, especially what was more or less affectionately known as Welles's Statue of Liberty costume, with points shooting out of his chunky crown:

> To give you a better picture of Charlie. He had so many of his
> friends talk to him about *Macbeth* that he now doesn't know
> what to think. He has memorised the *Life* article and cannot help
> but quote it to make a point. In other words, he's now
> beginning to believe the *Life* article . . . his suggestions . . . are
> directly opposed to your pitch in your letter that the cure is not
> to file down the roughness. His sensitivity to costumes, sound,

witches, voice etc. are all of a kind: intended to soften and make smooth the production.

Wilson was convinced that Feldman never passed on to Republic any of Welles's proposals. Herbert Yates himself was consistently sympathetic and encouraging, but insisted (not unreasonably) that any changes should be effected as soon as possible. Wilson was convinced that Yates had an essential optimism about the movie 'based on his personal belief in it. He has also, I feel, a sincere feeling of loyalty to you and the project which,' he added point-edly, 'has now become precarious.' Yates was wavering on how to sell it, feeling that the artistic high ground had been taken by Olivier. 'He's a bit wistful about "the greatest gangster the world has ever known" type of approach.' The 'Exploitation boys' were frustrated by not having got an endorsement ('they can't get anyone to "come out" for it'); there was no review good enough to quote, except foreign ones. Receipts were down everywhere; legally speaking, Republic could – should they be so minded – seize the picture from Literary Classics. A psychological impasse had been reached whereby the sales department felt that it was impossible to sell the picture in its present form. A decision was taken not to put it on general release till autumn of the following year.

It is interesting to note that the Scottish accents, which before long became an overriding obsession, are not mentioned here as a central problem. But soon the question was all-engrossing; under huge pressure, re-recording of certain lines, nominally supervised by Dick Wilson, was attempted. Welles offered this objection and that, while Wilson valiantly mediated with the studio, trying to interpret Welles's instructions on snatched transatlantic calls or via the erratic mail. Welles's own contributions, recorded in London, were not always properly synchronised. Eventually, and apparently impulsively, he decided that it must be all or nothing, and briefly came back to Hollywood to put the final touches to the re-recording of virtually all the dialogue, and the elimination of most traces of the accent. In the attractive vein of mellow reminiscence he so often adopted with Peter Bogdanovich, he told him, 'Feldman had been so nice about everything that, when he asked for the Scottishness to be muffled, I muffled it. That meant post-synching, of course, and made splendid nonsense of my whole proud exper-iment in miming to playback.' It was a rather different story at the time, a constant battle of wills, with Welles deploying his favourite tactic of hide-and-seek.

Then, in the autumn of 1949, Welles suddenly took control of making an entirely new version of *Macbeth*, redubbing and recutting the whole picture. He did it in Rome, himself, and entirely to his own scheme, removing twenty-one minutes (nearly a quarter of the film) from the running time. He took absolute responsibility for this version, publicly claiming it as his own work. 'They asked me to take out two reels,' he told Bogdanovich, 'and I did – but *I* cut the two reels, they didn't. I thought they shouldn't have been cut out, but I'm the one that cut it. Not some idiot back at home.' This was the version that was finally released in 1950, rather more than three years after that legendarily swift twenty-three-day shoot, and this was the version that formed the basis of all subsequent critical discourse on the film.

The most significant innovation in the new version was the introduction of a spoken and written epigraph to the film, in fairly naked emulation of the opening of Olivier's *Hamlet* (which quotes a speech from the play, ending with the bathetic and somewhat misleading formula: 'Hamlet is the story of a man who could not make up his mind.' Olivier – as active an actor as ever lived – plays the least indecisive Hamlet imaginable. Welles's epigraph is at least a guide to the physical design of his film and an explanation of the presence of the Holy Father). The other cuts tighten the action to the point of incoherence, while undeniably adding to the nightmarish atmosphere; the redubbing retains some of the Scottish burr, but within a basically standard 'English' pronunciation. This version of the film has more or less disappeared from circulation: it stands in relation to the earlier cut as the editions of some Bruckner symphonies do to each other: there are gains in each version, and losses. The press that it received was interestingly less prejudiced than the 1948 reviews: the comparison with *Hamlet* had faded, and some sense of what had actually been achieved – of the film Welles had been trying to make – was beginning to seep through. Bosley Crowther of the *New York Times* said, '. . . it has a great deal in its favour by way of feudal spectacle and nightmare mood . . . Mr Welles deploys himself and his actors so that they move and strike the attitudes of tortured grotesques and half-mad zealots in a Black mass or an ancient ritual.' He discerns in Welles's Macbeth – 'much given to pondering' – a 'monstrous quality. Except that he offers the suggestion that this fatally ambitious man took rather heavily to drinking in the later phases of his bloody career, he accomplishes no illumination of the classical character.' Jeanette Nolan was 'a pop-eyed and haggard dame . . .'; there was – and here it is hard to disagree – 'no real sexual tension between them'. Crowther finds that the whole purpose of the production seemed to be 'to create the vicious moods, the ruthlessness and the superstitions of the warriors in Scotland in Macbeth's day'; *c'est magnifique*, seems to be the verdict, *mais ce n'est pas* Macbeth, a not unreasonable judgement. For Welles, an annoying feature of the reviews was the occasional assumption that he had borrowed from Olivier 'the device of speaking the soliloquies while his lips do not move' (*Broadcast* magazine), though the films had been shot at exactly the same time, with the Atlantic Ocean between them. 'This is not so effective as it has been in Sir Laurence's Shakespearean films,' *Broadcast* bitchily noted, 'mainly because the predominance of Mr Welles's countenance obtrudes.'

It is a notable feature of these 1950 reviews that it has clearly been generally agreed among the critical fraternity that Welles was a figure about whom anything could be said, any casual rudeness indulged; he had been elected to the position of critical sitting duck, always good for a pot-shot. 'They don't review my films any more, they review me,' lamented Welles a little later. The critics were baffled by Welles, and remained so for the rest of his life, all too aware of the flaws in his work, but conscious of a certain magnificence about the failures that somehow made them more interesting than the films they had acclaimed. The reviews of *The Lady from Shanghai*, which Harry Cohn had finally released in 1948, had precisely followed this pattern: under the heading A WELLES DIVIDED, the *Herald Tribune* called it:

> an imaginative and highly stylised film which is at the same time one of the most inept celluloid dramas of this or any other season. His glaring effects and camera magic cannot be dismissed lightly by any lover of the cinema; unfortunately they have a selfish existence of their own, smothering the story and making it appear even more false and posy than it is. Like a fine car in which the maker has forgotten to put a steering apparatus, *The Lady from Shanghai* is a pretty silly piece of infernally good work . . . there is no coherence worth mentioning and as a result no picture. In disdaining to make an imitative or conventional film, Welles sometimes exaggerates his values out of all bounds, and sometimes hits on a tremendously effective idea . . . certainly Hollywood needs as much imagination as it can get into picture-making and the creative touches in *The Lady from Shanghai*,

though impossibly uncontrolled, indicate that Welles is still the man who can supply the much needed stimulant.

In the *New York Times*, Bosley Crowther, noting that the film could have been 'a terrific piece of melodramatic romance', continued, 'no sooner has Mr Welles the director deposited this supercharged group in . . . San Francisco . . . than Mr Welles the author leaves him in the lurch . . . Mr Welles might better have fired himself – as author that is – and hired somebody to give Mr Welles the director a better script.' The *ad hominem* attack then inevitably follows: 'and he certainly could have done better than use himself in the key role of the guileless merchant sailor . . . no matter how much you dress him up in rakish yachting caps and open shirts, Mr Welles simply hasn't the capacity to cut a·romantic swath . . . indeed his performance in this picture – and his exhibitionistic cover-ups of the story's general untidiness – give ironic point to his first line "When I start out to make a fool of myself, there's very little can stop me."' Welles had been asking for it, of course.

Macbeth was released in Britain the following year, and the reviews are significant, because by now Welles had become a considerable European presence – he had acted in two other films, including the one in which he finally became a film star, *The Third Man*, and had made the first of a number of false starts on his next Shakespeare film, *Othello*. Though the British reviewers were as grudging as their transatlantic counterparts, they grasped something about the film that had eluded the American press. Predictably, the verse-speaking and indeed the acting in general were given short shrift. 'Though Mr Orson Welles's film is very far from being *Macbeth*,' said the *Times* silkily, 'it is of great interest to students of Shakespeare and the cinema. They will certainly wish to see for themselves why a man of proven imagination should fail so lamentably with the play of Shakespeare's that would seem, of all the tragedies, the one most readily adaptable to the screen.' Not unreasonably, the uncredited reviewer discerns in 'the unlocalised, unromantic impressionist settings' a debt to the post-First World War German cinema: 'halls stretching away from the spectator with the improbable spaciousness of an ice-rink'. Campbell Dixon of the *Telegraph*, revisiting the film in its trimmed version after his exposure to the earlier version in Venice, was still disappointed in 'the brilliant Mr Welles': 'I should like to praise something, but what? The acting?' No one, he says, is really 'at home in the great Shakespearean tradition'. But elsewhere the tide had turned: 'The temptation with the long-awaited *Macbeth* is to go through it making ribald and incongruous comparisons,' wrote Richard Mallet in *Punch*. 'Going prepared to be interested, I was interested and stimulated.' Over-concentration, he felt, was the problem (which it certainly is in the eighty-minute version). *Sight and Sound* suggested that 'a more powerful effect might have been achieved if the film, properly, had been silent; simply a series of blood-curdling illustrations to a series of anonymous declamations from the sound track'. Caroline Lejeune, doyenne of British film criticism, wrote: 'It is uncouth, unscholarly, unmusical, historically unsound, and almost without exception, abominably acted; but even at its worst it has a sort of power; it is often horrid, but never negligible.'

Virtually all the English critics understood that Welles was pushing towards a new use of the medium and a new approach to Shakespeare. 'Welles's *Macbeth* is nothing if not of the cinema,' wrote Henry Raynor in *Sight and Sound*, claiming, in a striking and accurate parallel, that it was 'as complete a translation into another medium as [Robert] Helpmann's ballet of *Hamlet*'. Or, he might have said, Verdi's opera *Macbeth*: disappointing as a response to the play, but remarkable as a piece in its own right. In a cool consideration of Olivier's *Hamlet* and Welles's *Macbeth* as attempts at filming Shakespeare, Raynor acknowledges that both films, neither entirely satisfactory, show, in varying degrees, the immense possibilities of the medium, but continues: 'We do not know if the visual imagery of the cinema will or can ever develop the power of suggestion, the unmistakeable force and the subtlety of Shakespeare's imagery.' He concludes with a striking perception: 'So far, in *Macbeth*, we have only had Shakespeare's play adapted and filmed by one whose imagination has not progressed beyond the stage of Christopher Marlowe' – in other words, Welles is interested in rhetoric, in the epic, in the sensational, none of which goes to the heart of Shakespeare. (On the other hand, a Marlovian film is scarcely a thing to be sniffed at.)

By the time Raynor's words appeared, Welles had shot *Othello*, a film that is unquestionably Shakespearean, and an altogether richer achievement than *Macbeth*. It was made over some years, in almost comically adverse circumstances, and the result is profoundly flawed from a technical point of view; but its surface limitations are turned to advantage, have become part of the fabric of the film in a way that seems intended rather than fortuitous. Welles had begun to take control of more and more elements of the production; he dubs a number of characters, far from inaudibly; sound has become entirely a matter for post-production; his editing procedures have become increasingly individual. He was now an *auteur* in the most literal sense of the word, the author of every frame, dependent on no one except those from he could extract the money to shoot the next scene. In Paris in 1949 he commented on Hollywood from afar: 'What is needed is more pictures which frankly criticise the shortcomings and weaknesses of America, because nothing stops criticism like self-criticism.' But he himself was not interested in providing those pictures, having embarked on another project, both broader and more specific, that would preoccupy him for some years, amounting to nothing less than a private exploration into the very heart of film.

Meanwhile, in July of 1948, when the first version of *Macbeth* was close to completion, the warehouse storing the scenery and props from *Five Kings*, *Shoemaker's Holiday*, *Caesar* and *Heartbreak House* demanded long-overdue back payment of $100 a week; if not received, they threatened to sell the stuff. There was no money available, so they did. Across the letter Dick Wilson has scrawled: 'So we have lost it! End of era!' It was indeed, for Welles, in many senses. And it was for Wilson, too. At the height of the struggle to get *Macbeth* completed, Wilson made a private decision that he must leave Welles's employ; he was being destroyed by being Johnny-in-the-middle, torn between a director who was behaving capriciously and a studio that was blinkered and rigid. Nor was he being paid; the company's income was too erratic to guarantee regular wages for him. But money was the least of it for Wilson. Some years later, in the British magazine *Sight and Sound*, he admitted that he feared – all too understandably – that he was being engulfed by Welles. His dream of a partnership with his errant employer proved to be a fantasy; and Mercury Productions, though it remained on the letterhead for a few more years, was never to be the force for innovation in theatre and film that he had returned from his war service to create. Partnership was not a concept of any relevance for Welles; he was indeed the Welles of Onlyness.

Another epoch-ending note was the final loss of the *It's All True* material. In September of 1947, the distributor Jerome Hyams of Commonwealth Pictures wrote to Wilson offering to buy the footage from RKO if Welles would finish it. Wilson wrote back excitedly, saying that he felt that it represented 'Welles's finest work in the medium. It remains a great love of Welles's and one on which he someday intends to lavish a lot of love and labour.' He summarised the material, emphasising the Carnival sequence ('there are at least four hit tunes included'), not mentioning the extraordinary *Four Men on a Raft* footage; clearly, like RKO, he felt that it was the film's entertainment value that was central to its appeal, not the epic of Brazilian life. Welles, Wilson said, referring to the treatment Welles called *Carnaval*, has 'a good story for it which changes it . . . to a full feature'. This elaborate new version proposes a framing structure in which the central character, an American engineer, has been shot down. Awakening in the shack of a British missionary, he catches sight of his watch; the past (centring, of course, on the Rio Carnival of 1942) begins to return to him. He dreads remembering, because everything he recalls implies tragedy and an end of the happiness he dimly recollects. Loss of memory and attendant loss of identity; the relationship of the present and the past; what one was and what one has become — these were recurring and highly significant preoccupations of Welles's throughout his career; during this same period, indeed, he was also working on a screenplay drawn from the greatest of all plays about amnesia, Luigi Pirandello's *Henry IV*. (The central character in his version had become, piquantly enough, an American expatriate.) But *It's All True* was not to be realised as *Carnaval* or in any other form. 'Our current schedule would preclude immediate work on it,' Wilson ended. 'However, as a future project it is close to our hearts.'

Nothing happened. There were too many future projects, too many new dreams. As well as that doomed enterprise, and the virgin spools of *Macbeth*, Welles left behind him some emotional detritus when he left for Europe. His second marriage finally and formally came to an end. Rita Hayworth pithily observed that although she had been married to Welles, she never felt that she had a husband. (She also, gamely, claimed that she 'couldn't put up with his genius any more', a pleasant piece of PR.) The next film on which she worked had a resonant title: *Down to Earth*. Welles himself made no public comment on the matter, which was, after all, no more than legal confirmation of a well-established fact. For some years he had been having an active, varied and glamorous sex life, bedding (among others, according to Mrs Leaming) a young Judy Garland and a very young Marilyn Monroe; in Europe he had a series of romances with some exceptionally beautiful actresses. It is hard, nonetheless, to view the failure of his marriage to Rita Hayworth as just one of those things, two people who didn't quite hit it off. Its demise has some parallels with the ruin of his career (and there is no question, however complex the reasons, that his career in Hollywood was now a wreck).

Welles's relationship to Hayworth and to Hollywood were not dissimilar. In marrying Rita Hayworth, he attained what millions of men all over the world could only dream of. He set out to get her and he did, effortlessly. She fell deeply in love with him and put herself at his entire disposal. And then he immediately became restless. True, she had proved somewhat neurotic, unexpectedly demanding and not necessarily the ideal conversational partner. But within months – weeks, he told Barbara Leaming – he started to play the field again, unwilling to make any concession to married life or to engage in any significant way with the remarkable and complex woman to whom he had supposedly committed himself. The marriage started to unravel; within two years it was in serious trouble. There is no intention of censoriousness in recording these matters. Such things happen. But the pattern of flight is unmistakable, one repeated from his relationship with Dolores del Rio, who – by contrast with Rita Hayworth – was emotionally mature, socially brilliant and a fine artist in her own right. She was neither neurotic nor needy; she simply required commitment from him. And that he would not give. Any form of limitation, obligation, responsibility or enforced duty was intolerable to him, rendering him claustrophobic and destructive. He could only function as a free agent, untrammelled by partners, children, wives, administrators, accountants, producers, studios, political mentors. He must go his own way. His motto might have been Aleister Crowley's 'Do what thou wilt shall be all the law'. In terms of his work as a director, that meant that he had, inevitably, to become an independent film-maker. Confinement, whether personal or professional, was unbearable to Orson Welles. His exploratory urges were central to his nature; he indulged them unceasingly for the rest of his life. Occasionally, something close to a masterpiece would result. But that was not the purpose of his journey through life. The doing was all. And America in 1947 – when he embarked on his long, if sporadically broken, exile – was not the place in which to do it.

The Stage Productions

The Mercury Wonder Show

Autumn 1943
Hollywood

Music by Professor Bill and the
Circus Symphony
Script by divers hands, edited by
Orson Welles

Cast: Marlene Dietrich, Joseph
Cotten, Agnes Moorehead,
Lola Leighton, Merry
Hamilton, Tony Hanlon,
Sampson MacDonald, Mary
Rouland, Peggy Vaughn, Shifra
Haran, Jean Gabin.

Around the World

31 May–3 August 1946
Adelphi Theatre, New York
Tour: Boston, New Haven,
Philadelphia

Adapted by Welles from the novel
Around the World in Eighty Days
by Jules Verne. Music and
Lyrics: Cole Porter.
Choreography: Nelson Barclift.
Settings: Robert Davison.
Costumes: Alvin Colt. Circus
Arrangement: Barbette. Music
Director: Harry Levant.

Cast: Arthur Margetson (Phileas
Fogg), Larry Laurence

(Passepartout, Groom Clown),
Orson Welles (Dick Fix,
Dynamite Gus), Brainerd
Duffield (Bank Robber,
Benjamin Cruett-Spew, Second
Arab Spy, Oka Saka, Sol), Guy
Spaull (Police Inspector, Ralph
Runcible, Maurice Goodpile),
Jack Pitchon (London Bobbie),
Genevieve Sauris (Lady), Stefan
Schanbel (Avery Jevity, Arab
Spy, Mother Clown, Medicine
Man), Julie Warren (Molly
Muggins), Bernard Savage (Sir
Charles Mandiboy, British
Consul, Medicine Man), Billy
Howell (Lord Upditch, Sam,
Medicine Man, Station
Attendant, Sinister Chinese,
Dancing Gentleman), Bruce
Cartwright (Serving Man,
Fireman Clown, Mexican
Dancer, Dancing Gentleman),
Gregory McDougall (Serving
Man, Dancing Gentleman),
Dorothy Bird (Merrahlah,
Mexican Dancer), Myron Speth
(Dancer Fella, London Bobbie,
Dancing Gentleman), Lucas
Aco (Dancer Fella, Fakir,
Sinister Chinese, Jim, Dancing
Gentleman), Eddy Di Genova
(Snake Charmer, Monkey Man
Clown, Bartender, Singing
Gentleman), Victor Savidge,

Stabley Turner (Snake Charmers), Spencer James (Sikh, Jake), Mary Healy (Mrs Aouda), Arthur Cohen (High Priest), Phil King (Sinister Chinese, Dancing Gentleman), Jackie Cezanne (Lee Toy, Dancing Lady), Lee Morrison, Nancy Newton (Daughters of Joy), The Three Kanasawa (Foot Jugglers), Adelaide Corsi (Rolling Globe Lady), Miss Lu (Contortionist), Ishikawa (Hand Balancer), Mary Broussard, Lee Vincent, Patricia Leith, Virginia Morris (Aerialists), Ray Goody (Slide for Life), Jack Pitchon, Tony Montell (Roustabouts), Nathan Baker (Father Clown, Dancing Gentleman, London Bobbie, Sinister Chinese), Bernie Pisarski (Child Clown), Cliff Chapman (Bride Clown), Arthur Cohen (Minister Clown), Jack Cassidy (Policeman Clown), Allan Lowell (Kimona Man, Jail Guard, Singing Gentleman), Gordon West (Fireman Clown, Dancing Gentleman, London Bobbie), Daniel DePaolo (Dragon), Stanley Turner (Attendant), Victoria Codova (Lola), Kenneth Bonjukian, Jack Cassidy, Arthur Cohen, Stabley Turner (Singing Gentlemen), Florence Gault, Natie Greene, Arline Hanna, Marion Kohler, Rose Marie Patane, Genevieve Sauris, Gina Siena, Drucilla Strain (Singing Ladies), Mary Broussard, Elinore Gregory, Patricia Leith, Virginia Morris, Lee Morrison, Nancy Newton, Miriam Pandor, Virginia Sands, Lee Vincent (Dancing Ladies).

The Radio Broadcasts

*Shrendi Vashtar/Hidalgo/An
Irishman and A Jew*
15 September 1941. Lady Esther.
Featuring Welles, Dolores del
Rio, Hans Conried, Osa Mason.
Music by Meade Lux Lewis.

*The Right Side/The Sexes/Murder
in the Bank/Golden
Honeymoon*
22 September 1941. Lady Esther.

*The Interloper/Song of
Solomon/I'm a Fool*
29 September 1941. Lady Esther.

*The Black Pearl/There's a Full
Moon Tonight/Annabel Lee*
6 October 1941. Lady Esther. By
Norman Foster, Edgar Allan Poe.

*If In Years to Come/Dorothy Parker
Poetry*
13 October 1941. Lady Esther.

*Romance/Shakespearean
Sonnet/Prisoner of Assiout*
20 October 1941. Lady Esther.

Wild Oranges
3 November 1941. Lady Esther.

*That's Why I Left You/The
Maysvill Minstrel*
10 November 1941. Lady Esther.

The Hitch Hiker
17 November 1941. Lady Esther.
Fletcher.

A Farewell to Arms
24 November 1941. Lady Esther.

*Something's Going to Happen to
Henry/Wilbur Brown, Habitat:
Brooklyn*
1 December 1941. Lady Esther.

Between Americans
7 December 1941. Gulf Screen
Guild Theatre.

*Symptoms of Being Thirty-
Five/Leaves of Grass*
8 December 1941. Lady Esther.

The Great Man Votes
15 December 1941. Cavalcade of
America. Acting only.

President's Bill of Rights
15 December 1941. We Hold
These Truths.
    Mutual Broadcasting System.

*St Luke, Chapter Two/The
Happy Prince/Christmas
Poetry*
22 December 1941. Lady Esther.

There are Frenchmen and Frenchmen
29 December 1941. Lady Esther. Guest: Rita Hayworth.

The Garden of Allah
5 January 1942. Lady Esther.

The Apple Tree
12 January 1942. Lady Esther. Guest: Geraldine Fitzgerald.

My Little Boy
19 January 1942. Lady Esther.

American Laughter
25 January 1942. Red Cross Program.

The Happy Hypocrite
26 January 1942. Lady Esther.

Between Americans
2 February 1942. Lady Esther.

Pan American Day
14 April 1942. Broadcast from Brazil.

President Vargas' Birthday
18 April 1942. Broadcast from Brazil.

The Hitch Hiker
2 September 1942.

Information Please
18 September 1942. Panel game.

Juarez: Thunder from the Mountains
28 September 1942. Cavalcade of America.

Radio Reader's Digest
11 October 1942.

Admiral of the Ocean Sea
12 October 1942. Cavalcade of America.

Texaco Star Theatre
18 October 1942. Guest appearance. Featuring Fred Allen, Portland Hoffa, Alan Reed, Benay Venuta. CBS (rebroadcast on the Armed Forces Radio Service).

In the Best Tradition
26 October 1942. Cavalcade of America.

Flying Fortress
9 November 1942. Ceiling Unlimited.

Brazil
15 November 1942. Hello Americans.

Air Transport Command
16 November 1942. Ceiling Unlimited.

The Andes
22 November 1942. Hello Americans.

The Navigator
23 November 1942. Ceiling Unlimited.

The Islands
29 November 1942. Hello Americans.

Wind, Sand and Stars
30 November 1942. Ceiling
    Unlimited.

Alphabet: A to C
6 December 1942. Hello
    Americans.

Ballad of Bataan
7 December 1942. Ceiling
    Unlimited.

Alphabet: C to S
13 December 1942. Hello
    Americans.

War Workers
14 December 1942. Ceiling
    Unlimited.

Slavery – Abednego
20 December 1942. Hello
    Americans.

Gremlins
21 December 1942. Ceiling
    Unlimited.

The Bad-Will Ambassador
27 December 1942. Hello
    Americans.

Pan American Airlines
28 December 1942. Ceiling
    Unlimited.

Latin Music
3 January 1943. Hello Americans.
    Lud Gluskin substitutes for an
    indisposed Welles.

Anti-Submarine Patrol
4 January 1943. Ceiling Unlimited.
    Edgar G. Robinson substituted
    for a still indisposed Welles.

Mexico
10 January 1943. Hello
    Americans.

Finger in the Wind
11 January 1943. Ceiling
    Unlimited.

Feed the World
17 January 1943. Hello
    Americans.

Letter to Mother
18 January 1943. Ceiling
    Unlimited.

Ritmos de las Americas
24 January 1943. Hello
    Americans. Welles in-
    disposed. Latin American dance
    music conducted by Lud
    Gluskin.

*Flyer Come Home with your
    Wings/Mrs James and the Pot
    of Tea*
25 January 1943. Ceiling
    Unlimited.

Bolivar's Idea
31 January 1943. Hello
    Americans.

The Future
1 February 1943. Ceiling
    Unlimited.

The Jack Benny Program
14 March 1943. Welles substitutes
    for ailing Benny.

The Jack Benny Program
21 March 1943. Welles substitutes
    for ailing Benny.

The Jack Benny Program
28 March 1943. Welles substitutes for ailing Benny.

The Jack Benny Program
4 April 1943. Welles substitutes for ailing Benny.

The Jack Benny Program
11 April 1943. Welles substitutes for ailing Benny.

Reading Out Loud
3 September 1943.

Mercury Wonder Show
Interview
7 September 1943.

The Most Dangerous Game
23 September 1943. Acting only.

The Pepsodent Show
27 September 1943. Starring Bob Hope. Guest appearance.

Philomel Cottage
7 October 1943. Acting only.

Orson Welles Almanac
26 January 1944. Guest: Groucho Marx.

Orson Welles Almanac
2 February 1944. Guest: Lionel Barrymore.

Orson Welles Almanac
9 February 1944. Guest: Ann Sothern.

Orson Welles Almanac
16 February 1944. Guest: Robert Benchley.

Orson Welles Almanac
23 February 1944. Guest: Hedda Hopper.

Orson Welles Almanac
1 March 1944. Guest: Victor Moore.

Orson Welles Almanac
8 March 1944. Guest: Lucille Ball.

Orson Welles Almanac
15 March 1944. Guest: Charles Laughton.

Orson Welles Almanac
22 March 1944. Guest: Betty Hutton.

Orson Welles Almanac
29 March 1944. Guest: Mary Boland.

The Chase and Sanborn
Program
2 April 1944. Featuring Edgar Bergen and Charlie McCarthy. Guest Appearance.

Orson Welles Almanac
5 April 1994. Guest: Dennis Day.

Orson Welles Almanac
12 April 1944. Guest: Monty Woolley.

The Marvelous Barastro
13 April 1944. By Ben Hecht. Acting only. Featuring William Spier.

Orson Welles Almanac
19 April 1944. Guest: George Jessel.

Orson Welles Almanac
26 April 1944. Guest: Carole
   Landis.

Three of a Kind
27 April 1944. Special appearance
   in a programme produced on
   behalf of the US Treasury
   Department.

Orson Welles Almanac
3 May 1944. Guest: Lucille Ball.

The Dark Tower
4 May 1944. Acting only.

Orson Welles Almanac
10 May 1944. Guest: Jimmy
   Durante and Aurora Miranda.

Orson Welles Almanac
19 May 1944. Guest: Ann
   Sothern

Donovan's Brain (Part I)
18 May 1944. Acting only.

Orson Welles Almanac
24 May 1944. Guests: Lee Wilde,
   Lyn Wilde, Lois Collier.

Donovan's Brain (Part II)
25 May 1944. Acting only.

The Chase and Sanborn Program
28 May 1944. Featuring Edgar
   Bergen and Charlie McCarthy.
   Guest appearance.

Orson Welles Almanac
31 May 1944 Guest: Marjorie
   Reynolds.

Jane Eyre
5 June 1944. Lux Radio Theatre.

Featuring Loretta Young.
Directed by Cecil B. DeMille.

Orson Welles Almanac
7 June 1944. Special D-Day
   programme.

Fifth War Loan Drive
12 June 1944. Written by Welles.
   Featuring Welles, Walter
   Huston, Agnes Moorehead.

Orson Welles Almanac
14 June 1944. Special Tex-Arkana
   programme.

Fifth War Loan Drive
19 June 1944. Chicago.

Orson Welles Almanac
21 June 1944. Guest: Martha
   O'Driscoll.

Orson Welles Almanac
28 June 1944. Guest: Lynn
   Bari.

Orson Welles Almanac
5 July 1944 Guest: Lana Turner.
   Featuring *The Mercury Wonder
   Show*.

Orson Welles Almanac
12 July 1944. Guest: Susan
   Hayward.

Orson Welles Almanac
19 July 1944. Guest: Ruth Terry.

*The Chase and Sanborn
   Program*
13 August 1944. Featuring Edgar
   Bergen and Charlie McCarthy.
   Guest appearance.

Break of Hearts
11 September 1944. Featuring
Welles, Rita Hayworth.
Produced by Cecil B DeMille.
Lux Radio Theatre.

The Dream
23 September 1944. The Inner
Sanctum. Acting only.

Now is the Time
6 October 1944.

Philco Radio Hall of Fame
8 October 1944. Hosted by
Welles. Armed Forces Radio
Service.

The Dark Hours
15 October 1944. The Kate
Smith Show.

*False Issues and the American
President*
18 October 1944.

*The Chase and Sanborn
Program*
29 October 1944. Featuring Edgar
Bergen and Charlie McCarthy.
Guest appearance.

Round Table Political Broadcast
1 November 1944. Sponsored by
the Democratic National
Committee.

The Chase and Sanborn Hour
5 November 1944. Featuring
Edgar Bergen and Charlie
McCarthy. Guest appearance.

Philco Radio Hall of Fame
24 December 1944. Armed Forces
Radio Service.

*Lobbying/G.I. Bill of Rights/
New Year's/Post
War/Epiphany/Shut
Eye/Grable/Inauguration*
Eight programmes recorded for
Eversharp but never broadcast.

All-American Jazz Concert
16 January 1945. Sponsored by
Esquire. Guest appearance.

Heart of Darkness
13 March 1945. This Is My Best.
Sponsored by Cresta Blanca.

Miss Dilly Says No
20 March 1945. This Is My Best.
Featuring Welles, Francis X.
Bushman. Guest: Ann Sothern.

A Tale of Two Cities
26 March 1945. Featuring Welles,
Verna Felton, Rosemary de
Camp. Produced by Cecil B
DeMille. Lux Radio Theatre.

Snow White
27 March 1945. This Is My Best.
Featuring Jane Powell. Based
on the Walt Disney film.

The Diamond as Big as the Ritz
3 April 1945. This Is My Best.

The Master of Ballantrae
10 April 1945. This Is My Best.
Featuring Welles, Ray Collins,
Agnes Moorehead, Alan
Napier.

I'll Not Go Back
17 April 1945. This Is My Best.

Anything Can Happen
24 April 1945. This Is My Best.

Special V-E Day Program
7 May 1945.

New York – A Tapestry for Radio
10 July 1945. Columbia Presents Corwin.

French Press: The Liberation of Paris
19 July 1945. Narrator.

What Does the British Election Mean to Us?
9 August 1945. America's Town Meeting. Special appearance.

Fourteen August
14 August 1945. Columbia Presents Corwin. Written by Norman Corwin.

God and Uranium
19 August 1945 Columbia Presents Corwin. Featuring Welles, Olivia de Havilland.

Victory Extra
2 September 1945. Command performance. Special V-J Day production. Armed Forces Radio Service.

Orson Welles Commentaries
16 September 1945. Sponsored by Lear Radios.

Orson Welles Commentaries
23 September 1945.

Orson Welles Commentaries
30 September 1945.

Orson Welles Commentaries
7 October 1945.

Orson Welles Commentaries
14 October 1945.

Orson Welles Commentaries
21 October 1945.

Orson Welles Commentaries
28 October 1945

Orson Welles Commentaries
4 November 1945.

Orson Welles Commentaries
11 November 1945.

Orson Welles Commentaries
18 November 1945.

Orson Welles Commentaries
25 November 1945.

Orson Welles Commentaries
2 December 1945.

Orson Welles Commentaries
9 December 1945.

Orson Welles Commentaries
16 December 1945.

Orson Welles Commentaries
23 December 1945.

Orson Welles Commentaries
6 January 1946.

Orson Welles Commentaries
13 January 1946.

Orson Welles Commentaries
20 January 1946.

Orson Welles Commentaries
27 January 1946.

Orson Welles Commentaries
3 February 1946.

Orson Welles Commentaries
10 February 1946.

Orson Welles Commentaries
17 February 1945.

Orson Welles Commentaries
24 February 1946.

Orson Welles Commentaries
3 March 1946.

The Fred Allen Show
3 March 1946. Guest appearance.

Orson Welles Commentaries
10 March 1946.

Orson Welles Commentaries
17 March 1946.

Orson Welles Commentaries
24 March 1946.

Radio Reader's Digest
31 March 1946.

Orson Welles Commentaries
28 April 1946.

Orson Welles Commentaries
5 May 1946.

Orson Welles Commentaries
12 May 1946. George Hays
  substitutes for a sick Welles.

Orson Welles Commentaries
19 May 1946.

Orson Welles Commentaries
26 May 1946.

Orson Welles Commentaries
2 June 1946.

Around the World in Eighty Days
7 June 1946. Mercury Summer
  Theatre.

Orson Welles Commentaries
9 June 1946.

The Count of Monte Cristo
14 June 1946. Mercury Summer
  Theatre.

Orson Welles Commentaries
16 June 1946.

The Hitch Hiker
21 June 1946. Mercury Summer
  Theatre. By Lucille Fletcher.

Orson Welles Commentaries
23 June 1946.

Jane Eyre
28 June 1946. Mercury Summer
  Theatre. Featuring Welles, Alice
  Frost. Adapted by Norman
  Corwin from the novel by
  Charlotte Brontë. Music by
  Bernard Hertmann.

Orson Welles Commentaries
30 June 1946.

A Passenger to Bali
5 July 1946. Mercury Summer
  Theatre.

Orson Welles Commentaries
7 July 1946.

The Search for Henri Le Fevre
12 July 1946. Mercury Summer
  Theatre.

Orson Welles Commentaries
14 July 1946.

Life With Adam
19 July 1946. Mercury Summer
    Theatre.

Orson Welles Commentaries
21 July 1946.

The Moat Farm Murder
26 July 1946. Mercury Summer
    Theatre.

Orson Welles Commentaries
28 July 1946.

Golden Honeymoon
2 August 1946. Mercury Summer
    Theatre.

Orson Welles Commentaries
4 August 1946.

Hell on Ice
9 August 1946. Mercury Summer
    Theatre.

Orson Welles Commentaries
11 August 1946.

Abednego the Slave
16 August 1946. Mercury
    Summer Theatre.

Orson Welles Commentaries
18 August 1946.

I'm a Fool/The Tell-Tale Heart
23 August 1946. Mercury
    Summer Theatre.

Orson Welles Commentaries
25 August 1946.

Moby-Dick
30 August 1946. Mercury
    Summer Theatre. By Herman
    Melville.

Orson Welles Commentaries
1 September 1946.

The Apple Tree
6 September 1946. Mercury
    Summer Theatre. By John
    Galsworthy.

Orson Welles Commentaries
8 September 1946.

King Lear
13 September 1946. Mercury
    Summer Theatre. By William
    Shakespeare.

Orson Welles Commentaries
15 September 1946.

Orson Welles Commentaries
22 September 1946.

Orson Welles Commentaries
29 September 1946.

Orson Welles Commentaries
6 October 1946.

Anniversary Program
29 May 1947 Command perform-
    ance. Five-year anniversary of
    the Armed Forces Radio
    System.

The Films

The Magnificent Ambersons

RKO (Radio-Keith-Orpheum) Pictures. A Mercury Production. 88 minutes. Premiere: 13 August 1942.

Director and Screenplay: Welles, adapted from the novel by Booth Tarkington.

Associate Producers: Jack Moss, Richardson Wilson.

Cinematography: Stanley Cortez.

Editors: Robert Wise, Mark Robson.

Music: Bernard Herrmann (uncredited). Additional Music: Roy Webb.

Art Director: Mark Lee Kirk.

Sets: Al Fields.

Special Effects: Vernon L. Walker.

Sound: Bailey Feser, James G. Stewart.

Costumes: Edward Stevenson.

Assistant Director: Freddie Fleck. Additional footage directed by Norman Foster, Robert Wise, Freddie Fleck, Joseph Cotten, Jack Moss.

Cast: Tim Holt (George Minafer), Joseph Cotten (Eugene Morgan), Dolores Costello (Isabel Amberson), Anne Baxter (Lucy Morgan), Agnes Moorehead (Fanny Minafer), Ray Collins (Uncle Jack Amberson), Richard Bennett (Major Amberson), Don Dillaway (Wilbur Minafer), Erskine Sanford (Roger Bronson), J. Louis Johnson (Sam), Charles Phipps (Uncle John), Gus Schilling, Georgia Backus (additional cast), Narrator (Welles).

Journey into Fear

RKO (Radio-Keith-Orpheum) Pictures. A Mercury Production. Premiere: 12 February 1943. 68 minutes.

Director: Norman Foster.

Producer: Welles.

Screenplay: Joseph Cotten, based on the novel by Eric Ambler.

Cinematography: Karl Struss.

Music: Roy Webb.

Art Directors: Albert S. D'Agostino, Mark-Lee Kirk.

Sets: Darrell Silvera, Ross Dowd.

Special Effects: Vernon L. Walker.

Sound: Bailey Fesler, James G. Stewart.

Editor: Mark Robson.

Costumes: Edward Stevenson.

Cast: Joseph Cotten (Howard Graham), Dolores Del Rio (Josette Martel), Jack Moss (Peter Banat), Everett Sloane (Kopeikin), Welles (Colonel

Haki), Ruth Warrick
(Stephanie Graham), Frank
Readick (Mr Mathis), Jack
Durant (Gobo), Agnes
Moorehead (Mrs Mathis),
Eustace Wyatt (Dr Haller),
Shifra Haran (Mrs Haller),
Edgar Barrier (Kuvetli), Hans
Conreid (Magician), Richard
Bennett (Captain), Stefan
Schnabel, Robert Meltzer,
Herbert Drake, Bill Roberts
(additional cast).

The Stranger

The Haig Corporation. An
International Pictures
Production. Distributed by
RKO. 95 minutes.
Director: Welles.
Producer: Sam Spiegel (credited
S. P. Eagle).
Screenplay: Anthony Veiller.
Story: Victor Trivas, Decla
Dunning.
Cinematography: Russell Metty.
Editor: Ernest Nims.
Production Design: Perry
Ferguson.
Music: Bronislaw Kaper.
Costumes: Michael Woulfe.
Assistant Director: Jack
Voglin.

Cast: Welles (Franz
Kindler/Charles Rankin),
Loretta Young (Mary
Longstreet), Edward G.
Robinson (Inspector Wilson),
Philip Merivale (Judge
Longstreet), Richard Long
(Noah Longstreet), Konstantin
Shayne (Konard Meinike), Billy
House (Potter), Byron Keith
(Dr Lawrence), Martha

Wentworth (Sarah), Pietro
Sosso (Mr Peabody), Erskine
Sanford (Party Guest).

The Lady from Shanghai

Columbia Pictures. 86 minutes.
Director and Screenplay: Welles,
based on Sherwood King's If I
Die Before I Wake.
Associate Producers: Richard
Wilson, William Castle.
Cinematographer: Charles
Lawton Jr.
Music: Heinz Roemheld.
Song 'Please Don't Kiss Me' by
Roberts and Fisher.
Editor: Viola Lawrence.
Art Directors: Stephen Goosson,
Sturges Carne.
Sets: Wilbur Menefee, Herman
Schoenbrun.
Sound: Lodge Cunningham.
Costumes: Jean Louis.
Special Effects: Lawrence Butler.
Camera: Irving Klein.
Assistant Director: Sam Nelson.

Cast: Welles (Michael O'Hara),
Rita Hayworth (Elsa
Bannister), Everett Sloane
(Arthur Bannister), Glenn
Anders (Grisby), Ted de Corsia
(Sidney Broom), Gus Schilling
(Goldie), Erskine Sanford
(Judge), Evelyn Ellis (Bessie),
Louis Merrill (Jake), Harry
Shannon (Taxi Driver), Wong
Show Ching (Li), Sam Nelson
(Captain), Carl Frank (District
Attorney), Richard Wilson
(DA's Assistant).

Macbeth

Republic Pictures. A Mercury

Production. 112 minutes
(Welles's cut), 89 minutes
(revised cut).

Director and Screenplay: Welles,
based on the play by William
Shakespeare.

Producer: Charles K. Feldman.

Associate Producer: Richard
Wilson.

Cinematography: John L. Russell.

Editor: Louis Lindsay.

Art Director: Fred Ritter.

Sets: John McCarthy Jr, James
Redd.

Music: Jacques Ibert. Conducted
by: Efrem Kurtz.

Dialogue Director: William
Alland.

Special Effects: Howard Lydecker,
Theodore Lydecker.

Sound: John Stranksy Jr, Garry
Harris.

Second Unit Director: William
Bradford.

Assistant Director: Jack Lacey.

Optical Effects: Consolidated Film
Industries.

Costumes: Adele Palmer, Fred
Ritter, Welles.

Hair: Peggy Gray.

Cast: Welles (Macbeth), Jeanette
Nolan (Lady Macbeth), Dan
O'Herlihy (Macduff), Roddy
McDowell (Malcolm), Alan
Napier (Holy Father), Edgar
Barrier (Banquo), Erskine
Sanford (Duncan), John
Dierkes (Ross), Keene Curtis
(Lennox), Peggy Webber (Lady
Macduff, Voice of Witch),
Lurene Tuttle (Gentlewoman,
Voice of Witch), Christopher
Welles (Macduff's son), Jeffy
Farber (Fleance), Archie
Heugly (Young Siward), Gus
Schilling (Porter), Brainerd
Duffield (First Murderer, Voice
of Witch), William Alland
(Second Murderer).

The Writings

'His Honor, the Mayor', *The Free Company Presents* . . . Text of the radio broadcast (R108), Dodd and Mead, 1941.

Anonymous, 'The Sleepy Lagoon Murder Case' (pamphlet). Mercury Press, 1942. Welles wrote the introduction to this reactionary essay on a Hispanic man who was unjustly accused of murder.

'Moral Indebtedness', *Free World*, October 1943.

'Unknown Soldier', *Free World*, December 1943.

'The Good Neighbor Policy Reconsidered', *Free World*, March 1944.

'Habits of Disunity', *Free World*, May 1944.

'Race Hate Must Be Outlawed', *Free World*, July 1944.

'War correspondents', *Free World*, August 1944.

'American Leadership in '44', *Free World*, September 1944.

'Liberalism – Election's Victor', *Free World*. December 1944.

'Orson Welles Almanac, Orson Welles today', *New York Post*, 1945.

'G.I. Bill of Rights', *Free World*, January 1945.

'In Memoriam: Mankind Grieves for Our Late President', *Free World*, May 1945

'Now or Never', *Free World*, September 1945.

The Records

The Liberation of Paris
Asch Records, 1944
Political speeches and
commentary.

In the American Tradition
Decca Records, 1945
Political speeches and
commentary.

The Happy Prince
Decca Records, 1946

No Man is an Island
Decca Records, 1946
Literary/political speeches and
commentary featuring the works
of John Donne, Pericles, Patrick
Henry, John Brown, Abraham
Lincoln and Émile Zola.

References

All references in the text to Barbara Leaming are to be found in her book *Orson Welles: A Biography*; all references to Peter Bogdanovich are to be found in his book *This is Orson Welles*.

PREFACE

pp.xv–xvi 'By enlarging the field of causal explanation beyond the studio career of Orson Welles . . .' from *Persistence of Vision*.

p.xvi 'what matters is the homage Welles rendered to Flaherty . . .' ibid.

p.xvii 'incomparable bravura personality'. Kenneth Tynan, *Profiles*.

CHAPTER ONE
Orson Ascendant

p.4: 'like a Prussian riding master . . .' Betty Lasky, *RKO: The Biggest Little Major of Them All*.

p.4: 'big, robust bulldog . . .' ibid.

p.4: 'Your triumph is one of the greatest accomplishments . . .' *Hollywood Reporter*.

p.5: 'I just had a hot tip . . .' Betty Lasky, op. cit.

p.6: 'the Wizard of RKO . . .' Joseph V. Breen Press Conference, March 1941.

p.7: '*projectitis* . . .' Dusan Makavejev in Simon Callow, *Shooting the Actor*.

p.8: 'I hereby sell . . .' Agreement between Orson Welles and Charles Chaplin, 24 July 1941.

p.9: 'All the stories we do for Welles . . .' Letter from John Fante, n.d., quoted in Stephen Cooper, *Full of Life*.

p.10: 'part of the whole Broadway–Browder axis . . .' Quoted in Michael Denning, *The Cultural Front*.

p.11: 'a modern form of education . . .' Speech by Orson Welles, 6 March 1943.

p.11: 'I've never been anywhere else on time . . .' Duke Ellington, *Music is my Mistress*.

p.13: 'my own conception of the picture . . .' Memorandum to Joseph Breen, 10 July 1941.

p.14: 'MY FACE FILLS THE FRAME . . .' From draft for *The Way to Santiago*.

p.15: 'I took the right-wing . . .' Eric Ambler, quoted in Michael Denning, *Cover Stories*.

p.17: 'an unnamed picture has taken precedence . . .' RKO report, 17 July 1941.

CHAPTER TWO
Pampered Youth

p.18: 'The RKO lawyers did shudder . . .' Frank Brady, *Citizen Welles*.

p.25: 'extraordinary . . . one of the most interesting actors . . .' Peter Bogdanovich, *This is Orson Welles*.

p.26: 'I'd been such a breathless fan of his in the theatre . . .' ibid.

p.27: 'You have made me – happy . . .' Letter from Richard Bennett to Orson Welles, 8 March 1942.

p.30: 'I can think of nothing . . .' Orson Welles lecture to motion picture students of New York University, 20 October 1942.

p.30: 'It can be chalked up as another . . .' Letter from Robert Gessner to Richard Wilson, 24 October 1941.

p.33: 'I LOVE YOU.' Telegram from Orson Welles to Norman Foster, 27 September 1941.

p.33: 'Personally, I shall never . . .' Telegram from Norman Foster to Orson Welles, 2 October 1941.

p.33: 'WE ALL MISS YOU TERRIBLY . . .' Telegram from Orson Welles to Norman Foster, 3 October 1941.

p.33: 'the tremendous investment . . .' Richard Wilson account of telephone conversation with Reg Armour, 8 October 1941.

p.34: 'YOU ASKED ME TO BE BRUTALLY FRANK . . .' Telegram from Orson Welles to Norman Foster, 18 October 1941.

p.34: 'YOU REALLY ARE A SWEET GUY . . .' Telegram from Norman Foster to Orson Welles, 19 October 1941.

p.34: 'Charles Higham reports . . .' Charles Higham, *Orson Welles: The Rise and Fall of an American Genius*.

p.35: 'He had eight sets upstairs and downstairs . . .' Stanley Cortez in Charles Higham, *Sources of Light*.

p.35: 'This is the second case of the Welles company . . .' Memorandum from Bill Eglinston.

p.36: 'Immediately, said Cortez . . .' *Sources of Light*.

p.36: 'People said I was much too arty . . .' ibid.

p.37: 'she was quite unfocused . . .' Peter Bogdanovich, op. cit.

p.38: 'There I was to meet him . . .' *Daily Telegraph*, 15 March 1943.

p.38: 'Jim, it's too static . . .' Interview with James Stewart, *The RKO Story*, BBC Television, 1987.

p.38: 'CROSBY IS INDULGING IN TOO MUCH REFLECTOR . . .' Telegram from Orson Welles to José Noriega, 30 October 1941.

p.38: 'RETAKE HEAD-ON CLOSE SHOT . . .' Telegram from Orson Welles to Norman Foster, 8 November 1941.

p.39: 'SENOR ORSON WELLES DEAR PATRON . . .' Telegram from Norman Foster to Orson Welles, 9 November 1941.

p.39: 'Several times we were afraid . . .' Telegram from Norman Foster to Orson Welles, 2 December 1941.

p.39: 'how really and truly important and beautiful . . .' Telegram from Orson Welles to Norman Foster, 10 December 1941.

p.39: 'the greatest tour-de-force of

my career . . .' Barbara Leaming, *Orson Welles*.

p.40: 'Orson must have overheard . . .' *Sources of Light*.

p.40: 'while poor Tim Holt . . .' Interview with Agnes Moorehead, *Kurtain Kall*, 1 July 1973.

p.41: 'AGNES MOORHEAD DOES . . .' Telegram from George Schaefer to Orson Welles, 3 December 1941.

p.41: 'hastened to thank you . . .' Memorandum from Joe Breen to Orson Welles, 2 December 1941.

p.41: 'This film will be one of the outstanding pictures . . .' Memorandum from Phil Reismann to Orson Welles, 2 December 1941.

p.41: 'It is extraordinarily dramatic and beautiful to look at . . .' Letter from Herb Drake to Arnold Weissberger, 5 December 1941.

CHAPTER THREE
The Best Man in Hollywood

p.43: 'an imperialistic war for world markets . . .' FBI report, 16 April 1943.

p.45: 'the eager beaver to end all eager beavers . . .' Quoted in Culver and Hyde, *American Dreamer*.

p.45: 'Rockefeller may also . . .' Frank Brady, *Citizen Welles*.

p.45: 'They [the Brazilians] feel . . .' Letter from Phil Reismann to Joseph Breen, 11 December 1941.

p.46: 'Here is sensational news . . .' *A Noite*, 12 December 1941.

p.46: 'GIVE ASSURANCES TO ALL CONCERNED . . .' Telegram from Norman Foster to José Noriega, 24 December 1941.

p.47: 'That is good publicity for the school . . .' Letter from Richard Wilson to Roger Hill, 17 December 1941.

p.47: 'PLEASE SHUT UP FOR A FEW DAYS . . .' Telegram from Roger Hill to Orson Welles, 20 December 1941.

p.47: 'Everybody talks about it . . .' Letter from Roger Hill to Orson Welles, 23 December 1941.

p.47: 'It is probably difficult for you to realise . . .' Letter from Ellen Cole Fetter to Orson Welles, 16 December 1941.

p.48: . . . 'this goes to you as an expression of our government's . . .' Letter from George Schaefer to Orson Welles, 22 December 1941 (drafted by Joseph Breen).

p.48: 'there should be nothing sex-suggestive in the line . . .' Memorandum from Hays Office to RKO, 8 January 1942.

p.48: 'For your information and guidance . . .' Memorandum from William Gordon to Norman Foster, 3 January 1942.

p.49: 'There was a Mercury style of acting . . .' Peter Bogdanovich, *This is Orson Welles*.

p.51: 'I'm pretty awful in it . . .' ibid.

p.52: 'whoever was nearest the camera . . .' ibid.

p.53: 'Who's he?' Minute of meeting at RKO, 12 January 1942.

p.54: 'These *jangadeiros* are almost legendary figures . . .' OI-AA Memorandum to John Hay Whitney, 19 January 1941.

CHAPTER FOUR
Carnival

p.57: 'He has left the country furious with yours truly . . .' Letter from Herb Drake to Tom Pettey, 4 February 1942.

p.57: 'colder than a producer's heart . . .' Letter from Tom Pettey to Herb Drake, 22 January 1942.

p.58: 'The first thing on arrival . . .' Letter from Lynn Shores to Walter Daniels, 3 February 1942.

p.58: 'would like for Orson Welles to film some of the daring exploits . . .' Press Release by Tom Pettey, 29 January 1942.

p.59: 'I'll go nuts with another inactive week . . .' Letter from Ned Scott to Herb Drake, 7 February 1942.

p.59: 'We were on our own . . .' Joe Biroc interviewed in The RKO Story, BBC Television, 1987.

p.59: 'BECAUSE OF THE ENORMOUS AMOUNT OF WORK . . .' Telegram from Orson Welles to Jack Moss, 6 March 1942.

p.60: 'RECEPTION OF ORSON WELLES . . .' Telegram from Phil Reismann to George Schaefer, 12 February 1942.

p.60: 'this enormously sympathetic big boy . . .' A Noite, 11 February 1942.

p.60: 'The moment the Producer-Director-Writer arrived . . .' Press Release by Herb Drake, 12 February 1942.

p.61: 'Welles and Phil Reismann . . .' Memorandum from Tom Pettey to Herb Drake, 17 February 1942.

p.61: 'It must be remembered . . .' Memorandum from Orson Welles to RKO front office, 25 May 1942.

p.62: 'The human element in particular . . .' ibid.

p.63: 'Carnival isn't a religious observance . . .' Orson Welles Alamanac, 4 November 1944.

p.64: 'for 1942 the order is FORGET THE WAR!' Life, 18 March 1942.

p.65: 'a director of the movie production . . .' Press release by Tom Pettey, 18 February 1942.

p.66: 'a combination of crinolines . . .' Life, op. cit.

p.66: 'I am enclosing a sort of day-to-day report . . .' Letter from Lynn Shores to Walter Daniels, 16 February 1942.

p.67: 'The problem of shooting carnival . . .' Memorandum from Orson Welles to RKO front office, op. cit.

p.68: 'What made carnival what it was? . . .' Letter from Orson Welles to Bob Meltzer, 23 June 1942.

p.69: 'he was like a lighthouse . . .' Interview with Geraldine Fitzgerald, quoted in The Road to Xanadu.

p.69: 'The humiliated, the timid, the unsatisfied . . .' Rui Costa in research document, n.d.

p.75: 'ideas he might wish to look into . . .' Tom Pettey to Herb Drake, 22 February 1942.

p.76: 'no other personality from the United States . . .' A Noite, 23 February 1942.

p.76: 'We're working too hard down here . . .' Letter from Orson Welles to George Schaefer, 25 February 1942.

p.76: 'You may have heard . . .'

Letter from Orson Welles to John Hay Whitney, 25 February 1942.

p.76: 'positively Brazilian . . .' Letter from Phil Reismann to John Hay Whitney, 25 February 1942.

p.77: 'PLEASE ORSON . . .' Telegram from George Schaefer to Orson Welles, 27 February 1942.

CHAPTER FIVE
Only Orson and God

p.78: 'GET IN NORMAN JO DOLORES . . .' Telegram from Orson Welles to Jack Moss, 28 February 1942.

p.78: 'RESULTANT INTERNATIONAL PUBLICITY . . .' Telegram from Orson Welles to George Schaefer 2 March 1942.

p.79: 'With respect to Orson Welles . . .' Memorandum from Charles Koerner, 12 March 1942.

p.79: 'EVERYTHING HERE PROCEED-ING BEAUTIFULLY . . .' Telegram from Orson Welles to George Schaefer, op. cit.

p.79: 'AS FAVOR TO ME . . .' ibid.

p.79: 'I have a lot of things on my mind . . .' Letter from Lynn Shores to Walter Daniels, 9 March 1942.

p.80: 'everyone . . . will forget about us . . .' Letter from Tom Pettey to Herb Drake, 3 March 1942.

p.80: 'The glimpse into the future . . .' Press release by Tom Pettey, 4 March 1942.

p.81: 'a night of relaxation . . .' Letter from Tom Pettey to Herb Drake, op. cit.

p.81: 'I believe Welles's intentions . . .' Letter from Lynn Shores to Walter Daniels, 3 March 1942.

p.82: 'MOST IMPORTANT THIS BE THOROUGHLY UNDERSTOOD . . .' Telegram from George Schaefer to Phil Reismann, 4 March 1942.

p.82: 'It is all very grand and exciting . . .' Letter from Lynn Shores to Walter Daniels, op. cit.

p.82: 'The weather remains cloudy . . .' Letter from Tom Pettey to Herb Drake, 10 March 1942.

p.83: 'LOST JUNGLES . . .' Telegram from Tom Pettey to Herb Drake, 11 March 1942.

p.83: 'MOST COLORFUL ADVEN-TUROUS . . .' ibid.

p.84: 'Beautiful shots Rio . . .' Memorandum dictated by Orson Welles, 11 March 1942.

p.84: 'THAT THERE IS NOTHING IN THE WORLD I WON'T DO . . .' Telegram from Orson Welles to Phil Reismann, 15 March 1942.

p.84: 'THAT HE IS NOT TO MAKE ANY PICTURE . . .' Telegram from Phil Reismann to George Schaefer, op. cit.

p.85: 'Line up translators . . .' Memorandum from Orson Welles to Richard Wilson, 14 March 1942.

p.85: 'SURE YOU REALISE IMPOR-TANCE . . .' Telegram from George Schaefer to Orson Welles, 16 March 1942.

p.85: 'EAGER HEAR REACTIONS . . .' Telegram from Orson Welles to George Schaefer, 18 March 1942.

CHAPTER SIX
Pomona

p.86: 'PROBABLY EASTERN EXECUTIVES . . .' Telegram from Robert Wise to Orson Welles, 16 March 1942.

p.86: 'He ordered me to prepare picture . . .' ibid.

p.87: 'It should be shelved . . .' Report cards from Pomona showing 17 March 1942.

p.88: 'Much better than *Citizen Kane* . . .' Report cards from Pasadena showing ibid.

p.88: 'I did not want to cable you . . .' Letter from George Schaefer to Orson Welles, 21 March 1942.

p.89: 'UNSATISFACTORY REACTION . . .' Telegram from Jack Moss to Orson Welles, 23 March 1942.

p.89: 'You asked for a more detailed report . . .' Letter from Robert Wise to Orson Welles, 31 March 1942.

p.90: 'doubtless the most faithful adaptation any book . . .' Letter from Joseph Cotten to Orson Welles, 28 March 1942.

p.91: 'SURE I MUST BE AT LEAST PARTLY WRONG . . .' Telegram from Orson Welles to Jack Moss, 25 March 1942.

p.91: 'It is a lazy land and I'm afraid . . .' Letter from Tom Pettey to Herb Drake, 20 March 1942.

p.92: 'Once a year in December . . .' Letter from Lynn Shores to Walter Daniels, 21 March 1942.

p.92: 'We still haven't done any of the script stuff . . .' Letter from Tom Pettey to Herb Drake, 31 March 1942.

p.93: 'no assurance that our trek . . .' Memorandum from Walter Daniels to Reg Armour, 24 March 1942.

p.93: 'Just why I cannot seem to find out . . .' Letter from Lynn Shores to Walter Daniels, 28 March 1942.

p.93: 'it looks like Orson is going to make . . .' Letter from Tom Pettey to Herb Drake, op. cit.

p.93: 'BE SURE AND LEAVE HIM A REASONABLE . . .' Telegram from Phil Reismann to Orson Welles, 28 March 1942.

p.94: 'TELL JACK IT'S MORE IMPORTANT . . .' Telegram from Orson Welles to Norman Foster, 31 March 1942.

p.94: 'ALL EXPECTATIONS SURPASSED . . .' Telegram from Orson Welles to Phil Reismann, 30 March 1942.

p.94: 'I WANT YOU TO BELIEVE THAT I AM PERSONALLY ON THE HOOK . . .' Telegram from George Schaefer to Orson Welles, 31 March 1942.

p.94: 'he neither wished to go to jail . . .' Letter from Richard Wilson to Orson Welles, 9 April 1942.

p.94: 'THESE COMMITMENTS VALID . . .' Telegram from Orson Welles to George Schaefer, 12 April 1942.

p.94: 'On the Lynn Shores matter . . .' Memorandum from Richard Wilson to RKO front office, 27 April 1942.

p.95: 'the negro and low class element . . .' Letter from Lynn Shores to Alberto Pessao, 11 April 1942.

p.95: 'Mr Welles knows what to do with his own picture . . .' Memorandum from Richard Wilson to Orson Welles 14 April 1942.

p.96: 'CARIOCA CARNIVAL IS GOING TO BE VERY DARK . . .' *A Noite*, 2 April 1942.

p.102: 'Fact and fiction are served forth in unusual combination . . .' Memorandum from Mercury group to RKO front office, 28 May 1942.

CHAPTER SEVEN
Turning a Bad Koerner

p.104: 'a 100% natural . . .' Letter from Herb Drake to Orson Welles, 5 March 1942.

p.104: 'THERE ISN'T A BETTER DIRECTOR ON EARTH . . .' Telegram from Orson Welles to Norman Foster, 13 March 1942.

p.104: 'COMPLETELY AGREE WITH CABLED . . .' Telegram from Norman Foster to Orson Welles, 14 March 1942.

p.104: 'Everything I have seen of *Journey into Fear* . . .' Letter from Orson Welles to Joseph Cotten, 4 April 1942.

p.104: 'The dialogue, you will immediately note . . .' Letter from Orson Welles to Norman Foster, 4 April 1942.

p.105: 'THEY LOVED EVERYBODY . . .' Telegram from Jack Moss to Orson Welles, 18 April 1942.

p.105: 'Jo to turn into Dick Tracey . . .' Letter from Norman Foster to Orson Welles, 21 April 1942.

p.105: 'I can't be very intelligent about *Journey* . . .' Letter from Orson Welles to Norman Foster, 3 May 1942.

p.106: 'I love you, more than I even realised . . .' Letter from Norman Foster to Orson Welles, 21 April 1942.

p.106: 'At dinner tonight I complained . . .' Letter from Orson Welles to Norman Foster, 3 May 1942.

p.106: 'I think constantly of being with you . . .' Letter to Orson Welles from John Berry, 30 April 1942.

p.106: 'NEVER REALISED I WOULD MISS ANY MALE COMPANION . . .' Telegram from Phil Reismann to Orson Welles, 28 March 1942.

p.107: 'We have now finally decided . . .' Memorandum from Reg Armour to Jack Moss, 24 April 1942.

p.107: 'HAVE VERY SWELL NEW FAST CHEAP JOURNEY FINISH.' Telegram from Orson Welles to Jack Moss, 31 May 1942.

p.108: 'Did you find [Welles] easy to get on with? . . .' Quoted in Stephen Smith, *A Fire at Heart's Center*.

p.109: 'Use *Toujours ou jamais* as directed . . .' Memorandum from Orson Welles to Constantin Bakaleinikoff, quoted in ibid.

p.110: 'absence of melody . . .' Kathryn Kalinak, 'Text of Music: *The Magnificent Ambersons*', *Cinema Journal*, Summer 1988.

p.111: 'Am convinced . . . in view of man's temperament . . .' Memorandum from Gordon Youngman, 23 June 1942.

CHAPTER EIGHT
Four Men on a Raft

p.113: 'Each time the robust and handsome fiancé . . .' *Rio Cine-Radio Jornal*, 20 May 1942.

p.114: 'rehearsal: shooting Urca . . .' Activities report, 5 May 1942

p.114: 'our period of wholehearted co-operation was over . . .' Report by Richard Wilson to Orson Welles, 12 April 1942.

p.114: 'No threats, bribes, or payments . . .' ibid.

p.115: 'I HAVE NEVER READ ANYTHING . . .' Telegram from Phil Reismann to Orson Welles, 27 April 1942.

p.115: 'PR: [Welles] is a tough baby . . .' Minutes of conversation, 27 April 1942.

p.116: 'Here I am in New York . . .' Letter from George Schaefer to Orson Welles, 29 April 1942, delivered personally by Phil Reismann on arrival, 8 May 1942.

p.117: 'Did you get my birthday cable? . . .' Letter from Maurice Bernstein to Orson Welles, 14 May 1942.

p.119: 'A three-fold attack . . .' Letter from Arnold Weissberger to Orson Welles, 14 May 1942.

p.120: 'OUT OF FILM . . .' Telegram from Lynn Shores to Walter Daniels, 15 May 1942.

p.121: 'LEADING BRAZIL RAFTMAN DIES . . .' New York Times, 20 May 1942.

p.121: 'They got drunk with the fame . . .' Aino Da Noite, 20 May 1942.

p.121: 'WHAT AMOUNT WE COVERED IN STATES . . .' Telegram from Lynn Shores to Walter Daniels, 19 May 1942.

pp.121–2: 'working like a dog . . .' Letter from Phil Reismann to George Schaefer, 25 May 1942.

p.122: 'he still stays awake nights . . .' Letter from Lynn Shores to Walter Daniels, 5 June 1942.

p.122: 'but it all gets back to the main difficulty . . .' Letter from Phil Reismann to George Schaefer, op. cit.

p.122: 'Best wishes for a merry Xmas . . .' Letter from Lynn Shores to Walter Daniels, 5 June 1942.

p.122: 'You have got to come home the right way . . .' Letter from Herb Drake to Orson Welles, 1 June 1942.

p.123: 'FACT IS THAT ORSON IS DOING . . .' Telegram from Berent Friele to Phil Reismann, 21 April 1942.

p.123: 'as can be seen, it is already . . .' Report from Brazil division of OI-AA, 27 May 1942.

p.123: 'About a year ago . . .' Letter from Herb Drake to George Schaefer, 2 June 1942.

p.124: 'we will eliminate . . .' Memorandum from Charles Koerner to George Schaefer, 1 June 1942.

p.124: 'in a form not approved . . .' Memorandum from Reg Armour to Ross Hastings, 1 June 1942.

p.124: 'No notice is necessary . . .' ibid.

p.125: 'I AM ENTITLED TO BETTER . . .' Telegram from Jack Moss to George Schaefer, 3 June 1942.

p.125: 'PLEASE TRY TO FIND IT IN SCHAEFER'S . . .' Telegram from Gordon Youngman to Ned Depinet, 17 June 1942.

p.125: 'Wise tells me that this will in no way . . .' Letter from Charles Koerner to George Schaefer, 3 June 1942.

p.125: 'I think it is important . . .' Memorandum from George Schaefer to Reg Armour, 16 June 1942.

p.125: 'The natural conclusion can only be . . .' Letter from Jack Moss to Charles Koerner, 15 June 1942.

p.126: 'Dear Jack, Believe me . . .' Letter from Charles Koerner to Jack Moss, 16 June 1942.

p.126: 'The editing and the cutting of the picture . . .' Letter from Joseph Cotten to Charles Koerner, 19 June 1942.

p.128: 'the moment Schaefer's resignation was received it was accepted . . .' Louella Parsons, 2 July 1942, quoted in Betty Lasky, *RKO: The Biggest Little Major of Them All.*

p.128: 'what is necessary to terminate further operations by Mercury Productions . . .' Memorandum from Ross Hastings to Charles Koerner, 27 June 1942.

p.128: 'the Mercury files, a mimeograph machine . . .' *New York Times*, 12 July 1942.

p.128: 'I agree with Phil . . .' Memorandum from Charles Koerner, 1 July 1942.

p.129: 'GRANDE OTELO: He is a natural . . .' Memorandum from Robert Meltzer, 1 June 1942.

CHAPTER NINE
Look Who's Laughing

p.130: 'WELLES GROUP LEFT NORTH OKAY . . .' Telegram from Lynn Shores to Phil Reismann, 16 June 1942.

p.130: 'ORSON WELLES ANGRY . . .' *A Noite*, 16 June 1942.

p.130: 'And he threw a small coffee table . . .' Peter Bogdanovich, *This is Orson Welles.*

p.131: 'SHORES AGAIN SERIOUSLY SABOTAGING . . .' Telegram from Orson Welles to Phil Reismann, 25 June 1942.

p.131: 'ABSOLUTELY NO MORE MONEY . . .' Telegram from Phil Reismann to Orson Welles, 26 June 1942.

p.131: 'SHORES NOW SUCCEEDED GETTING PROCESS . . .' Telegram from Orson Welles to Phil Reismann, 26 June 1942.

p.131: 'The office is haunted daily . . .' Letter from Lynn Shores to Reg Armour, 26 June 1942.

p.132: '70% of them were very happy . . .' ibid.

p.132: 'Orson is making this picture . . .' Frank Daugherty, *Christian Science Monitor*, 26 June 1942.

p.133: 'I'm a total chameleon . . .' Unpublished interview with Kathleen Tynan, 12 February 1983.

p.134: 'he spoke to Fanto . . .' Interview by the author with George Fanto, July 1988.

p.134: 'he taught me everything I know about framing.' Interview by the author with Chico Albuquerque, February 2002.

p.135: 'the Co-ordinator's office told me . . .' Letter from Lynn Shores to Walter Daniels, 11 July 1942.

p.135: 'PROMPT ACTION NECESSARY . . .' Telegram from Lynn Shores to Phil Reismann, 14 July 1942.

p.136: 'any act done by Mr Welles . . .' *Aviso*, 20 July 1942.

p.136: 'Shores and gang . . .' Letter from George Fanto to Richard Wilson, 29 July 1942.

p.136: The project was 'hazed . . .' Letter from Ray Joseph to unknown correspondent, 5 August 1942.

p.137: 'the movie that Welles, the

incredible . . .' *Daily News*, 2 July 1942.

p.137: 'a marvellous three-week trip . . .' Peter Bogdanovich, op. cit.

p.138: 'A spanking is an inspiriting thing . . .' *Time*, 20 July 1942.

p.138: 'Welles has a picture that's distinctly not attuned . . .' Bosley Crowther, *New York Times*, 1 July 1942.

p.139: 'packed with cinematic power . . .' *Herald Tribune*, 14 August 1942.

p.139: 'In a world brimful of . . .' Thomas M. Pryor, *New York Times*, 14 August 1942.

p.139: 'TIME THE MAGNIFICENT . . .' Telegram from Jack Moss to Orson Welles, 18 July 1942.

p.139: '*The Magnificent Ambersons* is a magnificent movie . . .' *Time*, 20 July 1942.

p.140: 'WELLES VERSUS HOLLYWOOD AGAIN.' *New York Times*, 12 July 1942.

p.140: 'ROLLING UP FROM RIO.' Theodore Strauss, *New York Times*, 30 August 1942.

p.141: 'That was the end of the film . . .' Peter Bogdanovich, op. cit.

p.141: 'If RKO does not wish to continue . . .' Statement from Office of Inter-American Affairs, 1 September 1942.

p.142: 'It is my studied opinion . . .' Memorandum from William Gordon, 2 July 1942.

p.142: 'it is my definite feeling . . .' Letter from Orson Welles to Nelson Rockefeller, 20 October 1942.

p.142: 'I naturally hesitate . . .' Letter from Nelson Rockefeller to Orson Welles, 10 November 1942.

p.143: 'Nelson Rockefeller's definition . . .' Henry Wallace, quoted in Culver and Hyde, *American Dreamer*.

p.143: 'If on your own responsibility . . .' Letter from Peter Rathvon to Orson Welles, 12 November 1942.

p.143: 'Homeric proportions.' Letter from Orson Welles to Ferdinand Pinto, 26 March 1943.

p.143: 'He's ready to leave elaborate . . .' From treatment for *It's All True* material, 2 September 1943.

p.145: 'Possibly this outline can . . .' Memorandum from William Gordon to Charles Koerner, 10 September 1943.

p.147: 'I have a degree of faith in it . . .' Letter from Orson Welles to Ferdinand Pinto, op. cit.

p.148: 'now agrees . . .' Anonymous memorandum to Charles Koerner, 10 December 1942.

p.148: 'I believe that probably the greatest attribute . . .' Memorandum from Charles Koerner to Peter Rathvon, 30 June 1942.

p.148: 'This new set-up . . .' *Hollywood Reporter*, 4 June 1942.

p.149: 'Welles was offering Americans . . .' Betty Lasky, *RKO: The Biggest Little Major of Them All*.

p.150: 'Although *The Magnificent Ambersons* . . .' Theodore Strauss, 'The Return of the Hero', *New York Times*, 16 August 1942.

p.150: 'before it was common to be so . . .' David Kamp, 'Magnificent Obsession', *Vanity Fair*, 1 February 19?.

CHAPTER TEN
Ceiling Unlimited

p.156: 'You probably heard from my secretary . . .' Letter from William S. Paley to Orson Welles, 15 October 1942.

p.157: 'The radio is realising its potency as an educator . . .'. Speech given by Orson Welles, 6 March 1943.

p.157: 'I didn't know until Jack told me . . .' Letter from Arthur Miller to Orson Welles, 18 October 1942.

p.157: 'then genius won.' Newsweek, 9 November 1942.

p.158: 'all Welles and a yard wide.' ibid.

p.159: 'The best good-will propaganda . . .' Letter from Orson Welles to Nelson Rockefeller, 20 October 1942.

p.159: 'Orson is working harder . . .' Letter from Jack Moss to J. Hillpot, 15 December 1942.

p.159: 'I would like to say . . .' Letter from Jackson Leighter to Orson Welles, 11 January 1943.

pp.159–60: 'One first hears the rhythmic beat of jungle drums . . .' Bret Wood, Orson Welles: A Bio-Bibliography.

p.160: 'NATURALLY WE ARE UPSET . . .' Telegram from J. Hillpot to Orson Welles, 11 March 1943.

p.160: 'You will go to Hollywood . . .' Letter from Peter Rathvon to Orson Welles, 19 October 1942.

p.161: 'WE BELIEVE YOUR REVISED . . .' Telegram from Al Galston to Orson Welles, 3 September 1942.

p.162: 'if we do in motion pictures . . .' Memorandum from David O. Selznick to Alfred Hitchcock, 12 December 1938.

p.163: 'he must not deviate . . .' Letter from Loyd Wright to Jack Moss, 24 December 1942.

p.163: 'I should like also to urge you . . .' Memorandum from David O. Selznick to William E. Goetz, 10 December 1942.

p.164: 'general disbelief . . .' Letter from David O. Selznick to Joe Schenk, 15 July 1943.

p.168: 'the worst accorded to an American actor since . . .' Letter from Orson Welles to Robert Stevenson, 10 May 1944.

p.168: 'certain over-emphases . . .' Hollywood Reporter, 2 February 1944.

p.168: 'declamatory delivery'. Variety, 2 February 1944.

p.168: 'road-operatic sculpturings . . .' James Agee, Nation, February 1944.

p.169: 'There are about eight or nine . . .' Los Angeles Daily News, 15 February 1943.

p.169: 'This may be the last time I write a column . . .' New York Post, 10 February 1943.

p.171: 'Quiet on the set!' Jack Benny Show, 14 March 1943.

p.172: 'NOW THAT YOU HAVE QUALIFIED . . .' Telegram from William S. Paley to Orson Welles, 16 March 1943.

p.172: 'I know that you agree . . .' Letter from Orson Welles to Davidson Taylor, 21 September 1943.

p.172: 'You may not know the difficulties it caused.' Letter from Davidson Taylor to Orson Welles, 24 September 1943.

p.172: 'Mr Bryson and I are not

strangers . . .' Letter from Orson Welles to Davidson Taylor, 28 September 1943.

p.173: 'We cannot with much hope . . .' Letter from Lyman Bryson to Orson Welles, 5 October 1943.

p.173: 'I am sorry to have been advertised as a speaker . . .' Speech by Orson Welles, 16 October 1942.

p.174: 'All educators, whether they like it or not . . .' Speech by Orson Welles to Adult Education Conference, Los Angeles, 5 February 1943.

p.174: 'We admired tremendously your broad views . . .' Letter from Yvonne Ramus, 7 March 1943.

p.175: 'stage and screen performers . . .' Letter from Orson Welles to Helen Bryan, 25 September 1943.

p.175: 'My part in this free meeting . . .' Speech by Orson Welles, 11 September 1943.

p.176: 'that it was one . . .' Letter from Muriel Miller to Orson Welles, 11 September 1943.

p.176: 'You were confronted . . .' Letter from Charles W. Ward to Orson Welles, 13 September 1943.

p.176: 'you're a red-hot potato . . .' ibid.

p.176: 'liberal and courageous remarks . . .' Letter from an officer of the Packinghouse Workers to Orson Welles, 12 September 1943.

p.176: 'I'd give anything to know . . .' Letter from Polly of the United Automobile Aircraft and Agricultural Implement Workers to Orson Welles, 15 September 1943.

p.177: 'PLAIN TALK BY THE MAN FROM MARS . . .' *Trade Union Press*, n.d.

p.177: 'The armies of our united . . .' Speech by Orson Welles at Overseas Press Club, 2 November 1943.

p.177: 'the debt our theatre . . .' Memorandum by Orson Welles, 3 November 1943, outlining his forthcoming speech at Soviet-American Congress.

p.178: 'he speaks for his nation to all the nations . . .' Speech by Orson Welles to Soviet-American Congress, 8 November 1943.

p.179: '"Elsa," Welles told . . .' 'Lesson in Morals', Elsa Maxwell Column, *New York Post*, 7 November 1943.

p.179: 'I thought I was going to be . . .' Unpublished interview with Kathleen Tynan, 12 February 1983.

CHAPTER ELEVEN
It All Comes Out of the
Tent of Wonder

p.180: 'America must undertake now . . .' Henry Luce, *Time*, 17 February 1941.

p.181: 'This is a fight between a slave world . . .' Speech by Henry Wallace, 8 May 1942.

p.185: 'Despite being a political dictatorship . . .' Louis Dolivet, 'Shaping Tomorrow's World', *Free World*, 1946.

p.186: 'The Good Neighbor policy . . .' Orson Welles editorial, 'Good Neighbor Policy reconsidered', *Free World*, March 1944.

p.187: 'Very probably . . .' Orson

Welles, 'The Unknown Soldier', *Free World*, October 1944.

p.188: '"I got a tip," he said . . .' *Los Angeles Times*, 7 May 1943.

p.188: 'the fool who makes a deliberate choice . . .' Letter from Orson Welles to Robert Stevenson, 10 May 1944.

p.190: 'WOULD LIKE START WORK . . .' Telegram from Orson Welles to Alexander Korda, 26 June 1943.

p.190: 'personally, I am up to my neck . . .' Letter from Sergei Mihailovich Eisenstein to Alexander Korda, 3 October 1943.

p.192: 'the slightest noise . . .' Orson Welles introduction to *Magic* by Bruce Elliot.

p.193: 'with my lousy presentation . . .' Letter from Richard Himber to Orson Welles, 14 January 1942.

p.194: 'It's taken me a lot longer . . .' Orson Welles publicity blurb, August 1943.

p.194: 'The tent . . .' *Collier's Magazine*, August 1943.

p.195: 'a bewildered, slightly bitter expression . . .' *Vogue*, October 1943.

p.197: 'Miss Hayworth also works . . .' *Hollywood Reporter* 5 August 1943.

pp.198–9: 'The case of Orson Welles . . .' ibid.

p.198: 'and the harrowing and beautiful experience in Brazil . . .' *Collier's Magazine*, op. cit.

p.200: 'AS YOU KNOW I HAVE BEEN . . .' Telegram from Orson Welles to Alexander Korda, 10 March 1944.

CHAPTER TWELVE
Unrehearsed Realities

p.202: 'February 2nd is Ground Hog day . . .' Letter from Orson Welles to the show's writers, 28 January 1944.

p.202: 'You say that people . . .' Letter from Orson Welles to Bob Presnell, 18 February 1944.

p.203: 'YOU ALSO HAVE TENDENCY . . .' Telegram from John McMillan to Bob Presnell, 4 March 1944.

p.204: 'rashly put into my hands . . .' Telegram from Orson Welles to John McMillan, 5 March 1944.

p.204: 'the main intention was comic . . .' Telegram from Orson Welles to Leonard Lyons, 1 March 1944.

p.204: 'That'll be all . . .' *Orson Welles Almanac*, 8 March 1944.

p.205: 'many of you listening . . .' *Orson Welles Almanac*, 15 March 1944.

p.206: 'relax and leave us be . . .' Letter from John McMillan to Orson Welles, 22 March 1944.

p.207: 'To renew or not renew?' Letter from Dick Compton to William Collier, 16 May 1944.

p.208: 'I am sure you will be very helpful . . .' Letter from Henry Morgenthau to Orson Welles, 16 May 1944.

p.208: 'WON'T YOU PLEASE WRITE AS A PRAYER OR A DEDICATION . . .' Telegram from Orson Welles to Carl Sandburg, 15 May 1944.

p.208: 'I WOULD LIKE MUSIC FOR THIS . . .' Telegram from Orson Welles to Bernard Herrmann, 20 May 1944.

p.208: 'DELIGHTED . . .' Telegram

from Bernard Herrmann to Orson Welles, 20 May 1944.

p.209: 'BE SURE TO KEEP TEXARKANA . . .' Telegram from Fred Smith to Orson Welles, 19 May 1944.

p.209: 'NOW HERE'S A JOB FOR YOU . . .' Telegram from Orson Welles to Fred Smith, 22 May 1944.

p.209: 'Today we talk of the sacrifices . . .' Letter from Orson Welles to Fred Smith, 22 May 1944.

p.210: 'I want you to know . . .' Letter from Henry Morgenthau to Orson Welles, 27 June 1944.

p.210: 'It was a business decision . . .' Letter from Dick Compton to Orson Welles, 12 June 1944.

p.210: 'repainting dressing room defaced by you'. NBC, 14 June 1944.

p.211: 'To the fighting armies . . .' Speech by Orson Welles to the Hollywood Free World Association, 6 July 1944.

p.211: 'WE FILMMAKERS REALISE . . .' Telegram from Orson Welles to Time, 12 February 1944.

p.212: 'I send you herewith . . .' Letter from Orson Welles to Hedda Hopper, 28 January 1944.

p.212: 'GENUS GENIUS . . .' Hedda Hopper, Photoplay, May 1944.

p.213: '"Henry Wallace," Welles said . . .' Speech by Orson Welles to Independent Voters' Committee for Arts and Sciences for Roosevelt, 21 September 1944.

p.214: 'There is something to thank God for . . .' Article by Orson Welles, 'American Leadership in '44', Free World, 30 July 1944.

p.215: '"they" would try to get . . .' Speech by Orson Welles to the Hollywood Democratic Association, 1 September 1944.

p.215: 'What happened to the men . . .' Speech by Orson Welles at Registration Week Luncheon, 10 October 1944.

p.216: 'This is Orson Welles speaking . . .' Broadcast speech for American Labor Party, WABC, 11 October 1944.

p.216: 'I cannot believe . . .' Speech by Orson Welles, Herald Tribune Forum: False Issues and the American Presidency, 18 October 1944.

p.217: 'They are both suffering from . . .' Letter from Maurice Bernstein to Food Rationing Board, 28 October 1944.

p.217: 'I HAVE JUST LEARNED . . .' Telegram from Franklin D. Roosevelt to Orson Welles, 23 October 1944.

p.217: 'Dear Mr President . . .' Letter from Orson Welles to Franklin D. Roosevelt, 25 October 1944.

p.217: 'At such a time as this . . .' Unused campaign speech by Orson Welles, 6 November 1944.

p.218: 'You can sell that . . .' PM Magazine, 22 October 1944.

p.219: 'I AM AFRAID I DON'T . . .' Telegram from Donald Ogden Stewart to Orson Welles, 18 May 1944.

p.219: 'It is precisely for this reason . . .' Speech by Orson Welles, Herald Tribune Forum, op. cit.

p.220: 'The racist and all the other liars . . .' Article by Orson Welles, 'Significance of the Election', Free World, November 1944.

p.220: 'Dear Mr Welles . . .' Letter

from Franklin D. Roosevelt to Orson Welles, 25 November 1944.

p.221: 'Dear Mr President . . .' Letter from Orson Welles to Franklin D. Roosevelt, 23 December 1944.

p.221: 'I know she can't help . . .' Telegram from Harry S. Truman to Orson Welles, 24 February 1945.

CHAPTER THIRTEEN
Actor Turns Columnist

p.224: 'a kind of licensed jester'. Unpublished interview with Kathleen Tynan, 12 February 1983.

p.225: 'as excited as hell'. Letter from Ted Thackrey to Jackson Leighter, 15 November 1944.

p.225: 'What is it that makes a man . . .' Leonard Lyons Column Guest, *New York Post*, 1 December 1944.

p.226: 'to fuss'. Letter from Orson Welles to Ted Thackrey, 7 December 1944.

p.226: 'ALMANAC VERY LUSTY . . .' Telegram from Ted Thackrey to Orson Welles, 13 December 1944.

p.226: 'It looks as if the administration . . .' Letter from Geneva Cranston to Orson Welles, n.d.

p.226: 'Our Astrology department . . .' *Orson Welles Almanac, New York Post*, 22 January 1945.

p.227: 'The sting of a bee . . .' ibid., 23 January 1945.

p.227: 'ACTOR TURNS COLUMNIST . . .' *Time*, 29 January 1945.

p.228: 'This column is so important . . .' *New Yorker*, 27 January 1945.

p.228: 'The editor of this *Almanac* . . .' *Orson Welles Almanac, New York Post*, 30 January 1945.

p.229: 'I visited our State Department . . .' ibid., 31 January 1945.

p.229: 'This war is not all destruction . . .' ibid., 1 March 1945.

p.230: 'The general was the finest . . .' ibid., 26 March 1945.

p.231: 'Bursting up out of the bloody crust . . .' ibid., 7 March 1945.

p.231: 'we loved the man this side of idolatry . . .' ibid., 1 February 1945.

p.232: 'the rest of his life was an anti-climax . . .', 15 February 1945.

p.232: 'Chaliapin used to hold me on his knee . . .' ibid.

p.232: 'The me-only boys . . .' ibid., 27 February 1945.

p.233: 'Every season for quite some time now . . .' ibid., 2 February 1945.

p.233: 'It isn't as slick as . . .' ibid., 25 January 1945.

p.234: 'If it was his plan . . .' ibid., 5 February 1945.

p.234: 'The villainous customs official . . .' ibid., 6 March 1945.

p.234: 'Mrs Pankhurst and her lady friends . . .' ibid., 2 March 1945.

p.234: 'Rub bacon fat . . .' ibid., 7 March 1945.

p.234: 'it should be sent in a plain wrapper . . .' ibid., 2 March 1945.

p.235: 'I know that Orson . . .' Memorandum from Robert Hall of *New York Post* Syndicate Department, 22 February 1945.

p.235: 'the fantastic Mars genius . . .' Letter from Geneva Cranston to Orson Welles, 14 February 1945.

p.235: 'People have heard . . .' Letter from Geneva Cranston to Orson Welles (undated).

p.235: 'Ghost writer . . . is a member . . .' FBI report, 25 April 1945.

p.236: 'Then, in a little bit of a giveaway . . .' Letter from Jackson Leighter to Ted Thackrey, 9 March 1945.

p.236: 'These German newspapers which live . . .' *Orson Welles Almanac, New York Post*, 8 March 1945.

p.237: 'I've read most of Noël's book . . .' *Orson Welles Today, New York Post* 10 April 1945.

p.238: 'Remember that there is no choice . . .' ibid., 3 April 1945.

p.238: 'there is no doubt that this leadership . . .' Article by Louis Dolivet, 'Shaping Tomorrow's World', *Treasury for the Free World*, Arco, 1945.

p.238: 'Personally it would make me most happy . . .' Telegram from Orson Welles to Franklin D. Roosevelt, 8 February 1945.

p.238: 'April will be . . .' Message from Franklin D. Roosevelt 3 March 1945.

p.239: '"This newsletter" he wrote . . .' Orson Welles in Free World daily paper, 6 June 1945.

p.239: 'The heaped-up dead . . .' *Orson Welles Today, New York Post*, 8 May 1945.

p.240: 'Mr Roosevelt isn't 29 years old . . .' Broadcast, January 1945.

p.241: 'No, not for a moment . . .' Unpublished interview with Kathleen Tynan, 12 February 1983.

p.241: 'Today another servant of the Lord . . .' CBS broadcast speech by Orson Welles, 12 April 1945.

p.242: 'Something is on its way from Georgia . . .' Speech by Orson Welles, 13 April 1945.

p.243: 'I am going to ask that you be as co-operative . . .' Letter from Wayne Tiss to Jackson Leighter, 15 March 1945.

p.243: '*my best* in every sense of the word . . .' Letter from Orson Welles to Arthur Pryor, 30 May 1945.

p.244: 'Editors did not expect . . .' Letter from Robert Hall to Orson Welles, 19 May 1945.

p.244: 'Frankly I haven't recovered from the shock . . .' Letter from Orson Welles to Robert Hall, 30 May 1945.

p.245: 'a young woman had leaped up . . .' *Orson Welles Today, New York Post*, 23 April 1945.

p.245: 'it's the darnedest thing . . .' ibid., 23 May 1945.

p.246: 'Jack Benny's black sidekick . . .' ibid., 4 June 1945.

p.247: 'in which you are a recognised authority'. Letter from Bob Hall to Orson Welles, 26 June 1945.

p.247: 'Without question, the daily task . . .' Letter from Ted Thackrey to Orson Welles, 5 July 1945.

p.248: 'For three weeks . . .' Letter from Orson Welles to Ted Thackrey, 31 July 1945.

p.249: 'HOW WAS LAST COLUMN? . . .' Telegram from Orson Welles to Ted Thackrey, 1 September 1945.

p.249: 'His Gorgeousness, the Bey

. . .' *Orson Welles Today, New York Post*, 9 September 1945.

p.250: 'Clifton's. A marvellous place . . .' ibid., 22 September 1945.

p.251: 'It's always "Labor trouble" . . .' ibid., 29 September 1945.

p.251: 'we're figuring on . . .' ibid., 9 October 1945.

p.251: 'We are the world's greatest production . . .' ibid., 19 March 1945.

CHAPTER FOURTEEN
An Occasional Soapbox

p.252: 'EITHER LATIN AMERICA . . .' Telegram from Louis Dolivet to Orson Welles, 1 October 1945.

p.252: 'FROM MARTIAN BROADCAST . . .' *Free World*, Special Peace Issue, 7 September 1945.

p.253: 'We know that for some ears even the word "action" . . .' Article by Orson Welles, ibid.

p.253: 'YOUR APPEARANCE WILL MAKE . . .' Telegram from Will Rogers to Orson Welles, 26 February 1944.

p.253: 'We are in complete sympathy with . . .' Letter from Ray Pierre to Orson Welles, 26 January 1945.

p.253: 'Mr Thomas Martin Wentworth . . .' *Glamour*, 3 March 1945.

p.254: 'on the contribution of the Negroes . . .' FBI report, 14 December 1944.

p.255: 'had your speech put into Braille . . .' Letter from Helen Keller to Orson Welles, 26 October 1944.

p.255: 'considerable evenings engaged . . .' FBI report, 9 April 1945.

p.257: '[an] expert blending of the humorous . . .' Letter from William Lear to Orson Welles, 19 November 1945.

p.257: 'commentary on affairs of national interest . . .' Contract for Lear programme, 16 July 1945.

p.257: '"Hello", he says . . .' *Orson Welles's Commentary*, 16 September 1945.

p.259: 'I'll bet it is an interesting experience . . .' Quoted in letter to Orson Welles from Kirk Tuttle of Kudner Agency, 21 September 1945.

p.259: 'Mr Welles brings his views . . .' *Orson Welles's Commentary*, 30 September 1945.

p.261: 'inasmuch as [he] felt that Carlson . . .' Peter Bogdanovich, *This is Orson Welles*.

CHAPTER FIFTEEN
The S. T. Ranger

p.265: 'its attempt to tie in . . .' Letter from Helen Straus to Jackson Leighter, 27 February 1945.

p.266: 'we should like to organise . . .' Letter from Iris Barry to Orson Welles, 9 May 1945.

p.277: 'Orson has genius but in this film . . .' Edward G. Robinson, *All My Yesterdays*.

p.277: 'Tell me, Orson . . .' Hedda Hopper, *Los Angeles Times*, 28 October 1945.

p.278: 'Our new President . . .' *Orson Welles Today, New York Post*, 18 April 1945.

p.279: 'some daredevil instructor . . .' ibid., 4 November 1945.

CHAPTER SIXTEEN
Full, Complete and
Unrestricted Authority

p.281: 'the crazy and unusual . . .'
Cole Porter quoted in William
O'Brien, *Cole Porter*.

p.283: 'His attitude is pleasant; his
remarks . . .' Bertolt Brecht,
Journals, 10 December 1945.

p.283: 'the more scared I become
. . .' Letter from Charles Laughton
to Alfred Lunt, early 1946, quoted
in James K. Lyon, *Bertolt Brecht
in America*.

p.283: 'Dear Charlie . . .' Letter
from Orson Welles to Charles
Laughton, undated, late
April/early May 1946.

p.284: 'I said to him one day . . .'
Peter Bogdanovich, *This is Orson
Welles*.

p.284: 'So you find my confidence
in my own charm . . .' Letter
from Orson Welles to Charles
Laughton, op. cit.

p.284: 'OUR CHOICE IS SIMPLE . . .'
Telegram from Orson Welles for
World Peace Rally, 1 November
1945.

p.285: 'Peace is possible without
appeasement . . .' Speech by
Orson Welles, 24 September
1946.

p.285: 'NATIONAL COMMITTEE TO
ABOLISH . . .' Telegram from
National Committee to Abolish
Poll Tax to Orson Welles, 16
January 1945.

p.285: 'CITY BEING VERY BACKWARD
NEEDS OUTSTANDING . . .'
Telegram from Brotherhood
Rally Committee to Orson
Welles, 26 January 1946.

p.286: 'IMPOSSIBLE TO CONSIDER . . .'
Telegram from Orson Welles to
Lloyd F. Saunders, 2 March 1946.

p.286: '"Dear Orson," wrote the
photographer . . .' Letter from
Brent Gallagher to Orson Welles,
30 January 1946.

p.287: 'I can't say it any better . . .'
Letter from Marc Blitzstein to
Orson Welles, 3 April 1946.

p.287: 'Laugh it off. / This little
thought . . .' Text of *The Airborne
Symphony* by Marc Blitzstein.

p.287: 'The scenery and mechanical effects . . .' Quoted in the
programme booklet for *Around
the World*.

p.289: 'and a maid to help the
maid'. From Arthur Margetson
'Orson and I' (unpublished
article).

p.290: 'I've decided I simply can't
afford you . . .' Mike Todd,
reported in 'The Nine Lives of
Mike Todd', *Herald Tribune*, 13
November 1958.

p.290: 'part of luck is a pet superstition . . .' ibid.

p.290: 'It became apparent . . .' ibid.

p.290: 'a Mercury offering . . .'
'Mercury Theatre Planning
Return', *New York Times*, 7
March 1946.

p.291: 'The theme of this picture is
sex in the raw . . .' Memorandum
from Harry Cohn, early 1946.

p.292: 'We are the prey of drunken
stage hands . . .' Letter from Cole
Porter to Sam Stark, 1 May 1946.

p.293: 'the Orson Welles genius
. . .' *Boston Daily Globe*, 29 April
1946.

p.294: 'A good theatrical plot . . .'
Eliot Norton, *Boston Post*, 29
April 1946.

p.294: 'Orson has been a tower of

strength . . .' Letter from Cole Porter to Sam Stark, op. cit.

p.295: 'in a fashion typical of his past . . .' *Boston Post*, op. cit.

p.296: 'a miniature extravaganza . . .' Eliot Norton, 'Second Thoughts of a First-Nighter', *Boston Daily Globe*, 6 May 1946.

p.296: 'This is the greatest thing . . .' Bertolt Brecht, quoted in James K. Lyon, *Bertolt Brecht in America*.

p.296: 'With your kind indulgence . . .' Arthur Margetson, op. cit.

p.298: '*Around the World* bears the eccentric . . .' *Philadelphia Daily News*, 15 May 1946.

p.298: 'The show has about everything in it . . .' Edwin Schloss, *Philadelphia Record*, 15 May 1946.

p.299: 'I never heard of a show . . .' Orson Welles interviewed by John Wilson, *PM*, 29 May 1946.

p.300: 'the dump of all dumps'. William Craxton quoted in Nicholas van Hoogstraten, *Lost Broadway Theatres*.

p.301: 'HOW WELLES'S "WORLD" GOES ROUND . . .' Murray Schumach, *New York Times*, 30 May 1946.

p.301: 'In hot weather . . .' *Fanfare*, quoted in *Lost Theatres of New York*.

CHAPTER SEVENTEEN
Wellesafloppin'

p.303: 'There is hardly a word . . .' Vernon Price, *New York Post*, 1 June 1946.

p.303: 'as amorphous as a splash of mud . . .' Irving Cahn, 1 June 1946.

p.303: 'only eighty days? you ask yourself . . .' Robert Garland, *New York Journal-American*, 1 June 1946.

p.303: '*Around the World* is Orson Welles . . .' *Time*, 4 June 1946.

p.304: 'When the guffawing Mr Welles . . .' Lewis Nichols, *New York Times*, 1 June 1946.

p.304: Orson in casting himself . . .' Radie Harris, *Variety*, 1 June 1946.

p.304: 'a fine musical cheese dream . . .' Wolcott Gibbs, *New Yorker*, 8 June 1946.

p.304: 'Out of the same mould as the British . . .' William Hawkins, *New York World-Telegram*, 1 June 1946.

p.304: 'These products of showmanship . . .' Lewis Nichols, op. cit.

p.304: 'I, on the other hand . . .' John Chapman, *Sunday News*, 9 June 1946.

p.305: '[the show] needs discipline . . .' Lewis Nichols, *New York Times*, 8 June 1946.

p.305: 'Mr Davison has been prodigal . . .' John Chapman, op. cit.

p.305: 'and as the world tour progresses . . .' ibid.

p.305: 'Cole Porter's tunes have a way . . .' ibid.

p.305: 'if God will forgive me . . .' Wolcott Gibbs, op. cit.

p.306: 'The production at the Adelphi . . .' John Chapman, op. cit.

p.306: 'the recent arrival of *Around the World* . . .' Lewis Nichols, *New York Times*, 8 June 1946.

p.306: 'There are mischievous rumours . . .' Wolcott Gibbs, op. cit.

p.306: 'Unless some means are found . . .' Burns Mantle, *Theatre Year Book*, 1946.

p.307: 'HATE TO KEEP HECKLING YOU . . .' Telegram from Orson Welles to Walter Winchell, 7 June 1946.

p.307: 'this wild-and-woolly wunderkind . . .' Billy Rose, *New York Times*, 10 June 1946.

p.308: 'Orson tells me that if necessary . . .' John Chapman, op. cit.

p.308: 'I was thrilled, entranced . . .' Elsa Maxwell, *New York Post*, 13 June 1946.

p.309: 'I think the theatre is suffering . . .' *Orson Welles's Commentary*, 15 June 1946.

p.311: 'your production is fresh, witty . . .' Letter from Joshua Logan to Orson Welles, 14 June 1946.

p.311: 'I have been to see the show . . .' Letter from Oliver Smith to Orson Welles, 25 June 1946.

p.312: 'that . . . altruistically minded . . .' Burns Mantle, op. cit.

p.314: 'YOU COULDN'T KILL HIM WITH A CLUB . . .' Robert Sylvester, *Sunday News*, 28 July 1946.

p.315: '4): am enclosing . . .' Memorandum from Lolita Herbert to Orson Welles, 26 July 1946.

p.316: 'would have been a big and substantial hit . . .' Letter from Richard Wilson to Charles Laughton, 25 July 1946.

p.316: 'directing *Galileo* is only half . . .' ibid.

p.317: 'I do not appreciate your habit . . .' Letter from Charles Laughton to Orson Welles, 26 July 1946.

p.318: 'It seems that Brecht is our man . . .' Letter from Charles Laughton to Alfred Lunt, early 1946, quoted in James K. Lyons, *Bertolt Brecht in America*.

p.321: 'YOUR TRAGIC NEWS ARRIVED THIS MORNING . . .' Telegram from Cole Porter to Orson Welles, 29 July 1946.

p.322: 'REGRET IMPOSSIBLE SECURE . . .' Telegram from Sir Charles Cochran to Orson Welles, 17 September 1946.

p.322: '"I thought," Dick Wilson wrote . . .' Letter from Richard Wilson to Morris Halpern of London Films, 20 August 1946.

p.322: 'The show flopped . . .' Stanley Kauffmann, *New Republic*, September 1985.

CHAPTER EIGHTEEN
Officer X

p.323: 'SOUTH CAROLINA COP . . .' *Daily Worker*, 13 July 1946.

p.325: 'My Dear Mr Welles . . .' Letter from Edna Fraser to Orson Welles, 13 July 1946.

p.325: 'Dear Mr Welles . . .' Letter from Mary Houston to Orson Welles, 12 August 1946.

p.327: 'hate-filled orgy . . .' Langston Hughes, *Fight for Freedom*.

p.327: 'the inevitable, inescapable . . .' Walter White, quoted in Oliver Harrington, *Why I left America*.

p.327: 'the bestial gouging out . . .' ibid.

p.327: 'At a time when our statesmen . . .' ibid.

p.328: 'It was on Friday night . . .' Letter from Orson Welles to

Congresswoman Helen Gahagan Douglas, 12 October 1946.

p.328: 'I, Issac Woodard . . .' Affidavit by Isaac Woodard, 23 April 1946.

p.329: 'Down South they think . . .' Speech by Isaac Woodard, 7 July 1946.

p.329: 'GET THAT COP! . . .' *Daily Worker*, 17 July 1946.

p.330: 'I, Isaac Woodard . . .' *Orson Welles's Commentary*, 28 July 1946.

p.333: '"Orson," Les Lear, his former sponsor . . .' Letter from Les Lear to Orson Welles, 29 July 1946.

p.333: 'as soon as your broadcast . . .' Letter from Al Laster to Orson Welles, 30 July 1946.

p.333: 'Yes, Mr Welles, you spoiled . . .' Letter from Sol Stein to Orson Welles, 28 July 1946.

p.333: 'A FORMER FAN . . .' Anonymous letter to Orson Welles, 30 July 1946.

p.333: 'Since your Sunday night broadcast . . .' Letter from Odell Weeks to Orson Welles, 30 July 1946.

p.334: 'some people feel that Mr Truman . . .' *Orson Welles's Commentary*, 4 August 1946.

p.336: 'Isaac Woodard is on the conscience of America . . .' Statement by Orson Welles read by Joe Louis, 18 August 1942.

p.337: 'HOSPITAL RECORDS AMAZINGLY BRIEF . . .' Telegram from NAACP to Orson Welles, 14 August 1946.

p.337: 'the actual celluloid driven out of the city . . .' *Orson Welles's Commentary*, 12 August 1946.

p.338: 'I grabbed it away from him . . .' Statement by Lynwood Shull 17 August 1942.

p.338: YOUR TRULY GREAT COMMENTARIES . . .' Telegram from Oliver Harrington to Orson Welles, 21 August 1946.

p.338: 'The crying need of the minorities . . .' Letter from Samuel Procter to Orson Welles, 25 August 1946.

p.338: 'it seems that I was fighting in the wrong place'. Anonymous letter to Orson Welles, 25 August 1946.

p.338: 'Thousands of years ago . . .' Anonymous letter to Orson Welles, 20 August 1946.

p.338: 'Please don't come to Georgia . . .' Anonymous letter to Orson Welles, 12 August 1946.

p.338: 'COME OVER HERE . . .' Telegram from John Willingham to Orson Welles, 24 August 1946.

p.339: 'OUR NEWS DEPARTMENT . . .' Telegram from Adrian Samish to Orson Welles, 20 August 1946.

p.339: 'The place was Batesburg . . .' *Orson Welles's Commentary*, 18 August 1946.

p.340: 'a commercial spot . . .' Letter from Adrian Samish to Orson Welles, 2 October 1946.

p.340: 'I'm being sued for $2 million . . .' *Orson Welles's Commentary*, 25 August 1946.

p.341: 'ACTION OF JUSTICE DEPT . . .' Telegram from Oliver Harrington to Orson Welles, 27 September 1946.

p.341: 'You will all be disappointed . . .' Letter from Orson Welles to Helen Gahagan Douglas, 12 October 1946.

p.341: 'alarmed at the increased . . .'

J. Waties Waring, quoted in Tinsley E. Yarborough, *A Passion for Justice*.

p.342: 'We're told that we should . . .' *Orson Welles's Scrapbook*.

p.343: 'ORSON WELLES NEEDS HELP!' Advertisement taken out by Hollywood Independent Citizens Committee of The Arts, Sciences and Professions, 26 August 1946.

p.343: 'We, the People . . .' Anonymous letter to Orson Welles, 30 August 1946.

p.343: 'You mustn't quit – don't quit . . .' Anonymous letter to Orson Welles, 29 September 1946.

p.344: 'His Summer Theatre version . . .' *Mercury Summer Theatre of the Air*, 30 August 1946.

p.345: 'If Larry wishes to play Herod . . .' Letter from Richard Wilson to Alexander Korda, 11 September 1946.

p.345: 'Korda, asking for preliminary sketches . . .' Telegram from Alexander Korda to Orson Welles, 27 September 1946.

p.345: 'No, wired back Welles . . .' Telegram from Orson Welles to Alexander Korda, 28 September 1946.

p.345: 'COMPLETELY HEART-BROKEN.' ibid.

p.345: 'We regret having to report . . .' Letter from Joseph Breen, 4 September 1946.

p.346: 'MY TIME IS GETTING SHORT . . .' Telegram from Alexander Korda to Orson Welles, op. cit.

CHAPTER NINETEEN
If I Die Before I Wake

p.347: 'May I direct your attention . . .' Letter from Nichols and Phillips to Orson Welles, 13 September 1946.

p.348: 'I have written to Orson . . .' Letter from Ted Thackrey to Richard Wilson, 26 December 1946.

p.348: 'as the audience is caught in the grip . . .' Hermine Rich Isaacs, *Theatre Arts*, June 1946.

p.349: '"Dear Bill," he wrote to Castle . . .' Letter from Orson Welles to William Castle, n.d., quoted in *Step Right Up!*.

p.356: 'Glennie darling, get on the next . . .' ibid.

p.358: 'Orson, an insomniac . . .' William Castle, *Step Right Up!*.

p.358: 'Flynn joked, cajoled, needled . . .' Memorandum by Richard Wilson, n.d., from internal evidence, c. November 1946.

p.359: 'there's too much stalling . . .' Interview with Orson Welles by Thomas A. Brady, *New York Times*, 8 December 1946.

p.361: 'we have nothing to fear but Fier himself'. Barbara Leaming, *Orson Welles*.

p.361: 'something off-centre, queer, strange'. Memorandum from Orson Welles to Harry Cohn, n.d., mid-1947.

p.366: 'Rudolph [Maté] took a whole day . . .' Memorandum by Richard Wilson, op. cit.

p.366: 'I have a small public . . .' Interview with Orson Welles by Thomas A. Brady, op. cit.

p.377: 'According to Mary Pacios . . .' Mary Pacios, *Childhood Shadows*.

p.378: 'The Scar never fails . . .' Anonymous letter sent to Rita Hayworth, quoted in *If This was Happiness*.

CHAPTER TWENTY
The Forces of Darkness

p.382: 'RE POSSIBILITY OF YOUR APPEARING . . .' Telegram from Vinton Freedley 24 January 1947.

p.386: 'Shakespeare was very close to the origins . . .' Interview with Orson Welles by *Cahiers du Cinéma*.

p.389: 'the greatest thing that ever happened to Utah'. Press release 28 May 1947.

p.389: 'His sense of theatre . . .' Jeannette Nolan interviewed by François Thomas in 'Mésaventures d'un Bande Sonore'. *Positif*, July/August 1992.

p.390: 'last night's show was about as much . . .' Gladys Goodall, *Salt Lake Telegram*, 29 May 1947.

p.390: 'Shakespearian stand-by Macbeth . . .' *Variety*, 4 June 1947.

p.390: 'The Wellesian stage settings . . .' *New York Times*, 29 May 1947.

p.391: 'Jeanette Nolan "of the radio" . . .' ibid.

p.392: 'ANTA has completed a project . . .' Press release, 28 May 1947.

p.392: 'OUR APPRECIATION . . .' Telegram from Helen Hayes to Orson Welles, 28 May 1947.

p.392: 'offered an opportunity . . .' Programme note from Salt Lake City production.

p.393: 'Again I urge . . .' Memorandum from Orson Welles to Richard Wilson.

p.396: 'to "everyone" . . .' Peter Bogdanovich, *This is Orson Welles*.

p.399: 'RUN! Don't walk! Remember, this is . . .' Alan Napier quoted in Richard Maurice Hurst, *Republic Studios*.

p.399: 'One eye was on you . . .' Roddy MacDowall interviewed by the author, Los Angeles, June 1990.

p.400: 'The important thing to me . . .' Letter from Jerry Wald to Orson Welles, 14 July 1947.

p.400: 'From the human side . . .' Letter from Herbert J. Yates to Orson Welles, 18 July 1947.

CHAPTER TWENTY-ONE
The Welles of Onlyness

p.403: 'DEAR ORSON . . .' Telegram from Gregory Ratoff to Orson Welles, 8 September 1947.

p.403: 'BELIEVE ME AS YOUR FRIEND . . .' Telegram from Johnny Maschio to Orson Welles, 15 September 1947.

p.403: 'You will readily see . . .' Letter from Michael Curtiz to Orson Welles, 20 September 1946.

p.403: 'John Perry of the West End Management . . .' Telegram from John Perry to Orson Welles, 29 August 1947.

p.404: 'SORRY, Welles replied . . .' Telegram from Orson Welles to John Perry, 30 August 1947.

p.404: 'I HOPE GALILEO IS . . .' Telegram from Orson Welles to Charles Laughton, 30 July 1947.

p.404: 'ARRIVING SEPTEMBER 15TH . . .' Telegram from Orson Welles to Alexander Korda, 4 September 1947.

p.404: '"Please answer, urgently . . .' Letter from Maurice Bessy to Orson Welles, 6 October 1947.

p.404: 'IT IS ALMOST CERTAIN . . .'

Telegram from Alexander Korda to Orson Welles, 15 January 1947.

p.404: 'YOU TOLD ME YOU COULD . . .' Telegram from Alexander Korda to Orson Welles, 3 March 1947.

p.406: 'Q: Mr Welles . . .' Transcript of court case, 8 May 1947.

p.406: 'largely because your name topped . . .' Letter from Stella Holt to Orson Welles, 17 June 1946.

p.407: 'The people is heroic and suicidal . . .' Recorded speech made by Orson Welles c. July 1946.

p.408: 'to let the people of the world know . . .' Speech by Henry A. Wallace, 19 May 1947.

p.408: 'literally seared the ears off . . .' Gordon Kahn, Hollywood on Trial.

p.409: 'TERRIBLY SORRY BUT MY MONEY IS SPENT . . .' Telegram from Orson Welles to Citizens Committee on Displaced Persons, 9 June 1946.

p.409: 'THE MIGHTY "WE" LIKE YOU . . .' Telegram from Citizens Committee on Displaced Persons to Orson Welles, 17 June 1946.

p.409: 'after weeks of haggling begging bargaining . . .' Letter from Orson Welles to Louis Dolivet, undated, c. December 1946.

p.410: 'HOLLYWOOD STARS ARE BLASTED . . .' Hollywood Reporter, 30 September 1946.

p.411: 'I shall continue in the future . . .' ibid., 2 December 1946.

p.411: 'I definitely intend . . .' ibid.

p.411: 'a grave injustice has been done . . .' ibid.

p.412: 'Shall the studios remain open . . .' ibid.

p.412: 'the group of bigots . . .' Speech by Henry A. Wallace, Los Angeles, 19 May 1947.

p.412: 'THIS INDUSTRY IS NOW DIVIDING ITSELF . . .' Telegram from Billy Wilder, William Wyler and John Huston to Orson Welles, 2 October 1946.

p.413: 'the year 1947 was dominated by . . .' Eric Barnouw, The Golden Web.

p.413: 'with a small-town Robespierre . . .' John Cromwell, quoted in Gordon Kahn, Hollywood on Trial.

p.413: 'even my few remaining friends . . .' Letter from Orson Welles to Arthur Margetson, 24 February 1947.

p.413: 'FROM THE WAY YOU SOUND . . .' Telegram from Bruce Elliott to Orson Welles, 3 September 1947.

CHAPTER TWENTY-TWO
The Charm's Wound Up

p.414: 'All of this stuff of lighting candles . . .' Letter from Orson Welles to Richard Wilson, 3 September 1947.

p.414: 'Good news is that picture . . .' Letter from Orson Welles to Bernard Herrmann, 12 September 1947.

p.414: 'Some of the individual scenes . . .' Orson Welles, quoted in Frank Brady, Citizen Welles.

p.415: 'Being a director at heart . . .' Memorandum from Warren Doane to Edward Small, 23 April 1948.

p.416: 'There is too much footage

. . .' SoundScriber message from Orson Welles to Richard Wilson, 4 November 1947.

p.416: 'Several sections of Republic . . .' Letter from Richard Wilson to Orson Welles, 14 November 1947.

p.417: 'the whole lot – executives and artisans . . .' ibid.

p.418: 'for Christ's sake write! . . .' Letter from Richard Wilson to Orson Welles, 26 November 1947.

p.418: '"Dearest Chuck," he calls him . . .' Letter from Richard Wilson to Orson Welles, 10 February 1948.

p.418: 'low and generally confused . . .' ibid.

p.419: 'When I talked to Feldman . . .' Letter from Richard Wilson to Orson Welles, 24 March 1948.

p.419: 'Please send some generalisations at least . . .' Letter from Richard Wilson to Orson Welles, 14 March 1948.

p.420: 'Dear Old Hank Cinq . . .' Letter from Richard Wilson to Orson Welles, 19 April 1948.

p.420: 'For your information, Charles K. Feldman . . .' Letter from Richard Wilson to Orson Welles, 13 March 1948.

p.420: 'There's no reason why the witches . . .' Memorandum from Norman Corwin to Orson Welles, n.d, c. June 1948.

p.421: '[Welles's] own opinion . . .' Daily Telegraph, 6 September 1948.

p.421: '[It] . . . grabs the audience . . .' Il Tempo, quoted in Frank Brady, op. cit.

p.422: 'Coiffed with horns and crowns . . .' Jean Cocteau, The Art of Film.

p.422: 'fake light and cardboard settings'. Robert Bresson, quoted in Frank Brady, op. cit.

p.422: 'It may come as something . . .' Bosley Crowther, New York Times, 30 September 1948.

p.423: 'The scene opposite is not . . .' Life, 11 October 1948.

p.424: 'If Welles has failed utterly . . .' Newsweek, 18 October 1948.

p.424: 'There is no doubt . . .' Fortnight, 5 November 1948.

p.424: 'had exhausted themselves . . .' Letter from Richard Wilson to Orson Welles, 10 October 1948.

p.424: 'Of course I think the whole thing . . .' ibid.

p.426: 'for the first time in my life I got . . .' Peter Bogdanovich, This is Orson Welles.

p.427: 'What I am trying to do . . .' Cahiers du Cinéma, September 1958.

p.427: 'he that plays the king . . .' Foreword to He That Plays The King by Kenneth Tynan, 1950.

p.428: 'a prehistoric universe . . .' André Bazin, Orson Welles.

p.436: 'I don't think films made on a small budget . . .' Quoted in Peter Noble, The Fabulous Orson Welles.

p.436: 'I have had the considerable disillusionment . . .' Letter from Richard Wilson to Orson Welles, 7 May 1949.

p.438: 'it has a great deal in its favour . . .' New York Times, 28 October 1950.

p.439: 'They don't review my films any more . . .' Profile by Kenneth Tynan in Show, October/November 1961.

p.439: 'an imaginative and highly

stylised . . .' *Herald Tribune*, 28 December 1950.

p.440: 'a terrific piece of melodramatic . . .' *New York Times*, 10 January 1948.

p.440: 'though Mr Orson Welles's film . . .' *The Times*, 23 May 1951.

p.440: 'the brilliant Mr Welles . . .' *Daily Telegraph*, 28 May 1951.

pp.440–1: 'The temptation with the long-awaited . . .' *Punch*, 6 June 1951.

p.441: 'a more powerful effect . . .' *Sight and Sound*, September 1951.

p.441: 'It is uncouth, unscholarly, unmusical . . .' *Observer*, 27 May 1951.

p.441: 'Welles's *Macbeth* is nothing if not . . .' Henry Raynor *Sight and Sound*, June 1952.

p.442: 'What is needed is more pictures . . .' Quoted in Peter Noble, *The Fabulous Orson Welles*.

p.442: 'Some years later . . .' Henry Raynor, op. cit.

p.442: 'Welles's finest work . . .' Letter from Richard Wilson to Jerome Hyams, 16 September 1947.

p.443: 'couldn't put up with his genius any more . . .' *Daily News*, 10 November 1947.

Bibliography

Books

Agar, Herbert, *The Unquiet Years*. Rupert Hart-Davies, 1957.
Ambler, Eric, *Journey into Fear*. Hodder & Stoughton, 1940.
Anderegg, Michael, *Orson Welles, Shakespeare and Popular Culture*.
    Columbia University Press, 1999.
Barnouw, Eric, *The Golden Web*. Oxford University Press, 1968.
Bazin, André, trans. Jonathan Rosenbaum, *Orson Welles: A Critical
    View*, Elm Tree Books, 1978.
Behlmer, Rudy (ed.), *Memo from David O. Selznick*. Samuel French, 1999.
Bogdanovich, Peter, & Welles, Orson, *This is Orson Welles*. Harper-
    Collins, 1992.
Brady, Frank, *Citizen Welles*, Charles Scribner's Sons, 1989.
Brecht, Bertolt, ed. John Willett, *Journals 1934–1955*. Methuen, 1993.
Brogan, Hugh, *Penguin History of the United States*. Penguin, 1986.
Carringer, Robert, *The Magnificent Ambersons: A Reconstruction*.
    University of California Press, 1993.
Castle, William, *Step Right Up!* Putnam, 1976.
Collier, Peter, & Horowitz, David, *The Rockefellers*. Holt, Rinehart &
    Winston, 1976.
Cooper, Stephen, *Full of Life: John Fante*. North Point Press, 2000.
Culver, John C., & Hyde, John, *American Dreamer*. W.W. Norton, 2000.
Denning, Michael, *The Cultural Front*. Verso, 1997.
    Cover Stories. Routledge, Kegan & Paul, 1987.
Eels, George, *The Life That Late He Led*. 1967.
Ekirch, Arthur, Jr, *Ideologies and Utopias*. Quadrangle Books, 1969.
Ellington, Duke, *Music is my Mistress*. W.H. Allen, 1973.
French, Philip, *The Movie Moguls*. Weidenfeld & Nicolson, 1969.
Harrington, Oliver, *Why I Left America and Other Essays*. University of
    Mississippi Press 1994.
Higham, Charles, *The Films of Orson Welles*. University of California
    Press, 1970.
    Orson Welles: The Rise and Fall of an American Genius. St Martin's
    Press, 1985.
    Sources of Light. Indiana University Press, 1970.

Hodel, Steven, *Black Dahlia Avenger*. Arcade Publishing, 2003.

Hoogstraten, Nicholas van, *Lost Broadway Theatres*. Princeton Architectural Press, 1991.

Hughes, Langston, *Fight for Freedom: The Story of the NAACP*. Berkeley Publishing Corporation, 1962.

Hurst, Richard Maurice, *Republic Studios*. Scarecrow Press, 1979.

Jewell, Richard B., & Harbin, Vernon, *The RKO Story*. Arlington House, 1982.

Kahn, Gordon, *Hollywood on Trial*. Boni & Gaer, 1948.

Lasky, Betty, *RKO: The Biggest Little Major of Them All*. Prentice-Hall, 1984.

Latham, Earl, *The Communist Controversy in Washington*. Harvard University Press, 1966.

Leaming, Barbara, *Orson Welles: A Biography*. Viking, 1985.
If This was Happiness: Rita Hayworth. Viking, 1989.

Leiter, Sam, *Encyclopaedia of the New York Stage, 1940–1950*. Greenwood Press, 1992.

Lyon, James K., *Bertolt Brecht in America*. Princeton University Press, 1980.

May, Larry, *The Big Tomorrow*. University of Chicago Press, 2000.

Naremore, James, *The Magic World of Orson Welles*. Revised edn, Southern Methodist University Press, 1989.
More Than Night. University of California Press, 1998.

Noble, Peter, *The Fabulous Orson Welles*. Hutchinson, 1956.

Pacios, Mary, *Childhood Shadows*. 1st Books Library, 1999.

Raeburn, Ben (ed.), *Treasury for the Free World*. Arco, 1945.

Rivas, Darlene, *Missionary Capitalist*. University of North Carolina Press, 2002.

Sherwood King, R., *If I Die Before I Wake*. Simon & Schuster, 1938.

Smith, Stephen, *A Heart at Fire's Center*. University of California Press, 1991.

Straight, Michael, *After Long Silence*. W. W. Norton 1983.

Suskin, Steven, *Opening Night on Broadway*. Schirmer, 1990.
Show Tunes, New York. Dodd, Mead & Company, 1986.

Swanberg, W. A., *Luce and his Empire*. Scribner's, 1972.

Tarkington, Booth, *The Magnificent Ambersons*. Doubleday, Page & Company, 1918.

Thomson, David, *Showman: The Life and Times of David O. Selznick*. Alfred A. Knopf, 1993.

Tynan, Kenneth, *He That Plays the King*. Longman, Green & Co., 1950.

Wood, Bret, *Orson Welles: A Bio-Bibliography*. Greenwood Press, 1990.

Woodress, James, *Booth Tarkington: Gentleman from Indiana*. Lippincott, 1955.

Yarbrough, Tinsley E., *A Passion for Justice*. Oxford University Press, 1987.

Articles

Benamou, Catherine, 'It's All True as Document/Event', *Persistence of Vision*, Number 7. Film Faculty of University of New York, 1989.

Kamp, David, 'Magnificent Obsession'. *Vanity Fair*, January 2002

Kulinak, Katherine, 'Text of Music: *The Magnificent Ambersons*'. *Cinema Journal*, Summer 1988.

Margetson, Arthur, 'Orson Welles and I' (unpublished)

Ryan, Susan, 'Context for an Unfinished Text', *Persistence of Vision*, Number 7. Film Faculty of University of New York, 1989.

Stam, Robert, 'Orson Welles, Brazil and the Power of Blackness', *Persistence of Vision*, Number 7. Film Faculty of University of New York, 1989.

Thomas, François, 'Orson Welles' Turn from Live Recording to Post-Synchronization: A Technical and Aesthetic Evolution', in Philip Brody (ed.), *Cinesonic: Cinema and the Sound of Music*. Australian Film, Television and Radio School, North Ryde, 2000. 'Mésaventures d'un Bande Sonore'. *Positif*,

Interviews

Tynan, Kathleen. Unpublished.

'Les mésaventures d'une bande sonore: les deux *Macbeth* d'Orson Welles', *Cinémathèque*, Number 6, Autumn 1994. Interview with Jeanette Nolan, *Positif*, Number 449–450, July/August 1998.

Acknowledgements

As with *The Road to Xanadu*, pride of place in the acknowledgements must go the superb Lilly Library and its crack team under Saundra Taylor, as efficient, calm and helpful when I last visited it in 2005 as when I first did, in 1989. It is a real sadness to me that the span of the third and final volume of this biography leaves behind the period covered by the Lilly. Would that there were a similarly streamlined collection to cover the rest of Welles's life! Other American university libraries have been extraordinarily helpful: Ned Comstock at the University of Southern California and Ann Caiger at the University of California have both pointed me to unexpected corners of their respective collections.

I have naturally depended on the trail-blazing work of my predecessors, Roy Alexander Fowler (Welles's first chronicler), the late Peter Noble, Barbara Leaming, Frank Brady and Charles Higham. Robert Carringer's studies of *Citizen Kane* and *The Magnificent Ambersons* have been deeply stimulating, as has V S Perkins's BFI monograph on the latter film. Michael Anderegg's *Orson Welles: Shakespeare and Popular Culture* is a particularly original approach to Welles. The key Wellesian study remains, as it has since publication, James Naremore's *The Magic World of Orson Welles*, unmatched in its sensitivity to the cultural and political resonances of the work. Professor Naremore was one of an informal group of readers who read the present volume in manuscript form and all of whom offered invaluable reactions and positive suggestions: any merit the book may have owes a great deal to Naremore, to Simon Gray, Sir David Hare, Fiona Maddocks, Ann Mitchell and Angus Mackay. The book was also read avidly, chapter by chapter as I wrote it, by its dedicatee, Paula Laurence, who lived to read the last sentence of the final page. Helen of Troy to Welles's Dr Faustus, she was one of the first people to whom I spoke about him, and those early conversations were the foundation stone of an incomparably rich and loving friendship.

Other people – too many of them now gone to the great cutting room in the sky – who offered especial illumination on this period of Welles's life, some of whom also became good friends, were Roddy MacDowall, George Fanto, Rogério Szangerla, Chico Albuquerque, Miles Kreuger, François Thomas, Kent Hägglund, Norman Corwin, Robert Davison, Alvin Colt. Henry Jaglom and Peter Bogdanovich, staunchly loyal to their friend, were nonetheless extremely cordial to someone with whose views they often strongly disagreed. I must most warmly thank my copy-editor, Chuck Elliott, ever-vigilant on matters grammatical, orthographic and literary, and himself a great source of information about American life in the nineteen-forties; Alex Milner, who collated and coordinated the sprawling manuscript; Dan Franklin, whose reckless faith in the project sustained us all through the book's more than elephantine gestation; and, yet again, Maggie Hanbury, my agent, who so often understood what I was trying to do better than I did myself. Two secretaries have cheerfully endured the process, Karen Lichkin for nine years and Jane Tomlinson for one; my forbearing partner Daniel Kramer has never known a life with me which didn't have Orson in it too, but he has never once complained.

In the end, of course, the book has depended on its primary material, in this case, as I indicated in the Preface, of almost bewildering richness. Here, I owe a supreme debt to the generosity and assiduousness of Rosemary Wilton, producer of the excellent six-part BBC series, *The RKO Story*, who gave me unlimited access to the fruits of her long and hard researches. My old chum Richard France and my slightly newer one, Robert Fischer-Ettl, superb Welles scholars both, shared with me the magnificent research they did on the Isaac Woodard case for a documentary which it is fervently hoped will shortly be made, while Kent Hägglund guided me from his Swedish base through the complexities of Welles's radiophonic output. Conrad Black, at a moment when he was under a certain amount of pressure, took time to clarify some details concerning Welles's relationship with Roosevelt not referred to in his magisterial biography. By far the largest corpus of material is, of course, the Mercury archive lodged at the Lilly Library. I should like to pay heartfelt tribute to the man we must thank for its survival, Richard Wilson, who served Orson Welles nobly from his apprenticeship in the thirties through to the late forties when he finally and with a great wrench liberated himself from Welles's employ, to become a successful producer and director in his own right. Even though technically no longer employed by Welles, he continued to protect and foster his reputation: in my dealings with him I found him deeply sensitive to the memory of a man who did so very little to protect himself or his reputation. It is more than likely that Welles would prefer some of the contents of the Mercury archive to have fallen by the wayside, but if posterity finally appreciates his full complexity and originality, it will be thanks in no small measure to Richard Wilson.

The author and publishers are grateful for permission to reprint the following: excerpt from 'Airborne Symphony', words and music by Marc Blitzstein © 1946 Chappell & Co. Inc. Administered by Warner/Chappell Music Ltd, London w6 8bs. Reproduced by permission; excerpt from 'Wherever They Fly the Flag of Old England', words and music by Cole Porter © 1946 (renewed) Chappell & Co. Inc. Administered by Warner/Chappell Music Ltd, London w6 8bs. Reproduced by permission; excerpt from 'The Blinding of Isaac Woodard' by Woody Guthrie © Copyright 1965 (renewed) by Woody Guthrie Publications, Inc. All rights reserved. Used by permission.

Index

99th Pursuit Squadron 324
Abbey Theatre (Dublin) 168
Abbott and Costello Meet the Invisible Man
   (film) 415
ABC 290, 309, 339, 340, 342
Abednego (radio) 343
Acapulco 356, 362–3, 370, 404
Adelphi Theatre (New York) 300–1, 306,
   308, 310, 318, 322, 323, 326
Admiral of the Ocean Sea (radio) 156
Adorno, Theodor 423
Agee, James 168
Aiken (South Carolina) 328–9, 333–5, 337,
   338, 339
Aino Da Noite (newspaper) 46, 96, 121
Airborne Symphony 287
Albuquerque, Chico 134
All That Money Can Buy (Dieterle) 5
Alland, William 'Bill' 356, 385, 388, 394, 432
Allen, Fred 203
Allenberg, Bert 315
Ambler, Eric 6, 13–14, 50
American National Theatre and Academy
   (ANTA) 382, 391–3, 403, 424
American Student Union's Peace Ball 10
Americans All (documentary) 64
Amsterdam News 336
Anderegg, Michael, *Orson Welles: Shakespeare
   and Popular Culture* 429
Anders, Glenn 356, 367
Anderson, Dame Judith 396
Andrei Rublev (film) 427
Andreyev, Leonid 27
Annie Get Your Gun (musical) 311
Anouilh, Jean 311
Antheil, George 362
Antigone (Anouilh) 311
Antony and Cleopatra (Shakespeare) 418
Argentina 136
Armour, Reg 33, 93, 94, 96, 107, 115, 124,
   131

Around the World in Eighty Days (musical)
   xiii, 287–302, 290, 323, 334, 343, 357,
   392, 424; cost of production 305–6,
   321–2, 348; critics views of 303–5, 308,
   310–11; failure of 303–22; inception and
   production 280, 281, 283–4, 284, 285;
   Todd's abandonment of 316–19; Welles's
   promotion of 308–10
Art of Illusion, The 192
Atkinson, Brooks 391
Atlas Mountains 83
Atlee, Clement 239
Aviso newspaper 135

Bahia 135, 147
Bainter, Fay 385
Bakaleinikoff, Constantin 109
Bakhtin, Mikhail 386, 387
Ball, Lucille 204–5
Ballad for Americans (song) 10
Ballet Russes de Monte Carlo 288, 296
Bankhead, Tallulah 396
Barbette 289, 298–9
Barclift, Nelson 288–9
Barlow, Joyce 389
Barnes, George 166–7
Barnouw, Eric 413
Barra Da Tijuca 120, 132
Barrier, Edgar 17, 309, 388, 391, 433
Barry, Iris 266
Barrymore, John xvii, 26, 231–2
Batesburg (South Carolina) 336, 339, 341
Batista, Linda 129
Baxter, Anne 27, 88, 112
BBC 96
Beaton, Cecil 345
Beck, Martin 289
Ben-Hur (film) 269
Benamou, Catherine xvi, 74, 379
Bennett, Barbara 27
Bennett, Constance 27

www.vintage-books.co.uk